ADMINISTRATIVE DISTRICTS

Petrograd

I	Admiralty	VII	Moscow
II	Kazan	VIII	Aleksandr-Nev
III	Kolomenskaia	IX	Narva
IV	Spasskaia	X	Vasilievskii Isla
V	Liteinaia	XI	Petrograd
VI	Rozhdestvo	XII	Vyborg

Suburbs
1 Okhta

GOVERNMENT INSTITUTIONS

1 Winter Palace
2 Admiralty: Ministry of the Navy
3 Ministry of War
4 Marinskii Palace: Council of Ministers, State Council
5 Tauride Palace: State Duma
6 Senate
7 Holy Synod
8 General Staff Bldg.: Army General Staff, Ministry of Foreign Affairs: Ministry of Finance
9 Ministry of Trade and Industry
10 Ministry of Agriculture
11 Corps of Gendarmes
12 Ministry of Internal Affairs
13 Gradonachal'stvo
14 Central Post-Telegraph
15 Ministry of Education
16 Ministry of Justice
17 Circuit Court
18 House of Detention
19 Kresty Prison
20 Petrograd Women's Prison
21 Lithuanian Castle: Petrograd Correction Prison
22 Petrograd Exile Prison
23 Ministry of Transport
24 Nikolaevskii Station
25 Warsaw Station
26 Baltic Station
27 Tsarskoe Selo Station
28 Finland Station
29 Fortress of Peter and Paul
30 Central Telephone station
31 City Duma

BARRACKS

1 Lithuanian Regiment
2 Preobrazhenskii Regiment
3 Volynskii Regiment
4 Sixth Engineer Battalion
5 Moscow Regiment
6 Grenadier Regiment
7 Pavlovskii Regiment
8 Finland Regiment
9 Izmailovskii Regiment
10 Petrograd Regiment
11 Keksholm Regiment
12 Semenovskii Regiment
13 First & Fourth Cossack Regiment

MAJOR FACTORIES

Vyborg District
1 Aivaz
2 New Lessner
3 Nikol'skaia Cotton
4 Baranovskii II
5 Erikson
6 Parviainen
7 Sampsonievskaia Cotton
8 Nobel
9 Lebedev Jute
10 Russian Renault
11 Old Lessner
12 Promet II
13 Petrograd Cartridge I
14 Arsenal
15 Phoenix
16 Petrograd Metal Factory
17 Rosenkrantz

Petrograd District
18 Vulkan
19 Diuflon
20 Langenzippen
21 James Beck
22 Stetinin

Vasilievskii Island
23 Siemens-Haliske
24 Petrograd Pipe Factory
25 Laferm
26 Military Horseshoes
27 Siemens-Schückert
28 Donetsko-Iurievskii
29 United Cable
30 Baltic Shipyard

Liteinaia, Admiralty, Kolomenskaia
31 Orudinskii
32 Admiralty Shipyard I
33 Franco-Russian Factory

Aleksandr Nevskaia
34 Neva Shipyard
35 San-Galli

Narva
36 Petrograd City Gas
37 Treugol'nik
38 Dinamo II
39 Neva Shoes II
40 Skorokhod
41 Petrograd Wagon
42 Siemens-Schückert

Peterhof
43 Putilov
44 Putilov Shipyard

OTHER IMPORTANT PLACES

1 St. Isaac's Cathedral
2 Kazan Cathedral
3 Mikhailovskii Palace
4 Anichkov Palace
5 Summer Garden
6 Mars Field
7 Mikhailovskii Castle
8 Tauride Garden
9 Smol'nyi Institute
10 Aleksandr Nevskaia Monastery
11 Gostinyi Dvor
12 Public Library
13 Evropeiskaia Hotel
14 Hotel Astoria
15 Kazan Square
16 Znamenskaia Square
17 Theater Square
18 Petrograd Imperial University
19 Mining Institute
20 Bestuzhev Women's College
21 Technological Institute
22 Women's Medical Institute
23 Military Medical Institute
24 Forestry Institute
25 Narva Gate
26 Moscow Arch of Triumph

Publications on Russia and Eastern Europe
of the School of International Studies
Volume 9

Sponsored by the Russian and
East European program of
the School of International Studies

THE FEBRUARY REVOLUTION:
PETROGRAD, 1917

TSUYOSHI HASEGAWA

University of Washington Press

Seattle and London

Library of Congress Cataloging in Publication Data
Hasegawa, Tsuyoshi, 1941-
    The February revolution, Petrograd, 1917.

    (Publications on Russia and Eastern Europe of the School of International Studies ; no. 9)
    Bibliography: p.
    Includes index.
    1. Russia—History—February Revolution, 1917.
I. Title. II. Series: Washington (State). University.
School of International Studies.
Publications on Russia and Eastern Europe ; no. 9.
DK265.19.H37   947.084'1   80-50870
ISBN 0-295-95765-4

For Kim and Stephen

CONTENTS

ILLUSTRATIONS

PREFACE

This book seeks to describe and analyze the complex political process of the February Revolution in Petrograd during the nine days from February 23 to March 3, 1917. The importance of the February Revolution in Russia is self-evident. It put an end to tsarist autocracy and opened the floodgate to the Russian Revolution, which was to sweep the Bolsheviks to power in October. It was the watershed between the old and the new eras of Russian history—the culmination of the political development of prerevolutionary Russia and the beginning of the popular unrest that was to tear apart the fabric of the Russian state and society for the next few years. A discussion of the February Revolution must, therefore, look both backwards and forwards, back to the basic causes of the collapse of the tsarist regime, and forward to the seeds of the social strife of 1917.

Despite its historical significance, there have been few monographs that attempt a comprehensive analysis of the February Revolution, although some specific aspects of the revolution have been thoroughly researched.[1] There is only one in English—George Katkov, *Russia,*

---

1. V. S. Diakin, *Russkaia burzhuaziia i tsarizm v gody pervoi mirovoi voiny,* E. D. Chermenskii, *IV gosudarstvennaia duma i sverzhenie tsarizma v Rossii,* and Raymond Pearson, *The Russian Moderate and the Crisis of Tsarism, 1914-1917,* describe the relationship between the liberal opposition and the government during the war and the role of the liberals in the February Revolution. On the formation of the militia, see V. I. Startsev, *Ocherki po istorii Petrogradskoi Krasnoi gvardii i rabochei militsii;* on the formation of the Petrograd Soviet, see Iu. S. Tokarev, *Petrogradskii sovet rabochikh i soldatskikh deputatov v marte-aprele 1917 g.;* on Order No. 1 and the formation of the soldiers' committees, V. I. Miller, *Soldatskie komitety russkoi armii v 1917 g.,* and on the workers' strike movement

1917: The February Revolution—and five serious monographs in
Russian—the books by E. I. Martynov, E. Genkina, E. D. Chermenskii,
S. P. Mel'gunov, I. I. Mints, and E. N. Burdzhalov.[2] The works of
Martynov and Genkina, which were published in the 1920s, are seriously outdated in view of the materials made available since then.
The two émigré historians, Katkov and Mel'gunov, are concerned
with "high politics"—the actions of the liberals and the military leaders—that led to the end of the monarchy. We owe a great deal to their
pioneering work for our understanding of the political forces that
ultimately brought about the abdication of Nicholas II and Grand
Duke Mikhail Aleksandrovich. But their total neglect of the mass
movement, which, in my opinion, was the fountainhead of the specific
actions of the liberals and the military leaders, has rendered their interpretation one-sided. On the other hand, the Soviet historians, including
Burdzhalov, the author of the best monograph to date on the February
Revolution in any language, have maintained that the February Revolution took place, despite the opposition of the liberals, the military,
and the Socialist "compromisers", because of the overwhelming forces
of the revolutionary masses, largely under the guidance of the Bolshevik
party. In my view, neither is accurate.

The February Revolution was an eruption resulting from the fundamental contradictions inherent in the political conditions of prerevolu-

---

during the war and the February Revolution, see the various articles written by
I. P. Leiberov, and his still unpublished doctoral dissertation, *Petrogradskii proletariat v Fevral'skoi revoliutsii 1917 goda*. Also two collections of papers presented
at scholarly conferences offer valuable information on the focus and direction
of contemporary Soviet scholarship on the February Revolution: I. I. Mints,
L. M. Ivanov, et al., *Sverzhenie samoderzhaviia: sbornik statei*, and *Nauchnaia
sessiia, posviashchennaia 50-letiiu sverzheniia samoderzhaviia v Rossii*. The February Revolution has been a subject of discussion in many works of broader scope.
For instance, Michael T. Florinsky, *The End of the Russian Empire*, and Bernard
Pares, *The Fall of the Russian Monarchy*, describe the February Revolution in the
last chapter. William Henry Chamberlin, *The Russian Revolution, 1917-1921*,
and Leon Trotsky, *The History of the Russian Revolution* are two classics on the
Russian Revolution. The most recent monographs on the Russian Revolution
are Marc Ferro, *La révolution russe de 1917;* John L. H. Keep, *The Russian Revolution: A Study in Mass Mobilization*.

2. E. I. Martynov, *Tsarskaia armiia v fevral'skom perevorote;* E. Genkina,
"Fevral'skii perevorot," *Ocherki po istorii Oktiabr'skoi revoliutsii*, ed. M. N.
Pokrovskii, vol. 1; E. D. Chermenskii, *Fevral'skaia burzhuazno-demokraticheskaia
revoliutsiia 1917 goda v Rossii;* S. P. Mel'gunov, *Martovskie dni 1917 goda;* I. I.
Mints, *Istoriia Velikogo Oktiabria*, vol. 1, *Sverzhenie samoderzhaviia;* and E. N.
Burdzhalov, *Vtoraia russkaia revoliutsiia: Vosstanie v Petrograde* and *Vtoraia
russkaia revoliutsiia: Moskva, front, pereferiia*. To this list, I should also add Wada
Haruki, "Nigatsu kakumei," in *Roshia kakumei no kenkyu*, ed., Eguchi Bokuro.

tionary Russia. During the nine days of the revolution, various political
groups—the masses of workers and soldiers, the revolutionary parties,
the liberal politicians, the military leaders, and the defenders of the
monarchy—stepped onto the stage and enacted their own roles in that
intense drama. The role each one played was conditioned by his position in the political reality prior to the revolution, and the actions
of one actor were closely connected with those of the others. The
general outcome of the revolution was the result of the sum of these
actions. That is why it is necessary to reconstruct the revolutionary
process in its totality and assess the significance of specific issues in
that context.

We can discern two basic forces at work during the revolution:
the revolt of the masses against established order and the rejection by
the liberal elements in society of continued rule by the tsarist autocracy. The February Revolution began with the revolt of the masses, and
this factor continued to determine the basic nature of the revolution,
providing the general framework. But the revolt of the masses alone
did not make the victory of the revolution inevitable. Only when this
revolt touched off a chain of reactions that involved the liberals and the
military leaders was the victory of the February Revolution assured
and the general character of the revolution determined. Nor was there
any unity of goals and actions between the two forces that overthrew
the tsarist regime. While pursuing that overthrow, the liberals and the
masses often worked in opposition. Moreover, within each force there
existed substantial differences in tactics. The military leaders reacted
to events differently from the liberals, and even among the liberals and
among the military there was no unity of policy. Similarly, the leaders
of the mass movement disagreed on the fundamental nature of the
revolution and the policy to be pursued to achieve its goals. Contrary
to the argument presented by Soviet historians, who generally discount
the actions of all groups other than the Bolsheviks and the insurgents
as counterrevolutionary, these differences are precisely what determined the specific course of the February Revolution.

This book is an attempt to reconstruct the events from February
23 to March 3 by analyzing the actions of each group and the relationships among the various groups. Political conditions from the outbreak of World War I to the eve of the revolution will be discussed
in Parts I and II. The purpose of these chapters is to single out two
overriding causes of the February Revolution that had been brewing
in prerevolutionary Russia. The first was what Soviet historians term
krizis verkhov, "crisis of power", which was characterized by erosion
of the regime's authority and by the increasing alienation of the tsarist
government from the educated element of society. The second was

the growing radicalism of the masses, particularly the industrial workers. I do not pretend to claim my research in these introductory chapters to be original and exhaustive, since generally I rely on secondary sources to draw a general picture. I do believe, however, that the hypothesis I present on the relationship between the government and the liberals is somewhat original. I reject, on the one hand, the liberal interpretation represented by Michael Florinsky and Bernard Pares that pictures the liberals as unsung heroes mistreated by the short-sighted, ever corrupt tsarist government. On the other hand, I disagree with Katkov's view that the liberals successfully conspired to take over the tsarist government. The liberals were not so powerful as presented by Florinsky, Pares, and Katkov, and in this respect I am inclined to agree with the conclusion recently drawn by Michael Hamm and Raymond Pearson that the liberals were powerless to do anything against the regime.[3] A part of the reason for this powerlessness came from their fear of the revolt of the masses, as Soviet historians correctly emphasize.[4] But another important reason stemmed from the growing interdependence of the government and the liberals for the war effort. I submit that this mutual concern was an important reason why neither the government nor the liberals could break with each other despite their growing political estrangement.

The development of the labor movement during the war and the influence of the revolutionary parties among the working classes are subjects grossly neglected in western historiography. Although my research on these subjects is based on more primary sources than the account of the wartime relationship between the liberals and the government, it is far from extensive. The only contribution I can claim for these chapters would be the presentation of a comprehensive picture based on recent, scattered evidence on more specific problems.

My original research begins with Part III, which deals with the February insurrection that began with the workers' strike movement on February 23 and culminated in the soldiers' insurrection on February 27. Here I have attempted to describe the intense human drama as accurately as possible. It is my belief that a historian describing a revolution is as responsible for conveying the excitement and atmosphere in the streets as for analyzing the general tendencies of the mass movement. I hope that my attention to details will not tax the patience of the reader. I may only repeat here what Trotskii wrote

3. Pearson, *The Russian Moderates;* Michael F. Hamm, "Liberal Politics in Wartime Russia: An Analysis of the Progressive Bloc," *Slavic Review* 33, no. 3 (September 1974):453-68.

4. See V. S. Diakin, *Russkaia burzhuaziia* and E. D. Chermenskii, *IV gosudarstvennaia duma.*

in his introduction to volumes two and three of his classic, *The History of the Russian Revolution:*

You can present a photograph of a hand on one page, but it requires a volume to present the results of a microscopic investigation of its tissues. . . .In this struggle for details we were guided by a desire to reveal as concretely as possible the very process of the revolution. In particular it was impossible not to try to make the most of the opportunity to paint history from the life. . . .The heroine of Proust requires several finely-wrought pages in order to feel that she does not feel anything. It would seem that one might, at least with equal justice, demand attention to a series of collective historic dramas which lifted hundreds of millions of human beings out of non-existence, transforming the character of nations, and intruding forever into the life of all mankind.[5]

In these chapters I hope the reader can see how the revolution was made by real people blundering around without knowing exactly what to do, but that contrary to the traditional picture of the February Revolution as a "spontaneous, leaderless revolution," there did exist a group of experienced revolutionary workers determined to transform a labor demonstration into a revolution.

The relationship between the masses and the liberals, on the one hand, and between the masses and the revolutionary party leaders, on the other hand, are discussed in Part IV. These chapters describe an intricate drama in which the liberals' Duma Committee was forced to take revolutionary action to arrest the further development of revolution, and in which the overwhelming support of the insurgent masses transformed the Petrograd Soviet into something different from what the Socialist intelligentsia had intended. I also discuss the negotiations between the Duma Committee and the Petrograd Soviet leaders in their desperate attempts to extricate themselves from their respective predicaments. One finds the origins of "dual power" in these tripartite relationships among the Duma Committee, the Petrograd Soviet leaders, and the insurgents.

The political process that finally led to Nicholas II's abdication is the main concern of Part V. It deals with the Duma Committee's policy toward the monarchy, its dealings with the military leaders, and the military's reaction to the revolution. Part VI describes the formation of the Provisional Government and the abdication of Grand Duke Mikhail Aleksandrovich. These two parts cover the area to which Mel'gunov and Katkov devoted their main attention and my study is heavily indebted to their findings. Although we all have similar views on a number of issues, I have attempted to add new dimensions to the abdication drama, sometimes with the use of the Soviet archival

5. Trotsky, *The History of the Russian Revolution* 2:iv.

sources that were not available to Mel'gunov and Katkov. Moreover,
I have one fundamental disagreement with the émigré historians.
While they treat the actions of the Duma liberals and the military
leaders as political intrigues against the monarchy, I discuss this problem in the general framework created by the insurrection of the masses.
The actions and policies of the Duma Committee leaders and the
military leaders are presented, not as conspiracies, but as their reaction
to the over-all revolutionary situation in the capital.

In the preparation of this book, I was often asked if I could really
offer something new that had not been said before. I am confident
that I have provided a number of minor reassessments and reinterpre-
tations of events and factual problems, but I cannot claim that my
work will totally reshape everything hitherto believed about the revolution. My hope has been to present a total picture of the revolution
on the basis of extensive primary and secondary materials that have
not been synthesized previously. It is the first such attempt in English
and the general picture that emerges is considerably different from
those offered by Soviet historians.

My description is mainly limited to the events in the city of Petrograd. I am well aware that the February Revolution was nation-wide,
involving Moscow, Kiev, and other major cities, as well as the front,
the provinces, and the nationality minorities.[6] But the revolution outside Petrograd is beyond the scope of this study. This omission does
not mean that I attach little significance to the revolutionary process
elsewhere other than in Petrograd. On the contrary, I believe that
until a more comprehensive study of the revolutionary process of such
different areas is done, the true nature of the February Revolution will
not emerge. I might add that there are encouraging signs of emergence
of excellent studies on provinces, the Moscow workers, the Baltic
Fleet sailors, the soldiers in general, and the militia organizations.[7]

6. For the February Revolution in Moscow and other cities, at the front, and
in the provinces, see Burezhalov, *Vtoraia russkaia revoliutsiia: Moskva, front,
periferiia.*

7. For instance, Keep, *The Russian Revolution;* Norman Saul, *Sailors in Revolt:
The Russian Baltic Fleet in 1917;* David A. Longley, "Officers and Men: A Study
of the Development of Political Attitude among the Sailors of the Baltic Fleet
in 1917," *Soviet Studies* 25 (1973):29-50; David Longley, "Some Historiographical
Problem of Bolshevik Party History (The Kronstadt Bolsheviks in March 1917),"
Jahrbücher für Geschichte Osteuropas 27, No. 4 (1974):494-514; Diane Koenker,
"Urban Families, Working-Class Youth Groups, and the 1917 Revolution in Moscow," in *The Family in Imperial Russia: New Lines of Historical Research,* ed.
David L. Ransel, pp. 280-304; Diane Koenker, "The Evolution of Party Consciousness in 1917: The Case of the Moscow Workers," *Soviet Studies* 30, no. 1 (1978):
38-62. Books soon to be published include Diane Koenker's study of the Moscow

My justification for limiting the scope of this study to Petrograd is
that the events in Petrograd were decisive in shaping the basic pattern
of the revolution on the national scale and that there was a need to
reconstruct and analyze these events.

This book is the result of almost fifteen years' research. From the
time I began to study the Bolsheviks in the February Revolution for
my senior thesis at Tokyo University in 1963, I have been continuously
working on the February Revolution. In 1969, I completed my doctoral dissertation on this topic at the University of Washington. Although my dissertation became the foundations of the present book,
my subsequent research and the materials that have become available
since its completion made it necessary for me to rewrite it completely.
During these fifteen years I have examined the materials in the libraries
in Tokyo, in various parts of the United States, and in London, Helsinki, Moscow, and Leningrad. In addition to the published materials,
the archival materials at the Hoover Institution and at the various
archival administrations in the Soviet Union constitute a large body
of the materials used. As far as I know, I am the first historian outside
the Soviet Union who has made extensive use of the Soviet archival
materials on the February Revolution.

I do not intend to suggest that this is the only possible interpretation of the February Revolution. I am aware that there are still
many questions that are begging historians' further research. Nor do
I believe that there is only one path that leads to the truth. I am as
sure that there are some sources I have overlooked and that new materials will be introduced as I am that it is possible to reach different
conclusions from these same materials. It is my hope that this book
will help stimulate further discussion on various aspects of the February
Revolution.

I have followed the Library of Congress transliteration system with
some modifications in the text. Soft signs before *ev* was rendered *i*.
Thus Kondrat'ev and Ignat'ev are rendered Kondratiev and Ignatiev.
However, the Library of Congress transliteration is strictly observed
in footnotes and bibliography with the exception of the translated
works. Throughout the text, original Russian names are retained
(thus Pavel N. Miliukov, not Paul N. Miliukov) with the following
exceptions: names of obvious foreign origin are rendered into foreign

---

workers and Rex Wade's study on the militia. After the submission of the manuscript three works that discuss the problems dealt with in this book have been
published: Allan K. Wildman, *The End of the Russian Imperial Army* (Princeton:
Princeton University Press, 1980); I. P. Leiberov, *Shtrum na samoderzhaviiu* (Moscow, 1980): and Michael M. Boll, *The Petrograd Armed Workers' Movement in
the February Revolution* (Washington D.C.: University Press of America, 1979).

spelling (thus Schmidt, not Shmidt). I used also Nicholas II instead of Nikolai II and Maxim Gorky rather than Maksim Gor'kii. Geographical names present the most difficult problem. My preference is to retain the original Russian names. Thus I used Frantsuzskaia naberezhnaia instead of French Embankment. Most of the adjectives are retained except in obvious cases. I used Nikolaevskii Station rather than Nikolaev Station, Kolomenskaia District rather than Kolomna District, Marinskii Palace rather than Marian Palace. But I used Tauride Palace rather than Tavricheskii Palace, Kazan Square rather than Kazanskaia Square, and Moscow and Lithuanian Regiments rather than Moskovskii and Litovskii Regiments. Admittedly, it is inconsistent, but I decided to follow my own instinct rather than to suffer the artificiality of strict consistency. All dates in the text are given according to the Old Style, which is thirteen days behind the western calendar in the century in which our events took place. One further note—the archival materials given in abbreviated form in the footnotes are identified fully in the archival section of the bibliography.

ACKNOWLEDGMENTS

Many persons and institutions have assisted me in the preparation of this book. Don Treadgold, under whom I had a good fortune to study as a graduate student, directed my dissertation, from which the present work had developed, and has given me every possible assistance and encouragement at every stage. My understanding of Russian history was immensely enriched under his training, and I learned from him not only the techniques of historical research and writing, but also a high standard of professionalism. Marc Szeftel's bibliographic knowledge and command of the details of Russian history have never ceased to amaze me, and have been a constant source of information. John Keep was willing to discuss various aspects of the Russian Revolution with a budding graduate student. He might recognize that a term paper I wrote for him has found its way into a part of this book. The Far Eastern and Russian Institute, now the School of International Studies, and the Department of History at the University of Washington have offered me various assistance. I was fortunate to spend five years from 1964 to 1969 in the company of dedicated teachers and talented graduate students, who provided me with constant intellectual excitement. I am particularly grateful to Imre Boba, Robert Butow, Herbert Ellison, Solomon Katz, Kenneth Pyle, Peter Sugar, Dan Matuszewski, Bob Nichols, Joe Sanders, and Gary Ulman. It is my added pleasure, therefore, to renew my association with the University of Washington through this publication.

This book originated from my undergraduate thesis, which I completed in 1964 at Tokyo University. I owe a great personal debt to my mentor, Professor Saito Takashi, who guided my thesis and had a decisive influence in choosing my career as historian. Passionate historical debates exchanged at the meetings at the *Roshia-shi kenkyū-kai* kindled the interest of a young undergraduate student. Although my interpretations and historical approach have changed since then, my book represents long years' search for the answers to the questions raised by the Japanese historians on Russia in the early 1960s. I am particularly indebted to the pioneering work done by Wada Haruki. Professor Eto Shinkichi was responsible for providing me with the opportunity to study in the United States. I hope that the publication of this book will serve in a small way as a repayment of a long-neglected debt to these Japanese scholars.

David Danahar, Alex Rabinowitch, Ron Suny, Don Treadgold, Allan Wildman, and George Yaney have read the manuscript in its entirety in various stages. Their criticisms of my interpretation, presentation of facts, and style have immensely enhanced the quality of this book. Diane Koenker, Mark Kulikowski, David Longley, Ron Petrusha, Lewis Siegelbaum, Rex Wade, and Howard White have read parts of the manuscript, commented on various aspects and corrected numerous errors. I owe a special debt to Diane Koenker and Lewis Siegelbaum, whose willingness to share ideas over the years has been a constant source of encouragement. I am also grateful to John Bushnell, Michael Hamm; Peter Kenez, and William Rosenberg for their generous help. It would be amiss not to mention two scholars, George Katkov and Leopold Haimson, whose ideas greatly inspired me and whose personal encouragement had a greater impact than they themselves realize.

The International Research and Exchange Board (IREX) supported my first trip to the Soviet Union in 1973; the IREX and the Fulbright-Hays Research Abroad supported my research in Leningrad and Moscow in 1976-77; and the State University of New York provided me with the opportunity to study in the Soviet Union on its exchange program with the Moscow State University in 1979-80. Without their generous financial support this work would have been of much more meager quality. The Ford Foundation offered me its generous scholarship during my entire graduate training, and financed my numerous trips to the Hoover Institution. The Research Foundation of the State University of New York offered me its research fellowships in 1972, 1973, and 1976. The Institute of the Russian and East European Studies at the University of Illinois at Champaign-Urbana gave me a small financial assistance during my stay at its research laboratory in 1976.

I would also like to express my gratitude to many librarians and archivists. A great bulk of my research was conducted at the Henry Suzzallo Library at the University of Washington, the Hoover Institution at Stanford University, the Olin Library at Cornell University, the Lenin Library in Moscow, the Academy of Sciences Library (BAN) in Leningrad, the Saltykov-Shchedrin Public Library in Leningrad, the Central State Historical Archives (TsGIA) in Leningrad, and the Central State Archives of the October Revolution (TsGAOR). I owe a special debt to Ruth Kirk of the Interlibrary Loan at Suzzallo Library, Arline Paul at the Hoover Institution, and Serafima Egorovna Varehova at TsGIA, whose professional dedication was always a great inspiration to this author. I also visited the libraries at the following: University of Illinois, the New York Public Library, the Library of Congress, the British Museum, the University of Helsinki Library, the State Public Historical Library (GPIB) in Moscow, and Leningrad State Historical Archives (LGIA). The Interlibrary Loan Division of the Penfield Library at State University of New York at Oswego has been also helpful in obtaining numerous materials for me. I was especially fortunate to have access to the enormous archival materials in the Soviet Union through the willingness and cooperation of the *sotrudnitsy* at TsGIA, TsGAOR, and the archival division of the Lenin Library; I only wish that the same cooperation had been extended by other Soviet archival depositories.

I am indebted to many Soviet historians. Valentin Semenovich Diakin of the Institute of History at the Academy of Sciences in Leningrad and Evgenii Dmitrievich Chermenskii of Moscow State University were always willing to answer my various queries. Vladimir Petrovich Iakovlev of Leningrad State University not only helped me to locate various obscure materials, but also his love and knowledge of the city of Leningrad contributed to my better understanding of the history of the city. Leningrad State University and Moscow State University were most helpful during my stays in the Soviet Union. The State Historical Museum in Moscow was generous in reproducing photographs of the February Revolution.

Writing in a nonnative language presented me with one of the greatest obstacles I have had in the preparation of this book, and the English language has often had the upper hand with me in my constant struggle with its idiosyncrasies. Fortunately many people have been generous in offering assistance. I an grateful to Leila Charbonneau, David Danahar, and Susan Roth for their help in various stages of the manuscript. I owe, above all, a great debt to my editor, Margery Lang, whose thoroughness, rigor, and good taste have immeasurably improved the quality of this book. She has treated my manuscript with a love and care that could not be expected from any other editor. Her astute criticisms were directed not merely at my style but also at the contents; they led me to revise some concepts and correct inconsistencies. The

personal interest she took in my manuscript and her patience have
made the otherwise onerous task of editing, proofreading, and indexing
less painful. I have come to have great respect and admiration for
the publications staff of the School of International Studies of the
University of Washington, especially Jean Chatfield, Cynthia Louie,
and Felicia Hecker, who have been responsible for the book's composition. I am also grateful to the University of Washington Press for its
confidence and courtesy. Needless to say, no one other than myself is
responsible for any errors that might occur in the book.

I am also indebted to *Slavic Review* for its permission to use my
article, "The Formation of the Militia in the February Revolution,"
which appeared in the second issue of 1973; also to Penguin Books,
Ltd. for permission to use poems of Aleksandr Blok, "Those who were
born in years of stagnation," and Anna Akhmatova, "July 1914,"
Penguin Book of Russian Verse, ed. Dimitri Obolensky (rev. ed. London: Penguin Poets, 1965), pp. 284-85, 318-20.

My friends in various parts of the world, particularly three cities
I love—Seattle, Moscow, and Leningrad—have supported and encouraged me during the long, often difficult years of the preparation of
this book. I am particularly grateful to Jeff and Karen Brooks, Julie
Brown, Paul Bushkovich, Richard and Cathy Butler, David Danahar,
Mab and Lorraine Huang, Tom and Blanche Judd, Paul and Pat Morman,
Mary Shadoff, Michael and Veronica Urban, and Birgit Veit. I feel
no less gratitude to the Soviet friends whose names remain unmen-
tioned.

I deeply regret that two men, my father and my brother Kimihiro,
who would have been as pleased as I with the publication of this book,
are no longer alive to read it.

Those who were born in years of stagnation
Do not remember their way.
We, children of Russia's fearful years,
Can forget nothing.

Years that burnt everything to the ashes!
Do you bode madness, or bring tidings of hope?
The days of war, the days of freedom
Have marked our faces with a blood-red glow.

We are struck dumb; the tocsin's clang
Has made us close our lips.
In our hearts, once full of fervour,
There is a fateful emptiness.

Let the croaking ravens soar
Above our death-bed—
May those who are more worthy, O God, O God,
Behold Thy Kingdom!

                                        Aleksandr Blok

PART I

RUSSIA AND THE FIRST WORLD WAR

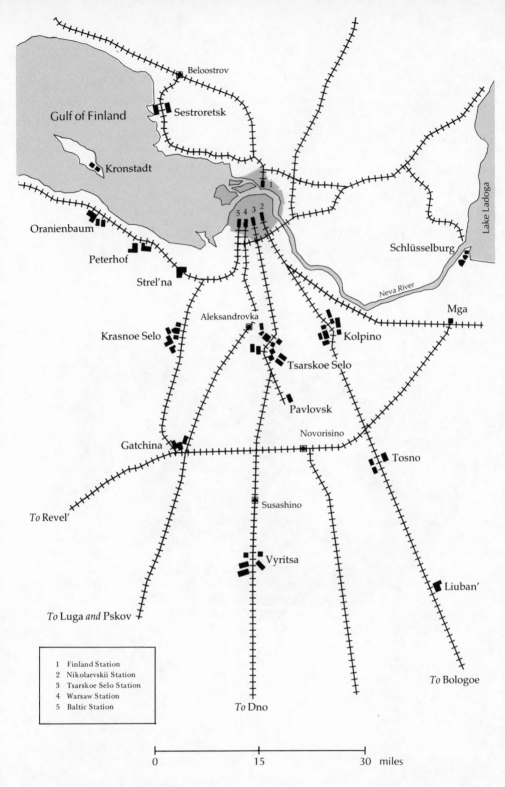

Gulf of Finland

Beloostrov

Sestroretsk

Kronstadt

Lake Ladoga

1

5 4 3 2

Oranienbaum

Schlüsselburg

Peterhof

Strel'na

Neva River

Mga

Aleksandrovka

Krasnoe Selo

Kolpino

Tsarskoe Selo

Pavlovsk

Novorisino

Gatchina

Tosno

To Revel'

Susashino

Vyritsa

Liuban'

To Luga *and* Pskov

To Bologoe

1   Finland Station
2   Nikolaevskii Station
3   Tsarskoe Selo Station
4   Warsaw Station
5   Baltic Station

To Dno

0   15   30   miles

Railways in Petrograd and environs; *preceding page*, Baltic refugees in Petrograd
(State Historical Museum, Moscow)

1

RUSSIA ENTERS THE WAR

 In 1914 Russia was hit by a severe drought. Not a drop of rain fell between Easter and the summer in most of European Russia. The crops died. A smell of burning trees and grass hung in the air. Dust blown from dry fields yellowed the city streets. Frightened, superstitious people whispered to one another that this was a bad omen for the years to come. Capturing this mood, Anna Akhmatova wrote in her poem, "July 1914":

> The sun has become a sign of God's disfavor;
> Since Easter no rain has sprinkled the fields.
> A one-legged passer-by came and,
> Alone in the courtyard, said:
>
> "Terrible times are drawing near.
> Soon the earth will be packed with fresh graves.
> You must expect famine, earthquakes, pestilence,
> And the eclipse of the heavenly bodies. . . ."[1]

On July 19, 1914, Nicholas II declared war against Germany to "preserve the honor, dignity, and unity of Russia." Thus Russia plunged into the First World War—the fateful war that was to lead to revolutions and a brutal civil war. During the seven years' savagery, Russia underwent unprecedented social and political convulsions. She entered the war as an

---

1. Anna Akhmatova, "July 1914," *Penguin Book of Russian Verse*, ed. Dimitri Obolensky (London: Penguin Books, Ltd., 1965), pp. 318-20.

obsolete autocracy, and left it as the world's first socialist state. The complexion of the world order and the lives of millions of people in Russia were to be affected by the changes that took place during this period.

But in July 1914 few foresaw the catastrophe ahead. After the declaration of war the nation was swept by a patriotic euphoria. On the day that Tsar Nicholas issued the manifesto declaring a state of war, people assembled in front of the Winter Palace in St. Petersburg carrying portraits of the tsar and holy icons. The tsar and tsarina came out onto the balcony to greet the crowds filling the massive Palace Square and spilling over into the side streets. Only a decade earlier in that same square, crowds carrying the tsar's portrait and holy icons had been fired upon by the tsar's troops. The incident, known as "Bloody Sunday," had marked the beginning of the 1905 Revolution and had shattered the naïve trust of the Russian people in the tsar. But now the hurrahs of the crowd echoed in the square. Some knelt and crossed themselves. For a brief moment Nicholas felt that tsar and people were one again.

Spontaneous patriotic demonstrations continued for a week in Petersburg, which was then renamed the more Russian sounding Petrograd. People gathered in front of the Winter Palace, the War Ministry, and the British and French embassies. Anti-German sentiment was rampant. Crowds ransacked the stores and offices owned by Germans, or by those with the misfortune to have German surnames. On July 20 a huge demonstration was staged in front of the German Embassy in Marinskaia Square near St. Isaac's Cathedral. They rampaged inside the building, throwing papers and furniture from the windows, built a huge bonfire in the square, and finally, amid the enthusiastic cheers of the crowd, knocked down the ornamental structure atop the building. One embassy employee was killed in the mêlée. The poet Zinaida Gippius noted in her diary: "Everyone went insane." The government was frightened by such outbursts, even if in support of the government, and the *gradonachal'nik* of Petrograd, Prince A. N. Obolenskii, banned further demonstrations.[2]

Patriotism pervaded all segments of society. The liberal opposition centered in the Duma (the Russian parliament), which since its inception in 1906 had been at loggerheads with Nicholas's bureaucracy,

2. *Birzhevyia vedomosti*, July 23 and 24, 1914; Gippius quoted in S. Mel'gunov, *Na putiahk k dvortsovomu perevorotu*, p. 13. The *gradonachal'nik*, appointed by and directly responsible to the minister of internal affairs, was entrusted with the task of securing peace and order in the city. He controlled the police, gendarmerie, and the secret police network, known as the *Okhrana*. The Petrograd *gradonachal'stvo*, the office of the *gradonachal'nik*, was located at the corner of Gorokhovaia and the Admiralty Prospekt.

decided to withdraw its criticism of the government for the sake of national unity. A one-day session of the Duma and the State Council, the upper house, was convened on July 26. Before the session, the members of both houses were invited to the Winter Palace where the emperor implored the members of the parliaments to do their duty to the end. His speech was greeted enthusiastically. Mikhail V. Rodzianko, chairman of the Duma, replied: "With a firm belief in the grace of God, we will grudge no sacrifices until the foe is vanquished and Russia's honor vindicated." Nicholas made the sign of the cross. A hymn, "Lord, Save Thy People," spontaneously resounded in the sumptuous Nikolaevskii Hall. Back in Tauride Palace, the site of the Duma, the entire membership, with the exception of a small number of Socialist deputies, solemnly pledged their support of the government. The Central Committee of the Kadet party, center of the liberal opposition, had voted almost unanimously their unconditional support of the government and suspension of criticism. Only F. I. Rodichev had raised an objection: "Do you really think that those fools could bring us a victory?" The Kadets' statement, written by its leader, Pavel N. Miliukov, proclaimed: "We are united in this struggle; we set no conditions and we demand nothing. On the scales of war, we simply place our firm will for victory." The "sacred union" was, it appeared, a strong bond.[3]

Patriotic fervor seized the workers as well. Their strike movement, which had gained momentum after the massacre at the Lena gold mine in 1912, had reached its peak on the eve of the war. At the beginning of July a general strike had been declared in St. Petersburg, and barricades had been erected in the streets. After the declaration of war, however, the strikes quickly dissipated.[4] Patriotic sentiment was so widespread among the workers that the Bolshevik activists admitted that it was physically dangerous even to speak against the war. The arrest of the Bolshevik deputies in the Duma, who stood against the war, did not provoke any serious protest among the workers.

In July 1914, Russia was a nation united. The liberal opposition and the workers' movement, which before the outbreak of the war had appeared to be bringing the country toward revolution, came forward to stand behind the government. The liberals pledged to withdraw their criticism and the workers flocked to volunteer for the

3. M. V. Rodzianko, *The Reign of Rasputin: An Empire's Collapse*, pp. 109–11; for the liberal political parties in Russia, see below, pp. 14–18. Rodichev quoted in Mel'gunov, *Na putiakh*, p. 14; Paul N. Miliukov, *Vospominaniia, 1859-1917* 2: 190; also see the abridged translation, Miliukov, *Political Memoirs, 1905-1917*, p. 306.

4. M. G. Fleer, *Rabochee dvizhenie v Rossii v gody imperialisticheskoi voiny*, pp. 5-8.

army. This picture of national unity brought tears to Nicholas's eyes. Such was the hypnotic hold of the war's outbreak, and it lasted until the first major defeat.

Yet while the crowds roamed the streets of Petrograd in a frenzy of support for the war, Akhmatova, moved by her uncanny premonitions, predicted the coming of a holocaust:

> A sweet smell of juniper
> Comes floating from the burning woods.
> The soldiers' wives bend over their children and moan,
> The weeping of widows echoes through the village.
>
> Not in vain were the prayers offered;
> The earth yearned for rain.
> The trampled fields were sprinkled
> With warm and red moisture.
>
> The empty sky is low, so low
> And the voice of the one who prays sounds soft:
> "They are wounding Your most holy body,
> And casting lots for Your garments."[5]

Akhmatova's poetic imagery of a one-legged peasant forecasting the savagery of modern warfare was a fitting picture of Russia's entry into the war, during which the old and the new clashed more fiercely than in any other country—a clash that was eventually to tear the nation apart. In the last decade of the nineteenth century Russia underwent spectacular industrialization under the leadership of Minister of Finance Sergei Witte that lifted Russia from slumbering backwardness and plunged her onto the path of modernization. The first wave of industrialization was financed mainly by foreign loans and by the government's "squeezing the peasant savings." The success of industrialization thus led to two of the organic weaknesses of Russian economy: foreign dependency and exhaustion of the peasants' resources. The latter weakness was manifested in the increase in peasant uprisings from 1900 to 1907. Progress itself engendered social instability.

Economic modernization also sharpened what Leopold Haimson calls "dual polarization of urban Russia: the polarization between government and society (*vlast'* and *obshchestvennost'*) and the polarization between the privileged class and the masses."[6] The "parting

5. Akhmatova, "July 1914."
6. Leopold Haimson, "The Problem of Social Stability in Urban Russia, 1905-

of the ways" of the educated class in Russia between the official
bureaucracy and the "superfluous" intelligentsia had occurred already
in the early half of the nineteenth century, but the impact of modernization made the conflict much sharper. To the liberal intelligentsia
modernization meant change not merely on an economic level, but a
wholesale westernization, of which political reform involving con-
stitutionalism and establishment of a national representative body
would be a *sine qua non*. Moreover, the emerging Russian middle class
increasingly demanded political influence commensurate with its
economic power. While the bureaucracy jealously guarded its obsolete
system of government, society groped for reforms of the political
system to bring it into the twentieth century. The tug of war between
government and society constituted one of the fundamental conflicts in
tsarist Russia.

Modernization also deepened another fundamental schism of
Russian society. Industrialization had created a new class—the industrial
proletariat. Most workers came from the village and kept their close
ties with the village communes. Many returned to the countryside
at harvest time, and some retained their land while working in the
cities. In the unfamiliar urban environment, they tended alien machinery for more than ten hours a day, and lived in crowded, unsanitary
urban ghettos. The wall that separated the poor from the privileged
was more visible in the cities than in the villages. The workers saw
the world divided into the poor who had to work and the privileged
who profited from their work—a world view basically similar to the
one they had held in the villages. Their hunger to achieve a higher
cultural level together with the spread of literacy reinforced even
more their dark anger and envy of the world from which they were
excluded. But unlike village life, urbanization brought the former
peasants a dynamic new element. Factories and workshops brought

---

1917," *Slavic Review* 23, no. 4 (1964): 619-42; 24, no. 1 (1965): 1-22. *Vlast'*
literally means "power," and it was used to mean the absolute, arbitrary power
of the tsar and his bureaucracy. *Obshchestvennost'* is an abstract noun derived
from *obshchestvo*, which is often translated as "society." On the one hand, it
was the society that existed outside *vlast'*, but on the other, it excluded the workers
and the peasantry. Specifically, the Duma, the zemstvos, the municipal self-government, industrialists, and all sorts of professional classes were included in *obshchestvo*. The adjective *obshchestvennyi* means "of *obshchestvo*," but there is no
satisfactory English equivalent. The *obshchestvennye deiateli*, for instance, were
activists who attempted to extend the power of *obshchestvo* by restricting the
absolute power of *vlast'*. In translating *obshchestvennyi* I have often used the
adjective "liberal," and at times "of society." The reader should be warned that
in most cases the term "liberal" is used in place of *obshchestvennyi*, but does
not neatly fit the definition of political liberalism in Western Europe.

the workers together, welding them into a cohesive, volatile class, and the concentration of workers in a few large cities, particularly St. Petersburg and Moscow, contributed to the rapid growth of class consciousness. After its attempt to organize the workers' movement under police tutelage failed, the tsarist government clumsily resorted almost exclusively to repressive measures, reinforcing the workers' sense of alienation from the established social order. As a result, the Russian workers became a uniquely radical social class.

The "dual polarization" had ripped Russian society apart in 1905. In this first Russian revolution two revolutions were simultaneously taking place: a revolution of society against autocracy and the revolt of the masses against the privileged class. But the tsarist regime managed to prolong its life by promising a limited constitutional concession. Nicholas issued the October Manifesto, in which he guaranteed basic civil rights to all citizens and promised to establish a national legislative body known as the State Duma. What followed after the October Manifesto was, however, a series of political backlashes that culminated in the Fundamental Laws in 1906. Contrary to the expectations of the liberals, the legislative body was to be bicameral. Together with the State Duma, the State Council was created, with half of its members directly appointed by the tsar. The Duma was encumbered by all kinds of restrictions. One of the glaring examples of the Duma's powerlessness was Article 87 of the Fundamental Laws, which gave the government emergency power to enact a law while the legislative chambers were not in session. The Duma had no power over the appointment and dismissal of ministers, which remained the exclusive right of the tsar. The Council of Ministers was not responsible to the parliament. The Duma had no legal power to check the conduct of the tsar and his bureaucracy.

It was not surprising, therefore, that the political concessions did not satisfy the liberals, but rather contributed to their intensified frustration. The first two Dumas were stormy confrontations with the government and were quickly dissolved long before they completed their terms. Anxious to create a Duma willing to cooperate with the government, Petr A. Stolypin, the powerful chairman of the Council of Ministers and minister of internal affairs, rewrote the electoral law on June 3, 1907, in such a way to assure a conservative majority—an act known as Stolypin's coup d'état. The Third Duma, in which the moderate Octobrists replaced the liberal Kadets[7] as a majority party, satisfactorily met Stolypin's expectation and dem-

7. For discussion on the liberal political parties, see below, pp. 14-18.

onstrated more willingness than its predecessors to cooperate with the government. It was the only Duma that completed its full term. But the rapprochement between government and society never materialized. Stolypin was assassinated in 1911. Although the election for the Fourth Duma in 1912 returned the Octobrists to the majority party again, it did not assure the continued cooperation between the Duma and the government. The leader of the Octobrist party, Aleksandr I. Guchkov, openly advocated reopening the attack on the government. Within the Kadet party, which never forgave the government for the change of the electoral law, the left wing that voiced the return to a more radical program gained momentum. The celebrated Beilis case, in which a Jewish carpenter was victimized by the inept, corrupt, anti-Semitic juridical system, became a rallying point for the liberals against the government. It appeared that after 1912 government and society were again on a collision course.

Resurgence of social tension was taking place against the background of rapid social transformation. Russian industry, which had suffered a setback after 1900, experienced a sudden upsurge after 1910. The second wave of industrialization was characterized by a more balanced development, growth of a mature business community, and less involvement and initiative on the part of the government. One of the factors that contributed to the second wave of industrialization was Stolypin's agrarian reform, which made excess labor in the countryside available to industry. For the first time the tsarist government attacked the village communes, which lay at the foundation of the agrarian question in Russia. Stolypin attempted to dismantle the village communes in the effort to create conservative farmers who could be counted on to support the regime. The village communes were dissolved, individual peasants appropriated lands, and some even consolidated them. But in the process thousands of peasants who could not share the advantage of the reform migrated to the city. The sudden influx, though helpful to industry, had an immensely negative effect on the social stability of urban Russia. The embittered peasants were more than eager, together with the young urban proletariat, to join radical action against established order.[8] The workers' strike movement, which had been suppressed during the "period of reaction" under Stolypin, who had not hesitated to employ draconic measures to restore peace and order after the havoc of the 1905 Revolution, was suddenly revitalized after the government troops' shortsighted firing on the mine workers at the Lena gold mine.

In protest against the Lena massacre, close to 100,000 workers

8. See Haimson, "The Problem of Social Stability," 23: 62-42.

in St. Petersburg and 250,000 in the nation struck between April 14 and 22. The workers continued to carry the momentum of the strike movement in 1913 and 1914 up to the outbreak of war. Not only did the number of strikes and participants in strikes increase, but also the workers' radicalism was demonstrated in the increasing violence against the authorities and in the growing influence of the Bolsheviks among the workers at the expense of the Mensheviks. The climax of the revived labor movement came two weeks before the outbreak of war in the Petersburg workers' general strike. The leadership of the strike shifted to younger, more impatient activists, and even the Bolsheviks were losing control of the militant workers. According to Haimson:

Many thousands of workers had then clashed with the police—at times fighting them with clubs, or hailing them with rocks from behind improvised barricades. Women and children had joined in building these barricades—out of telephone and telegraph poles, overturned wagons, boxes, and armoires. No sooner was a demonstration dispersed, or a barricade destroyed, than the workers, after evacuating their wounded, would regroup, and clashes would start all over again. Whole districts were without light, their gas and kerosene lamps having been destroyed.

Order was not restored until July 15, only four days before the outbreak of war.[9] One is struck by the uncanny resemblance between July 1914 and February 1917.

But why did the workers' strike not develop into a national revolution in July 1914 as it did in February 1917? The obvious reason was the outbreak of war. Patriotic fervor engulfed the entire society, including a large segment of the working class. The war and the "sacred union" gave the government an excuse to suppress the workers' movement. But as Haimson points out, even without the war it would have been doubtful that the Petersburg general strike could have led to a national revolution. First, it failed to set off a nation-wide political strike and remained a local labor unrest. Second, it failed to mobilize active support among other groups in society. Although the polarization between state and society had reached an impasse by 1914, the liberals sensed that they were alienated from the masses. Frightened by the violence of their revolt, they shrank from alliance with the working class against tsarism.[10] The war gave liberals, at least initially, a respite in which they could find an escape from the impasse in their confrontation with the regime, on the one hand, and from that narrow, dangerous spot in the corner where they would have to choose between

9. Ibid., 23: 642.
10. Ibid., 24: 1, 12.

revolution and counterrevolution, on the other. There was also another factor that made the difference between 1914 and 1917. Prior to July 1914, the army remained generally unaffected by the increasing social and political tensions outside, although to the extent that the army reflected the social reality of Russia, there existed within it a potentiality of dual polarization.

The question of whether the war retarded or facilitated the revolutionary process must be examined in this context. The outbreak of war contributed to a lessening of tensions: the strike movement dissipated, and the liberals pledged the "sacred union." But it was merely temporary. In the final analysis it was the war that ripened the revolutionary crisis far beyond its level in July 1914. The strike movement soon regained its prewar vitality, and the peculiar wartime conditions sharpened its intensity. The revolutionary parties gradually restored their organizational strength, more hardened and determined by the repression of the tsarist police. The *krizis verkhov* reached such a point that a reconciliation between state and society was no longer possible, and the liberals sensed with trepidation that the dreadful moment they would be forced to choose between revolution and counterrevolution was approaching every day. Finally, the war made the military more vulnerable to tensions from outside. The masses of new recruits in the army brought with them the same kind of radicalism that the uprooted peasants had brought to the cities. If city life reinforced the peasants' simplified world view of the division between the rich and the poor, the soldiers' life was more directly reminiscent of the prereform life of serfs on the landlord's estate. Moreover, polarization between state and society had progressed during the war to such a point that a majority of the officers' corps had, at least psychologically, deserted the regime. These developments of the revolutionary crisis during the war will be examined in more detail in subsequent chapters.

The challenge that the new era posed to Russia was more enormous, complex, and dangerous that any other in her recent history. Unfortunately, however, she was headed by a tsar with limited ability to face the problems with courage, energy, and imagination. If Russia had developed a system of government, either a constitutional monarchy or a *Rechtstaat,* in which a continuity of policy was assured regardless of the personal ability of the monarch, Nicholas's limitations would have mattered little. But the tsar retained privileges unknown to sovereigns in Western Europe. All executive authority throughout the empire was concentrated in him; the appointment and dismissal of ministers were matters of his will alone; the Council of Ministers, equivalent to a cabinet, was responsible only to him. Moreover, unlike the British cabinet, the Council of Ministers had no corporate responsibility. Each minister answered individually to the tsar, a system that contributed to jealousy and intrigues among them. Although the parliamentary system imposed a restriction on his absolute power, he still enjoyed vast privileges in dealing with the Duma. No laws became effective without his approval; he was assured of the conservative majority in the State Council with the right to appoint half of its members; he had the right to dissolve or prorogue the Duma whenever he deemed necessary; and he could ignore the Duma entirely with his prerogative to use Article 87.[11]

There was no question that Nicholas granted the constitutional concession in 1905 reluctantly, only under the pressure of the revolution, and that he considered the Duma a thorn in his notion of the invincibility of autocracy. Nevertheless, dissatisfied as he was with the new institution, he appears to have learned how to live with it and even at times preferred to use the Duma for his purposes. It is difficult to describe Nicholas's own political philosophy, since he did not reveal his thoughts even to his closest advisors. Historians would look in vain in his diary and his personal correspondence for clues to his ideas. Nonetheless it appears that he vacillated between advisors favoring cooperation with the Duma and reactionary advisors who advocated a hostile policy toward it; he appears to have skillfully manipulated the two camps of advisors to fit the needs of each particular time. His intellectual limitations may have prevented him from addressing himself squarely to the fundamental questions that faced Russia and he may have lacked the strategy to win the war, but he displayed an amazing array of sophisticated tactical skills to win many battles. In this limited sense, Nicholas II should be rehabilitated from the traditional interpretation that pictures him as a hopeless reactionary who had little understanding of political reality.

One of the most influential of his reactionary advisors was Nicholas's wife, Aleksandra Fedorovna. Born in a small German principality, Aleksandra came to Russia to marry Nicholas in 1894. Outwardly shy but inwardly quite strong-willed, she immediately alienated her future relatives and the St. Petersburg aristocracy. On her first day in Russia, immediately after the sudden death of Alexander III, Aleksandra saw how the relatives were slighting her weak-willed fiancé. Henceforward, Aleksandra became Nicholas's chief counselor, passionately committed to the preservation of autocracy.

Loathing the frivolous upper class in St. Petersburg, Aleksandra withdrew to a small private life centering around her family and a

---

11. See Paul P. Gronsky, *The War and the Russian Government*, pp. 3-25. The best work on the constitution in Russia is Marc Szeftel, *The Russian Constitution of April 23, 1906.*

few friends. Her inclination toward religious mysticism was heightened by the birth of their hemophiliac son, Aleksei. Stricken by guilt and driven by despair because modern science offered no cure for her sick boy, Aleksandra sought a remedy in mysticism. It was under these circumstances that Grigorii Rasputin, an illiterate *starets* (holy man) from Siberia, appeared at the imperial court. The tsarina's trusted friend, unhappy, ugly, crippled Anna Vyrubova, who was a devoted admirer of Rasputin, often served as liaison between Aleksandra and Rasputin. The *muzhik* from Siberia with his sensual goatlike body odor, hypnotic eyes, and insatiable sexual appetite, immediately hit it off well with the corrupt upper class. Rasputin discredited the authority of the tsar, but to the consternation of the decent elements in society, "Our Friend," as the imperial couple called him, remained a "man of God" to the empress. She acquired the habit of viewing the world in terms of We and They. Those who dared to speak against Us became They. Although Nicholas did not share Aleksandra's fanatical belief in the "holy man," he adamantly refused to yield to public pressure to get rid of Rasputin, since he believed that this was a family matter in which the public had no business meddling. As the Beilis case had become a rallying point of public outcry, the *Rasputinshchina* (bad era of Rasputin) became the symbol of tsarist intransigence. The tsarist power appeared to make a mockery out of the indignant public outcry and began to alienate the very section of society with which it should have allied to counter the approaching storm from below. The *krizis verkhov* had begun.

Nicholas's government at the outbreak of war was headed by the tsar's faithful servant, I. L. Goremykin. But the power of the chairman of the Council of Ministers, a position equivalent to premier or prime minister, was overshadowed by two powerful men in the cabinet, the reactionary minister of internal affairs, Nikolai A. Maklakov, and the progressive minister of agriculture, A. V. Krivoshein. After the unsatisfactory Duma election in 1912, official circles had discussed the possibility of abolishing the Duma altogether or depriving it of its legislative functions. Nikolai Maklakov was the champion of this policy. After the outbreak of war, Maklakov strongly argued in favor of dissolution of the Duma in wartime apart from ceremonial functions. But Krivoshein favored cooperation with the Duma, and proposed to reconvene the Duma not later than February 1, 1915. In the end the Council of Ministers adopted a compromise policy, accepting Krivoshein's proposal with a possibility of further postponement. Nicholas approved this decision. As long as the Duma overwhelmingly supported the "sacred union" and did not protest dissolution after its one-day session in July, there was no reason to adopt Maklakov's policy and risk arousing a sleeping dog.[12] While adopting Krivoshein's moderate policy on the reconvening, however, Nicholas allowed Maklakov to pursue a repressive policy against the liberal opposition. Censorship was introduced the day that Russia declared war; the ministry of internal affairs harassed the voluntary organizations; and two moderate liberals, Vasilii A. Maklakov (Nikolai Maklakov's own brother) and Petr B. Struve, were imprisoned for their defense during the Beilis trial in 1913. But the Duma accepted its dissolution without a whimper. When the Bolshevik deputies were arrested and deported to Siberia in flagrant violation of the parliamentary immunity extended to the members of the Duma, no protest was raised among the liberal politicians. In Pearson's words: In late 1914 the government achieved what it had failed to do in peacetime—it reduced the Duma in practice from a legislative to a consultative assembly.[13]

The composition of the Duma was (in order of ideological spectrum from the Left): Bolsheviks, 5, Mensheviks, 7, Trudoviks, 10, Progressists, 47, Kadets, 57, Octobrists, 85, Center, 33, Progressive Nationalists, 20, Nationalists, 60, and Rights, 64.[14] The Bolsheviks and the Mensheviks were Marxist revolutionaries, and the Trudoviks, led by Aleksandr F. Kerenskii, formed an independent Duma faction that stood close to the Socialist Revolutionary party. The Centrists, Nationalists, and the Rights constituted the right wing of the Duma, and stood for the monarchist principle, Russian nationalism, and the protection of landlords' interests. The largest bloc in the Fourth Duma was the liberals—Octobrists, Kadets, and Progressists.

The October Manifesto issued by Nicholas II in the 1905 Revolution had divided the Russian liberal movement. Those who accepted Nicholas's concessions, which promised basic freedoms and the creation of the parliamentary system, formed the "Union of October 17" or the Octobrist party, while the radical wing of the liberals, who refused to accept the October Manifesto as the basis of the Russian constitutional government, created the Constitutional Democratic party, the Kadets. The Octobrists, supported by the liberal-minded landowning class as well as the industrialists, was headed by one of the most colorful figures in Russian politics in the early twentieth century, Aleksandr I. Guchkov. Born to a wealthy merchant family in Moscow, Guchkov was closely connected with Moscow financial and industrial circles. Adventurous by temperament, he had participated as a volunteer in the Boer War and in the uprising in Macedonia

    12. Raymond Pearson, *The Russian Moderates and the Crisis of Tsarism, 1914-1917*, pp. 12-13.
    13. Ibid., p. 30.
    14. Ibid., p. 15.

in 1903. When the Octobrist party gained the majority in the Third Duma, he became the Duma chairman, contributing to the stabilization of the relationship between the government and the Duma. Guchkov and Stolypin respected each other and established a good working relationship, but Guchkov attacked Rasputin and earned the everlasting enmity of the imperial couple. After he fought a duel with Colonel S. N. Miasoedov (of whom more will be mentioned), Guchkov was forced to resign as chairman of the Duma in 1912, but continued to lead the Octobrist party. During the war Guchkov was one of the central figures in liberal politics both as a leader in the War Industries Committee and as one of the originators of the conspiratorial schemes for a palace coup.

The Octobrists supported the realization of basic freedoms but opposed the right of workers to strike and to form trade unions in defense industries and in those industries that vitally affected people's lives. Reflecting the landowners' interest, the Octobrists opposed the alienation of the landlords' land. Its conservative orientation was also reflected in its opposition to any kind of national autonomy within the empire. The Octobrists became the majority party in both the Third and the Fourth Dumas, but the election for the Fourth Duma increased the number of the more progressive industrialists within the party. Although in the Third Duma the Octobrists had cooperated with the government, Guchkov and his supporters including twenty Duma deputies departed from this policy in 1913, and voiced strong criticism of the government. A more conservative group of Octobrists, sixty-five Duma deputies, protested this radical direction and split from the party, forming the "Zemstvist-Octobrists." This group was led by Mikhail V. Rodzianko, who succeeded Guchkov as chairman of the Duma. A heavy-set landowner from Ekaterinoslav, nicknamed the "Bear," Rodzianko lacked Guchkov's adventurous spirit and constantly defended parliamentary method in achieving liberal reforms. During the war his moderation frustrated the more radical liberals but became a source of hope among the conservative elements of society. The split greatly weakened the Octobrist party and the process of disintegration continued during the war. Although the Octobrists provided the key to a formation of any majority in the Duma, they quickly lost their influence outside the Duma. In 1915, they ceased publication of their newspaper and the Central Committee of the party seldom met. The party members splintered into various groups centered around such leaders as Guchkov, Rodzianko, S. I. Shidlovskii, and I. V. Godnev.[15]

15. For an account of the activities of the Octobrist party, see V. S. Diakin,

The Kadets, the party of the liberal intelligentsia, represented the radical wing of the Russian liberal movement, standing for the achievement of fundamental freedoms and the end of discrimination based on class, nationality, or religion. Unlike the Octobrists, who believed that a constitutional system could be built on the October Manifesto, the Kadets maintained that to achieve this goal it would be necessary to create a "responsible government"—a government responsible to the parliament, elected on the basis of a universal, direct, equal, and secret ballot. Furthermore, they advocated independence and increased power for the local self-governments, the zemstvos. In their social policy, the Kadet party advocated a progressive income tax, an eight-hour working day, the workers' right to strike and to form trade unions, compulsory government health insurance, and the expropriation of land with compensation to the landowners.[16] It supported the autonomy of nationality minorities but opposed any move toward independence from the empire.

According to William Rosenberg, two principles were foremost in the Kadet party: a commitment to "the welfare of Russian society as a whole, rather than to the advancement of any particular social class or socioeconomic interest," and "a veneration of Russia as a state." The party perceived itself as transcending all narrow class interests and striving to achieve its ends for the welfare and freedom of all people. The Kadets advocated a social harmony in which "worker and peasant interests could not be advanced at the expense of the gentry and bourgeoisie, while Russia's upper classes could not exploit her workers and peasants."[17] They were also passionate nationalists, advocating a strong international position against Russia's adversaries. Therefore, the Kadets enthusiastically supported Russia's participation in the war and maintained that all citizens of Russia, regardless of class and nationality, should exert themselves to the utmost to win the war. Ultimately, however, the Kadets' fundamental posture of transcending class interests put them at a disadvantage: the conservatives accused them of being too radical, while Socialists and the working class viewed them as representing the interests of the Russian bourgeoisie.

Yet, from its inception in October 1905, the Kadet party provided an unmistakable intellectual leadership within the Russian liberal

Russkaia burzhuaziia i tsarizm v gody pervoi mirovoi voiny, pp. 30-33; Pearson, *Russian Moderates*, pp. 16-17. See also two recent monographs, Geoffrey A. Hosking, *The Russian Constitutional Experiment: Government and Duma, 1907-1914*; Ben-Cion Pinchuk, *The Octobrists in the Third Duma, 1907-1912*.

16. William G. Rosenberg, *Liberals in the Russian Revolution*, pp. 15-17.
17. Ibid., pp. 13-17.

movement. The party was led by Pavel N. Miliukov, a former history professor at Moscow University, well known as the author of numerous monographs on various aspects of Russian history. Brilliant, dogmatic, and arrogant, Miliukov exerted a dominant leadership over the party, maintaining a precarious unity threatened by the struggle between its right wing, represented by Vasilii Maklakov and Petr Struve, and its left wing, led by Nikolai N. Nekrasov and Prince D. I. Shakhovskoi. Later during the war Miliukov became the acknowledged leader of the Progressive Bloc, the Duma's liberal coalition formed in the summer of 1915.[18] The challenge to Miliukov's leadership came from the Left, led by Nekrasov. Dissatisfied with Miliukov's moderate policy and strict adherence to parliamentary politics, the Left Kadets called for return to earlier radical programs. Threatened by the challenge from the Left, with which the provincial Kadets and Moscow faction had increasingly sympathized, Miliukov welcomed "sacred unity" not only for patriotic reasons but also for saving the party from internal schism.[19]

The Progressist party was, according to Soviet historian V. S. Diakin, "in its composition the most bourgeois party of all."[20] The industrialists and financial leaders in Moscow, who had become disenchanted with the political and economic policy of the government, formed the party in 1911. It is important to note that a growing sense of independence as a bourgeois class was most keenly felt in the textile industry, which was least influenced by the government. Two Moscow industrialists, P. P. Riabushinskii and Aleksandr I. Konovalov, and liberal intellectual Ivan N. Efremov were the leading figures of the newly founded party. Owner of a large textile company and a large Moscow bank, Riabushinskii became spokesman for the growing Russian national bourgeoisie. In 1909 he began publication in Moscow of *Utro Rossii*, a newspaper proclaiming itself to be the organ of "the third estate of contemporary Russia," which intended to take over the nobility and bureaucracy. Konovalov, owner of textile concerns in Kostroma and Moscow, was a strong advocate of social peace between capital and labor, to be achieved by giving the workers the right to strike and form trade unions. He had formulated a plan for the joint struggle between the bourgeoisie and the proletariat against the tsarist

18. On Miliukov, see Thomas Riha, *A Russian European: Paul Miliukov in Russian Politics*. Also see Miliukov, *Vospominaniia*, and the abridged translation, *Political Memoirs*.

19. Pearson, *Russian Moderates*, pp. 18-19; Haimson, "The Problem of Social Stability," pp. 3-4.

20. Diakin, *Russkaia burzhuaziia*, p. 33.

regime, and for that purpose had created an Information Committee in 1914, in which even the Bolsheviks briefly participated.[21]

But the dream of Riabushinskii and Konovalov to create a party that would embody the interests of the entire Russian bourgeoisie did not materialize. This failure can be attributed to the impossibility of uniting two groups with vastly differing political outlooks: the financial and industrial oligarchs in St. Petersburg, and the Moscow industrialists supported by smaller provincial industrialists. The first group formed the conservative St. Petersburg Association of Factory Owners, led by such financial magnates as A. I. Putilov (head of the Russo-Asian Bank) and A. I. Vyshnegradskii (head of the International Bank). This group proved to be more docile politically, preferring to gain profit from their close cooperation with the bureaucracy. In contrast, the Moscow and provincial industrialists, who were generally excluded from the special favors extended by the government to the St. Petersburg magnates, were critical of the government. The Progressist party not only failed to lure the St. Petersburg oligarchs into the party, it could not even mobilize the provincial industrialists. According to Progressist P. A. Buryshkin, the party organization did not exist outside the Duma, and if the Progressist party played some role in the liberal politics during the war, it was not owing to its strength but to the energetic leadership of the two leaders, Konovalov and Efremov.[22]

During the war the liberals had two avenues through which they expressed their opinions: the Duma and the so-called voluntary organizations. Following a one-day session in July 1914, the Duma members met privately under the leadership of Rodzianko, and decided to establish a Provisional Committee for the Relief of the Wounded and Sick Soldiers and War Sufferers. This committee, originally designed for relief work, gradually acquired political significance. During the recess of the Duma it was the only organ of the Duma, "which, though sanctioned by no law and brought into existence *de facto*, remained

---

21. Haimson, "The Problem of Social Stability," pp. 4-8.
22. P. A. Buryshkin, *Moskva kupecheskaia*, p. 284; Pearson, *Russian Moderates*, pp. 17-18. See also an unpublished dissertation by Lawrence W. Lerner, "The Progressists in the Russian State Duma, 1907-1915." For the division of the Russian industrialists, see Ruth A. Roosa, "Russian Industrialists and 'State Socialism,' 1906-17," *Soviet Studies* 23, no. 3 (1972): 395-417; James White, "Moscow, Petersburg, and the Russian Industrialists," *Soviet Studies* 24, no. 3 (1973): 414-20; Ruth A. Roosa, " 'United' Russian Industry," *Soviet Studies* 24, no. 3, (1973): 420-25; Lewis Siegelbaum, "Russian Industrialists and the First World War: The Failure of the National Bourgeoisie," *Slavic and Soviet Series* 2, no. 1 (1977): 31-48.

. . . the guardian of the interests of the Duma."[23] It is important to remember that during the February Revolution, faced with the prorogation of the Duma and with the revolutionary crisis, the Duma delegates were to follow this precedent by creating a Duma committee. Usually the Provisional Committee met twice a week and discussed a number of current problems, but there soon emerged a demand for convening a long-term session of the Duma. Rodzianko was urged to use his "right of personal report" to the emperor to present this demand. Henceforth Rodzianko emerged as the spokesman for the Duma and for public opinion.

Another arena for the liberals' activities was in the voluntary organizations. On July 30, 1914, a congress of zemstvo representatives was held at which the zemstvo activists created the All-Russian Union of Zemstvos for the relief of the sick and the wounded. A little later the municipal self-governments followed suit by forming the All-Russian Union of Towns. These two voluntary organizations were headed respectively by two Progressists, Prince G. E. L'vov and M. L. Chelnokov, and were concerned with providing relief for the wounded and the sick, supplying sanitary trains and hospitals, aiding evacuees, combating epidemics, and getting food to the populace. Despite the practical tasks they set for themselves, patriotism was not the only motive behind the zemstvo and municipal self-government activists' participation in war efforts. Katkov's indictment of the voluntary organizations as a Trojan horse from which the liberals attempted to take over the entire state machinery may be an exaggeration, but he has a valid point: some activists in the Union of Zemstvos and the Union of Towns clearly sought to make them instruments of political reform. It is precisely for this reason that Minister of Internal Affairs Maklakov had opposed the creation of the voluntary organizations and that after their establishment attempted to curtail their activities. When Rodzianko requested permission to hold a meeting of the zemstvo representatives to discuss the supply of boots for the army, Maklakov refused on the grounds that the zemstvos would, under this guise, demand a constitution.[24] Despite Maklakov's objections

23. Gronsky, *War and the Russian Government*, pp. 28–29.

24. George Katkov, *Russia 1917: The February Revolution*, pp. 3–11; Diakin, *Russkaia burzhuaziia*, p. 68. See also an insightful article, Thomas Fallows, "Politics and the War Effort in Russia: The Union of Zemstvos and the Organization of the Food Supply, 1914–1916," *Slavic Review* 37, no. 1 (1978): 70–90. For the activities of the Unions of Zemstvos and Towns, see an unpublished dissertation, William E. Gleason, "The All-Russian Union of Towns and the All-Russian Union of Zemstvos in World War I: 1914–1917." For Rodzianko and Maklakov, see Rodzianko, *Reign of Rasputin*, pp. 119–20.

and obstructions, however, the Union of Zemstvos and the Union of Towns became deeply involved in war efforts, particularly in the food supply. The more deeply involved they became, the more these voluntary organizations depended on government subsidies and direction. From the government's point of view, too, the activities of the voluntary organizations became such an integral part of the war effort that it could no longer ignore them. This mutual dependence at the time when polarization between state and society was progressing to an irrevocable point became the unique characteristic of the relationship between the liberals and the government during the war.

The First World War glaringly revealed the schism between the new century into which the world was plunging and the old era from which it was emerging. It was the first modern war for which the entire industrial resources of a country were mobilized and the economy restructured. It was fought with armaments produced by the most advanced technology. Tanks, airplanes, and poison gas made their first appearance in warfare. The technological advances in artillery and rifles made traditional military strategy obsolete. When infantry rifles could fire up to fifteen rounds a minute at a range of two miles, a cavalry became useless. On the first day of the war, a Russian cavalry commander wept at the sight of the total annihilation of his unit. Yet tanks were too slow and too vulnerable, so despite severe limitations, armies had to continue to rely on horses for mobile attack. Military historian Norman Stone noted recently:

In general, the First World War was marked by an extreme, and extraordinary, dichotomy between weight and mobility, the two vital principles of warfare. Armies had been able to benefit from the economic strides of the nineteenth century, but not yet from those of the twentieth. Agriculture and railways had developed far enough for the supply and maintenance of millions of men to become possible. . . . But though these could be given lavish armament and supply, there was not much to make them mobile once they got beyond railheads. There was, in other words, a twentieth-century delivery-system, but a nineteenth-century warhead.[25]

Eventually Russia was knocked out of the war, not because her military technology was inferior to the enemy's, but rather because her sociopolitical system could not stand the strain of protracted modern warfare. To paraphrase Stone, her defeat was caused by the conflict between a twentieth-century war and a nineteenth-century body politic. The military themselves were hopelessly divided between "Sukhomlinovites" and "anti-Sukhomlinovites," front commanders and War Ministry, War Ministry and General Staff, northwestern front

25. Norman Stone, *The Eastern Front*, pp. 45, 50.

and southwestern front, and artillerists and infantry.[26] The Russian army, though equipped with the most advanced armament, continued to be plagued by its traditional organizational weakness. The Stavka, the general headquarters, was created, but it was powerless to resolve these divisions. Grand Duke Nikolai Nikolaevich, the tsar's uncle, was appointed commander in chief, and General N. N. Ianushkevich his chief of staff, but they were merely figureheads and had little influence over the conduct of war. The war minister, V. A. Sukhomlinov, under the aegis of the tsar himself, was powerful, but not powerful enough to silence his opponents.

Early in the war the Russians suffered a defeat at Tannenberg—a defeat in which 100,000 Russian soldiers and 400 guns were captured by the Germans, and during which General Samsonov, who led the offensive, shot himself. At the Galician front, where the Russians faced a less capable enemy, they achieved some success. At the beginning of 1915, the Russian army began an ill-prepared offensive through the Carpathians toward Hungary under the commander of the southwestern front, General N. I. Ivanov. But as soon as the German counteroffensive led by General August von Mackensen began in April, the Russians suffered defeat after defeat. The Great Retreat had begun. By summer all of Russian Poland, Lithuania, and a part of Belorussia, together with a large industrial region including Warsaw, L'vov, and Vilnus, fell into enemy hands. The defeat on the battlefield gave the Russians a rude awakening and drastically changed the political climate of the nation. The liberals began to criticize the government and the workers showed the first signs of restlessness.

An acute shortage of ammunition was blamed for the crushing defeat of the Russian army in 1915. That such a shortage existed is undeniable. Sukhomlinov and the Artillery Administration had grossly underestimated the demand for shells and rifles, partly because no one had foreseen that the war would last so long. The Franco-Russian General Staff agreement had assumed that the war would be over in six weeks. But they were wrong not only about the length of the war, but also about the consuming need for shells and rifles in modern warfare. A reserve of seven million shells—a figure based on the expenditures of the Russo-Japanese War—was expected to last the entire war. That amounted to about a thousand rounds per field gun, and as it turned out that was not enough in 1916 to keep a gun going for ten days. Sukhomlinov and the Artillery Administration were guilty of making no preparations for mobilizing Russian industries to cope with the great demand. They had relied exclusively on the

26. Ibid., passim.

existing state factories, the production capacity of which was absurdly low. In the Sestroretsk Weapons Factory only 4,530 rifles were manufactured in 1913, and shortly before the war began, production had stopped completely. Not until July 1914 was production resumed and 19 rifles produced. The Tula Gun Factory, the largest in the empire, manufactured only 16 rifles in seven months of 1914. As a result, in the first year of the war an entire army, or 140,000 soldiers, were left without rifles. It is estimated that the Stavka's minimum demand for shells was five times greater than the production norms of 1914.[27]

By the end of 1914 the shell and rifle shortage was finally recognized by Sukhomlinov and the Artillery Administration. They decided to solve the crisis by placing orders with foreign weapon companies rather than developing the war industries in Russia. They had little confidence in Russian industry and mistakenly concluded that going outside would be faster and less costly. "If these foreign firms had done their work," concludes Stone, "there would have been neither shell nor rifle crisis." But there were endless delays. An English firm, Vickers, which had received forty million rubles in advance, failed to deliver the promised shells, and only 9 percent of the Winchester order and 12 percent of the Remington and Westinghouse orders for rifles from the United States were honored. By relying on foreign firms, Russia fell deeply in debt for armaments she did not receive. More important, she forfeited valuable time in developing her own industries to meet the needs of the war.[28]

Yet the shell shortage was merely one aspect of the complex shortcomings of the Russian army. The division within the army and the obsolete, unimaginative military thinking of the commanders contributed equally to the defeat. For instance, the artillerists had insisted on the value of fortresses. Accepting their argument over Sukhomlinov's objections, the army had poured enormous resources and had concentrated large number of guns and shells in these strategic strongholds, which turned out to be nothing but useless military museums. More important, the army structure began to show signs of collapse as early as 1915. The annihilation of forty thousand officers in 1914, the cream of the officers' corps, contributed to a widening chasm between officers and men. There were not enough personnel to train the new recruits, who arrived at the front ignorant and undisciplined. Officers complained incessantly of the poor quality of

27. Ibid., pp. 45, 146; A. L. Sidorov, *Ekonomicheskoe polozhenie Rossii v gody pervoi mirovoi voiny*, pp. 11-12.

28. Stone, *Eastern Front*, p. 160; Sidorov, *Ekonomicheskoe polozhenie*, p. 262.

soldiers, "who held rifles like peasants with a rake." As a result, unnecessarily harsh measures were imposed on the soldiers. But the officers, fresh from a few weeks' of rushed training, were themselves often incompetent and the soldiers responded with insolence, inertia, and passive resistance. This chasm was to grow wider in the years to follow.[29]

The surge of patriotism at the outbreak of war hypnotized Russian society, which united behind the tsar. For the common struggle against the external enemy, people seemed to forget and forgive internal discord. But peace did not last long. As soon as the Russian army suffered a humiliating defeat, the monster of internal strife that was put to rest only temporarily raised its head. The liberals began to criticize the government. The workers in Petrograd were awakening from their somnolent inertia.

29. For the relationship between officers and soldiers, see chap. 8.

2

THE POLITICAL CRISIS
OF SUMMER 1915

 The dissatisfaction of the liberals with the government in the spring of 1915 was expressed in three demands: to allow increased participation in the war effort by representatives of society, to reopen the Duma, and to dismiss some of the unpopular ministers. Faced with a humiliating military defeat, Nicholas was forced to make concessions. He created a special council for national defense in which representatives of society were invited to participate. He also reconvened the Duma in July and dismissed four ministers. But the worsening situation on the battlefield hardened the liberals' stand. In the summer of 1915, those in the Duma coalesced into the Progressive Bloc, demanding moderate internal reforms. Adding a third component to the existing voluntary organizations, the disgruntled industrialists formed the War Industries Committee and stepped up their attacks on the government. Alarmed by the liberals' increasing voice in the making of decisions and suspicious of their demands for political reforms, Nicholas refused to yield to their pressure. In the summer of 1915, his differences with the liberals created the first serious political crisis since the outbreak of the war.

The retreat of the Russian army wounded the pride of patriotic Russians, who believed the shell shortage to be the cause of the defeat. In the spring and summer of 1915, the shortage was at its most critical point—reserves were exhausted and new orders failed to arrive. At this point the Russian industrialists took the initiative and began to organize the nation's economy for the war effort. Liberal leaders such as Rodzianko and Guchkov took inspection tours of the front for a firsthand view. Sukhomlinov complained: "A. I. Guchkov is basically thrusting his paws into the army. In the Stavka they must know this, but they take no measures against it. . . . In my opinion this can create a very dangerous situation for our existing state order."[1] Not only did the Stavka take no measures against the visits of Guchkov and Rodzianko, but it enthusiastically supported Rodzianko's plan to solve the shell shortage. The Octobrists who had close connections with the financial and industrial magnates in Petrograd had discussed the possibility of creating a special council composed of representatives of the War Ministry, the Duma, and the industrialists to coordinate and supervise economic activities. In early May, Rodzianko and the supporters of this idea, V. P. Litvinov-Filanskii and two financial magnates, Vyshnegradskii and Putilov, petitioned the tsar to create such a council. Nicholas accepted their petition and on May 14 the Special Council for Improvement of Artillery Supplies for the Active Army, composed of the chairman and three representatives of the Duma (three Octobrists), representatives from the War Ministry, and Vyshnegradskii and Putilov representing private industry, had its first meeting.[2] This concession by Nicholas was the beginning of a period of reconciliation.

The industrialists presented a demand at the council meetings for better coordination between the artillery administration and private industry. A major part of the discussion by the council was devoted to drafting a plan for government orders for armaments from private industry. According to Sidorov, "this was a major economic and political victory of the bourgeoisie."[3] The formation of the special council was a tactical victory from the government's point of view as well, because it split the industrialists into two opposing forces and thus weakened the chance of a concerted effort by the industrialists against the government. By allowing the conservative Petrograd industrial magnates to participate in the special council, the government succeeded in preventing them from joining with the liberals in opposition to the government. The Petrograd oligarchs, who were making tremendous profits from government contracts, completely dropped out of the political struggle.

The Kadets refused to participate in the special council on the grounds that it was headed by Sukhomlinov, whom they considered responsible for the shell shortage.[4] Instead they prepared a legislative

1. A. L. Sidorov, *Ekonomicheskoe polozhenie Rossii v gody pervoi mirovoi voiny*, p. 56.

2. M. V. Rodzianko, *The Reign of Rasputin: An Empire's Collapse*, pp. 130-34.

3. Sidorov, *Ekonomicheskoe polozhenie*, pp. 62-63.

4. Rodzianko, *Reign of Rasputin*, p. 134.

bill for the creation of a centralized body to deal with all war supply matters—a body that was to be under the tighter control of the Duma. In responding to these criticisms, the government countered with an attempt to reorganize the special council. It created four special councils under four different ministries: the Special Council for Defense under the War Ministry, a council for transportation under the Ministry of Transport, a council for food supply under the Ministry of Agriculture, and a council for fuel under the Ministry of Trade and Industry. The government made concessions to the liberals by extending the membership on these councils to the representatives of the Duma, industry, the War Industries Committee, the Union of Zemstvos, and the Union of Towns. Nevertheless, the government firmly maintained bureaucratic control over the councils, chaired by the respective minister, who had veto power.

The Moscow industrialists and other smaller provincial industrialists had resented that they were initially excluded from the special council created in May. This frustration led them to establish the War Industries Committee to mobilize the smaller industrialists in the war effort. On May 26, the Ninth Congress of the Representatives of Industry and Trade was held. Its major theme was the "mobilization of industry," a slogan advanced by Moscow industrialists and supported by the Kadets and the provincial industrialists. The congress decided to create local committees for the conversion of local industries to war industries. "To coordinate all work of various localities and groups and to accommodate this work with the activities of the higher governmental agencies," a Central War Industries Committee was created. The Moscow industrialists, who championed the opposition to the Petrograd magnates, succeeded in taking over its leadership and elected Guchkov chairman of the Central War Industries Committee and Konovalov vice-chairman.[5]

Although the War Industries Committee played an important role politically by voicing sharp criticism of the government, its economic role was minuscule. It merely served as an intermediary between government agencies and provincial industrialists. Financially the committee was almost exclusively dependent on state subsidies. Important issues dealing with the organization of a war economy were determined by the special councils and the War Industries Committee was limited

5. V. S. Diakin, *Russkaia burzhuaziia i tsarizm v gody pervoi mirovoi voiny*, pp. 91-94; Lewis Siegelbaum, "Russian Industrialists and the First World War: The Failure of the National Bourgeoisie," *Slavic and Soviet Studies* 2, no. 1 (1977): 40-41; Raymond Pearson, *The Russian Moderates and the Crisis of Tsarism, 1914-1917*, pp. 34-35.

to exerting some influence in these councils in behalf of the provincial industrialists. During their first two years, the military orders received by the War Industries Committee from government agencies constituted no more than 3 to 5 percent of the total orders. Actual fulfillment of orders amounted to even less. The special councils, therefore, had ample reason to complain about the poor performance of the War Industries Committee. The government, disturbed by the increased involvement of the War Industries Committee in political matters, even considered cutting off government subsidies. The shrill voices of the leaders of the War Industries Committee called not for the takeover of the entire function of the state, as Katkov argues, but for concessions from the government. This group had no intention of overthrowing the government upon which their existence depended.[6]

As soon as the Russian army began its humiliating retreat, the liberals began looking for scapegoats. They directed their criticism at the ministers hostile to the liberals. In mid-May, during an audience with the tsar, Rodzianko recommended the dismissal of four—Maklakov (minister of internal affairs), I. G. Shcheglovitov (justice), V. K. Sabler (procurator of the holy synod), and Sukhomlinov (war). At the same time, the liberals demanded the reopening of the Duma, which was suspended since the outbreak of the war except for a three-day session to pass the budget in January 1915. At the end of May the All-Russian Congress of the Representatives of Industry and Trade passed a resolution calling for immediate convocation of the Duma. The Unions of Zemstvos and Towns passed a similar resolution.[7] The liberal campaign for the convocation of the Duma and the dismissal of unpopular ministers found sympathetic ears even in the government. Seven ministers led by Krivoshein, meeting at the apartment of Foreign Minister S. D. Sazonov, decided that the Duma should convene as quickly as possible and, to achieve cooperation with the Duma, the four ministers should be dismissed. This opinion was later supported by Goremykin, who made the recommendation to Nicholas.[8]

On June 5, Nicholas signed the imperial rescript dismissing Maklakov. Nikolai Maklakov, a reactionary monarchist who consistently opposed liberal forces and attempted to block encroachment by society in the affairs of government, was singularly hated by even

6. Sidorov, *Ekonomicheskoe polozhenie*, pp. 191-212; Norman Stone, *The Eastern Front*, pp. 194-211; George Katkov, *Russia, 1917: The February Revolution*, pp. 7-11.

7. Rodzianko, *Reign of Rasputin*, p. 132; Diakin, *Russkaia burzhuaziia*, p. 75.

8. E. D. Chermenskii, *IV gosudarstvennaia duma i sverzhenie tsarizma v Rossii*, p. 87; Pearson, *Russian Moderates*, p. 41.

conservative Octobrists. Since the outbreak of the war he had sent
repeated warnings to the governors about the evil intentions of the
voluntary organizations and instructing the governors to discourage
their meetings. At the Council of Ministers' meeting he strongly opposed the formation of the special council, since it included the representatives from the Duma and industry. The day before his dismissal
some liberal leaders, including Petr Struve and Maklakov's own liberal
brother, Vasilii, gathered: "We racked our brains whom to dispatch
to the tsar to present a petition to persuade him to dismiss Maklakov."
On the following day, the liberals rejoiced at the news of his dismissal.[9] Now they directed their attention toward another target,
Sukhomlinov.

Sukhomlinov had a bad press. To be sure, he was corrupt and
politically reactionary, as most of the tsarist government's ministers
were. (If, in general, greed and politics are twin brothers, one would
be hard pressed to name one Russian high official at the turn of the
century who was above bribery.) Sukhomlinov was held responsible
for the catastrophic shell shortage in 1915, and Russia's unpreparedness for war in general. But as Stone points out, Sukhomlinov's arguments for modernizing the army, which had been rejected by his
political enemies in the army, made more sense than has been recognized. As for the shell shortage, it would have taken a clairvoyant
to foresee the length of the war and the demand for shells in modern
warfare. The real causes for the defeat of the Russian army lay in
areas for which Sukhomlinov was not directly responsible. The vicious
attacks against Sukhomlinov in the spring of 1915 were politically
motivated. The liberals wanted a pound of flesh from the government
for the humiliating defeat, and no one was better suited to be that
scapegoat than Sukhomlinov, a favorite of the tsar and the tsarina.
The liberals' demand was supported by anti-Sukhomlinovites in the
army who were resentful of the army reforms he had carried out—
reforms that led to the loss of their political influence in the army.
Those leaders in the Stavka and on the southwestern front were actually more responsible for bringing about the catastrophic defeat
than Sukhomlinov himself, but creating the impression that the
defeat was caused by a shell shortage, which was in turn caused by
Sukhomlinov's incompetence, served to cover up their own responsibility. The liberals eagerly accepted the explanation of the anti-Su-
khomlinovite generals. In February Sukhomlinov's slipping prestige
was dealt a heavy blow by the arrest of his protegé, Colonel S. N.
Miasoedov. Suspected of being a German spy, Miasoedov was tried

9. Chermenskii, *IV gosudarstvennaia duma*, p. 88.

by a military tribunal and executed, although there was actually no evidence to substantiate the charge against him. The affair was, as Polivanov later confessed, a "judicial murder," carried out by Sukhomlinov's enemies, one of whom was Sukhomlinov's successor, General A. A. Polivanov. The liberals, who had shown great courage for the cause of human rights in the notorious Beilis case, this time lent a hand to the miscarriage of justice. It marked the beginning of a vicious whispering campaign that contributed, with its innuendos and inflated, unsubstantiated charges appealing to the popular imagination, to Sukhomlinov's downfall and eventually to the loss of prestige of the imperial government. The argument went: If Miasoedov was a proven German spy, Sukhomlinov a proven traitor, then what is the empress? After all, she is a German woman, isn't she?[10]

In the face of mounting pressure from the liberals, the army generals, and now a majority of his own government, Nicholas regretfully parted with the war minister. "It is for him much better to avoid a scandal," he confided to his wife.[11] On June 11, unable to tell Sukhomlinov the bad news personally, Nicholas had a letter of dismissal delivered to his home. On the following day, Sabler, a staunch supporter of Rasputin, and Shcheglovitov, one of the organizers of the Beilis case, were dismissed. Public vindictiveness did not end with Sukhomlinov's dismissal. In 1916 he was arrested, tried on the charge of treason, and found guilty. Sir Edward Grey cryptically remarked to the visiting Duma delegates in England: "Brave is a government that decides at the time of war to try a War Minister for treason."[12] Sukhomlinov's personal enemy, A. A. Polivanov, was appointed the new minister of war, despite the empress's strenuous opposition. The only reactionary minister left in the cabinet was its chairman, Goremykin. The period of reconciliation was in full swing.

Besides dismissing the four ministers, Nicholas made another concession to liberal demands. The Duma was convened on July 19. The liberals, however, were not united on tactics to be employed in the new sessions. Progressist Ivan N. Efremov attacked Miliukov and advocated pressure to force Goremykin out.[13] The split between Left and Right had become more serious within the Kadet party. The

10. Stone, *Eastern Front*, pp. 17-43, 197-98; S. Mel'gunov, *Na putiakh k dvortsovomu perevorotu*, pp. 20-29. Stone rehabilitates Sukhomlinov, who has been considered a corrupt, incompetent minister of war and largely responsible for the Russian defeat in the spring of 1915. Polivanov is quoted in Stone, *Eastern Front*, p. 198; on the Miasoedov affair, see Katkov, *Russia, 1917*, pp. 119-32.

11. Quoted in Diakin, *Russkaia burzhuaziia*, p. 79.

12. Quoted in Mel'gunov, *Na putiakh*, p. 28.

13. Pearson, *Russian Moderates*, pp. 42-43.

left-wing Kadets criticized Miliukov's leadership and his inaction in the face of the mounting crisis in the country. They insisted on reviving the Kadet legislative plans, which included a demand for establishment of a "responsible ministry," namely, one responsible to the Duma. Miliukov strongly opposed such demands. In his opinion, it would be impossible to pursue the war without the cooperation of the government and its continuation should be the foremost task of the Kadets, one to which all other demands should be subordinated. He countered their demand with one for the establishment of a "ministry of confidence." The difference was not merely semantic: a "ministry of confidence" meant the acceptance by the liberals of the bureaucracy with a change of its personnel, a "responsible ministry" would have meant the replacement of the bureaucracy by the liberals, which would have been possible only through a drastic constitutional change. Vasilii Maklakov stated: "the slogan of a responsible ministry is at this moment revolutionary."[14] Miliukov and Maklakov feared that stepping up political demands would contribute to the revival of a mass movement. As early as July there was a sharp increase in strikes. According to Miliukov, "not to support the government now would mean to play with fire." In the Kadet conference held on June 6 to 8, Miliukov's opinion was supported overwhelmingly. Dissatisfied with the leadership, the left-wing Kadets sought mass support by devoting their energy to organizing social welfare departments in the cities and the labor exchanges. These organizations became points of contact between the liberal intelligentsia and the representatives of the workers' movement led by the moderate Socialists, although the Kadets did not have much success in achieving mass support among the workers.[15]

The Duma session opened as the military situation worsened. On July 24 Warsaw was taken. Then the fortresses of Brest, Novogeorgievsk, Ossovets, and Kovno, which had been considered invincible, fell one after another. On July 16, the new war minister declared that the nation was in danger, which brought two reactions from the liberals. One group, represented by Miliukov, considered that the demand for change required more caution; the more radical liberals, such as Nekrasov, concluded that it was now time to attack the government more aggressively. Nekrasov suggested to his Kadet colleagues that it

14. Quoted in Chermenskii, *IV gosudarstvennaia duma*, p. 85.
15. Quoted in Diakin, *Russkaia burzhuaziia*, pp. 82-83, 85-86. Miliukov reversed the Kadets' previous policy of nonparticipation in the Special Council for Defense after Sukhomlinov's dismissal. In protest, Nekrasov resigned from the Party Central Committee. Pearson, *Russian Moderates*, p. 47.

was time to be prepared to "take all power and all responsibility into our hands." Miliukov, on the other hand, appealed to the government: "Remove the road block, give the public organizations a way, give the nation internal peace." Despite the Progressists' insistence on the establishment of a responsible ministry, a majority of the Duma liberals accepted Miliukov's moderate demand: the formation of a ministry of public confidence.[16]

The political crisis in August 1915 involved two issues: Nicholas's decision to assume the supreme commandership and the government's attitude toward the newly formed Progressive Bloc in the Duma. Nicholas's decision to assume the supreme command was prompted by his concept of the duties of the sovereign in time of war, and by the empress's jealousy of Grand Duke Nikolai Nikolaevich. Aleksandra believed that the grand duke harbored ambitions to replace the emperor and was playing a dangerous game with Duma liberals. This decision had a positive aspect. The emperor's assumption of the supreme command would eliminate the division of authority between the civilian government and the military authorities, a division that had been a constant source of conflict in the theater of war. Since it was expected that the actual command of the army would not be taken by the emperor, who knew little about military operations, the military leaders were not concerned with the possibility of his meddling in military matters. In fact, the Stavka in Mogilev under the new chief of staff, General N. V. Alekseev, who replaced General Ianushkevich, was a remarkable improvement over Grand Duke Nikolai Nikolaevich's Stavka.[17] There were, however, grave dangers in this decision. Any defeat would taint the prestige of the emperor, who would be responsible as commander-in-chief for military strategy. More important, the new task would require Nicholas to stay in Mogilev, thus giving the empress and her friends in the capital more opportunity to meddle in government policies. It was for these reasons that when Polivanov broke the news of the tsar's decision on August 6 at the meeting of the Council of Ministers, a majority of the ministers were opposed. During the Council of Ministers' meetings from August 9 to 11 various ministers expressed their concern about the worsening political situation. Kharitonov stated: "The army and the population are resting their hope, not on us, but on the State Duma and the War Industries

---

16. Diakin, *Russkaia burzhuaziia*, p. 96; Miliukov quoted in Chermenskii *IV gosudarstvennaia duma*, p. 90; see also p. 91, and Pearson, *Russian Moderates*, pp. 47-48.

17. Stone, *Eastern Front*, pp. 191-93. For Nicholas's assumption of the supreme commandership and the cabinet members' reaction to his decision, see Pearson, *Russian Moderates*, pp. 54-56.

Committee." Shcherbatov remarked: "The government is hanging in the air, having no support from either below or above." Asked by Goremykin how to combat the revolutionary movement, Shcherbatov replied: "How do you want me to combat the growing revolutionary movement when I was denied the cooperation of the troops on the grounds that they are unreliable and that it is uncertain to make them shoot at crowds. With police alone it would be impossible to pacify the whole of Russia." Krivoshein, the most outspoken leader of the ministers who opposed the tsar's assumption of power, came to the conclusion that the only way out of this political crisis would be to reach a compromise with the Duma. But for this purpose he considered it necessary to form a majority in the Duma, composed of the monarchist faction from the Right to the Kadets.[18]

On August 11 and 12 the representatives of the Duma and the State Council met together and discussed a common platform to pursue. They decided to form a Progressive Bloc, which comprised two thirds of the Duma, excluding only those from the extreme Right and the Left. The program the Duma liberals agreed upon, according to an American historian, Michael Hamm, "offered at least a token for everyone: for peasants, equalization of rights; for workers, restoration of labor union activities and the labor press; for national minorities, an end to repression and exploitation."[19] But to reach a compromise with more conservative elements, the Kadets, the driving force of the Progressive Bloc, had to withdraw their platform: nothing was mentioned about social reforms; nationality questions were skirted. The only important point of the Progressive Bloc's program rested with its demand for the formation of a ministry of confidence. Even here the Kadet leadership had to oppose a more radical demand from the Left Kadets and the Progressists for the formation of a responsible ministry. Politically, the Progressive Bloc was characterized more by a willingness to reach a compromise with the government than by hostility toward it. As Miliukov, its foremost leader, stated, the formation of the Progressive Bloc was a "safety-valve of the drowning monarchy," and

18. Chermenskii, *IV gosudarstvennaia duma*, pp. 96, 109; Diakin, *Russkaia burzhuaziia*, p. 110. For the Council of Ministers' meeting during the political crisis in the summer of 1915, see A. Iakhontov, "Tiazhelye dni: Sekretnyia zasedaniia Soveta Ministrov—16 juliia-2 sentiabria, 1915 goda," *Arkhiv russkoi revoliutsii* 28 (1926): 5-136, and the translation, Michael Cherniavsky, *Prologue to Revolution: Notes of A. N. Iakhontov on the Secret Meetings of the Council of Ministers, 1915.* See also Pearson, *Russian Moderates*, pp. 49-50. The necessity of forming such a majority was also expressed in Struve's letter to Krivoshein.

19. Michael F. Hamm, "Liberal Politics in Wartime Russia: An Analysis of the Progressive Bloc," *Slavic Review* 33, no. 3 (1974): 455.

"the last measure to find a peaceful way out of the situation, which was from day to day growing more and more threatening." Their Socialist colleagues in the Duma, who had hoped that the liberals would take a more militant stand against the government, were disappointed. Kerenskii commented: "We do not judge you, we do not wish to fight with you, and we will calmly wait until you are disillusioned . . . and come to us for help."[20]

In the middle of August, anticipating the reorganization of the government, the liberal circles were busy formulating lists of cabinet members acceptable for a ministry of confidence. The Progressists' newspaper in Moscow, *Utro Rossii,* published on August 13 a list of of prospective ministers consisting of Rodzianko (premier), Guchkov (internal affairs), Miliukov (foreign affairs), Shingarev (finance), Nekrasov (transport), Konovalov (trade and industry), Krivoshein (agriculture), Polivanov (war), Savich (navy), Efremov (state comptroller), Ignatiev (education), and V. L'vov (procurator of the holy synod).[21] One should not take these busily circulated rumors as evidence of efforts by the liberals to take over power from the government. Such an ambition was far from being the goal of the liberal politicians in August 1915. Miliukov stated: "We do not seek power now. . . . It is now only necessary to change the head of the government with a wise bureaucrat." According to Vasilii Maklakov, the government could not be formed by the liberals alone, "because we don't know

20. Quoted in Thomas Riha, *A Russian European: Paul Miliukov in Russian Politics,* p. 227. For the program of the Progressive Bloc, see also Pearson, *Russian Moderates,* p. 51.

21. Chermenskii, *IV gosudarstvennaia duma,* p. 98. This list reflects the Progressists' thinking. Chermenskii gives still three other lists, which he discovered in Nicholas II's archives. According to this, the Kadets favored the following lists: G. E. L'vov (chairman), G. E. L'vov (internal affairs), Miliukov (foreign affairs), Polivanov (war), Savich (navy), Maklakov (justice), Ignatiev (education), V. N. L'vov (procurator of the holy synod), Konovalov (trade and industry), Dobrovol'skii (transport), and Pokrovskii (finance). The Octobrists' candidates consisted of the following: Guchkov (chairman), G. E. L'vov (internal affairs), Sazonov (foreign affairs), Guchkov (war), Savich (navy), Manukhin (justice), Kovalevskii (education), V. N. L'vov (procurator of holy synod), Konovalov (trade and industry), Nemeshev (transport), and Shingarev (finance). The members of the Progressive Bloc in the State Council favored the following list: Shcherbatov (chairman), V. I. Gurko (internal affairs), Miliukov (foreign affairs), Polivanov (war), Manukhin (justice), Ignatiev (education), V. N. L'vov (procurator of holy synod), Konovalov (trade and industry), Nemeshev (transport), and Shingarev (finance). These differences indicate that there was little agreement among the members of the Progressive Bloc on who should be the members of a ministry of confidence.

anything about the governmental matters. We don't know the techniques. And we don't have time to learn now."[22]

The cabinet was split on the two issues—the decision of Nicholas to assume the supreme command and the attitude toward the Progressive Bloc. In the background of the political crisis was the specter of the rapidly growing workers' movement in Petrograd. Finally jarred from dormancy, the workers in Petrograd rose in August, in the first large political strike since the outbreak of war, to protest the killing of workers in Ivanovo-Voznesensk. A strike that had begun in the city's largest plant, Putilov Factory, at the beginning of September developed into a general strike involving more than 82,000 workers.[23] It seemed imperative for the majority of ministers to seek a compromise with the Duma liberals to avoid a crisis. Nicholas's assumption of the supreme command and his rejection of a compromise with the Progressive Bloc, they feared, would drive the liberals to the side of revolution against the government. To Nicholas and his loyal servant Goremykin, the principle of autocracy should be all the more uncompromisingly upheld in the face of the mounting pressure, whether it came from the workers' strike movement or from the Progressive Bloc in the Duma.

The majority of the cabinet members wanted to petition Nicholas not to assume command, but Goremykin emphatically rejected the majority opinion, declaring that he would rather resign than join such a mutiny. Finally, the majority went ahead without Goremykin and composed a joint statement to the tsar. Signed by eight of the thirteen members of the cabinet, the letter recommended Goremykin's dismissal and concluded: "We venture once more to tell you that to the best of our judgment your decision threatens with serious consequences Russia, your dynasty, and your person."[24] They favored a compromise with the Progressive Bloc, but on this issue as well they met Goremykin's opposition. To split the fragile Progressive Bloc, Goremykin invited the representatives of its conservative wing to a meeting and asked them to form a conservative bloc. But they refused. Shul'gin, one of the deputies invited to this meeting, added

22. V. V. Shul'gin, *Dni*, p. 147.

23. See chap. 5.

24. Quoted in Bernard Pares, *The Fall of the Russian Monarchy* (New York: Vintage Edition, 1961), p. 276. Also see Pearson, *Russian Moderates*, p. 56. Polivanov and Grigorovich did not sign the petition because of their special obligations of military service to the emperor, although they fully supported the statement. The minister of transport, S. V. Rukhlov, was ill at that time, but he also supported the letter. Thus, only two members of the cabinet, Goremykin and Khvostov, opposed the joint statement.

insult to injury by unceremoniously recommending Goremykin's resignation instead. Goremykin now favored prorogation of the Duma. Meanwhile, ignoring him, other ministers decided to negotiate with the Progressive Bloc. On August 28, the Council of Ministers, after a preliminary talk with the Progressive Bloc, decided with a majority against Goremykin to recommend to the tsar that the present cabinet be replaced by one enjoying the trust and confidence of the Duma.[25] Goremykin immediately left for the Stavka, not to inform the tsar of this decision but to privately recommend immediate prorogation of the Duma and dismissal of the disloyal ministers.

The mood of the Progressive Bloc remained optimistic. The Duma was united and enjoyed the support of a large sector of the State Council. The Bloc's demands were modest and accepted by the majority of the cabinet ministers. As Pearson states, "It did not seem possible for the Bloc to be refused when so many factors were in its favour."[26]

Nicholas's assumption of the supreme command demonstrated his determination to prevent further erosion of the principles of autocracy. When he reluctantly dismissed Nikolai Maklakov, the latter had warned him that the slightest concession to the liberals would open a floodgate to further demands. Now this warning seemed to be borne out. He agreed to let the representatives of the public organizations participate in the special councils, dismissed, though reluctantly, the unpopular ministers, and opened the Duma. Despite all these concessions, it appeared that the liberals' voice against the government was growing louder. Even worse, criticism of his policy was now raised by his own ministers. On August 22, in the opening ceremony of the special councils in the Winter Palace, Nicholas stated: "I needed the Duma for securing defense. Now all the programs have been accomplished. The rest will be done by Article 87."[27] On the following day, the same day that the ministers dispatched their collective petition to the tsar, he left for Mogilev to assume supreme command. Two factors contributed to Nicholas's hardening attitude toward the liberal opposition. First, Alekseev, the new chief of staff, had succeeded in getting the last Russian troops out of the "Polish pocket." The Great Retreat was over. The supply of shells and artillery was increasing. With the improved military situation, Nicholas could afford to ignore internal criticism. Second, liberal criticism of the government invited a backlash from the right wing. On August 20 and 22

25. S. I. Shidlovskii, *Vospominaniia* 2:37-40; Chermenskii, *IV gosudarstvennaia duma*, pp. 117-18; Diakin, *Russkaia burzhuaziia*, p. 115; Pearson, *Russian Moderates*, pp. 53-54.

26. Pearson, *Russian Moderates*, p. 57.

27. Chermenskii, *IV gosudarstvennaia duma*, p. 111.

the Council of the United Nobility held its meeting. A. N. Naumov, future minister of agriculture, expressed his dissatisfaction with the government's permissiveness in allowing the liberal elements to influence policy. Its chairman, A. P. Strukov, wrote a letter to Goremykin on August 23, warning that concessions to liberal demands would endanger existing state order.[28] The change in the military position, the support from the conservative nobility, and the rising strike movement all led Nicholas to conclude that it was time to stop any nonsense about concessions to the liberals.

Goremykin returned to Petrograd on September 2 and informed his colleagues of the tsar's decision: to prorogue the Duma immediately for an indefinite time, and to refuse the collective resignation of the ministers, ordering them to remain at their posts. The ministers exploded. Polivanov warned that the prorogation of the Duma would be the beginning of a general strike. But Goremykin reminded him that the workers' movement had developed independently of the relationship between the government and the Progressive Bloc. Sazonov shouted: "Tomorrow blood will flow in the streets and Russia will plunge into an abyss." To this, Goremykin replied: "The Duma will be prorogued on the appointed date, and no blood will flow anywhere." The chance for reconciliation between the government and the liberals was lost forever. Miliukov's biographer, Thomas Riha, concludes: "The monarchy's last chance for survival had been missed in 1915, when discussion was still possible. Once the people began to make their demands in the streets, it was too late to rely on the Bloc, which had been the tool of evolution, not of revolution." The cabinet was paralyzed by the hopeless division between Goremykin and the majority of the anti-Goremykin ministers.[29]

If Goremykin's opponents in the cabinet proved to be right in the long run, the strategy of Nicholas and Goremykin had immediate success. The liberals swallowed the humiliation of the prorogation of the Duma in silence. The Progressists' proposal for a boycott of the special councils was rejected by other parties, and the Progressists themselves in the end decided to stay on. Behind their inaction was fear of a mass movement. The liberals wished to avoid any action that might ignite a fire among the masses. Maklakov stated: "If Russia went on strike, the government would perhaps yield, but I would not want such a victory." Even Nekrasov spoke of the necessity to

---

28. Ibid., pp. 114-15; Diakin, *Russkaia burzhuaziia*, p. 117.

29. Chermenskii, *IV gosudarstvennaia duma*, p. 133; Diakin, *Russkaia burzhuaziia*, p. 118; Cherniavsky, *Prologue to Revolution*, pp. 226-43; Riha, *A Russian European*, p. 235.

stick to the parliamentary method of struggle: "First of all we must prevent internal disorders." The Duma spent the last day of its session on September 3 in a businesslike manner without a murmur of protest. "The Bloc went into voluntary liquidation," Pearson states, "until the morale of its members recovered from the brutal shock of rejection of its campaign.[30]

On September 7 to 9 in Moscow the congresses of the Unions of Zemstvos and of Towns discussed the strategy of how to react to the government's action. In the Union of Towns the left-wing representatives introduced a resolution calling for a series of internal reforms, the convocation of the Duma, and the establishment of a responsible ministry, but this resolution was defeated by an overwhelming majority. Guchkov declared that he was afraid of "energetic words" in addressing the government, since "they might have a destructive influence on the masses." In the end, the congresses of the two unions decided to send a delegation for the establishment of a ministry of confidence and the convocation of the Duma. According to Guchkov, the congresses adopted the idea of a delegation, "not for a revolution, but for the very reason of strengthening the government and for the purpose of defending the fatherland from revolution and anarchy." When the delegation, which included such liberal activists as Prince L'vov, Chelnokov, and Riabushinskii, made a formal request to be received by the emperor, Nicholas refused to meet them, coldly remarking: "I, of course, will not receive such self-proclaimed plenipotentiaries."[31]

In the beginning of September, Aleksandra bombarded Nicholas with her appeals to dismiss the ministers who had dared to defy the emperor's will. To resolve the hopeless division within the cabinet, Nicholas called a Council of Ministers meeting at the Stavka for September 16. The proposed meeting disturbed the empress, who feared that in its course her husband might change his mind. She instructed him to have a preliminary meeting with Goremykin. Just prior to the meeting she sent another telegram, in which she implored her husband: "Don't forget before the meeting of the ministers to hold the icon in your hand and to comb your hair a few times with His [Rasputin's] comb."[32] The icon and Rasputin's comb must have done the wonder, since during the meeting Nicholas maintained uncharacteristic force-

---

30. Chermenskii, *IV gosudarstvennaia duma*, p. 120; "Progressivnyi blok, 1915-1917," *Krasnyi arkhiv* 50-51, nos. 1-2 (1932): 155; Diakin, *Russkaia burzhuaziia*, pp. 119, 121; and Pearson, *Russian Moderates*, pp. 58-59.

31. Diakin, *Russkaia burzhuaziia*, pp. 121-22, 125; Chermenskii, *IV gosudarstvennaia duma*, pp. 125, 127, 130; and Pearson, *Russian Moderates*, pp. 60-61.

32. Quoted in Diakin, *Russkaia burzhuaziia*, p. 125.

fulness. The "rebel" ministers were not even invited to the customary dinner with the tsar. The hungry ministers were compelled to grab something to fill their empty stomachs at the buffet at the Mogilev railway station. At the meeting Nicholas began his speech by expressing disappointment with the conduct of the majority of the ministers during the August crisis: "You prophesied an ill omen if I assumed the command of the army, but only good came of it. You believed that there would be a revolution if the Duma were prorogued, but nothing of the sort happened. How can I believe you after such an incorrect understanding of the present moment?"[33] On September 26 Shcherbatov and Samarin were dismissed. This was followed by the dismissal of the leader of the "liberal" ministers, Krivoshein, who was considered to be the most likely candidate to head a ministry of confidence. Thus began the "ministerial leapfrog"—perennial dismissals and appointments of ministers. To top it all, on September 27, Rasputin, who had been banished from the capital, was allowed to return to Petrograd. Thus ended the period of reconciliation in the spring and summer of 1915, in which Nicholas made some attempts to bridge the gap between bureaucracy and society.

The political crisis in the summer of 1915 demonstrated the fundamental powerlessness of the Russian liberals. The powerlessness was expressed in a satirical fable by Vasilii Maklakov, "A Tragic Situation," that appeared in *Russkie vedomosti* on September 15. In this fable Maklakov pictures an imaginary situation in which a mad chauffeur is driving a car down a steep hill at an uncontrollable speed. The passengers know that he is driving everyone to inevitable doom. But no one can grab the steering wheel, because one false move will surely send the car into the abyss. The driver knows this and mocks the anxiety and helplessness of the passengers: "You will not dare touch me." Maklakov continues: "He is right. You will not dare touch him, for even if you might risk your own life, you are traveling with your mother, and you will not dare endanger your life for fear she too might be killed. . . . So you will leave the steering-wheel in the hands of the chauffeur. Moreover, you will try not to hinder him—you will even help him with advice, warning, and assistance. And you will be right, for this is what has to be done."[34] Maklakov's fable explains the dilemma of the liberals during the war except for one factor he failed to include and without it the picture of wartime politics—the

33. Chermenskii, *IV gusudarstvennaia duma*, p. 131; Pearson, *Russian Moderates*, p. 59.

34. Katkov, *Russia, 1917*, pp. 178-79; B. B. Grave, ed., *Burzhuaziia nakanune fevral'skoi revoliutsii*, p. 65.

relationship between the mad chauffeur (the tsar) and the passengers (the liberals) rushing together down a steep, winding road (the war) —is not complete. The car also contains a time bomb (the mass movement) that might explode at any moment. Neither the chauffeur nor the passengers can control the bomb, and the passengers are as afraid to move for fear of exploding the bomb as they are in fear of the chauffeur's mad driving. After the crisis of the summer of 1915, the government and the liberal opposition drifted apart. The government's unyielding, unwise policies frustrated and angered the liberals. But never once did they lift a hand against the government. They sat in the passenger seat, frozen and helpless.

3

THE GOVERNMENT
AND THE LIBERALS, 1916

 After the political crisis in the summer of 1915, the relationship between the government and the liberals was like a bad marriage. Reconciliation was no longer possible, and as time went on, their mutual distrust grew stronger and their communication more acrimonious. But neither side wanted to make a clean break. The government continued to ignore the liberals' demands, but it stopped short of declaring total war on them. The liberals were outraged by its senseless policy, but they never once raised a hand against the government. However sour and rancorous their relationship had become, the war and the fear of a revolution from below kept their marriage together.

Their relationship after the summer of 1915 can be conveniently divided into three successive periods by the tenures of the three ministers of internal affairs: A. N. Khvostov, B. V. Stürmer, and A. D. Protopopov.[1] Each period was marked by the progressive deterioration of the integrity of the government and the increased influence of the court camarilla represented by Rasputin and Aleksandra. This deterioration manifested itself in "ministerial leapfrog." During the eighteen months from September 1915 to February 1917, Russia had four

---

1. A. N. Khvostov (26 September 1915-3 March 1916), Stürmer (3 March-9 July 1916), and Protopopov (16 September 1916-27 February 1917). A. A. Khvostov briefly assumed the post from 9 July to 16 September 1916, but for the sake of convenience, I have treated this period as a part of the Stürmer period, since Stürmer continued to dominate the political scene as chairman of the Council of Ministers.

prime ministers, five ministers of internal affairs, three ministers of foreign affairs, three ministers of war, three ministers of transport, and four ministers of agriculture—an extremely high turnover in vital posts of a government engaged in a fateful war. The military situation improved remarkably in 1916, but signs of strain were appearing in the nation's economy, particularly in the food supply. The economic crisis immediately invited a social dislocation. The workers' strike movement, temporarily stopped by the war, began to surface again, and the threat of a large-scale civil disturbance loomed.

After the failure of the Progressive Bloc to reach a compromise with the government, the liberals subsided into inaction. Their movement, once united around the Progressive Bloc, splintered in many directions. The most conservative industrialists detached themselves completely from the liberal movement, preferring to make a separate deal with the government. The Progressive Bloc pursued a cautious, even timid, policy of moderation under Miliukov's leadership and refrained from sharply attacking the government. Dissatisfied, the Left openly sought ways to influence the masses. One of the policies designed for this purpose was the creation of the workers' group under the War Industries Committee. But the flirtation with the labor movement backfired, further alienating the industrialists from the liberals. It was only in the fall of 1916, when the supply of food reached a serious situation and labor unrest had recovered its prewar vitality, that the liberals slowly began to raise their voices against the government. Nonetheless, their attacks, sharp as they were, remained verbal. By the end of 1916 the liberals had lost hope and they saw no way out of the stalemate.

The first to take Maklakov's place as minister of internal affairs was A. N. Khvostov, nephew of the minister of justice, A. A. Khvostov. Unlike his conservative but forthright uncle, he was somewhat of a scoundrel and had been elevated to his new post through his connections with V. N. Voeikov, the tsar's palace commandant, Rasputin, and Anna Vyrubova. The new minister of internal affairs stated that politics was a matter of "stomachs," and regarded the solution of the problem of the high cost of living as the first of his priorities. His proposed solutions were to concentrate all economic power in the hands of the Ministry of Internal Affairs and to form a consumers' union based on reactionary patriotic organizations. The first measure created even more chaos in the food supply mechanism, and the only tangible result of the second measure was an alarming increase in pogroms against the Jewish population. Hostile to the liberals,

Khvostov engineered the postponement of the Duma session scheduled for November and banned the congress of the Union of Zemstvos and Towns. He declared: "The demand for a ministry enjoying public confidence is tantamount to interference in the monarch's prerogatives." He made preparations for the election of the Fifth Duma, and wrote the "Khvostov Memorandum," which was designed to exclude all parties left of the Zemstvist-Octobrists from the next election.[2]

The liberals, still in a depression from the events of the summer of 1915, were unable to react effectively to Khvostov's attacks. N. I. Astrov, Kadet, stated: "We have reached the fateful border, beyond which there is no path for constitutional society. We will not be able to become revolutionaries." V. A. Bobrinskii, an Octobrist, noted: "The government is worse, but what can we say? I cannot find an answer, and the convocation of the Duma frightens me." The bureau of the Progressive Bloc did not meet at all until October. At the end of October, Miliukov called together the leaders of the Progressive Bloc and the voluntary organizations. But the meeting only revealed the internal divisions of liberal circles. The right wing of the Bloc from the State Council threatened to withdraw if radical political activities were accelerated, while the left wing led by the Progressists insisted on an active campaign against the government. On November 23, the government postponed the Duma session. Miliukov and the Progressive leadership faced a dilemma, but in the end decided to stage a mild protest. This decision immediately led to the formal withdrawal of the State Council delegates from the Progressive Bloc. "Far from purging the Bloc of its least reliable elements," Pearson states, "and clearing the way for an energetic campaign, this defection only impressed more deeply upon the Bloc's remaining adherents the fragility of the coalition and the necessity of most careful consideration before the smallest action. The secession of the Council Centre faction shocked the Bloc back into nonactivity and it was a full two months before the members mustered the courage to call a fresh meeting."[3]

Such inaction dissatisfied the left-wing liberals. In November, the Progressists led by Efremov proposed to the other members of the Bloc that they boycott the special councils. Their proposal was

2. Thomas Riha, *A Russian European: Paul Miliukov in Russian Politics*, p. 238. Raymond Pearson, *The Russian Moderates and the Crisis of Tsarism, 1914-1917*, p. 66.
3. V. S. Diakin, *Russkaia burzhuaziia i tsarizm v gody pervoi mirovoi voiny*, pp. 128-39, 140-43; Pearson, *Russian Moderates*, p. 70.

rejected, and the Progressists unilaterally withdrew from the special councils, although some of their representatives continued to partici- pate as leaders of the War Industries Committee. Efremov's militant line was, however, eminently unpopular even among the Progressists. The industrialist members of the party, fearing government reprisals in military contracts, switched their party affiliations to the Kadets. In December a group of Progressist deputies in the Duma, led by Prince E. N. Trubetskoi, joined the Kadet party.[4] A more important split was taking place among the Kadets. The radical rank and file and provincial members of the party had insisted on the need to extend their influence to the masses of workers, fearing that otherwise the workers' movement would destroy society. For this reason they groped for a way to make an alliance with moderate Socialists. In August 1915, an Okhrana agent reported that the labor exchange (a sort of unemployment office) in Petrograd was becoming a point of contact between the workers' movement and the liberals. By August, various labor exchange offices in Petrograd had created a single central organ, with the purpose of uniting the working class into one organized force. The ideological leaders of the new movement, which aimed at organizing the workers through the labor exchange, were A. A. Isaev (Kadet), Shapirovich (Menshevik), and Zagorskii and Ermalaev (Social- ist Revolutionaries). The leaders of the labor exchange even discussed the possibility of creating a militia and a provisional government in case the government decided to evacuate the capital.[5]

The radicalism of the rank-and-file Kadet members at the time of political crisis and in the face of military defeat was quite under- standable. But in the fall, in direct contrast to the inaction of their leaders, their radicalism grew even stronger. After the Progressive Bloc's failure to wring a concession from the government, the left-wing Kadets continued to move leftward, attempting to establish contact with the workers. In October 1915, these Kadets provided the main force behind the movement to create a residents' committee in each city district in Petrograd. Initially, the idea was proposed as a solution for the crisis in the food supply but the proponents clearly envisioned this body as more than a food supply committee. According to the plan, the city's economic and police functions would be transferred to these local self-governments, democratically elected by residents and representing such municipal agencies as the social welfare agencies (*popechitel'stvo*), labor exchanges, and the city duma, as well as

4. Pearson, *Russian Moderates*, p. 73.
5. Report of the chief of the Okhrana to the director of the police depart- ment, 22 August 1915; TsGIA, f. 1405, op. 530, d. 1058, *ll*. 50-55.

such workers' groups as workers' cooperatives, sick-fund organizations, and trade unions. These committees were to secure food for the people in each district, were to be empowered to regulate commercial activities, and were to provide each district with a militia to maintain peace. The left-wing Kadets, supported by the Mensheviks, pushed for this plan in the city duma. Two Kadets, Andronikov and Izmailov, boldly declared that they were willing to "take power from those who could not keep it." The Okhrana agent stressed that "the present campaign by the Kadets to create district residents' committees is being undertaken with the purpose of organizing wide circles of the population and the city self-government for seizure and concentration of power in their hands."[6] Eventually, this idea was overruled by the majority of moderates in the city duma, but it is significant that as early as the fall of 1915 the left-wing liberals were thinking of alternatives to the tsarist state organ. It is therefore no accident that during the February Revolution, as soon as the normal channels of the government became paralyzed, the liberals were quick to step in and organize the food supply committee and the city militia.

The leaders of the War Industries Committee also attempted to organize labor by creating the workers' group under the War Industries Committee. This attempt was most vigorously pursued by Konovalov, who feared that unless the workers' movement was organized by moderate leaders, its explosion would wipe out the fragile bases of the Russian capitalist system. Konovalov stated: "On the next day after the war a bloody internal war will begin among us. . . . We have nothing to hope for in the government; and we will be confronted, face to face, with the workers. And their force and our powerlessness are completely unquestionable. Wouldn't it be better in such a case to take a path of agreement, a path of sensible concessions from both sides?" Konovalov's proposal was enthusiastically supported by Guchkov, who, despite his membership in the conservative Octobrist party, had shifted his position from the staunch supporter of the "sacred union" to the advocate of radical action by the liberals. The War Industries Committee organized the election campaign for the workers' group in August and September in various factories in Petrograd and other cities. The Socialists were split into two groups: the Bolsheviks opposed the participation of workers' representatives in the War Industries Committee, the Mensheviks advocated participation. In the end, the Mensheviks managed to win the election, as the leaders of the War Industries Committee had hoped, forming the workers' group within the War Industries Committee.[7]

6. Report of the chief of the Okhrana to the director of the police department, 9 October 1915, TsGIA, f. 1405, op. 530, d. 1059, ll. 35-39. Also see Diakin, *Russkaia burzhuaziia*, p. 153; Pearson, *Russian Moderates*, pp. 67-68.

7. B. Grave, ed., *Burzhuaziia nakanune fevral'skoi revoliutsii*, p. 140; see

The formation of the workers' group, however, did not lead to the reconciliation of labor and capital, as the leaders of the War Industries Committee had wished. Two factors worked against it. First, even the moderate leaders of the workers' movement felt that there had been no cessation of a class war. A majority of the Mensheviks who formed the workers' group were motivated by their desire to establish a legal channel through which to defend the interests of the working class. They represented constituents who were becoming more radical in the face of worsening economic conditions. As the masses of workers were increasingly swayed by the radical slogans of the Bolsheviks, the workers' group had to demonstrate to them, to gain their trust, that they were not a tool of the capitalist class. Second, the creation of the workers' group was not supported by the industrialists, a majority of whom considered the flirtation of the War Industries Committee with the working class dangerous. Konovalov's proposals for legalizing trade unions, creating conciliation boards to solve labor disputes, reinstituting the system of factory elders, creating a labor exchange, and regulating labor wages outraged the industrialists. A member of the workers' group, G. E. Breido, denounced the industrialists: "As soon as we approach a question concerning your pocket, you shout: Watch out!"[8]

The era of Khvostov came to a quick end, not because of liberal criticism but because of the power struggle within the ruling circles. Khvostov had dreamed of replacing Goremykin as chairman of the Council of Ministers, as Goremykin's high-handed opposition to the Duma began to worry the tsar.[9] But Rasputin, who was once Khvostov's benefactor, was in the way of his ambition. To get rid of this obstacle, Khvostov engineered a seamy intrigue that involved his hired agent in a plot to assassinate the "holy man." Rasputin became suspicious of Khvostov, and the Rasputin clique both at the court and within the cabinet turned against him. When Nicholas finally dismissed Goremykin in February, it was not Khvostov, but his enemy, B. V. Stürmer, closely associated with Rasputin and strongly supported by Aleksandra, who took over the vacant post. The police chief, S. P. Beletskii, a key figure in Khvostov's assassination plot, betrayed his master, and the entire plot became known to the Rasputin clique and eventually to the public. Khvostov was dismissed, and Stürmer took over the Ministry of Internal Affairs as well, as recommended by Rasputin. The sordid scandal further contributed to the erosion of authority of the tsarist government.

Stürmer's appointment as chairman of the Council of Ministers

---

chap. 6. For Guchkov's shift of policy, see Pearson, *Russian Moderates*, p. 71.

8. Diakin, *Russkaia burzhuaziia*, p. 175.

9. For the differences between Nicholas and Goremykin, see Pearson, *Russian Moderates*, pp. 75-76.

on the eve of the convocation of the Duma was meant to appease the liberal opposition, since unlike Goremykin Stürmer advocated some cooperation with the Duma. Nicholas feared that the retention of Goremykin, who had proposed to postpone the scheduled Duma session, might provoke a stormy protest of the liberals. On February 9, when the Duma opened, to the pleasant surprise of the liberals Nicholas made an extraordinary gesture of good will by appearing personally. A few meaningless words uttered by the emperor were enough to soften the tone of the speeches of the Duma liberals and to raise hopes that this conciliatory gesture would be followed by further concessions. But Stürmer's declaration immediately dampened these hopes, for it was a repetition of the government's refusal to make internal reforms as long as the war continued. Confused and disappointed, the liberals did not know how to act. In the summer of 1915 the defeat of the army had driven them to action, but in the winter of 1916 the military situation was stabilized. Many industrialists and other liberal supporters had defected from political action, and the right-wing members of the Progressive Bloc wondered aloud if their policy in the summer of 1915 might not have been a mistake. Miliukov noted in his Duma speech: "I know where the exit is, but I do not know how to get there. We have no means for solving this question by our own forces, and we are no longer prepared to appeal to the wisdom of the government's power."[10] During the relatively long session, which lasted from February 9 to June 20, the Duma accomplished little. Whenever it discussed internal reforms, it revealed irreconcilable differences within the Progressive Bloc. Even on the Jewish question, the Progressive Bloc failed to support the rights of the Jewish population. Miliukov was absent in the latter part of the Duma session, since he elected to join the Duma deputation to Western Europe, despite the opposition of the Kadet Central Committee. A Menshevik Duma deputy, A. I. Chkhenkeli, remarked: "The Progressive Bloc is dead. Long live the regressive Bloc."[11]

The right-wing swing of the Progressive Bloc, however, did not prevent the conservative industrialists from deserting the liberal cause. The industrial magnates in the metallurgical industry formed the Council of Metal Factory Owners. In March the bankers followed suit, forming the Congress of Bankers. These organizations took a critical view of the War Industries Committee and the Progressive Bloc, disassociating · themselves from the liberal opposition. The chairman of both organizations was A. D. Protopopov, an Octobrist and

10. Diakin, *Russkaia burzhuaziia*, pp. 163-70.
11. Michael F. Hamm, "Liberal Politics in Wartime Russia: An Analysis of the Progressive Bloc," *Slavic Review* 33, no. 3 (1974):455.

vice-chairman of the Duma, who became the spokesman of the conservative industrial and financial oligarchs.[12]

Sensing the disarray of the liberal opposition, the court camarilla
took vengeance on the "rebel" ministers who had dared to show
sympathy with the liberals in the summer of 1915. In March, Polivanov
fell victim to a vicious campaign spearheaded by Aleksandra. In July
Sazonov was dismissed. Stürmer took over the Foreign Ministry, giving
up the Ministry of Internal Affairs to A. A. Khvostov (not to be confused with his scandalous nephew). In addition to Sazonov's dismissal,
the other news that brought some excitement among the liberals in the
summer of 1916 was Guchkov's famous letter to General Alekseev,
chief of staff. In this letter Guchkov characterized the state of government as complete bankruptcy. In his opinion, the liberals were totally
powerless to do anything about the situation: "Our methods of struggle
are double-edged, and under the rising temper of the masses, particularly of the working masses, they could become the first spark
to ignite a fire, the dimensions of which no one can predict or
localize." Guchkov hoped that Alekseev would recognize that in
the face of the powerlessness of the liberals, the military would be
the only force viable enough to exert influence on the tsar. Whatever Guchkov's intention was, the wide circulation of the letter
embarrassed Alekseev, who was questioned by Nicholas about his
correspondence with the "known enemy of the monarchy." This
episode must have increased Alekseev's suspicion of politics in general. The contents of Guchkov's letter were certainly not sensational
and if it became much talked about among the liberals, it was, as
Diakin states, because the liberals had very little to talk about that
summer.[13]

Whether or not Guchkov's letter had any effect on the military
leaders, the latter were becoming increasingly concerned with the
internal political situation, which was beginning to affect the morale
of the soldiers in the trenches and the barracks. There is evidence that
some of the military leaders had espoused the notion, even suggesting
it to the tsar, that a ministry of confidence should be formed to re-
unify the nation in the war effort. On June 15, Alekseev recommended
to Nicholas the establishment of a dictatorship to solve the nation's
economic problems. This recommendation reflected the military's
growing concern with the deterioration of the system of food supply,

12. Diakin, *Russkaia burzhuaziia*, p. 187.

13. V. P. Semennikov, ed., *Monarkhiia pered krusheniem*, p. 282. George
Katkov, *Russia, 1917: The February Revolution*, pp. 183-86; Diakin, *Russkaia
burzhuaziia*, p. 15. Katkov interprets Guchkov's letter as one of his conspiratorial
maneuvers to involve the military against the monarchy.

which had become worse in the cities and was also beginning to affect the provisions of the army.[14]

Russia, like most other countries, was not prepared for the war's profound impact on the national economy. As it continued, the economic structure had to be adjusted to the war effort, and each economic readjustment was accompanied by social and political implications. We have seen the readjustments made in the war industries and the political realignments that accompanied them. Equally important was the economic readjustment brought about by the food supply problem—a matter that vitally affected all segments of society: the government, which assumed the ultimate responsibility for feeding the army and the population; the army, which depended upon the government's ability to feed the soldiers; the liberals' voluntary organizations and self-governments, which were drawn into the food supply mechanism; the peasants, the providers; and the urban population, the consumers. At the outset, it must be said that, considering that foreign trade was virtually stopped and economic patterns were significantly changed by the war, the tsarist government's over-all performance in handling this enormous task of food supply was not as bad as is often argued. The mechanism the government created, despite important shortcomings, on the whole worked well. After all, the army did not suffer from lack of provisions, and no one in the cities starved. The collapse of the mechanism for supplying food actually came after the February Revolution.

The central coordinating body of all food supply matters was the Special Council for Food Supply, created in August 1915 and headed by the minister of agriculture. The special council involved in its supply network not only representatives of the bureaucracy—from the Ministries of Agriculture, Finance, Internal Affairs, State Bank, etc.— but also those from zemstvos, city dumas, and other nongovernmental agrarian and financial organizations. In fact, cooperation between bureaucracy and society *(obshchestvo)* was one of the most striking features of this special council. An overwhelming majority of the food commissioners at the provincial and district levels were persons who represented society, especially those from zemstvos.[15] To be

14. In General N. I. Ivanov's archives there is one document concerning the imperial rescript to grant a ministry of confidence dated sometime in the summer of 1916. "Proval popytki Stavki podavit' Fevral'skuiu revoliutsiiu 1917 goda v Petrograde," *Voprosy arkhivovedeniia*, no. 1 (1962), p. 104; Semennikov, *Monarkhiia pered krusheniem*, pp. 259-66.

15. K. I. Zaitsev, S. S. Demosthenov, *Food Supply in Russia during the War with Introduction of Peter B. Struve*, pp. 4-5. See also Thomas Fallows, "Politics and the War Effort in Russia: The Union of Zemstvos and Organization of the Food

sure, there were some occasions, particularly after the fall of 1916, in which the relationship between the government and the liberals became extremely strained, or in which the liberals used the council network as a forum for their political offensive against the government. But on the whole, bureaucracy and society worked well together on a practical level. The special council also had the good fortune to be headed by competent ministers of agriculture: Krivoshein, A. N. Naumov, A. A. Bobrinskii, and A. A. Rittikh. These men successfully maintained the basic framework of the supply network, and staved off the ever-present intervention of other bureaucratic agencies, particularly the Ministry of Internal Affairs.

Nevertheless, the food situation had reached crisis proportions by the summer of 1916. Its most critical aspect was the shortage and phenomenal increase in prices in Petrograd and Moscow. The crisis is often attributed to decreased agricultural production, but on the whole more than enough was produced to feed the army and the population at least until the end of 1917. Another cause was believed to be the paralysis of railway transportation. But, as Stone argues, "It was not trains, but timetables that offered problems." In other words, "trains chased grain, not the other way about."[16]

The most important cause of the breakdown in supply was the change in economic patterns during the war. Russian industry, which had converted to war industries, provided little for the peasants in exchange for their products, and when it did, the industrial goods came at an enormously high price. As a result, the peasants were unwilling to take their products to market; this, in turn, caused the price of foodstuffs to skyrocket, and provided ample room for speculation. The government gingerly experimented with price controls, but the fixed price was not used uniformly in various localities but rather coexisted with the free market price mechanism. Even if the government had enforced a rigorous, uniform fixed price, as the Kadets were insisting, it is doubtful that it would have solved the food supply crisis. The peasants would have hoarded their products or converted them to other uses or simply produced less. Another solution would have been forced requisition at a price dictated by the government. The special council actually experimented with this method half-heartedly in the form of Rittikh's requisition (razverstka). Rittikh's experiment was interrupted by the February Revolution, but the earlier indications

---

Supply, 1914-1916," *Slavic Review*, vol. 37, no. 1 (1978).

16. N. D. Kondrat'ev, *Rynok khlebov i ego regulirovanii vo vremia voiny i revoliutsii*, pp. 38-71; Norman Stone, *The Eastern Front*, pp. 292-95, 298.

were that it would have been a failure. Forced requisition, as the Bolsheviks were to learn during the Civil War, would have reduced agricultural production to a subsistence level. The problem was more complex than the special council alone could have handled. Nor could any panacea have been found in a simple policy such as the fixed price and requisition, or in bureaucratic reorganization that would concentrate food supply matters in the hands of the Ministry of Internal Affairs or in voluntary organizations. Under the circumstances, the special council's policy of limited governmental intervention while allowing the market mechanism to function was probably the best course of action. Shortcomings such as the acute food shortage in Petrograd and Moscow could have been handled by drastically rearranging priorities, although that would not have provided an ultimate solution. But before these measures could be implemented, the social and political fabric of society was torn apart.[17]

Given the complexity of the food supply crisis, the dictatorship proposed by General Alekseev could not have performed the necessary miracle to solve the crisis. Nicholas supported Alekseev's proposal, and granted Stürmer a "dictatorial power." But "Stürmer's dictatorship" was only nominal. Its only result was an increase in Stürmer's power over the supply of food. A new agency, the Committee to Combat the Cost of Living Increase, was created under the chairman of the Council of Ministers. The result, however, was even greater bureaucratic confusion in dealing with the complicated tasks that had been handled more expertly by the Special Council for Food Supply. Meanwhile, as the food crisis worsened in the fall of 1916, the workers' strike movement picked up momentum. It was only at this point that the liberals finally raised their voices against the government. The liberal newspapers demanded the convocation of the Duma. The Progressive Bloc entrusted Rodzianko with the task of seeking an audience with the tsar to press this demand, but Nicholas refused to receive him. As the capital began to show signs of restlessness, the moral decay of the government became more manifest. Stürmer's private secretary, A. A. Manasevich-Manuilov, a journalist connected with the Rasputin clique, was arrested for bribery and extortion, on the order of A. A. Khvostov, now minister of internal affairs. In this incident Rasputin's name loomed again. Stürmer's "dictatorship" was dealt a heavy blow, and Nicholas lost his enthusiasm for Stürmer. After Manasevich-Manuilov's arrest, Stürmer's intrigue against Khvostov

17. For a different interpretation on the causes of the food supply problem, see Fallows, "Politics and the War Effort in Russia," pp. 72-73. Fallows believes the government failure to develop an efficient mechanism to be the main cause of the problem.

intensified. Khvostov had already incurred the disfavor of the tsarina for having Sukhomlinov brought to trial despite her repeated entreaties to release him from prison. On September 16, Khvostov was dismissed, but instead of Stürmer, A. D. Protopopov was named acting minister of internal affairs.

Simbirsk, a small, poor province along the middle Volga, is said to have given the Russian Revolution three gifts: Lenin, Kerenskii, and Protopopov. Protopopov, a landowner in Simbirsk, a member of the Octobrist party and vice-chairman of the Duma, was the first representative of society to head the Ministry of Internal Affairs. Chairman of the newly formed Council of Metal Factory Owners as well as of the Congress of Bankers, he was closely associated with the conservative Petrograd financial and industrial magnates. He harbored a secret desire to assume a governmental post—an ambition in itself not unique among the public men who chose a political career. After all, Miliukov, Rodzianko, and Guchkov had such ambitions. What was unique, however, was that Protopopov did not hesitate to use the influence of the court camarilla to achieve his ambition. From 1903 he had maintained a secret association with a Tibetan doctor, P. A. Badmaev, whose circle Rasputin and other court dignitaries also frequented. Through Badmaev, Protopopov was acquainted with Rasputin. Already the business circles represented by Putilov and Vyshnegradskii had urged his candidacy for minister of finance through Rasputin. Unaware of this maneuver Rodzianko recommended that Nicholas appoint Protopopov minister of trade and industry. As it became obvious to Nicholas and the court camarilla that Stürmer's "dictatorship" would not solve the food supply crisis, Protopopov's proposal to get the help of the business community in solving the crisis caught their attention. In the face of growing signs of militancy among the liberals, Nicholas wished to muzzle their criticism by broadening the base of the government by inviting the participation of the most conservative element of society.

The liberals' initial reaction to Protopopov's appointment was overwhelmingly favorable. The liberal press expressed a hope that Protopopov would be instrumental in implementing liberal reforms. Rumors spread that Protopopov's appointment would be followed by Rodzianko's appointment as chairman of the Council of Ministers. Believing this rumor, Rodzianko went as far as to set the terms of acceptance, which included the deportation of the empress to Livadia, a resort in the Crimea. Even Konovalov believed that in a few months a Miliukov cabinet might be formed.[18]

18. M. V. Rodzianko, *Reign of Rasputin*, pp. 213-214; For the reaction of

Although Protopopov is often pictured as an unprincipled careerist, somewhat unstable mentally, he had a comprehensive plan for internal reform. His policy included land reform, granting peasants the land confiscated from the German colonists, zemstvo reforms, removal of the restrictions on the Jews in industry and trade (a plan that earned the ire of the reactionaries), and the institution of a mechanism of governmental checks and balances by making the executive branch responsible to a judiciary organ instead of the Duma. On the food supply question, he proposed the elimination of the fixed price and of governmental interference in commercial transactions for agricultural products. On labor questions, he proved to be a reactionary, opposing any attempts by the War Industries Committee to organize the workers.[19]

The liberals' enthusiasm about Protopopov's appointment, however, soon turned into anger as he began to behave more like a representative of Rasputin than a representative of society. Rodzianko was irritated by Protopopov's secret dinner appointments with Vyrubova and Stürmer. Moreover, to the consternation of his liberal colleagues in the Duma, the former vice-chairman tactlessly appeared before the Duma Budget Commission in the uniform of the chief of gendarmerie—a symbol of tsarist oppression. Attempting to recover the confidence of his former colleagues, Protopopov asked Rodzianko to arrange a meeting with the liberal leaders, where he was assailed with sharp denunciations. Miliukov declared that the liberals could not be friendly with "the person who serves with Stürmer, [the person] who sets Sukhomlinov free, the person who persecutes the liberal press."[20] Deeply offended, Protopopov never again tried to reach a compromise with the liberals but rather took vengeance through such repressive measures as banning all public gatherings without the presence of police. The liberals could not forgive the defector who had crossed over to the enemy camp, and heaped vicious

the liberals to Protopopov's appointment, see Diakin, *Russkaia burzhuaziia,* pp. 230-32; E. D. Chermenskii, *IV gosudarstvennaia duma i sverzhenie tsarizma v Rossii,* pp. 199-200.

19. For the traditional interpretation of Protopopov, see Bernard Pares, *The Fall of the Russian Monarchy,* pp. 376-91; Michael Florinsky, *The End of the Russian Empire,* pp. 90-92. Diakin rehabilitates Protopopov as a politician with a serious plan for comprehensive internal reforms who reflected the conservative segment of industrial and financial circles in Petrograd. For Protopopov's policy, see Diakin, *Russkaia burzhuaziia,* p. 233; idem, "K voprosu o 'zagovore tsarizma' nakanune Fevral'skoi revoliutsii," *Vnutrennaia politika tsarizma,* pp. 376-77; Chermenskii, *IV gosudarstvennaia duma,* pp. 198-99.

20. A. Shliapnikov, *Kanun semnadtsatogo goda* 2: 115-24. Also see TsGAOR, f. 102, d. 307a, t. 2, 1916 g., ℓℓ. 41-43.

invectives on him. The Octobrist party formally stripped him of membership.

On October 15, Protopopov proposed his food policy at the Council of Ministers' meeting. Prior to the meeting, the chairman of the Special Council for Food Supply, Count A. A. Bobrinskii, had taken measures to extend participation of the local self-governments in the procurement of grain. Alarmed by growing liberal influence in the supply mechanism, Protopopov, through a counter-proposal, attempted to concentrate all food supply matters in the hands of the Ministry of Internal Affairs. Despite objections raised by Bobrinskii and P. N. Ignatiev (minister of education), Protopopov's proposal gained support from the majority of the ministers. But when Protopopov made his proposal more elaborate at the next meeting, a majority began to have second thoughts, realizing that it would provoke opposition in the Duma. Nicholas, however, supported Protopopov, approving the elimination of the liberal elements in the food supply mechanism. As soon as Protopopov's proposal reached the ears of the liberals, their reaction was quick and unanimous; the Budget Commission on October 18 unanimously adopted a resolution denouncing the proposed policy. The prospect of a liberal offensive on the eve of the convocation of the Duma session led Protopopov to waver at the last moment. His assistant, General P. G. Kurlov, director of the Police Department, warned him that if he should adjourn the Duma in response to its criticism of his policy, it might provoke a large-scale mass disturbance. To the disappointment of Rasputin and Aleksandra, Protopopov had to withdraw the proposal.[21]

The food crisis, the awakening of the strike movement, and Protopopov's provocation raised the temper of the liberals on the eve of the new session of the Duma scheduled for November 1. The Progressists led by Efremov and Konovalov and the Left Kadets criticized Miliukov's policy of moderation, demanding the adoption of a slogan for the establishment of a responsible ministry and advocating an ultimatum to the government from the Progressive Bloc on the opening day. Against these radical opponents Vasilii Maklakov argued that the Duma was not capable of creating a responsible ministry in view of the fundamental differences on the basic issues among the various parties within the Progressive Bloc. "If we want to go all the way,

21. For Protopopov's proposal at the Council of Ministers' meeting, see TsGIA, f. 1276, op. 12, d. 1288b, ℓℓ. 2-5, 6-10, 12-13, 14-17, 20-28, 40; TsGIA, f. 1276, op. 12, d. 1790, ℓℓ. 168-78. For the discussion of the food supply question in the Budget Commission, see TsGIA, f. 1278, op. 5, d. 330, ℓℓ. 2-534; its resolution against Protopopov's policy, ℓℓ. 516-19. Diakin, *Russkaia burzhuaziia*, pp. 239-40; Chermenskii, *IV gosudarstvennaia duma*, p. 201.

we must talk about more than a responsible ministry," he said, "but we will not talk about that." Shul'gin stated: "Fight we must; the government is rotten. But since we are not going to the barricades, we cannot egg others on. The Duma must be a safety valve, letting off steam, not creating it." The only matter they agreed on was their opposition to Stürmer and Protopopov. On this basis Miliukov and Shul'gin set out to prepare a draft declaration, from which a demand for a responsible ministry was conspicuously dropped. This was too much for the Progressists, who withdrew in protest from the Progressive Bloc. The left-wing Kadets threatened to follow.[22] It was necessary for Miliukov to do something to prevent the collapse of the Progressive Bloc by keeping the left Kadets within the Bloc.

Miliukov's speech on November 1 was, therefore, intended to restore the moral authority of the Duma in the eyes of the critics of his leadership and to prevent further defection by the left-wing Kadets from the Progressive Bloc. On this opening day, Shidlovskii, an Octobrist and the formal head of the Progressive Bloc, read the declaration of the Bloc, written by Miliukov and Shul'gin, which called for Stürmer's resignation. Then Miliukov dropped the bombshell. He attacked Stürmer, insinuated his rumored intrigue for a separate peace, and ended each paragraph with the rhetorical question: "Is this stupidity or treason?" The speech was certainly a broadside, as Katkov calls it, since Miliukov had no factual evidence to prove Stürmer's treason. Miliukov himself later admitted that it was not his intention to prove Stürmer's treason, which he did not believe in the first place. The speech, however, caused an immediate sensation. Although stricken from the official stenographic record on the government censor's order, it was printed clandestinely and widely circulated among the urban population as well as among the soldiers at the front. At a time when scandal was clouding the government, Miliukov's speech fed the population what they wanted to believe: the government's treason. It was basically motivated "not by the guilt or incompetence of Stürmer but the complex predicament of the Progressive Bloc in the developing revolutionary climate of Russia in late 1916," but as Pearson aptly states, what had been intended to "let off steam" of the revolutionary movement had an effect of "making steam."[23]

Although Stürmer had no advance knowledge of Miliukov's vituperation, he had gotten wind of the adverse mood of the Progressive

22. "Progressivnyi blok," *Krasnyi arkhiv* 56, no. 1 (1933): 87, 114. For the discussions in the Progressive Bloc in October, see ibid., pp. 82-117; Pearson, *Russian Moderates*, pp. 108-15.

23. Katkov, *Russia, 1917*, pp. 190-93; Miliukov, *Vospominaniia* 2:276-77; Pearson, *Russian Moderates*, pp. 115, 117.

Bloc prior to the opening of the Duma. Although Nicholas had given him the authority to adjourn the Duma if it should make too much noise, that was not enough for Stürmer. He asked the tsar for the authority to dissolve it entirely and order a new election. Nicholas hesitated, but finally acquiesced, granting Stürmer an imperial manifesto to dissolve the Duma, only with the warning that he should use it wisely and only in an extreme case.[24] On November 1 Stürmer suffered the humiliation of having to sit and listen to Miliukov's tirade. Immediately after reading the government's declaration, Stürmer, pale with anger, walked out of the hall. Later that day, at a cabinet meeting, Stürmer in a fury declared that either the Duma or he must go. All the ministers except three, however, thought that if either had to go, it should not be the Duma. By this time Nicholas himself was inclined to agree with the majority in the cabinet.

Nicholas hesitated to take strong measures against the Duma in November, despite Miliukov's speech, for two reasons: pressure from the military leaders and pressure from his own relatives. After the demise of Alekseev's recommendation for the establishment of a dictatorship, Alekseev and his commanding staff at the Stavka had sympathized with the Progressive Bloc's demand for a ministry of confidence. Alekseev strongly advised Nicholas against measures to repress the Duma because such measures would lower the morale of the soldiers. According to Chermenskii, it was at Alekseev's urging that Nicholas had finally decided to convene the Duma. It is interesting to note that in November Alekseev allegedly agreed to take part in a plot engineered by Prince G. E. L'vov to deport the tsarina.[25] Whether or not Nicholas was aware of such a plot, the pressure from the military was something to be reckoned with. Presumably at Alekseev's urging, Minister of War D. D. Shuvaev, and Minister of the Navy I. K. Grigorovich, appeared at the Duma, imploring the Duma liberals to get down to the practical tasks of national defense. The moderate leadership of the Progressive Bloc, already frightened by what the government's reaction might be to their sharp attacks, gave a sigh of relief at the appearance of the two ministers in the Duma.

Nicholas's relatives were greatly disturbed by the meddling of Rasputin and Aleksandra in internal politics, which reached its apogee in the fall of 1916. At the end of October Nicholas took a trip to Kiev, where he was confronted by critical relatives that included his own mother, Aleksandr Mikhailovich, Pavel Aleksandrovich, and Mariia

24. TsGIA, f. 1276, op. 10, d. 7, ℓ. 97.

25. A. I. Denikin, *Ocherki russkoi smuty* 1:35; Chermenskii, *IV gosudarstvennaia duma*, pp. 214–15. See chap. 10.

Pavlovna. His mother, Dowager Empress Mariia Fedorovna, had sworn that she would never set foot in Petrograd as long as Aleksandra was there. After Nicholas returned to Mogilev, Nikolai Mikhailovich, an accomplished historian and the only intellectual in the imperial family, who had various connections with the moderate liberals, visited the tsar and handed him a letter advising him in the strongest terms to rid himself of Rasputin's influence and to be cautious of his wife's advice: "The words she utters are the outcome of clever intrigue. They are not the truth. If you are powerless to rid yourself of such influences at least be always on your guard against the the unceasing and systematic intriguers who use your wife as a tool." However, Nicholas's loyalty to his wife was unbending. He immediately sent this confidential letter to Aleksandra, who wrote back: "Why didn't you stop him in the middle of the conversation, and tell him that if he talks again about this subject or about me, you will send him to Siberia, because this borders on a state treason. . . . He is a shady character, a grandson of a Jew!" On November 5, Grand Duke Nikolai Nikolaevich, former commander in chief, visited the tsar at the Stavka, and strongly recommended the establishment of a ministry of confidence. During the conversation Nicholas did not utter a single word, and at the end he shrugged his shoulders and ushered his uncle out of the room. The grand duke sensed that the fate of the monarchy was sealed.[26]

Under these pressures Nicholas decided to dismiss Stürmer. On this Aleksandra agreed. She wrote to Nicholas: "Since Stürmer plays the role of a red flag in this madhouse, it is better to force him to resign." At this time Nicholas made an attempt to free himself of the influence of his domineering wife. He resented receiving a list of candidates from Aleksandra and Rasputin, and wrote back: "Only I ask you. Don't let Our Friend [Rasputin] interfere. I assume the responsibility, and therefore, I wish to be free in the selection." On November 9, he dismissed Stürmer, and over the objections of his wife, appointed A. F. Trepov his successor. Stürmer's downfall was greeted by the Progressive Bloc as a victory. Miliukov's tactics worked. Without making any constitutional demands as the Progressists and the left Kadets had insisted, Miliukov restored the prestige of the Progressive Bloc and the Duma as a leading center of the opposition movement against the government. After his speech Miliukov's popularity reached its zenith.[27]

26. Nikolai Mikhailovich's letter quoted in Victor Alexandrov, *The End of the Romanovs*, pp. 119-20; Diakin, *Russkaia burzhuaziia*, p. 244; Andrei Vladimirovich, "Iz dnevika A. V. Romanova za 1916-1917 gg.," *Krasnyi arkhiv* 26, no. 1 (1928): 197.

27. Diakin, *Russkaia burzhuaziia*, pp. 246, 261; Pearson, *Russian Moderates*, pp. 116-17.

Trepov, who had been minister of transport prior to the appointment to the premiership, was a conservative but honest bureaucrat, not connected with the Rasputin clique. For that reason Aleksandra opposed the appointment of an enemy of "Our Friend." Unlike his predecessors Trepov saw the necessity of cooperating with the Duma and was interested in establishing in the Duma a new right-wing majority willing to work with the government. He attempted to lure the conservative elements of the Progressive Bloc into this majority, thus crippling the strength of the liberal opposition. To achieve this, he was prepared to sacrifice Protopopov, who had become by this time the bête noir of the liberals. Trepov succeeded in gaining the tsar's approval of Protopopov's dismissal. He also made an unsuccessful attempt to bribe Rasputin to leave the capital.[28]

The liberal's reaction to Trepov varied. While the right wing of the Progressive Bloc welcomed him as a second Stolypin, the Progressists complained that nothing had changed with Trepov's appointment and insisted on continuing the attack. Miliukov and the leadership of the Progressive Bloc, however, welcomed Trepov and considered it possible to cooperate with his government as long as it dropped Protopopov. When the new chairman of the council of ministers appeared in the Duma on November 19 to read the declaration of his cabinet, the Socialist deputies led by N. S. Chkheidze and A. F. Kerenskii booed and jeered him for forty minutes, preventing him from reading the declaration. The liberals, who would have nothing to do with such a disruptive tactic, voted to remove the Socialist deputies from the floor. Menshevik Chkhenkeli declared: "You must realize that a struggle is going on between the government and the people, and as long as you want to take part in this struggle, you must completely break with the government and turn to the people."[29]

The liberals' verbal attacks were now heaped on Protopopov, but they were careful not to criticize Trepov and his government. The most sensational attack on the government came from totally unexpected quarters. The right-wing deputy, M. V. Purishkevich, a founder of the reactionary Union of the Russian People and a staunch monarchist, delivered an impassioned speech in which he attacked, amid the hushed audience, the "dark forces" led by "Grisha Rasputin" that had infiltrated the court and the government in the interests of the enemy, and termed the perennial appointments and dismissals of the ministers as "ministerial leapfrog." This speech was welcomed by the liberals enthusiastically. Miliukov stated: "Better late than never. Purishkevich opened his eyes, admittedly belatedly, but

28. Diakin, "K voprosu o 'zagovore' tsarizma," p. 373.
29. Chermenskii, *IV gosudarstvennaia duma*, p. 223.

nonetheless he opened his eyes. This fact itself is extremely important."[30]

Purishkevich's speech represented the opinion of the conservative
element of the nation, which because of its firm belief in the monarchy,
was all the more disturbed by Rasputin's influence and Aleksandra's
meddling. On November 26, the State Council, the usually conservative
upper house, known as "the gravedigger" of the Duma's legislative
initiatives, passed a resolution urging Nicholas to remove the "dark
forces" from the government. The United Nobility, which held its
congress from November 27 to December 1, also passed a resolution
attacking the "dark forces" and calling for the establishment of a
government that could cooperate with the legislative chambers.[31]
Little more than a year had passed since the United Nobility had
expressed its dissatisfaction with the government's flirtation with the
Duma. Pressure from the grand dukes also continued. At the end
of November a family gathering took place in Grand Duke Andrei
Vladimirovich's house. Grand Duke Pavel Aleksandrovich, as doyen
of the family, was entrusted with the task of persuading the tsar again
to change his policy. Grand Duke Pavel was received by Nicholas on
December 3 but his plea to give the nation a constitution, or at least
a ministry of confidence, fell on deaf ears. "What you ask is impossible," Nicholas declared, "the day of my coronation I took my oath
to the Absolute Power. I must leave this oath intact to my son."[32]

Although Nicholas had showed signs of independence from his
wife for a flicker of a moment, once Aleksandra began her relentless
letter-writing campaign, he easily gave in. When Nicholas was contemplating the possibility of dismissing Protopopov, she urged: "My dear,
look at their faces—Trepov's and Protopopov's. Is it not clear that
the face of the latter is purer, more honest, and more upright?" It
was not simply a matter of Protopopov, she insisted, but a matter of
autocracy. It was about time to show the nation who was boss—to
show that it was he who was the autocrat, not the Duma. Suspicious
of her husband's strength of will, she visited him at the Stavka one
day, and succeeded in reversing his decision to dump Protopopov.
As for Rasputin's influence, Aleksandra wrote: "Oh, my dear, I pray
to God so passionately to convince you that in Him [Rasputin] lies
our salvation. If He weren't here, I don't know what would become

30. TsGIA, f. 1276, op. 10, d. 7, ℓ. 386.

31. Chermenskii, *IV gosudarstvennaia duma*, pp. 228-29; Pearson, *Russian
Moderates*, pp. 125-26. The government also recognized that it was losing the
support of the conservative majority in the State Council. See TsGIA, f. 1276,
op. 10, d. 7, ℓ. 413.

32. Princess Paley, *Memories of Russia, 1916-1919*, pp. 24-27.

of us. He is saving us with His prayers and His wise advice." She went on: "He [Rasputin] lives for you and for Russia. We must hand to the Baby [Aleksei] a strong country and cannot be weak for his sake; otherwise, it will be much more difficult for him to reign." She encouraged her wavering husband: "Be like Peter the Great, Ivan the Terrible, and Emperor Paul" (fine examples of monarchs who used the cruelest punishments on their subjects). She expressed intense anger against the enemies of autocracy by suggesting that the tsar should send opponents such as Miliukov, L'vov, Guchkov, and Polivanov to Siberia.[33] These outbursts were enough to make the weak-willed sovereign capitulate.

While the Progressive Bloc timidly followed the parliamentary path charted by Miliukov, the voluntary organizations became increasingly vociferous in their attacks on the government. Both the Union of Zemstvos and the Union of Towns planned a congress for the beginning of December, and also attempted to hold an All-Russian Congress of Food Supply in Moscow, inviting the representatives of liberal as well as labor organizations. By this time the rank and file of the voluntary organizations had become so radicalized that they were insisting, over the objections of L'vov and Chelnokov, that if the government banned the congresses, the meetings should be held illegally. Some openly advocated the overthrow of the regime in cooperation with the masses of workers. Such radicalism frightened the heads of the unions, who were relieved when they received the government's order to ban meetings. On December 9 the police entered the building in Moscow where the representatives of the Union of Towns and the Union of Zemstvos had gathered and dispersed them before their meetings could begin. Having anticipated the police repressions, however, the Union of Zemstvos had previously adopted a resolution, which was made public by Prince L'vov. The resolution declared that the nation was in danger, called for the Duma to stop cooperating with the government, and demanded the immediate establishment of a responsible ministry. Just as Miliukov had found it necessary to attack the government on November 1 to prevent further defection of the Left Kadets from the Progressive Bloc, Prince L'vov used strong language to placate the radical workers of the voluntary organizations.[34]

33. "Perepiska Nikolaia Romanova s Aleksandroi Fedorovnoi," *Krasnyi arkhiv* 4, no. 4 (1923): 174, 184, 187; Diakin, *Russkaia burzhuaziia*, p. 261.
34. TsGAOR, f. DPOO, d. 27, ch. 46, 1916 g., ℓ. 30. For the radicalism of rank-and-file workers in the Unions of Towns and their conflict with the leaders, see William E. Gleason, "The All-Russian Union of Towns and the Politics of Urban

Faced with mounting criticism, Protopopov attempted to muzzle the liberals by closing down all the proposed meetings. The congresses of the Union of Towns and the Union of Zemstvos and the Congress of the Food Supply Question were not the only meetings banned by the police. Others included the meetings of pediatricians, the polytechnical society, dental school assistants, and the historical circle of Shniavskii People's University.[35]

The Progressive Bloc, which other liberal organizations expected to play the central role in the struggle against the government, continued to drag its feet. Konovalov, who had already walked out of the Bloc, proposed to his liberal colleagues that they combat the government through a general strike of liberal organizations. This would include the self-prorogation of the Duma and the resignations of L'vov and Chelnokov from the Unions and Towns and of Zemstvos. Konovalov's proposal, however, was received coldly and, even worse, snickered at by his liberal colleagues as a quixotic gesture. An Okhrana agent reported: "If the government would show the slightest sign of concession, the Kadets would come around to meet it." Despite the sensational speeches delivered by Miliukov and Purishkevich, the Duma accomplished little and adjourned for Christmas recess on December 16. On the last day of the Duma session Miliukov stated: "Our goal has not been fulfilled, and this must loudly be admitted. To the same degree that the faith in the popular representation is being lost, other forces, gentlemen, are entering into action. We are now experiencing a terrible moment. Before our very eyes, the liberal struggle is getting beyond the framework of strict legality and like in 1905 illegal forces are again emerging. The atmosphere is full of electricity. One can feel in the air the approach of thunder. No one knows, gentlemen, where and when lightning will strike."[36]

Several hours after this speech was delivered in the Tauride Palace, on the other side of the city a flash of lightning struck in the elegant house of Iusupov on the Moika River—a flash, which, to be sure, did not immediately bring a storm, but nonetheless foreshadowed its approach. Rasputin had been invited by young Prince Iusupov, married to Nicholas's niece Irina, to his house on the pretext that his stunningly beautiful wife, who was actually vacationing in the Crimea, wished the privilege of meeting the holy man. His weakness for women this time proved fatal for Rasputin, for the conspirators— Purishkevich, Prince Iusupov, Grand Duke Dmitrii Pavlovich (Nicholas's

Reform in Tsarist Russia," *Russian Review* 35, no. 3 (1976): 290-302.

    35. Diakin, *Russkaia burzhuaziia*, p. 259.

    36. Chermenskii, *IV gosudarstvennaia duma*, pp. 231-32.

cousin), and a few others—brutally murdered him and dumped his body into the frozen Neva. The names of the assassins was telling evidence of how rotten the foundations of the tsarist regime had become. They were not revolutionary bomb throwers but the staunchest monarchists, who believed that the only way to save the monarchy was to get rid of Rasputin. Rasputin was removed, but his removal did not change the political climate. Rather it cast an ominous shadow on the future.

The "sacred union" between the government and the liberals, formed at the outbreak of the war, had degenerated into mutual distrust by the end of 1916. Theoretically, there were various options open to both sides, which would ultimately have led to the total and final split between the two. The government could have dissolved the Fourth Duma, ordered a new election to the Fifth Duma, or suspended the Duma entirely during the war. It could also have disbanded all voluntary organizations, expelled the representatives of society from the special councils, and monopolized the food supply system. It could have arrested the Miliukovs and Guchkovs and shipped them to Siberia. These measures were in fact proposed by individual ministers and various reactionary groups, and some of them were seriously contemplated. But the government never took a decisive step that might once and for all have ruptured the relationship with the liberals.

Nicholas's actions during the war, at least from the tactical point of view, were skillful manipulations of the conflicting advice he received from the two opposing camps of advisors. By rejecting the reactionary policy favoring a virtual declaration of war against society, Nicholas kept the illusion of the internal reforms alive among the liberals, thereby preventing the liberals from taking radical action against the government. And yet he never allowed his concessions to go beyond the limit he could tolerate for the preservation of the integrity of autocracy. Nicholas's "stick and carrot" emasculated the liberal opposition and won him a tactical victory. But he did not realize that beneath the inaction of the liberals there was deep despair and anger that psychologically paved the way for their rejection of the regime. The tactical victory, thus, in a long run cost him the war.

On the other hand, the liberals could have taken more decisive action. They could have boycotted the special councils, passively resisted the government by withdrawing support of government policies, and made an alliance with the workers. Such a course was advocated by Konovalov and other left-wing liberals, and, from outside, was strongly urged by the moderate Socialists, who wanted to see the Russian bourgeoisie lead a struggle to overthrow the tsarist regime

in the same way that the French had toppled the monarchy and accomplished a "bourgeois-democratic revolution." The liberals, however,
refused to take any decisive action against the government, quite
apart from attempting to overthrow it.

One factor that prevented the final breakup of the bad marriage
was the mutual fear of a revolution in time of war. Despite the unfounded rumor about the government's intrigue for a separate peace,
both the government and the liberals were deeply committed to the
continuation of the war. Not only would a revolution be fatal to the
war effort, but it would threaten their very existence. The government
was, therefore, not anxious to throw the liberals to the other side
of the barricade. And the liberals were careful not to ignite an explosive
mass movement by making their criticism of the government too inflammatory.

There was another aspect that explained the avoidance of the final
breakup. Although the political relationship between the government
and the liberals became strained, the war brought the two closer together in terms of economic organization. To meet the economic
needs created by the war, the government relied more and more on
the initiative of the industrialists, the voluntary organizations, and
municipal and local self-governments. By the same token, the latter
needed the centralized guidance of the government. To take one
example, the food supply system represented the close relationship
and interdependence between government and society. The government
could not feed the army and the population without cooperation from
the zemstvos and city dumas; and without the centralized bureaucratic
mechanism and the guidance of the bureaucracy, the liberals could
not have handled the enormous task of food supply. Their mutual
hatred and distrust, combined with the mutual dependency, made
their relationship peculiarly ambiguous. And this ambiguity would
ultimately color the nature of the February Revolution.

4

PETROGRAD DURING THE WAR

 During the years of the war, Petrograd stood, in melancholy beauty, silent witness to the madness: the patriotic fever that seized the people in the streets at the outbreak of the war, Rasputin and the debauchery of the aristocratic ladies, the oppressive silence of the long queues in front of the bakeries, angry mobs of workers on strike, underground revolutionaries conspiring around dim lamps, the mounted police whipping fleeing demonstrators with their nagaikas, armed robberies committed by juvenile delinquents, an epidemic of suicides, the prosperity of whorehouses. A city of decadence and depravity, it smelled of blood, lust, and anger. The Soviet historical novelist Aleksei Tolstoi described Petrograd during the war:

Two centuries had passed like a dream: Petersburg, standing at the end of the earth, on the marshes and wastelands, had been lost in reverie of unlimited glory and power. Like visions in a delirium, palace coups, murders of emperors, triumphs, and bloody executions passed in a flash. Weak women seized a semidivine power. Sturdily built youths arrived with hands still black with dirt, and dared to climb up on the throne in order to share power, bed, and Byzantine luxury.

The neighbors looked around with horror to see these mad explosions of fantasy. With despondency and fear the Russian people surrendered to the delirium of the capital. The country fed Petersburg with its own blood, but never satisfied her appetite.

Petersburg lived a night life, satiated and shivering with excitement. Phosphorous summer nights, insane and voluptuous, and sleepless winter nights, green tables and a rustle of gold, music, twirling couples behind the windows, mad troikas, gypsies, duels at dawn, in the whistle of icy wind and the shrill sound of the flute—a parade of troops in front of the Byzantine eyes of the Emperor, which conjured up horror—thus lived the city.

In the past decade grandiose enterprises had been established with incredible speed. Millions of fortunes appeared as if from thin air. With crystal and cement they built banks, music halls, skating rinks, and magnificent saloons, where people became deadened by music, reflections of mirrors, half-naked women, light, and champagne. Hurriedly, gambling clubs, whorehouses, theaters, movie houses, and luna parks were opened. Engineers and capitalists worked for a project for a new construction, which would surpass the luxury of the capital, in an inhabited island not far from Petersburg.

In the city there was an epidemic of suicides. Courtrooms were filled with crowds of hysterical women, greedily demanding bloody and stimulating trials. Everything was possible—luxury and women. Debauchery was everywhere. It struck the palace like an infection.

And an illiterate *muzhik* with mad eyes and mighty masculine power reached the palace and the imperial throne, and mocking and sneering, began to defame Russia.

Petersburg, like any other city, lived a single life, tense and worried. The central power led this movement, but it did not go along with what could be called the spirit of the city. The central power strove to create order, peace, and expediency, while the spirit of the city strove to destroy this power. The spirit of destruction was in everything, saturating with its deadly poison the grandiose machinations of the stock market by famous Sashka Sakelman, the dark anger of a worker in a steel mill, and the broken dreams of a fashionable poetess, sitting after four o'clock in the morning in the artists' basement of "Red Bells,"—even those who were supposed to fight against it, unaware of it themselves, did everything to reinforce and quicken the destruction.

It was the time when love, and good, healthy feelings were considered banal and obsolete. No one loved, but everyone longed, like the poisoned, to press himself to everything so sharp that it would lacerate internal organs.

Girls concealed their virginity, wives their fidelity. Destruction was considered good taste, and neurasthenia a sign of refinement. This was preached by popular writers who emerged in one season from obscurity. People schemed up vices and perversions only to desire new ones.

Such was Petersburg in 1914. Tormented by sleepless nights, and numb with anguish caused by wine, money, unloved love, and the tearing and hopelessly emotional sounds of the Tango—a hymn of death—she lived as if in expectation of the fateful and terrible day. And that was a sure premonition—something new and incomprehensible was crawling out of every crack.[1]

Petrograd, the largest metropolis in the Russian Empire, was the center of everything. It was the seat of government, the economic and industrial center, and the mecca of cultural activities. All the government's buildings were concentrated in the center of the city. The sumptuous Winter Palace overlooked, on the one side, the Great Neva and the Small Neva, which split at the point of Vasilievskii Island, and across the Great Neva, the Fortress of Peter and Paul. On the other side, across Palace Square, it faced the massive General Staff building, where in addition to the main administration of the General Staff,

1. Aleksei Tolstoi, *Khozhedenie po Mukam, izbrannye sochineniia* 3 (Moscow, 1951): 8-10.

the Ministries of Foreign Affairs and of Finance were housed together. On the west side of the Winter Palace along the Neva stood the Admiralty with its high spire. Across from the Admiralty on the south the *gradonachal'stvo*, the headquarters of the Okhrana, occupied the corner of Gorokhovaia Street and on its west side, two stone lions guarded the yellow building of the War Ministry. Further west on the Neva, across from the statue of the bronze horseman in Senate Square, stood the buildings of the Senate and the Holy Synod. Next to the War Ministry on the south towered St. Isaac's Cathedral, the tallest building in Petrograd. If one stood by the statue of Nicholas I on horseback in the middle of Marinskaia Square in front of St. Isaac's, one would see on the east the Ministry of Agriculture next to the Hotel Astoria, one of the most luxurious hotels in Petrograd (which was commandeered by the military authority for officers on leave and officers of Allied Nations) and on the south, the Marinskii Palace, the seat of the Council of Ministers and the State Council. A short walk from the Winter Palace to Marinskaia Square, which would not take more than half an hour, would be enough for one to be overwhelmed by the power of the tsarist regime.[2]

The most famous street in Petrograd was the Nevskii Prospekt. Along this boulevard, stretching three and one-half kilometers from the Admiralty to the Aleksandr-Nevskaia Monastery, there were banks, stores such as Eliseev's, Martens, the office of Singer Sewing Machine, the most famous department store, the Gostinyi Dvor, many hotels, including the luxurious Evropeiskaia, and expensive restaurants and cafes. There were also palaces: the Anichkov Palace, the Stroganov House, the Palace of Grand Duke Dmitrii Pavlovich, who took part in Rasputin's assassination, and the Mikhailovskii Palace just off the Nevskii. The Kazan Cathedral stood in stark neoclassical grandeur on the north side of the Nevskii. Between Kazan Cathedral and Gostinyi Dvor, across from Hotel Evropeiskaia, stood the City Duma with its tall spire. The building next to Gostinyi Dvor across Sadovaia Street was the public library; and between the library and Anichkov Palace, behind the statue of Catherine the Great, was the magnificent Royal Alexander Theater. In sum, the Nevskii Prospekt was the symbol of the wealth and power of the privileged. People who could not afford proper attire usually did not venture into it. There were occasions, however, when the poor did invade the Nevskii, disrupting

2. The most important reference book for geographical locations in Petrograd in 1917 is *Ves' Petrograd na 1917 god: adresnaia i spravochnaia kniga g. Petrograda*. The Ministries of Internal Affairs, Education, and Trade and Industry were scattered along the Fontanka.

the decorum of privileged society. Since 1876, when the first political demonstration was staged in Kazan Square by the Populists, including young Georgii Plekhanov, later to become the founder of Russian Marxism, the stretch of Nevskii from Kazan Square to Znamenskaia Square in front of the Nikolaevskii Railway Station had been the favorite target of political demonstrations. But because of heavy police protection, workers seldom succeeded in staging a demonstration there.

The population of Petrograd was approximately two and one-half million in 1917, an increase of 200,000 from the beginning of the war. Unfortunately, a breakdown of the population according to occupation during the war does not exist, since the last census was taken in 1910. The 1910 census indicated that of a total population of 1,881,000, workers numbered 504,000 or 27 percent and 234,000 of these were factory workers. The rest of the workers included clerks in commercial and financial organizations (77,000), transport workers (52,000), and waiters, waitresses, and cooks (25,000). In addition, 41,000 worked for the city transport, water, electricity, gas, and other city organizations. There were 58,000 artisans—shoemakers, tailors, carpenters, joiners, painters, cleaners, and so on—constituting 3 percent of the population. Approximately 260,000 worked as household or institutional servants, guards, stableboys, janitors, cooks, cleaning ladies, laundresses, gardeners, porters, butlers, and so on. These servants, about 14 percent of the total population, constituted the lower stratum in Petrograd.[3]

On the other side of the scale, the nobility numbered 138,000 or 7.2 percent. There were landowners such as the Sheremetievs and Iusupovs, who owned land all over Russia. The Sheremetievs, for instance, owned 800,000 dessiatines of land or 17,600,000 acres. But very few nobles could live solely on their estates. Many had to find other means of support: in the bureaucracy, in intellectual or professional work, or in business. Some nobles invested their wealth in business and became industrialists. Still a greater number, nobles only by title, were rapidly becoming déclassé.

The economic life of Petrograd was dominated by a handful of financial and industrial oligarchs. Altogether the number of businessmen in Petrograd was less than 1 percent of the total population, but these owners of large banks, joint-stock companies, and huge industrial plants exerted almost exclusive economic control over the city. They formed the Petrograd Association of Factory Owners, led by

---

3. E. E. Kruze and D. E. Kutsentov, "Naselenie Petrograd," *Ocherki istorii Leningrada* 3: 104-46; *Petrograd po perepisi 15 dekabria 1910 goda*, pt. 2.

A. I. Putilov and A. I. Vyshnegradskii. Putilov headed the great Russo-Asian Bank, which had fourteen affiliates and was one of the largest stockholders of the syndicates, Promet, and Putilov Factory, the Neva Shipyard, Baranovskii, the Petrograd Wagon Factory, and many others. In contrast to the Moscow industrialists, who became the backbone of the Russian liberal opposition, the Petrograd oligarchs were known by their close association with the government and by their political conservatism. In addition to the large industrialists, there were 21,000 owners of stores, shops, and restaurants.

Approximately seventy thousand persons worked in the bureaucracy. They included those officials who reached the highest rungs of what was known as the Table of Ranks, as well as those on the lowest levels, who could not be counted as nobility, but bore the humiliating title of "honorary citizen." It is presumed that the economic status of the lowest stratum of the bureaucracy was no better than that of the workers, but they refused to live in the workers' quarters and formed their own ghettos in the inner city. Various members of the intelligentsia and the professional class—writers, artists, university professors, lawyers, doctors, teachers, and so on—numbered roughly two hundred thousand or 11 percent. During the war the living standards of the lower middle class deteriorated sharply. According to a city teacher who wrote a letter of complaint to one of the Petrograd newspapers about the difficult lives of teachers, it was impossible to live a decent life on the salary they received. Out of a salary of one hundred rubles a month, at least twenty rubles had to go for rent, and it was almost impossible to find a room for such a low rent in the entire city. Since they could not afford to live in a boarding house, they were forced to eat their main meal in the students' dining halls or in the dining halls run by the city's welfare departments—a humiliation. This itself cost at least twenty-five rubles a month, and since one could not get by on only one meal a day, another thirty rubles had to be spent for breakfasts and evening snacks. Working among dirty children, the teachers needed at least fifteen rubles for laundry. That meant that they were left with only ten rubles for tea, sugar, paper, the theater, books, and clothes: "We shall not talk about the high price of boots and skirts, which the teachers dispensed with for three to five years." Consequently, many teachers were forced to find another job after school, despite strict regulations forbidding such practice. It was not rare that the teachers, the most educated of all Russian women, had not read a single page for months and had not gone to a theater for years. The writer of the letter bitterly asked: "What can a person, tired, half-sick, and not living a normal life, teach the children?"[4] The life of other lower middle-class people could not have been much different. Even the Okhrana agents complained about the high cost of living, as a result of which they could no longer afford to buy "any underclothes, which in the service of police spies wear out very quickly," and demanded an increase in their wages by five rubles a month.[5]

Petrograd was also an educational and cultural center. There were sixty institutions of higher education in Petrograd, with 40,000 students, including Petrograd Imperial University (7,000 students), Bestuzhev Women's College (6,000), the Mining Institute (2,000), the Polytechnical Institute (6,000), and Technological Institute (3,000). The first three were located in the academic complex that included the Academy of Sciences, the Academy of Artists, and the Zoological Museum on Vasilievskii Island, the center of learning. Another student district was the Vyborg District, which contained the Military Medical Academy, the Polytechnical Institute and the Institute of Forestry. Although through the years the composition of the student body was democratized, there was a preponderance of the children of the nobility. Of all the students in St. Petersburg in 1910 35.4 percent were from the nobility, 19.1 percent were children of honorary citizens and merchants, and only 10.4 percent were peasants. There were 150 secondary schools in 1914, including gymnasia and trade and commercial schools for men and women. In 1915 there were 16,000 male students in the secondary schools, 9,000 of whom were from the nobility.[6]

Petrograd was a segregated city, where the privileged and the poor rarely mixed. The boundaries of living quarters were clearly delineated. The nobility and the well-to-do lived in the center of the city: the Admiralty, Kazan, and Liteinaia districts, and the southern parts of Vasilievskii Island and Petrograd District. The embankments of the Neva, Moika, Fontanka, and Ekaterina Canal were occupied by the elegant houses of the grand dukes, nobles, and the wealthiest industrialists. The Petrograd District became a favorite residential area for the intelligentsia, while the petty bureaucrats preferred to live in the poorer neighborhoods of the Petrograd District, Vasilievskii Island, and above all in the Moscow District behind Gostinyi Dvor.

The workers and artisans lived on the outskirts of the city—the Vyborg District, the outskirts of the Petrograd District, and Vasilievskii

4. *Rech'*, February 11, 1917.

5. TsGAOR, f. DPOO, op. 5, d. 669 (1917 g.), ℓ. 235.

6. Workers also carried the passports that classified them as peasants. For education in St. Petersburg, see S. S. Volk, "Prosveshchenie i shkola v Peterburge," *Ocherki istorii Leningrada* 3: 551-52, 561-62.

Island and the south end of the Obukhov Canal, particularly in the Narva and Peterhof districts. Almost all large factories were located in these industrial sections of the city. The Vyborg District was the most developed industrial complex. Along the narrow strip surrounded by the Vyborg District's main boulevard, the Sampsonievskii Prospekt, and the Nevka Naberezhnaia, stood the gigantic metallurgical plants of New Lessner, Old Lessner, Erikson, Nobel, Baranovskii, and Parviainen. Along the Neva bank on the southeast, the Arsenal, the Cartridge Factory, the Petrograd Metal Factory, Promet, and Phoenix stood with their smokestacks. Other large plants were located in the northern part of the Petrograd District (Vulkan and Langenzippen), the eastern tip of Vasilievskii Island, known as the Harbor, or *Gavan'* (the Petrograd Cable Factory and the Baltic Shipyard), and its northern part (the Petrograd Pipe Factory). Another industrial complex was on the south side of the Obukhov Canal in the Narva District (Dinamo, Skorokhod, and Treugol'nik) and in the Peterhof District, where the largest factory in Russia, the Putilov Factory, which employed more than 24,000 workers, was located.[7] Many artisans and small factory workers lived in the Ligovskaia District south of the Nikolaev- skii Railway Station, the roughest neighborhood in the entire city, full of taverns and houses of prostitution, where violence was rampant and the underground Ligovskaia gangs terrorized the residents. Another center for vice was around the Sennaia Square, famous for the Hay- market, a neighborhood that had undergone little change from the days of Dostoevsky's *Crime and Punishment.* During the war the population of prostitutes increased four to five times, and the incidence of venereal disease reached epidemic proportions, particularly near the soldiers' barracks.[8]

No city in Europe displayed so glaringly the barriers between the privileged and the poor as Petrograd. The elegance and modern con- veniences of its center equaled those of any other city in Europe. The poor did not need to see the Winter Palace or the Iusupov house to be overwhelmed by wealth. Only a few minutes' walk to any fashion- able street could evoke a sense of rejection from the beautifully or-

7. For the number of workers and the location of the factories in Petrograd in 1917, the most reliable source is *Spisok fabrichno—zavodskikh predpriiatii Petrograda.* Petrograd was divided into the following administrative districts *(chasti)*: (1) Admiralty, (2) Aleksandr-Nevskaia, (3) Vasilievskii Island, (4) Vyborg, (5) Kazan, (6) Kolomenskaia, (7) Liteinaia, (8) Moscow, (9) Narva, (10) Petrograd, (11) Rozhdestvo, and (12) Spasskaia. In addition, the following districts *(uchastok)* were attached to the city: (1) Lesnoi, (2) Novaia derevnia, (3) Okhta, (4) Aleksan- drov, (5) Poliustrovo, (6) Peterhof, and (7) Schlüsselburg.

8. *Krasnyi arkhiv* 17, no. 4 (1926): 8.

namented walls of those houses. In the Admiralty and Kazan districts 90 percent of the dwellings were of stone, but on Vasilievskii Island the stone buildings, including the factories, constituted only 29.4 percent, in the Vyborg District, 11.9 percent, and the Narva District, Novaia Derevnia and Okhta combined, only 5 percent. The crowding of the poor grew worse during the war with the sudden influx of people. It was not rare for ten to twenty persons to share a room. One source of statistical data tells us that only 18 persons out of 205 single workers slept in a single bed. Often an entire household had to sleep in one bed.[9] But those who slept in bed must have considered themselves fortunate, since many workers had to sleep on a bench in the corner of a room. Comparing these conditions with the letter written by the teacher who complained about the difficulty of finding a single room at a price within reach, one realizes the differences between the two worlds.

In the center of the city the streets were paved with cobblestones or asphalt and lighted by electricity or gas, and these modern conveniences were made available for the households in that area. Public transportation was by streetcar, which had been introduced at the turn of the century. Automobiles were available by the time of the war, but they generally were used by officials or were the luxurious toys of the wealthy. Many still depended on horse-drawn carriages, and cabs which busily weaved through the city's streets, were exclusively horse-drawn. But these "modern conveniences" did not extend to the workers' quarters. Streets were generally not paved, and in the spring they turned into a sea of mud. No one on the outskirts enjoyed electricity or gas, but relied on kerosene lamps. Although the water station had been established in the 1890s, the city's water main did not extend to the workers' districts, a contribution to the frequent epidemics. Streetcars did not run in the workers' quarters.[10] It was progress that widened the gap between the poor and the privileged, and made the resentment of those who could not share its fruits bitterer and more violent.

Administratively the capital was under the thumb of the *gradona-chal'nik*, appointed by and directly responsible to the minister of internal affairs. The eyes and ears of the tsar, he controlled the police, the gendarmes, and the Okhrana, and served as the watchdog over

9. I. P. Leiberov, *Petrogradskii proletariat v Fevral'skoi revoliutsii 1917 goda* 1: 17, Kruze and Kutsentov, "Naselenie Petrograda," pp. 132-33.

10. See N. N. Petrov, "Gorodskoe upravlenie i gorodskoe khoziaistvo Petrograda," *Ocherki istorii Leningrada* 3: 900-901.

the conduct of the municipal self-government, known as the city duma. After the outbreak of war, Petrograd was placed in the war theater, and its security became the direct responsibility of the commander of the Petrograd Military District. The city's day-to-day functions were entrusted to the city duma, the members of which were chosen by electors who met property qualifications so high that only eleven to twelve thousand of the two and one-half million residents were qualified. The electors elected 150 city duma deputies, who in turn elected the city administration (gorodskaia uprava) and the mayor (golova). The city administration was responsible for the use of city land, the running of city enterprises, city sanitation, the organization of public health and other services, the management of transportation, and the administration of schools, hospitals, and welfare services (popechitel'stvo). In addition, during the war the onerous task of providing food for the city was thrust upon the city duma. Within the city duma there was a constant struggle between the conservative elements, which opposed the city's active participation in social services, and more progressive elements, led by the Kadets, which vigorously attempted to extend welfare, medical care, transportation, and other social services to the widest number of people. Despite constant harassment from the gradonachal'nik, and the obsolete municipal law, the city duma made some progress in providing services in the city.[11] But progress was excruciatingly slow compared with the rising expectations of the masses.

Excluded from participation in the decisions concerning their lives, cramped in stinking, dirty living quarters, always hungry and tired, the poor looked across the river with envy and resentment. Nor did the corrupt upper class set a fine example. "Respectable" ladies flocked to Rasputin's apartment. His orgies, visible from the street through curtainless windows, provided an exciting spectacle.[12] Yet Rasputin's frolics were but one sign of the decadence of the Russian ruling class. The poor envied them, but at the same time with righteous indignation condemned them.

Such was the Petrograd that was about to pass the halfway mark in the third year of the war. And as Blok's poem so well expresses, there stood in the city, as always, "Night, a street, a lamp, and a chem-

11. For the inadequacies of the municipal law, see Michael Hamm, "The Breakdown of Urban Modernization: A Prelude to the Revolution of 1917," in The City in Russian History, ed. Michael Hamm (Lexington: University of Kentucky Press, 1976), pp. 182-200.

12. "Poslednii vremenshchik poslednego tsaria," Voprosy istorii, no. 10 (1964), p. 124.

ists shop," with "a meaningless and dim light." There seemed to many, like Blok, "no way out."

5

THE WAR AND THE WORKERS

Nothing was more dangerous to the tsarist regime than the political and social isolation of the working class, which was outside the existing social order—never integrated into privileged society. The heavy concentration of workers in a few large cities, the preponderance of large plants, and the peculiar mixture of advanced technology with the backwardness of Russian industrial development all contributed to the explosive, destructive nature of the working class. If the workers welcomed the outbreak of the war, their patriotic enthusiasm soon gave way, with the military defeat and the government's corruption, to disillusionment and then to anger as the cost of living increased sharply. The government's repressive policy, which eliminated practically all legal avenues of protest, drove them to radical action. By the end of 1916, the workers, who had been silenced by the onset of the war, began to listen to the revolutionary agitators calling for an overthrow of the tsarist regime. It is important, therefore, to examine the source of the rapid radicalization of the workers in Petrograd.[1]

Petrograd was the largest industrial center in Russia. At the beginning of 1917, it had 8.3 percent of the nation's factories within its boundaries, producing 22 percent of the total industrial output. Also the greatest number of workers were concentrated in Petrograd. At the beginning of 1914 they numbered 242,600, or 9.1 percent of the

1. My research on the Petrograd workers is not exhaustive. My purpose in this chapter is to present some hypotheses and raise questions rather than to make definitive conclusions on a number of important issues.

total work force in Russia. In three years of war this number rose to
392,800, an increase of 62 percent. An additional 24,200 worked
in neighboring regions outside the capital, where such large plants
as Izhora, Sestroretsk Weapons, and Schlüsselburg Gunpowder Factories were located. Altogether, Petrograd and its neighboring regions had 417,000 workers or 11.9 percent of all the workers in
Russia.[2]

Such a rapid expansion of Petrograd industry was closely connected
with the war. By August 1916, 94 percent of the workers and 61 percent of the factories in Petrograd were engaged in military production.[3]
The war drastically changed the composition of the workers by trade
(see table 1). The number of metalworkers doubled to 237,400 or
60 percent of the total work force in Petrograd. Although their proportion declined during the war, textile workers were the second largest
group (44,100 or 11.2 percent). Third were chemical workers, who
had increased by 85 percent, numbering 40,100 or 10.2 percent.
Another important effect of the war was the increased number of

TABLE 1

COMPOSITION OF PETROGRAD WORKERS BY TRADE

Industry	Number of Workers (in thousands)		Increase (+) or Decrease (-) 1/1/1914 through 1/1/1917	
	1914	1917	(in thousands)	(in percentages)
Metal/Hardware	100.6	237.4	+136.8	+136
Chemical	21.6	40.1	+ 18.5	+ 85.6
Textile	40.1	44.1	+ 4.0	+ 10
Paper/Printing	27.5	26.5	- 1.0	- 3.6
Food	22.7	15.8	- 6.9	- 30.4
Wood processing	5.0	6.7	+ 1.7	+ 34
Leather/Shoe	8.0	12.6	+ 4.6	+ 57.5
Mineral processing	2.2	3.9	+ 1.7	+ 77.3
Others	14.9	5.7	- 9.2	- 61.7
Totals	242.6	392.8	+150.2	+ 62

SOURCE: I. P. Leiberov, "Petrogradskii proletariat v gody pervoi mirovoi voiny,"
Istoriia rabochikh Leningrada 1: 466.

2. I. P. Leiberov, "Petrogradskii proletariat v gody pervoi mirovoi voiny,"
Istoriia rabochikh Leningrada 1: 462; Z. P. Stepanov, *Rabochie Petrograda v
period podgotovki i provedeniia Oktiabr'skoi vooruzhennogo vosstaniia* (Moscow,
1965), pp. 25-26. Stepanov's figure of the total number of Petrograd workers
is 385,000, about 7,000 smaller than Leiberov's figure.
3. Leiberov, "Petrogradskii proletariat v gody pervoi mirovoi voiny," p. 463.

large plants. The average number of workers per factory rose from 536 in 1913 to 974 in 1917. At the beginning of 1917, 132 factories alone, comprising only 13 percent of all factories, employed 317,328 workers or 80.7 percent of the total work force in Petrograd. The average number of workers per factory in this category was 2,404.[4] The largest was the Putilov Factory, which employed more than 24,000, followed by the Petrograd Pipe Factory (19,046), Treugol'nik (15,338), Obukhov (10,600), Okhta Explosives (10,200), and the Petrograd Cartridge Factory (8,292). All were involved in war production and, with the exception of Treugol'nik, all were owned by the government.[5]

It should be noted that at the background of the revival of the workers' movement during the war, there was a tremendous expansion of Russian industry, particularly of those sectors connected with war production. This expansion created an acute labor shortage, especially of skilled metalworkers, and it was these metalworkers who participated most actively in the strike movement. They enjoyed relative security—in a labor market where they were in great demand, they could present their demands more forcefully than their comrades in other industries that did not share the prosperity created by the war boom. Shortly after the beginning of the war, the government discontinued the practice of drafting skilled workers into the army, and those who had been already drafted gradually came back to the factories.

It was not the privileged workers in the largest plants, where wages and fringe benefits were much better than those in lesser factories and where the government paid much closer attention both in "carrot" and "stick," that stood at the vanguard of the radical workers' movement. The most active participants in the strike movement during the war came from those metal manufactories in the Vyborg District that employed between 1,000 and 8,000 workers—New Lessner (6,500), Parviainen (7,300), Aivaz (4,000), Promet (3,000), Phoenix (1,940), Erikson (2,200), and Nobel (1,600). Although more definitive conclusions have to await further research, it appears that in the government-owned large munition factories the workers tended to be older and had worked in the same plant for many years, while the workers in these Vyborg factories tended to be younger and the turnover rate was higher. If this hypothesis is correct, it appears that the major impetus of the radicalization of the Petrograd workers came from

---

4. Stepanov, *Rabochie Petrograda*, p. 32.
5. *Spisok fabrichno-zavodskikh predpriiatii Petrograda*. The Putilov Factory was sequestered by the government in February 1916.

these highly skilled, confident, young metalworkers whose economic benefits were much better than those in other sectors in industry but not as good as the older, skilled workers in the large government plants. Also the size of these factories, not so big as to preclude rapid communication among the workers nor so small as to be suppressed easily by the factory administration and police, contributed to the rapid mobilization of the workers.

Geographically, almost 70 percent of the workers were employed in the industrial sections of the capital: Vyborg (18 percent), Vasilievskii (14 percent), Nevskii (11 percent), Narva (10 percent), Petrograd (10 percent), and Peterhof (9 percent) (see table 2). If we include Lesnoi and Poliustrovo, the two suburban districts adjoining the Vyborg District, almost 25 percent of Petrograd workers were concentrated in that region. An additional 20 percent were in the Narva-Peterhof region. In these industrial districts the metalworkers were a majority, constituting 84 percent of the Vyborg workers, 73 percent of the Vasilievskii workers, and 94 percent in the Peterhof District.[6] We can assume that the workers lived near the factories in which they worked. The heavy concentration of workers in the working-class district, segregated from other parts of the city, facilitated the consciousness of solidarity as well as of distinctiveness of their class from the other segments of society. The overwhelming preponderance of metalworkers injected into the other segments of the working class a distinct class consciousness.

The war also changed the social composition of the working class in Petrograd. The number of workers increased by 148,200 during the three years from 1914 to 1917. The new work force was supplied by peasants, women and children, refugees, soldiers, and the middle class. Although no statistical data are available, I. P. Leiberov, the foremost Soviet historian on the labor movement during the war, estimates that peasants constituted 50 to 75 percent of the newly recruited workers.[7] Despite this influx of peasants, Petrograd workers remained the most urban of all workers in Russia. According to the trade union census of 1918, before the October Revolution only 16.5 percent of the Petrograd workers owned land, compared with 31 percent in thirty-one other provinces, 35.7 percent in Ivanovo-Voznesensk, and 39.8 percent in Moscow Province. Only 7.9 percent of the Petrograd workers still maintained households in the villages, compared with 20.1 percent of the national average.[8]

6. Stepanov, *Rabochie Petrograda*, p. 30. See table 4.
7. Leiberov, "Petrogradskii proletariat v gody pervoi mirovoi voiny," p. 467.
8. Stepanov, *Rabochie Petrograda*, p. 39.

TABLE 2
REGIONAL DISTRIBUTION OF WORKERS IN PETROGRAD

Districts	Number of Workers				
	All industries		Metalworkers		
	absolute	percentage	absolute	percentage all workers in district	metal-workers
Petrograd proper					
Vyborg	68,932	18.2	57,978	84.0	24.5
Vasilievskii Island	51,876	13.7	37,530	72.0	15.9
Narva	38,784	9.9	6,549	16.7	2.7
Liteinaia, Aleksandr-Nevskaia	32,769	8.6	13,299	40.0	5.6
Petrograd	37,840	9.7	24,444	64.3	10.4
Moscow	21,079	5.4	11,012	52.5	4.7
Kolomenskaia	10,480	2.7	9,237	88.1	4.0
Admiralty, Kazan, Spasskaia	5,660	1.5	1,865	32.9	0.8
Rozhdestvo	10,233	2.6	2,063	20.5	0.9
Total	277,653	72.1	163,977	58.9	69.5
Suburbs					
Nevskii*	38,208	10.6	26,641	70.0	11.1
Peterhof	36,148	8.8	33,753	93.7	14.5
Lesnoi	6,811	1.7	6,015	88.1	2.5
Poliustrovo	18,931	4.8	1,262	6.6	0.5
Okhta	4,273	1.2	3,110	72.5	1.3
Novaia derevnia	3,083	0.8	1,631	52.7	0.6
Total	107,454	27.9	72,412	67.6	30.5
TOTAL, Petrograd and suburbs	385,107	100	236,389	61.4	100

SOURCE: Z. P. Stepanov, *Rabochie Petrograda v period podgotovki i provedeniia Oktiabr'skoi vooruzhennogo vosstaniia*, p. 30.

*Nevskii District was an administrative district south of Aleksandr-Nevskaia District. In the tsarist period it was called Schlüsselburg District and placed outside the city limits. After the October Revolution it was renamed Nevskii District and incorporated into the city.

The second source of new laborers was women and children (see table 3). The number of women increased in all sectors of industry. The predominance of women in the textile industry further intensified during the war, and in the food industry women supplied more than half the labor force. Even in the metal industry, where in peacetime there were few women workers, the increase of women workers to more than one-fifth was remarkable. Children were mostly employed as unskilled workers. The increase in the number of women and children, however, did not reflect a corresponding decrease in the absolute number of adult male workers in Petrograd (see table 4).[9] Also, compared with other cities, there was a smaller increase in the number of women and children working in Petrograd. In Moscow Province the percentage of women workers increased from 25.2 to 37.7 percent during the war, and in all Russia from 26.6 percent to 43.2 percent, but the increase in Petrograd was from 25.7 percent to 33.7 percent.

Refugees were the third element of the growing work force in Petrograd. As a result of German occupation of the Baltic provinces and Poland in 1915, a large number of refugees (84,100 in December 1915, and 400,000 in February 1916) registered in Petrograd. It is estimated that 40,000 to 50,000 of these refugees were factory workers. Despite this new influx, nationality minorities composed only a small fraction of Petrograd's work force: more than 84 percent were Great Russians, only 6 percent Poles, less than 3 percent Lithuanians and Latvians, and less than 2.5 percent Finns.[10]

The working soldiers were largely in the state munition factories: there were 11,129 in the state factories under the Main Artillery Administration. According the the information supplied by the Petrograd Association of Factory Owners, 27,426 soldiers worked in the factories belonging to this organization.[11] A majority of these soldiers were workers who remained in the factories as soldiers after they were mobilized. They were under military discipline and could be punished by a military tribunal for participating in a strike. On the whole, in the state-owned munition factories under the Main Artillery Administration, barracklike discipline was enforced, and workers were under the constant surveillance of the officers of the guard regiments.

The middle class was another source of labor. Squeezed by the sharp rise in the cost of living, some members of this class had to find

9. Ibid., pp. 34-36.
10. Ibid., p. 42.
11. Ibid.; TsGIA, f. 150, op. 1, d. 207, ℓℓ. 94-96.

TABLE 3

FEMALE AND CHILD LABOR

Industry	Year	Number of workers			Increase in women and children, 1913–1917 (in percentages)
		adult male	female	children	
		(in percentages)			
All industries	1913	66.2	25.7	8.1	7.7
	1917	58.5	33.3	8.2	
Metal/Hardware	1913	91.2	2.7	6.1	18.1
	1917	73.1	20.3	6.6	
Wood processing	1913	96.9	1.1	2.0	25.1
	1917	71.8	20.7	7.5	
Textile	1913	32.0	57.0	11.0	13.3
	1917	18.7	68.6	12.7	
Food	1913	51.8	40.7	7.5	29.6
	1917	22.2	66.0	11.8	
Leather/Shoe	1913	71.1	20.5	8.4	24.8
	1917	46.3	42.8	10.9	
Chemical	1913	56.1	41.6	2.3	9.3
	1917	46.8	46.7	6.5	
Mineral processing	1913	76.2	16.7	7.1	17.2
	1917	59.0	20.6	20.4	

SOURCE: Z. P. Stepanov, *Rabochie Petrograda v period podgotovki i provedeniia Oktiabr'skoi vooruzhennogo vosstaniia*, p. 34.

TABLE 4

MALE, FEMALE, AND CHILD LABOR

	Number of workers (in thousands)					
	adult male		women		children	
	absolute	percentage	absolute	percentage	absolute	percentage
January 1, 1914	158.4	100.0	61.6	100.0	22.9	100.0
January 1, 1917	231.2	152.1	129.8	210.6	31.8	138.8

SOURCE: Z. P. Stepanov, *Rabochie Petrograda v period podgotovki i provedeniia Oktiabr'skoi vooruzhennogo vosstaniia*, p. 36.

jobs in factories to support their families. Others chose to work in factories to avoid military service.[12]

The influx of the new labor force was important, not only because the relative weight of the original Petrograd workers from the prewar period was declining, but also because its number sharply declined in the absolute sense. Leiberov estimates that 40,000, or 17 percent, of the prewar industrial workers were mobilized from July 1914 to October 1916. Although this figure was much smaller than the mobilization figures in other cities, the removal of a proletarian core of such magnitude must have precipitated the decline of the strike movement immediately after the beginning of the war. Only 200,000 to 220,000 workers, or 50 to 52 percent of the total number of workers during the war in Petrograd remained in the factories. These figures roughly correspond to the data for the Phoenix Factory in the Vyborg District. At the beginning of 1917, approximately 50 percent of the Phoenix workers had been working in factories since the prewar period; 3 percent came from factories in Poland and the Baltic Provinces; 9 percent were children of 14 to 17 years of age; 10 percent were peasants, 17 percent were artisans, and another 13 percent had been servants. In the Aivaz Factory there were 2,063 adult workers from the fall of 1914 to the end of 1916. Altogether 754 workers were called up, but only 68 were actually sent to the front, while 686 received deferment.[13]

Petrograd workers led the nation in literacy. The trade union census of 1918 indicated that the literacy rate of the Petrograd workers was 88.9 percent for men and 64.9 percent for women, compared with the national average of 79.2 percent for men and 44.2 percent for women. It was highest among the Petrograd metalworkers, whose literacy rate reached 92 percent for men and 70 percent for women.

Primary education was gradually reaching working-class children. The data taken from 724 workers in the metal workshop of the Putilov Factory indicates that 5.5 percent were illiterate; 23.3 percent had gone to one-year parochial schools; 47.5 percent had finished two-year city, village, or parochial schools; 9.6 percent had received three years of district or four years of city elementary schooling; and only two workers had more than four years of schooling.[14] Vocational

12. O. I. Shkaratan, "Izmeneniia v sotsial'nom sostave fabrichno-zavodskikh rabochikh Leningrada, 1917-1924," *Istoriia SSSR*, no. 5 (1959), p. 24.

13. Leiberov, "Petrogradskii proletariat v gody pervoi mirovoi voiny," pp. 468-69; I. P. Leiberov and O. I. Shkaratan, "K voprosu o sostave Petrogradskikh promyshlennykh rabochikh v 1917 gody," pp. 47-54; Stepanov, *Rabochie Petrograda*, p. 43.

14. Stepanov, *Rabochie Petrograda*, pp. 43, 45.

training also became increasingly available to working-class children.

In her study of working-class youth in Moscow, Diane Koenker stresses the importance of education in the creation of an urban youth culture. In Petrograd as well as in Moscow the evening courses organized by progressive intelligentsia and cultural clubs in factories and the People's Houses became the most important gathering places for the working-class youth. "Familiarity with arts and literature," Koenker states, "became an important symbol of status for the most advanced young workers, who could be distinguished by the writing desks and portraits of authors with which they furnished their rooms."[15]

How did these changes in the composition of the working class in Petrograd affect the workers' movement? First of all, it should be emphasized that despite the significant additions, Petrograd workers remained the most urban, the most literate, and the least affected by the new influx of labor forces. More than half of the Petrograd workers during the war were those who had been working in the capital before the war began. To this core of the Petrograd proletariat were added the displaced proletarian evacuees from Poland and the Baltic provinces and a sizable number of urban youths who were growing into adulthood during the war. It seems certain that the revival of the labor movement came from this core of the proletariat; it was they who insured the continuity of radical tradition of the workers' movement.

But how did the influx of peasants, women, and children influence the radicalism of the workers' movement? Haimson states that the influx of the uprooted peasants during the war contributed to the growing element of *buntarstvo,* a penchant for direct radical action. Koenker, on the other hand, argues that the newly arriving peasants, unfamiliar with urban life, retained much of their rural culture and had little contact with the established workers.[16] It seems certain that the newly recruited peasants could not have been immediately mobilized into the strike movement. They had few skills to offer and thus could not work in the advanced factories from which the major impetus of the strike movement came. We are still in woeful lack of any sociological study that examines the peasants' assimilation into urban life. Were they so thoroughly overwhelmed and shocked by strange ways of city life, as Koenker argues, that they retired to

15. Diane Koenker, "Urban Families, Working Class Youth Groups, and the 1917 Revolution in Moscow," in *The Family in Imperial Russia,* ed. David L. Ransel, p. 289.

16. Leopold Haimson, "The Problem of Social Stability," *Slavic Review* 24, no. 1 (1965): 18; Koenker, "Urban Families," pp. 293, 301-2.

enclaves of "village communes"—a subculture in urban setting—independent and separate from urban-born workers? It does not seem unlikely, however, that the very nature of urban life—housing, transportation, factory—gradually drew them closer to their fellow workers. Loosely organized *zemliachestva* (associations of countrymen), to which newly arriving peasants looked for help, might have lessened the shock of transition from rural to urban life, and some *zemliachestva* were used for the express purpose of politicizing them. Having gone through the rapid social transformation in the village resulting from Stolypin's agrarian reform, from which they did not gain, they may not have been far from comprehending the language of class warfare in the cities. High cost of living, food shortages, crowded housing, long working hours—these new urban miseries must have made them embittered and resentful. They may not have been directly involved in the strike movement, but it is possible to argue that they constituted a reserve army of the more militant, politically conscious workers. An element of *buntarstvo* was manifested in late 1916 and in the beginning of 1917 in the attacks on food stores, which were almost always initiated by women and youths. As the February Revolution approached, the gap between the more organized strike movement and the element of *buntarstvo* narrowed. While organization drew the unorganized workers into the strike movement, direct action injected into it an explosive, violent character.

The war imposed a tremendous burden on working women, since the support of the family often fell on their shoulders, when husbands and fathers were sent to the front or were killed or wounded in the war. They worked long hours for a meager salary, and then had to do the household chores when they returned home. Child care was a problem. Some large factories established their own nurseries, and there was one cooperative day-care center in the Vyborg District.[17] Concerned with the high rate of infant mortality, the Petrograd Association of Factory Owners created a commission to investigate the matter. On January 18, 1917, the commission reported that the main causes of infant death and sickness were (1) poor nourishment and irrational care of babies, (2) unsanitary and "uncultured" care of infants by mothers, (3) the mother's undernourishment and exhaustion, and (4) unsanitary conditions, superstition, and poor attention to proper living conditions. The commission, however, concluded that the cost of establishing nurseries in each factory would be prohibitive, and recommended to the association that the factory owners might look into the possibility of creating "nursing rooms" for the working mothers.

17. Leiberov, *Petrogradskii proletariat v Fevral'skoi revoliutsii* 1: 76-77.

The absence of mothers at home also contributed to a sharp rise in the number of crimes committed by minors, which rose from 1,860 in 1913 to 1,987 in 1914, 2,197 in 1915, and 3,301 in 1916, an increase of 77 percent.[18]

If it is difficult to gauge the contribution of the peasants to the radicalism of the labor movement during the war, it is more difficult to examine how the sudden surge in the number of women in the labor force affected its outcome. On the one hand, almost one-half of the women workers in Petrograd had simply continued work in factories they had worked in prior to the war, and among the new recruits were those who had previously worked and who had been forced by war to return to factories. These women workers must have had some familiarity with the labor movement. On the other hand, despite the tremendous influx of female labor in Petrograd, women were predominantly employed in industrial sectors that did not participate in the strike movement until the beginning of 1917.

Both Haimson and Koenker agree that the main source of radicalization of the working class came from urban-born, working-class youths. Free from traditional family ties, thrust into adult life much earlier than their rural counterparts, and bound by a common educational background and a thirst for knowledge, the working-class youths created a uniquely urban youth culture. They had more skills, sophistication, and knowledge than the new workers from the peasantry and as a result they gained access to relatively better paying jobs. They attended evening classes and joined drama and reading circles. Some even dressed like members of the educated upper class on occasion. But the more they aspired to share the treasures of the privileged class, the more painfully aware they became of the unbridgeable gap that separated them from those they wanted to imitate. Envy of the culture and wealth that the privileged class commanded and yet pride in their own class became the distinct features of their class consciousness. Urban youths, thus alienated, looked for a community to which they could belong. For some, evening classes and cultural clubs satisfied their sense of belonging, but for others participation in the underground revolutionary parties offered another outlet. And the Bolshevik party, which preached the most radical action and the most intransigent rejection of the existing regime, was an attractive answer to the psychological needs of adventurous, alienated youths. As Koenker states, for the period after the February Revolution, "with no family responsibilities, few material possessions, and a low stock of human capital . . . youths were free to take

18. LGIA, f. 1278, op. 1, d. 183, ℓℓ. 5-7; *Rech'*, January 31, 1917.

risks with their futures," such as joining the Bolshevik party even during the repressive years of war. My study of the mid-level Bolshevik activists in 1917 indicates that while there was a sharp decline in membership of the intelligentsia, working-class youths joined the Bolshevik party during the war at a higher rate than previously.[19] It seems likely that the major strength of the Bolshevik party came from the young, skilled, urban-born workers.

The first factor that contributed to the revival of the workers' movement during the war was the deterioration of wages. Although the nominal wages of Petrograd workers were one and one-half times higher than the national average, the difference was eaten up by inflation. The real wages of Petrograd workers in 1916 were 90 to 95 percent of the 1913 level, and by February 1917, they had dropped an additional 15 to 20 percent. These figures, however, do not reveal the wide fluctuation among various industries as well as between skilled and unskilled workers. Only in two industrial sectors, the metal and chemical industries, did the real wages increase, by 20 and 13 percent, respectively. In the food and textile industries, where women and children were predominant, the wages were less than half those of metalworkers. The phenomenal increase in the cost of living was directly responsible for the decline in real wages. In October 1916 when prices were compared with those of 1913, rye and wheat flour went up by 243 percent and 269 percent, buckwheat by 320 percent, wheat by 308 percent, salt by 500 percent, butter by 845 percent, meat by 230 percent, sugar by 457 percent, and shoes and clothes by 400 to 500 percent.[20] It is no wonder that the most important economic demand of the workers during the war was for an increase in wages.

Leiberov and Shkaratan argue that there emerged during the war labor aristocrats who constituted the social basis for the moderate Socialists. The data of wage distribution of New Lessner indicate the following: 27 percent of all the workers received less than 60 rubles; 25 percent between 60 and 100 rubles; 20 percent between 100 and 140 rubles; 19 percent between 140 and 200 rubles; 5 percent between 200 and 240 rubles; and 4 percent more than 240 rubles a month. Leiberov and Shkaratan estimate that about 5 to 7 percent of Petrograd workers belonged to labor aristocrats who earned more than

19. Koenker, "Urban Families," pp. 280-94, 301-2; Tsuyoshi Hasegawa, "The Petrograd Bolsheviks in 1917: A Profile." (Paper presented at the Duquesne History Forum, Pittsburgh, 1975.)

20. Leiberov, "Petrogradskii proletariat v gody pervoi mirovoi voiny," pp. 470-71; Krasnyi archiv 17, no. 4 (1926): 11.

250 rubles a month.[21]   It is not likely, however, that amount of income inversely corresponded to the degree of participation in the strike movement. Young, skilled metalworkers who constituted the core of the strike movement may not have been the highest wage earners but they earned more than the average worker. Nevertheless, more precise conclusions must await a further statistical study.

Also contributing to the rise of the strike movement were the long working hours. The average work day in the metal industry was eleven to twelve hours, and some of the textile and leather workers frequently worked more than twelve to thirteen hours a day. This intensification of labor resulted in an increase of accidents and sickness to almost one and one-half to twice the 1913 level. In 1915 factory inspectors found 1,372 violations of health and security regulations, but ten factory owners only were fined a total of 385 rubles. In the same year there were 321,898 labor fines imposed on workers, exacting a total of 109,633 rubles. The neglect of security measures often led to tragic accidents. On April 16, 1915, an explosion in the Okhta Gunpowder Factory destroyed two workshops and eight neighboring residential buildings, killing 110 persons and wounding 220 more. On November 15, 1915, poor ventilation of a workshop in Treugol'nik led to the poisoning of 39 women workers, along with symptoms of hysteria—shouting, crying, and laughter. Five days later another 11 workers were affected by poisonous gas in the same workshop. In October 1915, 50 anonymous workers of Langenzippen sent a petition to factory inspectors requesting intervention on their behalf to have two ventilation pipes installed in the workshop, since "every worker complains of a headache" resulting from "smoke and the smell of oil." The factory management had refused their request, replying, "You don't need such pipes. You will get cold, since heat will escape and the air is harmful to you anyway."[22]

Factory workers endured a long work day under hazardous conditions, and they had little at home to provide ease or comfort. The crowded conditions in the workers' districts have already been mentioned. Because of the tremendous influx of new labor in Petrograd, the shortage of housing was acute—a situation that led the managements of large plants to build dormitories in the factory compounds. Rent skyrocketed—by the end of 1916 the average monthly rent had increased to twelve rubles, compared with three to four rubles before

21. Leiberov and Shkaratan, "K voprosy o sostave . . . ," pp. 55-56.
22. Leiberov, "Petrogradskii proletariat v gody pervoi mirovoi voiny," pp. 472-73; idem, *Petrogradskii proletariat v Fevral'skoi revoliutsii* 1: 66, 72.

the war.[23] Many tenants unable to pay the rent were literally thrown out into the streets.

But the most important question for the workers in Petrograd after the summer of 1915 was that of the food supply. The amount of flour transported to Petrograd Province dropped from 65 million poods in 1914 to 57 million in 1916, and to 28.6 million in 1917, or 44 percent below the 1913 level.[24] In the fall of 1915, wheat flour, meat, sugar, and butter disappeared from the market, and it became difficult to buy matches, soap, candles, and kerosene. Workers had to stand in long queues after work to buy a loaf of bread, and often by the time they got off work the bread had all been sold.

The government had no solution for the problems of the workers, but relied almost exclusively on oppression to keep them in hand. Trade unions were driven underground immediately after the outbreak of war. Workers' publications were closed down and their editors arrested. With the arrest of activists, the workers' sick-fund organizations were decimated, and the workers' group of the city-wide Insurance Council ceased to exist after the arrest of all but two members. An Okhrana agent proudly reported: "Until now in Petrograd there has been no work by trade unions, and the association of pharmacists is the only trade union functioning at the time of war." Strikes were outlawed and strikers were punished with hard labor of four months to four years. The Moscow *gradonachal'nik*, Klimovich, stated: "All strikes . . . which inevitably result in a slowdown of supply to the army, are a clear aid to our enemy, and cannot be other than a sinister betrayal of our brave soldiers and treason to the fatherland." On September 2, 1915, General Frolov, commander of the Petrograd Military District, issued a warning to workers that any participation in strikes would lead to a trial before a military tribunal and result in an indefinite period of exile.[25]

Repressive as these measures were, they did not stop the workers' strikes, which remained the only effective means to express grievances. When in the summer of 1915 the strike movement showed signs of revitalization, the government discussed the possibility of militarizing labor. On August 2, 1915, the minister of trade and industry presented a proposal to the Council of Ministers to place all industries engaged in war production under the jurisdiction of the War and Naval Ministries and to regulate workers by military discipline. Under this proposal

23. See chap. 4 and also *Krasnyi arkhiv* 17, no. 4 (1926): 11.

24. Leiberov, *Petrogradskii proletariat v Fevral'skoi revoliutsii* 1: 78; idem, "Petrogradskii proletariat v gody pervoi mirovoi voiny," p. 474.

25. M. G. Fleer, *Rabochee dvizhenie v Rossii v gody imperialisticheskoi voiny*, pp. 34-35, 43-44.

the workers "should be deprived of the right to leave or stop work or service." The Council of Ministers, however, decided not to adopt this measure for fear that such militarization of labor would provoke widespread protest.[26] In the fall of 1915 the strike movement gained impetus and at the beginning of 1916, the Council of Ministers returned to the question of militarization of labor. It decided to punish the strikers instead by sending them to the front. Leiberov and Shkaratan cite the following figures: 30 workers of New Lessner, Erikson, Neva Shipyard and others in July 1915; 80 workers of Lebedev in August 1915; 800 workers of Phoenix and Parviainen in February 1916; 172 workers of Neva Shipyard in April 1916; 130 workers of Petrograd Metal in May 1916; and 1,750 workers of major factories in October 1916; altogether 6,000 strike leaders were mobilized into the army during the period between July 1915 and December 1916.[27] From these figures it appears certain that the government systematically used this punitive measure to discourage strikes, not realizing that it was contributing to the spread of revolutionary sentiments in the army units.

Factory owners continued to use a system of "blacklisting"—the circulation of a list of political undesirables among the members of the Petrograd Association of Factory Owners as well as among military authorities. Although the factory owners pledged not to hire anyone on the list, the acute shortage of skilled workers and the ease with which the activists could conceal their identities rendered blacklisting ineffective.[28]

Despite police repression, Petrograd workers managed to maintain their legal and illegal networks of activities. During the war four types of legal organizations attempted to protect the workers' interests: insurance organizations, trade unions, workers' cooperatives, and cultural and educational clubs and circles.

The Insurance Law of 1912 gave the workers the right to establish a sick-fund office in factories, which in turn sent representatives to the provincial and city Insurance Councils. Although the Insurance Councils were made up mostly of representatives of the factory owners and were placed under the strict supervision of the minister of trade and industry, the workers were given a legal outlet through which they could protect their collective interests. From 1912 to 1914

26. Ibid., pp. 46-47.
27. Leiberov and Shkaratan, "K voprosy o sostave . . . ," p. 53; in addition, several hundred strikers at the Putilov Factory were sent to disciplinary battalions at the front. Fleer, *Rabochee dvizhenie*, p. 47; M. Balabanov, *Ot 1905 k 1917 godu: massovoe rabochee dvizhenie* (Moscow, Leningrad, 1927), pp. 392-93.
28. Fleer, *Rabochee dvizhenie*, p. 49.

the workers waged an insurance campaign, creating the workers' sick funds in factories, electing a workers' group in the Insurance Councils, and establishing a journal, *Voprosy strakhovaniia*. The campaign was organized under the influence of the Bolsheviks, and *Voprosy strakhovaniia* became the Bolsheviks' legal journal.[29] After the outbreak of the war, the government closed down *Voprosy strakhovaniia* and arrested leading activists of the insurance movement, which, however, did not completely eliminate all the insurance organizations. Although the workers' group in the Insurance Councils ceased to function, the sick funds at the factory level continued and provided the workers with their only viable legal organization. Early in 1915 the activists in the sick-fund organizations began to reestablish contact with each other and by February the workers' insurance group began functioning and *Voprosy strakhovaniia* reappeared. This campaign was, as in the prewar period, organized by the Bolsheviks, who again controlled the insurance journal and who used it to spread their influence among the Petrograd workers. Professional Bolshevik revolutionaries such as A. A. Andreev, S. Roshal', V. V. Kuibyshev, and M. I. Kalinin worked in the sick-fund organizations in various factories as "experts" in insurance matters. To fill the eleven positions vacated by the arrested representatives in the fifteen-member workers' group of the Insurance Council, the activists launched an election campaign from December 1915 through January 1916. The result was an overwhelming victory for the Bolsheviks, who elected ten, conceding only one to the Mensheviks. The Okhrana, with good reason, regarded the insurance organizations as "Social Democratic reserve battalions," and relentlessly persecuted the activists. From August 1914 to December 1916 the government conducted seventy-seven "search and destroy" operations in the sick-fund organizations. Since by the fall of 1916 four of the workers' representatives had been arrested and only two remained, another election was held in October 1916. The Bolsheviks took four of the five new seats.[30]

The workers' insurance movement provided workers with their legal organizational base and activists in the sick funds strove to achieve maximum protection for the workers, as provided by the Law of 1912. Although shackled by the government's censorship, they managed to publish a legal journal, which addressed itself, in between the censored blank pages, to the workers' economic issues. The

29. Zh. Z. Falkova, "Rabochaia gruppa strakhovogo soveta v gody pervoi mirovoi voiny," *Sbornik rabot Leningradskogo tekhnologicheskogo instituta pishchevoi promyshlennosti*, pp. 49-53.

30. Leiberov, *Petrogradskii proletariat v Fevral'skoi revoliutsii* 1: 415-17, 436; Falkova, "Rabochaia gruppa strakhovogo soveta," p. 63.

Bolsheviks, who led the insurance campaign during the war, took advantage of every opportunity to spread their political slogans through insurance activities. By the end of 1916 there existed in Petrograd eighty sick-fund organizations, which recruited more than 176,000 members, about 45 percent of the total number of Petrograd workers.[31]

Another organization the workers attempted to restore during the war was the trade union. The workers repeatedly petitioned the government for permission to re-form legal unions. Fifteen different trades presented such petitions between December 1914 and February 1917, but only five were permitted, and after August 1916 no new trade unions were allowed. During the war until February 1917, there existed in Petrograd eleven underground workers' trade unions and three legal nonproletarian trade unions (clerks in printing plants, pharmacists, and doormen). Even the largest, the Union of Metalworkers, had only 4,000 members out of a total of 237,400 metalworkers, and its functioning was constantly hampered by factional struggles between Bolsheviks and Mensheviks for control.[32] The rest of the trade unions organized a few hundred workers at most and, in general, their illegal existence made them almost meaningless. The activists therefore preferred to spend their energy in other legal outlets.

The never-ending inflation forced the development of another type of legal organization: the workers' cooperative. The first was established in November 1915, through the joint efforts of the factory owners (Old Lessner, Erikson, Nobel, and Phoenix) in the Vyborg District and the Menshevik leaders (Gvozdev, Breido, and Abrasimov). The main task of the cooperatives was to purchase food and other essential items and distribute them at low prices to the consumers. In less than a year eleven workers' cooperatives sprang up in various parts of the city and succeeded in recruiting 11,000 members and by February 1917 there were twenty-three cooperatives with 50,000 members.[33] If the insurance movement developed under the influence of the Bolsheviks, the cooperative movement was led by the moderate Mensheviks, who controlled *Trud,* the legal journal devoted to the cooperative movement. In April 1916 the Petrograd Union of Consumers' Associations was formed as a coordinating center of all the workers' cooperatives in Petrograd. The cooperative movement, how-

31. Leiberov, *Petrogradskii proletariat v Fevral'skoi revoliutsii* 1: 413.

32. Ibid., pp. 436-39; 444-45.

33. TsGIA, f. 150, op. 1, d. 673, ℓℓ. 63-64; Leiberov, *Petrogradskii proletariat v Fevral'skoi revoliutsii* 1: 460.

ever, did not remain merely an economic organization. The Mensheviks used the cooperatives as a point of contact between the workers' movement and the liberal opposition, as well as a basis to expand their influence among the wide masses of workers. In the beginning of 1916, an Okhrana agent reported: "The revolutionary-minded elements are attempting to use the cooperatives . . . exclusively as a form of legal possibility."[34]

Another network for the workers' movement comprised the cultural clubs and circles in factories and evening classes organized by liberal philanthropic activists at the People's Houses. In many large factories there were semilegal cultural clubs and reading circles. The reading materials and discussions in these clubs were avowedly political and designed to inculcate class consciousness among the masses of workers. They served also as centers for underground activists to recruit fellow travelers and were often used illegally as gathering places for strike organizers to plan strategy. It is not known how many such clubs and circles existed or how many workers participated, but their role in providing activists with a meeting place was not insignificant.

Nevertheless, the workers' greatest weapon remained the strike, although that movement quickly subsided immediately after the outbreak of war. On July 19, responding to the mobilization, the hard core of the workers' movement, around 27,000 in number from the large metal manufactories in the Vyborg District, staged a demonstration against the war, but they were quickly chased away by mounted police. Another contingent of about fifty demonstrators boldly marched on the Nevskii Prospekt only to be attacked by angry patriotic crowds. These two demonstrations were the last resonance of the strike movement that had climaxed in the general strike two weeks before the war. After that, the strike movement was moribund until the summer of 1915. While 110,000 workers had struck on January 9, 1914, the anniversary of Bloody Sunday, only 2,600 workers celebrated the traditional day of protest in 1915. When the Bolshevik Duma deputies were arrested in November 1914, no strikes occurred; and when they were brought to trial in February 1916, strikes were organized only in six factories, involving 340 workers (see tables 5 and 6).[35] The war had two psychological effects on the workers. First, patriotic fervor had seized a small segment of workers in Petrograd. To the consternation of the veteran underground revolu-

34. Ibid., pp. 457-66.
35. Leiberov's study is based on an enormous number of archival sources. Since I did not have access to all the archives that Leiberov used, I have no way

tionaries, these workers marched at the head of the patriotic demonstrations singing, "God Save the Tsar." "Our class struggle," lamented one of the Bolshevik activists, "went down the drain." In some factories workers demanded the firing of engineers and foremen with German names. Second, there was a pervasive fear among the workers that they might be drafted into the army. "The workers clung to the lathe, as a drowning man grabs a straw, in order to stay in the factory."[36]

The defeat of the Russian army in the spring and summer of 1915, however, drastically changed the workers' mood. On July 4, 1915, more than 1,500 workers of New Lessner went on strike for higher wages, thus signaling a new wave in the strike movement. Henceforward, the New Lessner workers stood at the forefront of every major wartime strike in Petrograd. Within a week the strike spread to other factories, including the Putilov Shipyard, Neva Shipyard, and Erikson. In the last two factories, illegal strike committees were formed by the

---

of verifying the accuracy of his statistics. Statistics of strikes were compiled basically by four organizations: (1) the Factory Inspectorate, which excluded the factories under the jurisdiction of the war and naval ministries; (2) the military authority and the Special Council for Defense, which recorded only those in the war industry under defense contract; (3) the Petrograd Association of Factory Owners, which recorded only those that happened in the factories of the association members; and (4) the Okhrana and police departments. In order to understand the strike figures during the war, one must be aware of three factors. First, the distinction between political and economic strikes was somewhat arbitrary. Demands for higher wages and improvement of working conditions were classified as economic, and there were obvious cases where the strikes were motivated politically, like the protest strikes in reaction to the Ivanovo massacre. But between these clearcut cases there were many strikes that could not be easily classified one way or the other. Second, the report of number of strikers was not really reliable. Some reported the precise figure to the last digit, but others were rough estimates such as 1,000 or 2,000 workers; in some cases the reported strike participants even surpassed the total number of workers employed in the particular factory. Therefore, what we are concerned about in the statistics of the number of strikers is not precise figures, but rather its general trend. Third, if the number of strikers cannot be precisely estimated, the number of strikes seems to be more accurate. There is no reason to believe that these agencies would falsify information as to whether a strike occurred in one factory. Therefore, the most accurate index of the basic trend of the strike movement during the war is the combined total of the number of economic and political strikes. The data compiled by Leiberov are the most detailed to date.

36. *Rabochee dvizhenie v Petrograde v 1912-1917 gg.*, pp. 145, 285-87; Leiberov, *Petrogradskii proletariat v Fevral'skoi revoliutsii* 1: 96; "Podpol'naia rabota v gody imperialisticheskoi voiny v Petrograde," *Krasnaia letopis'*, nos. 2-3 (1922), p. 130; and K. Kondrat'ev, "Vospominaniia o podpol'noi rabote," *Krasnaia letopis'*, no. 5 (1922), p. 229.

TABLE 5

POLITICAL AND ECONOMIC STRIKES IN PETROGRAD,
JULY 1914 - FEBRUARY 1917

Period	Date	Political Strikes			Economic Strikes			Totals		
		Number of			Number of			Number of		
		strikes	strikers	lost working days	strikes	strikers	lost working days	strikes	strikers	lost working days
	1914									
	7/1-18		160,099			580	160,679			
	7/19-31	26	27,400	48,540	18	10,942	76,914	44	38,342	125,454
	8	–	–	–	–	–	–	–	–	–
	9	1	1,400	280	3	905	1,180	4	2,305	1,460
	10	–	–	–	2	106	42	2	106	42
	11	2	3,150	1,260	3	785	785	5	3,935	2,045
I	12	–	–	–	2	1,020	1,240	2	1,020	1,240
	1915									
	1/	14	2,595	2,488.5	2	145	565	16	2,740	3,053.5
	2	6	340	183.5	2	120	85	8	460	268.5
	3	–	–	–	6	461	311	6	461	311
	4	–	–	–	7	4,064	9,988	7	4,064	9,988
	5	10	1,259	899	7	2,571	1,607	17	3,830	2,506
	6	–	–	–	9	1,141	531	9	1,141	531
	7	–	–	–	29	17,934	33,965.5	29	17,934	33,965.5
	8	24	23,174	24,514.5	16	11,640	15,879	40	34,814	40,393.5
	9	70	82,728	176,623.5	13	7,470	12,730.5	83	90,198	189,354
	10	10	11,268	34,911.5	21	13,350	69,031.5	31	24,618	103,943
	11	5	11,020	6,280	19	6,383	7,509.5	24	17,403	13,789.5
	12	7	8,985	5,624.5	26	13,284	15,261	33	22,269	20,885.5
	1916									
II	1	68	61,447	64,556	35	16,418	34,749.5	103	77,865	99,305.5
	2	3	3,200	170	55	53,723	220,026.5	58	56,923	220,196.5
	3	51	77,887	386,405.5	16	11,811	81,162.5	67	89,698	467,568
	4	7	14,152	87,019	48	25,112	47,758	55	39,264	134,777
	5	3	8,932	2,282	42	26,756	125,496	45	35,688	127,778
	6	6	3,452	3,062.5	37	15,603	72,191.5	43	19,055	75,254
	7	2	5,333	60,025	27	20,326	26,004	29	25,659	86,029
	8	4	1,686	2,761	18	6,259	10,934.5	22	7,945	13,695.5
	9	2	2,800	2,400	33	24,918	84,783.5	35	27,718	87,183.5
	10	177	174,592	452,158.5	12	15,184	12,912	189	189,776	465,070.5
III	11	6	22,950	8,283	24	18,592	30,204.5	30	41,542	38,487.5
	12	1	1,000	25	7	8,798	29,835	8	9,798	29,860
	1917									
	1	135	151,886	144,116	34	24,869	59,024.5	169	176,755	203,140.5
	2/1-22	85	123,953	137,508	14	19,809	62,647	99	143,762	200,155

SOURCE: I. P. Leiberov, *Petrogradskii proletariat v Fevral'skoi revoliutsii* 1: 82, 141, 184.

underground revolutionary activists, including the Bolsheviks and the Mensheviks. The sudden increase in strikes alarmed the authorities. The commander of the Petrograd Military District, General Frolov, warned that participation in strikes would be punished. On July 12, all the members of the strike committee of Neva Shipyard and 103 strikers of Erikson who refused to return to work were arrested by the police.[37]

In June, a strike in a large textile factory in Kostroma—a province northwest of Moscow—resulted in a police shooting that killed twelve workers and wounded forty-five. It did not immediately arouse a strong protest among Petrograd workers. But on August 10, the police, overreacting to a demonstration of textile workers in Ivanovo-Voznesensk, fired on them, killing thirty and wounding fifty-three. On August 17, when the news reached Petrograd, the workers at Aivaz Factory struck. In the following two days the strike spread to large factories in the Vyborg, Narva, and Peterhof districts, involving 22,500 workers in twenty-three factories, all in protest of the Ivanovo massacre. The political strikes in August coincided with the rise of economic strikes. For the first time since July 19, 1914, the strikers clashed with the police, and some cases of vandalism of food stores were reported. In Mozhaiskaia Street near the barracks of the Semenovskii Regiment, a crowd of women, joined by the newly recruited soldiers of the Eger Regiment, attacked the police and wounded twenty policemen. Military police had to be brought in to restore order.[38]

The authorities reacted to the strike movement in August swiftly. From August 29 to September 2 the police arrested underground revolutionaries and activists in the insurance movement. In the Putilov Factory alone thirty workers were arrested, including twenty-three Bolsheviks (five of whom were members of the Bolshevik Petersburg Committee), six Socialist Revolutionaries, and one Menshevik.[39] The mass arrest provoked a city-wide general strike. On September 2, more than 6,000 workers in the Putilov Factory struck. Workers from seven different Putilov workshops assembled in the factory courtyard and passed a resolution that included a number of demands: recall of Bolshevik deputies from exile; release of the arrested Putilov workers; establishment of a responsible ministry; drafting of policemen into the army; and a 15 percent increase in wages. They also protested

37. Leiberov, *Petrogradskii proletariat Fevral'skoi revoliutsii* 1: 104-6.

38. TsGIA, f. 1405, op. 530, d. 1058, ll. 43-47; Leiberov, *Petrogradskii proletariat v Fevral'skoi revoliutsii* 1: 108-11; idem, "Petrogradskii proletariat v gody pervoi mirovoi voiny," pp. 483-84.

39. Leiberov, *Petrogradskii proletariat v Fevral'skoi revoliutsii* 1: 113.

TABLE 6

AVERAGE MONTHLY POLITICAL AND ECONOMIC STRIKES IN PETROGRAD

Period [a]	Political Strikes			Economic Strikes			Total		
		Number of			Number of			Number of	
	strikes	strikers	lost working days	strikes	strikers	lost working days	strikes	strikers	lost working days
I Total	59	36,144	53,651	88	40,218	127,213.5	147	76,362	180,864.5
Monthly average	4.5	2,780.5	4,127	6.8	3,093.7	9,785.7	11.3	5,874	13,912.7
II Total	260	313,268	854,305	373	228,590	741,734	633	541,858	1,596,039
Monthly average	20	24,097.5	65,715.8	28.7	17,583.8	57,056.5	48.7	41,681.4	122,722.2
III Total	460	477,181	74,490.5	124	112,170	279,406.5	530	589,351	1,023,897
Monthly average	76.7	79,530.2	12,415.1	20.7	18,695	46,567.8	88.3	98,225.2	170,649.5

SOURCE: Leiberov, *Petrogradskii proletariat v Fevral'skoi revoliutsii* 1 : 181.

a For exact dates of periods, see table 5.

the threatened prorogation of the Duma. The contents of the resolution had strong Menshevik overtones. In response to the Putilov strike, an All-City Strike Committee was hastily created by the activists of various underground party organizations. It appealed to workers of other factories to support the Putilov strike and to create a soviet of workers' deputies. The Petrograd workers responded with a four-day strike, which involved 25,800 workers at four factories on September 2; 56,900 workers at thirty-seven factories on September 3; 71,700 workers at sixty factories on September 4; and 32,200 workers at sixteen factories on September 5. The four-day strike involved a total of 82,700 workers from seventy factories.[40]

It is interesting to note that the All-City Strike Committee endorsed the idea of the creation of a soviet of workers' deputies, which had played a dominant role in leading the workers' strike movement in St. Petersburg in the 1905 Revolution. Where the initiative to create a soviet originated during the September strike is not clear, but the Bolshevik Petersburg Committee as well as the Mensheviks supported the idea. In the absence of a viable workers' organization that could coordinate the strike and assume effective leadership over the workers' movement in the entire city, it was not surprising to see the revival of the notion of the soviet among activists, some of whom must have participated in the struggle during the 1905 Revolution. It was reported that workers in the Putilov Factory began electing their deputies to the soviet on September 2, and that on the following day an election was held in a number of Vyborg factories.[41]

The general strike, however, revealed wide differences among leaders of the workers' movement. The Socialist deputies in the Duma were afraid that a workers' movement beyond their control would frighten the fragile coalescence that was the Progressive Bloc away from active political struggle against the government. Thus, Skobelev, Chkheidze, and Kerenskii went around to the factories and attempted to persuade the striking workers to return to work. On the evening of September 5, the enlarged meeting of the All-City Strike Committee discussed whether to continue the strike. All groups but the Bolsheviks advocated calling it off. The September general strike was ended.[42]

40. TsGIA, f. 1405, op. 530, d. 1058, ℓℓ. 61-63, 68-71, 75-76; Leiberov, *Petrogradskii proletariat v Fevral'skoi revoliutsii* 1:115; idem, "Petrogradskii proletariat v gody pervoi mirovoi voiny," p. 485; *Rabochee dvizhenie v Petrograde*, pp. 336-46.

41. Leiberov, *Petrogradskii proletariat v Fevral'skoi revoliutsii* 1:113, 115-16.

42. Ibid., p. 120.

The sudden revival of the workers' strike movement in Petrograd coincided with the defeat of the Russian army and the political crisis involving the government's relationship with the Duma. To what extent did these events influence the strike movement? Were the workers' strikes a protest against the defeat of the Russian army? Were they staged in response to the government's repression of the Duma liberals and in sympathy with the liberal opposition? The three-day strikes from August 17 through 19 took place in direct response to the Ivanovo massacre. There is no evidence to indicate that the workers were concerned with the fate of the Russian army in the battlefield or that they had demonstrated their sympathy with the Progressive Bloc that was being formed. The proletarian solidarity and their utter indifference to the conflict between the government and the liberal opposition were indicative of the course that the labor movement was to take in the future. Also important to the strike movement in the summer of 1915 were the workers' economic grievances. If the defeat of the Russian army influenced the workers' movement, it created a crack in the "sacred unity," a slight show of weakness of which the workers took advantage to air their griev-ances.[43]

The second wave of the strike movement from the end of August to the beginning of September coincided with the prorogation of the Duma. But the government's repressive measure against the liberals was not a major factor—the movement was initiated as a protest against the arrest of the Putilov workers. Although the resolution adopted by the Putilov workers contains a protest against the prorogation of the Duma and a demand for formation of a responsible ministry, that seems to be an exception. Okhrana reports describing in detail the four-day strike contain no other mention of the Duma.[44] It ap-pears, therefore, that just as the three-day strike in August was in reaction to the Ivanovo massacre, the four-day strike in September was in reaction to the police arrest of the Putilov strikers. The workers' strike movement during the war had a distinct class nature. It developed independently of the liberal opposition and its struggle with the govern-ment. There was nothing in common between the liberals and the workers' movement, and Miliukov, Maklakov, and other moderate liberals who feared the workers' strike movement more than the gov-ernment's repression had a good reason for doing so.

Although political strikes sharply declined after the September strike, economic strikes sustained the new level achieved in July 1915.

43. *Rabochee dvizhenie v Petrograde*, pp. 329-31.
44. Ibid., pp. 336-44.

Economic strikes never surpassed ten a month between July 1914, and June 1915, but they fluctuated between thirteen and twenty-nine from July through December 1915. The workers not only demanded higher wages but also reinstitution of factory elders, the rehiring of fired workers, better working conditions (ranging from installation of a new ventilation system to repair of the roof and soap in the toilets), and polite treatment of workers by the management. It is significant also that many textile factories that had not been involved in political strikes participated in economic strikes in the latter half of 1915 (see appendix 2). Also in the fall of 1915, Petrograd workers were involved in lively discussions concerning the election of the workers' representatives to the War Industries Committee.[45]

The change in mood of the workers that had developed within a year was vividly manifested in the traditional January 9 strikes in 1915 and 1916: only 2,600 workers at fourteen factories struck on the anniversary of Bloody Sunday in 1915, but more than 61,000 at sixty-eight factories joined the strike in 1916. These figures are all the more remarkable if one considers that the moderate Mensheviks and the workers' group of the War Industries Committee opposed the strike on the grounds that the workers were not sufficiently united to strike decisively. On this day the workers displayed greater militancy than earlier in confronting the police. Unlike the year before, there was a small demonstration in the Vyborg District. As the demonstrators met on the Sampsonievskii Prospekt with the police, a military truck transporting soldiers drove into the mounted police who were attacking the demonstrators. The crowd cheered the incident.[46]

The strike movement peaked again in February and March 1916. On February 4,230 workers of the electrical workshop of the Putilov Factory struck, demanding an increase in wages of 70 percent. Their economic strike was immediately exploited by underground activists— the Bolshevik collectives, which numbered 80 to 100 in the Putilov Factory, in cooperation with the Mezhraiontsy and the radical wing of the Mensheviks, decided to expand the strike to the entire factory. A mass rally was held in the factory courtyard, where the Bolshevik orators, Egorov (member of the Petersburg Committee), Efremov, and I. I. Bogdanov (Mezhraionets), made fiery speeches appealing to the workers to support the electrical workers. The strike expanded

45. Ibid., pp. 369-88. See chap. 6.
46. Leiberov, *Petrogradskii proletariat v Fevral'skoi revoliutsii* 1: 142-44; *Rabochee dvizhenie v Petrograde*, pp. 396-406.

to three other workshops, involving more than 5,800 workers. On February 6, the factory administration shut down the factory and announced that workers who did not return to work would be immediately fired. The strike leaders met at the sick-fund office and decided to appeal to the other workers to support the Putilov strike. Egorov was dispatched to the Vyborg District to coordinate the workers' offensive between the Putilov strike and the Vyborg District. The rank-and-file workers in the Putilov Factory, however, were disturbed by the takeover of the strike movement by professional revolutionaries. Frightened by the possibility of losing their jobs, and induced by the administration's partial concessions to their demands, the workers returned to work on February 10. The general strike that the Bolshevik activists hoped to generate did not materialize.[47]

But the management's concession—a 3 to 28 percent wage increase for those who earned less than 100 rubles a month—did not satisfy the Putilov workers. On February 18, employees in the new-shell workshop struck with the demand for a wage increase of 70 percent. The strike quickly spread to other workshops. On February 22, the administration resorted to a lockout for the second time and fired the strikers. More than 2,000 Putilov strikers were ordered to report to military service. On February 29, the Special Council for Defense decided to sequester the Putilov Factory into the government's artillery administration. This drastic measure provoked an immediate reaction from the Vyborg workers and on February 29 the workers of New Lessner, Baranovskii, Nobel, and Parviainen staged a sympathy strike. On the next three days, March 1 to 3, the major factories in Petrograd went on strike, involving 73,000 workers at forty-nine factories.[48]

The New Lessner workers consistently led the strike movement in Petrograd in 1915 and 1916. Here among 6,000 workers was the strongest Bolshevik collective, numbering thirty to forty members, of whom four members in the Petersburg Committee—V. V. Schmidt, N. P. Komarov, P. R. Boiarshinov, and T. K. Kondratiev—led underground party activities. On March 17,650 workers of the instrument and small-shell workshops of New Lessner went on strike and demanded a wage increase of 10 to 60 percent. On the following two days 1,950 workers from other workshops joined the strike, demanding

47. TsGIA, f. 1405, op. 530, d. 1060, ℓ. 84; Leiberov, *Petrogradskii proletariat v Fevral'skoi revoliutsii* 1: 144–47; *Rabochee dvizhenie v Petrograde*, pp. 431-40.

48. Balabanov, *Ot 1905 k 1917*, p. 375; Leiberov, *Petrogradskii proletariat v Fevral'skoi revoliutsii* 1: 150; idem, "Petrogradskii proletariat v gody pervoi mirovoi voiny," pp. 494–96; *Rabochee dvizhenie v Petrograde*, pp. 441-52.

a wage increase, polite treatment, and better sanitary conditions. A five-member strike committee was established under the leadership of a Bolshevik, N. V. Kopylov, and on March 21 the entire factory was struck. The administration resorted to a lockout, and fired all the strikers, of which about six hundred were drafted into the army.[49] The defeat of the New Lessner strike was costly, since most political workers, including all the Bolsheviks, were driven out of the factory. With its defeat, the strike movement quickly abated.

The workers' strike movement had reached a new stage. According to Leiberov's study, during the thirteen months from July 1914 to July 1915, political and economic strikes had involved a total of 76,362 workers at 147 factories; but during the next thirteen months— from August 1915 to August 1916—the figures rose to 541,858 workers at 633 factories. The monthly average rose from 11.3 factories and 5,874 strikers in the first thirteen months to 48.7 factories and 41,681 strikers in the next thirteen months. In the following six months from September 1916 to February 1917, just prior to the February Revolution, the monthly average further rose to 88.3 factories and 98,225 strikers (see table 6).

The worsening food supply situation and the general "crisis of power" (krizis verkhov) undoubtedly contributed to the revival of the strike movement in the fall of 1916. The workers' anger with inflation and the food shortage reached such a point that usually moderate leaders of the workers' group in the Central War Industries Committee admitted that "one provocation would be sufficient to ignite a disorder in the capital which might result in sacrifices in the thousands and tens of thousands."[50] If the workers' group concluded from this that the leaders of the workers' movement should exercise restraint, the Bolsheviks attempted to exploit the food crisis for the general struggle against the tsarist regime. At the beginning of October, the Petersburg Committee instructed the party workers to "demonstrate to the masses that the problem of the cost of living increase is closely related to the struggle for a democratic republic and the end of the war."[51] In various factories, such as Phoenix, New Lessner, and Erikson, groups of workers had held meetings since October 13 to discuss the problems of inflation and the food shortage. Some of the workers attempted to stage a demonstration in the main streets only to be chased away by the police. This tremor led to a sudden eruption on October 17, when even to the surprise of the radical

49. Leiberov, "Petrogradskii proletariat v gody pervoi mirovoi voiny," pp. 498-99.
50. Rabochee dvizhenie v Petrograde, p. 483.
51. Listovki Peterburgskikh bol'shevikov: 1902-1917 2: 222.

activists, the workers of Parviainen, Russian Renault, and New Lessner went on strike, and staged a demonstration along the Sampsonievskii Prospekt. When the demonstrators approached the barracks of the 181st Infantry Regiment where a crowd of soldiers sympathetically watched the workers' demonstration through the barracks fences, the police attacked the demonstrators. This angered the soldiers, who threw rocks and bricks at the police. Shouting, "Beat the police," the soldiers jumped over and crawled under the barrack fences and joined the demonstrators. The demonstrators, now outnumbering the police, surrounded them and took away their sabers and revolvers. It was only after the Cossacks and the training detachment of the Moscow Regiment arrived at the scene that order was restored. According to one of the soldiers who took part in the demonstration, A. Ivanov, former Bolshevik worker in the Putilov Factory, there were in the 181st Infantry Regiment many former strike participants, like himself, who continued political agitation in the military units. The military authorities later arrested 130 soldiers, and the 181st Infantry Regiment was removed from Petrograd. By the end of the day, 27,300 workers from ten factories had participated in the strike in the Vyborg District. On the following day, October 18, the strike spread to 46,300 workers at thirty-four factories in the Vyborg, Petrograd, Vasilievskii, and Moscow districts, and on October 19 to 75,400 workers at sixty-three factories in all parts of the city.[52]

The three-day strike was followed by another wave of strikes at the end of October. The second was purely political, and it was called by the Bolsheviks. The Petersburg Committee decided to appeal to the workers to stage a political strike against the trial of the Bolshevik sailors in the Baltic Fleet who had been arrested because of their revolutionary activities, and against the arrest of the soldiers of the 181st Infantry Regiment. On October 26, the opening day of the trial, 25,800 workers at thirteen factories participated in the strike; it spread to 52,500 workers at forty-seven factories on October 27, and on the third day to 79,100 workers at seventy-seven factories.[53] If one remembers that the Petersburg Committee's strike call for the trial of the arrested Bolshevik Duma deputies attracted only 340 workers at six factories in February 1915, the strike figures in the second half of October clearly demonstrate the increased radicaliza-

52. A. Ivanov, "Volnenie v 1916 g. v 181-om zapasnom pekhotom polku," *Krasnaia letopis'* 10, no. 1 (1924): 172. Also see *Rabochee dvizhenie v Petrograde*, pp. 490-93; Leiberov, "Petrogradskii proletariat v gody pervoi mirovoi voiny," p. 501.

53. TsGIA, f. 1405, op. 530, d. 1060, ℓℓ. 87-90; Leiberov, "Petrogradskii proletariat v gody pervoi mirovoi voiny," p. 502.

tion of the Petrograd workers and the growing influence of the Bolsheviks. This in turn contributed to the radicalization of the workers' group, which, aware of their slipping influence, tried to recover the lost ground.

After October, the strike movement subsided. Such was the inevitable aftermath of every explosion of labor unrest. The leaders had been arrested, the networks of communications and organizations were broken, and the workers needed time to recover from the emotional strain. Those who had been fired needed to find other jobs, often by disguising their identities. Nevertheless, the ebb of the workers' movement in November and December 1916 did not mean that the workers became apathetic and inactive. Strikes subsided, but sporadic attacks on food stores became rampant. When the strike movement picked up momentum again in January 1917, after two months' lull, it was to engulf a wider segment of the Petrograd workers, and eventually to develop into a revolution.

Petrograd workers can be divided into four groups according to their participation in wartime strikes. The vanguard of the strike movement were the metalworkers of Aivaz (4,100), Baranovskii (1,300), Vulkan (1,100), Dinamo (2,100), Nobel (1,600), Promet (3,000), Parviainen (7,300), Old Lessner (1,100), New Lessner (6,500), Phoenix (1,900), Diuflon (820), and Erikson (2,200) (see appendix 2). These workers, approximately 33,000, were the backbone of every major strike during the war. Particularly important were the two factories, Parviainen and New Lessner. Of these twelve factories all but Dinamo (Narva District), Vulkan (Petrograd District), and Diuflon (Petrograd District) were located in the Vyborg District. All were privately owned factories. They were by no means the largest plants in Petrograd, but those employing between 1,000 and 8,000 workers (with the exception of Dinamo). With the exceptions of Diuflon and Erikson all were engaged in weapon and munitions production. Diuflon was producing electrical machines and instruments. Erikson specialized in the production of telephones, but during the war it had also expanded its production to weapon manufacturing.[54]

54. The number of workers was as of January 1917. The number of workers, description of products, and geographical locations are derived from *Spisok fabrichno-zavodskikh predpriiatii Petrograda.* For a slightly different compilation of statistical data and a different conclusion, see Wada Haruki, "Nigatsu kakumei," in *Roshia kakumei no kenkyu,* ed. Eguchi Bokuro, pp. 345-46. Wada states that 70,000 workers from 20 factories were the vanguard of the strike movement. The second wave of the strike movement after January 9, 1917, involved another 75,000 workers from an additional 50 to 55 factories. But prior to the February Revolution, the remaining 240,000 workers in 900 factories had not joined the strike.

The second group consisted of workers whose participation was primarily limited to economic strikes, although some of them sporadically joined the political strikes. Three distinctly different workers belonged to this group. First were the workers of the state-owned largest munition factories: Neva Shipyard (6,100), Obukhov (10,600), Petrograd Metal (6,700), Putilov (24,400), Franco-Russian (6,700), Baltic Shipyard (7,600), and Putilov Shipyard (4,200). But other munitions factories such as Arsenal (4,000), Petrograd Cartridge (8,300), Orudinskii (3,500), Cable (2,300), Admiralty Shipyard (4,500), Okhta Explosives (10,200), and Okhta Gunpowder (5,700) were involved in no strikes during the war. Second were workers of metal factories engaged in weapon production: Rosenkrantz (3,800), Langenzippen (2,500), Ekval' (300), Russian Renault (1,700), Semenov (700), Armaturnyi (1,000), Siemens-Schückert Electrical (2,000), Koppel (600), Petrograd Wagon (2,000), Puzyrev (200), Russian-Baltic Motor (400), Lebedev Aeronautics (1,100), Russian-Baltic Aeronautics (500), Sliusarenko (200), and Stetinin (2,000). Third were textile workers: Voronin, Liutsh, Chesher, Nikol'skaia Manufacture (1,500), Lebedev Jute (1,000), Leontiev (600), Nevka (2,700), Neva Cotton (2,000), Okhta Cotton (900), Pal' (1,800), Petrovskaia (1,700), Sampsonievskaia (1,600), and Northern Weaving (1,000). Altogether 100,000 workers of this group persistently fought for economic gains, but they were not always active supporters of political strikes. In particular, textile workers did not join political strikes until the beginning of 1917.

The third category comprised workers of factories who struck once or twice during the war, but on the whole remained inactive. This group include 16,300 metalworkers, 9,300 textileworkers, 2,200 in paper manufacturing, 1,100 wood processors, 17,900 in leather and shoe manufacturing, 4,700 food and tobacco processors, 1,800 chemical workers, and 1,000 others—altogether 54,300 workers. The total of these three categories was 187,400. Since these figures represent all the workers of the struck factories and therefore have an obvious upward bias, the actual participants in strikes are presumed to be much smaller. Even this inflated figure is only 47.7 percent of the total workers in Petrograd in January 1917. Thus more than half of the Petrograd workers remained in the fourth category, those who never struck during the war.

There is no reason to believe, however, that the silent majority of these workers accepted their misery meekly. The general trend of the strike movement clearly indicates that the movement led by the vanguard of the metalworkers was gradually drawing the often cautious workers of the largest plants as well as less organized sector of the working class. The political and economic strikes that had developed differently throughout 1915 and in the beginning of 1916 had shown a trend to merge into one in late 1916.

The workers in Petrograd were the fundamental source of instability in Russian politics during the war. The patriotism at the outbreak of the war was quickly dissipated as wartime reality hit. Excluded from the established order of society and deprived of legal organizations to air their grievances, yet asked to continue their sacrifices for "national honor and pride," the workers became receptive to the agitators' call for radical action.

6

THE WAR AND THE

REVOLUTIONARY PARTIES

 The war had a profound impact on the revolutionary parties. At its outbreak, many of their leaders were arrested and exiled, their organizations destroyed, and their legal and illegal publications suppressed. Okhrana agents infiltrated underground organizations, carefully monitoring activities. Countless arrests and "search and destroy" missions by the police demoralized the activists. Moreover, all the revolutionary parties were seriously divided by ideological differences about the war. In general the Socialists split into two groups on this issue. The first, the "defensists," saw the war as resulting from German aggression and argued that the duty of the proletariat was to defeat German militarism and defend the nation against aggression: the struggle against tsarism should be temporarily suspended, and the government's efforts to win the war should be supported. The second group, the "internationalists," opposed the war, and regarded it as competition of imperialists for markets, a conflict in which the proletariat had nothing to gain. Thus, they stood for peace "without annexations and indemnities," and advocated a continued struggle against the tsarist government. The most extreme group of internationalists went one step further. advocating the defeat of the country and calling for a struggle to turn the imperialist war into a civil war against the capitalists. The leader of these "defeatists" was Lenin, who accused not only the "defensists" but also the moderate internationalists of betraying the proletariat by not breaking completely with the chauvinists."[1]

1. For the impact of the war on the Socialist parties in Russia, see M. Fainsod, *International Socialism and the World War*, pp. 45 ff.; Branco Lazitch, *Lenine et la IIIe Internationale*, pp. 19-75.

Related to the war issue, but ultimately more important in dividing the revolutionary parties, was the method of struggle against the regime. With the exception of a small group of ultradefensists, most revolutionaries stood for the continuation of a struggle to eliminate tsarism. While the moderate Socialists believed that this struggle should be waged jointly with the liberal forces, the left-wing Socialists rejected cooperation with the "bourgeoisie," maintaining that the working class was the only force capable of overthrowing the regime.

During the war a gradual realignment of revolutionary groups occurred. The internationalists formed a loose coalition in which, with their numerical strength and better organization, the Bolsheviks emerged as the leader. The moderate Socialists, on the other hand, gravitated to the workers' group of the War Industries Committee. Two groups competed with each other for control of the workers' movement in Petrograd.

The Bolsheviks

The Russian Socialist Democratic Labor party was split into the Bolsheviks and the Mensheviks at the Second Party Congress in 1903. Behind the seemingly minor doctrinal differences on party organization there were deep philosophical differences. While the Mensheviks, led by Iurii Martov, advocated the formation of an open mass party, Lenin insisted that the revolutionary party should be composed of a handful of dedicated, closely knit, conspiratorial revolutionaries, since the workers themselves, without the guidance of these conscious revolutionaries, would never develop a proletarian consciousness. The revolutionary party, Lenin maintained, should not tail behind the "spontaneity" of the workers. The Mensheviks vehemently opposed Lenin's "elitism." They were optimistic about the workers' initiative and creativity and attempted to nurture their cultural as well as their political development. On the matter of revolutionary strategy the Bolsheviks and the Mensheviks also differed greatly. The Mensheviks believed that Russia, like any other country, could not defy the iron law of history as outlined by Marx; she must pass through the historically preordained stages from feudalism to capitalism, and from capitalism to socialism, with two separate revolutions when history jumped from one stage to the next. The first revolution should be a bourgeois-democratic revolution, in which the bourgeoisie would play the leading role. Only when material conditions were ripe and other democratic reforms were accomplished under capitalism could a socialist revolution be carried out by the proletariat. Lenin opposed such a dogmatic application of Marxism to Russian reality, arguing that a bourgeois-democratic revolution in Russia would be possible only under the hegemony of the proletariat in cooperation with the peasantry. The Russian bourgeoisie, owing to peculiarities of its development, would be incapable of fulfilling the historical task of carrying out its own revolution. Only the proletariat, Lenin insisted, had the power to overthrow tsarism. Strategically, the Mensheviks considered it crucial for the proletariat and the bourgeoisie to form a united front against tsarism—a struggle in which the workers' movement should play a secondary role. In a bourgeois-democratic revolution, the Mensheviks maintained, the proletariat and its representative, the Marxist party, should abstain from participating in a bourgeois government. Lenin was skeptical of the value of such a coalition. Instead of the bourgeois government envisioned by the Mensheviks, the Bolsheviks advocated the formation of a provisional revolutionary government composed of representatives of the insurgent masses. Such a government alone could ensure the convocation of a truly democratic Constituent Assembly, which was to become a vehicle of a bourgeois-democratic revolution.

In the two years prior to the outbreak of war, the Bolshevik party gained considerable influence among Petrograd workers. The central headquarters abroad led by Lenin moved to Kraków to have better communication with the party organizations in Russia. From there Lenin maintained close contact with the Russian Bureau of the Central Committee, which assumed the over-all leadership over the party organizations in Russia. After the election of the Fourth Duma in 1912, the five Bolshevik deputies utilized their legal status in establishing contact with illegal organizations, although one, Roman Malinovskii, was a paid police agent. The legal paper, *Pravda*, which had begun publication in 1912 with a circulation of 6,000, had expanded to 11,500 by July 1914 (2,800 to 3,200 copies were subscribed in St. Petersburg). In addition to *Pravda*, the Bolshevik party published several other legal periodicals, including the insurance journal, *Voprosy strakhovaniia*.[2] From 1912 to 1914 the Bolsheviks organized an insurance campaign, successfully placing many underground revolutionaries in the factory sick-fund organizations and controlling the workers' group in the Insurance Council. The Bolsheviks also increased their influence in the legal trade unions, including the largest, the Union of Metalworkers. The membership of illegal organizations in St. Petersburg rose from 600 in 1910 to between 5,000 and 6,000 in 1914.[3]

2. E. E. Kruze, *Polozhenie rabochego klassa Rossii v 1900-1914 gg.*, pp. 93, 213-37.

3. The membership for 1910 is given in ibid., p. 79; that of 1914 is given by I. P. Leiberov, *Petrogradskii proletariat v Fevral'skoi revoliutsii* 1: 35. For the Bolshevik party's growing influence among the Petrograd workers, see Leopold

The world war, however, dealt a severe blow to the Bolshevik party. Lenin was arrested by the Austrian authorities and exiled to Switzerland, where it became virtually impossible to keep close contact with the party organizations in Russia. All the legal Bolshevik publications were suppressed. After the July strike, the authorities arrested more than 1,500 Bolshevik activists, and drafted them into the army at the first mobilization. The leaders in the Russian Bureau of the Central Committee and the Petersburg Committee were deported from the capital. Finally, in early November, the Bolshevik Duma deputies were arrested and charged with treason. The membership of the party in Petrograd shrank to 100 immediately after the outbreak of the war.[4]

Moreover, the war brought confusion among the party activists. On July 26, the Bolshevik Duma deputies, together with the Mensheviks, issued a declaration against the war, stating that it was initiated by the imperialistic politics of the capitalist nations, that the proletariat of the world would stand against the war, and that there should be no unity between the tsarist government and the people. The Bolshevik and the Menshevik deputies walked out of the Duma meeting during the vote on war credit to demonstrate their opposition to the war. The declaration, however, included the phrase: "The proletariat, permanent defender of freedom and the interests of the people, will carry out its own duty at all times and will defend the cultural welfare of the people from all kinds of encroachments, wherever they come from—either from inside or outside." This position that the proletariat would defend the nation from outside aggression—"revolutionary defensism"—was to become the official position of the majority of the Mensheviks after the February Revolution. Lenin, on the other hand, developed a totally different approach to the war. In the resolution adopted at the Bolshevik conference in Berne, and later developed in his theses "The War and Russian Social Democracy," Lenin advocated that the task of the proletariat was to transform the world war into a civil war against the imperialists, insisting that the defeat of tsarist Russia would be desirable since it would increase the opportunity for revolution.[5]

To the Bolshevik activists, who faced the near-destruction of the party organizations on the one hand and the upsurge of patriotic

---

Haimson, "The Problem of Social Stability," *Slavic Review* 23, no. 4 (1964): 629-31.

4. Leiberov, *Petrogradskii proletariat v Fevral'skoi revoliutsii* 1: 80.

5. S. V. Tiutiukin, *Voina, mir, revoliutsiia: Ideinaia bor'ba v rabochem dvizhenii Rossii, 1914-1917 gg.*, pp. 20-21, 30-34.

fervor in all segments of society on the other, the acceptance of Lenin's theses appeared suicidal. Many intellectuals, such as the left-wing lawyer N. D. Sokolov, left the party, disagreeing with Lenin's defeatism. Maxim Gorky, who had supported the Bolsheviks, came out in support of the war, although he was to change his position within a year. After Lenin's theses began to circulate in Russia at the end of September, the Bolshevik leaders held a conference in Ozerki, just outside Petrograd, from November 2 to 4, to discuss how to respond to the letter from Vandervelde, a Belgian Socialist, who had entered the patriotic cabinet as a minister and was urging the Russian Socialists to support the war and the government. The Bolshevik leaders rejected Vandervelde's suggestion on the grounds that "Russian absolutism," as well as "semifeudal German militarism," was the main enemy of the proletariat and democracy. Their reply, although rejecting the outright defensist position, sharply differed from Lenin's concept of war. Bolshevik leaders in Russia made a distinction between the "German-Russian feudal forces" and "Anglo-French democracy." The implication was that they would support the war if Russian absolutism were eliminated—a position clearly leading to "revolutionary defensism." Instead of advocating the defeat of tsarist Russia, they stated that "strengthening the victorious tsarist monarchy is extremely dangerous." On the last day of the conference all the participants, including the four Duma deputies and L. B. Kamenev, were arrested by the police and charged with treason. When they were brought to trial in February 1915, however, all the defendants were quick to denounce Lenin's defeatism.[6]

It was the rank-and-file activists who accepted Lenin's radical position quickly. Although confused by the outbreak of war and isolated from the leadership, the Bolshevik activists stood adamantly against the war. At the end of July, a Bolshevik worker and a worker-writer, Mashirov, met at the Ligovskaia People's House with other activists, and distributed a leaflet in which they boldly advocated the internationalist position against the war. The leaflet stated: "The Russian proletariat will find a method against the war. And there is only one method: to strengthen its class organizations by oral and printed propaganda among the troops of the active army and among

6. Ibid., pp. 45-46; N. N. Krestinskii, "Iz vospominaii o 1914 godu," *Proletarskaia revoliutsiia*, no. 7 (1924), pp. 50-60; F. N. Samoilov, *Po sledam minuvshego*, pp. 272, 276; B. Dvinov, "Pervaia mirovaia voina: Rossiiskaia sotsial-demokratiia," *Inter-University Project on the History of the Menshevik Movement*, Paper 10, pp. 38-39; Tiutiukin, *Voina, mir, revoliutsiia*, pp. 46-47; D. Baevskii, "Partiia v gody imperialisticheskoi voiny," *Ocherki po istorii Oktiabr'skoi revoliutsii* 1: 353.

the workers and the peasants against militarism with the appeal for a general insurrection for a democratic republic."[7] They published illegally a workers' journal, *Rabochii golos,* with a clear antiwar position. Bewildered by the ideological confusion at the top and dissatisfied with the inaction of the Petersburg Committee, they groped for a direction that would satisfy their militant antiwar stand. They therefore welcomed Lenin's theses with enthusiasm. Kondratiev remembers the great impression created by the special issue of *Sotsial Demokrat* containing Lenin's theses on war. A small group of underground Bolsheviks read this issue over and over until the smuggled paper became so tattered and the printed letters so smeared they could no longer read it. Lenin's theses, Kondratiev stated, "gave us a fresh spirit, vindicated and inspired us, fired our hearts with an irresistible desire to go further, not stopping at anything." It gave them confidence that the direction they had taken was the correct path.[8]

The Bolshevik party maintained contact with the workers through these activists, who were the first to attempt to reconstruct party organizations. They met clandestinely, organized an illegal network of party organizations, recruited sympathizers, set up illegal printing presses—*tekhnika,* as they called them—in their apartments, printed leaflets, and distributed them among workers. They lived under constant peril of arrest, court martial, and exile. Police informers infiltrated the various Bolshevik organizations and the activists had to develop a sixth sense about whether they were being tailed or if their secret meeting place was under surveillance.

It should be remembered that the Bolshevik party during the war was not the monolithic, bureaucratic organization it was later to become under Stalin. The central leadership could not and did not extend a strong control over the local organizations. The Russian Bureau of the Central Committee did not exist most of the time during the war, and when it finally came into existence, it was too weak and its means too limited to assume effective leadership. The Petersburg Committee assumed virtual leadership over the Bolshevik organizations in Petrograd, but its members were subject to constant police repression, and the turnover rate of its membership was high. Thus, most of the day-to-day operations were left to the discretion of the local organizations. The rank-and-file activists freely exchanged

7. *Listovki Peterburgskikh bol'shevikov* 2: 115. For the underground work of the Bolshevik activists immediately after the outbreak of the war, see "Podpol'naia rabota v gody imperialisticheskoi voiny v Petrograde," *Krasnaia letopis',* nos. 2-3 (1922), pp. 117, 120, 122.

8. A. Kondrat'ev, "Vospominaniia o podpol'noi rabote," *Krasnaia letopis',* no. 5 (1922), p. 236.

opinions, unafraid of challenging directives from the center. It was thanks to such independent but dedicated party activists—united by a common repudiation of the war and hatred against the regime, and motivated only by their desire for revolution—that the Bolshevik party endured the trials and tribulations of the war.[9]

By spring of 1915 the Petersburg Committee had been gradually restored. It established contact with the First City District, Vyborg, Narva, and Nevskii district committees. In July they held the first all-city conference in Oranienbaum with 50 participants representing 500 members. By September the Petersburg Committee had added the Petrograd, Moscow, and Kolomenskaia district committees. In addition, the Latvian, Lithuanian, Estonian, and Polish organizations were granted the right to participate in the Petersburg Committee as a district committee. By this time a student Bolshevik group had emerged, and in October the activists in the Baltic Fleet succeeded in organizing a Bolshevik underground cell, establishing contact with the Petersburg Committee. Ideologically, by the spring of 1915 the Petersburg Committee had come to adopt Lenin's position on the war.[10] At the same time publication activities resumed. The underground journal, *Proletarskii golos,* which took over Kondratiev and Mashirov's illegal publications, appeared under the Petersburg Committee. In February 1915, *Voprosy strakhovaniia* reappeared, and many Bolshevik intellectuals who had withdrawn from party work came back to participate in this, the only legal Bolshevik journal.

Reconstruction of the party organization, return of the veteran underground revolutionaries such as V. V. Schmidt and V. N. Zalezhskii, and finally the sudden revitalization of the strike movement, touched off by the Ivanovo massacre, unrealistically raised the hopes of the Petersburg Committee. At the meeting held on August 22 and 23, it adopted a militant resolution calling for a general strike; the organization of a people's militia; armed attacks on the police headquarters, enterprises, government buildings, and railway stations; confiscation of essential foodstuffs; organization of a soviet of workers'

9. See "Podpol'naia rabota v gody imperialisticheskoi voiny v Petrograde," pp. 116-43.

10. Kondrat'ev, "Vospominaniia o podpol'noi rabote," pp. 32, 36-37; M. G. Fleer, "Peterburgskii komitet bol'shevikov v gody imperialisticheskoi voiny," *Krasnaia letopis',* no. 4 (1926), pp. 112-18. See also Iv. Egorov, "Matrosy-bol'sheviki nakanune 1917 g.," *Krasnaia letopis',* no. 3 (1926), pp. 5-29; no. 4 (1926), pp. 68-92; Leiberov, *Petrogradskii proletariat v Fevral'skoi revoliutsii* 1: 97-98 and Tiutiukin, *Voina, mir, revoliutsiia,* p. 42.

deputies; and recruitment of the soldiers and officers into the general strike.[11]

The militant stand of the Petersburg Committee alarmed the police. Fully informed of the new tendency of the Petersburg Committee by the police spy Chernomazov, a secretary of the New Lessner sick-fund organization and a militant member of the Petersburg Committee, the police conducted large-scale arrests of the strike activists at the end of August and the beginning of September, including five members of the Petersburg Committee. The remaining members met on September 2 with the representatives of various district committees as well as those of the Putilov Factory, and decided to join an all-city strike committee to assume leadership of the general strike. It was also decided to attempt to transform the strike committee into a soviet of workers' deputies, and it was reported that in some factories workers began electing their representatives to such a soviet. The establishment of the soviet did not materialize, however, since the strike movement did not develop into a protracted general strike. The idea of creating a soviet was again briefly revived in the Petersburg Committee in October 1915, but as the strike movement subsided, it dropped the idea. Although the concept of creating a soviet had no practical meaning in the fall of 1915, it is significant to remember in relation to subsequent events during the February Revolution that the Petersburg Committee had already envisaged the possibility of creating a center of the strike movement in the form of a soviet.[12]

The most important activity on which the Bolsheviks concentrated in the fall of 1915 was their campaign against the election of the workers' representatives to the War Industries Committee. Guchkov and Konovalov had proposed the participation of workers' representatives in the War Industries Committee. At first, they had appealed to the workers' group of the Insurance Council to send delegates, but the Insurance Council, under Bolshevik influence, had rejected their request. The leaders of the Central War Industries Committee then appealed directly to the factory workers to elect

11. Other members who returned from exile included Litvinov, Zima Endin, Sergei Orlov, and Sergei Bogdat'ev. B. Zalezhskii, *Iz vospominanii podpol'shchika*, pp. 124-25. See also Leiberov, *Petrogradskii proletariat v Fevral'skoi revoliutsii* 1: 111-12.

12. Leiberov, *Petrogradskii proletariat v Fevral'skoi revoliutsii* 1: 116-17; idem, "Petrogradskii proletariat v gody pervoi mirovoi voiny," p. 486. Lenin subsequently criticized the Petersburg Committee's slogan for the creation of the soviet as premature. According to Lenin, the slogan for the soviet should be raised only in connection with an insurrection.

representatives. In this attempt they had the full support of the moderate Mensheviks. During August and September an election campaign was launched in major factories in Petrograd, and lively discussions went on in a series of meetings. The election was to be conducted in two stages. First, workers were to choose electors on the basis of one for every 1,000 workers for those factories with more than 1,000 workers and one for each factory with 500 to 1,000 workers. Then the electors were to select ten delegates for the Central War Industries Committee and six for the Petrograd District Committee.[13]

The Bolsheviks strongly opposed participation of workers' representatives in the "bourgeois" organization. But the Petersburg Committee decided to take full advantage of the election campaign to propagate their antiwar stand and revolutionary slogans among the workers. At the end of August, the Petersburg Committee decided to participate in the election of electors to expose the moderate Mensheviks, but not to participate in the War Industries Committee. Also it decided to try to transform the election to the War Industries Committee into an election to a soviet of workers' deputies, if a sudden rise of the revolutionary movement occurred. It adopted the "instructions" *(nakaz)* drafted by a veteran Bolshevik, Bogdatiev, which stated the following positions: (1) participation in the War Industries Committee would betray the will of the proletariat and revolutionary internationalism; (2) the electors should boycott such participation; and (3) at the appropriate moment, the electors should declare themselves a soviet of workers' deputies.[14] During the next several weeks the Bolsheviks and the Mensheviks were involved in lively debate at the factories, uniquely free of police harassment, to gain control of the workers. By September 21, 1915, pre-election meetings had been held at 93 of the 101 eligible factories, and 218 electors representing 213,000 workers had been elected. Of these electors, 60 to 70 were Bolsheviks, approximately 80 were Mensheviks and Socialist Revolutionaries favoring participation, and about 60 took a neutral position between them.[15]

When the electors finally met on September 27 to decide whether the workers should send their delegates to the War Industries

13. The author is indebted to Lewis Siegelbaum's unpublished manuscript "Class Collaboration in the First World War: The Central War-Industries Committee and the Workers' Group in Petrograd." This is the most judicious treatment of the subject in any language. Also see Zalezhskii, *Iz vospominanii podpol'shchika*, pp. 130-31.

14. Tiutiukin, *Voina, mir, revoliutsiia*, p. 209. TsGIA, f. 1405, op. 530, d. 1059, ℓℓ. 3-5; *Rabochee dvizhenie v Petrograde*, pp. 348-50.

15. Zalezhskii, *Iz vospominanii podpol'shchika*, p. 134.

Committee, the Bolsheviks scored a brilliant strategic victory. Two veteran professional revolutionaries, Bogdatiev and Zalezhskii, smuggled themselves into the meeting, pretending to be electors from the Putilov Factory, and spearheaded the Bolshevik attack on the advocates of participation. Zalezhskii made a fiery speech supporting the Leninist position to transform the war into a revolution. Apparently the Mensheviks, comfortable with their numerical strength, were not prepared for such an attack. According to the Okhrana report, the left-wing Socialist Revolutionaries, who had remained neutral, were swayed to the Bolshevik position. At the end of the meeting there were ninety-five votes for the Bolshevik resolution rejecting participation in the War Industries Committee and eighty-one against it.[16]

The victory of the Bolsheviks at the September 27 meeting, however, should not be taken as an accurate measure of their strength among the Petrograd workers. The outcome was obviously influenced by the highly charged atmosphere in the aftermath of the Ivanovo massacre and the September general strike as well as the workers' innate distrust of the employers' organization. Numerically, the moderate Mensheviks gained more votes than the Bolsheviks in the electors' election. Also, elections at the factory level were so confused that in some factories workers elected Menshevik electors with the Bolshevik instructions, and vice versa.[17]

After this unexpected defeat, the Mensheviks immediately struck back. Kuz'ma Gvozdev, a metalworker from Erikson and a Menshevik defensist, complained in an open letter to the workers that the Bolsheviks had violated a democratic electoral process by sending two pretenders to the meeting. Gvozdev's protest was obviously supported by the leaders of the War Industries Committee, and a second meeting was organized on November 29. By this time the strike movement had declined sharply and some of the Bolshevik electors had been arrested. So the Bolsheviks changed their strategy. After the meeting opened, the Bolshevik electors read a four-point declaration reiterating that participation in the War Industries Committee would be tantamount to betrayal of the working class, and then they walked out. The Socialist-Revolutionary delegates followed suit. According to the Okhrana report, of the 213 electors

16. Ibid., pp. 135-37; according to an Okhrana report, the vote was 90 for and 81 against. TsGIA, f. 1450, op. 530, d. 1058, ll. 18-19, 21-22.

17. Siegelbaum, "Class Collaboration," p. 7; Tiutiukin, *Voina, mir, revoliutsiia*, p. 211. Zalezhskii admits that during the election campaign the Bolsheviks suffered a shortage of good speakers who could compete with the Mensheviks. Thus, the Bolsheviks concentrated only on large factories. Zalezhskii, *Iz vospominanii podpol'shchika*, p. 133.

only 153 attended the meeting, and as a result of the walkout, only 74 remained at the meeting—hardly enough to make a quorum. But after Guchkov made a credentials check it was reported, rather miraculously, that 109 electors were present.[18]

Many Mensheviks spoke in support of participation in the War Industries Committee, but the meeting was not without further excitement. A Bolshevik who remained at the meeting, A. I. Dunaev, viciously attacked the Menshevik leadership: "You attack Goremykin, but support Guchkov . . . but whom are you struggling against with Guchkov? Not Goremykin, because he owns no factory, but Guchkov does. It is not Goremykin but the Association of Factory Owners that put the workers in such a situation. . . . Instead of appealing to the workers, you went to Guchkov, and today you drink his tea and tomorrow eat his sandwiches. These elections are lies . . . and by going there [to the Central War Industries Committee] you are deceiving the workers, as Guchkov's friend, Gvozdev, is deceiving them already." This speech caused an uproar. Electors jumped up and shouted obscenities at Dunaev, demanding that he be kicked out. Gvozdev ordered him to stop speaking and warned that a further outburst would force him to call the guards to remove him. Dunaev left the rostrum with a mocking smile, saying: "I am leaving, since I now see with whom I am dealing here. You would appeal to someone in the Okhrana or the police. By cooperating with Guchkov, you have come thus far to benefit from this."[19] In the eyes of the workers, the picture of some of their representatives silencing another with the aid of the police must not have been reassuring. After all the speakers had finished, election of the representatives to the War Industries Committee was held, but not before eight more Socialist Revolutionaries walked out. Finally, ten delegates were elected to the Central War Industries Committee and six to the Petrograd District Committee. The workers' group thus came into existence.

As Lewis Siegelbaum has said, this was certainly a Pyrrhic victory for the workers' group. The Bolsheviks' relentless campaign against them—unfairly labeling them "Gvozdevites," as "renegades" and "class collaborators"—did them much damage. In some factories, presumably under leadership of Bolshevik activists, workers held meetings protesting election of the workers' group. In Erikson and New Lessner the workers passed a resolution urging their electors to withdraw from the workers' group and threatening that, if they refused, they would be carted out of the factory in wheelbarrows—

18. TsGIA, f. 1405, op. 530, d. 1059, 𝓁. 79.
19. Ibid., 𝓁. 82.

one of the most humiliating punishments meted out to offenders against working-class interests.[20]

Although in the end the Bolshevik campaign for boycott of the election to the War Industries Committee proved unsuccessful, they took fullest advantage of the freedom for propaganda purposes. During the campaign the party grew in membership and extended its underground network. By the fall of 1915 the Petersburg Committee controlled eight city district committees and four neighboring regional committees (Sestroretsk, Kolpino, Schlüsselburg, and Kronstadt). The membership of the party, which had dwindled to 100 immediately after the war, rose to 1,200. In the middle of September, Aleksandr G. Shliapnikov arrived from Sweden on Lenin's instructions, and by the middle of November had succeeded in restoring the Russian Bureau of the Central Committee. The Russian Bureau concentrated for several months on organizing the workers' movement in Petrograd, transporting illegal party literature from the capital to the provinces, and establishing contacts with various local organizations, but the arrest of its members in March destroyed it.[21]

After the campaign against the election to the War Industries Committee, the Petrograd Bolsheviks concentrated on preparations for the strike of January 9, 1916. Since the workers' group opposed a strike on this anniversary of Bloody Sunday, it became the first test of the relative strength of the workers' group and the Bolsheviks among the Petrograd workers. Each district committee was instructed to create an organizational collegium under reliable leaders of the district committee by drawing its members from various party organizations in the district. The collegium was to fulfill the following functions: (1) expansion and reinforcement of the local party organizations, (2) restoration of contacts with the organizations that had been destroyed by the police, and with other districts, (3) organization of new groups, and (4) preparation of party literature. According to the Okhrana report, the collegia served the Bolsheviks as propaganda centers as well as training schools for new organizers.[22] The Petersburg Committee itself was preparing one leaflet urging the workers to stage a demonstration and strike on January 9 to protest the war and another leaflet specifically directed at the soldiers. S. G. Roshal'

20. Siegelbaum, "Class Collaboration," p. 8. Also see *Rabochee dvizhenie v Petrograde*, p. 363.

21. Leiberov, *Petrogradskii proletariat v Fevral'skoi revoliutsii* 1: 132. Also see A. Shliapnikov, *Kanun semnatdsatogo goda* 1: 92-94; 182-83; I. M. Dazhina, "Russkoe biuro TsK RSDRP v gody pervoi mirovoi voiny," in *Pervaia mirovoi voina, 1914-1918*, ed. A. L. Sidorov, L. M. Ivanov, et al., pp. 277-80.

22. TsGIA, f. 1405, op. 530, d. 1059, ℓ. 102.

was assigned to write the leaflets. However, at the end of December most of the members of the Petersburg Committee were arrested by the police when they were meeting in a restaurant in the Petrograd District. The Bolsheviks also advocated armed resistance to the police. "We will defend ourselves," became the party's slogan, and for this purpose the party organization in Old Lessner acquired 80 Browning rifles. In the Petrograd Metal Factory an illegal strike committee was created, and it was decided that this committee would consider itself a "fighting detachment."[23] On January 9, 1916, over 61,000 workers in sixty-eight factories joined the strike—impressive evidence of the Bolsheviks' growing influence among Petrograd workers.

The Bolsheviks, however, overextended themselves in the Putilov strike in February and the city-wide strike that followed in March. After the costly defeat of the New Lessner strike at the end of March, the most important bulwark of the Bolshevik organizations in Petrograd was well-nigh destroyed. Also in March the Russian Bureau of the Central Committee became defunct with the arrest of its members. After May the Petersburg Committee ceased its illegal printing activities.[24] It was not until October 1916 that the Petrograd Bolsheviks became active again in propaganda activities among the workers. When the food supply problem became acute, the Petersburg Committee instructed party activists to exploit this crisis for a new revolutionary offensive. The October strike, directly caused by the workers' dissatisfaction over the shortage of food and the never-ending rise in the cost of living, went far beyond the Bolsheviks' expectations, and developed into the largest political strike in Petrograd during the war. Taking advantage of this situation, the Bolsheviks attempted to stage a purely political strike in support of Bolshevik sailors in the Baltic Fleet, who were brought to trial, and soldiers of the 181st Infantry Regiment who had joined the demonstration and had been arrested by military authorities. Responding to the Bolsheviks' call, the workers staged a three-day strike, involving almost 80,000 workers on the third day. The October strike proved two things. First, given the combination of the right timing and a careful choice of slogans, the Bolsheviks were capable of mobilizing the masses of workers. Yet it would be a mistake to conclude that workers by and large came to accept the Bolshevik platform. An Okhrana report stated that although the masses of workers reacted to the food shortage and inflation, the Bolsheviks had a

23. Ibid., ℓℓ. 103-7.
24. *Listovki Peterburgskikh bol'shevikov* has only one leaflet published between May and October 1916. See *Listovki Peterburgskikh bol'shevikov* 2: 218-30.

hard time gaining support for their Social Democratic slogans.[25] Also it proved the unpredictability of the workers' movement. By October 1916 the workers were desperate, but the activists had no way of knowing when and how their mood could be translated into action.

According to Leiberov, the membership of the party dropped to between 100 and 120 in the period from July to December 1914; it rose to 1,200 by the end of 1915, then to 2,000 by September 1916; and on the eve of the February Revolution the membership of the Bolshevik party in Petrograd was 3,000. The number of party cells rose from 55 in February 1915, to 109 in September and October 1915, and to 110 in January 1917. At the end of 1916 and the beginning of 1917 the Petersburg Committee included nine city district committees, three national organizations, four neighboring regional committees, and a student Social-Democratic group.[26]

Because of constant police harassment, which led to the frequent breakup of the Petersburg Committee, the Petersburg Committee's leadership and influence were not strong. Therefore, it was the district committees that often directed day-to-day operation of the party. The Vyborg District Committee, with a membership of 500 to 600, and the Peterhof-Narva District Committee, with about 800 members, were the most important. Although with a smaller membership, the Vyborg District Committee was the more active and it was in some factories in that district that Bolshevik strength lay: New Lessner (80 to 100), Rosenkrantz (80), Parviainen (50), Old Lessner (30 to 40), Russian-Baltic Aeronautics (30), Petrograd Metal Factory (15 to 20), Erikson (15), and Promet (15). The chairman of the Vyborg District Committee at the beginning of 1917 was Ivan Dmitrievich Chugurin. A Mordovian born in 1883, he had been actively involved in underground party work since 1902 and had participated in the armed uprising in Sormovo during the 1905 Revolution. An experienced tinsmith, he had worked in various parts of Russia—Sormovo, Nizhnii Novgorod, Perm, Kiev, Moscow, and Petersburg. Although he had only three years' formal schooling in elementary school, he attended Lenin's party school at Longjumeau, France. In November 1916, he returned to Petrograd, and headed the Vyborg District Committee while serving on the Petersburg Committee. He had been arrested six times, twice exiled to Siberia, and had been in prison for two years.[27]

25. *Krasnyi arkhiv* 17, no. 4 (1926): 27-28; Leiberov, *Petrogradskii proletariat v Fevral'skoi revoliutsii* 1: 337-38.

26. Leiberov, *Petrogradskii proletariat v Fevral'skoi revoliutsii* 1: 339; "Iz proshlogo Leningradskoi organizatsii VKP (b)," *Krasnaia letopis'* 42, no. 3 (1931): 33-35.

27. Leiberov, *Petrogradskii proletariat v Fevral'skoi revoliutsii* 1: 340, 362.

The Vyborg District Committee often assumed the functions of the Petersburg Committee when its members were arrested. Another curious fact of the Vyborg District Committee was the large majority of its members who had been connected through the *zemliachestvo* (association of countrymen) of Sormovo and Nizhnii Novgorod. When the workers came to big cities, they often relied on connections with those who came from the same villages, districts, and provinces to find a job and a place to live. In an alien environment, the *zemliachestvo* was the most reliable source of assistance. In the spring of 1916, D. A. Pavlov,[28] V. N. Kaiurov, I. M. Gordienko, and N. F. Sveshnikov, all veteran Bolsheviks and experienced metalworkers, founded a *zemliachestvo* of Sormovo countrymen. Since many of the Bolshevik activists were skilled metalworkers who had fought in the 1905 Revolution in Sormovo, and later in the upsurge of the labor movement after 1912 in Sormovo and Nizhnii Novgorod, the *zemliachestvo* immediately became the stronghold of militant Bolshevik activists. Around twenty-five Bolsheviks joined the association, including Antiukhin, Gordienko, Kaiurov, K. I. Lebedev, N. I. Nazarov, V. N. Narychuk, D. A. Pavlov, Chugurin, and A. K. Skorokhodov. The members met once a week and discussed political matters, read leaflets and newspapers, and exchanged information. Five members of the *zemliachestvo* belonged to the Vyborg District Committee and three to the Petersburg Committee. In other words, the *zemliachestvo* of Sormovo became the unofficial inner circle of the Bolshevik underground leadership. Not only did it camouflage their illegal gatherings, but it also provided the Bolsheviks with the best defense against infiltration by police agents.[29]

The second important district committee was the Peterhof-Narva, with 800 members. The largest contingent was in the Putilov Factory with 150 party members and 26 party circles. The sick-fund organization in the Putilov Factory became the center of the Peterhof-Narva District Committee, which was led by Fedor Andreevich Lemeshev, a metalworker in the Putilov Factory and a member of the Petersburg Committee since 1916. Born in 1891, he had been an active Bolshevik member since 1914, and had been arrested twice—the second time in early January 1917. The Vasilievskii District Committee numbered

28. D. A. Pavlov was a modelmaker at Russian-Baltic Aeronautic and later worked under the famous aviation engineer, I. I. Sikorskii. He made a great contribution to aviation technology. His apartment, House 35 in Serdovol'skaia Street in the Vyborg District, was the headquarters of the Russian Bureau of the Central Committee (ibid., p. 42).

29. Ibid., pp. 342-43; I. Gordienko, *Iz boevogo proshlogo (1914-1918 gg.)*, pp. 44-46.

300, while the Petrograd District Committee headed by Skorokhodov had around 80 to 100 members. In both districts contacts with the factories were much weaker than in the Vyborg and Narva districts. Other district committees had a membership somewhere between 40 to 70.[30]

The district committees were subordinate to the Petersburg Committee, whose composition constantly changed during the war because of police arrests. The biographical data of the fifteen members of the Petersburg Committee at the end of 1916, given by Leiberov, offer a glimpse of the sort of activists that emerged during the war as the leaders of the Bolshevik party in Petrograd.[31]

The most obvious characteristic of the Petersburg Committee was its youth. The average age in 1917 was 27.3; only one member (Vinokurov) was over 40; five members were in their thirties—Zalutskii (30), Skorokhodov (37), Chugurin (34), Schmidt (31), and Shutko (33); the remainder were in their twenties. Working-class predominance was apparent: seven members were metalworkers, one member was a tram worker, two were clerks in the sick-fund organizations, one was a doctor, one a student, and one an underground professional revolutionary. In length of party membership, seven had joined before 1907, six between 1912 and 1914, and only two after the war. Only six members had higher than a secondary education, and the rest had finished elementary school. Despite their youth the Petersburg Committee members had been arrested a total of forty-four times and exiled eleven times—proof that they were experienced revolutionary leaders.[32]

Police repression was the most serious threat to Bolshevik organizations. According to Leiberov's study, from July 19, 1914, to February 15, 1917, the police arrested 743 Bolsheviks, 553 nonparty activists, 51 Mezhraiontsy, 34 anarchists, 79 Mensheviks, and 98 Socialist Revolutionaries.[33] Police agents infiltrated many of the Bolshevik organizations—M. E. Chernomazov, who worked in the

30. Leiberov, *Petrogradskii proletariat v Fevral'skoi revoliutsii* 1: 344–48.

31. They are: Nina Ferdinandovna Agadzhanova, Nikolai Kirillovich Antipov, Stepan Ivanovich Afanas'ev, Konstantin Nikitich Blotkin, Aleksandr Nikolaevich Vinokurov, Ernst Krishevich Eisenschmidt, Petr Antonovich Zalutskii, Petr Trofimovich Koriakov, Anna Profirovna Kostina, Fedor Andreevich Lemeshev, Aleksandr Kastrovich Skorokhodov, Nikolai Gur'evich Tolmachev, Ivan Dmitr'evich Chugurin, Vasilii Vladimirovich Schmidt, and Kirill Ivanovich Shutko. There was another member, Ia. Ia. Ozol'-Osis, but Leiberov excludes him because he was a police spy.

32. Leiberov, *Petrogradskii proletariat v Fevral'skoi revoliutsii*, pp. 357–63.

33. Ibid., pp. 368–69.

sick-fund organization in New Lessner, and Ia. Ia. Ozol'-Osis, a worker from Reikhel, both members of the Petersburg Committee, were police spies. A member of the Vyborg District Committee, V. E. Shurkanov, was also an informer. Chernomazov had a considerable following in the Petersburg Committee for his radical position, and Shurkanov, who used the name of Limonin in correspondence with the Okhrana, wrote highly intelligent reports.

In October 1916, Shliapnikov returned to Petrograd from abroad, and together with P. A. Zalutskii, who also had returned from exile by this time, and V. M. Molotov, a former student of the Polytechnical Institute, reestablished in November the Russian Bureau of the Central Committee. Shliapnikov headed the Russian Bureau and was in charge of establishing contacts abroad. Zalustskii entered the Petersburg Committee, representing the Russian Bureau. And young Molotov, still a flaming radical far from the gray bureaucrat he was to become under Stalin, was responsible for the bureau's publications.[34] The reestablished Russian Bureau was not strong enough to assume effective leadership over revolutionary activities in Petrograd. It lacked manpower, and, moreover, the Petersburg Committee, which had proudly continued to lead the rank-and-file Bolsheviks, did not easily submit to the Russian Bureau's instructions. The Russian Bureau, which considered reconstruction of the nation-wide organizations as the most pressing task, was more keenly aware of the Bolsheviks' unpreparedness for a revolutionary offensive. Naturally their strategy tended to be more moderate than the Petersburg Committee's. The differences were to be reflected in their respective attitudes toward the February 14 demonstration and subsequently in their strategies during the February Revolution.

Throughout the war the Bolsheviks consistently held a militant position against the war and against the tsarist government. Their view was at first unpopular among the workers, but as the workers grew increasingly disenchanted with the war, the Bolsheviks successfully extended their influence. The claim of the Soviet historians that the Bolsheviks alone were responsible for the development of the labor movement may be an exaggeration, but the existence of 3,000 hard-core Bolsheviks—dedicated, determined, and scattered throughout Petrograd—was certainly important to the dynamic development of the workers' movement during the war.

34. Shliapnikov, *Kanun semnadtsatogo goda* 1: 249-50; 35-42; Dazhina, "Russkoe biuro TsK RSDRP," pp. 281-82.

The Mensheviks

The outbreak of the war had an even more adverse effect on the Mensheviks than on the Bolsheviks. Iu. O. Martov was in Paris, F. I. Dan was arrested on the first day of the war and exiled to Siberia, and only A. N. Potresov of the Menshevik troika remained in Petrograd. While the Bolsheviks were united around Lenin's thesis, the Mensheviks became hopelessly divided on the issue of war. One of the radical Mensheviks, O. A. Ermanskii, stated: "The party, as a single Menshevik organization, did not exist. It did not exist at the very bottom." Another leading Menshevik, A. S. Martynov, later admitted: "After the declaration of war, a complete collapse took place among the Mensheviks."[35]

The Defensists

The extreme rightist position was taken by Gregorii Plekhanov, the father of Russian Marxism. He advanced the most blatant defensist position, stating that the victory of Western democracy over German militarism would be in the best interest of the Russian proletariat and, therefore, the task of the proletariat should be to suspend all internal struggle and cooperate with the tsarist government to win the war.[36]

Plekhanov's position, however, did not receive much support among the Mensheviks in Russia. The intellectuals gathered around the journal *Nasha zaria* took a defensist position somewhat different from Plekhanov. The intellectual force behind this ideology was Potresov. While Plekhanov advocated unequivocal support for the war, Potresov's position was: "We do not oppose the war." As long as the war was imposed on the Russian proletariat by Germany, it would be the obligation of the proletariat to defend itself. In the beginning of 1916 those Mensheviks who stood for this position published a collection of articles, *Samozashchita*. Such Menshevik intellectual luminaries as Potresov, Evgenii Maevskii, B. O. Bogdanov, F. A. Cherevanin, V. Levitskii, and P. Maslov belonged to this group. Kuz'ma Gvozdev, head of the workers' group, also joined the *samozashchita* group. Potresov declared in the introduction that internationalism and self-defense were not mutually exclusive but united, and remained the only practical policy. The main difference between

35. O. A. Ermanskii, *Iz perezhitogo (1887-1921 gg.)*, p. 121; Tiutiukin, *Voina, mir, revoliutsiia*, p. 51.

36. Tiutiukin, *Voina, mir, revoliutsiia*, p. 57. For Plekhanov's position also see Dvinov, "Pervaia mirovaia voina," pp. 30-32, 68-79.

Plekhanov and the *samozashchita* group was in their attitudes toward the tsarist regime. The latter saw it as a major obstacle to victory and that the proletariat should, therefore, join with the bourgeoisie in a common struggle to overthrow the tsarist regime.[37]

Centrists and the Duma Faction

The positions of both Plekhanov and Potresov were strongly opposed by the Menshevik leading center, the Organizational Committee, led by Martov. Its secretariat abroad considered either kind of defensism a betrayal of the international solidarity of the proletariat. They stood for peace without annexations and indemnities, and joined the antiwar international socialist conferences held in Zimmerwald and Kienthal.

After the arrest of the Bolshevik deputies of the Duma, the Menshevik Duma faction centered around N. S. Chkheidze and M. I. Skobelev became the only group in the Duma that represented the interests of the working class. Both Chkheidze and Skobelev considered themselves internationalists and viewed the war as an imperialist struggle between imperialist nations. Thus, at the outbreak of war, the Menshevik Duma deputies, in cooperation with the Bolsheviks, issued a joint declaration and walked out without voting for the war credits. Unlike Martov's unequivocal advocacy of proletarian internationalism, however, they advocated defense of the cultural heritage and of the interests of the working class against external aggression.[38] Thus, the difference between the Duma faction and the Menshevik defensists in Russia was a matter of degree, and there was already a theoretical common ground in their acceptance of "revolutionary defensism."

The Duma faction also took a view similar to the *samozashchita* group on the matter of internal struggle against tsarism. Unlike Plekhanov, the Duma faction also saw the necessity of waging a struggle against the tsarist government. In conformity with their theoretical understanding of the Marxist law of history, they viewed this struggle as one leading to a bourgeois-democratic revolution, in which the bourgeoisie should play a dominant role. They encouraged the liberals to join in the struggle and often attempted to restrain the workers from taking action that might frighten the liberal opposition.[39] There

37. For Potresov and the *samozashchita* group, see Dvinov, "Pervaia mirovaia voina," pp. 168-74; Leo Linde, "The Mensheviks in 1917," in *The Mensheviks from the Revolution of 1917 to the Second World War*, ed. Leopold Haimson, pp. 6-7.

38. Tiutiukin, *Voina, mir, revoliutsiia*, pp. 59-61.

39. Dvinov, "Pervaia mirovaia voina," p. 60.

was again a difference in emphasis between the Duma faction and the Menshevik defensists. While the latter's primary attention was focused on continuation of war to a victorious end, the former was more interested in the internal struggle against tsarism. But the difference was again a matter of degree, and despite their disagreement with the defensists, therefore, Chkheidze and the Duma deputies continued to cooperate with the defensists.

The leader of the Menshevik Duma faction was Chkheidze, a Georgian Menshevik. Although a fiery orator whose speeches in the Duma were often censored by the government, Chkheidze was by temperament a compromiser. Ermanskii commented: "Chkhiedze was constantly obsessed by the fear of making a mistake. He was afraid to take any definite position, against which an opposition could be raised. . . . Chkhiedze was afraid, as if he were afraid of fire, to take responsibility for a definite decision in serious questions."[40]

The Menshevik leaders exiled in Siberia also adhered to Martov's stand for internationalism, and later pledged their support for internationalism as manifested in the resolution at the Zimmerwald conference. The "Siberian Zimmerwaldists," as they were called, were led by I. Tseretelli, another Georgian Menshevik, who was to be prominent in the Petrograd Soviet after the February Revolution. It appeared on surface, therefore, that the Menshevik party was basically split into two groups: the internationalists—the Secretariat Abroad of the Organizational Committee, the Duma faction, the Siberian Zimmerwaldists, and the initiative group (see below)—and a small group of defensists. But this split was not decisive, and on the practical level realignment took place around the formation of the workers' group in the War Industries Committee.

The Workers' Group

The realignment of the Menshevik groups centered around the formation of the workers' group in the War Industries Committee. The defensists welcomed the formation of the workers' group as the proletariat's positive contribution to defense. In fact, the intellectual force behind the workers' group came from the defensists. Gvozdev was its chairman, and two brilliant Menshevik intellectuals, Bogdanov and Maevskii, joined its secretariat. Nonetheless, it would be erroneous to label the workers' group as a defensist organization. The Duma faction and the Siberian Zimmerwaldists favored the formation of the workers' group for two reasons. First, the working class would gain a legal organization to protect its class interests. Second,

40. Ermanskii, *Iz perezhitogo*, p. 120.

the workers' group would become an important vehicle through which the workers could wage a war, together with the bourgeoisie, against the tsarist regime.[41] To the overwhelming majority of lower echelon party workers the issue of war was inconsequential and the need to create a legal organization outweighed any other consideration.

The workers' group was created as a result of the election on November 29, 1915. The following members were elected: to the Central War Industries Committee, K. A. Gvozdev, chairman (Erikson), I. I. Emel'ianov (Pipe Factory), G. E. Breido (Lessner), F. Ia. Iakovlev (Pipe Factory), E. A. Kuz'min (Pipe Factory), G. N. Komarov (Obukhov), V. N. Abrasimov (Promet), E. A. Gudkov (Promet), E. A. Anasovskii (?), and Ia. Ia. Iakovlev (Putilov)—all Mensheviks; to the Petrograd District War Industries Committee, A. A. Ershov (Baltic Shipyard), A. V. Kochalov (Putilov), N. V. Vasiliev (Aivaz), V. M. Boshevol'nov (Nobel), Ia. S. Shilin (Petrograd Metal) and A. S. Ostapenko (Okhta Gunpowder)—the first three were Mensheviks, and the last was a Socialist Revolutionary.[42] Abrasimov was a police spy. From this list it is obvious that the strength of the workers' group lay in the state-owned large munition factories.

If the defensists had a secret desire to turn the workers' group into an instrument of class collaboration for the sake of national defense, they must have concealed this desire for tactical purposes, since during the discussion on November 29 the workers' group presented a consistently international argument on the war, and defended their participation in the War Industries Committee on two counts: the political expediency of acquiring a legal organization, and the need to create a common arena for the political struggle waged jointly with the bourgeoisie against tsarism. Ignoring Guchkov's plea for class collaboration, Gvozdev stated: "We have no desire to destroy Germany, and we shall not enter into the [War Industries] Committee for this purpose." The workers would participate in them for "the organization of society's forces and the struggle with the internal enemy." But Gvozdev criticized the Bolsheviks for insisting on establishing socialism immediately: "Socialism is not on our agenda yet, but the present task is the transfer of power from the hands of the nobility into the hands of the capitalists. In economic questions the bourgeoisie is our enemy, but in political questions it would go

41. Dvinov, "Pervaia mirovaia voina," pp. 84-85. Linde states that Potresov's group of defensists stayed away from the workers' group. Linde, "The Mensheviks in 1917," p. 7. Potresov himself was not involved in the workers' group, but Maevskii and Bogdanov, who took a position similar to Potresov, became important members in the secretariat of the workers' group.

42. TsGIA, f. 1405, op. 530, d. 1059, ll. 85-86.

along with us, hand in hand, since it needs the conditions of free political life as much as we do."[43]

The point that the workers' group would take advantage of their legal position to form a united front with the bourgeoisie against tsarism was more forcefully made by Emel'ianov. According to this worker from the Pipe Factory, the workers should stand for peace without annexations and indemnities. To the workers the most dangerous enemy was not Germany but the Russian government, which had brought the nation to the brink of ruin. The only way out would be a "radical change in the life of society and the democratization of the governmental structure." To achieve this, "our struggle must be conducted in conjunction with all the forces in society"—revolutionary appeals alone would not be enough. They should strive for agreements with all classes of society: "It is necessary to have an alliance with other classes—with the bourgeoisie. We will win with them, but without them we will suffer a defeat."[44]

The resolution of the workers' group, adopted on November 29, stated these aims: (1) to oppose any attempts to drag the working class into the war; (2) to consider the war harmful to the working class, since its purpose was to conquer markets for capitalists; (3) to demand peace without annexations and indemnities; (4) to conclude that the hopeless situation in which the nation found itself was the result of the government's policy; (5) to blame the Duma for having supported the government and for lacking the courage to seek the support of the people; (6) to struggle for the convocation of a constituent assembly and for freedom of the press and unions; (7) to demand an end to suppression of nationalist organizations and recognition of their right to self-determination; (8) to demand an eight-hour work day and land for peasants; and (9) to achieve the democratization of zemstvos and municipal self-governments.[45]

The motivation behind the participation of the workers' group in the War Industries Committee was further clarified by the "instructions" they formulated after the election of the workers' group: (1) to inform the Central War Industries Committee how the workers of Petrograd viewed the present situation of the country and the conditions for its salvation; (2) to declare to the Central War Industries Committee that the workers of Petrograd would not assume any responsibility for the work in the War Industries Committee in view of the composition of the committee and the impossibility

43. Ibid., ℓℓ. 80-81.
44. Ibid., ℓ. 81.
45. Ibid., ℓℓ. 84-85.

of participation by the working class; (3) to make a decisive protest against the election law of June 3, 1907, which was discriminatory against workers; and (4) to inform the Central War Industries Committee that to organize all the workers in Russia it would be necessary to convene an All-Russian Workers' Congress, which alone could decide conclusively the question of participation of the representatives of the working class in the work of the Central War Industries Committee. The "instructions" defined the tasks of the workers' group: (1) to maintain a separate workers' group within the Central War Industries Committee; (2) to have close contact with workers at the factory level through factory meetings and commissions; (3) to restore immediately trade unions, cultural clubs, and a workers' press; and (4) to attempt immediately to convene an All-Russian Workers' Congress. The meeting also adopted a political resolution protesting the prorogation of the Duma and the government's repression of voluntary organizations and the workers' press and cooperative organizations. It stated: "We maintain that the government in its struggle against the working class takes advantage of wartime to deprive the workers of rights achieved after decades of struggle. The organizations of industrialists also support and encourage this policy at present as well as in peace time despite their hypocritical phrases of national unity."[46]

The discussions and the resolution adopted at the November 29 meeting clearly show that Bolshevik accusations that the workers' group were supporters of the war and class collaboration were groundless. The group stood for the internationalist position of peace without annexations and indemnities. To be sure, class collaboration was the fundamental goal of Guchkov and Konovalov in inviting the workers' representatives in the War Industries Committee. In February 1916 Guchkov wrote an open letter to Gvozdev, requesting that the workers' group intervene in the labor dispute to achieve peace between labor and capital—a prerequisite for their common interest of national defense. Gvozdev rejected this request outright, stating that class collaboration was not their aim and pledging to protect the working-class interests.[47] Fully aware of the intentions of the leaders of the War Industries Committee, and risking the danger of being labeled class collaborators, the workers' group nonetheless defended its participation. In the leaflet distributed to the workers, they stated: "Our understanding of the interests of the nation and our under-

46. Ibid., ll. 86-86.
47. For Guchkov's letter and Gvozdev's reply, see TsGAOR, f. 570, op. 1, d. 2844, ll. 4-5; Dvinov, "Pervaia mirovaia voina," pp. 147-48.

standing of the way to save the nation from ruin make it imperative for us to remain in these institutions playing an exclusive role under the extraordinary conditions of wartime and to protect energetically the workers' interests from all attempts to reduce our hard-won gains."[48]

One of the most important goals of the workers' group was the convocation of an All-Russian Workers' Congress. The workers' group felt that while other classes had their all-Russian organizations, such as the United Nobility, the Union of Towns, the Union of Zemstvos, and the War Industries Committee, the workers had none. From its point of view an All-Russian Workers' Congress would serve two purposes: the workers would be given a legal national organization to protect their interests, one that would render the common struggle with the bourgeoisie against tsarism more effective and broader in nature. Moreover, the recognition of the workers' group at such a congress would legitimize their existence, removing the basis of the Bolsheviks' accusation that the workers' group had betrayed the workers' real wishes. The demand for the convocation of an All-Russian Workers' Congress was presented at the Second Congress of the War Industries Committee in February 1916 and was supported by the leaders of the Central War Industries Committee. The government, however, never allowed such a congress.

As a practical measure to protect working-class interests, the workers' group attempted to establish a mechanism through which the workers could present their demands. They advocated the re-establishment of the *starosta* system (factory elders) and the creation of conciliation boards. The workers had been given the right to elect elders in the Law of 1903. According to this law, the workers had the right to present a list of candidates to the factory administration, who would choose their elders from the list, subject to the approval of the governor of each province. The elders were not to interfere with the employers' prerogatives of hiring and firing, and often after labor disputes the elders found themselves on the list of workers fired from the factory. Even such limited labor representation incurred the disfavor of many factory owners, and the *starosta* system had for all practical purposes become a dead issue. Thanks to the efforts of the workers' group, however, the *starosta* system suddenly acquired popularity among the workers in 1916. The Central War Industries Committee at its Second Congress in February 1916 approved the demand to reestablish the *starosta* system in every factory.[49]

48. TsGIA, f. 1405, op. 530, d. 1059, *l*. 123.
49. "Deiatel'nost' Rabochei gruppy TsVPK," February 15, 1917, TsGAOR,

The idea of conciliation boards had been in the minds of the leaders of the Central War Industries Committee long before the workers' group was formed. Guchkov, for instance, had made a proposal to establish such a channel for labor negotiations to the Special Council for Defense, and had negotiated with the minister of trade and industry, Prince Shakhovskoi, for concrete measures to put the idea into practice. The workers' group after its formation immediately picked up the idea, worked out a detailed proposal, and presented it at the Second Congress of the War Industries Committee in February 1916.[50] The joint efforts by the workers' group and the leaders of the Central War Industries Committee immediately provoked strong opposition from the industrialists. A Moscow industrialist, Iu. P. Guzhon, declared: "They will bring such harm, allowing the workers' representatives of committees to be engaged in politics." The Petrograd and Moscow Associations of Factory Owners as well as the Council of Metal Factory Owners strongly opposed the *starosta* system and the conciliation boards. Even the Progressist, Riabushinskii, opposed this flirtation with workers' demands, stating that the institution of conciliation boards was the task of trade unions, which, as Riabushinskii well knew, did not exist. Rejected by the government and opposed by the industrialists, the *starosta* system and the conciliation boards remained largely on paper until the February Revolution. In Petrograd the *starosta* were elected and operated only in Erikson, Aivaz, and the Pipe Factory.[51]

The workers' group was also concerned with the improvement of the workers' living conditions. It initiated the workers' dining hall *(stolovaia)* campaign and actively participated in the workers' cooperative movement. These activities served dual purposes. Not only were they attempts to improve the workers' living conditions, but also they were intended to be a focal point where the workers' movement and the liberal opposition coalesced. In the fall of 1916 the workers' group presented a demand to the Petrograd City Duma to establish public dining halls managed by the workers' organization in conjunction with the city self-government. At the initiative of the workers' group, eighty persons from the sick funds and the workers' cooperatives met in September 1916 and created a special commission for the creation of public dining halls. This commission demanded

---

f. 579, op. 1, d. 2235, pp. 19-21. Also see TsGAOR, f. DPOO, d. 347/1917, ll. 11-12 (a circular of the workers' group, September 19, 1916).

50. "Deiatel'nost' Rabochei gruppy TsVPK," pp. 17-19.

51. V. S. Diakin, *Russkaia burzhuaziia*, pp. 196-97; "Deiatel'nost' Rabochei gruppy," p. 21.

that the city administration make funds and space available—a demand that eventually led to the city duma's decision to open such eating facilities in Petrograd.[52] As a more fundamental solution to the food supply problem, the workers' group, believing that the crisis could be solved only by society taking over the distribution of food, supported the idea of convening an All-Russian Congress of Food Supply, to which representatives of all classes of society would be invited. This concept was strongly endorsed by the liberal activists in the Unions of Zemstvos and of Towns. The congress, scheduled to meet in early December, was banned by Protopopov.

The workers' group considered the workers' offensive in strikes and demonstrations premature and in the long run harmful when the workers were not fully organized under its leadership and other forces of society were not ready for decisive action. It would provoke police repression and nullify whatever gains the workers had made in the difficult time of war. Emel'ianov stated: "A political struggle is not an appeal for strikes, not a meeting in a factory, not a noisy resolution or a shout, but a long preparation for a struggle."[53] This view conveniently merged with the defensists' view that the workers should exercise self-restraint for the sake of self-defense. To Maevskii self-defense was the most important task of the proletariat, and "strikism" would be harmful to self-defense and ultimately to revolution. Only in the effort to defend itself against the external enemy had the working class a possibility of gaining political rights.[54]

Whether for self-defense or for forming a united action with other classes in society, the workers' group often attempted to dissuade workers from joining what it considered to be ill-prepared strikes. For instance, it opposed the strike of January 9, 1916. During the Putilov strike in February 1916, the workers' group issued a leaflet appealing to workers to stop the strike, since an isolated, spontaneous outburst would "weaken and destroy the developing conflict of all Russian society with the government," bringing harm to the interests of the working class. During the October strike in 1916, the workers' group issued a similar leaflet, characterizing the strike movement as organized by "irresponsible elements wishing to push it to extreme activities." It recommended that workers return to work and petitioned military authorities to open the factories.[55]

The workers' group also intervened in labor disputes, not because

52. "Deiatel'nost' Rabochei gruppy," pp. 21-23.
53. Shliapnikov, *Kanun semnadtsatogo goda* 2: 88.
54. Evg. Maevskii, *Kanun revoliutsii* (Petrograd, 1918), pp. 4, 7-8.
55. "Deiatel'nost' Rabochei gruppy," pp. 9, 14-16.

it actively sought peace between labor and capital, as the Bolsheviks constantly charged, but rather because there was no legal organization representing the workers, and the striking workers turned to the workers' group for assistance. In most cases, it proved powerless to resolve conflicts.[56]

Such activities invited strong criticism from the initiative group, radical wing of the Mensheviks. After the Second Congress of the War Industries Committee, K. S. Grinevich, one of the initiative group leaders, wrote a letter to the Menshevik Secretariat Abroad, complaining of the workers' group's strong leaning toward defensism. The Menshevik internationalists abroad, led by Martov and Larin, wrote a letter to the workers' group, severely reprimanding its members for their betrayal of the internationalist position and threatening their expulsion from the Menshevik internationalist group.[57] Not only the Mensheviks abroad but also the Duma deputies and the initiative group began raising a strong voice against the workers' group. A series of violent meetings were held in March, and at the beginning of April, defying all criticism, the workers' group boldly declared: "The leaders abroad went insane and until now have considered themselves leaders of the Russian proletariat. Such time was long gone, and a sharp and decisive outcry is necessary so that they will retire to the background and occupy their place."[58] The initiative group decided to break completely with the workers' group, openly seeking a new path for the left-wing internationalist alliance.

The workers' group's moderate policy, restraining the workers' penchant for direct action, eventually cost the group its popularity. It became increasingly clear to its leaders that they were losing ground to the more radical elements. During the insurance campaign in the summer of 1916, Gvozdev received only seventeen votes in his own "fiefdom," Erikson Factory, and Breido only fourteen votes in Lessner, where he had received more than 1,000 votes in the election campaign for the workers' group in the fall of 1915.[59] Alarmed by the loss of their influence, the workers' group finally changed their strategy in a radical direction in December 1916. On December 13 to 15 in Petrograd, the workers' group held a conference in which representatives of other workers' organizations also took part. The resolution adopted at this conference reiterated the proletariat's dual goals:

56. Ibid., pp. 4-16.

57. Tiutiukin, *Voina, mir, revoliutsiia*, p. 220; TsGAOR, f. 579, op. 1, d. 2844, ℓ. 7; Dvinov, "Pervaia mirovaia voina," p. 131.

58. Tiutiukin, *Voina, mir, revoliutsiia*, p. 221.

59. Ibid., p. 222.

peace without annexations and indemnities, and struggle with the internal enemy, the tsarist government. Viewing the current situation as a general crisis, in which all classes of Russian society, including the Unions of Zemstvos and of Towns, the War Industries Committee, the Duma, and even the nobility, had joined forces against tsarism, the workers' group concluded that the workers' task would be to join this struggle. Its task was not to alienate the privileged class, but to persuade it to move more decisively in the struggle against the regime, a struggle for "decisive overthrow of the existing regime and the establishment in its place of a Provisional Government based on the organized, independent, and free people."[60] The workers' group decided to launch a campaign for the workers' strike movement at the opening of the Duma after the Christmas recess. Although it had opposed the strike on Janurary 9, 1916, it now actively supported the workers' offensive in the anniversary of Bloody Sunday in 1917, and urged the workers to join the strike.

The workers' group represented the only viable alternative to the Bolsheviks—the only other group with substantial influence among the workers in Petrograd. Their history clearly reveals the nature of labor politics in the tsarist regime and proves that even their moderate programs were impossible to achieve in the context of tsarist labor politics. None of the workers' group's pet programs—the convocation of an All-Russian Workers' Congress, the *starosta* system, the establishment of conciliation boards, the public dining halls, and an All-Russian Congress of Food Supply—was successfully implemented. Not only were they vetoed by the government, they were not approved by the industrialists either.

All the Mensheviks who participated in the workers' group had a fundamental belief in the essential revolutionary character of the Russian bourgeoisie and in its ability to replace the tsarist regime. They held, further, that it would be possible to form a united front of the bourgeoisie and the proletariat. But as we have seen, the Russian liberals were far from revolutionary, always more afraid of revolt from

---

60. TsGAOR, f. DPOO, op. 17, d. 45, 1917, ℓℓ. 40-46. Tiutiukin advances a remarkable interpretation, unorthodox among Soviet historians, that the new direction adopted by the workers' group "objectively contributed" to the revolutionary situation, influencing the "defensist-oriented" workers to act decisively in the struggle against the tsarist regime. This view, indirectly hinted at in his book, *Voina, mir, revoliutsiia,* is more forcefully developed in the symposium devoted to the February Revolution. See S. V. Tiutiukin, "Rabochaia gruppa TsVPK nakanune Fevral'skoi revoliutsii," *Nauchnaia sessiia posviashchennaia 50-letiiu sverzheniia samoderzhaviia v Rossii,* sec. 1, pp. 45-48.

below than the government's repression. And the workers, seeing no results from participation by the workers' group in the War Industries Committee but a request from the group to put a brake on the strike movement, became increasingly disenchanted. Their strike movement then developed independently, and was not, as the workers' group envisaged, a part of the *obshchestvennye* forces against the tsarist regime, but rather a force in itself, outside of and against all other forces in society.

By the end of 1916, the leaders of the workers' group themselves became convinced that none of the programs they had advocated could be achieved as long as the tsarist regime continued. Moreover, they realized the group was rapidly losing its influence among the workers and finally came to advocate the wholesale overthrow of the tsarist regime.

Although Guchkov and Konovalov defended the workers' group as a moderate wing of the labor movement striving to inject peace in labor strife, in the final analysis Protopopov and his police were justified in concluding that it was ultimately revolutionary, with the goal of overthrowing the government. It proved impossible for the government and the workers' group to coexist. Konovalov's dream of organizing labor so that it would not become revolutionary not only failed but also backfired. Contrary to the general contention of Soviet historians, the workers' group had its share of deepening the revolutionary crisis.

The Initiative Group

The initiative group was the radical internationalist wing of the Mensheviks. From the beginning of the war, it consistently stood against the war. In November 1915, during the height of the election campaign for the War Industries Committee, the initiative group issued an appeal to the workers, and called for refusal to support the defensists, boycott of the election to the War Industries Committee, and opposition to the militarization of labor. Although they opposed participation in the War Industries Committee, the main attack during the election campaign was directed against the Bolsheviks, who did not hesitate to employ opportunistic tactics to discredit their fellow Mensheviks. They explained to the Bolsheviks that their friends would participate in the War Industries Committee, not for national defense, but for organizing the working class.[61] Even after the formation of the workers' group, the initiative group refused to break its organiza-

61. Leiberov, *Petrogradskii proletariat v Fevral'skoi revoliutsii* 1: 138-39; Dvinov, "Pervaia mirovaia voina," p. 149.

tional tie with them, but watched their cautious activities with growing concern. The "revolutionary defensism" of the workers' group dissatisfied the initiative group, which considered such a position tantamount to capitulation to defensism. Finally, at the end of June 1916, convinced that further negotiations with the workers' group would be useless, it decided to call for their withdrawal from the War Industries Committee. In August, it issued a leaflet attacking the workers' group and appealing to the workers not to support it. As relations between the two groups broke down completely, it sought a left-wing alliance with the group standing for the internationalist position. The initiative group had around four to five hundred members at the end of 1916 and party cells existed in twenty-five to thirty factories.[62]

Mezhraiontsy

The Mezhraiontsy belonged to a faction of the Russian Social-Democratic Labor party that stood for the reunification of the Bolsheviks and the Mensheviks. At the outbreak of war, this group adopted the internationalist position and issued a leaflet with a slogan against the war and for the overthrow of the tsarist regime. The group was led by a former Bolshevik, I. Iurenev, and cooperated with the internationalist faction of the Mensheviks around Trotskii, who was a member after his return to Russia in May 1917, until he and other Mezhraiontsy formally joined the Bolshevik party. Immediately after the war their organizational strength lay in Vasilievskii Island and the Narva District, where their membership at one point exceeded that of the Bolsheviks. By the end of 1914, the Mezhraiontsy numbered around three hundred to three hundred fifty.[63]

In the spring and the summer of 1915 the Mezhraiontsy were the focus of police repression. The membership dwindled to between 60 and 80. According to an Okhrana agent, the organization was reduced to "the state that one cannot talk about its existence." It was not until February 1916 that the Mezhraiontsy resumed their organizational activities in Vasilievskii Island, Petrograd, Moscow, and First City districts. In the fall of 1916 they began publication of a weekly magazine, *Rabochie vedomosti*, three issues of which

62. Tiutiukin, *Voina, mir, revoliutsiia*, pp. 221-22; Leiberov, *Petrogradskii proletariat v Fevral'skoi revoliutsii* 1: 407.

63. I. Iurenev, "Mezhraionka (1911-1917)," *Proletarskaia revoliutsiia*, no. 1 (1924), pp. 115-17, 123-25, 127-36; A. Popov, "Stranichka vospominanii o rabote v 'Mezhraionke,' " *Proletarskaia revoliutsiia*, no. 10 (1923), p. 96.

subsequently came to light. The membership was restored to 150 by the fall of 1916.[64] By the end of 1916 the Mezhraiontsy had seven district committees, and party cells existed in sixteen enterprises as well as in Petrograd Imperial University and the Psychoneurological Institute. The Mezhraiontsy's uniqueness lay in their energetic publishing activities. While the Bolshevik illegal printing presses were often destroyed by the police, the Mezhraiontsy managed to maintain theirs, and isssued a series of antiwar leaflets.

The Mezhraiontsy were important in transforming the antiwar groups into a front united in opposition to the workers' group. In November 1916 one member wrote a letter to L. M. Karakhan, an arrested and exiled leader of the Mezhraiontsy from the Psychoneurological Institute, who was later to become a famous Soviet diplomat. In this letter the reporter stated optimistically that the internationalist groups, joined by the Bolshevik Petersburg Committee, Mezhraiontsy, and the Menshevik initiative group, were considering a joint publication in the style of *Rabochie vedomosti*. An informal organ was being created that would have the task of "elaborating on the fundamental questions of theory and practice from the internationalist point of view, of struggling for the union of all internationalist groups along the line of the Third International and of severing all ties with the social chauvinists and of waging a struggle against them." This organ would be, it was emphasized, strictly on private initiative. The letter cautioned that the top leaders of these parties were still skeptical of organizational unity, but "at the factory level all the activities are discussed and taken jointly." The letter continues: "A dark spot in the bright background is the Gvozdevites, but they are constantly losing ground."[65]

It was not easy to bring together the Bolsheviks and the Mensheviks, who differed greatly in outlook and ideology, and who had in the past heaped abuse on each other. It was to the credit of the Mezhraiontsy, who served as a go-between, that the antiwar groups, despite their differences, gingerly formed a loose coalition.

64. Early in 1915 the police made a chain of arrests touched off by the arrest of an inexperienced activist of the Mezhraiontsy group at the Nikolaevskii Station, who was carrying, rather conspicuously, a big sack containing illegal printing equipment. For the fascinating details of how the police workers destroyed the network of the Mezhraiontsy, see TsGIA, f. 1405, op. 530, d. 1058, ll. 9-24. Also see Leiberov, *Petrogradskii proletariat v Fevral'skoi revoliutsii* 1: 136.

65. Bil'iaminov's letter to Lev Mikhailovich Karakhan, November 15, 1916, TsGAOR, f. DPOO, op. 17, d. 45, 1917, l. 49.

Socialist Revolutionaries

The war caused a serious split in the Socialist Revolutionary party, which, unlike the Bolsheviks and the Mensheviks, had rejected Marxism and had inherited the traditional *narodniki* (Populist) revolutionary ideology. At the outbreak of the war, the famous terrorist Boris Savinkov announced: "I am a Russian with all my heart. With all my heart I wish the victory of Russia." In an open letter printed in the Socialist Revolutionary journal, *Mysl'*, in Paris, Savinkov declared: "We do not set any conditions. We demand nothing. We simply acknowledge that the task for which the government is struggling at the present moment is our task as well. And all the time during the war we shall disarm ourselves, lay down our arms, and with all our means cooperate for the success of our task."[66] On August 22, 1914, in a small town near Lausanne, Switzerland, the Socialist Revolutionary party leaders abroad held a conference to discuss their policy toward the war. The conference revealed a serious internal split. A majority led by N. D. Avksentiev and Bunakov took a defensist position, while a small minority led by Viktor Chernov, the party's founder, advocated the internationalist position. In Russia also, a majority of the SR organizations took the defensist position. The leaders of the SR organizations in Petrograd, which had been decimated by police repression in the spring of 1914, decided to abstain completely from any political action during the war.[67]

This position, however, was sharply criticized by a small group of radical internationalists in the party. In late August and early September 1914, a serious conflict took place between the remaining Petersburg Committee of the Socialist Revolutionary party, which had decided to withdraw from activity, and the Narva District autonomous group of SRs, which began independently to circulate a leaflet against the war among the workers of the Putilov Factory and the soldiers in the barracks in the Narva District. At the beginning of September about one hundred SR workers held a meeting outside the Neva Gate and adopted a resolution in which they warned the party leaders that if they took no action against the war, the SR workers would join the Bolshevik party. Disgusted by the inaction of their leaders, some of the SR workers did actually join in Bolshevik activities.[68]

66. Tiutiukin, *Voina, mir, revoliutsiia*, pp. 67-68.
67. Ibid., p. 72.
68. Ibid., p. 74; *Petrogradskie rabochie v gody imperialisticheskoi voiny*, p. 93.

By the summer of 1915 the internationalist wing of the Socialist Revolutionaries had resumed active propaganda work among the workers in Petrograd. Their circles existed in four districts: the Vyborg, Nevskii, Vasilievskii, and Kolpino. In the Vyborg District the SR workers formed the initiative organization of the Petrograd group of Socialist Revolutionaries. By the beginning of 1916 thirty to thirty-five SR cells existed with five- to six-hundred members. Their strength lay in the Baltic Shipyard (four cells with forty to fifty members), the Pipe Factory (two cells with thirty members), the Neva Shipyard, Obukhov, and the Putilov Factory.[69] This radical wing of Socialist Revolutionaries formed an alliance with the Bolsheviks in opposition to the election campaign to the War Industries Committee in the fall of 1915. At the meeting of November 29, after the Bolsheviks walked out, an SR worker, Koriakin, read the resolution of the SR internationalists, which stated that "only the institution created by the forces and the will of the toiling people could decide on the question of defense of the country in the interest of democracy," and that the participation in the Central War Industries Committee "would be a single blow to all the workers' democracy."[70] After Koriakin read the declaration, the SR internationalists also walked out.

Openly criticizing the SR leaders influenced by Kerenskii, who had supported the Menshevik workers' group and their participation in the War Industries Committee, the SR internationalist organization, the Petrograd group of Socialist Revolutionaries, composed an open letter to the Bolsheviks, demonstrating their solidarity with the latter. The open letter written by a student SR leader Aleksei Sadikov, stated:

(1) We, the Socialist Revolutionary Internationalists, greet you, who were the first ones to raise a voice against those who consciously violated the elementary rules of party discipline and comradely ethics; (2) together with you, we shall fight against the disruptive action and attempts to appeal to the bourgeoisie to solve our internal questions; (3) together with you, we consider the meeting on November 29 illegal, and denounce those who took part in the votes and by so doing sanctioned the meeting and those who subsequently approved the results of the meeting.[71]

Unlike the Bolsheviks, however, the Socialist Revolutionary internationalists were numerically weak, inexperienced in protecting their underground organizations, and, more important, had never succeeded in creating a center of leadership comparable to the Bolsheviks' Petersburg Committee. Police repression in the spring and the summer of

69. Leiberov, *Petrogradskii proletariat v Fevral'skoi revoliutsii* 1: 137.
70. TsGIA, f. 1405, op. 530, d. 1059, ℓ. 79.
71. Ibid., ℓℓ. 91-93.

1916 had weakened their organization. The Okhrana agent proudly reported in October 1916: "As for the strictly narrow work of local organizations of the Socialist Revolutionaries, after the liquidation of the leaders of the Petrograd Committee on the night of July 31 this year, they are at the present moment in complete disorder, despite some unsuccessful attempts of new leaders to reestablish it."[72] Another Okhrana report was more categorical: "The Socialist Revolutionary party is completely disorganized and as a properly functioning organization, united with a central leadership, does not exist."[73] In the summer of 1916, Petr Aleksandrovich clandestinely returned to Petrograd from abroad. On the eve of the February Revolution, he participated in a series of joint meetings with the Bolsheviks, Mezhraiontsy, and the initiative group, presumably representing the Socialist Revolutionaries, but it appears that his group was composed of no more than a handful of activists.

The right-wing Socialist Revolutionaries, who stood for the defensist position, were led by A. F. Kerenskii. Until the summer of 1915, when the underground revolutionary organizations were destroyed by the police, Kerenskii was the center of revolutionary activities. On July 16 and 17, Kerenskii invited the Socialist Revolutionary activists, including Chaikovskii and Peshekhonov, to his apartment. Around thirty representatives attended the Congress of Socialist Revolutionaries, which passed a resolution calling for the convocation of a constituent assembly, a change in the state structure, and formation of a united front of all revolutionary forces. The resolution recognized the powerlessness of the Duma in solving the current crisis, and urged that "the Duma should serve merely as a body to unite the people's forces until the convocation of the constituent assembly." The resolution pointed out the necessity of uniting the Duma SR organization with the underground activities. After this "congress" a series of meetings of the Petrograd Socialist Revolutionaries were held in the outskirts of Petrograd, at which the possibility of creating a soviet of workers' deputies was suggested.[74]

Kerenskii was an ardent believer in the alliance between the Socialist parties and the liberal opposition for the struggle to overthrow tsarism. It was for that reason that he became active in the masonic organization, through which he established personal connections with the liberal activists.[75] His activities and speeches in the Duma

72. *Krasnyi arkhiv* 17, no. 4 (1926): 30.
73. Tiutiukin, *Voina, mir, revoliutsiia*, p. 66.
74. TsGIA, f. 1405, op. 530, d. 1058, ℓℓ. 40-42, 34-35.
75. For the problem of the Freemasons and the February Revolution, see chap. 27.

were all appeals to the liberals to assume more active leadership of the masses in the revolutionary struggle against the government. When the workers' movement became enlivened in the summer of 1915, Kerenskii became fearful of its adverse effect on the liberals. Thus, on September 4, Kerenskii made a speech at the meeting of the Trudoviks in the Duma, stating that they must not give the government an excuse for either military defeat or for internal repression. They should assume a waiting tactic and appeal to the workers "not to strike, not to waste their efforts on an aimless offensive but to maintain them for a general revolutionary offensive in the near future under better conditions." For the next couple of days, the Trudoviks and the Mensheviks, who had adopted a similar position, went around to the Petrograd factories to persuade the workers to return to work.[76]

During the election campaign for the War Industries Committee, the right-wing Socialist Revolutionaries supported the participation of the workers' representatives in the War Industries Committee. As we have seen, their policy provoked a strong protest from the left-wing SRs. The split between the Right and the Left became wider. While the Right, together with the workers' group, opposed the strike on January 9, 1916, the radical wing in the Vyborg District supported the strike, and together with the other internationalist groups, engaged in propaganda work among the workers for strike.[77]

While the left-wing SRs moved closer to the Bolsheviks, Kerenskii and the Trudoviks approached other radical intellectuals to form a Left Bloc. Thirteen intellectuals and one worker were invited to Chkheidze's apartment on October 9, 1916, to discuss the possibility of forming such an alliance. As for the attitude toward the war, a majority of the participants, with the exception of Sokolov, accepted the principle of the internationalist position of peace without annexation or indemnities. The participants were concerned with the growing indifference among the masses to the Duma and its activities, and with the Duma's loss of prestige, and with their own lack of control over the masses—a situation that was being exploited by extremists. To exert more influence among the masses, the participants decided to create a Left Bloc. The resolution, drafted by Peshekhonov and adopted at the meeting, stated that because of the "definite decline of influence of the progressive-liberal political tendencies headed by the Kadets," the "complete bankruptcy of the Duma and the Progressive Bloc," and the "unquestionable confusion of the central

76. TsGIA, f. 1405, op. 530, d. 1058, ℓℓ. 98-99.
77. *Rabochee dvizhenie v Petrograde*, p. 405.

government," the radical intellectuals had decided "to strive for the creation of a Left Bloc to take advantage of an expedient moment and to achieve political liberation of the country." It should be remembered that at the same time the Progressists led by Konovalov seceded from the Progressive Bloc, advocating closer cooperation with the leaders of the workers' movement.[78] Although documentary evidence is lacking, it appears that the proposal for the creation of the Left Bloc was made with the knowledge and the support of the Progressists, particularly of Konovalov. The Left Bloc, however, did not come into existence as a political group with definite platforms and programs. It did not go beyond a group of Socialist intelligentsia who met from time to time to discuss the current political situation and exchange information.

Realignment of the Revolutionary Parties

During the war there was a realignment of the revolutionary parties. The internationalists—the Bolsheviks, Mezhraiontsy, initiative group of the Mensheviks, and left-wing SRs—slowly formed a loose alliance. Since their ideological differences were still too great and their mutual distrust, hostility, and jealousy too strong to overcome, this alliance was never a formal one, but, nonetheless, after the fall of 1915, they earnestly attempted to coordinate their activities. It appears that willingness to form such an alliance was much stronger at the lower level. In the factories these antiwar groups acted in harmony in deciding to strike or call a factory general meeting. The Bolshevik Petersburg Committee was willing to enter into such an alliance on an ad hoc basis, but the Russian Bureau of the Central Committee was never enthusiastic about cooperation with other groups. Details of the formation of the internationalist alliance are still obscure and await further historical research.[79]

There is no question that the Bolsheviks were the dominant force among the internationalist groups, with their organizational strength, ideological unity, and tactical militancy. The Bolshevik party survived the severe test during the war—the near destruction of the party organization, the initial ideological confusion on the attitude toward the war, constant police repression, and infiltration of police agents. Against these odds, the party grew and gained in-

78. *Krasnyi arkhiv* 17, no. 4 (1926): 29-30; see chap. 3.
79. Recently Soviet historians have emphasized the importance of the alliance of left-wing internationalists. See Leiberov, *Petrogradskii proletariat v Fevral'skoi revoliutsii*, passim, and Tiutiukin, *Voina, mir, revoliutsiia*, pp. 226-43.

fluence among the workers, particularly among the young radicals.

The other Socialist groups standing in opposition to the Bolsheviks gravitated toward the workers' group. While the Bolsheviks and other internationalist groups had no confidence in the liberals to wage a struggle against tsarism, the workers' group considered the joint struggle with the bourgeoisie against the tsarist regime the most urgent task of the moment, one to which all other considerations should be sacrificed. Their political goal was to integrate the workers in a joint struggle headed by the liberals, but it became obvious that this policy had little appeal to the workers. By the fall of 1916, the workers' group was obviously losing ground to the Bolsheviks and to regain its lost influence among the workers, the workers' group turned leftward in December 1916, sharpening its attack on the government and advocating a decisive offensive for its overthrow. Thus, two opposing forces in the workers' movement, in spite of their vast tactical and ideological differences, came to stand in direct opposition to the regime, whose overthrow they both desired and worked for. The active members of the revolutionary parties combined constituted no more than 2 percent of the total number of Petrograd workers, but with the indifference of the vast majority of workers to the doctrinal differences separating the parties, they found it significant that both camps stood for overthrow of the regime. The differences assumed practical importance only after the February Revolution, not before.

The workers' group also created an important buffer zone between the liberals and the workers' mass movement. If the workers' movement had been under the complete influence of extremists like the Bolsheviks, the liberals would have had no choice but to turn their backs completely on the mass movement. The liberals tried until the last moment to avoid a revolution, and the majority, with a few exceptions, refused to lend their support even to the workers' group. The existence of the workers' group, however, contributed to the liberals' psychological acceptance of revolution. If revolution was unavoidable, they would not have to stand in complete opposition to it and join in a counter-revolution, because they could count on the moderating influence of the workers' group. In this sense, the existence of the workers' group provided a vital link between the liberals and the revolution.

At the end of 1916 Russian politics was in stalemate. The government was singularly unpopular and isolated from all segments of society, with the possible exception of a handful of hopelessly reactionary organizations. The conservatives, who repeatedly tried to persuade the tsar to change his policy so that the monarchy and the nation might be saved, were helpless before his obdurate refusal. The liberals had abandoned the government but did not know how or with what to replace it. They feared that one false move on their part might unleash an uncontrollable popular uprising that might sweep them away as well. The main current of the liberals led by Miliukov stubbornly clung to the parliamentary method, which became increasingly ineffective. Out of desperation, some liberals leaned toward a palace coup, while others sought an alliance with the moderate leaders of the workers' movement in the hope that the mass movement would be guided by "more responsible" elements. In the end, neither course was successful. The liberals' indecisiveness during the war rose from their dual desires: first, they wanted a fundamental change in the government's policy and personnel, whether that meant a ministry of confidence, a responsible ministry, or the abdication of Nicholas; second, they wanted to avoid a popular uprising. This immobilizing dichotomy was to determine the fundamental nature of the February Revolution.

The government's policy toward the workers' movement was limited exclusively to police repression. It offered no constructive means of dealing with the causes of the workers' grievances, nor did it attempt to integrate the workers into established society by allowing them their own legal organizations. The government's policy naturally drove the masses of workers to turn receptive ears to the propaganda of the underground revolutionary activists, who attempted to channel the workers' specific grievances into a general struggle to overthrow the government. The increasing radicalization of the workers' movement during the war revealed the impracticability of the dream nurtured by Konovalov and Guchkov of injecting a moderate element into the workers' movement to achieve peace between labor and capital. The workers' group created for this purpose was turned into an instrument of revolution by the moderate Socialists themselves. Thus, two forces, the Bolsheviks and the workers' group, contributed to the workers' participation in the revolutionary movement. Nonetheless, the vast majority of the workers remained beyond their firm control. The leaders of the workers' movement generally felt that the atmosphere in the factories was becoming highly charged, but even the activists in closest contact with the workers did not know where or when a spark would ignite the explosion.

PART II

ON THE EVE

Upper left, General N. V. Alekseev; *upper right*, M. V. Rodzianko; *lower left*, A. I. Guchkov; *lower right*, P. N. Miliukov (all from Hoover Institution); *preceding page*, Nicholas II, Aleksandra, and family (Hoover Institution)

7

THE TSAR, THE TSARINA,
AND THE GOVERNMENT

The assassination of Rasputin did not eradicate the ills of the Russian government. The tsar and tsarina now barricaded themselves within their small world and, shut off from reality, reacted to the outside with increased suspicion and hostility. Instead of rejoicing at Rasputin's disappearance, the Russian upper class were apprehensive that his violent death would be a prelude to something more catastrophic. Fearing that Nicholas's stubborn refusal to adopt reforms would bring the entire aristocracy to its doom, they intensified their efforts to change his mind. But the more they talked about reform, the wider the gulf separating the throne from the aristocracy became.

Nicholas was in Mogilev on December 17 when he received the letter from Aleksandra telling him of Rasputin's murder. He immediately left Mogilev for Tsarskoe Selo to console his distraught wife, who was crushed by the death of the *starets*. In his letter to her, he said that he was "shocked and shaken," but close observers noted that he was "gay and good-humored to a degree he had not been for a long time past." Secretly he might have felt relief to be free of Rasputin, who had not inspired in him the blind attachment his wife felt, and who had caused him to break ties with many loyal servants. But when it came to a question of loyalty, he would stand firmly behind his wife. Aleksandra, on the other hand, was completely shaken by Rasputin's death. Pierre Gilliard, tutor of the tsarevich, noted: "I shall never forget what I felt when I saw the Czarine again. Her agonized features betrayed, in spite of all her efforts, how terribly she was suffering. Her grief was inconsolable. Her idol had been shattered. He who alone could save her son had been slain. The period of waiting began—that dreadful waiting for the disaster which there was no escaping. . . ."[1]

On the tsarina's order Rasputin's body was brought to a chapel outside Petrograd, where his female admirers held a small funeral service. The tsarina came with her daughters. Kneeling in front of the coffin, she prayed and wept for a long time. Rasputin was buried three days later, December 22, in Tsarskoe Selo. The service was at three o'clock in the morning—an odd hour for a burial—as if to hide the event from the public. Nicholas, Protopopov, and V. N. Voeikov were pallbearers. Aleksandra wept bitterly and desperately. Grand Duke Andrei Vladimirovich sardonically noted in his diary: "It was so touching that no commentary is necessary."[2]

The involvement of Grand Duke Dmitrii Pavlovich in the assassination drew the rest of the imperial family together. Although Purishkevich escaped to the front and Prince Iusupov retired to his private estate, Dmitrii Pavlovich was put under house arrest on December 18 at the tsarina's command. Many of the grand dukes considered this action illegal, since she had no authority to issue such an order without the tsar's consent. Dmitrii's father, Grand Duke Pavel Aleksandrovich, and other relatives intervened and requested that the tsar release Dmitrii. But Nicholas adamantly refused. Such a "severe" punishment shocked the rest of the family. Dmitrii's request to talk with the tsar personally was "brutally" rejected and he remained under house arrest, forbidden to receive any visitors, including his own father. On December 23, he was deported to Persia to serve in the army. On Nicholas's special order no one was allowed to bid him farewell at the station. The shocked grand dukes and grand duchesses composed a joint petition to Nicholas, requesting his permission to transfer Dmitrii to a place with a better climate in view of his bad health. On December 31 Nicholas rejected this petition: "No one is given the right to be involved in a murder. I know that conscience will not give many peace, since Dmitrii Pavlovich is not the only one involved in this. I am surprised that you addressed such a petition to me."[3]

In the eyes of Nicholas's relatives, the imperial couple was acting

1. *The Letters of the Tsar to the Tsaritsa, 1914-1917*, p. 312; Princess Paley, *Memories of Russia*, p. 35; Pierre Gilliard, *Thirteen Years at the Russian Court* (London: Hutchinson, n.d.), p. 183.

2. Andrei Vladimirovich, "Iz dnevnika A. V. Romanova," *Krasnyi arkhiv* 24, no. 1 (1928): 188.

3. Paley, *Memories of Russia*, pp. 32-35; Andrei Vladimirovich, "Iz dnevnika A. V. Romanova," pp. 186, 191-92; Nicolas Mikhailovitch, *La fin du tsarisme: Lettres inédites à Frédéric Masson (1914-1918)*, p. 136.

out of vengeance. Not only was Dmitrii, whose motives had been "pure" and "patriotic," deported brutally against the wishes of most of his relatives, but those who dared to criticize the tsar and tsarina, even privately, were exiled from Petrograd. Grand Duchess Mariia Pavlovna, a half-sister of Dmitrii and daughter of Pavel Aleksandrovich and Princess Paley, was put under house arrest because she had dared to bid her brother farewell at the station. On December 31 Grand Duke Nikolai Mikhailovich, a well-known historian, was punished by expulsion from the capital for speaking out against the tsarina privately at a yacht club. On New Year's Day he left Petrograd for his private estate instead of attending the traditional New Year's celebration at court. Nicholas had specifically ordered him not to appear. At the beginning of January Kirill Vladimirovich was banished from the capital. Finally, the axe fell on Andrei Vladimirovich, the center of the grand ducal movement. Colonel A. N. Linevich, a close friend of Grand Duke Andrei Vladimirovich, was summoned by the tsar and asked about the "antigovernment activities" of his friend. Nicholas stated: "It is a pity that he talks too much and speaks ill of me. I was so satisfied with him, appointed him field hetman, and sent him to Persia to the Shah, a mission which he had performed well. What on earth does he have against me? It seems that I have paid sufficient attention to him."[4] In a few days Andrei Vladimirovich was also deported from Petrograd.

The tsar's relatives saw in these acts the intrigue of the tsarina, the "Hesse woman," as Nikolai Mikhailovich called her, a foreigner and an intruder. "This is no longer a desire for vengeance," uttered one of the grand dukes in despair, "but sadism in the vengeance." "The emperor's orders," writes Nikolai Mikhailovich, "remind me of the vulgar Florentine nobles in the epoch of the Borgias and the Medicis."[5] The historian's instinct was not far from the truth.

The failure to "talk sense into the tsar" led some of the grand dukes to rest their hopes on the moderate wing of the liberal movement. During the crisis after the assassination of Rasputin the grand dukes frequently met with Rodzianko. They were radicalized enough to see a compromise with the Duma and the establishment of a ministry of confidence as the only way to turn back the approaching storm. Some even discussed the possibility of a palace coup. According to the French Ambassador, Maurice Paléologue, on December 22, at a party given by the industrialist Bogdanov, Grand Duke Gavriel Kon-

    4. Paley, *Memories of Russia,* pp. 39-40; Andrei Vladimirovich, "Iz dnevnika," pp. 192, 193-94; Nicolas Mikhailovitch, *La fin du tsarisme,* pp. 139-40.
    5. Nicolas Mikhailovitch, *La fin du tsarisme,* p. 138.

stantinovich promised the other industrialists present that he would talk with his relatives about the possibility of removing Nicholas and establishing a regency. Presumably Grand Dukes Kirill, Boris, and Andrei Vladimirovich wanted to establish a regency under Grand Duke Nikolai Nikolaevich.[6] According to Duma deputy Demidov, the grand dukes discussed a plan to remove the tsarina from power by using troops of a guard regiment supposedly led by Grand Duke Dmitrii Pavlovich, but the latter would not agree to the plan. The mother of Kirill, Boris, and Andrei, the Grand Duchess Mariia Pavlovna, suggested to Rodzianko that the tsarina should be forcibly removed. As Diakin notes, the grand dukes' "conspiracy" reveals more their despair than a serious plan.[7] But it is important to note that the majority of Nicholas's relatives had already deserted him before the revolution.

If Nicholas was relieved by the disappearance of Rasputin, his relatives' interference on behalf of the murderer and their increased outcry against his wife angered him and brought the royal couple even closer together. Refusing to understand the world outside, Nicholas and Aleksandra secluded themselves in their private retreat, frightened by a mystical premonition that they were doomed, but unable to do anything to escape this fate.

The removal of Rasputin did not end the influence of the court camarilla. On December 20, Protopopov was promoted from acting minister of internal affairs to minister and was to become the target of public hatred, the role vacated by Rasputin. Trepov, who had striven to achieve some compromise with the Duma liberals, was dismissed on December 26. Prince N. D. Golitsyn, an old bureaucrat with close connections to the tsarina, became the new chairman of the Council of Ministers. Golitsyn, a retired member of the State Council, had been the chairman of the Committee for the Relief of the Wounded, of which the tsarina was honorary chairman. On December 25 he was suddenly summoned by the tsar and commanded to succeed Trepov. The old man, who had considered himself retired from active duty, was dumfounded and declined to accept the offer on the pretext of illness, but finally had to surrender to the will of the sovereign. Though an honest man with no connections to the Rasputin clique, Golitsyn had no political programs, a fact he himself later confessed.[8]

6. Maurice Paléologue, *An Ambassador's Memoirs* 3: 139-40.

7. *Poslednye novosti*, September 2, 1924, quoted in V. S. Diakin, *Russkaia burzhuaziia i tsarizm v gody pervoi mirovoi voiny*, p. 264; M. V. Rodzianko, *The Reign of Rasputin*, p. 247.

8. Deposition of Golitsyn, *Padenie tsarskogo rezhima* (7 vols. Moscow, Leningrad, 1924-1927) 2: 256.

The dismissal of Trepov, the appointment of Golitsyn, and the promotion of Protopopov—all indicated that Nicholas's government had moved further to the Right. It became apparent when Nicholas changed the composition of the State Council on January 1, 1917. With a single stroke of the pen, the tsar purged the appointed members of the Progressive Bloc in the State Council and replaced them with members who had right-wing credentials. As a result, the right wing increased from 58 to 70 members. If the government continued to rely on the support of the right-center (23 members) and counted on the nine ministers who had the right to vote in the State Council, the right wing now regained the majority, with 102 votes against the 96 votes of the Progressive Bloc.[9] Reflecting the right-wing swing of the State Council, it elected the notorious former minister of justice, I. G. Shcheglovitov, as chairman of the State Council.

Despite this coup in the State Council, the right wing was seriously split. The more enlightened of the bureaucracy believed that the nation was headed blindly toward catastrophe and sought a way out through compromise with Duma liberals. During the Christmas vacation, A. V. Krivoshein, General A. A. Polivanov, Count A. A. Bobrinskii, and A. S. Taneev were involved in a series of meetings with the Duma liberals. Regarding themselves as prime candidates to head a government, they were receptive to the idea of the formation of a ministry of confidence.[10] On the other hand, the more reactionary element around Nikolai Maklakov and A. A. Rimskii-Korsakov encouraged the tsar to take a firmer stand against the Duma by dissolving it and ordering a new election to purge the liberals. Rimskii-Korsakov's memorandum, which was handed to Protopopov on January 15, included the following proposals: change the laws governing the Duma in such a way as to increase the right-wing element, purge the undesirable elements from the state apparatus, increase the right wing in the State Council, assist the right-wing press, suppress "draconically" the liberal press and the activities of the Unions of Towns and of Zemstvos, and increase the police force.[11] Some of his recommendations, such as changing the composition of the State Council and increasing the police force, had already been implemented.

The split in the right wing was reflected in the division within

9. *Utro Rossii*, January 1, 1917.

10. For the series of meetings between the representatives of the liberals and the bureaucracy, see TsGAOR, f. DPOO, d. 307a, t. 2, 1916 g., ℓℓ. 76v-76g; ibid., d. 341, ch. 57/1917 g., ℓ. 1; ibid., f. POO, 1917 g., d. 669a, ℓℓ. 2-3; Maklakov's letter to Konovalov, ibid., f. DPOO, op. 343, ZS 57, ch/1917 g., ℓℓ. 20, 22.

11. "Programma soiuza russkogo naroda pered Fevral'skoi revoliutsii," *Krasnyi arkhiv* 20, no. 1 (1927): 243-44.

the Golitsyn cabinet. On January 3, the Council of Ministers discussed the date of the opening of the Duma after Christmas recess. Originally it was scheduled to open January 13. Attempting to show his concilia- tory attitude toward the Duma, Golitsyn had already made a statement that the new cabinet would reconvene the Duma as scheduled. But at the Council of Ministers' meeting, Protopopov proposed to postpone the Duma opening until February 14. Eight ministers supported Protopopov and only six sided with the premier. The proposals of the cabinet meeting were referred to Nicholas, and he accepted Protopopov's.[12] The minority in the cabinet wanted to make a con- ciliatory gesture to the Duma liberals, although they were not willing to go as far as Krivoshein and Polivanov, who were prepared to accept the opposition's demand for the establishment of a ministry of con- fidence. On the other hand, the majority of the cabinet took a hostile position toward the Duma liberals, but they, too, were not willing to go as far as the extreme reactionaries, such as Rimskii-Korsakov, who advocated complete dissolution of the Duma and a change in the electoral law to assure a new right-wing majority in the Duma.

With Trepov's dismissal and Nicholas's semiretirement, there was no question that it was Protopopov who was running the show. Unlike the archreactionaries, who believed in the unswerving loyalty and patriotism of the masses, Protopopov did not underestimate the danger of a mass movement. For that reason he attempted to strengthen the police force and was particularly concerned with security measures in Petrograd.[13] Nevertheless, he was not free of a misconception common among the reactionary politicians of the time, that a revolution would be possible only at the instigation of a group of subversive elements. His main method of combating the revolutionary movement was thus to emphasize police repression of underground revolutionary organizations. At the end of Decem- ber 1916 and the beginning of January 1917, Protopopov's police raids on Bolshevik underground organizations decimated the Petersburg Committee. A small band of anarchists were totally annihilated by the arrest of their leaders after an amateurish attempt at a bank robbery. The Socialist Revolutionaries were splintered and remained inactive. In January 1917, the group that Protopopov considered most dangerous was the workers' group of the Central War Industries Committee. He was alarmed by their growing radicalism and saw in the appeal of the workers' group to support the Duma a dangerous

12. TsGIA, f. 1276, op. 10, d. 7, ℓℓ. 449-50.
13. See chap. 8.

possible link between the workers' movement and the liberal opposition. A press campaign against the workers' group began with the
accusation that it was advocating the overthrow of the government
and the establishment of a Socialist Democratic republic. In early
January General S. S. Khabalov, commander of the Petrograd Military
District, served notice that henceforward his representative would
sit on every meeting of the workers' group. Members of the workers'
group in Moscow and Samara were arrested. On January 17 and 19
the police broke into their office on Liteinyi Prospekt and searched
for evidence of illegal activities. Finally, on January 27, Protopopov
made a decisive move by having his police arrest the members of the
workers' group in Petrograd.[14] Protopopov had feared that such drastic
measures might lead to a large-scale strike movement among the
workers. When that did not happen, he became more convinced that
since he had successfully eradicated the potential troublemakers,
he had also eliminated the possibility of the immediate outbreak
of revolution. He paid little attention to the more disturbing signs,
often pointed out by his own Okhrana agents, that the despair and
frustration of the workers might impel them to take action on their
own.

If Protopopov acted decisively in dealing with the workers' movement, he was more careful in his move against the liberal opposition.
He shared with various archconservatives the opinion that the Duma
should ultimately be dissolved and that a new election should be
conducted in a way that would assure a right-wing majority. For
that purpose he sent a circular in December to the governors, requesting
information concerning the composition of the electorate in each
province and the likely results if an election were held soon.[15] On
February 2, he commented approvingly on Markov II's recommendation to change the electoral law in the same fashion that
Stolypin had changed it on June 3, 1907. Immediately after the arrest
of the workers' group, Nicholas entrusted Nikolai Maklakov with
the job of composing a draft manifesto for the dissolution of the
Duma and the preparation of a new election. Maklakov willingly
fulfilled this task, stating in his letter to the tsar: "More than at any
other time power [*vlast'*] must be concentrated, convinced, and welded
together by a single purpose to restore state order at any cost and
must be confident in victory over the internal enemy which has long
been growing more dangerous, more savage, and more impudent than

14. See chap. 11.
15. Deposition of Protopopov, *Padenie tsarskogo rezhima* 2: 293-94.

the external enemy."[16] Maklakov accused the Duma of engaging in a "political struggle against the government" instead of solving the practical problems facing a nation at war. Since the nation needed action, "not speeches disturbing the people's spirit and shaking state order," the tsar was to order the dissolution of the Duma and set a new election for December 1, 1917. It should be noted, however, that even Maklakov's draft manifesto did not mention anything about a change in the electoral law. Presumably a policy advocated by irresponsible reactionaries such as Markov II and Rimskii-Korsakov was too provocative for such a conservative as Maklakov.[17]

Protopopov, however, did not agree with Maklakov on the timing of the dissolution of the Duma. As a former Octobrist, he was more aware of the volatility of the liberal opposition, among whom rumors of a palace coup were widely circulating. An ill-timed dissolution of the Duma might push them to action. True, he took some repressive measures. On January 11, he sent the governors a letter instructing them to prohibit the local zemstvos and city dumas from discussing political questions. Also he attempted to undermine the effectiveness of the voluntary organizations by curtailing government subsidies and recruiting employees of these organizations into the military. He engineered the postponement of the Duma opening until February 14, and organized a campaign against the liberal opposition, heavily subsidizing right-wing organizations such as the Fatherland's Patriotic Union and the Union of the Russian People. A campaign of letters and telegrams, carefully orchestrated by the Ministry of Internal Affairs, gave the tsar and tsarina the illusion that they were indeed supported by the overwhelming majority of the Russian people. Protopopov, however, avoided a major showdown with the liberals, and opposed the immediate dissolution of the Duma.[18]

Protopopov's policy did not satisfy the conservatives. Maklakov and Shcheglovitov criticized him as "soft" on the liberals, while those who accepted the liberals' demand for the establishment of a ministry of confidence believed that Protopopov was leading the government into headlong clash with the opposition. The net result was the further disarray of the right wing and the government. In fact, the government all but ceased to exist in the last two months of the tsarist regime. Relying more and more on his unofficial but more effective channel

16. V. P. Semennikov, ed., *Monarkhiia pered krusheniem*, pp. 97-98.

17. TsGAOR, f. 601, op. 1, d. 1003, *ll.* 1-2; E. D. Chermenskii, *IV gosudarstvennaia duma i sverzhenie tsarizma v Rossii*, p. 247.

18. Diakin, *Russkaia burzhuaziia*, p. 269; according to Protopopov, Nicholas was contemplating the possibility of arresting Guchkov. Protopopov advised against it. TsGAOR, f. ChSK, d. 460, *l.* 158.

of political influence through Vyrubova and the tsarina, Protopopov stopped attending the meetings of the Council of Ministers. Golitsyn could not stand Protopopov, who had made him look like a fool in the matter of the postponement of the Duma session and unsuccessfully attempted to dismiss him by petitioning the tsar. But Protopopov was firmly entrenched under the tsarina's protection. The "ministerial leapfrogging" continued. P. N. Ignatiev, minister of education, was dismissed at the same time as Trepov. When the new minister, Kul'chitskii, was appointed on January 27, two deputy ministers of the ministry of education resigned in protest at this third-rate appointment. The minister of war, D. S. Shuvaev, a critic of Rasputin, was dismissed also. The tsarina's obedient servant. M. A. Beliaev, was appointed in January. Some ministers went on sick leave with real or pretended illnesses. The minister of finance, P. L. Bark, had been off duty since December on sick leave and was in no hurry to return to the capital. His resignation or dismissal was rumored in the papers. Also the minister of the navy, Admiral I. K. Grigorovich, fell ill, and was more often at home than in his office. The minister of trade and industry and the minister of foreign affairs, V. N. Shakhovskoi and N. N. Pokrovskii, expected to be dismissed because of their opposition to Protopopov. Only the ministers of agriculture and transport, A. A. Rittikh and E. B. Kriger-Voinovskii, continued to work energetically to solve the problems of food supply and transportation. The top-level bureaucrats in the ministries of education, justice, finance, foreign affairs, and trade and industry stopped working on major policy proposals because they had no idea how long their ministers would be in office. The high officials of the Ministry of Internal Affairs did not know where to address their reports since Protopopov and his deputies refused to accept them. Two of his deputy ministers finally gave up and walked out on Protopopov. The post of deputy minister remained unfilled in the ministries of foreign affairs, justice, internal affairs, transport, and education. Thus, while the tsar helped to wipe away the tears of his grief-stricken wife, his government stopped functioning, leaderless and demoralized.[19]

Sensing that the country was going to pieces, even the traditionally conservative elements of the nobility took an unprecedented step. On January 12, the assembly of the provincial nobility was convened in Novgorod and passed a resolution calling for the removal of the

19. It should be pointed out that during the war "ministerial leapfrogging" was accompanied by "gubernatorial leapfrogging." In 1914 only 12 new governors were appointed, but in 1915 the number rose to 33, and in 1916 to 43. See Diakin, *Russkaia burzhuaziia*, p. 275.

"dark forces" from the government and stressing the importance of the unity of tsar and people. The governor of Novgorod was immediately dismissed for having allowed such a resolution. A similiar resolution was adopted by the assemblies of provincial nobility in Simbirsk (Protopovov's own province), Iaroslav, Samara, and Moscow provinces.[20] It was Rodzianko who emerged as the rallying point for the discontented nobility and the grand dukes. He tried to mobilize them into concerted action to persuade the tsar to form a ministry of confidence. On January 3 Rodzianko asked A. D. Samarin, chairman of the Council of the United Nobility, and P. A. Bazilevskii, marshal of nobility of Moscow province, to meet him in Petrograd. Before this meeting Rodzianko had met with Grand Duke Mikhail Aleksandrovich, Nicholas's brother. After his departure Rodzianko explained to the two Moscow nobles that the grand duke had agreed that two measures would be necessary to save Russia from the present situation: the formation of a ministry of confidence headed by Rodzianko himself, and the removal of the tsarina from politics. According to Rodzianko, the liberal forces could not be counted on. The Duma would sooner or later be dissolved, and constant government repression had rendered the Unions of Zemstvos and of Towns powerless. In his opinion, the United Nobility was the only remaining voice that could influence the tsar. Rodzianko then requested that Samarin and Bazilevskii seek an audience with the tsar in an attempt to talk some sense into him.[21]

On January 7 Rodzianko himself met with the tsar, but Nicholas was in no mood to listen to him and accused the Duma of being busily engaged in libelous propaganda against such a talented man as Protopopov. Three days later Samarin sought an audience with the tsar and presented the resolution passed by the Twelfth Congress of the United Nobility, which requested that the tsar appoint a ministry responsible to the tsar but willing to work in cooperation with the Duma. This recommendation also made no impression on Nicholas.[22] Bazilevskii's audience with Nicholas took place on February 9. The marshal of nobility of Moscow province described the desperate food problem in Moscow, the acuteness of which was evident merely by "seeing early in the morning the queues in front of bakeries and listening to the complaints of women, who stand all night in the cold and go away empty-handed." The tsar expressed the hope that the situation

    20. Rodzianko, *The Reign of Rasputin*, p. 256; Diakin, *Russkaia burzhuaziia*, p. 296.

    21. OR GBL, Dnevnik P. A. Bazilevskogo, p. IV, ed. khr. 1, ℓℓ. 78-79.

    22. Chermenskii, *IV gosudarstvennaia duma*, p. 268-69.

would soon be improved thanks to Rittikh's energetic efforts. Bazilevskii pointed out that the people no longer believed in a government that had brought the nation to such chaos, and presented to the tsar the resolution of the Moscow nobility calling for the formation of a ministry capable of cooperating with the Duma. Nicholas made no reply, changed the topic, and said at the end of the conversation: "Send the Moscow nobility my sincere appreciation for the prayers and expressions of feelings. Also tell them that no one is more grieved than I with the internal situation in such a moment when we must still fight with the enemy and when a close unity is necessary to deal him a final blow." The tsar then politely shook hands and departed with his characteristic smile.[23]

On the following day, February 10, Rodzianko was again received by the tsar. In what turned out to be his last report, Rodzianko begged him not to dissolve the Duma, which alone, in his opinion, could prevent the outbreak of a revolution since it alone had a restraining influence on the people's passions. But Nicholas proved to be more aggressive than at the previous audience. Responding to Rodzianko's fear of an impending revolution, he said: "My information indicates a completely different picture. As far as the mood of the Duma is concerned, if the Duma allows itself to make such sharp attacks as the last time, then it will be dissolved." Rodzianko came home with the depressing feeling that nothing would change Nicholas's mind.[24]

On the same day, the imperial couple received Grand Dukes Aleksandr Mikhailovich and the tsar's own brother, Mikhail Aleksandrovich. Aleksandr Mikhailovich stated that although he himself was an enemy of the parliamentary system he could see no alternative other than the formation of a ministry acceptable to the Duma to relieve the tension in the Duma. The empress, smiling cynically, interjected: "What you are talking about makes me laugh! Nicky is an autocrat! How could he share his God-given right with anyone else?" In desperation Aleksandr Mikhailovich yelled at Aleksandra: "I see you are ready to perish with your husband. But don't forget us. Must we all suffer from your blind foolishness? You don't have the right to bring your relatives along to the abyss."[25]

At the center of all these collective pressures was Rodzianko.

23. Dnevik Bazilevskogo, ℓℓ. 89-91.

24. Rodzianko, The Reign of Rasputin, pp. 259-61; Deposition of Rodzianko, Padenie tsarskogo rezhima 7: 163-65; "Dnevnik E. A. Naryshkina," Poslednie novosti, May 10, 1936.

25. Aleksandr Mikhailovich, Kniga vospominanii 1: 280-81.

The conservative elements of society, sensing the impending storm, came to regard the moderation of the Duma's chairman as the last and only hope. Rodzianko, in turn, solidified his strength with the aristocracy to counterbalance his slipping popularity among the liberals. Grand Duke Mikhail Aleksandrovich provided him with a vital link to the rest of the grand dukes. Although Nicholas's brother worked closely with Rodzianko, he also kept in touch with another wing of the liberal movement represented by Prince G. E. L'vov, Rodzianko's rival. The link between L'vov and the grand duke was A. A. Klopov, a retired minor bureaucrat who had obtained the privilege of writing directly to the tsar. Klopov, who had recommended a dictatorship headed by General Alekseev at the end of 1916,[26] in January 1917, suddenly began to advocate the formation of a ministry of confidence headed by Prince L'vov. Between January 19 and February 13 Klopov wrote a series of letters to the tsar, imploring, before the opening of the Duma, the formation of a ministry "responsible to the tsar and to the people." He also urged the tsar to make a personal appearance at the Duma on February 14 to symbolize his unity with his people. On January 29 and February 6 he obtained permission to have an audience with the tsar and expounded his opinions directly. Klopov's move was closely coordinated with L'vov and Mikhail.[27] His petitions, however, met with Nicholas's stone wall, like other petitions.

The frantic efforts of the grand dukes and the nobility to influence the tsar stemmed from their fear that disaster was imminent. Many awaited the opening session of the Duma with trepidation. The workers' demonstration was expected the same day, and rumors of a palace coup were rampant. On the morning of February 14, Rodzianko hurried to see the acting chief of staff, General Gurko, and informed him that he had reliable information that a palace coup was being planned and would be carried out. Gurko immediately took a train to Tsarskoe Selo and requested an audience with the tsar. One of the court officials, Z. V. Arapov, was sitting in the next room. He heard nothing for the first fifteen minutes, then suddenly he heard Gurko thundering: "Your Imperial Majesty, you are willfully preparing yourself for the gallows. Do not forget that the mobs will not stand on ceremony. You are ruining yourself and your family." Nicholas's answer was inaudible, but in a few seconds Gurko stormed

26. For the role of Klopov, see Diakin, *Russkaia burzhuaziia*, pp. 245, 265, TsGIA, f. 1099, op. 1, d. 16, *ℓ*. 1.

27. TsGIA, f. 1099, op. 1, d. 15, *ℓℓ*. 1-3, 8-9, 12, 13-25; ibid., d. 20, *ℓℓ*. 1-4; ibid., d. 17, *ℓℓ*. 1-2; ibid., d. 3, *ℓℓ*. 1-2.

out of the room, pale and trembling, and muttered: "We are done with."[28]

All the petitioners were struck by both the inflexibility and the calm with which Nicholas refused their recommendations. They would have understood better if the tsar had angrily dismissed them, deriding their softness toward the liberal opposition and threatening them for defying the autocrat. But they were baffled by his impeccable observance of court etiquette, by his patience, and by the personal charm he extended to them. Yet he refused to yield an inch. Many felt that an invisible wall separated them from the sovereign, who did not seem to comprehend what they were saying. In a way their impression was correct: since Rasputin's assassination Nicholas was living in a world far removed from reality. There was something intensely personal in his understanding of the responsibility of a sovereign. To Nicholas politics could not be separated from his own personal morality and religion. While his critics presented a compromise with the Duma as a political alternative, to Nicholas there could be no such alternative, since it would strike at the heart of his moral and religious convictions. He could not accept it without breaking his sacred obligations to God.

Not long before the revolution, the tsarina attended a religious celebration in Novgorod. She was greeted with speeches by the governor and the city mayor, and the crowds at the railway station welcomed her with a thunderous hurrah. She remarked: "Apraksin always frightens me with all sorts of popular disturbances, and is convinced of some sort of dissatisfaction among the people. Now he heard how warmly people and the city mayor, not a government official, greeted me, and saw how much love could be felt in the people toward the tsar and his family."[29] The tsar and tsarina relied more and more on such organized popular support for assurance that the people and the tsar were still one.

Nothing happened on February 14 to disturb the peace. It seemed to Nicholas that all these panic-stricken conservatives had fallen victim to alarmism. He was impressed with Protopopov for his sound advice and superb job of keeping the security of Petrograd. Relieved by this turn of events, and with renewed faith in the minister of internal affairs, Nicholas finally decided to end his vacation and resume his

28. Dnevnik Z. V. Arapova, RO GBL, f. 12, papka 1, d. 9, ℓℓ. 85-87, quoted in Chermenskii, *IV gosudarstvennaia duma*, p. 274. My request to use this archive was rejected.

29. RO GBL, f. 218, no. 306, B. A. Engel'gardt, "Potonuvshii mir: Vospominaniia," ed. khr. 3, ℓ. 82. I was not allowed to read three chapters devoted to the period prior to the February Revolution of Engelhardt's memoirs.

duty as supreme commander in chief in Mogilev. On February 22, after
two months' stay, he left his family in Tsarskoe Selo. On the way,
he dispatched a telegram to his wife: "Am traveling well. In thought
with all of you. Feel lonely and sad. Am grateful for letters. Embrace
all. Good night. Nicky."[30] By the time this telegram reached Tsarskoe
Selo, the workers in the Vyborg District were out in the streets,
demanding bread. The February Revolution had begun.

30. *Letters of the Tsar to the Tsaritsa*, p. 312.

8

THE SECURITY OF PETROGRAD

 "Armed insurrection in some form or other," writes Katharine Chorley, "is the classic method of making a revolution, and . . . it is bound to imply a clash with professionally trained troops equipped with all the gear of scientific warfare. History shows that, in the last resort, success or failure hinges on the attitude which those armed forces of the *status quo* government will take toward an insurrection."[1] An insurrection is not likely to succeed against a regime that can muster the full allegiance of its armed forces. Its success is possible only when the ineptitude of an existing regime reaches the point where it is unable to make use of its full military resources.[2]

Thanks to an abundance of accurate information dispatched by the omnipresent Okhrana agents, the tsarist government was by no means blind to the rapidly growing public furor against the regime. Anticipating major disturbances, the government began to take precautionary measures in late 1916. These measures, however, suffered basic weaknesses that clearly revealed that decay had gone so far that the regime was no longer capable of preserving itself.

The men in charge of the security of Petrograd in the civilian branch of the government were the minister of internal affairs, Protopopov, the director of the police department, A. T. Vasiliev, and the Petrograd *gradonachal'nik,* Major-General A. P. Balk. But

1. Katharine C. Chorley, *Armies and the Art of Revolution* (London: Faber & Faber, 1943), pp. 11, 16, quoted in Chalmers Johnson, *Revolutionary Change* (Boston: Little, Brown, 1966), pp. 99-100.

2. Crane Brinton, *The Anatomy of Revolution* (revised and expanded edition; New York: Random House, 1965), pp. 86-88.

because Petrograd was designated as part of the theater of war, civilian authorities were relegated to a secondary role and it was the military branch of government that was primarily responsible for maintaining the security of the city. At the end of January 1917, the Supreme Command separated Petrograd and vicinity from the front and formed an independent Petrograd Military District under the commander of the district, Major-General S. S. Khabalov. Lack of coordination between the civilian and military authorities hindered effective enforcement of security measures. The difficulty was further compounded by the ambiguous division of jurisdiction between two military authorities, the commander of the Petrograd Military District and War Minister General M. A. Beliaev.

At first glance one is struck by the mediocrity of those men to whom the safety of the largest city of Russia was entrusted. Unable to command respect even from his colleagues in the cabinet, Protopopov was a symbol of the regime's corruption and intransigence as well as the focus of public hatred for the government after Rasputin's death. Although he was aware of the danger of a mass movement, he believed that elimination of the revolutionary underground would be sufficient to prevent a major disturbance. Vasiliev owed his promotion to the position of director of the police department to his acquaintance with Protopopov. He had an influential friend, P. A. Badmaev, who was reputed to know the secret lore of Tibetan medicine, and whose house both Rasputin and Protopopov had frequented. Upon his appointment, Vasiliev gave Protopopov his assurances: "I shall never do anything behind your back; I shall always consult you and submit to your instructions."[3]

Balk, former assistant to the chief of police in Warsaw, became Petrograd *gradonachal'nik* on Protopopov's recommendation, replacing Prince Obolenskii, who had lost favor with the tsarina and Protopopov. Obolenskii was, in Protopopov's opinion, "too self-confident and inactive." In addition, Aleksandra was outraged by his sister's remarks attacking her close relationship with Rasputin. In November 1916, Obolenskii was dismissed, and Balk, Protopopov's classmate in the First Corps of Cadets, and whom Badmaev and Rasputin also knew, was appointed.[4] Balk himself well knew that he was not qualified to fill this important position, but the offer was too good to refuse. According to Vasiliev, Balk was a "stern, upright man, a chief familiar with every detail of the police department." But the regime needed more than a police chief familiar with the details of bureaucratic procedure.

3. A. T. Vassilyev, *The Okhrana: The Russian Secret Police* (Philadelphia and London: J. B. Lippincott, 1930), pp. 143-46.
4. TsGAOR, f. ChSK, d. 460, ℓℓ. 161-62; Vassilyev, *The Okhrana*, p. 197.

What mattered most, however, was the incompetence of Petrograd's military leaders since they had the ultimate responsibility for security. The man who was in direct command of troops was Major-General Khabalov, who had spent his entire career in military administration without ever commanding troops on a battlefield. What the regime needed to cope with a major disturbance was a commander who could accurately assess the psychology of his enemy as well as of his own troops and deploy his forces efficiently and with determination. According to Balk, Khabalov was "incapable of leading his own subordinates and, above all, of commanding troops."[5]

Equally unimpressive was War Minister Beliaev, whom Nicholas once described as "an extremely weak man who always gives way in everything and works slowly." Like Khabalov, he had spent his entire military career behind a desk. The world war gave him a chance for rapid promotion. After serving as chief of the General Staff in Petrograd and member of the Military Council, he was appointed war minister on January 3, 1917, replacing General D. S. Shuvaev, who had irritated the tsarina by his outspoken opposition to Rasputin. In this unusually quick promotion Beliaev undoubtedly took advantage of his connections with the court camarilla. His narrow bureaucratic mind obviously could not compensate for Khabalov's inexperience. A. I. Verkhovskii, future minister of war in the Provisional Government, was more uncharitable: "Cold careerism and military illiteracy were combined in him with a supreme contempt for people and the willingness to sacrifice thousands of lives, if it was necessary for his personal success."[6]

Had Khabalov obtained assistance from capable officers, his inexperience might not have been catastrophic. In the formulation of security measures, it was assumed that Lieutenant-General A. N. Chebykin, who enjoyed the confidence of other officers, would take the actual command of the troops in Petrograd. Chebykin, however, fell ill in early January, necessitating Khabalov's hasty appointment of Colonel V. E. Pavlenkov of the Preobrazhenskii Regiment as a temporary replacement. This was a poor choice, since Pavlenkov, who had arrived in Petrograd from the front only at the beginning of February, "was not familiar even with the topography of the capital and did not know at all the sentiments of the army units."[7] Moreover, Pavlenkov suffered

5. A. Balk, "Poslednie piat' dnei tsarskago Petrograda: Dnevnik posledniago Petrogradskago gradonachal'nika" (Belgrade, 1929, unpublished manuscript, Hoover Institution), p. 5b.

6. Nicholas, quoted in Sir Bernard Pares, *The Fall of the Russian Monarchy*, p. 327; E. I. Martynov, *Tsarskaia armiia v fevral'skom perevorote* (Moscow, 1927), p. 61; A. I. Verkhovskii, *Na trudnom perevale*, p. 145.

7. N. O. Akaemov, "Agoniia starago rezhima," *Istoricheskii Vestnik* 148 (1917): xi.

a mild heart attack shortly before the outbreak of the February Revolution and had to conduct most business from bed. Khabalov thus found himself commanding troops without the help of more experienced field officers.

These were the men in positions of major responsibility—mediocre, ailing, unimaginative, lethargic, and incompetent. But the weakness of security authority went deeper than the personalities of its leaders. It was essential that good communication exist between Petrograd and the high command at the front for obviously if the disturbances went beyond the ability of the Petrograd authorities to handle alone, reinforcements would have to be brought in. But the relationship between Petrograd and military leaders at the front was marred by hostility and distrust. One can trace this mutual animosity to the way the Petrograd Military District had been detached from the northern front.

It was inevitable that a conflict of interests would arise between the commander of the northern front, General Ruzskii, and the men in charge in Petrograd—Khabalov and Beliaev. As a front commander, Ruzskii regarded the transfer of necessary supplies and provisions from industrial regions in Petrograd to the front as of highest priority. On the other hand, Khabalov and Beliaev were concerned with provisions not only for the reserve unit but also for the workers in war industries. As the supply of goods, particularly foodstuffs and fuel, fell sharply during the first months of 1917, the two men in Petrograd began to complain bitterly, with legitimate reason, that Ruzskii was endangering the security of Petrograd by giving the front unduly favorable treatment. This was a minor problem of priorities that any country engaged in total war encounters and an efficient government would have made a rational readjustment of priorities without impairing the integrity of the government as a whole. Not so in Russia. Khabalov and Beliaev chose intrigue, employing the political influence of Protopopov and the tsarina.

Relations between Protopopov and Ruzskii had been strained since November when Ruzskii had objected to Protopopov's food policy. This objection had coincided with the liberals' outcry against Protopov's policy and had increased the minister of internal affairs' suspicion of the "liberal" commander of the northern front. It seemed more important to place the Petrograd Military District under his direct control, not subject to the military intelligence network. Ruzskii, on the other hand, reacted with irritation to Protopopov's meddling in military censorship. Declaring that military intelligence had different goals and purposes, he refused to downgrade it to a tool of the political police. As for the allocation of provisions, Ruzskii considered the Petrograd Military District a "burden" to the northern front, and in principle did not object to its detachment from his jurisdiction. What he did object to was the way it was detached.[8]

Supporting Khabalov and Beliaev, Protopopov relayed their complaints to the tsarina, and engaged in a vicious attack on Ruzskii's character, while insisting to the tsar that for security reasons the Petrograd Military District should be separated from the northern front.[9] Whether or not Aleksandra's bedroom propaganda or Protopopov's argument as an expert on the security of Petrograd prevailed, Nicholas decided to detach the Petrograd Military District. It was the dubious manner in which this decision was made, more than the decision itself, that angered army leaders. If this incident reinforced their contempt of Protopopov and the tsarina, they were also embittered by the disgraceful conduct of Khabalov and Beliaev.

It is therefore not surprising that the elaborate contingency plan drafted by the Petrograd security authorities did not include assistance from the front. The security forces consisted of the police and the reserve soldiers. In Petrograd there were 3,500 policemen assigned to sixteen precincts. The police were singularly unpopular with the populace, who saw the oppression of the state not in actual laws and executive orders, but in their implementation by the police. It was obvious that 3,500 police would not be able to cope with large-scale labor unrest. Naturally, the security authorities hoped to rely on the enormous number of reserve soldiers stationed in Petrograd. Although the statistics do not provide an accurate figure, there were said to be between 160,000 and 271,000, made up of five groups: guard units, infantry, cavalry, technical units, and cadets in military schools.[10] The guard units were the most important of the security force in the capital. Altogether there were 99,000 guard soldiers assigned to fourteen battalions representing fourteen guard regiments.

8. TsGAOR, f. ChSK, d. 460, 𝑙. 164; Andrei Vladimirovich, "Iz dnevnika A. V. Romanova," *Krasnyi arkhiv* 24, no. 1 (1928): 202-3.

9. TsGAOR, f. ChSK, d. 460, 𝑙. 164.

10. According to Martynov and Shliapnikov, the number of soldiers in Petrograd was approximately 160,000. Martynov, *Tsarskaia armiia v fevral'skom pereverote*, p. 58; A. Shliapnikov, *Semnadtsatyi god* 1: 160. According to Kochakov, it was 271,000. This figure is based on the data of the commissary section of the army and inflated, since it included servicemen in administrative units. B. M. Kochakov, "Sostav petrogradskogo garnizona v 1917 g.," *Uchenye zapiski Leningradskogo universiteta, seriia istoricheskikh nauk*, no. 205, p. 61. According to the data given by the Military Commission of the State Duma, it was 170,000. According to the materials in the Extraordinary Investigation Commission of the Provisional Government, there were 180,000 soldiers as of February 1, 1917. See E. N. Burdzhalov, *Vtoraia russkaia revoliutsiia: Vosstanie v Petrograde*, pp. 96-97.

The cavalry was divided into Cossacks, who numbered 3,200, and regular cavalry units composed of 4,700 soldiers. The soldiers in the technical units included a bicycle battalion, an armored car division, engineer units, railway battalions, and artillery units. There were approximately 10,000 military students in and around Petrograd. In addition to the soldiers stationed in Petrograd, the military authorities counted on the soldiers in nearby cities. There were 69,800 in Tsarskoe Selo to protect the Imperial Palace; 70,300 in Peterhof, Oranienbaum, and Strel'na; 33,900 in Krasnoe Selo; and 21,700 in Gatchina. All were within thirty miles of Petrograd. Thus in Petrograd and its immediate vicinity there were perhaps 322,000 to 466,800 soldiers available.[11] The enormous concentration of reserve soldiers in Petrograd warrants the statement: "The whole city had been turned into a military camp." This large number apparently gave the authorities the illusion that Petrograd was invulnerable to any internal threat. In addition, there were 42 army corps in Finland, Vyborg, and Kronstadt Military districts, subordinated to the northern front.[12]

Anticipating great labor unrest in response to the strike calls of various revolutionary organizations for February 10 to February 14, a military commission headed by Khabalov, but actually led by Lieutenant-General Chebykin, mapped out a contingency plan in cooperation with the *gradonachal'nik*. The city was divided into sixteen military districts, identical with the police precincts, and a battalion of guard regiments was assigned to each. The contingency plan would be carried out in three stages. In the first, police alone would cope with a disorder, with minimal assistance from the Cossacks. Since this stage was not considered a military situation, the *gradonachal'nik* would remain the commander of the security forces. If the police could not handle the situation, the second stage—a military one—would be declared. The commander of troops in Petrograd would take over the command of all security forces from the *gradonachal'nik*, while in each district the commander of a guard battalion would replace the precinct police chief and command both police and soldiers. Guard battalions would be mobilized to assigned positions to safeguard public buildings, banks, palaces, and railway stations from insurgents. At this stage, however, only cavalry units, mostly Cossacks, would be used for direct confrontation. The soldiers would be prohibited

11. Kochakov, "Sostav petrogradskogo garnizona," p. 61; Burdzhalov, *Vtoraia russkaia revoliutsiia*, p. 95.

12. Viktor Shklovsky, *A Sentimental Journey: Memoirs, 1917-1922*, trans. Richard Sheldon, p. 7; I. P. Leiberov, *Petrogradskii proletariat v Fevral'skoi revoliutsii* 2: 4.

from using firearms except in self-defense. If measures taken at the second stage proved to be insufficient, Khabalov had the authority to proceed to the last stage. Infantry and guard units would then launch an all-out attack on the recalcitrant crowds, using firearms and machine guns. It was presumed that this last stage would be sufficient to suppress any disturbance.[13] Curiously, the contingency plan did not mention when the authorities of Petrograd should seek forces from the front.

The government did not realize that the enormous number of soldiers in Petrograd was in itself a double-edged sword. As long as the army could maintain discipline, the government would not have to worry about the possibility of major disturbances. However, a swing in the soldiers' allegiance would radically alter the balance of power in the capital. The Russian army, like any army, could not exist in a vacuum, independent of society. Increasing social tensions during the war were inevitably bound to reflect on military life as well. As John Bushnell points out, life in the Russian army reminded the peasant recruits of serf life before the emancipation. As they were taught to "speak, look, and turn and more with military precision," they were also exposed to the vices of the tsarist army— beatings, extortion, theft by the officers. Since a regiment was self-sufficient economically as well as being a military unit, the soldiers were required, in addition to performing military duties, to function as tailors, cobblers, carpenters, caterers, cooks, gardeners, stableboys, and so on. They also worked in the officers' clubs and sometimes in the officers' private households as singers, musicians, church attendants, butlers, and lackeys. In a reserve unit, more than half of the soldiers were detailed to such nonmilitary duties. Officers addressed soldiers as "thou" (ty), as masters addressed serfs, and soldiers responded to the officers using the honorific "Your Excellency." Officers treated soldiers as inferior in social caste. Striking an ordinary recruit was a matter of course, but it was unthinkable to beat an educated volunteer. The officers spent little time with their men, did not understand them, and did not care to understand them.

The soldiers organized their barracks in the only way they knew how —in a traditional peasant *artel'* (peasant communal unit). The practice of drafting recruits from the same region into the same unit facilitated the existence of peasant communes in the army and because the

13. TsGAOR, f. POO, op. 5, d. 669, 1917 g., ll. 190-91; *Rabochee dvizhenie v Petrograde*, pp. 534-39; Martynov, *Tsarskaia armiia v fevral'skom perevorote*, pp. 63-65; Deposition of Khabalov, *Padenie tsarskogo rezhima* 1: 184; Supplementary deposition of Protopopov, *Padenie tsarskogo rezhima* 4: 92-93.

soldiers' pay was low, their economic existence depended on the *artel'*. Since a regiment was supposed to be self-sufficient, and financial support from the commissariat was always insufficient, a practice known as "voluntary labor" *(vol'nye raboty)* was developed in which soldiers were sent to a branch of the civilian economy to earn money. It was the soldiers' *artel'* that contracted the voluntary labor. The officers' position was quite delicate in the units' economic existence. They were not merely the soldiers' military superiors, but they were also masters of their unit's economy, which depended on the soldiers' voluntary labor. Those officers who tried to assert their leadership over the soldiers' economic activities were most resented. Economic mismanagement by officers was rampant, but even when there were clear cases of theft and extortion the soldiers had no recourse, because the offenders were also their military superiors. But even when such corruption did not exist, in the eyes of the soldiers the officers were always outsiders who tried to live off the soldiers' labor.

In sum, a soldiers' life was to most of the peasant recruits a serfdom in uniform. Herein lay the basic source of soldiers' rebellion. It was not surprising, therefore, that when the revolt did take place during the February Revolution, it was primarily directed against the officers, and two of the most important demands were elimination of the servile relationship of the soldiers under the yoke of the officers and the soldiers' control of the economy of the military units.[14]

If the officers left the soldiers more or less alone, noncommissioned officers had daily contact with the soldiers. The NCOs rose to their positions from the ranks and displayed most blatantly the brutal practices of beating, extortion, and theft. Nonetheless, the NCOs themselves were conscious of the social wall separating them from the officers and were much closer to the soldiers in social and cultural background. Promotion to officers' rank was still difficult, even during the war. NCOs were not permitted to enter the officers' clubs and continued to live with the soldiers. Because of their background and precisely because of their proximity to the privileged officers' rank, which they could not enter, the NCOs were more resentful of the officers than the soldiers. They had risen because of their talent, leadership, and initiative, and these qualities combined with resentment against the established order made them often at the forefront of the soldiers' rebellion.

14. For the description of the soldiers' life in the army, I relied extensively on John Bushnell's excellent paper, "Peasants in Uniform: The Tsarist Army as a Peasant Society," unpublished paper presented at the Mid-Atlantic AAASS Conference, Ithaca, N. Y., April, 1979.

In addition to these fundamental chasms that separated the officers from the soldiers and the NCOs there were certain disturbing factors that ultimately contributed to the breakdown of military discipline.

After the outbreak of war military authorities could no longer indulge in the luxury of carefully selecting the soldiers to be stationed in the major cities. After the most reliable guard soldiers were sent to the front, reserve guard units, once noted for their unswerving loyalty to the regime, came to be filled with dissatisfied soldiers in their forties, called *sorokoletnye*. They were embittered and disgruntled at having to abandon their families and adjust to the regimented life of the barracks. Another large group of reserve soldiers in Petrograd was made up of evacuees who had been sent back from the front because of illness or injury and reactivated into reserve units after a period of recuperation. After living close to death at the front and witnessing the corruption in the rear, these evacuees began to reflect upon whether the danger, fatigue, and loneliness at the front were justified. Their antiwar sentiment grew stronger as the day approached to depart again for the front.[15]

These frustrations and grievances were further aggravated by the petty regulations of the barracks. The dreariness and monotony, the dull repetition of drills, the strict enforcement of curfew and reveille, and the difficulty in acquiring a pass—all these contributed to a repressed anger. There was also an explosive element among the reserve soldiers: the presence of former strike participants. Prior to 1916, the government had carefully avoided recruiting politically undesirable elements into the armed forces, let alone assigning them to such important cities as Petrograd and Moscow. By early 1916, however, in the face of a resurgence in strikes, the government had begun drafting strikers as punishment. Scarcity of training facilities and difficulties of transportation forced military authorities to train the strike participants where they were drafted. The result was that although they were not politically organized or in touch with revolutionary parties outside, some soldiers had carried their subversive ideas from the factories to the barracks. Chebykin himself acknowledged that the reserve battalions composed of factory workers were not reliable.[16]

15. Gerhard Wettig, "Die Rolle der russischen Armée im revolutionären Machtkampf 1917," *Forshungen zur osteuropäischen Geschichte* 12: 82-83; Martynov, *Tsarskaia armiia*, pp. 29-30; Shklovsky, *Sentimental Journey*, p. 7.

16. Alexandr Ivanov, "Volnenie v 1916 godu v 181-om Zap. Pekh. Polku," *Krasnaia letopis'* 10, no. 1 (1924): 171-73; TsGAOR, f. DPOO, d. 347/1917 g., ℓ. 33.

The soldiers often reacted to the police with utmost hostility. The police were granted a deferment from military service. The soldiers felt that the "Pharaohs," as the police were derogatorily called, beat up defenseless demonstrators instead of fighting the Germans. During confrontations between police and demonstrators, soldiers often ceased to be bystanders and attacked the police. One of the most famous of these incidents was the revolt of the soldiers of the 181st Infantry Regiment in October 1916.[17] According to Colonel B. A. Engelhardt, an Octobrist deputy of the Duma, "It was no longer the army in peace time, united in strict discipline under the commanding officers, whose interests were closely connected with the existing system. —No, it was armed mobs capable at any moment of exercising their own will and their demands. . . . [The reserve battalions] were not military units, but rather hordes of armed people. Not united in discipline under commanding personnel, they were more reserves of flammable material than a prop of the regime."[18]

Of the many mistakes committed by security authorities in Petrograd, misunderstanding the sentiments of the reserve soldiers was the most costly. The Ministry of Internal Affairs had established an elaborate internal spy network in every area of civilian life. Okhrana agents dispatched amazingly accurate reports on the political tendencies of all civilian organizations, but their network did not extend to the military forces. Army intelligence and the Okhrana frequently worked at cross-purposes. The former were largely amateurs—such as former engineers or instructors from military schools—whose efficiency left much to be desired, and military authorities often ignored communications from the Okhrana. When Protopopov questioned the reliability of reserve soldiers shortly before the outbreak of the February Revolution, Khabalov replied: "All troops will fulfill their duty," and rejected Protopopov's recommendation that some of the unreliable units be removed from Petrograd. This would be impossible, Khabalov replied, because there were insufficient barracks available outside Petrograd to house many battalions. In his opinion, the question of the reliability of soldiers was irrelevant, since he would use only training detachments to counter workers' demonstrations.[19] He had no doubt about the reliability of these detachments, which were designed to train noncommissioned officers. This argument, however, did not convince Protopopov, who recommended to the tsar that more dependable

17. See chap. 5.

18. B. A. Engel'gardt, "Potonuvshii mir," ed. khr. 3, ℓℓ. 101-2.

19. A. D. Protopopov, "Predsmertnaia zapiska A. D. Protopopova," *Golos minuvshago na chuzhoi storone* 15, no. 2 (1926): 190; Vassilyev, *The Okhrana*, p. 208.

troops be brought to Petrograd. Nicholas then requested General Gurko, acting chief of staff,[20] to send two cavalry divisions to Petrograd on leave status. Gurko rejected this request on the grounds that it would be physically as well as strategically impossible and sent instead a token number of naval service corps. Despite some misgivings, Protopopov did not expect "serious revolutionary tendencies" in the reserve battalions, and was convinced that in the event of a labor disorder the government could find support in the troops, whose loyalty to the tsar he did not question.[21]

If military authorities had doubts about the reliability of the troops in the reserve battalions in Petrograd, they did not realize how far the loyalty of their officers had been eroded. Between April 1914 and January 1917 the number of officers increased from 40,590 to 145,916, while the number of soldiers increased from 1.2 to 6.6 million. To appreciate the drastic increase in the number of officers, one must understand that the cream of the officers' corps had been annihilated in the first year of the war. By July 1915, officers' casualties had reached 60,000—undoubtedly the result of the admirably gallant but stupid tradition of the officers' literally marching at the head of advancing troops. This means that by January 1917 the army had recruited 170,000 new officers and at the time of the February Revolution less than 10 percent of the officers were regulars.[22]

The 60,000 casualties among the officers had two important consequences. First, replacements were of lower military quality. Thousands of retired officers were recalled to active duty. The Academy of the General Staff was closed, its students commissioned to command units or detailed to staff assignments, and almost three thousand soldiers who had the necessary educational qualifications were immediately promoted to officers' rank. A great majority of new officers, however, were graduates of accelerated courses in the military schools and the newly created ensign schools. The entrance requirements for these schools were lowered, and the accelerated courses lasted only four months. "Probably there was no European army of the period," Peter Kenez states, "in which the officers possessed as little general and military education as in the Russian."[23] Such officers could not be expected to possess ability deserving the

20. General Alekseev was on sick leave.

21. I. I. Mints, *Istoriia Velikogo Oktiabria*, vol. 1, *Sverzhenie samoderzhaviia*, p. 469; and TsGAOR, f. ChSK, d. 460, ℓ. 178.

22. Peter Kenez, "A Profile of the Prerevolutionary Officer Corps," *California Slavic Studies* 7 (1973): 145.

23. Ibid., pp. 148-49.

respect of the soldiers. Since better officers were immediately sent to the front, those who remained in the rear were either sick, or old, or incompetent.

Second, the dire need of officers facilitated the democratization of the officers' corps. Even prior to the war, the government had found it hard to maintain its social exclusiveness—such prominent generals as Alekseev, Kornilov, and Denikin had all come from poor families. The war opened up the opportunities for aspiring young men of humble social origin for quick promotion in the Russian army. In 1916 only 4 percent of the junior officers came from nobility, while 70 percent had peasant background.[24] Unlike the senior officers brought up in the tradition of the Academy of the General Staff with emphasis on narrow military mind and ignorance of political currents outside the military, these junior officers brought into the army acute political consciousness. The officers' corps reflected more and more the sentiments of the liberal opposition: even some members of the revolutionary parties—such as V. B. Stankevich (right-wing Populist), S. Matislavskii (SR), and A. Tarasov-Rodionov (Bolshevik)—could be found among the officers, despite the requirement of a security check before the commissioning of an officer.

Thus, on the eve of the revolution, the regime could no longer take it for granted that the officers, who had traditionally imposed strict discipline on the soldiers, would display unquestioned loyalty to the existing regime. In mid-January, Vasiliev brought a report to Protopopov concerning the mood of the officers in Petrograd. It gave accounts of two salons where officers gathered—that of Countess N. S. Sheremetieva, where opposition-minded officers gathered, and that of Countess S. S. Ignatieva, where right-wing officers met. But at both salons "revolutionary speeches" were delivered and derogatory words were often spoken about the tsar. The liberal-minded young officers in the Baltic Fleet were talking about the possibility of a palace coup and swore to each other that in case of revolution they would defy orders of the tsar.[25] What Crane Brinton calls "transfer of allegiance" had already taken place among the officers of the Russian army. A surprising fact was not that the officers did not remain loyal to the regime, but rather they were not more actively involved in political activities aiming to overthrow the regime.

Superficially, in February 1917, Petrograd appeared to be in a position to withstand internal disruption. The city was fortified with an enormous number of troops, and security authorities had

24. Ibid., p. 179.
25. TsGAOR, f. ChSK, d. 460, ℓ. 179; see chap. 10.

prepared elaborate plans to counter any serious disturbance. A close examination of the security measures, however, reveals that this appearance was completely deceptive. The men in charge lacked leadership, and the various agencies lacked coordination. Demoralization, apathy, and resentment seeped through to the garrison troops. Behind an impressive facade, the structure was rotting from within. Only a small push was needed to topple it.

9

THE LIBERAL OPPOSITION

 The crisis of power *(krizis verkhov)* that accelerated after the assassination of Rasputin and the sudden revitalization of the labor movement pushed the liberal opposition even further into desperation. Some saw the powerlessness of "words" and called for "action." But many dreaded cooperation with a mass movement. The center of the Progressive Bloc, led by Miliukov, barely succeeded in maintaining the leadership of the liberal opposition, confining its activities within the parliamentary process. Miliukov's line represented the mainstream of liberal opposition and he could no longer retain tight control over the liberals as a whole. On the eve of the revolution they were splintering into different groups. The most radical wing, particularly the lower echelon of the liberal workers in the voluntary organizations and municipal self-governments, began more actively to cooperate with the labor movement. The leaders of the Central War Industries Committee strove for a united action between the liberals and the workers' movement by exerting the influence of the workers' group on the Petrograd workers. Others began seriously discussing a plan for a palace coup to remove Nicholas from the throne. Frightened by this sudden radicalization, its right wing, represented by Rodzianko, desperately sought a compromise with the tsar by mobilizing the support of the grand dukes and the nobility.

In a tense political atmosphere during the Christmas recess the liberal politicians held a series of meetings. On December 21 and 22 the Central Committee of the Kadet party held its plenary conference. Responding to the growing demand for peace and direct action advocated by the lower echelon of the party, Miliukov obstinately defended the continuance of parliamentary tactics and the policy of supporting the war to a victorious end.[1] Unlike the Kadets, who ultimately accepted Miliukov's policy, the Progressists advocated a more radical one. On December 30 they gathered at P. P. Riabushinskii's apartment in Moscow and adopted a resolution not to accept the expected dissolution of the Duma. According to their plan, the Duma delegates would be asked to reassemble in Moscow and issue an appeal to the nation and the army to support the defiant Duma against the government.[2] But the other parties in the Progressive Bloc reacted to this appeal coldly, considering it a parody of the disastrous "Vyborg appeal," in which the liberal Duma deputies in the First Duma had attempted to persuade the nation to show a passive resistance to the government's dissolution of the Duma. In addition, Konovalov's group advocated closer cooperation with the leaders of the workers' movement and held a series of conferences with the moderate Socialists in Petrograd, Kiev, Kharkov, Tiflis, and Odessa, presumably in an attempt to form a Left Bloc.[3]

If Konovalov was deeply involved in an effort to form an alliance with the moderate Socialists, he was busy on the other front as well. During the Christmas recess he initated a diplomatic mission to representatives of the bureaucracy to sound out the possibility of mobilizing support among an enlightened element of the bureaucracy for a liberal campaign to form a ministry of confidence. His envoys, Vasilii Maklakov and D. A. Olsufiev, met with A. V. Krivoshein, A. A. Bobrinskii, and A. S. Taneev. Presumably they agreed in principle on the need to remove Protopopov and composed a list of candidates for a ministry of confidence acceptable to both camps. But beyond that nothing specific came out of these meetings.[4]

On January 7 the government announced that it had decided to postpone the opening of the Duma until February 14—another humiliation to the liberals, particularly when the new chairman of the Council

1. V. S. Diakin, *Russkaia burzhuaziia i tsarizm v gody pervoi mirovoi voiny*, pp. 288-89.

2. B. B. Grave, ed., *Burzhuaziia nakanune fevral'skoi revoliutsii*, p. 165.

3. E. D. Chermenskii, *IV gosudarstvennaia duma i sverzhenie tsarizma v Rossii*, p. 233.

4. How this mission came about is not known, but this policy was opposed by the Moscow Kadets. TsGAOR, f. DPOO, d. 27, ch. 46, 1916 g., l. 60; TsGAOR, f. DPOO, d. 341, ch 57/1917, l. 1; TsGAOR, f. DPOO, d. 307a, t. 2, 1916 g., ll. 76v-76g; TsGAOR. f. DPOO, 1917 g., d. 669a, ll. 2-3; for Maklakov's letter to Konovalov, describing his meeting with one of the representatives of the bureaucracy, see TsGAOR, f. DPOO, op. 343ZS, 57ch/1917 g., ll. 20, 22.

of Ministers, Golitsyn, had pledged to convene the session as scheduled. On the same day, at the initiative of the Kadets, the representatives of the liberal opposition, including the Octobrists, the Progressists, and the Trudoviks, met at Konovalov's apartment, and discussed what action they should take in response to the government's decision. The Progressists insisted on the abandonment of parliamentary tactics, and proposed that the Progressive Bloc should present an ultimatum to the government immediately, demanding the convocation of the Duma. If the government refused to comply with the demand, the liberals should boycott the Duma entirely. According to Konovalov, "the powerless Duma, the target of mockery by the government, is in the eyes of the people much worse than the absence of the Duma." Konovalov was supported by Kerenskii. Rodzianko strenuously objected to this radical position. "It is necessary," he insisted, "to maintain our self-control to the end, and whatever the cost, to fulfill our duty before our fatherland and the electors." Opposing the proposal of an ultimatum to the government, he advocated that the liberals open the Duma session with sharp attacks on the government in the manner they had opened the previous Duma session on November 1, 1916. Vasilii Maklakov also considered it premature "to throw down the gauntlet to the government and seek a path of nonparliamentary struggle." In his opinion, the task of the liberals was still to organize the forces of society. Only if the Duma were dissolved should "the first page of a new Russian Revolution be opened." Maklakov declared that there was no substantial disagreement between the radicals and the moderates in the liberal opposition. All were convinced that "a revolutionary path is inevitable." The disagreement revolved around the question of when they should open this struggle. The Kadets would insist, Maklakov continued, that the struggle would begin only when all parliamentary means were exhausted. It was impossible to find a middle ground between the radicals and the moderates in this meeting, and in the end the representatives decided not to adopt a rigid plan at that point.[5]

Maklakov's statement at this meeting demonstrated the powerlessness of the moderate liberal opposition. Forced into a corner, they felt that a revolution might indeed be at hand. Nevertheless, they decided not to act, fearing that a decisive act against the government might touch off a mass movement they knew they could not control. The workers' successful strike in Petrograd on January 9 appeared to confirm their fear. A radical action would also split the Progressive

5. TsGAOR, f. DPOO, d. 27, ch. 46, ℓℓ. 60-62; TsGAOR, f. DPOO, d. 171/ 1917 g., ℓℓ. 63-66.

Bloc—a result the liberals could ill afford, since the disintegration of the Progressive Bloc would mean the loss of the focal point of the liberal opposition.

At the beginning of January the workers' group began a campaign among the Petrograd workers to organize a strike and mass demonstration on February 14, the opening day of the Duma, in front of the Tauride Palace, to urge the Duma liberals to assume a more decisive leadership. Konovalov and Guchkov supported the new radical direction of the workers' group in the hope that the group would recapture its previous strength in the workers' movement, exert a moderating influence, and serve as a link between the workers and the liberal opposition. This hope, however, was crushed when Protopopov's police arrested the leaders of the workers' group on January 27. Two days after the arrest Guchkov called an emergency meeting of the liberal politicians and the activists of the workers' movement in the Central War Industries Committee. Altogether thirty-five to forty persons attended the meeting, including Guchkov, Konovalov, Abrasimov (the remaining member of the workers' group, who was a police spy), Kerenskii, Chkheidze, Miliukov, three members of the Moscow War Industries Committee, and the representatives of the Unions of Zemstvos and of Towns.

The first speaker, Miliukov, shocked the participants by his hostile speech against the workers' group. In Miliukov's opinion, the Duma should and could be the only center of opposition against the government. No other organization and no other class should have the right to act independently of the Duma. Miliukov attacked the involvement of the workers' group in politics, which went far beyond its competency under the law. In particular, he criticized its appeal to the workers to stage a demonstration in front of the Tauride Palace on February 14. Such a demonstration would be easily suppressed by the government and give Protopopov a further excuse for repressive measures not only against the workers' organizations but against the liberal opposition as well.

Miliukov's speech immediately provoked an outcry. Guchkov and Konovalov defended the workers' group for its service to national defense by intervening in conflicts between capital and labor. Miliukov's colleague in the Kadet party, M. S. Adzhemov, attacked his party leader for his strictly legalistic point of view. If Miliukov's accusations of the workers' group were justified, all the other voluntary organizations, such as the Unions of Zemstvos and of Towns and the War Industries Committee, were guilty of political involvement beyond their legal competency. Adzhemov continued: "A blow to the workers' group is in fact a blow to the entire Russian society. The arrest of the workers' group weakens the entire system of the forces of society in the country. The matter that stands before the allies of the workers' group is to seek a means by which to react to this blow in an appropriate way." This opinion was also supported by Kerenskii, who urged the War Industries Committee to take the challenge thrown by the government and fight. Chkheidze criticized Miliukov for being a man of words and not of action. He warned that Miliukov would "one beautiful day find himself behind the tail of events, since if everything continues as it is, it is easy and inevitable to see only the workers alone at the head of the political offensive and events." Professor Zernov of the Central War Industries Committee insisted that it was time to act. It was necessary, he argued, to create a center to coordinate all classes of society before the opening of the Duma to begin an open and decisive struggle with the government. Prince Drutskii indirectly proposed the creation of an illegal underground organ through which the opposition could transmit its decisions to the leading circles of the masses. P. N. Perverzev of the Moscow War Industries Committee supported this idea. In conclusion, the meeting adopted a proposal made by Zernov, Adzhemov, and Perverzev that a second meeting of the representatives of the opposition be held in the near future to discuss the political problem facing the nation, to create a special organ to inform the wide masses of the decisions and the intentions of the leading circles of the opposition, and to elect a committee to serve as a center for all opposition activities.[6]

Obviously, moderates like Miliukov were outnumbered at this meeting. The Octobrists and other right-wing parties in the Progressive Bloc had not been invited. The Progressists and the Socialists, who had been frustrated by Miliukov's inaction as leader of the Progressive Bloc, unleashed their pent-up frustrations. Many bold words were carelessly spoken, which might have provided them with a psychological catharsis, but had no practical significance. Despite the resolution adopted at the meeting, Guchkov and Konovalov made no attempt to call a second meeting. Presumably they concluded that with the destruction of the workers' group the last chance to link the liberal opposition to the workers' movement was gone forever.

The only action that the liberal opposition took in reaction to the government's arrest of the workers' group was Guchkov's open protest letter, which he made public on January 30 and in which

6. TsGAOR, f. DPOO, d. 34 3ZS, 57 ch/1917, ll. 15-17; TsGAOR, f. DPOO, d. 347, 46/1917, ll. 16-17; TsGAOR, f. DPOO, op. 5, 669a, ll. 17-19; Rabochee dvizhenie v Petrograde, pp. 180-84. This Okhrana report with slightly different variations was presumably written by Abrasimov.

he refuted the charges brought by the government against the group. In Guchkov's opinion, contrary to the government's accusation that the workers' group secretly advocated revolution, he felt it represented a more moderate wing of the workers' movement and constantly sought peace between labor and capital for the sake of national defense. If the workers' group had become involved in politics, that reflected the worsening political condition of the nation. Guchkov stated that the Central War Industries Committee, whatever disagreements it had with the workers' group, shared with it the opinion that the existing government, which had brought on the current political crisis, would be incapable of achieving a victory over the external enemy.[7] Guchkov's letter, however, sounded more like an epitaph than a battle cry. Beyond this protest letter, neither Guchkov nor Konovalov did anything to reestablish contact with the workers' movement. Deprived of that vital link, they sensed that the workers had gone completely beyond their control and henceforward relied exclusively on the possibility of a palace coup to effect a political change.

This did not mean, however, that the liberals on the whole abandoned attempts to establish a united front with the workers. Since the summer of 1915, the rank-and-file activists of the voluntary organizations and municipal self-governments had attempted an alliance with the leaders of the workers' movement. These radicals in the liberal movement had used the social service organizations of the municipal self-governments, the labor exchange offices, and the cooperative organizations as their points of contact. In their practical work in these organizations they had established a close working relationship with the activists of the workers' movement and it was at their insistence that the activist-workers and students had become involved in the practical activities. The more these liberal activists became involved in work to alleviate the misery of the poor, the more convinced they became of the impossibility of continuing without a fundamental restructuring of the state system.[8]

On the eve of the February Revolution food distribution had become a common cause for which the radical liberals could take united action with the moderate Socialists. Since the summer of 1915 the social service organizations of the city duma had been involved in the welfare program for the poor. On the other hand, the workers' group had launched a campaign to create local food committees.

7. TsGAOR, f. DPOO, d. 347, 46/1917, ℓℓ. 27-28; TsGIA, f. 1276, op. 13, d. 34, ℓ. 2; Shliapnikov, *Semnadtsatyi god* 1: 280-83.

8. For the radical actions of the rank-and-file liberal activists in 1915, see chap. 3.

These two movements from two different directions merged and demanded the creation of local committees consisting of all classes and groups of society. The liberals participated in the cooperative movement and created many organizations that included the workers as well as other classes of society. It was also reported that the Union of Zemstvos attempted to establish an organ for legal assistance to the masses, an attempt that an Okhrana agent saw as the radical liberals' effort to contact the masses.[9]

Although only fragments of evidence are available, it appears certain that the radical activists of the liberal opposition became more actively involved in efforts to form a united front with the workers. They were not successful in capturing a broad segment of the masses, but it is important to note that at the lower level there was substantial understanding and cooperation between radical liberals and moderate Socialists. In January an Okhrana agent reported that the left-wing liberals had already given up the possibility of a moderate approach. They pessimistically predicted that the country was headed toward "the inevitable experience of spontaneous and even anarchistic revolution, at which point there will already be no time, no place, and no basis for the realization of the Kadets' programs, and at which point there will be a basis for the transformation of Russia into a state free from tsarism, created on new social foundations." On January 18, another Okhrana agent reported that the left-wing Kadets now openly advocated a policy "to take part in a revolution in order to organize a new 'healthy' government, which could finish off the existing system, even in the form of its replacement by a democratic republic."[10]

If the dangerous possibility of the explosion of a mass movement prompted the left-wing liberals to move further to the Left, the same prospect led the moderates to act more cautiously. On January 18, despite the radical elements' demand for a boycott, the Budget Committee of the Duma resumed its normal function. At the same time, the liberal press reported, with a touch of wishful thinking, that Trepov might be reappointed chairman of the Council of Ministers.[11] When this proved to be a false rumor, the representatives of the Duma and the State Council in the Special Council for Defense entertained the idea of convening all the special councils with Nicholas's participation,

9. I. P. Leiberov, *Petrogradskii proletariat v Fevral'skoi revoliutsii* 1: 471-72; TsGAOR, f. DPOO, op. 343ZS, 57 ch/1917, ℓℓ. 9, 11, 13.

10. TsGAOR, f. DPOO, d. 307a, to. 2, 1916 b., ℓ. 76g; ibid., d. 171/1917, ℓ. 30.

11. M. V. Rodzianko, *The Reign of Rasputin*, p. 255.

and presenting at this joint meeting a petition to the tsar for a ministry of confidence. This proposal was approved by an overwhelming majority at the meeting of the Special Council for Defense, but its chairman, War Minister Beliaev, refused to submit this decision to the tsar. He instead recommended to the tsar not to convene such a meeting and not to be caught in the trap set by the liberals by attending the meeting of the Special Council for Defense.[12]

In the meantime, the Central Committee of the Kadet party met on February 4 and 5 for the last time before the February Revolution. The Left Kadet M. S. Adzhemov stated that the Kadets should support the workers' demonstration on February 14. N. K. Volkov opposed Adzhemov, arguing that the demonstration might provoke the government to close down the Central War Industries Committee. F. I. Rodichev also shared the opinion that the government was waiting for a chance for a bloody suppression of the entire opposition movement. He expressed fear that the February 14 demonstration might lead to the kind of repression they had seen on Bloody Sunday in 1905. Although unsaid, it was clear that what Rodichev feared was not only the suppression of the opposition movement but what might follow from it—a revolution. Miliukov agreed, saying that widespread sympathy among the workers in favor of the workers' group's call for a demonstration unfortunately did not exist. The demonstration would fail, in his opinion, unless it was organized by the police itself. A majority of the Kadets supported Miliukov's opinion, as always, that the Kadets should exert their utmost influence to dissuade the workers from participating in the demonstration.[13]

As for the tactics in the forthcoming session of the Duma, Adzhemov and N. I. Astrov proposed that the Progressive Bloc undertake a sharp attack on the tsarina at the opening session. Miliukov and Rodichev, on the other hand, insisted on a "businesslike" tone and opposed any political declarations. The Kadets in the end accepted Miliukov's opinion, and decided "not to deploy a frontal attack against the government on the first day." Concerning criticism of the tsarina, the Kadets decided to mention her only "by allusion."[14] This position was even more moderate than the one advocated by Rodzianko in January.

12. Diakin, *Russkaia burzhuaziia*, p. 294; Chermenskii, *IV gosudarstvennaia duma*, p. 267; Rodzianko, *The Reign of Rasputin*, p. 259.

13. Chermenskii, *IV gosudarstvennia duma*, pp. 264-65. This account is based on the minutes of the Central Committee of the Kadet party on February 4, 1917, RO GBL, f. 229, op. 1, papka V, ed. khr. 23a. My request to use this archive was rejected.

14. Diakin, *Russkaia burzhuaziia*, p. 295. This is based on the archival material cited in fn. 13.

On February 10 in the Kadet paper, *Rech'*, Miliukov's open letter to the workers was printed side by side with Khabalov's proclamation to the workers. Miliukov suggested that the appeal to stage a demonstration on February 14 in support of the Duma might have originated in "dark forces" under the influence of Germany. If the workers responded to this provocation, they would in fact play "into the hands of the enemy."[15]

Miliukov's policy to take no action against the government was prompted partly by fear that it might provoke a mass movement and partly by concern that support of the workers' movement would split the Progressive Bloc. The Octobrists had already been resentful of "Miliukov's dictatorial manner." To maintain unity in the Progressive Bloc, Miliukov had a series of meetings with various members and had moved further to the Right through these meetings to keep the Octobrists in the Bloc. An Okhrana agent noticed the growing influence of Miliukov on Rodzianko and Shul'gin.[16] Like the Kadets, the Progressive Bloc as a whole decided not to make an attack on the government on the opening day of the Duma. Miliukov flatly rejected the suggestion made on February 13 by a Kadet, V. A. Obolenskii, and supported by left-wing Kadets, that the Progressiv Bloc present a petition to the tsar on the opening day, requesting the formation of a responsible ministry. Such a move, in Miliukov's opinion, would be unconstitutional.[17]

The inaction of the Progressive Bloc led some of the liberals, notably Guchkov, Konovalov, and Prince L'vov, to believe that the only alternative open to the liberals would be a palace coup. On the eve of the opening of the Duma a rumor of a palace coup was spreading throughout Petrograd. Sensing the danger in this adventurous course and attempting to recover his slipping popularity among the liberal circles, Rodzianko was busily involved in attempts to mobilize the grand dukes and the nobility to persuade the tsar to form a ministry of confidence. These attempts, as we have already seen, had no effect.[18]

Aware of their own powerlessness, the liberals hoped that if internal pressure could not change the government's reactionary policy, external pressure from the Allies could be brought to bear. For this purpose they made a concerted effort to recruit the Allied representatives, who had assembled in Petrograd to attend the Inter-Allied Military Conference from January 29 to February 7.

15. *Rech'*, February 10, 1917.
16. TsGAOR, f. DPOO, d. 27, ch. 46/1916, ℓ. 58.
17. Chermenskii, *IV gosudarstvennaia duma*, p. 273.
18. See chaps. 7 and 10.

While the French ambassador, Maurice Paléologue, had a close association with the grand dukes and the conservative elements of the Progressive Bloc, the British ambassador, Sir George Buchanan, had sympathized with the moderate Kadets. The Russian-English Society, of which Buchanan was honorary chairman, included in its membership such liberal politicians as Miliukov, Maklakov, Guchkov, Shingarev, Tereshchenko, and Nekrasov.[19] The British ambassador from time to time stepped out of his competency and made recommendations to the tsar on internal affairs of Russia. As the political situation changed from bad to worse at the end of 1916, Buchanan was increasingly disturbed by the possibility of revolution, which would knock Russia out of the war. In this context, Buchanan made an unprecedented move at the end of December 1916. Having gained the reluctant permission of his home government, he requested an audience with the tsar, and advised him to drop Protopopov and form a ministry of confidence. Such a policy would, Buchanan implored, "break down the barrier that separates the Emperor from his people." To this Nicholas replied with sarcasm: "Do you mean that *I* am to regain the confidence of my people or that *they* are to regain *my* confidence?" The only result of Buchanan's act was that the British ambassador incurred more displeasure from the imperial couple.[20]

The Allied delegations arrived in Petrograd on January 16. They were received enthusiastically by liberal circles, which threw a series of banquets in their honor. Behind the scenes the liberals met separately with Lord Milner, the British chief representative, and G. Doumergue, his French counterpart, and requested their intervention in Russian internal matters. They argued that otherwise Russia would be plunged into a revolution. Liberal pressure notwithstanding, the Allied delegates avoided interfering. Lord Milner told the liberals that his mission to Russia was concerned merely with military matters. After he returned to Great Britain, he reported to the government that the situation in Russia was calmer than ever and that the tsar and his family enjoyed unusual popularity.[21] As for Doumergue, he was only interested in securing the Russian government's pledge to support the French claim to territory on the right bank of the Rhine

19. Diakin, *Russkaia burzhuaziia,* p. 305.

20. Sir George Buchanan, *My Mission to Russia and Other Diplomatic Memories* 2: 45-50.

21. Chermenskii, *IV gosudarstvennia duma,* p. 273. Katkov contends that Lord Milner acted on behalf of the liberals and made recommendations to Nicholas to carry out a political reform. This contention, however, is not supported by evidence. See George Katkov, *Russia 1917: The Russian Revolution,* pp. 223-28.

at the peace conference. At the meeting with the liberal representatives, hastily arranged by Paléologue, Doumergue replied to the liberals' desperate plea by saying that they had to be "patient" and learn to give the war top priority. The only act by the Allied delegation that was construed by the government as interference in internal affairs was the British delegates' request to extend their stay until the Duma session began, to witness the evidence of national unity. But this request was rejected by the government. If the British delegation stayed, the Duma would not be convened. The British delegates left Russia on February 8 without witnessing the "unity of the Russian people."[22]

On February 14, the Duma opened the new session. The workers responded with a one-day strike, but failed to stage a large-scale demonstration in front of the Tauride Palace in support of the Duma. The much talked-about palace coup did not take place. All in all, the opening day of the Duma was an anticlimax. The liberals were in disarray and did not know what to do. Rodzianko's opening statement was marked more by his sharp attack on the workers' demonstration than by criticism of the government. The government outmaneuvered the liberals in its opening gambit. Immediately after Rodzianko's opening statement, the minister of agriculture, Rittikh, exercised his ministerial prerogative and asked for the floor. He spoke of food distribution, defended his policy of requisition (razverstka), and asked for the cooperation of the Duma in his effort to solve the critical problem. Rittikh's move forced the Duma to begin its session with a discussion of food supply and distribution in a "businesslike" manner, and forestalled any possibility of Duma delegates attacking the government on a broader political question. Moreover, the government's choice of focusing on the food supply was a strategic success, since the Progressive Bloc was hopelessly divided on this question. The Octobrists and the Nationalists, who represented the interests of the landowning class, had sharply criticized the Kadets' insistence on rigid fixed prices. At the Duma session on February 20, Octobrist Kapnist II openly declared that the Octobrists were closer on this issue to Rittikh than to Miliukov, while his colleague N. V. Savich stated that they disagreed with the Kadets on economic questions. Shul'gin supported Rittikh, and attacked the Progressive Bloc's social and economic program.[23]

In contrast to the Duma, the usually more conservative State Council took a defiant stand against the government. On the opening

22. Maurice Paléologue, *An Ambassador's Memoirs* 3:188; Raymond Pearson, *The Russian Moderates and the Crisis of Tsarism 1914-1917*, pp. 134-35; Chermenskii, *IV gosudarstvennaia duma*, p. 272.

23. Diakin, *Russkaia burzhuaziia*, p. 316; Chermenskii, *IV gosudarstvennaia duma*, pp. 276-77.

day the left wing and the center of the State Council walked out in protest against the appointment of I. G. Shcheglovitov as its chairman without giving him a chance to end his opening speech. When Guchkov, newly elected to the State Council, made his first speech on February 21, it was received enthusiastically.[24]

The mood of the liberals was one of demoralization and despair. Only Miliukov remained undaunted, and criticized those who demanded action: "Our word is already our action. The word and the vote are still the essence of our single weapon." But many of his colleagues did not believe in this. Shul'gin wrote to Grand Duke Nikolai Mikhailovich: "The attack of the Duma is sluggish. Alas, no one believes in words any longer." Another member of the Progressive Bloc, A. I. Savenko, noted: "The deputies wander around like emaciated flies. No one believes in anything. Everyone's hands are down. All feel and know their powerlessness. The situation is hopeless."[25] Rodzianko's wife wrote a letter to Countess Iusupova: "The general tone [of the Duma] was a little dim after everything we waited for on the first day, but all the better. It is a dangerous time now; the smallest spark might ignite a fire." Attack on the government came only from the Left. On the second day of the reopened session on February 15, Kerenskii demanded the overthrow of the "tyrants" and criticized liberal inaction: "I say to you that your speeches on the necessity of calm at all costs are either the naïve sentiments of superficial thinkers or just an excuse to avoid the real fight, just a pretext to stay safely in your armchairs. . . . You don't want to listen to anybody but yourselves but soon you will have to listen, for if you do not hear the warning voices, you will encounter the harsh facts."[26] On February 22, the Duma deputies attended the funeral of their colleague, M. M. Alekseenko, former chairman of the budget commission. As the coffin was brought out of the Tauride Palace, Shul'gin could not dispel the gloomy thought that Alekseenko might after all be the fortunate one, for he would not have to see what was coming.

It seems to be no accident that on February 22, police recorded an unusually high number of suicides among the upper class: "A daughter of a colonel, E. V. Kritskaia, age thirty-three, by drinking liquid ammonia. At 8 A.M. a noble, Stanislav Iakovich, age fifty-five, by shooting himself in the head with a revolver. At 9 A.M. a staff-captain, P. Gehring,

24. *Rech'*, February 15, 21, 1917.
25. TsGAOR, f. 670, op. 1, d. 439, ℓ. 6; Chermenskii, *IV gosudarstvennaia duma*, p. 277.
26. "K stroii poslednikh dnei tsarskogo rezhima (1916-1917 gg.)," *Krasnyi arkhiv* 14, no. 1 (1926): 245-46. Kerenskii quoted in Pearson, *The Russian Moderates*, p. 137.

age twenty-eight, by shooting himself in the right temple with a revolver. At 12 noon, a student of the Women's College, Gebeksmann,
age twenty-seven, found dead by hanging herself."[27] The death knell
sounded also for Russian liberalism. The February Revolution was only
one day away.

27. TsGAOR, f. POO, op. 5, d. 669 (1917 g.), ℓ. 279. Pearson states that a
few days before the February Revolution, the Octobrists "abandoned pretensions
to independence and threw themselves on the mercy of the government." In
Pearson's opinion, "with the defection of its largest fraction, the Progressive Bloc
was finished." Pearson, *The Russian Moderates*, p. 138. It is unlikely, however,
that the Octobrists formally quit the Bloc. In fact, on February 27 Shidlovskii
still continued to act as its formal head. The Octobrists' eagerness to cooperate
with the government was nothing new and does not seem to represent any turning
point in the history of the Progressive Bloc.

10

THE LIBERALS, CONSPIRACIES,

AND THE FREEMASONS

 On the eve of the February Revolution rumors of a palace coup were circulating widely in Petrograd. There is no need to record all the references, since by the end of 1916 it had become fashionable at salons to speak against the government, and most of the talk about a palace coup was nothing but gossip, wishful thinking, or rumor. But there were two groups of conspirators who apparently went a little beyond salon talk.

The first group centered around Prince L'vov. According to the émigré historian, S. Mel'gunov, who was the first historian to focus on this obscure question by collecting material and interviewing those involved in the conspiracies, L'vov early in the war had begun to doubt Nicholas's ability to lead Russia to victory.[1] He became directly involved in the conspiracy for a palace coup in November 1916, when he proposed to General Alekseev a joint action to remove the pernicious influence of the tsarina. Although he was trusted by Nicholas and Aleksandra, General Alekseev had become concerned about the growing influence of the tsarina and Rasputin in internal politics. Aleksandra had once suggested to Alekseev that Rasputin be invited to the Stavka, but Alekseev had indignantly rejected the idea, declaring that if Rasputin set foot in the Stavka, he would resign his post. In November 1916 there was a rumor that Aleksandra was planning to come to live with the tsar at the Stavka to exert a stronger influence

1. S. P. Mel'gunov, *Na putiakh k dvortsovomu perevorotu*, p. 91; Grigorii Aronson, *Rossiia nakanune revoliutsii: istoricheskii etiudy*, p. 123.

on him. According to Mel'gunov, this finally led Alekseev to support L'vov's plan to remove the tsarina from the political scene. The plan was to arrest her in the train on her way to Mogilev, deport her to the Crimea, and force the tsar to form a ministry of confidence headed by L'vov. This plan was to be executed on November 30. But before that date Alekseev fell ill, and took a leave from the Stavka to convalesce in the Crimea. When L'vov came to the Crimea to confer with Alekseev, the latter refused to see him and rejected his proposal for a palace coup. According to Denikin, Alekseev considered it out of the question to stage a palace coup during wartime. Mel'gunov believes that Alekseev rejected L'vov's second proposal, since that proposal, which might lead to the forcible removal of the tsar himself, went further than he could tolerate.[2] Alekseev's involvement in L'vov's conspiracy, as explained by Mel'gunov, is based on hearsay and is difficult to substantiate with historical evidence.

Presumably Prince L'vov was involved in another plot. On December 9, 1916, after the police refused to permit the All-Russian Congress of the Unions of Towns and of Zemstvos to be held, a small group of conspirators headed by L'vov gathered in his apartment. At this meeting, attended by N. M. Kishkin, M. M. Fedorov, and A. I. Khatisov, L'vov revealed another plan for a palace coup that would remove Nicholas and install Grand Duke Nikolai Nikolaevich in his place. The conspirators were to use a small guard unit led by sympathetic grand dukes to arrest the tsar and deport him abroad, while they were to incarcerate Aleksandra in a monastery. L'vov revealed to those present that the army's support for this plan had been assured by General A. A. Manikovskii. The conspirators accepted L'vov's plan, and entrusted Khatisov, mayor of Tiflis and chairman of the Caucasian branch of the Union of Towns, with the delicate task of recruiting Grand Duke Nikolai Nikolaevich, former supreme commander in chief and viceroy of the Caucasian front, into the conspiracy.[3] When Khatisov revealed L'vov's plot to the grand duke, he did not reject the idea outright, but raised two questions. He asked how people with deep monarchist sentiments would react to the forcible removal of the tsar, and he wondered about the possible reaction of the army to such an act. The grand duke asked for two days to think it over. When Khatisov returned two days later, Nikolai Nikolaevich answered that he had decided not to join the plot, since his assistant, General Ianushkevich, believed that the army would not

2. Mel'gunov, *Na putiakh*, pp. 94-102; A. I. Denikin, *Ocherki russkoi smuty* 1: 37-39.

3. Mel'gunov, *Na putiakh*, pp. 105-17.

tolerate a palace coup.[4] Thus, L'vov's second plot collapsed in its initial stage.

Another conspiratorial group was led by Guchkov. Early in October, a meeting of the leaders of the Progressive Bloc was held in the office of M. M. Fedorov. Among the participants were Miliukov, V. Maklakov, Shingarev, Konovalov, Tereshchenko, Nekrasov, and Guchkov. Guchkov advocated the idea of a palace coup at this meeting, but the Kadets, led by Miliukov, strongly opposed it. The meeting adjourned without reaching any decision. After the meeting, however, Nekrasov and Tereshchenko came to see Guchkov, and expressed their agreement with Guchkov that a palace coup should be attempted. They formed a committee of three and elaborated a plan. It was agreed that they would seize the imperial train along the railway line between Tsarskoe Selo and Mogilev, possibly near a village formerly owned by Alexander I's notorious adviser, Arakcheev, in Novgorod Province. Prince D. Viazemskii was entrusted with mobilizing the guard unit stationed in this village for the plot. Also, General A. I. Krymov was involved in the plot, and was supposed to come to Petrograd to recruit some army units for the coup.[5] But preparations went slowly. The plot was to be acted upon in the middle of March and Krymov did arrive in Petrograd at the month's beginning. But before the conspirators could take action, the February Revolution broke out.

Historians differ on the question of how seriously one should take these conspiracies. To Katkov they represent one of many attempts by Russian liberals to overthrow the tsarist regime, and he sees in the February Revolution the fruition of their plots. To Chermenskii, they were nothing but the idle chitchat and wishful thinking of disgruntled liberals, who were neither willing nor able to carry out a coup because they were afraid of the revolutionary movement. Diakin grants that the two groups represented by L'vov and Guchkov had gone further than mere talk, but states that L'vov's plot had collapsed before January 1917, and that although Guchkov's plot was more serious than L'vov's, it did not go beyond the "embryonic stage."[6]

4. Ibid., pp. 108-9.

5. Ibid., pp. 148-54; A. I. Guchkov, "Vospominaniia," *Poslednie novosti*, September 13, 1936; Deposition of Guchkov, *Padenie tsarskogo rezhima*, 6: 261-62.

6. George Katkov, *Russia 1917: The February Revolution*, pp. 173-77, 215-17; E. D. Chermenskii, *IV gosudastvennaia duma i sverzhenie tsarizma v Rossii*, pp. 238-45; idem, "K voprosu o krizise verkhov v Rossii nakanune Fevral'skoi revoliutsii," *Nauchnaia sessiia po istorii perioda mirovoi voiny*, sektsiia 4, *bor'ba klassov i*

Another Soviet historian, V. Ia. Laverychev, presents the most interesting viewpoint. Laverychev believes that Guchkov's group, which included not only Nekrasov and Tereshchenko but also Konovalov and Efremov, seriously contemplated staging a coup to depose the tsar in early 1917. But for the successful operation of their coup, the conspirators needed the following conditions: (1) an agreement with authoritative representatives of Nicholas's relatives, (2) the consent of the military leaders, and (3) the backing of the leading liberal circles. The conspirators ran into various obstacles. First, their plot for a palace coup was strongly opposed by many liberal leaders such as Miliukov and Rodzianko. Second, the tsarist government had avoided serious confrontations with the liberals—a measure that gave the moderate liberals an illusion that a compromise with the government could be made. By January 1917, the conspirators had gained none of their conditions. After the government's arrest of the workers' group, however, the conspirators revived their discussions, but could not agree on the exact timing for a coup. When the strike movement began to expand rapidly, particularly after February 14, they tried to avoid a coup as long as the workers remained stirred up. They hoped that the wave of strikes would soon subside, as it had in the past. As it turned out, a palace coup was already impossible in February; the only chance for its success would have been in January, but "the political inertia and the limitations of the Russian bourgeoisie made it impossible for the conspirators to take advantage of this opportunity." In conclusion, Laverychev makes a startlingly unorthodox remark, usually not accepted by Soviet historians: "In the definite historical moment this conspiracy objectively aided the struggle of the proletariat for the overthrow of the monarchy. The conspiracy hastened the development of a revolutionary crisis and became one of the reasons for the quick victory of the February Revolution."[7]

In view of the lack of historical evidence, it appears premature to come to a definitive conclusion about conspiracies for a palace coup. However, it is possible to establish two facts—the conspiracies existed and a palace coup never took place—and to make a few provisional hypotheses.

---

partii v gody pervoi mirovoi voiny, pp. 147-58; idem, "IV gosudarstvennaia duma i sverzhenie samoderzhaviia v Rossii: k voprosu.o zagovorakh burzhuazii i tsarizma nakanune revoliutsii," *Voprosy istorii*, no. 6 (1969), pp. 73-79; V. S. Diakin, *Russkaia burzhuaziia*, pp. 298-304.

7. V. Ia. Laverychev, "Legendy, predpolozheniia i fakty o podgotovke dvortsovogo perevorota," *Nauchnaia sessiia posviashchennaia 50-letiiu sverzheniia samoderzhaviia v Rossii* 3: 81-86.

One cannot deny a certain amateurishness in these plots. For one thing, the conspirators talked too much. L'vov revealed to the liberal politicians who gathered at Chelnokov's apartment in early December 1916 that a palace coup would take place soon and the liberals should be prepared for it. Chelnokov, in his letter to Mel'gunov after the revolution, said that it was nothing but talk.[8] According to Rodzianko, General Krymov raised the possibility of a palace coup to the Duma politicians who came to Rodzianko's apartment to listen to his report on conditions at the front. At this meeting Tereshchenko advocated a coup so strongly that Rodzianko had to stop his speech. According to Mel'gunov, an unnamed important public figure went to see Guchkov at the Central War Industries Committee. He was greeted by Tereshchenko, who told the visitor that Guchkov was unavailable at the moment, since he was attending a meeting on the "conspiracy."[9] The talkativeness of the alleged conspirators of course makes one wonder about their seriousness. The dead earnestness of the *narodniki* bomb throwers simply was not to be seen among the liberal conspirators. Miliukov was right when he said: "We were inexperienced revolutionaries and poor conspirators."

Moreover, the existence of the conspiracies, though not the details, was well known to the police and the government. Colonel Globachev, director of the Okhrana, reported to Khabalov on January 19 that "our domestic Yüan Shih-k'ai" in the group of Guchkov, Konovalov, and L'vov intended to take advantage of unexpected events for their personal ambitions. A week later Globachev wrote a more specific warning that a group led by Guchkov, L'vov, S. N. Tretiakov (a Moscow industrialist and member of the Progressist party), Konovalov, and M. M. Fedorov "regard as unachievable their dream of seizing power under the pressure of the demonstration of the masses of the population, and all the more rest their hopes exclusively on the conviction of the inevitability in the near future of a palace coup, supported at least by one of the two army units sympathetic with this group." Nicholas entertained the notion of arresting Guchkov, the central figure of the conspiracies, but Protopopov, who believed that his arrest might provoke a more dangerous reaction than the conspiracy itself, talked him out of it.[10] Nonetheless, the police sent agents to keep the conspirators under surveillance. The conspiracies did exist,

8. Mel'gunov, *Na putiakh*, p. 105.

9. M. V. Rodzianko, *The Reign of Rasputin*, pp. 244-45; Mel'gunov, *Na putiakh*, pp. 151-52.

10. TsGAOR, f. DPOO, op. 1917, d. 669a, ll. 10, 14; f. ChSK, d. 460, l. 158.

but in spite of what Katkov believes, they do not seem to have been serious enough to threaten the tsar.

No conspiracy was actually put into effect, but that does not mean that the conspiracies were insignificant, as Chermenskii argues. Although a palace coup was not accepted as practical by most of the liberals at the beginning of 1917, it was presented as an alternative, though rejected, to Miliukov's parliamentary policy, which had brought the liberals up a blind alley. When the February Revolution erupted, even the liberals who had refused to accept the prospect of a palace coup had to change their minds to avoid a cataclysm. The notion of a palace coup was thus revived during the February Revolution in a different form for different purposes.

Also significant was the extent to which a wide segment of society, even those who supported monarchical principles, believed and accepted as a lesser evil the possibility of a palace coup. Grand Duchess Mariia Pavlovna suggested to Rodzianko the notion of the forcible removal of the tsarina, and was severely reprimanded by him for such irreverent remarks. Grand Dukes Nikolai Mikhailovich and Aleksandr Mikhailovich also suggested the possibility of a palace coup to none other than the prosecutor of the Petrograd Circuit Court, S. V. Zavadskii, who in turn did not conceal his sympathy for the idea.[11] Commenting on the grand dukes' willingness to accept a coup in which they themselves did not wish to take part, Maklakov stated: "The Grand Dukes are incapable of agreeing on a plan of campaign. Not one of them dares show the slightest initiative, and each of them claims to be working solely on his own behalf. They want the Duma to put the match to the powder. In other words, they are expecting of us what we are expecting of them."[12] When the marshal of the nobility of Moscow Province, Bazilevskii, arrived on February 6 in Petrograd, Prince Volkonskii, former deputy minister of internal affairs and the marshal of nobility in Petrograd Province, described the tense mood in Petrograd and hinted that "a decisive event must be started from above without the knowledge and participation of the people."[13] The pervasiveness of such rumors and the secret desire to welcome a palace coup indicate that Russian aristocracy had deserted Nicholas even before the revolution.

Since no liberal conspirators were prepared to throw bombs by themselves, an important element in their plots was the military.

11. Rodzianko, *The Reign of Rasputin,* p. 243; S. V. Zavadskii, "Na velikom izlome," *Arkhiv russkoi revoliutsii* 8 (1923): 40-41.
12. Maurice Paléologue, *An Ambassador's Memoirs* 2: 167-68.
13. OR GBL, f. 15, "Dnevnik Bazilevskogo," p. 87.

But with the notable exceptions of Krymov and Viazemskii, no one in the military seems to have been involved in the plot. Guchkov noted this in his letter to Mel'gunov written after the revolution: "I did a great deal for which I could have been hanged, but little of real achievement, because I could not succeed in involving anyone from the military."[14] The military's refusal to join a plot for a palace coup did not mean, however, that they stood firmly behind the tsar and his government. On the contrary, the military leaders also watched the deteriorating political situation with growing concern. Judging from General Alekseev's correspondence with Guchkov, L'vov's overtures to him concerning a palace coup, and his alleged support for L'vov's proposal, Alekseev's sympathies seem to have rested with the liberal opposition. According to Denikin, Alekseev opposed a palace coup, but he opposed it not because he was unswervingly loyal to the tsar, but because "at the time of war" such a drastic change would seriously affect the war effort. Alekseev's temporary replacement, General Gurko, appealed directly to the tsar to carry out internal reforms. General Ruzskii, commander of the northern front, allegedly said after the revolution that had he known of such a plot, he would have joined it. General Brusilov, commander of the southwestern front, also presumably declared: "If I had to choose between the Emperor and Russia, I would follow Russia."[15] Admiral Nepenin of the Baltic Fleet was said to have thought over the possibility of a palace coup on many sleepless nights. Even Nicholas's uncle, Nikolai Nikolaevich, took two days to think about the possibility of joining L'vov's plot, although he rejected it in the end. It seems clear that the high command was vaguely aware of a plot, and sympathized with it, but refused to join the conspirators. This psychological preparation for a palace coup by the military leaders is important to remember to understand their reaction to the February Revolution.

If the high command secretly sympathized with the plotters, though not with the plots themselves, young officers were less discreet. Young naval officers in the Baltic Fleet, centered around Captain I. I. Rengarten, discussed the possibility of direct action against the government on February 27. This action was to be led by some liberal leaders in cooperation with military leaders at the front. For that purpose the young officers decided to contact K. G. Zhitkov, editor of *Morskii sbornik,* who had been insisting on such an action for a long time, and who maintained close connections with the liberal politicians. On February 28, the officers met again. Prince Cherkasskii

14. Mel'gunov, *Na putiakh,* p. 149.
15. Ibid., p. 156; Rodzianko, *The Reign of Rasputin,* p. 245.

raised the question: "What should we do if a revolution begins on the ships?" Rengarten answered: "We must be prepared for everything. The Stavka, the tsar, can order the fleet to support the old order. Our admiral will then be in a dilemma, and we are obligated to do everything in our power to direct the admiral's decision toward the salvation of Russia, although it might go against instructions from above."[16] The revolution in Petrograd was already five days old, and it was to spread to the Baltic Fleet on the next day. Their "conspiracy" did not go beyond the talking stage, but it must be noted that on the eve of the revolution there were sentiments within the military favoring a palace coup.

Given such prevalent dissatisfaction, one of the curious aspects of the conspiracies is why the military was not actively involved in them. Two explanations are possible. First, the main goal of the military leaders was the continuation of the war to a victorious end. They were not willing to make sacrifices that might disrupt the war effort. The continuation of the bad policies of Nicholas's government, by which they were greatly disturbed, seemed to them a lesser evil than the unpredictable outcome of a forcible change in the midst of war. They were committed to the continuation of the war not merely because they were professional military men but because their patriotism was the foremost principle guiding their conduct. Even before the February Revolution their patriotism was divorced from their loyalty to the tsar and the monarchy. Compared with the inseparable unity of emperor worship and patriotism in every Japanese soldier, the mystique of tsarism did not have a strong enough hold on the highest Russian military leaders, who were supposedly the most important prop holding up the regime. Second, all the military leaders of the tsarist army were trained in the old school, which emphasized that military men were not to be involved in politics. Their inbred skepticism and disdain for domestic politics must have contributed to their refusal to join the conspiracies.

Another curious aspect of Russian wartime politics was the role of the Freemasons. In 1967 George Katkov presented the thesis that the February Revolution was partly inspired by the conspiracies of the masonic organization. According to Katkov the masonic lodges were created in the fall of 1915 explicitly for the political purpose of overthrowing the tsarist regime. The members of this secret organization had infiltrated everywhere—the bureaucracy, the voluntary organizations, and the political parties from the Kadets to the Bolsheviks.

16. I. I. Rengarten, "Fevral'skaia revoliutsiia v balticheskom flote," *Krasnyi arkhiv* 32, no. 2 (1929): 119, 120.

Also the Freemasons were behind every conspiracy for a palace coup. The leaders of the masonic organization were Kerenskii, M. I. Tereshchenko, N. V. Nekrasov, Konovalov, and I. N. Efremov. The military branch of the movement was headed by the Duma deputy, Count Orlov-Davydov, who maintained relations with both Kerenskii and Grand Duke Nikolai Mikhailovich, also a Freemason. Katkov continues: "The division between the initiated and the uninitiated cut straight across all party boundaries. Party allegiances and party discipline had to yield to the stronger tie of the masonic bond." When the Provisional Government was composed during the February Revolution, it was created under the influence of the masonic pressure group.[17]

Two facts must be stressed at the outset. First, the existence of masonic organizations and the masonic ties of some influential political activists during the war appear to be undeniable. Second, historical evidence concerning the masonic movement during the war is so limited that, as Nathan Smith states, any assumption on its role are not only "provisional" but "somewhat premature as well."[18]

A strong masonic movement appeared after the 1905 Revolution. Various lodges were established in Russia as branches of the French masonic organization. In Moscow the lodge Astre was led by a psychiatrist, N. N. Bazhenov, and in St. Petersburg the Cosmos was organized by the famous historian Maksim Kovalevskii and E. V. de Roberti, E. Anichkov, and Iu. Gambarov, and the Northern Star was headed by Kadet lawyer M. S. Margulies and managed by a police spy and Kadet member, Prince D. O. Bebutov. Vasilii Maklakov and journalist A. Amfiteatrov were alleged to be members of the Cosmos.[19] But these organizations apparently had gone out of existence before the war.

In the fall of 1915 the masonic movement experienced a sudden revival, no doubt related to the traumatic defeat on the battlefield. According to E. D. Kuskova, an active member of the movement and a political activist of long standing, who had taken a position between

17. Katkov, *Russia, 1917*, pp. 163-73. Soviet historians generally remain silent on the issue of the masonic movement, with the exception of N. N. Iakovlev, who accepts Katkov's thesis in his book intended as a rejoinder to Solzhenitsyn's *August, 1914*. But Iakovlev's masonic references obviously invited the ire of the authorities, and his book was immediately removed from the bookstores in the Soviet Union. See N. N. Iakovlev, *1 avgusta, 1914 g.* (Moscow, 1974), pp. 3-19.

18. Nathan Smith, "The Role of Russian Freemasonry in the February Revolution: Another Scrap of Evidence," *Slavic Review* 27, no. 4 (1968): 604. This is a translation of part of the unpublished memoirs of V. A. Obolenskii with Smith's commentary.

19. Mel'gunov, *Na putiakh*, pp. 181-83; Grigorii Aronson, *Rossiia nakanune revoliutsii: Istoricheskie etiudy*, pp. 112-13.

the liberals and the moderate Socialists, the new masonic organization had no connection with foreign lodges, had abolished all rituals and mysticism, and was political in nature. It was designed to revive the Union of Liberation, the liberal organization before and during the 1905 Revolution, and to work underground for the liberation of Russia. She explains that the masonic form of organization was necessary to recruit into the political movement members of the bureaucracy and the imperial court who would never have joined any open liberal political organization. Secrecy was one of the most important characteristics of the masonic movement during the war. Each member who was initiated in a lodge swore, in sacramental language, absolute secrecy and willingness to sacrifice his or her life (women were also admitted) for truth and freedom. Each lodge consisted of five members and had no knowledge of the existence of other lodges. All lodges were connected with a higher body, a regional council, and regional councils with the highest organization, the All-Russian Convention, which elected the Supreme Council consisting of three members. A Kadet member, V. A. Obolenskii, was a member of the Supreme Council.[20]

Another characteristic of the masonic organization during the war was that its members were drawn from various political groups of totally different political ideologies and persuasions. In addition to Kuskova and her husband, S. N. Prokopovich, the following political figures were said to be members: Prince L'vov (Progressist), A. F. Kerenskii (Trudovik), N. V. Nekrasov (left-wing Kadet), Vasilii Maklakov (right-wing Kadet), N. S. Chkheidze (Menshevik), N. D. Sokolov (former Bolshevik lawyer), A. I. Konovalov (Progressist), Grand Duke Nikolai Mikhailovich, and M. I. Tereshchenko (chairman of the Kiev War Industries Committee, Kadet). According to Kuskova, at least two Bolsheviks were also members.[21] The masonic organization actively attempted to recruit other public figures. Miliukov was approached, but this rationalist refused to join, saying: "I hate any kind of mysticism." S. Mel'gunov, a Popular Socialist (a right-wing group of Populists), also refused. In Mel'gunov's words, "I decisively refused to join the masonic organization, since for the genuine unification [of political groups] such a traditional appearance seemed unnecessary and anachronistic."[22]

20. Kuskova's letter to N. V. Vol'skii, November 15, 1955, in Aronson, *Rossiia nakanune revoliutsii,* pp. 119, 138; Smith, "The Role of Russian Freemasonry," p. 606.

21. Aronson, *Rossiia nakanune revoliutsii,* p. 110. Obolenskii denies the importance of the Bolsheviks. He states that he knew only one minor Bolshevik who was a member of the masonic organization. Smith, "The Role of Russian Freemasonry," p. 606.

22. Mel'gunov, *Na putiakh,* p. 186.

Kuskova claims that the influence of the masonic organizations was enormous. Its "own people" were everywhere: the Free Economic Society and Technological Society were completely taken over, and the Mining Institute was under its strong influence. Although Katkov accepts Kuskova's contention at face value, there is no evidence to verify her claim.[23] The three institutions she names were by no means the most important liberal organizations. One wonders if the masonic organizations were active in more important organizations such as the War Industries Committee, the Unions of Zemstvos and of Towns, the special councils, the city dumas and the State Duma, and if they were, as Katkov claims without much evidence, how they attempted to influence the decisions within those organizations.

Even if one accepts the existence of such a pervasive network encompassing various organizations and political parties, it is unlikely that its members were united by coherent political programs. Grand Duke Nikolai Mikhailovich's letters to his friend, Frédéric Masson, make it clear that he firmly stood for the monarchist principle.[24] In the Progressive Bloc's discussions during the war, Maklakov, on the one hand, and Nekrasov and Konovalov, on the other, always found themselves at opposite poles. Despite Katkov's contention that the masonic bond was stronger than party discipline, one of the leaders of the Petrograd masonic organization, Obolenskii, states the opposite: "I cannot imagine that it [the masonic organization] played a large role in revolutionary events because its members came from various mutually hostile political parties whose internal cohesion was very much stronger than masonic 'fraternity.' So strong was the enmity among the 'brethren' at this time that I, for example, as chairman of one of the Petersburg lodges, could not call a single meeting after the February Revolution because the members of my lodge simply would not be able to sit around a common table."[25]

Although it remains mere conjecture, the crux of the entire question of masonic conspiracies appears to be nothing more than the personal relations that were established between some—not all—of its members, particularly Kerenskii, Nekrasov, Tereshchenko, Konovalov, and

23. Kuskova's letter to Vol'skii, November 15, 1955; and Kuskova's letter to L. O. Dan, February 12, 1957, in Aronson, *Rossiia nakanune revoliutsii*, pp. 139, 141. Kerenskii denies that the masonic organizations played an important part in the revolution. See Alexander Kerensky, *Russia and History's Turning Point*, pp. 87-89. For Kerenskii and the masonic organizations, see Nina Berberova, *The Italics are Mine* (New York: Harcourt, Brace, & World, 1969), pp. 311-16. Katkov, *Russia, 1917*, pp. 172-76.

24. Nicolas Mikhailovitch, *La fin du tsarisme*, passim.

25. Smith, "The Role of Russian Freemasonry," pp. 607-8.

Efremov. About these men it is possible to speak, as Katkov does, of a personal bond stronger than "party discipline and allegiance," although this bond was not merely a masonic tie. Nekrasov championed the cause of the left-wing Kadets, who advocated the Progressive Bloc's abandonment of parliamentary tactics and the unification of the liberal opposition with the workers' mass movement. Konovalov and Efremov, the leaders of the Progressist party, likewise became disenchanted with Miliukov's moderate leadership of the Progressive Bloc. Having finally walked out of the Bloc, they began to advocate closer cooperation between the liberals and the workers' movement. Konovalov and Tereshchenko were the early advocates of the participation of the workers' group in the War Industries Committee. Kerenskii, on the other hand, became increasingly wary of the violent workers' movement, and believed that it should be restrained within a certain framework to help the liberals with the common struggle against tsarism. All these five men shared two basic political goals of the moment. First, in view of the powerlessness of the Progressive Bloc and other voluntary organizations to lead the struggle against the tsarist regime, it would be necessary to create a center for the opposition movement that would combine both the liberal and the radical left-wing forces. Second, a mass uprising would be dangerous and should be avoided. To control an explosive mass movement, the creation of a center would be imperative. These "five" were thus deeply involved in attempts to establish a Left Bloc in October 1916.[26] The masonic bond undoubtedly facilitated their efforts, but what brought them together were common political goals.

Nevertheless, the Left Bloc never went beyond a loose personal association of the radical intelligentsia, and never became a cohesive political body that could influence the workers' movement. It is possible to speculate that the group of "five" then concluded that the only way to effect a political change without a popular uprising would be through a palace coup. Nekrasov and Tereshchenko cooperated with Guchkov in plotting a palace coup, and the Okhrana reports list Konovalov's name among the conspirators. In January, Nekrasov unsuccessfully attempted to recruit Maklakov and Shul'gin into the conspiracy.[27] It seems unlikely, as Katkov contends, that all the members of the masonic organizations were deeply involved in this conspiracy, but it seems certain, and not surprising, that persons like Nekrasov, Tereshchenko, and Konovalov had finally come to choose a palace coup as the only viable alternative.

26. See chap. 6.
27. Mel'gunov, *Na putiakh*, p. 193; V. V. Shul'gin, *Dni*, pp. 127-29.

The conspiracies for a palace coup and the masonic movement grew out of the despair and powerlessness of the Russian liberals on the eve of the revolution. Guchkov and the "masonic five" believed that after all other means had been exhausted, a palace coup would be the only way to avoid a revolution, while Miliukov and other liberals opposed it for fear that such a coup might touch off a cataclysm they could not control. In the end, the difference did not matter, because a popular uprising struck first. But ironically it was the popular uprising itself that revived the idea of a palace coup and made it acceptable to most of the liberals during the February Revolution.

11

THE FOOD SUPPLY CRISIS
AND THE WORKERS

 The crack in the dike that eventually let in the deluge that swept away the old regime was the problem of food, which reached an alarmingly acute stage in the third winter of the war. When Protopopov's food policy ended in miscarriage in October 1916, Nicholas appointed A. A. Rittikh the new minister of agriculture. Rittikh, an able administrator who had once worked under Krivoshein, immediately began working energetically to solve the problem. On November 29 he launched a program of requisition *(razverstka)* that imposed a procurement quota on each province, district, and village. Although this program was interrupted by the February Revolution and not given a chance to reach completion, signs of failure were already apparent. The program obviously conflicted with the interests of the producers, who applied considerable pressure for the quota to be lowered. Even before the requisition was put into effect, the quota was lowered to 89 percent of the original plan prepared by the Special Council for Food Supply at the provincial level, 63 percent at the district level, and finally 52 percent at the village level. Moreover, producers gained another concession from Rittikh in raising the fixed price higher than the original plan. In addition, the stated purpose of the requisition policy was to provide the army and the war industries with food. The task of feeding the general population—among whom the shortage was most acute—still remained in the hands of the local self-governments.[1]

1. N. D. Kondrat'ev, *Rynok khlebov i ego regulirovanie vo vremia voiny i revoliutsii*, pp. 108-9.

Although Rittikh traveled from one province to another in January and February 1917 to drum up support for his program, the food supply in Petrograd did not improve. On the contrary, it got worse. On February 13, 1917, Petrograd *gradonachal'nik* Balk petitioned Golitsyn to improve the transfer of flour to Petrograd. He revealed that in the last week the shipments of flour had been reduced to 5,000 poods a day under the norm of 60,000 poods (1 pood = 16.38 kilograms or 36 pounds). By February 14, the reserves of rye flour in Petrograd had dwindled to 664,000 poods, and of wheat flour to 50,000 poods. This was barely enough to last twenty days on the assumption that each person would receive one funt (0.90 pound or 409.4 grams) of flour a day. With this amount the government was supposed to feed the two and one-half million people of Petrograd for at least two months.[2] Within ten days after February 14 the reserves of flour further dropped by 36 percent or to 460,000 poods of rye and wheat combined.

The supply mechanism in Petrograd suffered from the existence of two conflicting authorities. The commissioner of food supply under the *gradonachal'nik* was formally responsible for the distribution of food in the city. But since the *gradonachal'stvo* did not have resources and personnel to handle the job, the practical tasks of food supply were entrusted to the Food Supply Commission of the city duma. As the situation worsened, conflicts between the two authorities arose. Both the city duma and the *gradonachal'nik* tried to stop further deterioration of the food situation. The commissioner of food supply attempted to limit the consumption of flour by banning the baking and sale of buns, pies, cakes, and cookies; the city administration prohibited the sale of meat during *Maslenitsa* (a three-day religious holiday). To protect the dwindling reserves the *gradonachal'nik* prohibited the Petrograd Union of Consumers from selling flour to the workers' consumer cooperatives and the workers' dining halls—a policy that angered the workers.[3] The *gradonachal'stvo* also discussed the possibility of introducing rationing, but the overwhelming opinion was against it, since enforcement would be exceedingly difficult. On the whole, the *gradonachal'stvo* reacted lethargically and failed to adopt effective measures to improve the situation.

Dissatisfied with the inaction of the *gradonachal'stvo*, the liberals demanded that the entire food supply matter be handed over to the

2. TsGIA, f. 1276, op. 15, d. 48, ℓ. 72; *Rech'*, February 14, 1917; I. P. Leiberov, *Petrogradskii proletariat v Fevral'skoi revoliutsii* 2: 17.

3. *Rech'*, January 28 and February 4, 1917; Leiberov, *Petrogradskii proletariat v Fevral'skoi revoliutsii* 2: 26.

city duma. The city administration finally endorsed this demand, while
V. G. Groman and Petr Struve, representatives of the Union of Towns
in the Special Council for Food Supply, advocated the transfer of the
food supply matter completely to the municipal self-governments.
Another policy that was strongly advocated by the liberals was the
introduction of rationing. At the Petrograd City Duma on February 13,
a majority rejected the proposal to appeal to the populace to limit
consumption of flour on the grounds that such an appeal would cause
a panic, but the city duma unanimously approved the proposal to
introduce rationing. In mid-February the delivery of rye flour dropped
to a new low, and that further drained the reserves of the city administration. Faced with a crisis and constant pressure from the liberals,
the *gradonachal'nik* and the military authority finally decided to adopt
a rationing system, which was to be introduced at the beginning of
March.[4] After this decision was made on February 19, rumors spread
that food rationing, restricting the per capita consumption of bread
to one funt a day, would be introduced in the near future. This caused
a panic. Enormous queues formed in front of bakeries, and there
were scattered incidents of attacks on bakeries.[5]

The effects of the food supply crisis were most vividly described
in an Okhrana report written on the eve of the February Revolution.
According to this, food prices rose markedly over even the price indices
for December 16, 1916. The percentage of increase in the price of
various items is indicated in Table 7.[6]

TABLE 7

INCREASE IN FOOD PRICES,
DECEMBER 16, 1916-FEBRUARY 1917

(In percentages)			
Potatoes	25%	Bread	15%
Carrots, turnips	35	Chocolate	100
Cabbage	25	Sugar candy	75
Meat	20	Cookies, sweet rolls	100
Sausage	50	Apples	70
Ham	60	Pears, oranges	150
Butter	15	Fabric	50-60
Cheese	25	Shoes	30
Eggs	20	Underwear	25
Milk	40		

4. *Rech'*, February 9, 12, 14, 17, and 23, 1917.
5. Leiberov, *Petrogradskii proletariat v Fevral'skoi revoliutsii* 2: 33.
6. TsGAOR, f. POO, op. 5, d. 669 (1917) g., ll. 25-33.

The Okhrana agent pointed out that no one without personal connections had access to flour or bread, although in the newspapers optimistic assurances of sufficient reserves of flour were reported almost daily, and the people heard and saw with their own eyes that major bakeries were selling their surpluses to other merchants. Although people were starving, freshly baked white bread was always available in expensive restaurants. Before the war a bakery could sell 10,000 rolls a day, but now most bakeries sold no more than 800 rolls, which were usually gone in one or two hours. Lack of flour forced many bakeries to close. This meant that the housewives had to travel further across town to stand in long queues. Many items such as meat, ham, and sausage disappeared from the markets. Milk was priced so high that poor people could not afford it. Many workers' diets consisted of whatever small amount of bread they managed to buy and cabbage soup. Not only food items disappeared but other essential materials as well—boots, galoshes, fabric, soap, and medicine. Firewood was so expensive that many people were forced to decide whether they should heat their apartment and survive on near-starvation rations or whether they should eat and freeze to death. This was particularly hard on the children, who had been deprived of milk, eggs, sweet tea, and butter, and who were now in the precarious position of losing the last vital source of nourishment—bread. The Okhrana agent poignantly remarked:

Resentment is felt worse in large families, where children are starving in the most literal sense of the word, and where no other words are heard except, "Peace, immediate peace, peace at all costs." And these mothers, exhausted from standing endlessly at the tail of queues, and having suffered so much in watching their half-starving and sick children, are perhaps much closer to a revolution than Messrs. Miliukov, Rodichev and Co., and of course, they are much more dangerous, since they are the stockpiles of flammable material, needing only a spark to set them afire.[7]

Rents also went up considerably, eating up a major portion of the workers' wages. The agent observed that alcoholism had reached epidemic proportions among the workers since September 1916. There was a growing conviction among the more politically conscious workers that a peaceful solution of the food problem would be impossible, and that it would take a revolution for the workers to escape from this misery. The Okhrana agent ominously predicted: "The underground revolutionary parties are preparing a revolution, but a revolution, if it takes place, will be spontaneous, quite likely a hunger riot."[8]

7. Ibid., ℓ. 27.
8. Ibid., ℓ. 33.

It appears certain that the acute shortage of food contributed to the sudden revival of the strike movement at the beginning of 1917 after two months' lull. From January 1 through February 22, 1917, there were 268 strikes, involving 320,517 strikers, an average of 5.6 strikes and 6,048.6 participants a day.[9] Each strike was reported in the daily telephone reports of the Okhrana to the director of the police. There is no need to describe all such reports, which generally give the number of strikers and the nature of demands. Most of the strikes did not last more than one day and ended in failure, since the economic demands were far above what the employers could afford. Faced with a rapidly diminishing supply of raw materials, many factories were forced to curtail production, and employers were in no position to make increases in wages by 50 to 100 percent, which the workers felt perfectly justified in asking.[10] When the strike—the last resort—failed to help the workers improve their lot, they became receptive to propaganda of political agitators for more radical action.

Leiberov emphasizes two characteristics of the January-February strike movement. First, the distinction between economic strikes and political strikes, arbitrarily made by the factory inspectors, became increasingly useless. Second, although political strikes were spearheaded by experienced activists in large factories, economic strikes spread to factories that had never before been involved in the strike movement. The data in Appendix 2 further indicate two important trends of the 1917 strikes. First, although the metalworkers of factories employing between 1,000 and 8,000 workers continued to stand at the forefront of the strike movement, workers from smaller metal factories employing less than 1,000 began to participate. Second, political strikes began to involve workers of the largest munition plants as well as the textile workers who had generally abstained from the political strikes previously. One of the most protracted strikes took place in the textile mills Voronin, Liutsh, Chesher in the Vyborg District. The strike, which involved women workers almost exclusively, lasted more than a month. Whether this strike was sustained by particular leaders, or whether an organized political group attempted to inject leadership, is not known, but its duration indicates that discontent

9. See table 6. Of these, 132 political strikes with 147,655 strikers were on January 9.

10. For Okhrana reports on strikes in January and February, see TsGAOR, f. POO, op. 5, d. 669 (1917 g.), ll. 4, 5, 7, 8, 19-23, 45, 56, 60, 153-54, 255-56, 269, 278; TsGAOR, f. POO, 1917 g., d. 669a, ll. 20-23, 40-45, 51-52, 54-55, 62; TsGAOR, f. DPOO, d. 341, ch. 57/1917 g., ll. 5, 18, 27; TsGAOR, f. DPOO, d. 61, ch. 2, 1. B, 1917 g., ll. 1-2, 12, 14-24.

had reached the previously unorganized women workers in the textile factories.[11] Also the workers of another textile mill, Leontiev, were involved in a five-day strike in January. It is important to remember that there were women workers experienced in organizing a strike in these textile mills in the Vyborg District from which the strike movement that touched off the February Revolution was initiated.

The revolutionary organizations scrambled to control the workers under their influence. Wishing to exploit their discontent, all the revolutionary parties called for a one-day strike on January 9, the anniversary of Bloody Sunday. The workers' group, which had opposed a strike on January 9 the previous year, appealed to the workers to stage a strike and demonstration in support of the Duma in its struggle against the government. The Bolshevik Petersburg Committee also decided to concentrate its propaganda on the January 9 strike and demonstration, intending to lead the demonstration to a confrontation with the police. But the police moved fast and arrested leading Bolshevik activists on December 9, 10, 18, 19, and 28, and January 2. The December 28 raid practically annihilated the Petersburg Committee, with the arrests of F. A. Lemeshev, I. D. Andreev, eight other members, and the confiscation of their illegal printing press.[12] Despite this blow the hastily reconstructed Petersburg Committee continued propaganda among those workers promoting the strike, but only the Vyborg District Committee and the Latvian National Committee managed to issue leaflets. Although the police arrest temporarily slowed down Bolshevik propaganda, the Menshevik initiative group and the Mezhraiontsy, forming a united front with the Bolsheviks, took up the slack by issuing the leaflets. The initiative group appealed to the workers to strike against the war and the monarchy and for the establishment of a republican system and the convocation of a constituent assembly. In their leaflet the Mezhraiontsy attacked the workers' group, and urged the workers to stage a strike, not in support of "Prince L'vov, Miliukov, and Co.," as the workers' group encouraged, but against the war, tsarism, and the bourgeoisie. But unlike the Bolsheviks the Mezhraiontsy called for the unification of the Bolsheviks and the Mensheviks. Only under the leadership of a united Social Democratic party could the proletariat be victorious against tsarism and the bourgeoisie.[13]

11. Leiberov, *Petrogradskii proletariat v Fevral'skoi revoliutsii* 2:224; TsGAOR, f. POO, op. 5, d. 669 (1917 g.), ll. 19, 20, 45, 56; TsGAOR, f. POO, 1917 g., d. 669 a, ll. 22, 23, 44.

12. TsGAOR, f. DPOO, 1917 g., d. 5 ch. 57/1917 g., ll. 1-3, 18; *Rabochee dvizhenie v Petrograde*, pp. 520-23; "Iz proshlogo Leningradskoi organizatsii VKP (b)," *Krasnaia letopis'* 42, no. 3 (1931): 37-38.

13. TsGAOR, f. DPOO, 1917 g., d. 5 ch. 57/1917 g., l. 18; A. Shliapnikov,

On January 9, 1917, over 140,000 workers from at least 120 factories, or more than 40 percent of the total number of workers in Petrograd, participated in the strike. In the Vyborg and Nevskii districts it took on the character of a general strike. It was more than twice as large as the previous year's anniversary strike (67,000 workers of 55 factories), and even exceeded the 1914 strike, the largest one on January 9 until then (110,000 workers).[14] Although a great number of workers participated in the one-day strike, massive demonstrations did not take place. Some workers attempted to demonstrate in the Vyborg District, but they were easily scattered by the police. Petrograd security authorities were relieved by the lack of violence and proudly attributed this to the successful repression of the Bolshevik underground organizations.[15]

After the January 9 strike the revolutionary parties became embroiled in serious competition for control of the workers' movement in Petrograd. As their next move the workers' group planned a strike and a massive demonstration in front of the Tauride Palace on February 14 in support of the Duma. In mid-January the workers' group sent instructions to various workers' organizations in Petrograd, urging them to intensify propaganda work for the February 14 demonstration. This circular stated that the success of the general strike on January 9 was an indication that Petrograd workers considered a major confrontation between the bourgeoisie and tsarism to be inevitable. "This confrontation will be beneficial to democracy," the letter continued, "and in such a struggle, the proletariat will tip the balance of the scale by its organized activities." Gvozdev, Abrasimov, Breido, Emel'ianov, and other leaders busily went from factory to factory and spoke at mass rallies to drum up support for their plan.[16] On January 26 the workers' group adopted a resolution intended to be distributed among the workers. Responding to the accusation of the antiwar groups that the workers' group stood for the war, the workers' group replied

---

Semnadtsatyi god 1:264-68, 271-72.

14. For the strike figures on January 9, 1917, see TsGAOR, f. POO, op. 5, d. 669 (1917 g.), ℓℓ. 41-42; TsGAOR, f. DPOO, d. 158/1917 g., ℓℓ. 1-2; *Rabochee dvizhenie v Petrograde*, pp. 523-26. According to all these sources, 144,498 workers from 114 factories struck on this day. Leiberov adds the figures that are not included in the Okhrana reports and comes up with the following totals: 147,655 (or 42.8 percent of all workers) from 132 factories (or 14.6 percent of the total number of factories). Leiberov, *Petrogradskii proletariat v Fevral'skoi revoliutsii* 1:288. See also Appendix 2, col. 11.

15. Shliapnikov, *Semnadtsatyi god* 1:25; TsGAOR, f. DPOO, d. 158/1917 g., ℓℓ. 1-2, 3-4.

16. TsGAOR, f. DPOO, d. 347, 46/1917, ℓ. 9; TsGAOR, f. DPOO, d. 347, ℓ. 15.

that peace achieved by the present government would bring to the people even more unhappiness, misery, and slavery. The main task of the proletariat would not be to end the war but rather to overthrow the autocracy. The proletariat should, therefore, actively participate in the impending confrontation between the bourgeoisie and the autocracy on the opening day of the Duma. For that purpose the workers' group urged the workers to create factory strike committees.[17]

The leftward turn of the workers' group alarmed the government. On January 3 Khabalov wrote a letter to Guchkov, in which he complained about the workers' group's "subversive activities." According to Khabalov, the workers' group was trying to establish a Social Democratic republic by overthrowing a legitimate government. Protopopov considered the possibility of linking the workers' movement with the liberal opposition most dangerous, and began a press campaign against the workers' group.[18] But he feared that the arrest of its members might provoke a massive strike movement. He consulted the tsar on this matter, and Nicholas said: "What can we do? Arrest them."[19] Their resolution gave Protopopov a favorable excuse. On January 27 Protopopov's police raided the workers' group while its members were having a meeting in their office on the Liteinyi. Altogether eleven members, including its chairman, Gvozdev, secretary, Bogdanov, and the five workers who were present at the meeting, were arrested. It was only because of Guchkov's intervention that Gvozdev was released into Guchkov's custody, on the grounds of illness. Only three members of the group, a police spy, Abrasimov, and two others, Ia. S. Ostapenko and Anasovskii, escaped arrest. From then on Ostapenko and Anasovskii continued their propaganda as underground revolutionary activists on behalf of the workers' group, until they, too, were arrested on February 25.[20]

The arrest deprived the workers' group of its leaders, forced the activists to go underground, and destroyed the possibility of united action between the liberals and the working class. Despite this blow, the remaining members of the workers' group and the activists who supported it continued propaganda for the February 14 demonstration. An oratorial group was formed and engaged in intensified propaganda activities, particularly in Erikson, Obukhov, Arsenal, and other large state factories.[21] In view of the persistent rumor that Abrasimov was

17. Shliapnikov, *Semnadtsatyi god* 1:279-80.
18. TsGAOR, f. DPOO, d. 347/1917, ℓℓ. 2g., 21.
19. TsGAOR, f. ChSK, d. 460, ℓℓ. 154-57.
20. TsGAOR, f. DPOO, d. 347/1917 g., ℓℓ. 3-5.
21. TsGAOR, f. POO, op. 5, d. 669, 1917 g., ℓ. 25; Leiberov, *Petrogradskii proletariat Fevral'skoi revoliutsii* 2:318.

a police provocateur, the remaining members broke off relations with him.

The attempts of the workers' group to organize a political offensive on February 14 met with hostility from the antiwar groups. The initiative group, responding to the distributed leaflets, declared that the Duma, "anti-people in its composition and reactionary in its political demands, is not capable of carrying out a struggle for the interests of people and will in the decisive moment go with the government against the people rather than with the people against the government." The Duma stood for the continuation of the war against the wishes of the people, while in internal policies it "wants to maintain all the privileges of the propertied classes untouched." Thus the initiative group objected to the idea of the workers' group to "subordinate the interests of the working class to the interests of the bourgeoisie," and to use the workers' movement as an "instrument" of the bourgeois opposition.[22]

Going one step further than the initiative group, the Bolsheviks proposed an alternative move to disrupt the action organized by the workers' group. On February 2 the Petersburg Committee decided to organize a one-day strike on February 10 to commemorate the anniversary of the trial of the Bolshevik Duma deputies. The Petersburg Committee's decision, however, ignored a "small detail," as Shliapnikov pointed out. The three-day religious holiday, *Maslenitsa,* was to start on February 9, and on February 10 most of the factories would be either closed or on curtailed working hours.[23] Taking this into consideration, the Russian Bureau proposed a one-day strike on February 13, and if the movement received the overwhelming support of the workers, the Bolsheviks were to take the initiative in the strike movement on February 14 from the hands of the workers' group. The Russian Bureau's proposal, however, was too moderate for the members of the Petersburg Committee, since the former still subordinated its policy to the initiative of the workers' group. Despite the attempts of the Russian Bureau to talk them out of it, the Petersburg Committee went ahead with their original plan.

The Mezhraiontsy supported the Petersburg Committee's proposal to stage a one-day strike on February 10, but they were more cautious about "premature action" at a time when the working class was not yet organized under a united Social Democratic party and when the workers had not established solidarity with the soldiers.[24]

22. Shliapnikov, *Semnadtsatyi god* 1: 287-90.
23. TsGIA, f. 1405, op. 530, d. 1060, ℓℓ. 20-22; TsGAOR, f. POO, 1917 g., d. 669a, ℓℓ. 38-39; Shliapnikov, *Semnadtsatyi god* 1:41-42.
24. Shliapnikov, *Semnadtsatyi god* 1: 43-44.

The police were alarmed by the discussions of the workers' offensive as reported by the Okhrana agents, who were convinced that there would be a large-scale "disturbance" from February 10 to February 14. In preparation the security agencies of Petrograd mapped out an elaborate plan to suppress disorders and on February 9 a proclamation was issued in the name of Khabalov that any demonstration would be countered with severe measures by the police. On the following day Miliukov's statement, which attempted to dissuade the workers from strike and demonstration, was printed in Petrograd newspapers side by side with Khabalov's proclamation.[25] Miliukov insinuated that the appeal for the demonstration was the insidious work of German spies. If Miliukov's statement indicated a division of the Progressive Bloc in its attitude toward the workers' movement, it had no tangible effect on the workers' actions. The movement in Petrograd was to the point where neither Miliukov's prestige nor the ugly specter of German spies could stem its tide.

On February 10 most factories were closed at ten o'clock in the morning for the *Maslenitsa* holiday. In some factories it was payday. With the exception of a few political rallies held at the initiative of the Bolshevik activists, the Petersburg Committee's attempt to organize a strike was a complete fiasco. Only 424 workers of three factories struck on this day.[26] The failure of the February 10 strike divided the antiwar groups over what to do about the proposed February 14 strike. The Russian Bureau tried to regroup the demoralized Bolshevik activists for the February 13 strike, but could not get much cooperation from them. The Mezhraiontsy distributed a leaflet appealing to the workers not to participate in the demonstration on February 14, but decided to take part if spontaneous demonstrations sprang up. On the other hand, the initiative group decided to join the demonstration and to take the initiative from the hands of the workers' group. On February 13, at the students' political rallies attended by a small group of students at the Polytechnical Institute and the Psychoneurological Institute, a Bolshevik-inspired resolution for a strike on February 13 was passed, but this had no practical significance, and no workers responded to the Russian Bureau's strike call on that day.[27]

25. TsGAOR, f. POO, 1917 g., d. 669a, ℓℓ. 38-39; TsGIA, f. 1405, op. 530, d. 1060, ℓℓ. 20-22; TsGAOR, f. DPOO, d. 341, ch. 57/1917, ℓℓ. 6-7; see chap. 8. Also see *Rech'*, February 10, 1917.

26. Shliapnikov, *Semnadtsatyi god* 1: 311; Leiberov, *Petrogradskii proletariat v Fevral'skoi revoliutsii* 1: 327.

27. I. Iurenev, "Mezhraionka, 1911-1917 gg.," *Proletarskaia revoliutsiia* 25, no. 2 (1924): 131-33; R. Kovnator, "Nakanune 'fevralia': otryvki iz vospominanii," *Revoliutsionnoe iunoshestvo, 1905-1917*, p. 186; Shliapnikov, *Semnadtsatyi god* 1: 56, 312.

On February 14 more than 84,000 workers from 52 factories participated in the strike.[28] Aivaz, Petrograd Metal Factory, Putilov, and Obukhov, where the workers' group had concentrated its propaganda activities, were the major forces. A majority of strikers, however, quietly went home, although it was noted that in two areas—the Vyborg District and the Peterhof Chaussée—some attempts were made to stage a demonstration. But the demonstrations were easily crushed by the police. Security authorities took extraordinary precautions to protect government buildings, factories, and railway stations, and in accordance with the plan, in addition to the police, troops were assigned to prescribed positions.[29] Security was extremely tight near the Tauride Palace, where the workers' group had appealed to the workers to stage a massive demonstration. But on this day no one could get near the Tauride Palace. Shliapnikov, dressed as a respectable "bourgeois," took an inspection tour near the Tauride Palace and the Smol'nyi Institute, but he saw no "mass demonstration." Some residents gathered nervously near the palace, and servants and doormen stood sheepishly on street corners, expecting to see "disorders." Even the police were hidden from sight. Shliapnikov remarked: "Thus I was not fortunate enough to see the 'mass support' for the State Duma." It was reported that only two- to three-hundred demonstrators appeared near the Tauride Palace, but they were immediately chased away by the police.[30]

On many university campuses the students held political rallies, although classes went on as usual. At the Petrograd Imperial University, about three hundred students gathered in the famous long corridor. They attempted to disrupt lectures, but ran away at the sight of the police. Some of the students went to the Tauride Palace and others decided to stage a demonstration on the Nevskii. At Bestuzhev Women's College, six hundred students joined a rally, where they adopted a resolution calling for "the continuation of the war with the Allies in solidarity with the State Duma, but not in agreement with the policies of the government." At the Polytechnic Institute about two hundred students decided to stage a demonstration in Kazan Square on the Nevskii. A demonstration was attempted on the Nevskii, presumably inspired by the Bolshevik students eager to take

28. TsGAOR, f. DPOO, d. 341, ch. 57/1917, 𝑙. 8. According to another Okhrana report, there were 89,576 workers from 58 factories. TsGAOR, f. POO, 1917 g., d. 669a, 𝑙. 46. See also Appendix 2, col. 12.

29. See chap. 8. Leiberov, *Petrogradskii proletariat v Fevral'skoi revoliutsii* 1: 330-31.

30. Shliapnikov, *Semnadtsatyi god* 1: 56-57; TsGAOR, f. DPOO, d. 341, ch. 57/1917 g., 𝑙. 8; TsGAOR, f. POO, 1917 g., d. 669a, 𝑙. 46.

the initiative away from the leaders of the workers' group, but the demonstrators were quickly dispersed by the police. During the confrontation nine university students, seven high-school students, and four workers were arrested.[31]

The small turnout of strikers compared with the January 9 strike and lack of any massive demonstration in front of the Tauride Palace have led Soviet historians to conclude that the February 14 offensive proposed by the workers' group was a dismal failure.[32] But considering the enormous handicap inflicted by the arrest of almost all its leaders, the persistent opposition of the Bolsheviks, Mezhraiontsy, and the initiative group, and the scare tactics used by Miliukov and Khabalov, the workers' group proved its viability as a leading group in the workers' movement by bringing out more than half of the number of strikers in the January 9 strike. No doubt it would be a mistake to argue that all the strike participants on February 14 were supporters of the workers' group, as it would be incorrect to assume that all the workers who took part in the October strike in 1916 consciously supported the Bolsheviks. It appears that the fine doctrinal differences that separated the two groups of the workers' movement did not play an important part in the workers' decision. A majority of workers still remained well beyond the firm grasp of either group, but what the strike on February 14 proved was the willingness of many workers to act in response to the call to overthrow the regime.

After February 14 the strike movement quickly picked up tempo. In the latter half of February two huge plants, the Izhora Factory and the Putilov Factory, were struck. The Izhora, located in Kolpino, was one of the largest state weapons factories, where an underground Bolshevik organization had been actively organizing the factory workers. Various workshops in this factory had presented their economic demands between January 30 and February 3: an increase in hourly wages, an increase of overtime wages by 350 to 450 percent, the provision of heated latrines in the workshops, free medical aid for the workers and their families, and an eight-hour workday.[33] On February 8 the factory management conveyed its partial acceptance of the demands through the *starosta*, but the workers found this answer inadequate. On February 9 all the workshops except two were shut down. The workers, about three thousand in number, who set up a picket line near the factory gate, refused to admit other workers.

31. TsGAOR, f. DPOO, d. 341, ch. 57/1917, ℓ. 8; TsGAOR, f. POO, 1917 g., d. 669a, ℓ. 46; Shliapnikov, *Semnadtsatyi god* 1:312.
32. Leiberov, "Petrogradskii proletariat v gody pervoi mirovoi voiny," p. 511; E. N. Burdzhalov, *Vtoraia russkaia revoliutsiia: Vosstanie v Petrograde*, pp. 107-8.
33. TsGAOR, f. DPOO, d. 61, ch. 2 1B, 1917 g., ℓ. 14.

Two workers who ventured to break through the picket line had dirty machine oil thrown in their faces.[34] On February 13, Izhora employees resubmitted their demands, but the management refused to negotiate. The excited workers held a meeting at which a Bolshevik worker, Panov, spoke against the proposed strike call by the "Gvozdevites" on February 14. The management ordered the workers to return to work by February 15. Despite the Bolshevik workers' appeal not to strike, the workers continued the strike on February 14. The political rally held in the factory was broken up by the Cossacks, but according to the Okhrana, "in general there was an impression that the Cossacks were on the side of the workers."[35] In defiance of the administration's order, the workers did not report to work on February 15, and held a massive political rally in the factory courtyard. No sooner had the Bolshevik worker Panov begun his speech than the Kolpino police chief, accompanied by the Cossacks, attempted to arrest him. By the time they reached the speaker's platform, Panov was securely hidden among the crowd of workers. Another Bolshevik, Mareev, stood up on a piece of heavy machinery and began his speech. A Cossack officer attempted to stop him: "Russia is in danger, and you are appealing for strike. What are you doing? You must not do this." At this point, a representative from the Petersburg Committee sprang up on the railing and shouted at the officer: "Shame on you, Mr. Officer. You are the one who is ruining Russia. People are demanding bread." The meeting was broken up by the Cossacks, but the workers shifted the meeting place from one workshop to another through narrow passageways, where the Cossacks' horses could not go. On February 16 the factory administration declared a lockout.[36]

On the following day 478 workers of the gun-carriage punching workshop of Putilov Factory abandoned their work and demanded an increase in wages. Despite the administrator's threat that the workshop would be closed down, the workers continued the strike for three days. On February 20 the strike spread to 830 workers in the machine workshop and 850 workers in the boiler workshop, and on the following day to 1,000 workers in the assembly workshop. A huge rally was held in the factory courtyard in which speakers appealed to other workers to join the strike. Fearing that a factory general strike might be declared, the factory administration resorted to a lockout. On February 22 the factory gates were tightly secured, and the workers read the proclamation issued by the director of the factory,

34. Ibid., ℓ. 15; TsGAOR, f. POO, op. 5, d. 669, 1917 g., ℓ. 255.
35. TsGAOR, f. POO, d. 669 (1917 g.), ℓ. 255.
36. Ibid.

Major-General Dublitskii, declaring that "in view of the systematic disruption of order" the factory would be closed for an indefinite period.[37] Thus, 26,700 workers at the Putilov Factory were out of work. According to Putilov worker A. Grigelevich, the angered workers held a rally outside the factory gate. Some proposed that they break the gates and go into the factory, but others advocated that they go around the city in an attempt to draw other factories into the strike. Reportedly the workers elected a strike committee on the spot, marched along the Peterhof Chaussée toward the Narva Gates, and disrupted the work of Tentelev Chemical Factory on the way.[38] The lockout, however, deprived the Putilov workers of a gathering place, something they needed to sustain the momentum of the strike movement. In spite of the often repeated misconception that the Putilov strike touched off the February Revolution, the Putilov workers remained inactive until February 25, the third day of the February Revolution.

The strike movement crescendoed—on February 20, 1,486 workers of the Putilov Shipyard, 2,000 workers of the Petrograd Wagon Factory, and 1,200 workers of the Russian Cotton Manufacture struck for an increase in wages. On February 21, these factories were joined by 741 workers from the boiler workshop of the Obukhov Factory. Drivers and conductors of the city trams presented their demand to the city administration for a wage increase. On February 22, the strike spread to 700 workers in Perun in the Narva District, 600 workers in the Russian-Baltic Aeronautic Factory, 200 workers in the Franco-Russian Factory, 1,000 workers in Lebedev Jute, 80 workers in Baranovskii, and 300 workers in the Petrograd Pipe Factory. At Parviainen, 2,000 workers held a short meeting *(letnyi skhodka)* to discuss the food crisis. The textile workers of Voronin, Liutsh, and Chesher struck again, demanding a 50 percent wage increase and the establishment of a bread shop in the factory.[39] These strikes were still isolated from one another, but they were, like the rumbling of thunder, sure signs of an approaching storm.

---

37. TsGAOR, f. POO, 1917 g., 669a, ℓℓ. 51, 55; TsGAOR, f. POO, op. 5, d. 669, ℓℓ. 269-70, 278.

38. Burdzhalov, *Vtoraia russkaia revoliutsiia: Vosstanie v Petrograde*, p. 116.

39. TsGAOR, f. POO, 1917 g., d. 669a, ℓ. 54; TsGAOR, f. POO, op. 5, d. 669, ℓℓ. 154, 269-70, 278, 292-93. According to an Okhrana report, 7,500 workers of New Lessner and 1,500 workers of Russian Renault struck on February 22. Ibid., ℓ. 11. This must be a mistake. No other records mention strikes in these factories.

PART III

THE UPRISING

Demonstrators in the Nevskii Prospekt (Stinton Jones, *Russia in Revolution*); *preceding page*, insurgents firing at police (Hoover Institution)

12

THE BEGINNING:

FEBRUARY 23

Clara Zetkin, a famed German Social Democrat, proposed naming March 8 (February 23 on the Julian calendar) International Women's Day at the Second International Conference of Women Socialists held in Copenhagen in 1910. The first demonstrations in celebration of this day took place in Germany, Austria, Switzerland, and Denmark in 1911, but its significance soon became lost among the western Socialists in the holocaust of the World War. Russian Socialists celebrated this day first in 1913 in a miserably small demonstration in St. Petersburg, but unlike their colleagues in western Europe a small group of radical antiwar Socialists managed to keep the memory of this day alive even in the midst of the war by distributing leaflets against the war. Yet February 23 was not as well imbedded into the tradition of the workers' movement in Russia as May Day or January 9. Thus when International Women's Day approached in 1917, it is not surprising that none of the Russian Socialist parties greeted it with great enthusiasm and determination, though actually it was the spark that ignited the Russian Revolution of 1917.

From the end of December the Mezhraiontsy had tried to stage a united action with the Bolshevik Petersburg Committee and the Menshevik initiative group for the celebration of International Women's Day, but the three groups could not agree on slogans and decided to act independently. The initiative group devoted one issue of their journal, *Trud*, to celebration of the day.[1] The Mezhraiontsy were the most

1. I. Iurenev, "Mezhraionka, 1911-1917 gg.," *Proletarskaia revoliutsiia* 25, no. 2 (1924): 133-34; O. A. Ermanskii, *Iz perezhitogo*, pp. 138-39.

active, managing to distribute leaflets among the workers. The leaflet explained in simple language that the workers, particularly the
women, were victimized by the war, which continued only for profits
to capitalists. Stressing that their misery and hunger would not be
eliminated unless the capitalist system were overthrown, the leaflet
appealed to the workers: "The government is guilty; it started the
war and cannot end it. It is destroying the country and your starving
is their fault. The capitalists are guilty; for their profit the war goes
on. It's about time to tell them loud: Enough! Down with the criminal
government and all its gang of thieves and murderers. Long live peace!"
Despite its inflammatory language, the leaflet was intended to serve
no more than educational purposes; certainly it was not designed to
incite the workers to direct action in the streets. The Mezhraiontsy
held a series of "educational" meetings from February 20 to February 23 in Aivaz Factory and the workers' cooperative, Ob"edi-
nenie.[2]

The Bolsheviks failed to issue any leaflets at all on this day, since,
according to Shliapnikov, the printing office of the Petersburg Committee had been destroyed by the police raid.[3] The Bolshevik inaction,
however, was the result of the policy of the Russian Bureau of the Central Committee, led by Shliapnikov himself, rather than of the technical
difficulties. The bureau, considering the build-up of organizational
strength of the party its most urgent task, directed lower party organs
not to divert unnecessary energy for this relatively insignificant occasion
and to restrict their activities to propaganda among the workers. This
policy met some resentment from party workers in Vyborg District,
who advocated bolder action, calling for a strike.[4] On February 22,
a Bolshevik worker of Erikson Factory and a member of the Vyborg
District Committee of the Bolshevik party, V. Kaiurov, organized a
meeting of women workers, at which he explained the meaning of
Women's Day, the history of women's liberation movement, and above

2. A. Shliapnikov, *Semnadtsatyi god* 1:308; R. Kovnator, "Nakanune 'fevralia': Otryvki iz vospominanii," p. 184.

3. Shliapnikov, *Semnadtsatyi god* 1:74.

4. N. Sveshnikov, a Bolshevik worker in Old Lessner, and a member of the
Vyborg District Committee, mentions that the Vyborg District Committee adopted
a resolution on February 20 to take measures to have women abandon their work
on February 23. This seems to be unlikely, since a strike restricted to women
workers was impossible. Sveshnikov's account, however, indicates that some
Bolshevik workers were dissatisfied with Shliapnikov's directives. N. Sveshnikov,
"Vyborgskii raionnyi komitet RSDRP (b) v 1917 g.," *V ogne revoliutsionnykh
boev: Raiony Petrograda v dvukh revoliutsiiakh 1917 g.: sbornik vospominanii
starykh bol'shevikov-pitertsev*, p. 82; idem, "Otryvki iz vospominanii," *Petrogradskaia pravda*, March 14, 1923.

all, the significance of the struggle against the war. Kaiurov, however, strongly urged the audience to refrain from action and to follow only the directions of the Bolshevik party.[5]

The revolutionaries underestimated the despair and rage of the female workers. After their husbands and sons had gone to the front, all the burden of supporting families fell upon them. They worked from dawn to dusk, sometimes for as long as thirteen hours, to earn low wages that could not catch up with ever increasing prices and after the long day they stood in long lines in the freezing cold for hours just to get a loaf of bread. No propaganda was necessary to incite these women to action. A police officer in the second precinct of Vyborg District reported to the *gradonachal'nik* on February 22: "The masses of workers are extremely agitated by the shortage of food. Almost all the police officers hear every day complaints that they have not eaten bread for two, three days or more. Therefore it is easy to expect major street disturbances. The acuteness of the situation reached such a point that some who were fortunate enough to be able to buy two loaves of bread cross themselves and cry from joy."[6]

On the morning of February 23 illegal meetings were held in several textile factories in Vyborg District. Five of the largest—Nikol'skaia Cotton (1,497 workers), Vyborg Cotton (755), Nevka (2,748), Sampsonievskaia Cotton (1,592), and Lebedev Jute Factory (998)—were concentrated along the bank of the Neva and Sampsonievskii Prospekt. While the workers of other textile mills had not been drawn into the strike movement, the women in these factories had actively participated in the strike movement during the war.[7] They now abandoned work at the end of their meetings, and marched to the neighboring factories, shouting simply "Bread!"

Nevka Cotton Factory was located between two large metal factories, New Lessner and Erikson. The women moved to these factories, appealing to the metalworkers to join their strike, shouting: "Bread!" The spontaneous movement put the Bolshevik workers on the spot. On the one hand, they knew that the Russian Bureau of the Central Committee was reluctant to support direct action at this moment. On the other hand, they could not in good conscience ignore and isolate the fellow workers who had started the strike movement. When the news of

5. V. Kaiurov, "Shest' dnei fevral'skoi revoliutsii," *Proletarskaia revoliutsiia* 13, no. 1 (1923): 158.
6. TsGIA, f. 1278, 1917 g., op. 1, d. 741, ℓ. 114.
7. Wada Haruki, "Nigatsu kakumei," in *Roshia kakumei no kenkyu*, ed. Eguchi Bokuro, p. 393. See Appendix. For the location and the number of workers of these factories, see *Spisok fabrichno–zavodskikh predpriatii Petrograda*.

the women's strike reached Erikson Factory, Kaiurov and four other Bolsheviks met in a corridor. Kaiurov was angry with the breach of discipline of the workers he thought he had controlled. "I was extremely indignant with the actions of the strikers," writes Kaiurov. "Not only did they blatantly ignore the decisions of the party district committee, but also just the night before I had appealed to the women workers to maintain restraint and discipline. And suddenly this strike. It appeared that there were no goals and purposes, if we discount the ever-increasing bread lines, which were essentially the reason for the strike."[8] The Erikson Bolsheviks, unable to decide whether they should support the strike, wanted to wait and see what the other party activists in the factory would do. They met with the SRs and the Mensheviks in a joint meeting attended by about a dozen political leaders in the factory. A number of urgent questions were raised. Would the Erikson workers respond favorably to a strike call? If they went on strike, would there be any guarantee that other factory workers would join them also? Should they restrict themselves only to a strike or should they stage a demonstration in the streets? According to one of the participants in the meeting, an SR worker, I. Mil'chik: "Despite the absence of conviction as to whether other factories would join us, it was decided quickly and unanimously, which was usually not the case, to go on strike and go out into the streets with the slogans: " 'Down with the autocracy,' 'Down with the war,' and 'Give us bread.' " Kaiurov recalls: "My proposal was adopted that once we decide to act with protest, we must immediately lead all the workers without exception into the streets and we ourselves must stand at the head of the strike and demonstration."[9] The activists in Erikson thus gambled on direct action, overcoming their indecision and misgivings. The spontaneous strike movement with economic demands now began to be transformed into a highly political demonstration led by experienced, conscious elements of the working class.

No one worked in the workshops, although machines were still running. The workers formed various groups, anxiously awaiting the decision of their leaders. As usual, the young workers were first to learn of the strike decision. Whistling and shouting, they ran from one workshop to another: "Stop the work. To the meeting!" The machines stopped with a clanging noise. Workers grabbed their overcoats and hurried to the courtyard. Foremen suddenly disappeared behind the glass windows of their offices, and watched the workers

8. Kaiurov, "Shest' dnei," p. 158.

9. I. Mil'chik, *Rabochii fevral'*, pp. 60-61; Kaiurov, "Shest' dnei," p. 158.

"like frightened birds." Administrators also appeared in the courtyard, accompanied by the engineers, but they simply watched the workers' meeting with a curious look. The strike leaders spoke, instructing rather than agitating, and emphasized that the purpose of the demonstration was the overthrow of tsarism, and that under no circumstances should the workers resort to vandalism. The strike call was accepted with enthusiasm, and the workers went out of the factory gate to Sampsonievskii Prospekt. Kaiurov became convinced that "the idea of action has been long ripe among the workers."[10]

A similar process was repeated in New Lessner as well. A Bolshevik worker in the New Lessner Factory, I. Gordienko, recalls that on the morning of February 23, workers of the factory suddenly heard women's voices screaming for bread and against the war. Halting their work, they rushed to the windows. The women, filling the narrow streets below the windows, waved at them, shouting: "Come on out! Quit working! Join us!" Agitated, the workers ignored their foremen's threats, and held a political meeting in each workshop. *Strike* was the unanimous decision and the workers hurried out of the factory and into the streets to join the crowds moving along the Bol'shoi Sampsonievskii Prospekt. According to Chugurin, the appeal of the textile workers for strike caused a dilemma among the Bolshevik activists in New Lessner. But under strong pressure from young workers for strike, they, too, had to decide to join it. The demonstrators, joined by 4,500 workers from Erikson and 7,500 workers from New Lessner, moved to Russian Renault, where the workers also joined them. The demonstrators surged south along Sampsonievskii Prospekt, drawing workers from the factories along the way. According to Leiberov's calculation, by 10 A.M. ten factories and approximately 27,000 workers in Vyborg District struck. By twelve o'clock noon twenty-one factories and 50,000 workers had joined. Not all of the strikers were dedicated political activists, however. When the demonstrators reached the end of Sampsonievskii Prospekt, they numbered only 4,000; the rest of the strikers had gone home.[11]

About two thousand demonstrators moved toward another industrial complex along the bank of the Great Neva. The first target was the Arsenal, a large state munitions factory. The Arsenal workers were usually conservative, for they received a higher salary than workers

10. I. Mil'chik, *Rabochii fevral'*, pp. 61-62; Kaiurov, "Shest' dnei," p. 158.

11. I. Gordienko, *Iz boevogo proshlogo*, pp. 56-57; I. P. Leiberov, *Petrogradskii proletariat v Fevral'skoi revoliutsii* 2: 60-68; idem, "Nachalo Fevral'skoi revoliutsii (sobytiia 23 fevralia 1917 g. v Petrograde)," *Iz istorii velikoi Oktiabr'skoi sotsialisticheskoi revoliutsii i sotsialisticheskogo stroitel'stva v SSSR: Sbornik statei*, pp. 8, 12; TsGIA, f. 1282, 1917 g., op. 1, d. 741, ℓ. 111.

in other factories and a special pension for sickness and old age. Throughout the morning workers in the factory discussed in whispers the disturbances outside. During the lunch break the demonstrators approached the factory, appealing directly to Arsenal workers to quit
work. In one of the workshops, about forty workers led by an SR
member, I. Markov, left the workshop. Joining other workers coming
from other workshops, they went into the streets through the factory
gates, defiantly singing La Marseillaise. The administration of the
Arsenal could do nothing about this sudden mass walkout, though they
did rush to the factory gates to shout: "Come to your senses. What are
you doing?! You are aiding our enemy, the Germans! Traitors to
the fatherland!" The strikers retorted: "What about Sukhomlinov?
Miasoedov? The Empress herself is a Germany spy."[12]   Another SR
member, I. Mil'chik of Erikson Factory, who was among the demonstrators outside, told a different story. The demonstrators, who did not
expect the conservative Arsenal workers to join the strike voluntarily,
surrounded the factory and bombarded it with rocks and pieces of iron.
This tactic—forcible removal of workers—was to become common during
the strike movement in the February Revolution. The Arsenal workers
were forced to abandon work, but rather than joining the demonstration, most of them went straight home. After the Arsenal, the
demonstrators went to nearby Phoenix, "removing" the workers
from this factory also. Another group of demonstrators reached Petrograd Cartridge Factory on Tikhvenskaia Street around four o'clock
in the afternoon, another government-owned munitions factory with
more than 8,000 workers. The demonstrators broke the factory gate,
rushed inside the factory compound and, running from one workshop
to another, disrupted work. The police arrested nineteen demonstrators, but 5,000 workers were "removed." The demonstrators set
up a picket line in front of the Arsenal, Cartridge Factory, Phoenix,
and Petrograd Metal Factory to make sure that the night shift would
not resume work.[13]

Aivaz Machine Factory (4,000 workers) was located in Lesnoi,
far north of the major industrial complex in Vyborg District. Around
two o'clock in the afternoon, at the initiative of the women workers
in the factory, the workers met in the automation section. The women
workers complained about the inequality of women and appealed
to the men to support their demand for bread. The factory administrator promised to bake bread in the factory at the expense of the

12. I. Markov, "Kak proizoshla revliutsiia," Volia Rossii, no. 5/6 (1927),
pp. 69-70.

13. Mil'chik, Rabochii fevral', p. 65; TsGIA, f. 1282, 1917 g., op. 1, d. 741,
ℓℓ. 111, 112.

management and some speakers spoke against the strike, arguing that in view of the management's good will it would be counterproductive. But this voice of moderation was drowned out by the women's shouts: "Let's go home." By four o'clock, the workers quietly left the factory and went home.[14]

Although there were scattered incidents of strike in other parts of the city, the strike movement was mainly a local phenomenon in Vyborg District. By the end of the day the strike engulfed thirty-two large plants and more than 59,800 workers, or 61 percent of all the workers in Vyborg District.[15]

The first factories to strike in Petrograd District were Diuflon and Langenzippen. About three hundred workers of Langenzippen marched along Kamenoostrovskii Prospekt to Kronver Prospekt, disrupting work at a few factories along the way. They moved to the Kronver division of the Pipe Factory and to the Kahn factory, but were repulsed by police. On the northern side of Petrograd District about fifteen hundred workers of Vulkan assembled at the gate of the Machine Factory of the First Russian Society of Aeronautics, another munitions factory, and appealed to the workers to abandon their work. The police rushed to the scene and a police inspector, Vashev, ordered the crowd to disperse. No sooner had Vashev pulled his revolver to enforce his order than the angry mob surrounding him beat him with sticks and clubs. The demonstrators broke into the factory, and "removed" the workers. On this day, in Petrograd District, altogether eleven factories and 8,341 workers took part in the strike.[16]

The labor unrest of February 23 was limited mainly to these two districts. In Narva-Peterhof District the lockout of Putilov Factory continued, and Putilov workers did not take part in the strike.[17] In Kolomenskaia District, Franco-Russian Factory workers held a political rally, but a majority supported opinions against participation. The total number of strikers on February 23 was somewhere between

14. TsGIA, f. 1282, 1917 g., op. 1, d. 741, ℓ. 112.

15. Leiberov, *Petrogradskii proletariat v Fevral'skoi revoliutsii* 2: 75; idem, "Nachalo Fevral'skoi revoliutsii," p. 17. See Appendix 2, col. 14.

16. TsGIA, f. 1282, 1917 g., op. 1, d. 741, ℓ. 121; Leiberov, *Petrogradskii proletariat v Fevral'skoi revoliutsii* 2:76; idem, "Nachalo Fevral'skoi revoliutsii," p. 17; TsGAOR, f. POO, op. 5, d. 669, ℓ. 310.

17. Shliapnikov, *Semnadtsatyi god* 1: 81. Some historians erroneously credit the initiative of the strike movement on February 23 to the workers of Putilov Factory. Marc Ferro, *La révolution de 1917: La chute du tsarisme et les origines d'Octobre*, p. 64; Oskar Anweiler, *Die Rätebewegung in Russland, 1905-1921*, p. 128; Raymond Pearson, *The Russian Moderates and the Crisis of Tsarism, 1914-1917*, p. 140. Khabalov states that there was no trouble in the Putilov Factory. Deposition of Khabalov, *Padenie tsarskogo rezhima* 1:213.

78,000 and 128,000 or about 20 to 30 percent of the workers in Petrograd. The number of struck factories was about 50.[18] The number of strikers and the struck factories of the February 23 strike was much smaller in scope than the January 9 strike, and a little smaller or comparable to the February 14 strike.

What distinguished the February 23 strike from the previous large strikes during the war was not its size, but its militancy. In many factories the strike was not a voluntary decision by the workers, but rather forcible removal by the striking workers. Another important aspect was that the February 23 strike was accompanied by the workers' persistent attempt to stage a demonstration on the Nevskii. As soon as the news of the strike reached the *gradonachal'nik*, he assigned large police forces to Liteinyi Bridge, which connects Vyborg District to the center of the city, and to Liteinyi Prospekt, the main street leading from the Liteinyi Bridge to Nevskii Prospekt. The strategy of the police was first to prevent demonstrators from crossing the river, and secondly to drive them away from Liteinyi Prospekt, if some managed to break through the police lines at the bridge.[19]

The workers in Vyborg District moved to the Liteinyi Bridge from two directions: Bol'shoi Sampsonievskii Prospekt on the west side of Vyborg District, and Bezborodkin Prospekt-Simbirskii Prospekt, on the east. The first important confrontation between police and demonstrators took place on Liteinyi Bridge and the superiority of the organized police forces in such a restricted area was unmistakable. Although the demonstrators tried many times to charge the lines at the bridge, the police successfully held them back. Only a handful of demonstrators managed to break through.[20] There was one factor, however, that the police overlooked. The winter was severe, and the Neva was still frozen. At about four o'clock in the afternoon demonstrators began crossing the river on the ice. Since the use of

18. TsGIA, f. 1282, 1917 g., op. 1, d. 741, л. 118. According to the Okhrana report, the number of strikes and of the struck factories was respectively 78,444 and 43; according to the police report, respectively 87,534 and 50; according to Leiberov, 128,388 and 49. "Fevral'skaia revoliutsiia i okhrannoe otdelenie," *Byloe* 7, no. 1 ((1918): 162; Shliapnikov, *Semnadtsatyi god* 1: 78, 316; Leiberov, *Petrogradskii proletariat v Fevral'skoi revoliutsii* 2:86; idem, "Nachalo Fevral'skoi revoliutsii," p. 24; E. N. Burdzhalov, *Vtoraia russkaia revoliutsiia: Vosstanie v Petrograde*, pp. 128-29. Evidently the figures Leiberov gives include the strikers of Putilov Factory, who did not actively participate in the strike and the demonstration on February 23.

19. Deposition of Khabalov, *Padenie tsarskogo rezhima* 1: 183.

20. "Fevral'skaia revoliutsiia i okhrannoe otdelenie," p. 163; A. Kondrat'ev, "Vospominaniia o podpol'noi rabote," *Krasnaia letopis'* 7 (1923): 63; TsGIA, f. 1282, op. 1, d. 741, лл. 112, 142.

firearms was forbidden at this stage, the police were powerless. Some strikers went to the Petrograd District, reaching the center of the city from there through the Troitskii Bridge, where the police cordon was less tight. Nevertheless, no sooner had they reassembled on the left bank of the river than the police attacked them. Obviously the police had the upper hand this day.[21]

Once on the other side of the Neva, the workers divided into two groups. One moving toward the Fontanka Canal tried to reach Kazan Square on the west end of the Nevskii.[22] This was the first group to arrive at the Nevskii. The Kazan police precinct report states: "At 4:40 P.M. crowds of approximately one thousand people, predominantly women and youths, approached Kazan Bridge on Nevskii Prospekt from the direction of Mikhailovskaia Street, singing and shouting, 'Give us bread!' "[23] But the police and gendarmes immediately dispersed the crowds.

Another group moved along Liteinyi Prospekt toward Znamenskaia Square on the east end of the Nevskii. Along the way, approximately two hundred demonstrators broke the closed gates of the Orudinskii Factory, a munitions factory annexed to the Arsenal, inciting the workers there to join the demonstrators. The police pushed back the crowds, but 1,900 workers mingled with the demonstrators. Later, another group invaded the same factory from the direction of Shpalernaia Street, succeeding in completely stopping the work of three thousand workers in a cartridge workshop—a tactic of forceful removal. Swollen by the infusion of Orudinskii Factory, the crowd of about two thousand moved onto Liteinyi Prospekt. No sooner had they marched as far as Marinskaia Hospital, not far from the Nevskii, than the mounted police led by Colonel M. G. Shalfeev charged upon the demonstrators, and drove them away immediately. During the melee

21. Some historians underestimate the superiority of the police over the demonstrators on this day. For instance, Ferro, *La révolution de 1917*, p. 65, and Gerhardt von Wettig, "Die Rolle der russischen Armee im Revolutionären Machtkampf 1917," *Forschungen zur osteuropäischen Geschichte*, p. 88. Wettig writes: "The police were no longer the master of the situation." This was not the case on February 23, even in the Vyborg District.

22. Katkov writes that the street demonstrators were "centered mainly on the Znamenskaia Square at the eastern end of the Nevskii Prospekt." George Katkov, *Russia 1917: The February Revolution*, p. 247. Actually, together with Znamenskaia Square, Kazan Square was an important target for demonstrators. Ferro, *La révolution de 1917*, pp. 72-73. This map is misleading; the demonstrators reached Kazan Square not only from the direction of Znamenskaia Square, but also from the north along the Fontanka and the Ekaterina Canal. Also the main route they took to reach Znamenskaia Square was not Znamenskaia Street, but Liteinyi Prospekt.

23. Shliapnikov, *Semnadtsatyi god* 1: 87; TsGIA, f. 1278, 1917 g., op. 1, d. 741, ℓℓ. 143-44.

some demonstrators responded to the police attack by throwing rocks, wounding one of the policemen. The last attempt to reach the Nevskii was made by a small group of demonstrators from the direction of Suvorov Prospekt at 7 P.M., but the police easily broke up the demonstration.[24]

The demonstrators failed to achieve their primary aim of holding a mass rally either on Znamenskaia Square or on Kazan Square. Only a handful of them succeeded in reaching the Nevskii, and even those who did were easily chased away by the police. Nevertheless, the demonstrators managed to disrupt the movement of the streetcars. They took tram keys away, disconnected electricity, and sometimes toppled the cars over.[25]

The workers' strike coincided with a revolt of consumers. Around three o'clock in the afternoon about two hundred people, predominantly women and youths, who were standing in line in front of the Fillipov bakery in Bol'shoi Prospekt in the Petrograd District, heard the manager of the store announce that all the bread was sold. No sooner had this announcement been made than the crowd smashed the windows, broke into the store, and knocked down everything in sight, causing three- to four-thousand rubles of damage. At seven o'clock in the evening about one hundred youths marched along Suvorov Prospekt, breaking along the way windows of a candy store, a meat shop, and a vegetable store.[26] Such vandalism was to increase sharply in the following days. All the revolutionary activists, the Bolsheviks included, had counseled the workers against vandalism. It is interesting to point out that mostly women and youths were involved in such cases. The workers' strike movement, which began on February 23, was soon to absorb this element of society.

On this day an unusually high number of robberies were reported. Thousands of rubles were stolen from many stores in the center of the city. In a spectacular bank robbery of the Siberian Trade Bank, 35,000 rubles were stolen.[27] Although such information is not available for the subsequent days of the revolution, it is not hard to imagine that the crime rate went up in direct proportion to the number of strikes.

The anger of the demonstrators was directed against the police. A police officer, Kargelis, was struck on his head by the demonstrators

24. TsGIA, f. 1282, 1917 g., op. 1, d. 741, ℓ. 11; Shliapnikov, *Semnadtsatyi god* 1: 79-80.

25. TsGIA, f. 1278, 1917 g., op. 1, d. 741, ℓℓ. 10, 11.

26. TsGOAR, f. POO, op. 5, d. 669 (1917g.), ℓ. 289; TsGIA, f. 1282, 1917 g., op. 1, d. 741, ℓ. 126.

27. TsGAOR, f. POO, op. 5, d. 669 (1917 g.), ℓ. 292.

when he was arresting a young worker stealing a key from a tram driver. Another officer, Grotgus, was beaten unconscious at Finland Station, where he was arresting a worker. Altogether four policemen were reportedly assaulted.[28]

Detecting the reluctance with which the Cossacks were fulfilling their orders, the demonstrators reacted to them differently. The *grado-nachal'nik* himself noted the laxity of discipline among the Cossacks in the following instance during his inspection tour around the town:

On the Nevskii Prospekt, the demonstrators, moving from sidewalks into the middle of the street, began to assemble across the city duma. A platoon of police ordered them to disperse in vain. The crowds grew bigger and louder. Noticing half a company of the Cossacks under the command of an officer indifferently watching the crowds at the Kazan Cathedral, I got out of the automobile, approached the officer, told him who I was, and ordered him to take a position of concentration immediately in full gallop and drive away the crowds without using weapons. The officer, still quite young, perplexedly looked at me, and gave the command with a sluggish voice. The Cossacks formed a platoon formation and . . . moved slowly. Going together with them several steps, I shouted: "On gallop!" The officer turned his horse "on motion," and the Cossacks did the same, but the closer they got to the crowds, the slower their gallop became and finally they completely stopped. . . . But at the time the mounted police appeared from the Kazan Square and drove away the demonstrators.[29]

Such incidents remained isolated, but the demonstrators read vacillation and awkward hesitation on the Cossacks' faces. Hope grew in the activists' mind: "The soldiers are with us. They will not shoot." And it was this hope that inspired them for the next day's action.

The outbreak of the workers' strike movement coincided with the returning of the Duma deputies to the normal session after a two-day recess. The liberal opposition, which had opened the Duma session on February 14 with pessimism and a sense of powerlessness, was suddenly alarmed by signs of a popular rising. The Duma continued to debate the food shortage, but the focus of debate shifted to the general ineptitude of the government. A Kadet deputy, A. Shingarev, who was reputed to be the expert on agricultural affairs, criticized the speech made by Rittikh, minister of agriculture, in the Duma a few days before. "What we heard," he pointedly remarked, "was not

28. TsGIA, f. 1282, 1917 g., op. 1, d. 741, ℓℓ. 137-38; "Fevral'skaia revoliu-tsiia i okhrannoe otdelenie," pp. 163-64; N. O. Akaemov, "Agoniia starago re-zhima," pp. vii-viii; Shliapnikov, *Semnadtsatyi god* 1: 84-85; TsGAOR, f. DPOO, op. 341, ch. 57/1917, ℓ. 15.

29. A. Balk, "Poslednie piat' dnei tsarskago Petrograda: Dnevnik posledniago Petrogradskago gradonachal'nika," pp. 1-2.

the minister of agriculture, but an extremely irritated polemicist."
The mistake that led to the current crisis was not caused by isolated
economic factors such as the low fixed prices, Shingarev continued,
but by the government itself. "There was no uniform plan; I dare say
there was no governmental power that could carry out a solution
to the food problem systematically, seriously, thoughtfully and not
along its own inflexible path." Shingarev further pointed out that
although the various societal (obshchestvennye) organizations such
as All-Russian Union of Zemstvos and the Petrograd City Duma had
shown initiative in organizing the food supply and had offered cooperation with the government, their sincere attempts had been frustrated by the government's stubborn refusal. Further commenting on
Rittikh's plea not to play politics on this matter and to cooperate
with the government without "poisonous suspicion," Shingarev declared: "We are obliged to help the Russian state. We are doing this,
[Voice: 'Right'], and we did and shall continue to do that. But, gentlemen, why this puzzlement, as if we could go anywhere without politics,
and what is this politics?" Isn't Rittikh's speech in the Duma
itself, he asked, politics? Yes, "a completely definite politics and a
very old politics." The applauding audience from the Left added:
"Protopopov's politics."[30]

Rittikh's reply was almost drowned out by catcalls from the floor.
The minister of agriculture remarked that he was disturbed by Shingarev's speech, because the Kadet did not seem to understand the tragic
situation that the country found itself in—a situation that urgently
demanded a practical solution, not "I-told-you-so" rhetoric. "Gentlemen, it appears to me, and perhaps, everyone must feel this, that we
are experiencing a triumphant historical moment; perhaps, for the
last time, the hand of fate will turn the scale on which the future of
Russia weighs itself."[31]

Shingarev's criticism, however, was moderate, compared to the
speeches delivered by the Socialist deputies. Menshevik deputy Skobelev remarked that the country was, with catastrophic speed, rushing
head on to a dreadful upheaval. He continued: "What is happening
in the streets? These unhappy, half-starved children, mothers, and
wives, who had submissively and humbly stood in front of the bakeries
and waited for bread for more than two years, finally lost patience,
and perhaps helplessly, and even hopelessly, went out peacefully to
the streets, hopelessly calling out: bread." The food supply is not

---

30. Stenograficheskii otchet: Gosudarstvennaia duma, chetvertyi sozyv, sessiia
V (Petrograd, 1917), pp. 1572-73, 1587, 1591-92.
    31. Ibid., pp. 1594-95.

only a political question, he declared, but also a social question. This is the time when a wise government would have to devote all its energies to insure harmony of the classes, lest class antagonism and class struggle should disrupt the governmental forms. But such a policy cannot be expected from the Russian government, which brought to Russia nothing but "chaos, a Sodom and Gomorrah, and signs of corruption and decay erupting everywhere." Skobelev's violent denunciation invited such stormy applause from the Left and angry protests from the Right that Rodzianko had to warn the speaker to adhere to the subject in question and refrain from inflammatory words. Not heeding Rodzianko's repeated warnings, Skobelev went on: "We know in history many occasions when a government ruined a country once and for all by bringing the people to starvation, to the point where the enraged people harshly chastised those who were responsible for their starvation." The language was unmistakable; Skobelev was speaking of a revolution. When he further reminded the liberals on the floor of their "forefathers" in France and of their actions against the throne during the French Revolution, Rodzianko finally ordered, amid pandemonium from the floor, the speaker to stop his speech.[32]

Kerenskii, who followed Skobelev, pointed out that the current crisis was the inevitable consequence of the failure of the government to reorganize and revitalize national life at the beginning of the war, and warned that the *stikhiia* of the masses, who would not heed reason and words any longer, would overturn all political and social orders unless their demands were satisfactorily met. He remarked pessimistically that *stikhiia* had reached such a point that it would be impossible to establish a common language between the masses and the Duma. Responding to Kerenskii's statement, Shingarev remarked: "*Stikhiia*, gentlemen, is terrible; *stikhiia* should not control, but rather governmental intelligence should control the state in such a way that *stikhiia* would not be broken loose." What the liberal opposition had feared all along during the war was emerging in reality. Nevertheless, they had no answer except to plead to the government to have more intelligence. After the revolution, Miliukov stated: "We did not want this revolution. We did not wish particularly that it would come at the time of the war. And we had desperately struggled so that this would not happen."[33]

The Duma finally passed a motion presented by Miliukov that urged the government to take immediate measures to secure food for

32. Ibid., pp. 1642, 1645, 1647, 1649.
33. Ibid., pp. 1649-50, 1653-54, 1656; *Poslednie novosti*, March 12, 1917.

the people of the capital and other cities, to devote particular efforts to a solution of the food problem for the workers engaged in the defense industry, and to entrust the food matter to the city self-governments and other organizations of society.[34]

As the temperature sharply dropped in the evening, exhausted demonstrators quietly returned home. Altogether twenty-one demonstrators had been arrested, an amazingly small figure considering the extent of the strike and the demonstration. By seven o'clock in the evening the Nevskii became quiet again; or even quieter than usual, since people who would usually stroll along the boulevard had not appeared this day. A strong searchlight installed on the spire of the Admiralty illuminated the deserted Nevskii, making an eerie impression on the minister of internal affairs, who was taking an inspection tour around the city.[35]

But in the workers' quarters the atmosphere was lively. Workers spoke with one another about the strike in their factories, demonstration in the streets, and confrontation with the police. Their leaders, too, were busy assessing the significance of the events and planning the strategy for the next day. On this night a member of the Bolshevik Vyborg District Committee, Chugurin, called an extraordinary meeting of the Petersburg Committee and the Vyborg District Committee at the apartment of a Bolshevik member, I. Aleksandrov, on Golovinskaia Street on the outskirts of the Vyborg District. The participants included A. Skorokhodov, K. Shutko from the Petersburg Committee, P. Zalutskii representing the Russian Bureau of the Central Committee, I. Chugurin, N. Sveshnikov and other Vyborg Committee members. They came to several important decisions concerning the future course of action and adopted a resolution calling for a three-day general strike and intensification of propaganda activities among the soldiers. The resolution affirmed the continuation of demonstration on the Nevskii. The Bolsheviks were urged to "go to the factories and mills early in the morning without resuming work and after a short rally to lead as many workers as possible to the demonstration against the war at Kazan Cathedral." Upon learning the outcome of this meeting, Shliapnikov was disturbed by the radicalism of his subordinates. He thought that the call for a general strike was too mechanical and too irresponsible, for the party possessed neither resources nor strength to carry through an ill-prepared general strike.[36] However, he had

34. *Stenograficheskii otchet: Gosudarstvennaia duma, chetvertyi sozyv, sessiia V*, pp. 1657-60; TsGIA, f. 1276, op. 10, d. 7, ℓ. 468.

35. TsGAOR, f. POO, op. 5, d. 669, ℓ. 319; "Fevral'skaia revoliutsiia i okhrannoe otdelenie," p. 162; TsGAOR, f. ChSK, d. 466, ℓ. 170.

36. Sveshnikov, "Otryvki iz vospominanii"; "Vyborgskii raionnyi komitet,"

little control over the Vyborg Bolsheviks, who had begun to take independent action.

In the evening the Petrograd Union of Consumers called a meeting of the representatives of the cooperatives, sick funds, and other workers' representatives under the influence of the workers' group in the M. A. Semenov factory in Petrograd District. Some Bolsheviks, presumably as representatives of the sick funds, also attended. It was decided to urge the workers on the following day to stage a demonstration with the slogan "Bread and peace!" and to direct it to the Tauride Palace. The workers' group organized a special propaganda team of Menshevik activists, but the police moved quickly and arrested all its members.[37] It is significant that both the Bolsheviks and the workers' group decided to support the strike on the following day. Presumably these decisions were transmitted to their activists during the night.

While leaders of the workers' movement were planning the next day's strategy, security authorities were also busy discussing what measures to employ to restore order. In the evening Khabalov convened a meeting in the office of the *gradonachal'stvo,* headquarters of the security authorities during the February days. In addition to Balk *(gradonachal'nik),* Vasiliev (director of the police department), Colonel Pavlenkov (commander of troops in Petrograd), Major-General Globachev (chief of the Petrograd Okhrana), and Major-General Kazakov (commander of the gendarme division), commanders of various reserve battalions also attended the meeting.[38] Balk briefed them on the day's developments, calling particular attention to the dangerous signs of the Cossacks' reluctance to suppress the demonstration. Colonel Troilin, commander of the Cossack Regiment, explained that most of the Cossacks were inexperienced in the suppression of internal disorder and that their horses were unaccustomed to the hard pavement and narrow streets clustered with tall buildings. Furthermore, he continued, the Cossacks were not given the necessary equipment. How could they effectively attack demonstrators without nagaikas, he asked. Khabalov immediately ordered that each Cossack be given fifty kopeks to purchase a nagaika.[39] The meeting decided to make

p. 83; Shliapnikov, *Semnadtsatyi god* 1: 87.

37. Leiberov, *Petrogradskii proletariat Fevral'skoi revoliutsii* 2: 140; TsGAOR, f. POO, 1917 g., d. 669a, ℓℓ. 63-64.

38. Balk, "Poslednie piat' dnei," pp. 2-3.

39. Ibid., p. 3. A nagaika is a whip constructed of a stick about fifteen inches long with a leather thong of about twenty inches. At the end of the leather thong there are two small pieces of leather about an inch in diameter that enclose a piece of lead. A Cossack could use a nagaika with dexterity. He could brush a fly from one's face without touching the skin, or he could maim one for life. According

the second stage of the contingency plan fully effective. Troops would be deployed to assigned military districts to protect important positions of the city.

Protopopov was in constant touch with Vasiliev. The director of the police department assured Protopopov that the government need not worry about the movement overmuch, since it was spontaneous and lacked organized action by revolutionary forces. He predicted that by the next morning the workers would resume their normal work. Protopopov agreed, and conveyed this optimistic opinion to the empress in Tsarskoe Selo through the assistant commandant of the palace, General Groten.[40] Golitsyn also thought that they were simple street demonstrations that would be quickly dealt with by the police.[41] Those who watched the movement more closely, however, did not 'share such optimism. Okhrana agents accurately reported the general atmosphere in the streets, and warned the government that the movement might develop into an uprising. One of the reports stated: "The shortage of bread is driving the masses of workers to action. They are more and more convinced that an uprising is the only way out of this blind alley of the food problem. Now everybody in the street is talking about an uprising, as if it were near and inevitable." Another Okhrana report said that some soldiers in the Semenovskii Regiment openly spoke about their intention to shoot into the air had they received an order to fire upon the demonstrators.[42]

It is not difficult to see the direct cause for the strike on February 23—shortage of food. The slogan "Bread" drove the textile workers in the Vyborg District into the street. It united the striking workers with the women and the youths standing in a long queue, while it unnerved the soldiers sent to suppress the demonstrators. But the February 23 strike was not simply a hunger riot. The demand for bread was symbolic expression of their deep disapproval of the system itself. As soon as the strike began "spontaneously," the "conscious" elements of the experienced activists of the large metal fac-

---

to a British eyewitness, Stinton Jones, at one demonstration a Cossack attacked a young demonstrator with a nagaika. "In an instant his coat was cut through and soon the whole of that side was saturated with blood from the deep wound." On another occasion, a whip of nagaika "caught a face of a woman . . . and gashed it open to the bone." Stinton Jones, *Russia in Revolution, Being the Experiences of an Englishman in Petrograd during the Upheaval* (London: Herbert Jenkins, 1917), pp. 85-86.

40. Supplementary deposition of Protopopov, *Padenie tsarskogo rezhima* 4: 96; TsGAOR, ChSK, d. 466, ℓℓ. 169-70.

41. Deposition of Golitsyn, *Padenie tsarskogo rezhima* 2: 262.

42. Burdzhalov, *Vtoraia russkaia revoliutsiia*, pp. 134-35.

tories joined and assumed leadership of the strike and the demonstration. Although the strike movement remained on this day merely a local event in the Vyborg District and to a lesser degree in the Petrograd District, there emerged on that first day unmistakable signs. The strike spread in the Vyborg District more quickly and more violently than ever before and, moreover, it was accompanied by persistent attempts by the workers to stage a demonstration in the center of the city. No one noticed, but the February Revolution was already one day old.

13

THE SECOND DAY:
FEBRUARY 24

 The cold, misty morning of February 24 began as any other morning. Smokestacks and brick factories were silhouetted through a veil of that typical Petrograd rain that seemed to seep into the bones with its freezing wetness. But this day, instead of the repressive silence that usually fell upon the hordes of workers hurrying to the factories, an unusual excitement filled the workers' district. Behind the morning fog, the strike organizers, like ants, moved busily. No single revolutionary headquarters ordered them to organize a strike. Nor was there any organizational unity among the activists. But regardless of political persuasion, these activists acted as one body. The workers were greeted by the activists' speech for strike and demonstration at the factory gates. In many factories political rallies were organized even before nine nine o'clock.

In Aivaz Factory, which was controlled by moderate Socialists, more than thirty-five hundred workers gathered in the automation section. The orators stressed the importance of unity, while demanding the removal of the government and appealing to the workers to act in an organized fashion without resorting to irresponsible acts. The destination of the demonstration was said to be the Tauride Palace. The Bolsheviks were also busy; in Erikson they called for the continuation of the strike to protest against inflation, the shortage of bread, the war, and the autocracy. Further appealing to the workers to stage a massive rally in Kazan Square, they urged them to arm themselves with knives, hardware, and pieces of ice.[1] Not all the orators were experi-

---

1. TsGIA, f. 1282, 1917 g., op. 1, d. 741, ll. 159-60; TsGAOR, f. DPOO,

enced political activists, however. The strike movement itself created numerous leaders, who, acting independent of any political organization, gave the masses of workers a sense of direction. Okhrana agent Krestianov vividly recorded the speech and the actions of one of the otherwise anonymous leaders, a certain Petr Tikhonov, who delivered the following at a meeting in Stetinin Factory:

Comrades, as you all know, yesterday, February 23, the entire Vyborg District did not work. So, comrades, we must quit our work today, support union with other comrades and go to get bread by ourselves. Comrades, my opinion is this. If we cannot get a loaf of bread for ourselves in a righteous way, then we must do everything: we must go ahead and solve our problem by force. Only in this way will we be able to get bread for ourselves. Comrades, remember this also. Down with the government! Down with the war! Comrades, arm yourselves with everything possible—bolts, screws, rocks, and go out of the factory and start smashing the first shops you find.[2]

After this speech Tikhonov led the workers to a nearby factory. The invaders demanded that all the workers should quit work and threw rocks at those remaining in the building. Then Tikhonov's mob proceeded to Finland Station, stopping trains and driving passengers out of cars. Tikhonov then suddenly decided to lead to the Tauride Palace. They moved on to the Liteinyi Bridge, ransacking bakeries on their way.[3]

But the major force behind the strike movement on the second day came from the workers of New Lessner, Erikson, Parviainen, and Russian Renault. As on the previous day, they moved to the Arsenal, Petrograd Cartridge Factory, and Promet, removing all workers from these factories. In Vyborg District 74,842 workers of sixty-one factories, more than two thirds of the total work force, participated in the strike, constituting a third of the total strikers in Petrograd on this day.[4]

The demonstrators coming from Sampsonievskii Prospekt and Simbirskaia Street moved toward Liteinyi Bridge. By nine o'clock in the morning the crowds reached 40,000 people, more than half of the total number of the workers in Vyborg District. The protection of Liteinyi Bridge was even tighter this day. In addition to the police

op. 341, ch. 57/1917 g., ℓ. 96; "Fevral'skaia revoliutsiia i okhrannoe otdelenie," p. 165; I. P. Leiberov, "Vtoroi den' fevral'skoi revoliutsii (sobytiia 24 fevralia 1917 g. v Petrograde)," in Sverzhenie samoderzhaviia: sbornik statei, ed. I. I. Mints, L. M. Ivanov, et al., p. 101.

2. "Fevral'skaia revoliutsiia i okhrannoe otdelenie," p. 167.
3. Ibid., pp. 167-68.
4. TsGIA, f. 1282, 1917 g., op. 1, d. 741, ℓℓ. 16, 26; Leiberov, "Vtoroi den' fevral'skoi revoliutsii," p. 102.

under the command of Colonel Shalfeev, two and one half companies
of Cossacks and two companies of the Moscow Regiment, altogether
520 armed soldiers and police, awaited the arrival of the demonstrators.[5] As the crowd moved on Sampsonievskii Prospekt toward
the bridge, the officers suddenly commanded the Cossacks to attack
the approaching demonstrators. As soon as the demonstrators faced
the galloping Cossacks with unsheathed sabers, the festive mood that
had dominated the laughing and singing demonstrators changed to
sudden panic. There was nothing with which to protect themselves,
nor was there room to run away. The officers charged into the crowds.
Then galloping Cossacks followed the officers, filling the full width
of the streets. The terrified demonstrators must have expected bloodshed at any moment. But an amazing thing happened. The Bolshevik
Kaiurov recalls: "But, what joy! The Cossacks rushed in one line
through the 'hole' just made by the officers. Some of them smiled;
and one of them even winked at the workers." Jubilant cheers echoed
in the streets. No one was hurt. "This wink was not without meaning,"
Trotskii writes. "The workers were emboldened with a friendly, not
hostile, kind of assurance, and slightly infected the Cossacks with
it." In spite of repeated orders by officers, the Cossacks refused to
charge the demonstrators. After the same scene was repeated four
times, the officers, realizing the uselessness of the endeavor, gave up
hope of dispersing the crowds. The Cossacks returned to their former
position in front of the demonstrators.[6] Those who stood at the head
of the demonstration began talking with the Cossacks. Old women took
the first steps toward them and pleaded: "We have our husbands,
fathers, and brothers at the front. But here we have hunger, hard
times, injustices, shame. The government mocks us instead of helping
us. You also have your mothers, wives, sisters, and children. All we
want is bread and to end the war."[7]

The officers attempted to separate the Cossacks from the workers
by lining up the Cossacks across the street to block movement of the
workers forward. The emboldened demonstrators, however, dared
to dive under the feet of the Cossacks' horses. The Cossacks, still
mounted, made no attempt to prevent them. As Trotskii commented,
"The revolution does not choose its paths: it made its first steps toward
victory under the belly of a Cossack's horse."[8]

5. TsGIA, f. 1282, 1917 g., op. 1, d. 641, ℓ. 16.
6. V. Kaiurov, "Shest' dnei fevral'skoi revoliutsii," pp. 159-60; Leon Trotsky,
History of the Russian Revolution 1: 104.
7. I. Gordienko, *Iz boevogo proshlogo*, p. 57.
8. Kaiurov, "Shest' dnei," p. 160; Trotsky, *History of the Russian Revolution*
1: 105.

The demonstrators massed in front of the police and the Cossacks guarding Liteinyi Bridge. Shalfeev at first tried to persuade the crowds to disperse peacefully. But, realizing that the demonstrators were sneaking through the bridge by diving under the horses, he ordered the mounted police to attack. The police whipped those crossing the bridge with nagaikas, while the Cossacks stood neutral. Although the neutrality of the Cossacks made the attack of the police less effective—Kaiurov saw visible signs of confusion and apprehension in Shalfeev—it was nevertheless impossible for the demonstrators to break through the heavy cordon. Someone shouted: "Comrades, let's go on the ice!" About 5,000 people crossed the Neva on the ice to Liteinyi Prospekt. However, no sooner had they reached the street than the waiting police charged, driving them either toward the Circuit Court or to Voskresenskii Prospekt. The first group of demonstrators reassembled on Frantsuzkaia Naberezhnaia only to be scattered again by the combined forces of police and patrols of the Ninth Reserve Cavalry Regiment. The other group was further pushed back to the Vyborg side of the river by the gendarmes.[9] On this day, more demonstrators managed to reach the other side of the river much earlier than on the previous day, but they met stiff resistance by the police. The streets in the city's center were still under secure control of the police.

Although Vyborg District continued to be the center of the movement, the strike spread to all districts of the city. In Petrograd District, demonstrations originated in three areas. In the western part about forty-five hundred workers from six factories including Vulkan held a political rally and moved along Bol'shoi Prospekt and from there toward Kamenoostrovskii Prospekt. Also four thousand workers of five small factories in the southern section of the island and fifty-five hundred workers of the ten small factories in the north moved from the opposite direction to Kamenoostrovskii Prospekt. Many university students, high school students, and vocational students had joined the workers.[10] The demonstrators from these three directions converged into one group in the center of the district, and moved toward Troitskii Bridge to cross the Neva. At the corner of Kamenoostrovskii and Bol'shoi Prospekts, according to the police report, a few shots were fired from one of the houses at the demonstrators, killing an unidentified young woman who was watching the demonstration on the

9. TsGIA, f. 1282, 1917 g., op. 1, d. 741, ℓℓ. 23-24, 42; N. O. Akaemov, "Agoniia starago rezhima," p. xi; A. Shliapnikov, Semnadtsatyi god 1:91; Leiberov, "Vtoroi den' fevral'skoi revoliutsii," pp. 111-12.
    10. TsGIA, f. 1282, 1917 g., op. 1, d. 741, ℓ. 55.

sidewalk. She became the first victim of the February Revolution. Another worker was also shot in the rear, and testified that the shots came from the police. A seventeen-year old student of a vocational school was arrested for disseminating a "malicious, unfounded rumor" that the police had shot the demonstrators.[11] Reacting to the incident, the crowd attacked the police by throwing rocks and pieces of ice. The demonstrators moved toward the bridge, but the third squad of mounted police, which had formed a line across the street, charged the slowly approaching demonstrators, driving them to the sidewalk. In Petrograd District as well, police continued to control the situation. On February 24 in this district, 22,596 workers from forty factories participated in the strike. In contrast to the demonstration in Vyborg District, the demonstration in Petrograd District was accompanied by vandalism—police records show at least eight cases in this district alone. Bakeries, meat shops, milk stores, and other food stores were the main targets. The most violent attack took place on the city food store. Crowds, mostly women and youths, broke into the store, turned over the counters and shelves, destroyed cashiers' desks, and stole the money. The police arrived at the scene and arrested a young woman, but the excited crowd threw rocks and bottles at the police.[12]

Some of the striking workers of Vyborg and Petrograd districts broke through police cordons at Tuchkov and Birzha bridges on the Small Neva, and reached Vasilievskii Island. The first group of five hundred such workers moved along Malyi Prospekt toward the electrical manufacturing factory, Siemens-Haliske, but their attempt to break into the premises was thwarted by the police. As the reassembled Vyborg workers reached the factory gate, the activists in the factory (Bolsheviks, Mezhraiontsy, and SRs) succeeded in persuading their fellow workers to abandon their work. The strikers of Siemens-Haliske, joined by the workers in the neighboring factories, moved along Malyi Prospekt toward the harbor, the island's largest industrial complex.[13] When the demonstrators reached the 17th Line, they attacked the Military Horseshoes Factory by breaking windows; some broke in, disrupting work. The soldiers of Finland Regiment were brought in to restore order, but the disturbances lasted for four hours. Finally, the factory completely stopped work, and the workers went home.

11. Ibid., ℓℓ. 34-35; TsGAOR, f. DPOO, d. 341, ch. 57/1917, ℓ. 96.

12. Akaemov, "Agoniia starago rezhima," p. xii; Shliapnikov, *Semnadtsatyi god* 1: 96; Leiberov, "Vtoroi den' fevral'skoi revoliutsii," p. 104; TsGIA, f. 1282, 1917 g., op. 1, d. 741, ℓℓ. 14-15, 31-32, 58; TsGAOR, f. POO, op. 5, d. 669, ℓ. 319.

13. Leiberov, "Vtoroi den' fevral'skoi revoliutsii," p. 105.

During this confrontation, some demonstrators also attacked food stores on Srednyi Prospekt. One student of the Psychoneurological Institute was arrested for his inflammatory speech, and leaflets, presumably issued by the Mezhraiontsy, demanding the end of the war and the establishment of a Social-Democratic republic, were confiscated.[14]

In the harbor district on Vasilievskii Island, the military electromanufacturing factory, Siemens-Schückert, was the center of the strike movement. About three thousand workers led by the revolutionary underground activists abandoned work and actively engaged in the agitation in neighboring factories—Baltic Shipyard, Nail Factory, and Petrograd Cable Factory. More than 10,000 workers of these factories joined the strike. On Vasilievskii Island 23,248 workers of 28 factories struck, more than one third of the total number of workers in the district. Also, students of Petrograd University and Bestuzhev Women's College organized a political demonstration on Bol'shoi Prospekt.[15]

Strikes and demonstrations occurred in other districts as well. In Narva District the major factories, such as Siemens-Schückert, Skorokhod, Dinamo, and Moscow Tram Park, were occupied by soldiers of the Petrograd and Eger regiments. Moreover, the Putilov workers could not provide leadership, since the factory still continued the lockout. Nevertheless, more than 9,000 workers of 25 factories joined the strike.[16] In the Moscow District altogether 19,506 workers of 23 factories were involved in what were the most violent demonstrations organized. Police reported that young hooligans, mostly between the ages of 12 and 15, marched along Zvenigorodskaia Street, destroying the windows of the nineteen stores along the way. Also a tobacco store, a bakery, and a drugstore on Pushkin Street were attacked by 500 demonstrators, mostly women and youths.[17]

The strike movement spread further, not only to the outskirts of the city, Okhta, Nevskii District, and Novaia Derevnia, but also to its center. In Liteinaia District 6,000 workers in the Orudinskii Factory were "removed" again by the Vyborg workers, who had crossed the Neva. The Artillery Administration closed the factory in the morning.[18]

14. TsGIA, f. 1282, 1917 g., op. 1, d. 741, ll. 43, 52-53.
15. Ibid., ll. 43-44; Leiberov, "Vtoroi den' fevral'skoi revoliutsii," pp. 106-7.
16. TsGIA, f. 1282, 1917 g., op. 1, d. 741, l. 50; Leiberov, "Vtoroi den' fevral'skoi revoliutsii," p. 107. Leiberov's figures are 35,795 strikers of 26 factories, but they contain the Putilov Factory, which remained locked out. I subtracted 26,000 workers from Leiberov's figures.
17. TsGIA, f. 1282, 1917 g., op. 1, d. 741, ll. 13, 20-21.
18. Ibid., ll. 18-19, 23, 29-30.

In Kolomenskaia District workers of the Franco-Russian Factory held a meeting at seven o'clock in the morning in the machine workshop, where speakers spoke both for and against the strike. The factory's administration gave the workers an ultimatum to return to work by eleven o'clock, but by three o'clock in the afternoon only 50 workers out of 6,656 remained in the factory. In the Naval Admiralty Shipyard, a usually conservative state factory, out of 5,916 workers only 390 continued to work. In the three districts located in the heart of the city, 16,421 workers of 22 factories joined the strike. On February 24, the strike participants reached at least 158,000 and the struck factories 131, almost doubling the size of the strike on the previous day.[19] Never before during the war were so many people involved in a strike on a single day. The driving force of the strike movement was provided, as on the previous day, by veteran activists of the metal factories in the Vyborg District, but the strike spread to the gigantic munition factories as well as to small factories, those that had never before in the war joined a strike.[20] Looting and vandalism sharply increased, signifying that the attempts by conscious activists to organize strike and demonstration and the pent-up anger of the lower stratum of society were being forged into one combined force.

The first columns of demonstrators appeared in the Nevskii by eleven o'clock in the morning. Thousands, from all parts of the city, followed the first column, driving the well-dressed public from the street. According to Leiberov, during the day thirteen columns of demonstrations consisting altogether of 36,800 demonstrators marched in the Nevskii, Liteinyi, Suvorov, Zagorodnyi Prospekt, and Ligovskaia streets—an event unprecedented since 1905.[21]

The demonstrators held at least four rallies at Kazan Square: each time the police assisted by Cossacks and platoons of the Ninth Cavalry Regiment dispersed the crowds, but each time the demonstrators came back in great numbers, and each time it took the police longer and more reinforcements were needed. On the other side of the Nevskii at Znamenskaia Square as well a mass political rally was held. Speaker after speaker stood on the statue of Alex-

---

19. Leiberov, "Vtoroi den' fevral'skoi revoliutsii," pp. 109-10; this figure is based on the Okhrana records. "Fevral'skaia revoliutsiia i okhrannoe otdelenie," p. 164. According to the materials of the *gradonachal'stvo*, the number of strikers and of the struck factories were respectively 197,000 and 131. Akaemov, "Agoniia starago rezhima," p. xi; E. N. Burdzhalov, *Vtoraia russkaia revoliutsiia: Vosstanie v Petrograde*, p. 143. According to Leiberov, it was 214,111 and 22. Leiberov, "Vtoroi den' fevral'skoi revoliutsii," p. 111.

20. See Appendix 2, col. 15.

21. "Vtoroi den' fevral'skoi revoliutsii," p. 112.

ander III—the hippopotamus, as the workers called it—demanding bread and denouncing the war and autocracy. Speeches were largely incoherent, but as one of the participants, Mil'chik, stated, "logic and coherency were not needed by the people. . . . The first free speech under the open sky in front of the massive crowds in full view of the Cossacks and the police was perceived by heart and sounded like music."[22]

A platoon of a training detachment of the Volynskii Regiment arrived at Znamenskaia Square. The assistant commander was a noncommissioned officer, Sergeant T. Kirpichnikov, a sympathizer of the demonstrators. The crowds approached the officers pleading with them not to shoot and were assured by Kirpichnikov that the soldiers would not fire. He persuaded his commander to let the demonstrators pass as long as they moved down the sidewalk.[23]

Although the police and troops still managed to disperse the crowds, the demonstration clearly expanded in its effectiveness as well as in number. Onlookers showed their sympathy with cheers—wounded soldiers in the hospitals enthusiastically waved at the demonstrators. As they passed, residents along the Nevskii opened their windows and watched the unusual scene. On the Nevskii trams completely stopped, as tram drivers refused to drive even under police protection. Stores, restaurants, and cafes, which usually remained open until late in the evening, closed their doors early in the afternoon. The last demonstrators left the Nevskii at eight o'clock in the evening and as they left for their quarters, they reassured one another: "We will see you tomorrow on the Nevskii."[24]

The rapid development of the strike movement on this day encouraged the political activists. The Bolshevik Russian Bureau of the Central Committee held meetings several times during the day and decided to expand the movement to the soldiers "without restricting this offensive to any kind of mechanical resolution calling for a three-day general strike as was done by the Petersburg Committee." It further decided to dispatch a messenger to the Moscow organization

22. TsGIA, f. 1282, 1917 g., op. 1, d. 741, *ll*. 38–41; Shliapnikov, *Semnadtsatyi god* 1: 92–93; "Fevral'skaia revoliutsiia i okhrannoe otdelenie," p. 166; Akaemov, "Agoniia starago rezhima," p. xiii. According to Leiberov, six rallies involving 15,400 participants were held in the Nevskii. Leiberov, "Vtoroi den' fevral'skoi revoliutsii," p. 115. I. Mil'chik, *Rabochii fevral'*, p. 72.

23. T. Kirpichnikov, "Vozstanie 1.-gv. Volynskago polka v fevrale 1917 g.," *Byloe* 27/28, no. 5/6 (1917): 5–6.

24. Kaiurov, "Shest' dnei," p. 161; Shliapnikov, *Semnadtsatyi god* 1: 88, 90, 100; Claude Anet, *Through the Russian Revolution: Notes of an Eye-witness from 12th March–30th May*, p. 11.

to inform the Bolsheviks in Moscow of recent developments in Petrograd. The Vyborg District Committee met in Okhta in the evening with almost all the members participating. Sveshnikov states: "The atmosphere was exuberant, but we felt the absence of common leadership, and bad communication from other districts. The correct revolutionary direction of the Russian Bureau was really needed."[25] It demanded that the Russian Bureau issue a manifesto to the workers that clearly defined the political goals of the current strike movement. It also passed a resolution introduced by Chugurin calling for a general strike and intensified efforts in the struggle against the police and in the agitation among the masses.[26] In the evening Shliapnikov took an inspection tour on the Nevskii. Rather than arranging a meeting with the Petersburg and Vyborg committees, he returned directly to the Pavlovs' apartment, where he found the party activists in the Vyborg District—Kaiurov, Chugurin, Kuklin, Skorokhodov, and others—gathered and exchanging opinions. According to Shliapnikov, "To all it was clear that a revolution had begun and Russia had begun to move [*Rossiia tronulas'*]. The revolutionary movement involved such a wide range of circles that no one doubted that a decisive battle had begun."[27] It is unlikely, however, that the Russian Bureau of the Central Committee took it for granted that a revolution had begun. Actually, it continued to hesitate about throwing all its organizational support behind the strike movement. Chugurin must have pressed Shliapnikov to assert stronger leadership and, particularly, to issue a manifesto. Yet the Russian Bureau failed to draft a manifesto clarifying where it stood on the current strike movement. The inaction of the Russian Bureau deeply disappointed the party activists at the lower level.

Only the Mezhraiontsy managed to issue a declaration to the workers on this day. Their leaflet called for a strike in support of the Putilov workers, and stated: "Hunger will not be eliminated either by the destruction of stores or by marching to the Duma. Only a revolution will get us out of the blind alley of war and misery." It appealed for a democratic republic, socialism, and the creation of a provisional revolutionary government. Although this leaflet did not recognize the new stage of the strike movement, which surpassed the mere labor dispute of the Putilov Factory, distribution of the

25. Shliapnikov, *Semnadtsatyi god* 1: 87; N. Sveshnikov, "Vyborgskii raionnyi komitet RSDRP (b) v 1917 g.," p. 83; idem, "Otryvki iz vospominanii."

26. *Vospominaniia I. D. Chugurina* deposited in the Leningrad Party Archives, quoted in Leiberov, "Petrogradskii proletariat 25 fevralia," p. 37.

27. Shliapnikov, *Semnadtsatyi god* 1: 90.

leaflet itself was significant in giving the workers a sense of direction.[28]

It is difficult to establish the activities of other revolutionary organizations. A small number of radical Socialist Revolutionaries represented by Aleksandrovich and S. Maslovskii continued activities in cooperation with the Mezhraiontsy. The Mensheviks tried to organize a literary committee for the purpose of propaganda among the workers. A small number of the Menshevik intelligentsia gathered and contacted Chkheidze and Chkhenkeli in the Duma. A leader of the initiative group, Ermanskii, noted: "If someone had asked me what would be the outcome of this movement, I would not have been able to give him a definite answer. . . . As for our admittedly weak initiative workers' group, it did not meet during these days."[29]

The representatives of the workers' sick funds and cooperatives were more actively involved. On the previous day the activists under the influence of the workers' group had met at the Semenov Factory and had decided to support the strike and to direct the demonstration to the Tauride Palace. Only a small group of workers went to the Duma.[30] Nevertheless, this did not necessarily mean that a majority of the demonstrators favored the Bolsheviks and rejected the workers' groups' policy. Whether they staged a demonstration in the Nevskii or at the Tauride Palace did not have as much significance as some Soviet historians claim. Since February 14 police protection around the Tauride Palace was extremely heavy, and moreover, the barracks of the Preobrazhenskii, Volynskii, and Lithuanian regiments were located in between the Tauride Palace and Liteinyi Prospekt—an important deterrent to a demonstration at the Tauride Palace.

At the factory level considerable cooperation existed among various revolutionary party members. It appears that in the absence of any definite instructions from the central party organizations, interparty cooperation in the factories played a more important part in the strike movement during the February Revolution. Burdzhalov, recognizing the importance of this cooperation, states: "In the streets of Petrograd, the Mensheviks, SRs, and nonparty workers fought together with the Bolshevik workers. In the course of this struggle the unity of their aims took shape and the unity of their action was formed."[31]

28. Burdzhalov, *Vtoraia russkaia revoliutsiia*, p. 155; I. Iurenev, "Mezhraionka, 1911-1917 gg.," *Proletarskaia revoliutsiia* 25, no. 2 (1924): 140.

29. Burdzhalov, *Vtoraia russkaia revoliutsiia*, p. 156; TsGAOR, f. POO, op. 5, d. 669, ℓ. 315; O. A. Ermanskii, *Iz perezhitogo*, pp. 141-42.

30. Leiberov, "Vtoroi den' fevral'skoi revoliutsii," pp. 117-18.

31. Burdzhalov, *Vtoraia russkaia revoliutsiia*, p. 155.

While the workers waged demonstrations in the streets, the Duma continued its debate about food distribution. After the right-wing deputies denounced liberal and Socialist critics for utilizing the crisis for their sinister political purposes, Shingarev again led an attack upon the government. He outlined in more detail than on the previous day the efforts of the Petrograd City Duma to solve the food problem, and referred to the resolutions passed by the city duma as well as by the State Duma urging the government to transfer responsibilities to the local self-government. Bitterly criticizing the government's refusal to consider these resolutions, Shingarev declared: "We must demand from our government an immediate answer to the question. . . . what measures it will take and is taking to feed sufficiently the population in large cities in the country."[32] Shingarev repeated that the only way to supply food adequately would be to transfer all authority to the Petrograd City Duma.

F. I. Rodichev, a deputy from Petrograd and a member of the Kadet party, advanced the criticism further than his colleague. What is at issue is, he said, not only the matter of the government's handling of food distribution, but also the general competence of the government. He declared: "We demand at the present moment in the name of the people . . . to the government: Give us those people whom all Russia can believe. We demand above all the expulsion from it persons whom all Russia despises."[33] Rodichev's speech was greeted with prolonged applause from the floor.

The temper of the Duma was further excited by a speech delivered by Chkheidze, who pointed out the impossibility of reaching a compromise with the government. He stated: "The interests of this government are absolutely and diametrically in contradiction to the interests of the country and interests of the people. . . . We must say: it is impossible to enter into negotiations with this government on whatever repentance, whatever compromise, whatever agreements, and whatever slogans. What other conclusions can we draw from this? But, gentlemen, you are not making this conclusion."[34] Sooner or later, he continued, the struggle they were witnessing would reach the point where not only the government but also the fundamental structure on which it was based would be eliminated and replaced by a new system created by the people's own initiative. "I greet all sorts of radical resolutions of yours," but he pointed out that when people went out in the streets, declaring a civil war and prepared to face machine guns, passing resolutions would be futile. Chkheidze thus

32. *Stenograficheskii otchet: Gosudarstvennaia duma*, pp. 1704-7,1710.
33. Ibid., pp. 1713-14.
34. Ibid., p. 1721.

appealed to his liberal colleagues to establish contact with the movement in the street by asserting their leadership. In the streets there already existed "free organizations, arbitrary and without any sanction of legal institutions," arising spontaneously from the workers' movement. Lacking, according to the Menshevik vision of revolution, was the participation of the "bourgeoisie" in the movement.

Kerenskii followed Chkheidze's main theme, and urged the Duma liberals to create "truly democratic organizations of society, which now, today, will create a stronghold against the licentious passions of *stikhiia.*" Any appeal coming from this "legal institution" within the framework of the old political structure would have no meaning whatsoever. It was not words but actions that the current crisis demanded.[35]

A deputy from Samara Province, Krylov, reported to the audience the incident he had just witnessed at Znamenskaia Square. The crowds who filled the square greeted the Cossacks with resounding "hurrah" because the Cossacks chased away the police who had beaten an old woman with a nagaika. The audience on the Left greeted this news with prolonged applause and burst into exclamations: "Bravo," "Hurrah!"[36]

The Duma overwhelmingly passed Shingarev's motion to ask the government about the measures it was taking in trying to solve the food question. This day's debate demonstrated that the Duma shifted its emphasis from the discussion on food distribution to over-all denunciation of the government. A call for a revolution, which had been suppressed by the chairman on the previous day, was frequently heard on the floor this day and enthusiastically applauded by the audience.

To convey these sentiments of the Duma, Rodzianko met Golitsyn, urging him to call an emergency meeting of the government and the Duma representatives to solve the food problem. On the evening of February 24 this meeting, attended by the four cabinet ministers as well as by the representatives of the Duma and the State Council, unanimously decided to transfer the distribution of food in Petrograd to the jurisdiction of the Petrograd City Duma.[37]

While the workers effectively expanded the movement, the government reacted to the crisis in a most unimaginative fashion. The council of ministers held a meeting on this day at the Marinskii Palace from

35. Ibid., pp. 1726-28.
36. Ibid., p. 1730.
37. TsGIA, f. 1276, op. 10, d. 7, ll. 466, 469; *Rech'*, February 25, 1917; Deposition of Beliaev, *Padenie tsarskogo rezhima* 2:231; M. V. Rodzianko, "Gosudarstvennaia duma i fevral'skaia 1917 goda revoliutsiia," *Arkhiv russkoi revoliutsii* 4 (1922): 56.

one to six P.M. But as if nothing were happening in the streets, the ministers did not discuss the unrest. Protopopov did not even bother to attend the meeting.[38] The over-all objective of security authorities continued to be dispersal of the demonstrators. To achieve this objective, it was necessary to isolate the workers in various sections of the city and to keep them from joining together in the city's center. The police controlled the main bridges, but as on the previous day the frozen Neva nullified their effective protection. Khabalov failed to adopt any measure to prevent the workers from crossing the river. War Minister Beliaev, irritated by the same news of the demonstrators' crossing the river on ice, impetuously advised Khabalov by telephone to shoot at the crowds on the ice "in such a way that the bullets would hit the ice in front of them." Khabalov, rejecting this impossible advice, adhered to his original plan: at the second stage firearms would not be used.[39]

One can appreciate the ridiculousness of this inflexible adherence to the already mapped-out contingency plan when one learns that during these two days twenty-eight policemen were assaulted by demonstrators. On the second day, particularly, the demonstrators' attack on police grew more vicious, as instances of reported sniper fire demonstrated. Their most favored targets were policemen in sentinel posts. *Gradonachal'nik* Balk asked Khabalov for either more troop reinforcements to protect sentinel police or for complete withdrawal of policemen from sentinel posts. Khabalov agreed only to reduce the number of sentinel posts by half, while increasing simultaneously the number of policemen in each post to two.[40] A brilliant bureaucratic solution, but two policemen were as powerless as one before the outraged crowds.

Khabalov interpreted the unrest solely in terms of a shortage of bread. For this reason he considered it advisable to issue the following statement throughout the city:

For the past days the distribution of flour to bakeries for the purpose of production of bread in Petrograd has been at the normal level. There should not be any shortage of bread for sale. If in some stores bread is lacking, it is because many who are afraid of shortage of bread have bought it for stock. Rye flour is suffi-

38. A. I. Spiridovich, *Velikaia voina i fevral'skaia revoliutsiia, 1914-1917 gg.* 3:87.

39. E. I. Martynov, *Tsarskaia armiia v fevral'skom perevorote*, p. 72; Aleksandr Blok, "Poslednie dni starago rezhima," *Arkhiv russkoi revoliutsii* 4 (1922):26.

40. "Fevral'skaia revoliutsiia i okhrannoe otdelenie," p. 164; Akaemov, "Agoniia starago rezhima," pp. xiv, xvi; Martynov, *Tsarskaia armiia v fevral'skom perevorote*, p. 74.

ciently stocked in Petrograd. Supply of this flour comes in without interruption.[41]

The proclamation was far from true. Immediately after it was printed in the major newspapers on the following day, the delegates of the Petrograd bakers' union visited Khabalov, complaining that the flour they obtained amounted to a mere 3,000 poods, whereas they needed 5,000 poods to maintain sufficient production. Khabalov replied that under the circumstances it would be impossible to appropriate the amount of flour requested by the bakers.[42] Although aware of the untruth of the proclamation, Khabalov was in no position to admit a shortage of bread in the capital to the populace. The problem of the proclamation was that it was not accompanied by more energetic, concrete efforts by the government to make more bread available to the populace, even by exhausting the reserves in the city and diverting the portions earmarked for the military. Such expedients might have slowed down the strike movement but, unaccompanied by such concrete measures, the proclamation did not help. It left the stomachs of the demonstrators empty and, even worse, it fanned their anger.

As on the previous night, Khabalov called a strategic meeting in the office of the *gradonachal'stvo*. Members of the general staff raised the question of the Cossacks' reliability, some even proposing the transfer of undesirable elements to Finland and their replacement by more reliable Cossack units from Krasnoe Selo and Novgorod. Colonel Pavlenkov, however, considered such action premature. The conferees decided: (1) to tighten the supervision over bakeries so as to assure that all the flour given to them would actually be baked into bread and sold to the populace; (2) to arrest the revolutionaries who were instigating the disturbances; and (3) to strengthen the composition of the cavalry units by bringing in a battalion of guard regiments from Novgorod.[43] Nothing was changed in the basic orientation of the previous policy. From these decisions one can hardly detect a sense of urgency. They met with this crisis in the same lethargic manner as they had met others. Martynov summarizes the weaknesses of the authorities as follows:

The first two days revealed to an utmost degree the weakness of the government to which large troops were available. It failed to bring them into action, judging

41. *Rech'*, February 24, 1917.

42. Deposition of Khabalov, *Padenie tsarskogo rezhima* 1:184-85.

43. Akaemov, "Agoniia starago rezhima," p. xvi; Deposition of Khabalov, *Padenie tsarskogo rezhima* 1:188-89; Martynov, *Tsarskaia armiia v fevral'skom perevorote*, pp. 74-75.

that the police only were enough to suppress the disturbances, though it was obviously not enough to cope with the movement. It is true that the troops in the Petrograd Garrison were from the government's point of view not especially reliable. Nonetheless, in order to save the existing regime, they should have had no moment of delay, for as a result of the propaganda that had been developed, each additional day would make these troops more unreliable.[44]

Few predicted that the strike movement that had begun in Petrograd would ultimately lead to a revolution, but many felt as early as the second day that an unusual political crisis had arrived. The number of strike participants was greater than any other previous strike during the war, and workers succeeded in staging demonstrations and holding mass political rallies in the Nevskii for the first time since 1905. Demonstrations had become more violent, involving many assaults on policemen. Cossacks and soldiers reacted to the demonstrators sympathetically. All the revolutionary underground parties were united in their support of the strike and demonstration for the ultimate purpose of overthrowing the tsarist regime. In the face of this crisis, the Duma liberals finally gained a concession from the government concerning the jurisdiction of food supply in Petrograd. But this concession was as irrelevant as Khabalov's proclamation, since the movement that developed in the streets was not merely a bread riot. It was directed against the regime itself.

44. Martynov, *Tsarskaia armiia v fevral'skom perevorote*, p. 76.

14

THE GENERAL STRIKE:
FEBRUARY 25

 The battle was resumed early in the morning. A general strike had begun, spreading now to the workers who had stood aloof during the past two days. Middle-class elements such as students, white-collar workers, and teachers now joined the workers' demonstration. The Vyborg District was no longer the center of the movement—strikes and demonstrations took place all over the city. More than 200,000 factory workers joined the general strike.[1]

Petrograd was threatened with paralysis. Newspapers ceased publication; trams and cabs were nowhere in sight; and many stores, restaurants, and banks closed their doors. When *Gradonachal'nik* Balk noted that the movement "bore the character of an uprising,"[2] he was not exaggerating, for on numerous occasions Cossacks and soldiers began to support the demonstrators in action against the police, while the strike organizers began to coalesce into a single united center.

This day also the movement followed the established pattern of strike and demonstration, but on a larger scale and with increasing

---

1. The figure of the Okhrana report is 210,248; that of the *gradonal'stvo*, 240,000; Leiberov gives 300,000. See N. O. Akaemov, "Agoniia starago rezhima," p. xiii; E. I. Martynov, *Tsarskaia armiia v fevral'skom perevorote*, p. 76; E. N. Burdzhalov, *Vtoraia russkaia revoliutsiia: Vosstanie v Petrograde*, p. 143; I. P. Leiberov, "Petrogradskii proletariat vo vseobshchei politicheskoi stachke 25 fevralia 1917 g.," in *Oktiabr' i grazhdanskaia voina v SSSR: Sbornik statei k 70-letiiu akademika I. I. Mintsa*, p. 32.

2. A. Balk, "Poslednie piat' dnei tsarskogo Petrograda: Dnevnik posledniago," *Petrogradskago gradonachal'nika*, p. 5a.

effectiveness. The workers went to the factories, not to work but to attend political meetings. Orators with varying political opinions rose at the rallies, appealing for the overthrow of tsarism. The slogan "Bread" now became of secondary importance. A Bolshevik worker, Kaiurov, acquired two pieces of red cloth on which he boldly wrote: "Down with Autocracy" and "Down with the War."[3] A young student of the Psychoneurological Institute, Kovnator, who belonged to the Mezhraiontsy, was awakened at eight o'clock in the morning. On the previous night the Mezhraiontsy were instructed to go to the street to join the demonstration and it was Kovnator's responsibility to make a red banner. But it was difficult to find a large piece of red cloth, particularly without a single kopek in his pocket. Finally he went to his girl friend, and expropriated a red skirt. He made two banners out of it, sewing on them: "Down with Autocracy," and "Down with War. Long Live Revolution."[4] This day red banners with such radical demands would fill Nevski Prospekt.

Moderate leaders attempted to give the demonstration a more organized character, and appealed to the workers to refrain from looting and pillaging. The meeting in Aivaz Factory, for instance, adopted a resolution calling for "peaceful demonstration" in Nevskii Prospekt. Crowds packing a workshop of the New Parviainen Factory loudly applauded the speakers—Bolsheviks, Mensheviks, and the SRs alike—who appealed to the workers with equal passion to stage another demonstration on the Nevskii. Denouncing the war and tsarist oppression, they shouted: "We cannot live like this any longer. We are human beings, not animals."[5]

Their two days' experience, particularly the sharp pain of a blow of the nagaika, had taught the workers a lesson. They were prepared for the police, and wore heavy coats, sheepskin coats, heavy boots, and put on their shoulders and backs pads made of cotton, wool sweaters, towels, and underwear. They cut a piece of metal on a lathe to fit their heads, and wore it under their hats. Before their departure they filled their pockets with such "weapons" as nuts, bolts, screws, pieces of metals, and whatever they could find in the factory. During the night sharp nails were scattered in strategic positions to counter attack by the mounted police. Many workers carried knives and pieces of broken bottles for the purpose of stabbing the horses. Factory committees were formed in New Lessner, Old Lessner, and Promet,

3. V. Kaiurov, "Shest' dnei fevral'skoi revoliutsii," p. 162.
4. R. Kovnator, "Nakanune 'fevralia': Otryvki iz vospominanii," p. 188.
5. TsGIA, f. 1282, 1917 g., op. 1, d. 741, ll. 80-81; A. Shliapnikov, *Semnadtsatyi god* 1: 117; A. Kondrat'ev, "Vospominaniia o podpol'noi rabote v Petrograde," *Krasnaia letopis'* 7 (1923): 64.

the three factories that provided the driving force of the strike movement during the February Revolution. In at least three factories in Vyborg District—Aivaz, Erikson, and Old Parviainen—workers' fighting detachments were formed.[6]

The demonstrators moved toward Liteinyi Bridge from all directions. As on the previous day many crossed the river on the ice. But this day the confrontation on the bridge bore a different character. As the demonstrators approached the bridge, the police chief, Colonel Shalfeev, leading a platoon of mounted police and with his nagaika held high, charged headlong into the crowd. The veteran demonstrators who had suffered repeated humiliation from the whips of Shalfeev during the past two days were waiting for this. The crowd ran to the sides, making a wide opening in the middle. But no sooner had Shalfeev galloped through this path than they closed it after him, blocking the platoon of police and isolating Shalfeev in their midst. The chief of police tried to force his way out, desperately swinging his nagaika, but the demonstrators swarmed around him, pushed him off his horse, and seized both his nagaika and saber. One of the workers, taking a large piece of wood from a nearby cabman's coach, began to pound on the victim, while another, taking Shalfeev's revolver, shot him in the heart. During this melee, the Cossacks "retreated and left the chief of police lying on the bridge."[7] Immediately after this incident a large number of demonstrators were able to cross the bridge without much difficulty.

In Vyborg District, the outnumbered police became the targets of the demonstrators' vicious attacks. First, the demonstrators wiped out sentinel posts, taking away their sabers and revolvers. Emboldened, they attacked the police stations on Tikhvenskaia Street and Sampsonievskii Prospekt. By evening the telephone connections between the *gradonachal'stvo* and the police stations in Vyborg District were cut off. Many police officers could escape only by disguising themselves as soldiers. The workers had created a "liberated section" already on February 25.[8]

In Petrograd District, the Petrograd Machine Factory, Vulkan, on the west side and the Diuflon Factory on the east represented the two important gathering points for all the workers. About five thousand

6. Based on Leiberov's personal interviews with the participants in the February Revolution. Leiberov, *Petrogradskii proletariat v Fevral'skoi revoliutsii* 2: 158-59, 162-63.

7. TsGAOR, f. POO, op. 5, d. 669, l. 11; Kondrat'ev, "Vospominaniia o podpol'noi rabote," p. 64.

8. TsGAOR, f. POO, op. 5, d. 669, l. 12; Akaemov, "Agoniia starago rezhima," p. xix; Leiberov, "Petrogradskii proletariat 25 fevralia," pp. 37-38.

workers proceeded on Bol'shaia Spasskaia Street toward Bol'shoi Pros-
pekt only to be dispersed by the police. The crowds assembled in the
Diuflon Factory moved on Kamennoostrovskii Prospekt toward Troitskii
Bridge. The police with the assistance of the soldiers of the Grenadier
Regiment drove the crowds from the bridge, but they were powerless
to prevent the demonstrators from crossing the river on the ice.[9]

On Vasilievskii Island the Baltic Shipyard on the south end and the
Siemens-Haliske Factory on the north became the gathering centers.
From these two points the workers moved toward Bol'shoi Prospekt.
Crowds surrounded Petrograd Pipe Factory, the largest factory on
the island and the stronghold of the workers' group, which had stayed
out of the strike for the past two days. Some workers who resisted
joining the strike barricaded themselves in workshops. While demonstrators outside were trying to break into the factory, a violent battle
was waged inside between the strikers and anti-strikers. Some of the
anti-strikers were seriously wounded.[10] The director of the factory
called for a company of the Finland Regiment. When a company of
the reserve battalion under the command of Second Lieutenant Iossa
arrived at the scene, one of the workers, a certain Dmitriev, began
harassing the commander, shouting obscenities. The young commander
pulled his gun and shot the young worker without warning. The news
of this killing spread quickly, inciting the workers of the Petrograd
Pipe Factory to burst angrily into the streets. This also caused an
indignant reaction among the soldiers in the barracks of the Finland
Regiment, who discussed the incident and swore never to fire upon
the demonstrators.[11]

The demonstrators moving along Srednyi Prospekt stopped at
the Laferm tobacco factory. About fifty demonstrators broke into
the factory, turned off the electricity, smashed lamps, stopped machines, and threw protesting foremen into the streets. The demonstrators on Vasilievskii Island moved on toward Nikolaevskii Bridge,
which was guarded by a platoon of the Fourth Don Cossack Regiment.
As the crowds approached the bridge, the platoon sergeant remained
inactive, indifferently observing the marching crowds. The angered
commander of Vasilievskii Island, Colonel Khodnev, shouted at the
Cossacks to charge into the demonstrators. The Cossacks moved forward slowly, but instead of chasing the demonstrators away they
quietly let them cross the bridge.[12]

9. Leiberov, "Petrogradskii proletariat 25 fevralia," p. 38.
10. Leiberov, *Petrogradskii proletariat v Fevral'skoi revoliutsii* 2: 171.
11. "Vystuplenie leib-gvardii Finlandskogo zapasnogo polka," *Pravda,* April 11,
1917.
12. Leiberov, *Petrogradskii proletariat v Fevral'skoi revoliutsii* 2: 172; TsGIA,

For the first time since the beginning of the movement on February 23, Putilov workers joined the movement. Together with workers of nearby factories, they staged a mass demonstration along Peterhof Chaussée, recaptured the factory, and formed a factory committee. The workers' factory committee created a fighting detachment to disarm the police and to maintain order in the district.[13]

Like an avalanche the workers' movement engulfed other classes of society. The strike spread to the most unorganized sector of the working class—the workers of small factories, store clerks, waiters and waitresses, cooks, and cabdrivers. An Okhrana agent reported the conversation of the cabdrivers: "Tomorrow the cabbies will not take the general public, but only the leaders of the disorders."[14] The usually more conservative city employees—electricians, water and gas employees, postal workers, and the tram drivers and conductors—joined the strike, contributing to the city's paralysis. Printers also struck, stopping the publication of all newspapers in Petrograd. University professors found few students in their classrooms. The students of Petrograd University, the Polytechnical Institute, the Mining Institute, the Psychoneurological Institute, the Technological Institute, Bestuzhev Women's College and other smaller colleges absented themselves from classes and attended the political rallies held on their campuses instead. According to one figure, 15,000 students joined the strike.[15]

The common working men and women, clothed in greasy, worn-out jackets and overcoats, invaded the Nevskii. Among the workers' blue-visored caps and the scarves of women, one could see here and there the green and the light blue of students' caps. The crowds continuously sang revolutionary songs—*La Marseillaise, Varshavianka,* and *Boldly, Comrades, Keep Pace*—songs they had had to sing clandestinely only a few days before. Songs, shouts of slogans, and leaders' short speeches created a constant buzzing echo on the long stretch of the Nevskii. On the balconies of the buildings "burzhui ladies" waved handkerchiefs at the demonstrators. Kovnator unfurled the red banners made out of his girl friend's skirt; excited cheers rose from the demonstrators. At least fifteen columns of demonstrators marched on the Nevskii this day. They held at least four rallies there, each attended by more than a thousand people.[16]

f. 1282, 1917 g., op. 1, d. 741, ℓ. 105.

13. Leiberov, "Petrogradskii proletariat 25 fevralia," p. 39.

14. TsGAOR, f. POO, op. 5, d. 669, ℓ. 11.

15. Leiberov, "Petrogradskii proletariat 25 fevralia," p. 41; V. Baranovskaia, *Soldaty-Pavlovtsy* (Leningrad, 1968), p. 20.

16. Kondrat'ev, "Vospominaniia o podpol'noi rabote," *Krasnaia letopis'* 7 (1923): 65-66; Kovnator, "Nakanune 'fevralia,'" p. 189; Leiberov, "Petrogradskii

The aggressiveness of the demonstrators had sharply increased. Armed with whatever was available—rocks, broken bottles, sharp pieces of ice, they attacked the police sentinel posts. Occasionally revolver shots were fired at the police. As the number of arrests grew numerous, it became increasingly difficult for the police to transfer those arrested to proper detaining facilities. In many cases, the police temporarily detained those arrested in nearby houses appropriated for this purpose. Number 46 on the Nevskii, for instance, was converted into a prison, where about sixty arrested persons were held. Demonstrators gathered in front, demanding the release of the prisoners. When the police guard refused, demonstrators broke into the house, setting all the prisoners free.[17] Cossacks stationed nearby refused to come to rescue the police on the grounds that the house was located beyond their assigned territory.

About 6 P.M., on the Nevskii between Anichkov Bridge and Liteinyi Prospekt, a hand grenade exploded, killing a mounted gendarme and injuring his horse. Two home-made bombs were thrown at the corner of Liteinyi and Nevskii. One of the demonstrators shot a policeman at the intersection of the Nevskii and Vladimir Prospekt, but escaped arrest. Although Khabalov refused to grant permission for the use of firearms, some policemen had to use their revolvers in self-defense. On this day alone there occurred seventeen serious clashes between police and demonstrators.[18]

The crowds acted more boldly as they became assured that the soldiers would not interfere, and approached the barracks. They surrounded the patrols and the sentinels and appealed to the soldiers: "Tell your comrades to support us, not to go against us." Some soldiers approvingly nodded their heads. On Nevskii Prospekt, demonstrators temporarily stopped when they saw the Cossacks in front. A girl walked out of the ranks of the demonstration and moved forward toward the

---

proletariat 25 fevralia," p. 42.

17. TsGIA, f. 1282, 1917 g., op. 1, d. 741, ℓℓ. 94-95.

18. "Fevral'skaia revoliutsiia 1917 goda: Dokumenty Stavki verkhovnogo glavnokomanduiushchego i shtaba glavnokomanduiushchego armiiami severnogo fronta," Krasnyi arkhiv 21, no. 2 (1927):5; "Fevral'skaia revoliutsiia i ohkrannoe otdelenie," p. 169; TsGIA, f. 1282, 1917 g., op. 1, d. 741, ℓ. 157; according to Leiberov, among these seventeen incidents there were eleven in which demonstrators used weapons (seven cases involving revolvers, three of bombs, one of a hand grenade, and six of rocks, screws, and pieces of metal and ice). From these figures Leiberov concludes that the proletariat of Petrograd "transformed the peaceful struggle into an armed uprising on February 25." However, as Burdzhalov argues, it would be rash to view the whole movement as an armed uprising on the basis of these isolated incidents. Leiberov, "Petrogradskii proletariat 25 fevralia," pp. 42-43; Burdzhalov, Vtoraia russkaia revoliutsiia, p. 152.

Cossacks. A thousand eyes followed her. Suddenly she threw away wrapping paper and held out a bouquet of red roses to the officer, who leaned over and took the flowers. Mad, riotous shouts of hurrah were sounded.[19]

Both Cossacks and soldiers executed orders reluctantly. Colonel Khodnev, commander of the training detachment of Finland Regiment, complained about the conduct of the Cossacks: "The Don Cossacks acted with utmost inertia and irresolution. They blatantly refused to take action against the rebels; they even pointed their weapons at the defenders of the legitimate government and order. . . . More than once I heard them say threateningly: 'It is not 1905 now. . . . We will not act against ourselves and against the people.'"[20]

In some cases they expressed their sympathy with the demonstrators in direct action. At number 3 Kazan Street, about two dozen arrested demonstrators were detained under the surveillance of two policemen. About 2 P.M., as demonstrators gathered in front of the house demanding the release of their comrades, a platoon of Cossacks arrived at Kazan Square. Despite the request of the police, however, the Cossacks did nothing to disperse the crowds, insisting that their assignment did not include protection of the prison. The cheering crowds surrounding the Cossacks appealed: "Comrade Cossacks, join us. Help us to liberate our comrades!" The Cossacks assembled in a circle for discussion. All the eyes of the demonstrators were anxiously fixed on them. Suddenly the Cossacks galloped to the door of the house, chasing the guards away with shouts: "You bastards! You are serving only for money." The Cossacks opened the door and released all the prisoners.[21]

The most symbolic incident occurred in Znamenskaia Square. According to one version, thousands of demonstrators filled the square between the statue of Alexander III and Nikolaevskii Station. Orator after orator delivered passionate speeches, some against the war, others calling for support of the Duma and the establishment of a responsible ministry, while the Cossacks watched the rally indifferently. About three o'clock in the afternoon a platoon of mounted police led by an officer, Krylov, arrived at the scene. At Krylov's shrill command, police charged the crowds, who in panic ran in all directions. Krylov,

19. *Pravda*, March 12, 1919, quoted in Burdzhalov, *Vtoraia russkaia revoliutsiia*, p. 148; Aleksei Tarasov-Rodionov, *February 1917*, pp. 46-47.

20. Quoted in Burdzhalov, *Vtoraia russkaia revoliutsiia*, p. 149; "Fevral'skaia revoliutsiia i okhrannoe otdelenie," p. 169.

21. V. Shepelev, "Fevral'skie dni," *Ogonek*, no. 7 (1927); Akaemov, "Agoniia starago rezhima," pp. xix-xx; Shliapnikov, *Semnadtsatyi god* 1:111.

leading the attack, snatched a red banner from fleeing demonstrators and tore it in contempt. Some workers, caps in hands, approached the Cossacks and humbly pleaded for assistance: "Cossack brothers, help the workers in their struggle for peaceful demands. You see how the Pharaohs are treating us hungry workers. Help us!" The Cossacks exchanged glances in embarrassment. Next moment, they rushed into the crowds with unsheathed sabers. It first occurred to Kaiurov that they were hurrying to help the police, but instead they were attacking the the police who then galloped away in fright. The crowds ran back to join in the attack. After the tumultuous melee, the Cossacks returned to their former postion as if nothing had happened. But lying on the snow in the square were the bleeding remains of Krylov. It is impossible to determine who dealt the fatal blow, the Cossacks or the demonstrators. An examination of the body, ordered by Khabalov, showed wounds caused by both sabers and revolver shots.[22] According to another version, Krylov ordered the Cossacks to fire upon the crowds. When this order was ignored, the angered police chief swung his arm and slapped a Cossack on his cheek. At this instant, a Cossack junior officer, M. G. Filatov, a recipient of the order of St. George, who was mounting his horse next to the struck Cossack, unsheathed his saber and struck Krylov's head a violent blow.[23] Whichever version was correct, this incident reinforced the optimism of the insurgents that the soldiers would take their side.

After the incident on Znamenskaia Square, the crowds went to Kazan Square. Driven away from there, they again moved back on the Nevskii toward Znamenskaia Square, but this time armed soldiers of the Ninth Cavalry Regiment lined up in the Nevskii and the side streets, blocking the path of the demonstrators. Particularly heavy ranks were formed across Sadovaia Street near the Gostinyi Dvor. The demonstrators, convinced that the soldiers would not shoot, marched triumphantly. Finally, the first rank of the demonstration stopped as the soldiers pointed their bayonets at their chests. The crowds at the back, still singing revolutionary songs, continued to move forward. In the confusion at the front, women screamed tearfully: "Comrades, put down your bayonets. Join us." The soldiers, confused, threw quick glances at each other. Then, lifting their rifles to their shoulders, slipped in among the demonstrators. Thunderous cheers greeted the soldiers, whose gray overcoats were submerged in the sea

22. TsGIA, f. 1282, 1917 g., op. 1, d. 741, ll. 83, 89; Kaiurov, "Shest' dnei," pp. 162-63; Martynov, *Tsarskaia armiia v fevral'skom perevorote*, p. 79; Akaemov, "Agoniia starago rezhima," p. xxi.
    23. E. Efremov, "Podvig na Znamenskoi," *Neva*, no. 2(1926), p. 218.

of demonstrators. Securely protected, the first soldiers to abandon their posts marched with the workers.[24]

These isolated incidents indicated that the situation was moving rapidly toward a climax. As the confrontation intensified, it became more difficult for soldiers to maintain neutrality. In a dilemma between increasingly rigorous orders from above and persuasive pleas from the demonstrators, tension among the soldiers mounted to a breaking point. But how many would have the courage to defy their military orders? While scattered incidents showed that some soldiers helped the demonstrators, others had now begun to obey the order to shoot at the crowds.

Two platoons of a training detachment blocked the Nevskii near the City Duma, forming lines across the street on the bridge on the Ekaterina Canal. Kaiurov, Aleksandrovich, and other leaders ran ahead of the demonstration to test the sentiments of these soldiers. Having tried to convince the soldiers in vain not to shoot, they withdrew to the side, while the demonstrators approached the soldiers to a distance of no more than fifty steps. Suddenly, an officer gave the signal. The soldiers fired one volley, another, and a third. Standing near the soldiers, Kaiurov followed the direction of the rifles. They shot into the sky. The crowd hit the dirt, but realizing what happened, they got up with cheers. But the next moment, another volley was fired, this time into the crowd. The panic-stricken demonstrators ran to the sides, with screams of hysteria, leaving the bleeding and moaning victims on the street. Nine were killed, nine wounded.[25]

Another shooting incident took place on the Nevskii near the Gostinyi Dvor. A company of the Ninth Cavalry Regiment on guard ordered the demonstrators to disperse with a threat of shooting. As if answering this warning, some in the crowds fired several revolver shots at the soldiers, severely wounding one private. Immediately a platoon of dragoons dismounted and opened fire, killing three demonstrators and wounding ten others.[26]

While the crowds were occupying the streets, the Duma engaged in a debate on the food problem. Its irrelevance was obvious even in the eyes of the Duma deputies themselves. Rittikh solemnly announced that the government had decided to transfer food distribution matters

24. Baranovskaia, *Soldaty-Pavlovtsy*, p. 22; Kaiurov, "Shest' dnei," p. 163.

25. Kaiurov, "Shest' dnei," p. 164; Burdzhalov, *Vtoraia russkaia revoliutsiia*, p. 148.

26. Telegram of Khabalov to Alekseev, no. 3703; "Fevral'skaia revoliutsiia 1917 goda," *Krasnyi arkhiv* 21, no. 2 (1927): 5; Deposition of Khabalov, *Padenie tsarskogo rezhima* 1:189-90. According to Balk, four were killed and twelve wounded. Balk, "Poslednie piat' dnei," p. 5a.

to the jurisdiction of the city duma. His speech, however, was taken by the Duma critics as an affront rather than the government's sincere gesture for reconciliation with society. Shingarev was quick to point out that the government had made this compromise under the pressure of the current crisis only to withdraw the concession when the crisis was over. If transfer of the jurisdiction was legally possible, he asked, why had not the government carried out this reform in November of 1916, when the Petrograd City Duma had requested? How was it possible to accept this clever maneuver, when the government not only had not released the leaders of the workers' group of the War Industries Committee, but also had begun arresting other leaders influential among the workers? Shingarev warned that it would not be society but the government that would have to assume responsibility for what might happen in the streets.[27]

Kerenskii urged his colleagues to adopt a motion to dismiss the present cabinet, form a ministry of confidence, guarantee the freedoms of speech, assembly, organization, and personal inviolability, and place the food supply matter in the hands of the populace. Opposing this motion, Chkheidze declared that any proclamation addressed to the government would create an illusion among the populace that it would still be possible to solve the crisis within the existing political system.[28] Rodzianko, however, ruled Kerenskii's motion out of order, and adjourned the Duma meeting quickly until February 27.

The city duma, to which the entire responsibility of the food supply in Petrograd was suddenly entrusted by the government, had an emergency meeting in the evening. Since the city duma was located by Ekaterina Canal on the Nevskii, the center of the demonstrations, this meeting, attended not only by the city duma deputies, but also by the representatives of various public and workers' organizations, could not but bear a political character.

The first speaker, Senator S. V. Ivanov, stated that the meeting should not and could not be restricted to the discussion of food distribution in view of the crisis developing in the streets. After listening to Lelianov's report on the government's decision to transfer the task of food distribution to the city duma, Ivanov further remarked that despite the demand made a long time before by the city, the government did not respond until it was forced by this serious crisis. A member of the city duma, Major-General P. P. Durnovo, expressed skepticisim about the possibility of improving the food situation in Petrograd by transferring jurisdiction to the city government. In his

27. *Stenograficheskii otchet: Gosudarstvennia duma,* pp. 1745-46, 1749-52.
28. Ibid., pp. 1756-58.

opinion, unless the government promised to assure fifty wagons of
flour rather than thirty-five, the city duma should not take the task
upon itself and should inform the populace of the reality of the situation. M. S. Margulies reported that the city health department had
begun to organize district food committees. However, these committees
were running into difficulties since they could not establish contact
with the workers due to the minister of internal affairs' prohibition
on including workers' delegates in the committees. Because of this
the health department in Vyborg District refused to cooperate, protesting against the exclusion.[29] Despite the opinions counselling restraint, many speakers demanded resignation of the government.

The chairman of the Petrograd Union of Workers' Cooperatives,
I. G. Volkov, boldly declared that the solution of the food crisis would
be possible only under a democratic state order, and demanded not
only the resignation of the government but also a fundamental change
in the state structure.[30] Not only the workers' representative, but
also the Kadet liberal, Kogan, demanded a revolution. He stated that
it was time not to talk about the food supply problem, but to think
about the revolution that had started as a fact and to do everything
to lead it before other irresponsible elements assumed leadership.[31]
The appearance of Kerenskii further augmented the excitement. He
brought the news that the police had just arrested all the participants
in a public meeting of the workers' group of the War Industries Committee. The agitated audience burst into angry shouts and unanimously
decided to send the mayor of the city, Lelianov, and the State Duma
deputy, Shingarev, to the government to secure release of the arrested
workers. A worker of the Lessner Factory, Samodyrov, protested
against the arrest of the workers "in the name of the workers of all
Russia," saying, "The trouble does not lie in the Protopopovs, but
in the system itself. We would not change a thing if we patched up
the existing state system; we must destroy it from the foundations."
According to the Okhrana records, the atmosphere became revolutionary, much like the political meetings during the 1905 Revolution.[32]

The workers' movement thus induced the liberals to sharpen
criticism of the government. Some even openly advocated revolution.
There was no question in their minds that the crowds went to the
streets with a righteous cause and that the government was ultimately
responsible for the crisis. Yet it became increasingly clear that the

29. Shliapnikov, *Semnadtsatyi god* 1: 329-31.
30. Ibid., p. 332.
31. Quoted in P. P. Aleksandrov, *Za Narvskoi zastavoi: Vospominaniia starago
rabochego*, p. 126. Aleksandrov was a Bolshevik worker of the Putilov Factory.
32. Shliapnikov, *Semnadtsatyi god* 1: 329, 333-34.

liberals had no control over these unruly demonstrators. Their passionate speeches in the city duma as well as in the State Duma reflected
the increasing tension in the streets, but remained ineffective in influencing the masses and unheeded by the government. Moreover,
despite strong words uttered from the rostrum, few believed that the
crisis was truly serious enough to become a revolution. Both the State
and the city dumas decided not to hold a meeting on the following
day, Sunday.

The rapidly developing events in the city had a deep impact on
the activities of the revolutionary leaders. The activists keenly felt
the need to establish a center for the movement to coordinate activities,
and a proposal to set up an organization similar to the Soviet of Workers' Deputies in 1905 was widely discussed among various activists'
circles.[33]

As the street fighting became more intense, estrangement between
the Bolshevik Russian Bureau of the Central Committee and the lower
echelons of the party deepened. Some members of the Vyborg District
Committee now openly advocated an armed uprising, urging the Russian Bureau to issue a manifesto calling for an insurrection. In the
morning Sveshnikov called on Shliapnikov. According to this member
of the Vyborg District Committee, "Shliapnikov's mood and his account of the developing events surprised me a little. When I referred
to the events in the city as a revolution that had begun, Shliapnikov
said: 'What revolution is happening there?! Give the workers a loaf
of bread, and the movement would be gone.' " Needless to say, the
Vyborg District Committee was outraged by this statement. Some
now argued that they should take the initiative and make the manifesto
by themselves.[34] Categorically rejecting the Vyborg Committee's
recommendation, Shliapnikov adopted a draft leaflet with milder
content, which, in spite of all the diatribes against the war, tsarism,
and the bourgeoisie, failed to mention a concrete proposal for action.
The leaflet stated that to end the war the proletariat should overthrow
not only the government but also the bourgeoisie represented by the
Duma as well as the nobility represented by the zemstvos. Only one
line–"All to the struggle. To the streets! For yourself, for your children, and for your brothers," referred to action. Those Vyborg activists
who had demanded endorsement of the policy of an armed uprising
were deeply disappointed with this leaflet. They again turned to Shliapnikov, begging him to grant permission to seize arms. Some, like Chu-

33. See chap. 17.
34. Sveshnikov, "Vyborgskii raionnyi komitet," pp. 83-84. This part was
omitted in his previous article in *Petrogradskaia pravda*.

gurin, led a workers' fighting detachment to attack the police headquarters to seize weapons, without permission of the Russian Bureau.
Shliapnikov, however, stubbornly rejected such a request. In his opinion, such adventurism would hinder the cause of revolution. "I feared
that the reckless policy of obtaining weapons in such a manner could
do nothing but harm to the cause. Excited workers using a revolver
against a soldier could only provoke some army units and give an
excuse to the soldiers to attack the workers. Therefore, I definitely
refused to allow anybody to seek weapons and requested that they
try to draw the soldiers into the uprising in a most persuasive way
and to obtain weapons in this way for all the workers."[35] In the light
of what happened two days later, this was perfectly sound judgment.
The strike movement had gone as far as it possibly could. The key
to further development of the revolution, if this movement could
be developed into a revolution, would undoubtedly depend on the
attitudes of the soldiers. It would have been perfectly proper for Shliapnikov as a responsible revolutionary leader to cool the temper of
excited adventurists, who might provoke a reaction, and to put them
in line with an "objectively correct strategy." But one must remember
that Shliapnikov wrote his memoirs from history's vantage point.
He knew that the soldiers' insurrection had occurred on February 27.
It is difficult to know if he had held the same opinion on February 25
as he narrated in his memoirs. Trotskii states: "He wished in his
way to avoid bloody clashes between workers and soldiers, staking
everything on agitation. . . . We know of no other testimony which
confirms or refutes this statement of a prominent leader of those
days—a statement which testifies to sidestepping rather than fore-
sight."[36]

Shliapnikov's statement would have been more convincing had it
been accompanied by more energetic leadership over the strike and
the demonstration. As disgruntled members of the Vyborg District
Committee testified, the leadership of the Russian Bureau of the Central Committee left much to be desired. It did not think very highly of
the movement. During the past three days, none of the three members
of the bureau seems to have physically led or joined the movement.
They did not run from one factory to another, calling for strike, nor
did they face rifles pointed directly at them during the demonstration. They did not share the fear and exultation of the street fighting
with the actual strike organizers and the demonstration leaders like

35. Shliapnikov, *Semnadtsatyi god* 1: 102-5; Leiberov, *Petrogradskii proletariat
v Fevral'skoi revoliutsii* 2: 162.

36. Trotsky, *History of the Russian Revolution* 1: 120.

Kaiurov and Chugurin. It was only natural that Shliapnikov's instructions to draw the soldiers into uprising without seizing weapons was met with resentment, even with contempt, by those who had risked their lives in the streets.

Those who accurately sensed the pulse of the popular movement were the leaders who actually led the strike and the demonstration in the factories and the streets. Their demand for an armed uprising, adventurous though it might appear, was based on their intuitive observation of the soldiers' psychology. They realized that soldiers "are all tied together by a compulsory discipline whose threads are held, up to the last moment, in the officer's fist."[37] The experience of February 25 clearly demonstrated that when the officers effectively asserted their leadership, the soldiers would pull the trigger of their rifles at the demonstrators, despite their suppressed sympathy and pangs of conscience. Trotskii best describes the decisive moment when the demonstrators confront the soldiers:

The critical hour of contact between the pushing crowd and the soldiers who bar their way has its critical minute. That is when the gray barrier has not yet given way, still holds together shoulder to shoulder, but already wavers, and the officer, gathering his last strength of will, gives the command: "Fire!" The cry of the crowd, the yells of terror and threat, drowns the command, but not wholly. The rifles waver. The crowd pushes. Then the officer points the barrel of his revolver at the most suspicious soldier. From the decisive minute now stands out the decisive second. The death of the boldest soldier, to whom the others have involuntarily looked for guidance, a shot into the crowd by a corporal from the dead man's rifle, and the barrier closes, the guns go off of themselves, scattering the crowd into the alleys and backyards.[38]

The leaders of the demonstration learned from their experience that to draw the soldiers to their side they should get the officer before he pulled his trigger. For that reason, they demanded weapons. It was risky; it might provoke a reaction. But they were willing to take that risk.

The Petersburg Committee defiantly adopted a policy contrary to the Russian Bureau's instructions. Ignoring the leaflet issued by the Russian Bureau, it decided to issue its own.[39] Also it urged the

37. Ibid., p. 121.
38. Ibid., pp. 121-22.
39. The proceedings of this meeting were reported in the police record. See TsGAOR, f. DPOO, op. 5, ch. 57/1917 g., ℓℓ. 30-32; TsGAOR, f. DPOO, d. 341, ch. 57/1917 g., ℓℓ. 42-43. The first one is a handwritten report; the second is a typewritten report that corrected some factual mistakes in the first one. Also see E. K. Barshtein and L. M. Shalaginova, "Departament politsii o plane petrogradskikh bol'shevikov v fevrale 1917 g.," *Voprosy arkhivovedeniia*, no. 1 (1962), p. 112.

Bolsheviks to take measures for building barricades in the streets and seizing the electric power station, water supply station, and the telephone station. Responding to the widespread movement to establish a center of the movement, the Petersburg Committee decided to create a factory committee in each factory, which would dispatch its delegates to an "Information Bureau," which in turn would be transformed into a soviet of workers' deputies at an appropriate moment.[40] In defiance of the Russian Bureau, the Petersburg Committee considered the transition from general strike to armed uprising the most urgent of those tasks at hand. On this night the Petersburg Committee issued a leaflet addressed to the soldiers, appealing to them to join the workers' movement against the tsarist regime and the war.[41]

On the night of February 25-26 the Mezhraiontsy discussed how to have the workers react to Khabalov's order to return to work. The Mezhraiontsy did not question that the workers would not heed Khabalov's proclamation. However, "considering that the workers' revolutionary movement had not yet reached a decisive moment, at the same time wishing to partake in it, and above all fearing that this would eventually develop into spontaneous explosion of unorganized masses," the Mezhraiontsy decided to issue a leaflet appealing to the workers not to obey Khabalov's proclamation. Together with this leaflet, the Mezhraiontsy issued another leaflet directed to the soldiers, urging them to "follow the example of the Cossacks at Znamenskaia Square."[42]

40. TsGAOR, f. DPOO, op. 5, ch. 57/1917 g., l. 32; TsGAOR, f. DPOO, d. 341, ch. 57/1917, l.42.

41. Shliapnikov, Semnadtsatyi god 1: 101-2; Listovki peterburgskikh bol'-shevikov 2: 250-51; TsGAOR, f. DPOO, d. 341, ch. 57/1917 g., l. 44. The details of the Petersburg Committee's meeting on February 25 are obscure. According to Zalutskii, the Executive Committee of the Petersburg Committee held a meeting at an apartment on Kronver Street, attended by Skorokhodov, Shutko, Chugurin, Gan'shin, Zalutskii, and others. Skorokhodov, Shutko, and Chugurin declared that they decided to halt the workers' demonstration to avoid further bloodshed. Zalutskii explained to them that the military units were wavering and that a revolution would be impossible without blood. To Zalutskii's surprise the participants were persuaded by his argument and adopted a militant resolution calling for intensification of the struggle. Zalutskii himself was entrusted with the task of writing a short leaflet. P. Zalutskii, "V poslednie dni podpol'nogo petersburgskogo komiteta bol'shevikov," Krasnaia letopis' 35, no. 2 (1930): 37. Zalutskii's account, however, does not correspond with the police record of the Petersburg Committee's meeting or the general mood of the Bolshevik activists on February 25. The meeting Zalutskii described might have taken place on February 26.

42. See p. 253; I. Iurenev, "Mezhraionka," pp. 140-41.

The Menshevik activists and the leaders of the cooperative movement held a meeting that was attended by thirty to fifty delegates
from all districts of Petrograd. Chkheidze, F. A. Cherevanin (Menshevik-Defensist), and the two leaders of the cooperative movement,
I. G. Volkov and N. Iu. Kapelinskii, also attended. They decided
to create a soviet of workers' deputies and instructed the participants
to return to their respective organizations to organize elections to
the soviet.[43] In the evening, with Guchkov's permission, the two
remaining members of the workers' group, Ostapenko and Anasovskii,
called a meeting of the representatives of the workers' movement
in the office of the Central War Industries Committee on Liteinyi,
presumably to discuss the food crisis, but obviously intending to
discuss broader political questions. Kerenskii, Skobelev, and thirty
representatives of the workers attended the meeting. But on the
grounds that the two members of the workers' group on the search
warrant were among the participants, the police broke up the meeting
and arrested all the participants. Kerenskii and Skobelev were immediately released. The Okhrana report also mentioned that the Socialist Revolutionaries had decided to join the movement "to support
the revolutionary offensive of the proletariat," and that the anarchists
had also decided to "take advantage of the moment for their aims . . .
for terror against the government in the broadest possible ways,"
including setting bombs in the Okhrana and the provincial gendarme
administration.[44]

While the experience in the streets on February 25 made the
leaders who lived in the midst of the movement more radical, the
sensitive antennae of the Okhrana accurately caught the decisive
change in the atmosphere of the crowds. Indicating a dangerous align-
ment between the demonstrators and the soldiers, Kochgar warned:
"If a moment is lost and the leadership is transferred to the high
echelons of the revolutionary underground, the events will take the
widest scale."[45] One of the most intelligent and articulate Okhrana
agents, Limonin, who was actually Shurkanov, a member of the
Bolshevik Vyborg District Committee, reported to the *gradonachal'nik:*

The people became convinced that a revolution had begun, that its success
would be assured for the masses, that the government was powerless to suppress
the movement since the army units were not standing behind it, that a decisive

43. *Izvestiia Petrogradskogo soveta rabochikh i soldatskikh deputatov,* August 27, 1917. See chap. 17.
44. TsGAOR, f. DPOO, d. 341, ch. 57/1917 g., ℓℓ. 31–32.
45. "Fevral'skaia revoliutsiia i okhrannoe otdelenie," p. 169.

victory would be near, since the army units would openly go to the side of the revolutionary forces, if not today then tomorrow, that the movement which had started would not die down, but would grow without interruption to a victorious end and to an overthrow of the state order.[46]

The police forces clearly had to take a defensive position in the face of the massive, aggressive demonstration. This fact, coupled with the highly disturbing Okhrana reports, compelled security authorities to proceed to the last stage of the contingency plan—an active deployment of troops with the maximum use of firearms.

Nicholas's telegram to Khabalov provided the military authorities with the excuse to switch to an all-out offensive. The news of serious disturbances in the capital reached Nicholas in Mogilev for the first time on February 25 through the empress's telegram and the report of the palace commandant, Major-General V. N. Voeikov, who had kept in touch with Protopopov. On the night of February 25, Nicholas ordered Khabalov by telegram to "quell by tomorrow the disturbances in the capital which are inexcusable in view of the difficulties of the war with Germany and Austria." Later Khabalov testified before the Extraordinary Investigation Commission of the Provisional Government: "This telegram took me by surprise. . . . But what should I do? The emperor ordered: you must shoot. . . . It was a terrible blow. Because I could not see how this measure which I had been trying to avoid in the past days could without fail lead to a desirable result."[47] This testimony should not be taken too literally. The objective reality of February 25 plainly showed that the measures designed for the second stage of the contingency plan could no longer subdue the demonstrators. Even on this day, some officers found it necessary to use firearms to disperse the crowds, a violation of Khabalov's instructions in the second stage. It was plain, even without the emperor's telegram, that draconian measures would be needed to deal with the unrest if it were to be put down once and for all.

As usual, Khabalov convened a strategic conference at the *grado-nachal'stvo* at 10 P.M. After reading the emperor's telegram he announced that he would require the troops to fire upon recalcitrant demonstrators on the next day. Khabalov issued two proclamations to the populace that were posted throughout the city. One was addressed to all the workers, ordering them to return to their work by Feb-

46. Ibid., pp. 173-74. This report was dated February 26, but the content of the report was obviously concerned with the situation of February 25.

47. Deposition of Khabalov, *Padenie tsarskogo rezhima* 1: 190; TsGAOR, f. ChSK, d. 460, ℓ. 69.

ruary 28, Tuesday. He sternly warned that any violators of this ultimatum would have to face life in uniform at the most dangerous front.[48] The other served notice to the populace that "any gathering in the street is forbidden" and that Khabalov had given permission to the soldiers "to use arms for the restoration of order in the capital." The workers did not pay much attention to Khabalov's proclamations. One in the crowd gathered in front of the proclamation posted on a wall in Vyborg District commented: "It is interesting to see how he is going to send all of us to the front. Who is going to produce supplies for the army? He himself?"[49]

Protopopov and Vasiliev were alarmed by the development in the city, and sent the police during the night to arrest the activists. More than one hundred persons were arrested on this day, including the two members of the workers' group and five members of the Bolshevik Petersburg Committee. Most arrests were made in three districts: Vyborg, Narva, and Rozhdestvo.[50]

Although the security authorities decided to take rigorous measures against the demonstrators, they neglected to report the real situation in the capital to the high command at the front. Khabalov sent the first news of the unrest in Petrograd to the Stavka only on February 25. In this telegram, outlining the development of the unrest since February 23, Khabalov optimistically stated: "Today, February 25, the attempts of the workers to penetrate into the Nevskii were successfully thwarted. A part [of the demonstrators] who managed to penetrate thereto were driven away by the Cossacks."[51] That picture had no resemblance to what actually happened in the streets in Petrograd. Although he mentioned some of the serious incidents involving the killing of police officers, one would be given the impression that with the large reinforcements from the outskirts of Petrograd the capital was securely protected.

The two telegrams dispatched by Beliaev conveyed an even more

48. Deposition of Khabalov, *Padenie tsarskogo rezhima* 1: 191; Martynov, *Tsarskaia armiia v fevral'skom perevorote*, p. 82.

49. TsGIA, f. 1282, 1917 g., op. 1, d. 741, ℓ. 6; Gordienko, *Iz boevogo proshlogo*, p. 61.

50. The number of the arrested is not known precisely. On February 24 altogether 7,538 were in various prisons in Petrograd; on February 25 the number of prisoners rose to 7,652, an increase of 114. The increase in the Rodzhestvo police precinct probably resulted from the arrests of the participants in the meeting held at the initiative of the workers' group. TsGAOR, f. DPOO, d. 341, ch. 57/1917 g., ℓℓ. 24, 29. It would be extremely interesting to study the composition of the arrested activists, but unfortunately such material has not been discovered.

51. Telegram of Khabalov to Alekseev, no. 486, "Fevral'skaia revoliutsiia 1917 goda," *Krasnyi arkhiv* 21, no. 2(1927): 4-5.

optimistic picture, seriously distorting the real situation. Beliaev assured the tsar that since the military authorities were taking adequate measures to suppress the disturbances, order would be restored by the next day. In his telegram to Voeikov, Protopopov stated: "the commander of the military district is taking energetically all the measures to put an end to further disturbances."[52] In this way, security authorities in Petrograd tried to hide their embarrassment at allowing such a wide-scale disturbance in Petrograd on February 25, and left the Stavka in the dark as to the real situation in the capital.

The cabinet members met for the first time since the outbreak of the strike movement on February 23. Golitsyn convened a meeting at midnight at his apartment on Mokhovaia 41, just off Liteinyi Prospekt. Not only the cabinet members but also senior statesmen such as Trepov, Nikolai Maklakov, and Prince A. A. Shirinskii-Shikhmatov also took part in the meeting. The majority of the ministers expressed skepticism of Protopopov's optimism. After reading the imperial order, Khabalov assured the ministers that on the next day thirty thousand soldiers assisted by artilleries and armored cars would take a decisive offensive against the rebels. The minister of foreign affairs, N. N. Pokrovskii, interrupted. Could the government really expect to eradicate the fundamental cause for the unrest only by military means? Pokrovskii argued that it was about time to seek a political solution: resignation of all the ministers and the formation of a new cabinet through negotiations with the Duma. The minister of foreign affairs went as far as to suggest the names of persons who might successfully command the confidence of the nation: P. N. Ignatiev, A. A. Polivanov, and General M. V. Alekseev. This proposal met with the support of the minister of agriculture, A. A. Rittikh, and some others. But Protopopov bitterly opposed any compromise with the Duma, which was, in his opinion, the major instigator of the present unrest. Only two reactionary ministers, N. A. Dobrovol'skii, minister of justice, and N. I. Raev, procurator of the holy synod, supported Protopopov. The majority favored negotiations with the Duma. According to the secretary to the Council of Ministers, I. N. Lodyzhenovskii, the Council of Ministers also discussed Beliaev's proposal to declare a state of siege in Petrograd. But it did not take any action on this proposal. Having decided to delegate the responsibilities of negotiations with the Duma to Pokrovskii and Rittikh, the Council of Ministers adjourned the meeting at three o'clock in the morning. The popular rising thus succeeded in causing a crack in the tsar's cabinet.[53]

52. A. S. Lukomskii, *Vospominaniia* 1: 123; TsGAOR, f. ChSK, d. 460, ℓ. 20; Shliapnikov, *Semnadtsatyi god* 1: 136.

53. For the Council of Ministers meeting on February 25, TsGAOR, f. ChSK,

On the third day the strike movement developed into a general strike, engulfing all segments of society. Police and troops no longer controlled the crowds. The demonstrators' attack on the police became more violent and deliberate, and the soldiers more openly expressed their sympathy with the crowds. Many felt that a revolution had begun. Revolutionary underground organizations strove to create a center of the movement. While the tsar ordered military authorities in Petrograd to shoot to kill the demonstrators, his cabinet decided to avert the crisis by negotiating with the Duma. The situation was moving quickly toward a climax.

As the last demonstrators slipped out of the center of the city, Petrograd was restored to tranquillity. As the commotion and noise stopped, eerie silence crept onto Nevskii Prospekt. Only the lights of the Royal Alexander Theater shone brightly for the premiere of Lermontov's *Masquerade*. French Ambassador Paléologue took his secretary's wife, Vicomtesse du Halgouët, to a concert at the Marinskii Theater. The concert hall was almost empty. After glancing around the deserted hall "with eyes that were almost in tears," the violinist Enesco came close to the audience at the corner of the orchestra, and played a piece of Saint-Saëns. When Paléologue left the theater, the usually lively Theater Square was desolate. Their car, the only one in the square, passed through the deserted city. They saw the Moika Bridge and the Lithuanian Castle heavily guarded by the gendarmes and troops. Madame du Halgouët remarked: "Are we witnessing the last night of the regime?"[54] It was too hasty a remark: the regime had a few more nights to spare.

---

d. 466, ᴫᴫ. 119, 175; Deposition of Khabalov, *Padenie tsarskogo rezhima* 1: 192-94; Deposition of Golitsyn, ibid. 2: 231-33; Balk, "Poslednie piat'dnei," p. 6.
    54. Paléologue, *An Ambassador's Memoirs* 3:215-16.

15

BLOODY SUNDAY:
FEBRUARY 26

 Sunday, February 26, was a sunny winter day. The bright sun, the blue sky, the crisp air, and the soft snow that covered the ground during the night created a holiday spirit. In the heart of Petrograd, however, the morning sun unveiled an extraordinary scene. The streets had been turned into a military camp overnight. Soldiers formed pickets in front of buildings, at major intersections, bridges, and railway stations; sentinels paced watchfully in the streets with rifles on their shoulders. Mounted patrols and squads of cavalry trotted in the city streets, while soldiers of the Engineers Regiment rolled field telephone lines from one intersection to another. The policemen at sentinel posts were removed and police detachments armed with rifles took positions. In the courtyards the Red Cross established its headquarters and prepared sanitary wagons and stretchers. After eleven o'clock in the morning machine-gun units rolled onto the Nevskii and installed their guns at strategic intersections along the way.[1] No pedestrians nor trams and cabs were visible in the heart of the city. Cabmen took the yokes off their horses. All the city schools, together with many other private schools, were closed until Tuesday. No one was permitted to go out into the streets in the center, and those who had to go out were stopped by soldiers on patrol and asked for identification. All stores, restaurants, and cafes were closed. For the first time since February 23 all the bridges were raised to prevent demonstrators from crossing the Neva. Khabalov dispatched a telegram to the

1. RO GBL, f. 369, no. 16, d. 34, V. D. Bonch-Bruevich, "Fevral'skaia revoliutsiia," ll. 2-3.

Stavka: "Today, February 26, it has been quiet in the city since morning."[2]

This judgment was premature, however. This day gates were closed at most of the factories and, unable to use them as rallying points, the workers assembled directly in the major streets of their districts. The bridges were up, but it was no trouble to cross the Neva on the ice. It was not until late in the morning that the first demonstrators appeared on the Nevskii, marching triumphantly and festively, singing revolutionary songs, and shouting slogans. As soon as they reached the Nevskii the mood and the scene changed. Unlike the previous days, the soldiers systematically and ruthlessly fired upon the approaching crowd.

Four major shooting incidents took place. Soldiers of the Semenovskii Regiment, taking positions at the intersection of Nevskii and Vladimir Prospekts, fired on the crowd, killing and wounding several people.[3] Demonstrators approaching the intersection of Nevskii Prospekt and Sadovaia Street near the Gostinyi Dvor suddenly met with volleys of fire from the soldiers of the training detachment of the Pavlovskii Regiment. The crowds scattered behind the buildings, but many lay flat on the snowy street. They carried the dead and wounded to the city duma, leaving stains of dark blood on the snow. After a few volleys, the streets were empty. Altogether eighteen wounded demonstrators were brought into the city duma, which suddenly became a hospital, staffed with student volunteers wearing the arm bands of the Red Cross and doctors and nurses who had rushed to the scene.[4]

The third and the fourth incidents—more serious than the first two—involved the first and the second training detachments of the Volynskii Regiment that took positions on the south side of Znamenskaia Square. The commander of the detachments, Major Lashkevich, tried to enforce strict discipline among the reluctant soldiers. At first, he attempted to disperse the crowds by sending squads of mounted patrols, giving them an order to use nagaikas and sabers, if necessary. The patrol soldiers, however, begged the demonstrators to disperse

2. TsGIA, f. 1276, op. 8, d. 679, ch. 3, ℓ. 112; telegram, Khabalov to Alekseev, no. 3703; "Fevral'skaia revoliutsiia 1917 goda," *Krasnyi arkhiv* 21, no. 2 (1927):5.

3. TsGAOR, f. POO, op. 5, d. 669, ℓ. 357; E. I. Martynov, *Tsarskaia armiia v fevral'skom perevorote*, p. 85; "Fevral'skaia revoliutsiia i okhrannoe otdelenie," p. 170.

4. TsGAOR, f. POO, op. 5, d. 669, ℓℓ. 356-57; Martynov, *Tsarskaia armiia v fevral'skom perevorote*, p. 85; "Fevral'skaia revoliutsiia i ohkrannoe otdelenie," p. 170; O. A. Ermanskii, *Iz perezhitogo*, p. 172; I. Gordienko, *Iz boevogo proshlogo*, p. 60; V. Kaiurov, "Shest' dnei," p. 165; TsGAOR, f. DPOO, d. 341, ch. 57/1917 g., ℓℓ. 45, 46; TsGIA, f. 1276, op. 8, d. 679, ch. 3, ℓ. 112.

rather than using their weapons. The angered commander immediately had one private arrested for insubordination. On another occasion, Lashkevich abused a noncommissioned officer when the latter refused to strike an old woman who approached him and pleaded with him not to shoot. The soldiers sensed that the decisive moment was approaching. What should they do when ordered to shoot? They secretly asked Sergeant Kirpichnikov, a sympathizer with the demonstrators. Kirpichnikov answered: "If they make us shoot, shoot in the air. You cannot help obeying the order, otherwise they will shoot us."[5]

Unable to disperse the crowds in the square, Lashkevich finally decided to fire upon them. A bugle sounded as a warning signal, but the crowds remained, apparently not understanding what would come next. Second Lieutenant Vorontsov, commanding officer of the second training detachment, shouted: "Fire!" Sharp cracks echoed in the square. The panic-stricken crowds ran amock, seeking shelter and leaving their bleeding comrades behind. Some soldiers intentionally shot into the air. Vorontsov was enraged, snatched a rifle from one of the soldiers, and began shooting at the fleeing people. Forty persons were killed and more were wounded. Police dragged the dead bodies to the middle of the square and among them were two soldiers in uniform who had joined the demonstration. On the east side of the square, the first training detachment that took positions facing the intersection of Suvorov Prospekt and First Rozhdestvenskaia Street also fired on demonstrators gathering there, and killed ten persons and wounded several.[6]

Frightened crowds disappeared from the Nevskii behind buildings and inside houses. Some rushed into a cafe, which became filled with workers with visored caps. They, together with the regular customers—dandies in fine clothes and gold rings, well-dressed ladies, and prostitutes—spoke in frightened whispers and peered through the curtains at the streets. Someone said in a low voice: "It's the training detachment. The careerists!"[7] All the troops involved in the shootings on February 26 were the training detachments of the guard regiments—the special military units designed to train noncommissioned officers from specially selected soldiers.

5. T. Kirpichnikov, "Vozstanie 1.-gv. Volynskago polka v fevrale 1917 g.," *Byloe* 27-28, nos. 5-6 (1917):7-8.

6. TsGAOR, f. DPOO, d. 341, ch. 57/1917 g., ll. 45, 46; Kirpichnikov, "Vozstanie 1.-gv. Volynskago polka," p. 8; Martynov, *Tsarskaia armiia v fevral'skom perevorote*, p. 85; "Fevral'skaia revoliutsiia i okhrannoe otdelenie," p. 170.

7. Iu. Volin, *Rozhdestvo svobody: Pobrosok iz al'man: Revoliutsiia v Petrograde*, pp. 12-13.

After the shootings, the crowds viewed the police and the troops of the training detachments with extreme but wary hostility. As soon as the shooting stopped, people reappeared in the streets and threw rocks and pieces of ice at them. Some who had been chased away from Znamenskaia Square into the Old Nevskii Prospekt and Goncharnaia Street hid behind buildings and shot at the military patrols. Five policemen who were patrolling on Apraksin Street behind Suvorov Theater were suddenly attacked by sniper fire and barely escaped to nearby police headquarters.[8]

The revolution had now reached a new stage. From then on the demonstrators came out onto the streets fully aware of the danger of being gunned down. Would the movement continue to be supported by most of the workers or would it dissipate? The soldiers, cornered at last by the orders to shoot, had to choose between conscience and obedience. Could the government continue suppressing its conscience in the name of discipline? The fate of the revolution depended on these questions, as the events of February 26 clearly demonstrated that as long as the majority of the soldiers remained within the boundaries of military discipline, an insurrection would have no chance for success.

The shooting incidents unnerved the leaders of the demonstration. It appeared to Mil'chik "that the movement was destroyed, that tsarism had taken the upper hand, and that on the following day the soldiers would begin shooting at the workers in the workers' district." The Bolshevik worker Kaiurov believed: "The uprising is coming to an end. The demonstration had no arms, nothing with which to answer to the government, which had taken a decisive measure."[9] The Bolshevik Russian Bureau of the Central Committee held its meeting late at night. Chugurin again pleaded with Shliapnikov to call for the seizure of weapons and creation of a workers' militia. This militant Bolshevik insisted that armed workers would be able to turn the tide in their favor. But after the soldiers' shooting no one was convinced. Shliapnikov argued that the only hope for the revolution would lie in a transfer of the allegiance of the soldiers. The committee finally decided to continue the struggle, concentrating all the Bolsheviks' energy on propaganda among the soldiers.[10]

Members of the Vyborg District Committee, which assumed the function of the defunct Petersburg Committee, met in vegetable gardens outside the city limits. In the gloom of the meeting, many

8. TsGAOR, f. DPOO, d. 341, ch. 57/1917 g., ll. 46, 49.
9. I. Mil'chik, *Rabochii fevral'*, pp. 82-83; Kaiurov, "Shest' dnei," p. 165.
10. Shliapnikov, *Semnadstatyi god* 1: 127.

expressed the opinion that the Bolsheviks should bring the movement to an end.[11] Fatigue and the penetrating cold, however, prevented them from reaching a definite plan. The meeting adjourned after it was decided to meet at Kaiurov's apartment on the following day. Early next morning about forty representatives from various factories and a member of the defunct Petersburg Committee, K. I. Shutko, gathered at Kaiurov's apartment. Shurkanov, a police spy from the Aivaz Factory, presented the most radical opinion, calling for the continuation of the struggle and including the use of firearms. He was supported by the majority, who adopted a resolution calling for the continuation of the strike, a transformation of the struggle into an armed uprising, fraternization with the soldiers, seizure of weapons, and the prompt dissemination among the workers of a manifesto published by the Bolshevik party.[12]

Shurkanov's radical opinion may have been a provocation, but it also corresponded to the sentiment of the masses of workers. While the shooting incidents contributed to the gloomy pessimism of the movement's leaders, among the workers they provoked profound outrage and inspired a determination to fight. An Okhrana agent reported that on Vasilievskii Island "Socialists" held rallies, calling for the continuation of the strike with large-scale retaliation against those factories that resumed work. A joint meeting of the Bolsheviks and the Mezhraiontsy on the island produced a resolution appealing to the workers to continue the strike and the demonstration, to coerce movie theaters, billiard halls, and other entertainment facilities to close their businesses, and to seize weapons for the formation of a workers' militia.[13] Some activists openly advocated an armed uprising. A worker, Iu. Volin, heard an orator shouting: "Comrades! Tomorrow is the decisive day. Let's not be naïve any more. Let's go with weapons in hand! Pull down their fortresses. In arsenals and in weapons factories we will find revolvers, firearms, and cartridges. We will go to the Kresty, to the Fortress of Peter and Paul, to all the prisons, where our brothers are languishing, the fighters for freedom. Comrades! Now or never."[14]

11. Early on the morning of February 26, the Russian Bureau held an emergency meeting with the party members of the Vyborg District Committee. They discussed how to fill the gap of the defunct Petersburg Committee, whose members had been arrested with a few exceptions by the police. The Vyborg Committee was asked to take over the role of the Petersburg Committee. Shliapnikov, *Semnadtsatyi god* 1: 121-22; Kaiurov, "Shest' dnei," pp. 165-66.

12. Kaiurov, "Shest' dnei," p. 166; N. Sveshnikov, "Otryvki iz vospominanii," *Petrogradskaia pravda*, March 14, 1923.

13. "Fevral'skaia revoliutsiia i okhranoe otdelenie," p. 171.

14. Volin, *Rozhdestvo svobody*, p. 43.

As the Bloody Sunday of 1905 touched off a storm of revolutionary movement, the bloody Sunday of February 26 also prepared the way for an uprising of the workers in Petrograd.

A police report noted: "Now everything depends upon the direction of the army units; if they do not turn to the side of the proletariat, the movement will quickly subside; but if the troops stand against the government, nothing will be able to save the country from revolutionary upheaval."[15] Military authorities tightened regulations in the barracks by cutting contact between soldiers and the outside world. From the outbreak of the unrest soldiers were denied passes and the privilege of reading newspapers and using telephones, and were confined tightly within their barracks.[16] Nevertheless it was impossible to keep the news entirely from the soldiers—news from the streets spread quickly in the barracks.

The Pavlovskii Regiment barracks were located on the western side of Mars Field. Soon after the training detachment of this regiment fired upon the demonstrators on the Nevskii near the city duma, a group of workers rushed to the barracks and told the soldiers. Soldiers of the Fourth Company, who were predominantly evacuees, were outraged by the news and stormed into the company arsenal. Contrary to their expectations, however, they found only thirty rifles (for the training of one thousand soldiers) and no cartridges. Thus, more than a hundred mutineers went out into the streets unarmed. They moved along the Ekaterina Canal toward the Nevskii under the command of a noncommissioned officer, with only the vague notion that they had to make their comrades stop shooting at the demonstrators. As they moved along the canal, they encountered a squad of mounted police that suddenly appeared from behind Mikhailovskaia Square. The soldiers opened fire upon the police, killing one policeman and wounding another. This volley of fire exhausted all their cartridges.[17]

The revolt was immediately reported to Khabalov, who ordered Pavlenkov "to take all possible measures so as not to spread this further," and sent a company of the Preobrazhenskii Regiment to suppress it. The soldiers of the Preobrazhenskii Regiment, however, refused

15. Quoted in E. N. Burdzhalov, *Vtoraia russkaia revoliutsiia: Vosstanie v Petrograde*, p. 182.

16. V. Baranovskaia, *Soldaty-Pavlovtsy*, p. 25.

17. TsGAOR, f. DPOO, d. 341, ch. 57/1917 g., *l.* 48; Martynov, *Tsarskaia armiia v fevral'skom perevorote*, pp. 87-89; "Fevral'skaia revoliutsiia i okhrannoe otdelenie," p. 170; Shliapnikov, *Semnadtsatyi god* 1: 164-67; Deposition of Khabalov, *Padenie tsarskogo rezhima* 1: 195-202; Baranovskaia, *Soldaty-Pavlovtsy*, pp. 25-31.

to fire upon the mutineers. After the initial outburst of anger wore out, the insurgents faced cold reality: other demonstrators they might have joined were nowhere in sight and they had used all their ammunition. Sensing doom, they decided to return to their barracks and to incite rebellion among other soldiers.

In the meantime, not only officers of the Pavlovskii Regiment but also officers from other units rushed to the Pavlovskii barracks and walked from one bay to another between the soldiers' plank beds. They told the soldiers that the training detachment had been removed from the streets and the regimental chaplain gave a lecture on the soldier's duty to tsar and fatherland. As soon as the Fourth Company returned, the insurgents were disarmed and the entire company was placed under strict surveillance. Nevertheless, it turned out that twenty-one soldiers were still missing.[18] Officers and soldiers of the training detachment guarded the room and machine guns were installed at the door, their muzzles facing directly inside the bay.

The revolt of the Fourth Company gravely alarmed the military authorities. Beliaev demanded immediate execution of all participants without trial, but such draconic measures were not Khabalov's style. He had nineteen ringleaders arrested and imprisoned in the Fortress of Peter and Paul during the night. These nineteen imprisoned leaders and three other leaders who were classified as AWOL included fourteen privates, four privates in reserve (ratniki), one senior noncommissioned officer, and three platoon noncommissioned officers. The presence of four NCOs on this list indicates that the NCOs played a crucial role at the decisive moment of the soldiers' insurrection.[19] On the next morning Khabalov himself visited the barracks, warning the soldiers that only the death penalty would await those who might join a similar rebellion in the future. He had no way of knowing that in a few hours an even larger soldiers' uprising would begin.

At the critical moment, when the success or the failure of the revolution depended almost totally upon the attitude of the soldiers, the rebellion of the Pavlovskii Regiment was ominous. It was still an isolated action without a direct bearing on subsequent events, since the military authorities successfully kept the news from spreading. Yet this incident symbolized the effect the order to shoot had on

18. Baranovskaia, *Soldaty-Pavlovtsy*, p. 29.

19. Deposition of Khabalov, *Padenie tsarskogo rezhima* 1: 196; Martynov, *Tsarskaia armiia v fevral'skom perevorote*, pp. 88-90. Baranovskaia for the first time published the names of the twenty-one ringleaders. It would be interesting to study the background of these arrested soldiers, but Baranovskaia's list does not go beyond the rank of the soldiers. Baranovskaia, *Soldaty-Pavlotsy*, p. 31.

the soldiers. A rebellion of more than a hundred soldiers constituted a serious threat to the maintenance of order. Nevertheless, Khabalov and Beliaev decided not to report the incident to the Stavka, and sent optimistic information that did not mention the Pavlovskii rebellion.[20] Balk later commented on the shortsightedness of the military leaders, stating that despite having achieved "such brilliant success in restoring order in the streets" the military authorities led by "weaklings and confused people" failed to take advantage of their success.[21]

While the troops were firing on demonstrators, Rittikh and Pokrovskii met representatives of the Duma, N. Savich, V. Maklakov, P. Balashov, and I. Dmitriukov early in the morning of February 26. The Duma critics presented the formation of a ministry of confidence as a minimal condition of restoring order, although they disagreed among themselves as to the advisability of adjourning the Duma.[22] The success of the repression on February 26, however, hardened the government's attitude toward the Duma. The majority of the cabinet members, who had considered a compromise with the Duma as a necessary evil on the previous night, now saw a political solution as unnecessary. When Pokrovskii and Rittikh reported their negotiations with Duma delegates, the cabinet members listened with boredom and summarily dismissed the possibility of further negotiations. According to Protopopov, "a compromise was impossible, for the representatives [of the Duma] demanded a change of the government and the appointment of a new ministry composed of persons who enjoyed public confidence. . . . The demands of the representatives were deemed unacceptable." Instead, the Council of Ministers now decided to prorogue the Duma over the strong objections of Pokrovskii and Rittikh.[23]

As a small group of people gathered in front of the Tauride Palace, a young student made a speech to them in front of the closed gates. "Our deputies, the representatives of the people, have nothing to say," he accused. In a hoarse voice the student explained that he himself had been in the Duma and had heard the deputies' speeches:

20. A. S. Lukomskii, *Vospominaniia* 1: 124. It was not until early afternoon of the following day that Khabalov finally mentioned the revolt of the Pavlovskii Regiment. Telegram of Khabalov to the tsar, no. 56, "Fevral'skaia revoliutsiia 1917 goda," *Krasnyi arkhiv* 21, no. 2 (1927): 8.

21. Quoted in Burdzhalov, *Vtoraia russkaia revoliutsiia*, p. 176.

22. Ibid., p. 164. Miliukov states that he also attended the negotiations, but he does not recall what was discussed. P. N. Miliukov, *Vospominaniia* 2: 289.

23. TsGAOR, f. ChSK, d. 466, ℓ. 176; Supplementary deposition of Protopopov, *Padenie tsarskogo rezhima* 4: 99–100; TsGAOR, f. ChSK, d. 466, ℓℓ. 120, 121.

"those cowards" had said nothing about the demonstrations in the streets. He had seen a frightened Miliukov argue with Shul'gin. The Duma had ended debates three hours earlier than usual. "They decided, comrades, they decided to have the next meeting on Tuesday, February 28! Cowards! Liars! Chatterboxes! They are hoping that during these three days the soldiers will shoot the demonstrators, and then they will again begin pouring their own water! Then they will interrogate the government: on what basis did they shoot the unarmed demonstrators in the streets of Petrograd? Traitors! Comrades, there is nothing to hope for from them." Someone shouted: "Down with the Duma."[24]

The shooting had been equally unexpected to most of the Duma deputies and it had provoked a strong reaction. Although it was Sunday, many deputies gathered in the Tauride Palace in the evening, and demanded that the chairman of the Duma protest in the strongest terms. Rodzianko telephoned Khabalov and protested in trembling voice: "What is the firing for? Why the blood?"[25] On this day Rodzianko dispatched the first of a series of telegrams, with definite political designs, that were destined to influence the course of the revolution. In the telegram sent to the tsar, he stated:

The situation is serious. The capital is in a state of anarchy. The government is paralyzed. Transport service and the supply of food and fuel have become completely disrupted. General discontent is growing. There is wild shooting in the streets. In places troops are firing at each other. It is necessary that some person who enjoys the confidence of the country be entrusted at once with the formation of a new government. There must be no delay. Any procrastination is tantamount to death. I pray to God that at this hour the responsibility may not fall upon the Emperor.[26]

On receiving this telegram, Nicholas told the minister of the imperial court, Count V. B. Frederiks: "Again this fat Rodzianko has written me all sorts of nonsense, to which I will not even reply."[27] Thanks to this telegram Rodzianko has been credited with predicting what was to come on the following day. But on February 26, when the government for the first time took the upper hand in the situation, there existed no "anarchy," no cross fire among the soldiers, no paralysis of the government. The description of the situation was distorted to serve Rodzianko's political goal; the formation of a ministry of

24. Volin, *Rozhdestvo svobody*, pp. 17-18.
25. Deposition of Khabalov, *Padenie tsarskogo rezhima* 1: 214.
26. *Izvestiia revoliutsionnoi nedeli*, no. 1, February 27, 1917.
27. Quoted in N. Avdeev, ed., *Revoliutsiia 1917 goda: Kronika sobytii* (6 vols.; Moscow, 1923-1930) 1: 40.

confidence. On the basis of other sources of information that depicted the situation in Petrograd differently and more accurately, Nicholas rejected Rodzianko's telegram as a hoax.[28]

The chairman of the Duma sent another telegram to General Alekseev and General Ruzskii, stating: "The government is in a state of complete paralysis and completely powerless to suppress the disruption of order. Humiliation and disgrace are threatening Russia, for the war cannot be ended victoriously under such conditions." Capitalizing upon the grave disruption of the movement of war supplies resulting from the current crisis, Rodzianko concluded that the only solution would be to form a ministry of confidence and urged the military leaders to support his position before the monarch.[29] Again, it is impossible to describe the situation of February 26 as one of complete paralysis and powerlessness of the government. Rodzianko attempted to mobilize support from military leaders for his intended goal, appealing to their fear of major disruption of military operations. Generals at the front must have found themselves at a loss as to what to make of the two completely conflicting stories. Rodzianko's pessimistic news did not correspond at all to Beliaev and Khabalov's assurances that the situation was completely under control. What happened the next day appeared to the military leaders to vindicate the accuracy of Rodzianko's evaluation, despite the contrary in actuality—a factor that led the military leaders to accept Rodzianko's information uncritically for the following several days.

Late at night Rodzianko was invited to Golitsyn's apartment. The chairman of the Duma again protested the shooting of demonstrators by the loyal troops. Golitsyn's reply was more humiliating to the Duma chairman: he handed to Rodzianko the imperial decree of prorogation of the Duma. News of the prorogation drove the Duma deputies out of their beds to the Tauride Palace. The hastily convened meeting of the Bureau of the Progressive Bloc proposed that the Duma hold a special session on February 27, thus ignoring the imperial decree. Rodzianko, however, could not bring himself to accept this proposal, and maintained that the Duma had no power to violate the Fundamental Law. But he reluctantly agreed to hold a *senioren konvent* (Council of Elders) and a private meeting of Duma deputies.

28. Tsuyoshi Hasegawa, "Rodzianko and the Grand Dukes' Manifesto on 1 March, 1917," *Canadian Slavonic Papers* 18, no. 2 (June 1976): 158-59.

29. "Fevral'skaia revoliutsiia 1917 goda," *Krasnyi arkhiv* 21, no. 2 (1927), pp. 5-6. "Telegrammy i razgovory po telegrafu mezhdu Pskovom, Stavkoiu i Petrogradom, otnosiashcheisia i obstoiatel'stvam otrechenie ot prestola Gosudaria Imperator, s primechaniiami k nim general-ad"iutanta N. V. Ruzskago," *Russkaia letopis'* 3 (1923): 8 (hereafter, "Telegrammy Ruzskago").

While the Socialist deputies advocated that the Duma deputies should
go out onto the streets to assume leadership of the movement, the
conservatives, startled by the government's determination, urged
their colleagues to refrain from further attack on the government.[30]

Bloody Sunday of 1917 was the turning point of the February
Revolution. While the government's offensive temporarily weakened
the will of the leaders who had led the movement since February 23,
it strengthened the determination of the masses of workers to continue
the struggle. This day, unlike the previous day, government troops
had complete control of the streets in the heart of the city. But the
victory was deceptive. Khabalov's order to the unwilling soldiers to
fire upon the demonstrators pushed them further into moral dilemma.
Although it was an isolated case, without effect on the soldiers' insurrection on the following day, the unsuccessful revolt of the soldiers
of the Pavlovskii Regiment was ominous.[31]

The government won the battle on this day, but the director of
the police department, Vasiliev, began sleeping in his friend's apartment. At nine o'clock in the evening the city's electricity was shut off
at the government's order. Military patrols stood at street corners
and let no one go near the Nevskii Prospekt. From the darkness came
sporadic sounds of shooting echoed by the howling of dogs. No one had
ever heard dogs howl on the Nevskii before; it happened only on that
night of February 26.[32]

30. TsGIA, f. 1276, op. 8, d. 679, ch. 3, ℓ. 112; "Fevral'skaia revoliutsiia
i ohkrannoe otdelenie," pp. 172-73.

31. TsGAOR, f. ChSK, d. 466, ℓ. 176.

32. Volin, *Rozhdestvo svobody*, p. 22.

16

THE INSURRECTION:
FEBRUARY 27

 The shooting incidents in the Nevskii Prospekt on February 26 convinced both government officials and leaders of the demonstrators that the soldiers' bullets would soon silence the outcry of protest that had resounded in the streets of Petrograd for the past four days. But this impression was mistaken; they both underestimated the psychological impact of the shooting order on the soldiers, whose tension had reached the breaking point. The abortive attempt by the Fourth Company of the Pavlovskii Regiment indicated their desperate emotional state.

The soldiers who made the first decisive move for the historic insurrection were those of the training detachments of the Volynskii Regiment who were directly involved in the shootings on the Nevskii on the previous day.[1] One of the leaders of the uprising, Sergeant Kirpichnikov, describes how the rebels prepared for the insurrection.[2] On the evening of February 26, young noncommissioned officers of

1. The insurrection resulted from the independent decisions of the soldiers, not from the influence of the workers' propaganda in the barracks. The worker-activists concentrated their propaganda activities on the barracks of the Moscow Regiment in the Vyborg District. The insurrection began in the Volynskii Regiment, least influenced by the workers' propaganda activities. The soldiers of the Moscow Regiment did not join the insurrection until much later on this day. V. Kaiurov, "Shest' dnei," p. 166; E. N. Burdzhalov, *Vtoraia russkaia revoliutsiia: Vosstanie v Petrograde*, pp. 183-84.

2. T. I. Kirpichnikov, "Vozstanie 1.-gv. Volynskago polka v fevrale 1917 g.," pp. 10-16; idem, "Vosstanie Volynskago polka," *Ogonek*, no. 11, 1927. The latter is taken from the first article in *Byloe*. There is an important collection

this regiment returned in a gloomy mood to the barracks from the action in the streets and their conversation turned to the possibility of insubordination. Kirpichnikov and another noncommissioned officer, Mikhail Markov, who assumed leadership of the conspiracy, easily won the allegiance of the already frustrated platoon and squad leaders, who solemnly pledged not to obey the order to take positions at Znamenskaia Square on the next day. The conspirators quickly spread this decision to their trusted comrades, and took measures to seize available machine guns and to confine the soldiers tightly in their bays lest the secret should leak out. In the meantime, Kirpichnikov succeeded in obtaining cartridges by forging an order from the company commander, Lashkevich.[3]

The next morning the soldiers assembled in the large corridor of the second floor earlier than usual. Kirpichnikov revealed the decision: "Enough blood has been shed. It is time to die for freedom." This appeal to insubordination was enthusiastically met with hurrahs from the soldiers. Kirpichnikov's instructions were to answer orders from the company commander with cheers of "hurrah" and to obey only orders from Kirpichnikov.

At ten minutes to eight Second Lieutenant Kolokolov appeared. He detected no sign of rebelliousness among the soldiers, who quietly stood in platoon formation. At eight o'clock Lashkevich arrived. No sooner had he greeted Kirpichnikov than the soldiers loudly shouted: "Hurrah!" Unable to make out the meaning of these unexpected shouts, "he stopped and, maliciously smiling, asked what it meant." One of the soldiers shouted: "Enough blood!" Markov declared: "We will no longer shoot and we also do not wish to shed our brothers' blood in vain." Frightened as much as angered by the hostile protests, Lashkevich attempted to restore order by reading Nicholas's telegram

---

of memoirs, "Revoliutsiia 1917 goda: ocherk, napisannyi soldatami uchebnoi komandy Volynskago polka," *Biblioteka svobody* (1917). This material is unavailable to me. Kirpichnikov's background is not clear. According to Mints, he was a former Putilov worker, but Burdzhalov dismisses this theory. I. I. Mints, *Istoriia Velikogo Oktiabria* 1: 185; Burdzhalov, *Vtoraia russkaia revoliutsiia*, pp. 183-84.

3. Late at night Lashkevich telephoned Kirpichnikov inquiring whether everything was all right in the barracks. When he learned that Kirpichnikov had obtained cartridges in his name without his authorization, Lashkevich demanded an explanation. Kirpichnikov barely managed to avoid detection by replying that he was too eager to shoot those German spies in the streets to wait for his superior's authorization. Satisfied with this explanation, Lashkevich gave Kirpichnikov the instruction to give reveille at seven and wait for him in formation. Kirpichnikov, "Vozstanie 1.-gv. Volynskago polka," pp. 10-12.

ordering the suppression of disorder. This even further provoked the anger of the soldiers. Kolokolov sensed the approaching danger and slipped out of the building. Fearing that the second lieutenant would send for troops to suppress this insubordination, Kirpichnikov ordered Lashkevich to leave the building immediately. The commander hurried across the barracks yard, when the soldiers rushed to the windows and fired at him. Lashkevich was instantly killed.[4] The rebellion had begun.

The rebels ran out of the building. Having organized themselves in squad formation in the barracks yard, they scattered to other companies of the regiment to appeal to them to join the revolt. With the exception of the Fourth Company, however, a large majority of the soldiers refused to take part in the rebellion.[5] The rebellion of the soldiers of Volynskii Regiment thus failed to involve the entire regiment and, like the attempt by the soldiers of Pavlovskii Regiment on the previous night, it appeared at first as though it would end as an isolated, local episode. Yet there was one significant difference. While the barracks of the Pavlovskii Regiment were isolated from other regimental barracks, those of the Volynskii Regiment were located close to the barracks of three other units, the Preobrazhenskii Regiment, the Lithuanian Regiment, and the Sixth Engineer Battalion across a street. About nine o'clock, rebels of the Volynskii Regiment marched out of the gates of the barracks and moved toward the regiments along Vilenskii Lane. When the rebel soldiers approached the compound of the Preobrazhenskii Regiment the military drill being conducted on the field was immediately halted. As the rebels invaded the barracks yard, they encountered resistance. After the melee, the rebels, assisted by some of the soldiers of the Preobrazhenskii, cap-

4. Ibid., pp. 12-13; TsGAOR, f. POO, op. 5, d. 669, ℓ. 357.

5. We do not know the precise number of the rebel soldiers of the Volynskii Regiment, but it does not appear to be very large. The major contingent came from the soldiers of the training detachments. Kirpichnikov, "Vozstanie 1.-gv. Volynskago polka," p. 13; G. P. Perets, *V tsitadeli russkoi revoliutsii: Zapiski komandanta Tavricheskago dvortsa*, pp. 23-25; TsGAOR, f. POO, op. 5, d. 669, ℓ. 12. The last item cited above was the last Okhrana report before its disintegration. The mutiny of the Preobrazhenskii Regiment is more obscure than the revolt of the Volynskii Regiment. Since some companies of this regiment joined the loyal troops almost intact, it appears that the extent to which the soldiers joined the revolt was not large. According to Leiberov, there was some Bolshevik influence in the Preobrazhenskii Regiment. In the weapon workshop located at the corner of Grecheskaia and Gospital' streets, a Bolshevik, A. N. Paderin, former Putilov worker and activist in the sick funds, worked and maintained contact with the Bolshevik Narva District Committee. However, his role in the revolt of the Preobrazhenskii Regiment on February 27 is not clear.

tured the regimental arsenal and freed prisoners from the stockade. An officer who tried to defend the arsenal was killed by the insurgents.[6]

Soldiers of the Lithuanian Regiment were standing in formation in the regimental compound when they heard the commotion and noise from the barracks of the Volynskii Regiment. As soon as the rebels appeared, shouting "hurrah!" and shooting blank cartridges in the air, some immediately abandoned their posts and joined the revolt. Many vacillated as officers appealed to them to maintain neutrality, but not for long. Soon the entire barracks was in confusion with the blare of trumpets, clanging of the regimental bell, and rifle shots. Many soldiers ran into the streets to join the revolt.[7] The rebels, joined by some civilians, moved along Kirochnaia Street toward Liteinyi Prospekt, while some headed toward the barracks of the Sixth Engineer Battalion on Kirochnaia. Soldiers of this battalion heard the shooting and the shouts approaching their barracks while they were preparing for instructions. Suddenly the barracks gates were thrown open and the insurgents rushed in, shouting: "Hurrah, comrades, take rifles! Take cartridges!" The soldiers stormed the battalion arsenal and seized all the rifles. The battalion commander, Colonel Gehring, and several officers were killed on the spot. The soldiers of the Engineers marched out of the barracks with their band in the lead.[8] By noon the insurrection had thus spread to four regiments.

The insurgents marched along Kirochnaia, filling the entire width of the street. They fired volleys of shots at the barracks of the gendarme division, where the gendarmes had already deserted at the first news of the rebellion. The writer Mikhail Slonimskii, who served at the time in the Sixth Engineer Battalion, vividly remembers this first step toward revolution: "We marched forward to the unknown. The Engineer Officers' Training School, where I had received the first officer's title, had surrendered. A gendarme at the gate fired a shot, but immediately his rifle was taken away from his hands. Surrounded by the angry soldiers, he turned pale, and pleaded: 'Don't

6. "Fevral'skaia revoliutsiia i okhrannoe otdelenie," p. 176. The rebels captured 500 rifles and 5 machine guns in the Preobrazhenskii Regiment. Mints, *Istoriia Velikogo Oktiabria* 1: 538.

7. "Vpechatleniia soldata zapasnogo bataliona leib-gvardii Litovskogo Polka," *Pravda*, March 10, 1917; Burdzhalov, *Vtoraia russkaia revoliutsiia*, p. 186. The number of rebel soldiers in the Lithuanian Regiment is not known, but it appears that it provided the largest contingent at the initial stage of the insurrection.

8. O. Sipol', "Iz vospominanii," *Petrogradskaia pravda*, March 12, 1920, quoted in Burdzhalov, *Vtoraia russkaia revoliutsiia*, pp. 186-87; Kirpichnikov, "Vozstanie l.-gv. Volynskago polka," p. 14; Mikh. Slonimskii, *Kniga vospominanii*, p. 13.

kill me; I didn't know you had a revolution.' "[9] When the insurgents reached Liteinyi Prospekt, they turned to the right toward the Vyborg District.[10] Some of the soldiers broke into the Orudinskii Factory and completely disrupted the work. The rest of the rebels moved along toward Liteinyi Bridge, which was guarded by a training detachment of the Moscow Regiment.[11]

Early in the morning, still unaware of the soldiers' uprising on the other shore of the Neva, workers in the Vyborg District were continuing their strike. In Erikson and Aivaz, for instance, they held meetings and passed a resolution calling for continuation of the struggle against tsarism to complete victory. At nine o'clock in the morning more than a thousand workers gathered in Bol'shoi Sampsonievskii Prospekt and marched toward Liteinyi Bridge, singing revolutionary songs and waving red flags but were scattered by the Cossacks.[12] On this day the militant workers intended to do more than demonstrate. During the night Chugurin and his comrades of the fighting unit made a suprise attack on the armory in the Lesnoi District. Encountering little resistance, they seized rifles, revolvers, and bullets. Between ten and eleven o'clock workers of Phoenix, Rosenkrantz, and the Petrograd Metal Factory occupied the Petrograd Cartridge Factory and seized a large amount of ammunition stocked in the factory. Demonstrators attacked the police station on Tikhvinskaia Street after a short fight with the police.[13] After this uniformed police completely disappeared from Vyborg District—the chief of police had instructed his subordinates to disguise themselves in civilian clothes and disappear in the streets.[14] Then the workers moved on to attack Finland Station, where they disarmed the guard soldiers without any

9. Kirpichnikov, "Vozstanie 1.-gv. Volynskago polka," p. 14; Slonimskii, *Kniga vospominanii*, p. 14.

10. It is not known why they decided to go to the Vyborg District. Wada examines three reasons: spontaneous decision, the existence of large caches of weapons in the Vyborg District, and the conscious attempts by the Bolshevik activists. Wada Haruki "Nigatsu kakumei," in *Roshia kakumei no kenkyu*, ed. Eguchi Bokuro, p. 414. By this time the insurrection was already more than three hours old and many activists had joined the soldiers. Yet it was still an isolated event, and to expand the base of the insurrection and acquire more weapons, it was natural that the insurgents headed to the Vyborg District.

11. Kirpichnikov, "Vozstanie 1.-gv. Volynskago polka," p. 14.

12. I. P. Leiberov, "Petrogradskii proletariat v bor'be za pobedu fevral'skoi burzhuazno-demokraticheskoi revoliutsii v Rossii," *Istoriia SSSR*, no. 1 (1957), p. 64; TsGAOR, f. POO, op. 5, d. 669, ℓ. 357.

13. I. P. Leiberov, *Petrogradskii proletariat v Fevral'skoi revoliutsii* 2: 357; idem, "Petrogradskii proletariat v bor'be za pobedu . . . ," p. 64.

14. Burdzhalov, *Vtoraia russkaia revoliutsiia*, p. 192.

difficulty. About twelve o'clock noon the Vyborg workers attempted to move to the center of the city through the Liteinyi Bridge. The first group met with volleys of fire from the training detachment of the Moscow Regiment. The militant workers charged and overcame the resistance, killing the commander and some soldiers.[15] The first group of workers who broke through the bridge joined the insurgent soldiers on Liteinyi Prospekt.

As some workers were moving to the center of the city, the soldiers conversely were trying to reach the Vyborg District. Around one o'clock in the afternoon the soldiers led by Kirpichnikov and Markov approached the Liteinyi Bridge and were fired upon by the troops of the Moscow Regiment. Several were killed and wounded. Kirpichnikov and Markov, joined by other insurgent soldiers, reached the bridge, and by talking with the soldiers of the Moscow Regiment, cleared the "misunderstanding." The soldiers of the Moscow Regiment no longer obstructed passage, and the insurgents crossed the bridge safely.[16]

Soon Nizhegorodskaia Street from the Liteinyi Bridge to Botkin Street were filled with soldiers carrying rifles with red ribbons around their bayonets. The workers were enthusiastic in their greeting—surrounding them, they hugged and kissed the insurgent soldiers. But the soldiers were far from exuberant. According to SR worker Mil'chik, "There was no excitement among the soldiers; they were frightened and depressed." A Bolshevik worker, S. Skalov, also observed: "On the faces of the rebels despair and fear of impending reprisals were visible. . . . They powerlessly marked time. Their mood was extremely gloomy and depressing." But the appearance of the insurgent soldiers infected the workers with triumph. The crowd, joined by a few soldiers, attacked the weapon depot near Finland Station and armed themselves with whatever they could find. Bayonets were hanging from wadded overcoats—many filled their pockets with Colts and Nagans. Young workers came out, beaming, with a rifle, sometimes two, on their shoulders.[17]

The armed workers—the *sans-culottes*—as Mil'chik called them—"liberated" all the teahouses, cafes, restaurants, and dining halls, and declared them "property of the people." With jokes and facetious remarks, but "with revolutionary categoricalness," armed workers kicked out protesting owners and invited insurgent soldiers for a

15. "Dnevnik soldata v Vyborgskoi storone," *Pravda*, March 10, 1917.
16. Kirpichnikov, "Vozstanie 1.-gv. Volynskago polka," pp. 14-15.
17. I. Mil'chik, *Rabochii fevral'*, pp. 87-88; S. Skalov, "27 fevralia 1917 g. v Petrograde," *Krasnaia nov'*, no. 3 (1931), p. 116.

cup of tea. The soldiers, who were invited to one of these teahouses in Vyborg Street, were suddenly fired upon by a machine gun behind the church at the corner. The soldiers ran blindly, throwing away their rifles, to find cover. Some broke into the teahouse through a window. Inside, boiling water was toppled onto the floor, steaming up the house.[18]

To Skalov it was essential to lead these frightened soldiers to action before they began retreating, and to unite them with the revolutionary workers. Together with his two SR colleagues, Skalov suggested to the soldiers that they attack Kresty Prison and liberate the revolutionary leaders from the dungeon of tsarist oppression. However, only a few responded to this appeal, the remainder indifferently remaining at the same place. Those few rebels moved on Simbirskaia Street toward the prison. The crowd gathered at Finland Station disappeared into the building as the rebels appealed to them to join with them to attack the Kresty, and workers of the Petrograd Cartridge Factory also ignored the appeal. Only a small contingent of seventy to a hundred insurgents made the attack on the Kresty.[19]

The Kresty—officially the Petrograd Solitary Prison and the Women's Prison—were grim-looking brick buildings bounded by Arsenal Street and the Neva, where 2,400 prisoners—including political prisoners—were confined.[20] It offered little resistance. Despite their small number, the rebels destroyed the iron gates, disarmed the guards and set the prisoners free. They burned all the books and papers in a large bonfire in the prison yard.[21] Bund leader M. Rafes, an inmate of the Kresty, suddenly heard a deafening shot outside around two o'clock in the afternoon, then there was a continuing pounding of rifle butts on the prison gates. Inmates, responding, began hitting the bars in their cells with utensils. Suddenly the rebels appeared and opened the door of each cell. Finally, the door of Rafes's cell was opened, and there stood a soldier with a rifle and Rafes's fellow inmate, Breido, a Menshevik member of the War Industries Committee, who had been set free a moment before. Breido spoke in a voice of

18. Mil'chik, *Rabochii fevral'*, p. 90.

19. Skalov, "27 fevralia 1917 g.," p. 116; according to M. I. Kalinin, a member of the Bolshevik Petersburg Committee, the crowd gathered at Finland Station demanding action. Kalinin stood up on the platform and appealed to the crowd to attack the Kresty. "In an instant the idea was caught up and spread." M. I. Kalinin, *Za eti gody* (3 vols.; Moscow, 1929) 3: 432.

20. The number of prisoners was derived from TsGAOR, f. DPOO, d. 341, ch. 57/1917 g., ℓ. 29.

21. Skalov, "27 fevralia 1917 g.," pp. 116-17; Burdzhalov, *Vtoraia russkaia revoliutsiia*, p. 191.

disbelief: "These are the soldiers with rifles who liberated us." The freed prisoners in tears kissed and embraced each other. Outside the prison, the police spy, Abrasimov, a member of the workers' group of the War Industries Committee, also crying, walked around and kissed the liberated political prisoners. Among those who were set free was B. O. Bogdanov, a member of the Petersburg Committee of the Menshevik party and secretary of the workers' group of the War Industries Committee. The rebels carried Bogdanov on their shoulders, and asked him to make a short speech. Choked with emotion, Bogdanov uttered a few incoherent sentences and ended his speech quickly with the words: "Go continue your work. It is not the time for speeches."[22] Those freed included not only political prisoners but also a great number of criminals. Martynov admits: "Exactly from this moment the uprising in the city began to bear a bloody character; murders, pillage, arson, and various provocatory offenses had begun to be committed."[23] The rebels who had liberated the Kresty marched to the Tauride Palace.

The Vyborg District housed two military barracks, one for the Moscow Regiment and the other for the Bicycle Battalion—the two units that had maintained discipline relatively well. About four hundred rebels, including the remaining insurgents of the Volynskii Regiment led by Kirpichnikov, gathered in front of the Moscow Regiment barracks. Officers had prepared for the insurgents' attack by assigning a training detachment inside the barracks gate and machine guns were set in the second-floor windows of the officers' building. As the insurgents appealed to the soldiers of the Moscow Regiment to join the insurrection, volleys of shots were fired upon them. A young second lieutenant among the rebels shouted: "Those who endear freedom—march forward!" About twenty-five stalwarts including Kirpichnikov charged across the barracks yard. The troops of the training detachment retreated but a hail of machine gun and rifle fire met the charging rebels. The second lieutenant was instantly killed and the rest were forced to retreat.[24] The crowds responded by firing on the barracks, and some ran across the yard again. A Bolshevik worker, Kondratiev, among the first to reach the barracks, appealed to the soldiers to join the insurrection. The soldiers, however, were extremely reluctant. Only after being given an ultimatum—that the rebels would attack the barracks with heavy artillery—did they come out to join the rebels in the streets. Some officers ran away, while the

22. M. Rafes, "Moi vospominaniia," *Byloe* 29 (1922): 184-85.
23. E. I. Martynov, *Tsarskaia armiia v fevral'skom perevorote*, p. 100.
24. Kirpichnikov, "Vozstanie 1.-gv. Volynskago polka," p. 15.

rest confined themselves in the upper floor of the officers' hall, where they ceased their resistance when they exhausted their ammunition.[25] By three o'clock in the afternoon, the Moscow Regiment had capitulated to the rebels.

The Bicycle Battalion was the only armed unit in Petrograd that demonstrated substantial resistance to the mutineers on February 27. Because of the basic technical skills required of them, the soldiers of this battalion were in the main sons of the middle and upper classes. This helped ease the tension between officers and soldiers—a tension that rose from an irreconcilable class antagonism in other military units. The Bicycle Battalion was exceptional—the morale of the soldiers was high.[26]

When the insurgents who gathered at the barracks gate of the Bicycle Battalion attacked the officers on duty, soldiers of the battalion rushed to rescue them, shooting at the rebels. The commander, Colonel Balkashin, hurried from one barracks to another, personally inspecting the soldiers and encouraging them to stand firm against the rebels. He assigned two companies to guard the gates. About 6 P.M. the second wave of insurgents attacked. A large crowd moved along Sampsonievskii Prospekt, pushing the sentinel companies back toward the barracks. Colonel Balkashin then withdrew his troops, leaving only a small platoon at the gates. Instead, he installed machine guns on the ground pointing at the gates. Realizing the strength of resistance, the crowd no longer charged upon the soldiers. The resistance of the Bicycle Battalion proved that an organized military unit, led by a capable officer, could cope with larger numbers of disorganized rebels effectively. Yet the episode was an isolated one. Balkashin repeatedly and futilely attempted to telephone headquarters for advice. By the evening all telephone connnections with the center of the city had been cut off. Two intelligence officers dispatched by Colonel Balkashin to the headquarters never returned. During the night insurgents broke into the battalion armory, seizing all the cartridges there.[27] The defeat of this lone defense of the old regime became a matter of time.

Gradually the insurgent soldiers submerged into the crowds. Kirpichnikov could gather only fifteen soldiers of the Volynskii Regiment and five or six soldiers of the Lithuanian and Preobrazhenskii Regiment altogether. There was no semblance of order. The armed mob began

25. A. Kondrat'ev, "Vospominaniia o podpol'noi rabote," *Krasnaia letopis'* 7 (1923): 68; Mil'chik, *Rabochii fevral'*, p. 89.

26. Martynov, *Tsarskaia armiia v fevral'skom perevorote*, pp. 98-99.

27. Ibid., p. 101.

to control the streets. A Bolshevik worker, Gordienko, tried to organize them into military formation, but the soldiers reacted with utmost hostility to the civilian's order. Nevertheless, through the attacks on the prison and the military barracks, the rebel soldiers and the workers began establishing a sense of solidarity. "On the Sampsonievskii Prospekt," a worker, Mil'chik, recalls, "cleaving the crowd, an automobile packed with soldiers with rifles roared through. On the bayonets there was something we had never seen nor heard of: red flags were flying."[28]

In the heart of the workers' district along Sampsonievskii Prospekt near Erikson, the police headquarters were burned to the ground in the evening. The crowd built a huge bonfire in front of the burning building, which lit the workers and the youths "armed to the teeth" aglow. The crowd dragged policemen from "garrets and cellars, where they had hid themselves." They beat the helpless victims at intervals; they beat them, rested a while, and beat them again. Almost insane with terror, bloody, and with swollen and bruised eyes, the policemen repeatedly threw themselves at the knees of the crowd, pleading for mercy.[29]

It was out of the question for the insurgent soldiers to return to barracks for resting or sleeping. Workers took upon themselves to convert expropriated "property of the people" into temporary sleeping quarters. The "liberated" Petrograd Women's Prison was made into a huge hostel for the insurgent soldiers, who, understandably, refused to spend the night in the prison. In many of the workers' apartment houses hung hastily written signs: "Soldiers cordially invited for meals and lodging." The Vyborg Consumers' Association decided to give all food at its disposal to the insurgent soldiers.[30]

In the afternoon another contingent of soldiers and workers in the Vyborg District crossed the bridge to the center of the city. They marched toward the Tauride Palace, which was rapidly becoming the center of the insurrection. The insurgents attacked the House of Detention on Shpalernaia Street and freed 958 prisoners. They set fire to the Circuit Court; black smoke rose up in the winter sky. On the other side of the Circuit Court across Liteinyi Prospekt they broke into the Main Artillery Administration and the Arsenal adjacent to it. Having killed General Matusov, chief of the Arsenal, they captured 40,000 rifles and 30,000 revolvers and pistols. These weapons, in addition to those captured from regimental arsenals,

28. Mil'chik, *Rabochii fevral'*, p. 87.
29. Ibid., p. 91.
30. Ibid., pp. 90-91.

were freely handed to the workers and other civilians in the crowd.[31] During the rebels' attack on the Arsenal, a Japanese businessman who was negotiating for a weapon purchase agreement with the Artillery Administration was shot to death.[32] Rebel soldiers of the Armored Car Division reassembled the armored cars that had been disassembled on Khabalov's order and, draping them in red banners, careened through Liteinyi Prospekt.[33] Soldiers and workers armed with rifles, with cartridge belts across their shoulders, aimlessly shot in the air from the cars.

Soon the streets were filled with crowds holding newly acquired weapons like children with Christmas gifts. An English eyewitness saw a hooligan with an officer's sword fastened over his overcoat, a rifle in one hand and a revolver in the other. A worker was standing by, holding an officer's sword in one hand and a bayonet in the other. A young boy was walking with a large butcher knife on his shoulder. One man had a rifle in one hand and a tram-line cleaner in the other. A student was walking with two rifles and a belt of machine-gun bullets around his waist. And even a quiet-looking businessman held a large rifle and wore a cartridge belt around his business suit.[34]

A number of youths experimented with their new toys by firing off into any direction. Many innocent bystanders were killed when young boys threw cartridges into fires. One little boy of about twelve years of age was warming himself, together with a large number of soldiers, at one of the bonfires in the streets. Suddenly he pulled the trigger of the automatic rifle he was holding. One of the soldiers standing nearby fell dead. The shocked boy kept the trigger pulled back until all seven bullets were fired. Three soldiers were instantly killed, and four were wounded.[35] The value of human life had depreciated with alarming suddenness.

As the disorganized mob controlled the streets, anarchy and lawlessness became widespread. A young professor of Petrograd University, Pitirim Sorokin, witnessed more than once "groups of soldiers and street loafers looting wine-shops with no one to stop

31. Leiberov, "Petrogradskii proletariat v bor'be za pobedu . . . ," p. 63. More than 2,000 shells and 2,000,000 cartridges fell into the hands of the masses. Mints, *Istoriia Velikogo Oktiabria* 1:538.

32. Kikuchi Masanori, *Roshia kakumei to Nihon-jin*, pp. 12, 134, 158.

33. Viktor Shklovsky, *A Sentimental Journey*, p. 12. The armored car division had two garages: one on Kovenskaia Street near the barracks of the Preobrazhenskii Regiment and the other on Dvorianskaia Street near the Fortress of Peter and Paul in the Petrograd District.

34. Stinton Jones, *Russia in Revolution: Being the Experiences of an Englishman in Petrograd during the Upheaval*, pp. 119-20.

35. Ibid., p. 134.

them."[36] A gymnasium student noted in his diary that crowds broke into a bakery at Sadovaia and Bol'shaia Pod"iatskaia, and hurried home with their loot.[37] According to a Japanese student, two insurgent soldiers, who were staying in the same boarding house, returned with pictures, carpets, and a hunting dog they had expropriated from the wealthy, and threw a big orgy with prostitutes with the money they got by selling their loot.[38] Despite Soviet historians' attempts to ignore the criminal elements in the uprising, it would be pointless to argue that these destructive actions never took place or that they were committed only by the criminal element that had nothing to do with the revolution. Leiberov argues that from February 23 to February 27 altogether 97 stores were attacked and 29 people arrested. But most of those arrested were not the industrial proletariat and of those workers arrested, most were teenagers. From this Leiberov concludes that the criminal element had no connection with the organized revolutionary movement, and that 97 cases of vandalism committed out of a total of 6,827 stores in the city were miniscule.[39] Leiberov's figures are based on police archives up to February 26; on February 27, the police disintegrated and there was no record of pillaging and looting on this day. Contrary to Leiberov's contention, mob violence became pervasive. It was partly owing to the release of all the criminals from the prisons. According to a police record, as of February 26 the city's prisons held 7,652 prisoners.[40] It is not known how many of these were political, but those who were set free were not merely the political activists, but also murderers, arsonists, burglers, and rapists. To compound the situation, all the city's law-enforcement organs disappeared. But not all the criminal actions were committed by the criminals. What guided the rebels were not necessarily lofty ideals or cold rational political calculations but rather more primitive emotions—anger, fear, instinct for excitement. A criminal element and destructive impulses were an integral part of the revolutionary process. Trotskii stated: "A revolution is always distinguished by impoliteness, probably because the ruling classes did not take the trouble in good season to teach the people fine manners."[41]

Indeed, to some intelligentsia, even those sympathetic with the revolution, what emerged in the streets in Petrograd appeared to be *stikhiia*—an elementary, anarchical, primitive force of the oppressed

36. Pitirim Sorokin, *Leaves from a Russian Diary and Thirty Years After*, p. 13.
37. TsGIA, f. 1101, op. 1, d. 1195, *ll.* 4-5.
38. Kikuchi, *Rochia kakumei to Nihon-jin*, p. 193.
39. Leiberov, *Petrogradskii proletariat v Fevral'skoi revoliutsii* 2: 286-88.
40. TsGAOR, f. DPOO, d. 341, ch. 57/1917, *ll.* 24-29.
41. Leon Trotsky, *History of the Russian Revolution* 1: 133.

classes, to which any political articulation remained alien. V. B. Stankevich, who witnessed the unleashed *stikhiia* in the streets as an officer
as well as a Socialist stated:

With what slogans did the soldiers go out? They went out, obeying some mysterious
voice; and then with obvious indifference and coldness they afterwards allowed
themselves to hang all possible slogans upon themselves. Who led them when they
conquered Petrograd, when they burned the Circuit Court? Not a political thought,
not a revolutionary slogan, not a conspiracy, and not a mutiny. But an elementary
movement that suddenly reduced the whole old regime to ashes without leaving
anything. . . . Unknown, mysterious, irrational, welling up out of deepest layers of
popular feeling, suddenly the street overflowed with gray mass, bayonets sparkled,
shots rang out, and bullets whistled.[42]

The soldiers' insurrection spread to other parts of the city. In
Petrograd District the troops guarded all the bridges on the Neva
and the Nevka from early in the morning and effectively isolated
the island from both Vyborg District and the center of the city. Nevertheless, the people in this district learned the news of the uprising
and of its development by telephone, which was operating all day.
In the morning a large crowd gathered in the streets, particularly
on Bol'shoi Prospekt and Kamennoostrovskii Prospekt. They were
mostly in a festive mood, making no determined effort to break
through the heavy cordon on the bridges to make connections with
the center of the insurrection.[43] After three o'clock in the afternoon,
a crowd of about one hundred men and women, many of them young-
sters, assembled in front of the barracks of the Grenadier Regiment.
Waving a red flag, they appealed to the soldiers to join the insurrection.
The grenadiers watched curiously and when a few stalwarts attempted
to enter the barracks yard, they let them through the gates without
resistance. Inside the compound, the rebels demanded that the prisoners confined in the stockade be freed immediately. The soldiers
fulfilled this demand, but refused to join the insurrection.[44]

By evening the cordon at the Troitskii Bridge was broken, and
trucks carrying soldiers and workers armed with rifles and wearing
cartridge belts around their shoulders roared into the Petrograd District.
Immediately, they were directed to the police stations and the barracks
of military units. One of the trucks, in which a Bolshevik worker,
Gordienko, alertly took a position in front of a machine gun, moved
to the garage of the Armored Car Division on Dvorianskaia Street

42. V. B. Stankevich, *Vospominaniia, 1914-1919 gg.*, pp. 76-77.
43. A. V. Peshekhonov, "Pervyia nedeli: Iz vospominanii revoliutsii," *Na
chuzhoi storone* 1: 255-56.
44. Ibid., pp. 257-58; I. Golubuev, "Kak grenadery prisoedinilis' k narodu,"
Pravda, March 12, 1917.

near the Fortress of Peter and Paul. The soldiers of the Armored Car Division joined the insurrection with two armored cars, after volleys of machine guns were fired on the iron roof of the garage.[45] In the meantime, a second wave of demonstrators gathered in front of the barracks of the Grenadier Regiment, again appealing to the soldiers to abandon their posts. Some grenadiers slipped out of the gates, but the majority still remained in the barracks. As the third wave of demonstrators appeared, this time with armored cars, the soldiers finally broke into the regimental armory, seized all weapons, and joined the crowds. With a band of musicians in the lead, the insurgent grenadiers marched toward the Tauride Palace.[46]

The barracks of the Finland Regiment were located on Vasilievskii Island. The soldiers of this regiment had shown signs of agitation since Second Lieutenant Iossa, an officer of the regiment, killed a demonstrator on February 25. Since then, the soldiers were forbidden to approach telephones and a sentinel was placed at each telephone in the barracks. On February 27 a training detachment was sent to protect the bridges so as to isolate the island from both Petrograd District and the center of the city. Colonel Sadovskii ordered the soldiers of the training detachment to repulse at any cost the attack of "the revolutionaries" and to keep them from Vasilievskii Island. Yet after he learned the general situation in the capital, Sadovskii became disturbed and suddenly disappeared. The soldiers remaining in the barracks assembled in a large assembly hall, where junior officers of the companies appealed to the soldiers to be faithful to the fatherland and to their oaths. After the officers left, the soldiers secretly met and decided not to shoot at the insurgents and to join the insurrection when the rebels appeared. The insurgent soldiers and the armed workers staged a demonstration in the center of the district, but no serious attempt was made to break in the regimental barracks. It was not until the second day of the insurrection that the Finland Regiment joined the insurrection.[47]

The soldiers' insurrection spread to the south of the city, where the barracks of three regiments, the Semenovskii, the Izmailovskii, and the Petrograd were located. Thousands of Putilov workers in the Narva District moved toward the center of the city in the morning, seizing weapons on the way from a gun shop in Aleksandrovskii

45. I. Gordienko, *Iz boevogo proshlogo*, p. 63.

46. Golubuev, "Kak grenadery prisoedinilis' k narodu," *Pravda*, March 12, 1917.

47. Vasilii Starkov [Efreitov], "Prisoedinenie Finlandtsev," *Pravda*, April 1, 1917; "Vystuplenie leib-gvardii Finlandskago zapasnago polka," *Pravda*, April 11, 1917.

Market. In the center of the city additional weapons were handed to the workers. The armed workers now began attacks on the police stations, while others gathered near regimental barracks in an effort to draw soldiers into the insurrection.[48]

In the morning a company of Semenovskii Regiment was deployed to protect Moscow District from the insurgents, but the commander of the battalion decided to withdraw all the troops to the barracks, fearing that the insurgents might adversely influence his own soldiers. About eight o'clock in the evening, crowds assembled near the barracks; the entire machine-gun detachment, led by Sergeant Major Mel'nichukov, rushed out of the barracks with loud hurrahs. They, too, were led with a band, and marched to the police station in the district, where they ransacked the station and killed the police chief. The Semenovskii soldiers then moved toward the barracks of the Izmailovskii Regiment on Izmailovskii Prospekt.[49]

Soldiers of Izmailovskii Regiment had learned of the insurrection of the army units early in the morning. All anticipated that freedom would come and that they would be emancipated from the "cursed stone barracks." Finally, at about eleven o'clock in the evening, the rebel Semenovskii soldiers appeared, shooting in the air and shouting: "Brothers of Izmailovskii Regiment, come on out!" The insurgents easily disarmed the guards and, breaking into the barracks, freed prisoners from the stockade. The soldiers of the Izmailovskii Regiment rushed out with joyous hurrahs. All the officers disappeared. From there the crowd moved to the barracks of the Petrograd Regiment. A drunken officer fired on the crowd but was immediately captured. Joined by the soldiers of the Petrograd Regiment, the insurgent soldiers in the southern districts marched toward the Tauride Palace.[50]

The soldiers' insurrection that began in Volynskii Regiment early in the morning thus involved practically all the military units in Petrograd by the end of February 27. It is estimated that the participants in the soldiers' insurrection rose from 10,200 in the morning to 25,700 in the afternoon, and to 66,700 by evening. It further grew in the morning of February 28 to 72,700, by afternoon to 112,000, and in the evening, 127,000. By the afternoon of March 1, almost the entire garrison, 170,000 soldiers, took the side of the revolution.[51]

48. Leiberov, "Petrogradskii proletariat v bor'be za pobedu . . . ," p. 67.

49. I. N. Zhuravlev, "Prisoedinenie Semenovtsev," *Pravda*, March 17, 1917.

50. Ibid; S. D. Izmailovtsev, "Vystuplenie Izmailovtsev," *Pravda*, March 21, 1917.

51. A. K. Drezen, *Bol'shevizatsiia petrogradskogo garnizona v 1917 goda:*

What was the strength of this "revolutionary force"? If one were to organize the rebelling soldiers and armed workers into one revolutionary army to defend the revolution against the expected counter-revolutionary attempt by the old regime, one would find himself in an impossible situation. Once the soldiers abandoned their posts they became a disorganized, anarchical, unruly mob, heeding no authority, and taking an extremely hostile attitude toward any attempt to establish discipline and organization. Kirpichnikov noted that only two hundred soldiers out of the many he had led to rebellion reached Vyborg District.[52] Where did they go? They were in the streets, acting on their own. The mob created anarchy in the streets of Petrograd. They attacked barracks, police stations, and prisons, but left other strategically important positions in the city almost untouched; they made no conscious attempt to take over railway stations, the Ministry of Transport, the General Staff, the power station, or the water supply station. Shklovskii, who spent most of his time on this day at Nikolaevskii Station, suggested that the insurgents occupy the top floor of the Severnaia and Znamenskaia hotels so that they could keep the station covered. However, the necessary forces were not available. A guard hastily appointed from the soldiers running in and out immediately disappeared. Although insurgents attacked the central telephone station, they could not seize the office until midnight and telephone operations continued to function. Communications between Petrograd and the Stavka were never disrupted.[53] Nor did the insurgents ever attempt to spread the insurrection beyond the confines of Petrograd. To be sure, soldiers in surrounding areas joined the insurrection on the following days, but no conscious efforts of the Petrograd insurgents were responsible for this. The disarray and the absence of leadership of the insurgents were such that one of the Duma leaders, A. Bublikov, noted: "One disciplined division from the front would have been enough to quell the uprising. More than that, it would have been possible to pacify

---

Sbornik dokumentov (Leningrad, 1932), p. vi; Leiberov, Petrogradskii proletariat v Fevral'skoi revoliutsii 2: 489.

52. Kirpichnikov, "Vozstanie 1.-gv. Volynskago polka," p. 15.

53. Shklovsky, A Sentimental Journey, p. 15; A. Balk, "Poslednie piat' dnei tsarskago Petrograda: Dnevnik posledniago Petrogradskago gradonachal'nika," p. 9; N. O. Akaemov, "Agoniia starago rezhima," p. xxv. There were three special telegraph installations, known as the Hughes apparatus, which connected Petrogard directly with the Stavka and other fronts. These machines were installed in the Naval Staff, the General Staff, and the war minister's residence. The insurgents attacked none of these offices.

it by a simple blockade of railway movement from Petrograd."[54] A remarkable fact of the February uprising was that it succeeded at all. What prevented the tsarist government from putting it down?

When one looks into the uprising, one is struck with the extreme ineptitude of the security authorities. Not only could they not prevent the uprising from spreading throughout the city, but they also failed miserably to muster forces that could have rallied behind the tsarist government. The frightened, unnerved leadership made mistake after mistake, ultimately driving itself to total disintegration.

One of the peculiar aspects of the insurrection at its initial stage was the relative ease with which the rebels spread the rebellion to other military units. The rebel soldiers did not encounter any serious resistance, while many officers did not use force to keep the soldiers from joining the revolt, maintaining noncommittal neutrality as if they were indifferent bystanders. Certainly the revolt took them by surprise. At the sudden intrusion of the insurgents, the officers found themselves outnumbered as the reliability of the soldiers under their command suddenly became questionable. An officer of the Lithuanian Regiment who ordered his men to fire upon the rebels was stabbed to death by his own soldiers. Yet their inaction stemmed largely from their deep-rooted disillusionment with the regime, which they did not feel worth defending at the risk of their lives. In absence of clear-cut directions from the top of the hierarchy, they withdrew from action. When the mutineers came to the Armored Car Division, the officers told the soldiers: "Do what you think best."[55] Many officers simply took refuge in the officers' clubs and in apartments of acquaintances in the city.

One important cause for the officers' inaction was the failure of the commanding hierarchy in Petrograd to mobilize the officers, who were more rigorously bound to military discipline than the soldiers, against the insurrection. News of the uprising in the Volynskii Regiment reached the *gradonachal'svto* shortly after eight o'clock in the morning. *Gradonachal'nik* Balk immediately relayed the news to Khabalov and Protopopov. Khabalov instructed Colonel Viskovskii, commander of the Volynskii Regiment: "Do your best to prevent this from spreading. Make them return to the barracks and try to disarm them. Make them stay in the barracks." There is no evidence to indicate that Khabalov took any measures other than this extremely

54. Quoted in S. S. Ol'denburg, *Tsarstvovanie Imperatora Nikolaia II-go* 2: 251.

55. Kirpichnikov, "Vozstanie 1.-gv. Volynskago polka," p. 14; A. P. Kutepov, "Pervye dni revoliutsii v Petrograde: Otryvok iz vospominanii, napisannykh generalom Kutepovym v 1926 gody," in *General Kutepov: Sbornik statei*, p. 164; Shklovsky, *A Sentimental Journey*, p. 11.

ambiguous order to suppress the uprising at its incipient stage. As for Protopopov, after learning the news, he changed the subject and asked the *gradonachal'nik* what the latter thought about the imperial order of prorogation of the Duma. Met with Balk's negative estimation, Protopopov said: "Well, let's see what God will do by evening."[56]

When Khabalov arrived at the *gradonachal'stvo* about nine o'clock, he discovered the absence of Colonel Pavlenkov, who should have taken the necessary measures as commander of troops in the city of Petrograd. Khabalov immediately transferred the command to Colonel Mikhailichenko, commander of the Reserve Battalion of the Moscow Regiment.[57] This was the first of a series of mistakes Khabalov made on this day. Being a commander of a regimental battalion whose task had been limited to the security of one district of the city, Mikhail-ichenko did not have sufficient familiarity with the contents and the background of the troop deployment policy in the contingency plans nor with the over-all picture of troop strengths and morale. Moreover, the sudden change of command at this critical moment contributed to a grave breakdown of the commanding hierarchy. As one might expect, Mikhailichenko took no active part in the formulation of counter-insurgency measures. As a result, Khabalov found himself in the position of commanding the loyal troops unaided by any other experienced officer. The realization of this responsibility panicked Khabalov, whose confusion and irresolution led the loyal troops to chaos and disarray. One of the police precinct chiefs, Halle, was summoned to the *grado-nachal'stvo* on this morning supposedly for the task of familiarizing commanding personnel with the map of the city—a procedure that itself suggests the haphazard nature of the entire counterinsurgency policy. When Halle arrived at the *gradonachal'stvo,* no one bothered about the map of the city: there was utter confusion and Khabalov and other commanding officers nervously scurried about from room to room. Colonel Kutepov, who talked to Khabalov, observed: "I noticed that General Kabalov's lower jaw was quivering during the conversation." Mikhailichenko also admitted that after eleven o'clock no one knew who was commanding.[58]

56. Deposition of Khabalov, *Padenie tsarskogo rezhima* 1: 198; Balk, "Pos-lednie piat' dnei," p. 8.

57. It is not known where Khabalov was or what he was doing during the cru-cial period between the initial reception of the news at eight o'clock and his arrival at the *gradonachal'stvo* at nine. At any rate, inaction during this time cost him dearly. Deposition of Khabalov, *Padenie tsarskogo rezhima* 1: 198.

58. Burdzhalov, *Vtoraia russkaia revoliutsiia,* p. 194; Kutepov, "Pervye dni revoliutsii v Petrograde," p. 161; Leiberov, *Petrogradskii proletariat v Fevral'skoi revoliutsii* 2: 433.

By early in the afternoon police forces in Petrograd had disintegrated. At noon Balk had ordered removal of police patrols from the streets and all the policemen had returned to headquarters, waiting, with absolutely nothing to do, for further instructions. But none came. The superiors disappeared through back doors in civilian clothes. The police chief of the Moscow District precinct advised his men to change clothes and to disappear as quickly as possible. According to the police chief of the Aleksandr-Nevskii police precinct, Kargelis, in the absence of instructions from above, "we simply went home, leaving police headquarters, which were burned down by the evening of February 27 by the mobs."[59] Many police officers escaped by disguising as women. But even with a woman's dress, hat, and veil, many were discovered by the insurgents. Some were executed on the spot, and others were taken to a place of detention.[60] Crowds set fire to police stations—particularly spectacular was the one near Nikolaevskii Station. The building with its 150-foot tower was ablaze for several hours. Some of the police officers, however, refused to go home. They took their arms, and barricading themselves on the rooftops and the corners of high buildings, shot at the crowds at random. According to Gruzdev, commissioned to investigate the shooting incidents during the February Revolution by the Provisional Government's Extraordinary Investigating Commission, such scattered shooting incidents were almost exclusively caused by police. But contrary to popular belief, the police did not systematically use machine guns. The story of the machine guns installed on the rooftops on Protopopov's order belonged to one of the legends of the February Revolution.[61]

Since the elaborately constructed contingency plan did not anticipate a soldiers' uprising, Khabalov had to improvise counterinsurgency measures on the spot. Late in the morning, he made two decisions: to use armored cars against the insurgents, and to organize a punitive detachment from reliable troops. Immediately Captain Antonovskii, assistant to the commander of the Armored Car Division, was summoned to the *gradonachal'stvo*. Replying to Khabalov's order to get the armored cars ready to suppress the "disorder" in the streets, Antonovskii explained the "technicalities" involved. Only one out of the eight armored cars at his disposal would be ready immediately against the insurgents, the rest not until evening. Antonovskii added

59. Leiberov, *Petrogradski proletariat v Fevral'skoi revoliutsii* 2: 437-38; TsGAOR, f. ChSK, d. 460, л. 22.
60. Jones, *Russia in Revolution*, p. 164.
61. TsGAOR, f. ChSK, d. 466, л. 185.

further that not one soldier of the division could be counted on for use of the armored cars against the insurgents, and that it would be impossible to drive the cars with officers alone. Besides, he continued, the effectiveness of the armored cars against the insurgents would be limited. Antonovskii suggested that the order should be directly referred to the commander of the division, Lieutenant-Colonel Khaletskii. Khabalov was furious. Threatening to chop off his head at further defiance of his order, Khabalov told Antonovskii to get the cars ready. But by the time Antonovskii returned to his division, it had joined the revolution. All the cars had been put into operation, not against the revolution, but for the revolution.[62]

Khabalov attempted to form loyal forces from the soldiers available nearby and divided them into two detachments—one to protect headquarters and the other to attack mutineers. Colonel A. P. Kutepov was appointed commander of this hastily organized punitive shock detachment. Colonel Kutepov, a recipient of the Order of St. George, had been in Petrograd only for a week on leave when he received the order of his appointment. Despite Kutepov's repeated refusal on the grounds of his unfamiliarity with the situation, Khabalov high-handedly imposed the appointment.[63]

Kutepov was charged with clearing the area between Liteinyi Bridge and Znamenskaia Square of rebels, for which Khabalov gave him a company of the Keksholm Regiment and a machine gun. In addition, two companies of Preobrazhenskii Regiment and a company of the Machine Gun Regiment, which had just arrived at Nikolaevskii Station from Oranienbaum, joined the punitive detachment, which altogether consisted of 1,000 soldiers and fifteen machine guns.[64] The reliability of these soldiers left much to be desired. Soldiers of Preobrazhenskii Regiment complained that they had not eaten since the previous afternoon. The machine gunners sullenly refused to return Kutepov's greetings. Moreover, Kutepov discovered that neither the water nor the glycerin necessary to fire machine guns were available to the machine-gun company. Nevertheless, the important fact was that in the face of large-scale insurrection, these soldiers chose to remain within military discipline. Kutepov made the best of the situation—cajoling, intimidating, and encouraging. Despite reluctance, the soldiers followed Kutepov to the last moment, until resistance became meaningless.

62. Leiberov, *Petrogradskii proletariat v Fevral'skoi revoliutsii* 2: 433-34.
63. Kutepov, "Pervye dni revoliutsii v Petrograde," p. 161.
64. Deposition of Khabalov, *Padenie tsarskogo rezhima* 1: 214; Kutepov, "Pervye dni revoliutsii v Petrograde," p. 161; TsGAOR, f. ChSK, d. 460, л. 67.

About eleven o'clock, the punitive detachment left headquarters and marched on Nevskii Prospekt. The street that had been the center of activities during the past days was quiet and it seemed to Kutepov unbelievable that an uprising was taking place. But when the detachment reached Znamenskaia Square, Kutepov received the news from Khabalov's special emissary that, having set fire to the Circuit Court, the insurgents were approaching the Winter Palace.[65] Khabalov's plan was to clear the area along Liteinyi Prospekt, isolating the rebels in the Vyborg and Liteinaia districts and to secure the government-controlled area west of the Liteinyi while waiting for reinforcements from the front. However, the insurgents moved more quickly than he had anticipated, spoiling his plan to establish the front line in the Liteinyi. Accordingly, Khabalov ordered Kutepov to move the detachment back to the *gradonachal'stvo*.

Reasonable though it might have been, this sudden change of basic strategy further convinced Kutepov of the ineptitude of the commanding authority. Exploding in anger, he flatly declared to Khabalov's emissary that he would follow the first order, moving along Liteinyi and then returning to the Winter Palace through Mars Field.[66] This virtual insubordination of superior command caused a fatal lack of communication between the headquarters and the punitive detachment. Khabalov later testified:

Something impossible had happened on that day! The detachment proceeded with a brave and determined officer. But somehow it disappeared and there were no results. Something must have gone wrong: had it moved with determination, then it would have encountered this electrified crowd and the organized troops would have driven this crowd away to the corners of the Neva and the Tauride Gardens. . . . I sent [an envoy] but there was no news. . . . I sent another three platoons of Cossacks from those who were available to me. I have to say that after I sent this detachment I was left without any troops and had to gather another detachment in order to have something to resist with in case of further rebellion. I received only the information that Kutepov's detachment had gone as far as Kirochnaia, that it was moving along Kirochnaia and Spasskaia, but that it was impossible to move farther, and that it was necessary to send reinforcements.[67]

This testimony is largely responsible for the legend later created by historians, William Chamberlin, for instance, that the loyal forces dispatched to suppress the uprising "simply melted away as soon as they came into contact with the revolutionary mobs."[68] However, this does not exactly correspond to occurrences. It should be noted that Kutepov's troops demonstrated willingness to fulfill their com-

65. Kutepov, "Pervye dni revoliutsii v Petrograde," pp. 162-63.
66. Ibid., p. 163.
67. Deposition of Khabalov, *Padenie tsarskogo rezhima* 1: 198-99.
68. William Henry Chamberlin, *The Russian Revolution, 1917-1921* 1: 79.

mander's order. The punitive detachment maintained its cohesion, and put up a successful resistance against the insurgents until evening. But the isolation of Kutepov's forces reinforced Khabalov's sense of hopelessness.

Ignoring Khabalov's order, Kutepov moved his troops along Liteinyi Prospekt, where he encountered the insurgents for the first time. Kutepov decided to stay in the midsection of Liteinyi Prospekt, realizing that it would not be easy to clear the entire street of the insurgents, who were amassing in its northern section. He sent one of the officers to telephone Khabalov of this decision—the last communication, as it turned out, between the punitive detachment and headquarters. Kutepov's forces immediately cleared the small area near Preobrazhenskii Cathedral between Kirochnaia and Baseinaia, and established the house of Count Musin-Pushkin (Liteinyi, no. 17) as the headquarters and Preobrazhenskaia Square as the troops' assembling field.[69] A unit of the Keksholm Regiment led by Captain Davydov took position in the Officers' Club at the corner of Liteinyi Prospekt and Kirochnaia, and opened machine-gun fire at the demonstrators. One machine gunner, who refused to fire, was shot on the spot by Davydov.[70] An SR intellectual, N. Stepnoi, was standing on Liteinyi near the burning Circuit Court. A young teenager was making a speech in front of a small crowd, his eyes sparkling and his lean white face aglow with courage. As Stepnoi walked away, he heard a shot. He turned, and saw the young man lying on the ground with his skull blown off and blood gushing out.[71] The northern section of Liteinyi was the most dangerous part of the city on that afternoon.

But Kutepov's decision to squat in the midsection of Liteinyi precipitated the disintegration of the loyal troops. His objective was to clear Liteinyi Prospekt and to establish the front line for the government-controlled area on the west. Kutepov realized the impossibility of carrying out this assignment without substantial reinforcements, which, he was also well aware, would not be provided. The midsection of Liteinyi itself had insufficient strategic significance to stake the existence of the entire detachment. Kutepov's decision contributed to the suicidal isolation of his troops as well as to the significant reduction of the strength of the loyal troops, which became separated into two sections of the city with no communication.

While Kutepov's troops failed to expand the occupied territories, they successfully held them from the insurgent's attack. Despite their

69. Kutepov, "Pervye dni revoliutsii v Petrograde," pp. 163-64.
70. Leiberov, *Petrogradskii proletariat v Fevral'skoi revoliutsii* 2: 435.
71. N. Stepnoi, *Etapy velikoi russkoi revoliutsii*, p. 12.

grumblings and complaints of hunger and the lack of ammunition, the soldiers more or less obeyed Kutepov's order until they were completely surrounded. Kutepov's repeated requests for reinforcements and food remained unfulfilled. When he finally reached the *gradonachal'stvo* by telephone, no one answered, since headquarters had moved to the Admiralty without Kutepov's knowledge. Casualties among his troops as well as his officers increased. As darkness fell, insurgents filled the streets, smashing street lamps and shooting at the troops. At this point, the loyal troops began to defect. Kutepov finally realized that the end of his resistance had arrived. He noted with bitterness: "A large part of my detachment mingled with the crowds. I understood that my detachment could no longer resist. I returned home, ordered the doors closed but gave instructions that my soldiers be fed bread and sausages. Not a piece of bread had been given to these soldiers."[72] It was only then, after he had closed the doors behind him, that Kutepov's troops "melted away" among the insurgents.

In the meantime, Khabalov busily tried to bring the loyal troops together, ordering reserve regiments to send all available soldiers to the Palace Square. Not many regiments responded favorably to Khabalov's appeal, although two companies of Preobrazhenskii Regiment, an entire battalion of Pavlovskii Regiment, and three companies of Izmailovskii Regiment, among others, arrived in perfect composition, constituting the major core of the loyal forces.[73] The commander of the 181st Infantry Regiment answered that though his soldiers did not take part in the uprising, he could not expect them to join the loyal forces, while the commander of the Finland Regiment wanted to keep the reliable soldiers at his own disposal. The lack of weapons and ammunition created a serious problem, since the Arsenal and munition factories had fallen into the hands of the rebels. Khabalov asked the commandant of Kronstadt, Admiral Kurosh, to send reinforcements, and if not, at least ammunition. But the admiral refused; because of the imminent danger of Kronstadt sailors rebelling in response to the uprising in Petrograd he could not afford to comply with any of Khabalov's requests.[74] Thus, all Khabalov could do was hold on until reinforcement troops arrived from the front.

The situation, however, was not as hopeless in early afternoon

---

72. Kutepov, "Pervye dni revoliutsii v Petrograde," pp. 164-69.

73. In addition to the companies cited above, a company of the Third Rifle Regiment, three companies of the Eger Regiment, a company of the First Reserve Machine Gun Regiment and two artillery batteries (without shells, however) arrived at Palace Square. Martynov, *Tsarskaia armiia v fevral'skom perevorote*, p. 103; Burdzhalov, *Vtoraia russkaia revoliutsiia*, p. 196.

74. Deposition of Khabalov, *Padenie tsarskogo rezhima* 1: 200-201.

as Khabalov believed. The uprising of the soldiers was confined only to the Volynskii, Preobrazhenskii, Lithuanian Regiments, Sixth Engineer Battalion, and the Armored Car Division. Most of the other units still remained in the barracks, although they were reluctant to support the government. Kutepov's forces maintained cohesion in Liteinyi. The Fortress of Peter and Paul had not fallen to the rebels and could easily have become the stronghold of the loyal troops. In the city there were many pockets of loyal forces. The area surrounded by the Winter Palace, the General Staff, the Admiralty, and the *grado-nachal'stvo* was most secure under the protection of loyal forces, which assembled in support of the government. Hotel Astoria, the Ministry of Agriculture, and Marinskii Palace on Marinskaia Square were also protected by a small detachment and many officers who had fled to the Astoria. The Department of Police on the Fontanka held off the insurgents' attack. The training detachment of Finland Regiment, consisting of seventy soldiers led by five officers, controlled the Tuchkov, Birzha, and Palace bridges, thereby isolating Vasilievskii Island from the insurgents. The Stock Market was under its protection. The soldiers of the Keksholm Regiment occupied the insurance company, Zhizn', at the corner of Moika and the Kriukov Canal. Installing a machine gun on the window, they controlled the area near Theater Square. As Leiberov states, with better communication and better leadership, these forces could have become mobilized against the revolution.[75] But the panicked commanding authority never attempted to connect the loyal forces. Khabalov contemplated dispatching a detachment under the command of either Zankevich or Mikhailichenko to Vyborg District to make connection with the still resisting Moscow Regiment, but he abandoned this idea in view of the lack of ammunition.[76]

The only action Khabalov took was to request reinforcements from the front. He made this request in his telegram dispatched at 12:10 P.M. to the Stavka.[77] Although Khabalov gave assurances that he was taking "all measures necessary to suppress the rebellion," the request for reinforcements indicated the seriousness of the situation. An hour later, however, Beliaev dispatched the following telegram to Alekseev: "The disturbances which began in some army units from the morning are vigorously and energetically being suppressed by companies and battalions remaining faithful to their duty. It has not been successful so far to suppress the rebellion, but I am firmly con-

75. Leiberov, *Petrogradskii proletariat v Fevral'skoi revoliutsii* 2: 440.
76. TsGAOR, f. ChSK, d. 460, ℓ. 68.
77. Telegram of Khabalov to the tsar, no. 56, "Fevral'skaia revoliutsiia 1917 goda," *Krasnyi arkhiv* 21, no. 2 (1927): 8.

vinced of the rapid approach of tranquillity, the achievement for which merciless measures are being taken. The government is maintaining complete calm."[78]

In the light of the rapid expansion of anarchy and the constant deterioration of the government's resistance, one can only conclude that Beliaev's estimation of the situation was outrageously far from reality. His telegram, counterbalancing the urgency in Khabalov's telegram, greatly contributed to the delay of action on the part of the military leaders.

While the military authorities in Petrograd revealed their incompetency, the reaction of the cabinet members to the insurrection demonstrated an even more ignominious irrelevancy. War Minister Beliaev received the news of the insurrection at 8:30 in the morning and immediately relayed it to Golitsyn. The cabinet members gathered at Golitsyn's apartment on Mokhovaia Street, off Liteinyi, and exchanged their observations and impressions. No sense of urgency was felt in the discussion.[79] Faced with the rapid deterioration of the situation, however, the Council of Ministers met for the second time this afternoon, this time officially, at Golitsyn's apartment. It declared an emergency situation, placed Petrograd under martial law, and transferred all the power temporarily to the military command. About three o'clock in the afternoon Khabalov appeared at Golitsyn's request to brief the cabinet members. Khabalov's performance did not inspire the confidence of the ministers. Beliaev noted: "His hands were trembling; apparently he lost the balance necessary for providing leadership at such a serious moment." After Khabalov retired, Golitsyn requested Beliaev to visit the *gradonachal'stvo* to see to it that military authorities should take decisive measures against the rebels. When Beliaev went to the *gradonachal'stvo* at four o'clock and received reports from Colonel Mikhailichenko and other officers, he found an appalling situation; he realized that there was "complete absence of ideas, insufficient initiative of policies."[80] The war minister immediately tried to rectify the situation by interfering in the commanding authority. He formally dismissed Chebykin and appointed Colonel Zankevich, chief of the Petrograd General Staff, commander of troops in Petrograd. This appointment created utter confusion. Khabalov felt that his command was undercut by Beliaev's meddling, while Zankevich set out to make his own plans after inspecting the loyal troops gathered in Palace Square. No one knew any longer who

78. Telegram of Beliaev to Alekseev, no. 196, ibid.
79. Deposition of Golitsyn, *Padenie tsarskogo rezhima* 2: 263.
80. Deposition of Beliaev, ibid., pp. 239-40; TsGAOR, f. ChSK, d. 460, ℓ. 114.

had ultimate authority and Khabalov, Zankevich, and Beliaev kept issuing conflicting orders.[81]

In the evening, around seven o'clock, the Council of Ministers held what turned out to be the last meeting of the tsar's cabinet. Golitsyn's apartment was no longer safe, and the ministers moved to Marinskii Palace. *Gradonachal'nik* Balk asked for permission of the Council of Ministers to lead the police to Tsarskoe Selo to protect the imperial palace. His request sounded to most of the ministers like a request for desertion. Protopopov asked Balk why he had not turned to Khabalov for the request—the ultimate authority for security matters. Balk replied that Khabalov was nowhere to be found. Protopopov ordered Balk to remain in the city with the police, which had by this time completely disintegrated.[82]

The Council of Ministers decided to send the tsar a telegram requesting formation of a dictatorship headed by a popular general, a change of composition of the cabinet, including the dismissal of Protopopov, and a negotiated settlement with the Duma. Finance Minister Bark argued that since there was no time to wait for the tsar's answer, Golitsyn should exercise his prerogatives as chairman of the Council of Ministers, and act accordingly. It was decided to delegate all authority to the chairman of the Council of Ministers temporarily and to force Protopopov to resign on the pretext of his "illness."[83] Grand Duke Kirill Vladimirovich, who had arrived at the *gradonachal'stvo* from Tsarskoe Selo, had made a strong recommendation through Beliaev for Protopopov's dismissal.[84]

During the meeting they were told that Protopopov's apartment on the Fontanka was burned by the insurgents and his wife was barely saved by one of the servants. All the ministers expressed sympathy, but it did not prevent them from requesting his resignation. Golitsyn asked him "to make a sacrifice." Protopopov finally accepted his resignation. The ministers then asked Protopopov to leave Marinskii Palace immediately for fear that his presence might endanger their safety. To this request Protopopov replied: "It remains only for me to shoot myself." But he did not commit suicide; escorted by his

---

81. Deposition of Pertsov, quoted in Martynov, *Tsarskaia armiia v fevral'skom perevorote*, p. 104; Deposition of Khabalov, *Padenie tsarskogo rezhima* 1: 201, 203; Deposition of Beliaev, *Padenie tsarskogo rezhima* 2: 230, 239-40; TsGAOR, f. ChSK, d. 460, ℓ. 70.

82. TsGAOR, f. ChSK, d. 466, ℓℓ. 177-78.

83. Ibid., ℓ. 178.

84. Deposition of Beliaev, *Padenie tsarskogo rezhima* 2: 240; Deposition of Golitsyn, ibid., p. 267.

bodyguard, he went to the state controller's building, and slept overnight in the servants' quarters.[85]

Less than twenty-four hours after handing the Duma the imperial decree of prorogation, Golitsyn's government decided to resign. Golitsyn dispatched a telegram to the tsar, submitting resignation of his cabinet and requesting formation of a dictatorship in Petrograd. He made this decision, it appears, under the pressure of Grand Dukes Mikhail Aleksandrovich and Kirill Vladimirovich. The chairman of the Duma also came to Marinskii Palace to press Golitsyn for the formation of a ministry of confidence. While rejecting Rodzianko's demand, Golitsyn suggested the formation of a temporary dictatorship under the regency of Grand Duke Mikhail. Mikhail's plea to establish a dictatorship was, however, tersely rejected by Nicholas.[86]

By evening the area under the control of the loyal troops had shrunk further. The government held a small area surrounded by the *gradonachal'stvo,* the Admiralty, the Winter Palace, Palace Square, and the General Staff. Also Marinskaia Square was still secure and the Fortress of Peter and Paul remained untouched by the insurgents. But the Department of Police was completely surrounded by insurgents by two o'clock in the afternoon. The siege continued all night, and it was finally captured only early in the morning of February 28. The telephone station on Morskaia Street was heavily guarded by government troops. When the insurgents assembled on Morskaia and Kirpichnyi Lane, they were fired upon by machine guns. At midnight a detachment of insurgent workers and students sneaked into the building, and overcoming resistance, succeeded in stopping telephone operation. Students of the Military Automobile School took part in this attack, and among the attackers was young poet V. Maiakovskii, who served in the Military Automobile School.[87] The training detachment of Finland Regiment securely guarded the Birzha, Tuchkov, and Palace bridges, thereby continuing to isolate Vasilievskii Island from the revolution. The Stock Market was converted into a prison for arrested insurgents.[88] By evening, however, armed insurgents attacked the troops guarding Tuchkov Bridge. The loyal

85. TsGAOR, f. ChSK, d. 466, ℓℓ. 178-79; Leiberov, *Petrogradskii proletariat v Fevral'skoi revoliutsii* 2: 448.

86. Conversation between General Alekseev and Grand Duke Mikhail Aleksandrovich, "Fevral'skaia revoliutsiia 1917 goda," *Krasnyi arkhiv* 21, no. 2 (1927): 11-12. See chap. 22.

87. Leiberov, *Petrogradskii proletariat v Fevral'skoi revoliutsii* 2: 454, 455; Burdzhalov, *Vtoraia russkaia revoliutsiia,* p. 195.

88. Mints, *Istoriia Velikogo Oktiabria* 1: 547.

troops put up a furious resistance but, faced with endless waves of insurgents, they finally withdrew. The isolation of Vasilievskii Island was broken.[89]

Gradually pessimism pervaded headquarters. Balk noted: "The number of officers gathering in the *gradonachal'stvo* became greater and greater. The atmosphere was depressing. The agony of the government had begun. Sobbing started. A captain of Keksholm Regiment wept hysterically; its training detachment had just refused to carry out his orders."[90] With the loyal troops so few, Khabalov deemed it necessary to withdraw them from Palace Square, where they would be vulnerable to attack from all directions. At the meeting called by Khabalov three alternatives were discussed: (1) to move headquarters to the Admiralty, where the loyal troops could utilize the large space in front of it; (2) to transfer headquarters and the loyal troops to the Winter Palace and to resist to the last soldier for the preservation of monarchy; and (3) to flee from Petrograd to Tsarskoe Selo and to wait for the arrival of the reinforcements.[91] Khabalov supported the first proposal; Zankevich advocated the second. At nine o'clock the troops began to move from Palace Square to the Admiralty. Infantry occupied the corridors and lobby, while machine gunners prepared their guns at the windows of the upper floors. The cavalry were assigned to the barracks of the Mounted Guard Regiment of Morskaia Street.[92]

Under the circumstances the Admiralty gave the loyal troops the best protection with a large open space of the Aleksandr Garden in front and the Neva at the back. In addition, three main streets issued from the Admiralty to three major railway stations—Nikolaevski, Tsarskoe Selo, and Warsaw Stations—at which the reinforcement troops were expected to arrive.[93]

Apparently unable to comprehend that the government troops were surrounded by hostile rebels, Beliaev ordered Khabalov to issue a declaration to the populace proclaiming the entire city of Petrograd to be in a state of siege and announcing the dismissal of Protopopov. Beliaev had this proclamation printed in the Admiralty. The unfortunate task of posting the copies of the proclamation throughout the

89. Leiberov, *Petrogradskii proletariat v Fevral'skoi revoliutsii* 2: 455.

90. Balk, "Poslednie piat' dnei," p. 11.

91. Deposition of Khabalov, *Padenie tsarskogo rezhima* 1: 202; Akaemov, "Agoniia starago rezhima," p. xxiv.

92. Martynov, *Tsarskaia armiia v fevral'skom perevorote*, p. 106; Balk, "Poslednie piat' dnei," p. 12.

93. Deposition of Khabalov, *Padenie tsarskogo rezhima* 1: 202-3; Burdzhalov, *Vtoraia russkaia revoliutsiia*, p. 198.

city fell on Balk, who, realizing the ridiculousness of the assignment, declared that he would not carry out this order without heavy protection and glue and brushes, neither of which the government availed itself of. It was decided to throw them in the streets wherever possible.[94] More than a thousand copies of this proclamation were printed, but only a few copies were thrown in Aleksandr Garden in front of the Admiralty. Beliaev's obsession with issuing orders did not stop. He wanted Khabalov to impose a curfew on the populace. Khabalov ignored his request. Tiazhel'nikov and other officers saw Beliaev composing a telegram to be dispatched to the Stavka, in which he described the situation in Petrograd as "disturbing." The officers shook their heads, questioning the sanity of the war minister.[95]

This evening Khabalov dispatched a telegram to the Stavka, in which for the first time since the outbreak of the insurrection, he outlined the total disaster of the government troops: "I implore you to report to His Majesty the Emperor that I could not fulfill the order of restoring order in the capital. . . . By evening the rebels occupied considerable parts of the capital."[96] The telegram, which should have been written much earlier, brought a serious shock to the Stavka when it arrived there at 12:55 A.M. on February 28.

Nothing would reveal more blatantly the ineptitude of the military authorities than their treatment of the soldiers who came to the support of the government. They had been waiting for action for several hours without any food or any clear indication of leadership. Their complaints became increasingly vociferous. The companies of Pavlovskii Regiment deserted in disgust. Colonel Zankevich inspected the troops and discovered that even the soldiers of the Izmailovskii Regiment, whom he trusted most, were wavering. At eleven o'clock Zankevich ordered the loyal troops to move to the Winter Palace. The reasons for this unexpected move remained unknown; it could be that, sensing the pessimistic mood among the soldiers, Zankevich tried to boost morale by appealing for a heroic last struggle in the emperor's palace. Zankevich's order further alienated the soldiers. The soldiers of Preobrazhenskii Regiment slipped into darkness while moving to the Winter Palace and returned to their barracks. The only troops remaining for the government were three companies of Izmailovskii Regiment, one company of Eger Regiment, one company of the Rifle Regiment, two batteries of the Artillery Division, and one machine-gun company

94. Deposition of Khabalov, *Padenie tsarskogo rezhima* 1: 207; Akaemov, "Agoniia starago rezhima," p. xxviii; Balk, "Poslednie piat' dnei," p. 14.

95. TsGAOR, f. ChSK, d. 460, ℓ. 114.

96. Telegram of Khabalov to Alekseev, "Fevral'skaia revoliutsiia 1917 goda," *Krasnyi arkhiv* 21, no. 2 (1927): 14-15.

—altogether 1,500 to 2,000 soldiers including the remainders of the police and gendarmes, with 12 guns, 40 machine guns, and a small number of cartridges.[97]

The soldiers who still remained faithful to their oaths of allegiance were humiliated once more at the Winter Palace. As the tired, dirty soldiers arrived at the palace and prepared for bivouac, the palace commandant, General Komarov, was shocked at the appalling scene. How dare these dirty soldiers with strong body odor invade the tsar's palace? The immaculately shining floor was blemished with dirt from the soldiers' boots. The building and furniture might be damaged if a battle were to be engaged here. General Komarov bustled around, fuming and complaining about this blasphemous situation, determined to kick the soldiers out. He found a sympathetic ear in Khabalov, but Zankevich stubbornly refused to evacuate.[98] Though grumbling, Komarov had no choice but to give the troops temporary permission to stay. Shortly after midnight an automobile brought Beliaev and Grand Duke Mikhail Aleksandrovich to the Winter Palace. The soldiers who had felt uncomfortable after Komarov's outburst enthusiastically welcomed the grand duke who, they believed, courageously came to risk his life with common soldiers for the defense of the monarchy. Actually, Mikhail's visit to the Winter Palace was not motivated by such heroism. After meeting with Rodzianko and Golitsyn and offering to help his brother Nicholas in vain, it became too late for him to return to Gatchina. The safest place to spend the night happened to be the Winter Palace. Coolly ignoring the cheering soldiers, Mikhail hurriedly retired to his room without a word of greeting. Immediately Komarov sought an audience and bitterly complained about the soldiers' presence. Wholeheartedly agreeing with Komarov, Mikhail summoned Beliaev and Khabalov and ordered them to evacuate the soldiers from the palace immediately.[99]

Khabalov, Beliaev, and Zankevich discussed where to move the troops. The Fortress of Peter and Paul was a possibility but crossing the bridge now occupied by insurgents was out of the question, particularly when they did not have much confidence in the reliability of their own troops. Finally, they decided to return to the Admi-

97. Deposition of Khabalov, *Padenie tsarskogo rezhima* 1: 203; Burdzhalov, *Vtoraia russkaia revoliutsiia*, p. 198. According to Burdzhalov, the number of soldiers was only 600.

98. Deposition of Khabalov, *Padenie tsarskogo rezhima* 1: 203; Balk, "Poslednie piat' dnei," p. 14; Martynov, *Tsarskaia armiia v fevral'skom perevorote*, pp. 107-8.

99. Deposition of Khabalov, *Padenie tsarskogo rezhima* 1: 203; Balk, "Poslednie piat' dnei," p. 14.

ralty.[100] This decision outraged the soldiers who had jubilantly welcomed the grand duke only a few hours before. They naturally felt that they were being "kicked out like dogs" by the person they thought they were defending. To add insult to injury, the troops were ordered to march boldly from the Winter Palace to Senate Square around the Admiralty, instead of simply crossing the street, to show the strength and determination of the loyal troops.[101] This was too much for the hungry and angry troops who had faithfully fulfilled their duty. Soldier after soldier deserted his position; some simply returned to their barracks, and others, including even some gendarmes, marched to the Duma with red armbands on the sleeves of their overcoats. The loyal troops shrank to only four companies with very few cartridges, almost no food, and two artillery guns.[102] Without firing a shot at the insurgents and without encountering attack by insurgents, the loyal troops were reduced to zero. Zankevich noted: "There was no confrontation whatever with the [insurgent] troops or the people. I had the impression that by the evening of February 27 all the commanding personnel came to the conclusion that any struggle with the revolution would be hopeless."[103] Exhausted and broken-hearted, Khabalov, Beliaev, and Balk sat in silence at a large table in a room on the third floor of the Admiralty and waited for the representatives of the new government to appear for their arrest.

During the night the emperor dismissed Khabalov as the commander of the Petrograd Military District, and appointed General N. I. Ivanov as military dictator in Petrograd. To obtain the information necessary for his assigned operation against the insurgents, Ivanov asked Khabalov in a telegram from Mogilev a series of questions. The reply given by Khabalov revealed the extent of the collapse of the loyal troops in Petrograd. Almost all army units, with the exception of a few companies remaining in the Admiralty, had either joined the insurrection or remained neutral. All the railway stations had fallen to the insurgents. With the exception of the Admiralty all the city was controlled by the insurgents, or at least Khabalov could not establish contact with other parts of the city. All police forces had disintegrated. The insurgents had started arresting ministers. All the weapons, artillery, and military supplies went into the hands of the insurgents. With the exception of the chief of staff near the

100. Balk, "Poslednie piat' dnei," p. 15; Akaemov, "Agoniia starago rezhima," p. xxix.

101. Leiberov, *Petrogradskii proletariat v Fevral'skoi revoliutsii* 2: 446.

102. Deposition of Khabalov, *Padenie tsarskogo rezhima* 1: 204.

103. TsGAOR, f. ChSK, d. 460, l. 114.

Admiralty, Khabalov had established no contact with other military forces and staff.[104] However, this pessimistic picture reflected Khabalov's psychological state more than the real relationship between the loyal and the revolutionary forces. As we shall see in the next chapters, while Khabalov was busily moving his troops back and forth between the Admiralty and the Winter Palace, expecting an all-out attack from the insurgents, the revolutionary leaders were frightened at the prospect of counterattack by Khabalov's troops.

Disintegration of the loyal troops meant the immediate collapse of the cabinet. As the ministers in Marinskii Palace learned that the insurgents were approaching the palace, in spite of their decorations, medals, high ranks, and their respect for decorum, honor, and dignity, the primitive instinct of survival was the only faculty they could muster. Someone who thought that the insurgents' attack had begun in panic turned off all the lights of the palace, but when this news turned out to be false and the lights were turned back on, some members of the cabinet found themselves under the table, and glanced, embarrassed, at each other. Two other ministers hid themselves in a dark room of the court couriers.[105] There was no dignity or heroism in the last scene of the dying regime.

After leaving Marinskii Palace, Protopopov and his bodyguard were walking along the Moika, looking for a safe place to spend the night. Protopopov saw Prince Shakhovskoi, minister of trade and industry, walking on the other side of the street from the opposite direction, his face covered with the collar of his overcoat. The two ministers passed by without exchanging a glance, and pretended not to recognize each other. Like criminals, they were now hunted men.[106]

At midnight, the arrests of the ministers began. The insurrection had triumphed in Petrograd. Throughout the night crowds were running in the streets, waving red flags and singing revolutionary songs, while the sky was aglow from the burning buildings.

When women workers of Vyborg District abandoned their work early on the morning of February 23, no one realized that they were witnessing the movement that would overthrow tsarism. But to the chorus of the women's battle cries, the voices of other militant Petrograd workers were immediately added. The strike movement grew with astonishing speed. On the third day the general strike had paralyzed the

104. "Fevral'skaia revoliutsiia 1917 goda," *Krasnyi arkhiv* 21, no. 2 (1927): 20-21.

105. M. V. Rodzianko, "Gosudarstvennaia duma i fevral'skaia 1917 goda revoliutsiia," *Arkhiv russkoi revoliutsii* 6 (1922): 58.

106. TsGAOR, f. ChSK, d. 466, ℓ. 180.

capital. People in Petrograd had not seen such a large strike and demonstration since 1905. The police could no longer control the angered demonstrators in the streets. On the fourth day, however, the tsarist government took decisive steps to suppress the disorder and the troops fired upon the demonstrators. At that moment, the workers' movement appeared to be coming to an end.

Yet one significant difference existed between the movement in February 1917 and all the previous workers' disturbances during the war. The difference lay in the attitude of the garrison soldiers. By the third winter of the war the traditional loyalty that had bound the soldiers to the tsar and discipline had disappeared to be replaced with apathy and resentment. From the beginning of the unrest the soldiers sympathized with the demonstrators, and the government's order to fire upon the demonstrators, ironically, compelled the soldiers to make a final choice. On February 27, the soldiers revolted en masse.

The security authorities in Petrograd did not know what to do. Despite the availability of the loyal forces, they panicked, and in their confusion committed one mistake after another. The police disappeared. The punitive detachment was isolated. The ineptitude and the confusion of the commanding authority led to the final disintegration of the loyal troops without their firing a single shot at the insurgents.

The insurrection had triumphed in Petrograd. But the revolution was not won yet. Tsar Nicholas was alive and well in Mogilev, determined to crush the incipient revolution in the capital.

Above, Empress Aleksandra and Anna Vyrubova; *left*, Grigorii Rasputin; *right*, Grand Duke Dmitrii Pavlovich, one of the assassins of Rasputin (all photographs from the Hoover Institution)

Barricades in Liteinyi Prospekt (Hoover Institution)

Burned police records (Hoover Institution)

Insurgents gather at Tauride Palace (State Historical Museum, Moscow)

Above, insurgents from the Volynskii Regiment and other units in Liteinyi Prospekt, February 27, 1917 (State Historical Museum, Moscow); *left,* Sergeant T. I. Kirpichnikov, leader of the revolt of the Volynskii Regiment (Hoover Institution)

Young looters with captured
sabers and other booty (Hoover Institution); *below*, check-
ing a pass at Tauride Palace
(Hoover Institution)

Дни. революціи. 1917 г.
Предъявленіе пропуска при бъъздъ
въ Таврическій дворецъ.

Group of arrested officers (Stinton Jones, *Russia in Revolution*)

Insurgents arrest former police officer in disguise (Hoover Institution)

Insurgent soldiers march to Tauride Palace with a red flag (State Historical Museum, Moscow)

Showing the view of the Reception at Government House, Honolulu, May 1908 (?)

PART IV

THE PETROGRAD SOVIET
AND THE DUMA COMMITTEE

Above, N. S. Chkheidze delivers a speech to sailors in the Tauride Palace (Hoover Institution); *below*, a plenary meeting of the Petrograd Soviet of Workers' and Soldiers' Deputies in Tauride Palace (Hoover Institution); *preceding page*, insurgent soldiers and sailors gather in Tauride Palace (State Historical Museum, Moscow)

17

THE FORMATION OF
THE PETROGRAD SOVIET

 The sudden explosion of the soldiers' rising on February 27 completely destroyed the tsarist administrative network in Petrograd. The "former" ministers and generals now became fugitives from the triumphant insurgents. Yet, even though the rebels took the capital into their hands with unexpected ease, they had no idea of what to do next. Suddenly, at the height of the intoxication of liberation, fear chilled their passions. The rumor spread that counterrevolutionary troops sent by Nicholas II were approaching the capital from the front. While the soldiers had shaken off the chains of military discipline, they found no revolutionary authorities to give them direction. Soldiers who had broken their oaths to the tsar now sought an institution that would sanction their actions. The Duma, which had spearheaded the attack on the government from its rostrum, appeared to the masses of soldiers to be the institution to absolve them from the "crimes" they had just committed. The cry: "To the Tauride Palace!" leaped from soldier to soldier.[1]

The success of the insurrection also meant broadening the basis of the mass movement. The leadership that had provided the driving force in the strikes and the demonstrations before February 27 quickly eroded once the rebellion expanded beyond the confines of the workers' movement. For the first time since February 23 many private citizens joined the political movement, attacking police stations and prisons, or just going out to the streets to greet the soldiers. The leaders

1. E. N. Burdzhalov, *Vtoraia russkaia revoliutsiia: Vosstanie v Petrograde,* p. 202.

of the workers' movement could not extend their effectiveness to the newcomers. The Bolsheviks, trying to divert the massive support for the Duma as the center of the movement, appealed to the workers to establish Finland Station in the Vyborg District as a center. This attempt, however, went unheeded; workers and even the Bolsheviks themselves eventually joined the irresistible current flowing to Tauride Palace.

When the soldiers' rude boots stepped onto the carpeted floor of the palace built by Catherine the Great for one of her lovers, two groups were responding to the events outside—the Duma leaders and the Socialist leaders. From the former there emerged a Provisional Committee of the State Duma (the Duma Committee), a parent body of the Provisional Government, while the Socialists created the Petrograd Soviet of Workers' Deputies, to be renamed the Petrograd Soviet of Workers' and Soldiers' Deputies on March 1. Thus two conflicting authorities came into being. And it was during the first few days of the February Revolution that the two authorities established the strange ambivalent relationship of cooperation and antagonism, a relationship that lasted basically until September of this turbulent year.

From the point of view of revolutionary leadership during the February insurrection, two characteristics stand out: first, the movement had no leadership strong enough to organize the masses into some kind of revolutionary power. Secondly, the top leaders of the revolutionary parties took little part in the insurrection. The creation of the Petrograd Soviet might appear to have finally closed the gap between the masses and the revolutionary leaders. The insurrection seemed, on the surface, to have finally found a voice to dictate its will. Actually, however, the gap between the masses and the leaders was never bridged. The Petrograd Soviet created two faces: one aspect expressing the long suppressed desires of the masses for destruction of the existing system and the other representing the revolutionary intelligentsia, whose preconceived notion of revolution often clashed with the desires of the masses. These two faces remained like a double-exposed photograph, never merging into one clear image.

As Oskar Anweiler states, despite its short-lived existence, the St. Petersburg Soviet of 1905 had left a strong revolutionary tradition that was clearly imprinted on the consciousness of the St. Petersburg workers.[2] Although the revolutionary parties failed to incorporate

2. Oskar Anweiler, *Die Rätebewegung in Russland, 1905-1921*, p. 127 (English translation, *The Soviets: The Russian Workers, Peasants, and Soldiers Councils, 1905-1921*, trans. Ruth Hein [New York: Pantheon Books, 1974]).

the notion of the soviet integrally into their revolutionary programs after the defeat of the 1905 Revolution, they nevertheless left the possibility of its recreation open. In fact, in February 1917, they picked up where they had left off in 1905. The ideas on the soviet they developed in 1905 therefore influenced their respective attitudes toward the soviet in February and March of 1917.

The creation of the Soviet of Workers' Deputies in major industrial cities, particularly, in St. Petersburg, in the 1905 Revolution necessitated the evaluation by the revolutionary parties of the viability of this organ in the context of their over-all revolutionary theory. The Mensheviks assumed that the first revolution in Russia should be bourgeois-democratic, in which the bourgeoisie, not the proletariat, should play a leading role. At this stage, the Social Democrats should not join a bourgeois government, let alone seize power, but rather remain "the party of the extreme opposition," and exert pressure from outside to insure the completion of the bourgeois democratic revolution. This policy, however, did not preclude the possibility of "partial, episodic seizures of power and of forming revolutionary communes in this or that city or district, purely to further the spread of the uprising and the disorganization of the government."[3] The Mensheviks encouraged the revolutionary movement of the proletariat as long as it remained within the confines of the struggle against tsarism. The workers should take part in a struggle for the creation of a "revolutionary self-government"—a network of elected organs at county and provincial levels to be created by all classes of people, disregarding legal electoral procedures, for the purpose of convening an all-Russian constituent assembly. According to Martov, the leader of the Mensheviks, this was an attempt to "disorganize the tsarist administration from within through democratic upheaval and force the government to accept a constitutional concession."[4] And yet, the workers should not be submerged in the democratic movement, rather they should be organized in a separate class organization. To draw the workers, who had been denied participation in the political life of the state, into the mainstream of the political process and to transform the Social Democratic party from an illegal, secret party into one that was open and for the masses, the Mensheviks called for the establishment of the All-Russian Workers' Congress. According

3. Solomon M. Schwarz, *The Russian Revolution of 1905: The Workers' Movement and the Formation of Bolsehvism and Menshevism*, p. 8. Resolution adopted in the Menshevik conference held in Geneva in April/May 1905, quoted in ibid., p. 12.

4. Ibid., p. 168; quoted in Anweiler, *Die Rätebewegung in Russland*, p. 84.

to their program, the factory workers would elect their deputies to the city workers' congresses, which in turn would send their deputies to the All-Russian Workers' Congress.[5] As a revolutionary tactic, the notion of a revolutionary self-government and of the All-Russian Workers' Congress remained a naïve, highly unrealistic pipedream, which deserved to be attacked by Lenin as "good for nothing." As he pointed out, in a political reality in which revolutionary forces had to face the tsarist machine of oppression, these notions would be meaningless unless they were combined with an armed insurrection in its most concrete terms.[6] Furthermore, the Mensheviks never clarified the relationship between a bourgeois-democratic government and a locally formed revolutionary self-government. Would not a revolutionary self-government undermine the authority of the central government? Would it be possible for the workers to carry out a struggle against the remnants of tsarism, on the one hand, and to refrain from joining the central government, on the other? These ambiguities, which had provoked merely an academic interest, suddenly bore serious and practical consequences after the February Revolution. Yet behind this unrealistic formulation of their revolutionary program, one cannot but see the Mensheviks' overriding concern with democratic principles and with the necessity to insure the independence of the young and fragile labor movement.[7]

The creation of the soviets in 1905 compelled the Mensheviks to apply the notions of revolutionary self-government and of the All-Russian Workers' Congress in concrete situations. They conceived of the soviet as the embodiment of a revolutionary self-government as well as a transitional institution through which their goal of the All-Russian Workers' Congress would ultimately emerge. They never envisaged the soviet as a revolutionary power replacing the tsarist regime. This power could be organized only by a constituent assembly that would comprise all classes of the population, not by the soviet, which was an exclusive class organization restricted to the workers.[8] Although the Mensheviks paid but scant attention to the soviet after the defeat of the 1905 Revolution, their basic concept of the soviet remained unchanged.

While the Mensheviks' revolutionary theory was built on the assumption that the bourgeoisie should play a leading part in the

5. Ibid., p. 83.
6. V. I. Lenin, *Sochineniia* (4th ed.) 9: 161.
7. Anweiler, *Die Rätebewegung in Russland*, p. 85; Schwarz, *The Russian Revolution of 1905*, p. 13.
8. See Anweiler, *Die Rätebewegung in Russland*, pp. 86-89.

bourgeois-democratic revolution, the Bolsheviks denied the revolutionary role assigned to the bourgeoisie by the Mensheviks. The Bolsheviks maintained that after the overthrow of the tsarist regime a provisional revolutionary government composed of the proletariat and the peasantry should establish a dictatorship. Strongly opposing the Menshevik concept of a revolutionary self-government, Lenin called for the establishment of revolutionary committees. Unlike the Mensheviks' notion of revolutionary self-government as a spontaneous movement, Lenin's revolutionary committees would be organized under the strong influence of the Social Democrats and their task would be directly connected with an armed insurrection.[9] The Bolshevik's elitism and mistrust of the "spontaneity" of the workers' movement were clearly reflected in their attitude toward the soviets in 1905. As long as the Petersburg Soviet functioned as a strike committee, the Bolsheviks supported it, but after the strike was over, the Bolshevik organization in St. Petersburg was hostile toward the soviet. The central issue was the relationship between the party and the spontaneous mass movement. The Bolsheviks' representative to the Executive Committee of the Petersburg Soviet, Kunniants (Radin), declared that the existence of the soviet outside of Social Democracy was "harmful" and "a menace to the free development of the class movement toward Social Democracy." The Party Central Committee demanded that the soviet accept the program of the party or, if they refused, they would either leave the soviet entirely or remain in it only to expose "the absurdity of such political leadership."[10]

Unlike the Petersburg Bolsheviks, Lenin sensed the importance of the soviet as an organization that could draw a broader spectrum of the working class into the political struggle. He advanced this view for the first time in an article entitled "Our Tasks and the Soviet of Workers' Deputies" written in November 1905. Criticizing the narrow dogmatic view expressed by Radin, Lenin stated: "I must state . . . that it seems inexpedient to demand that the soviet adopt the programs of Social Democracy and join the Russian Social Democratic Labor party. It seems to me that for leading the political struggle the soviet . . . as well as the party are equally indispensable at the present moment." And yet Lenin clearly distinguished his idea from the Mensheviks' policy toward the soviet by associating this organ directly with the concrete task of insurrection and by relating it to the problem of a revolutionary power, although he came to the latter conclusion hesitantly. He stated: "Perhaps, I might be mistaken, but it seems to me

9. Ibid., pp. 92-93.
10. Schwarz, *The Russian Revolution of 1905*, pp. 180, 183-84.

. . . that in political relations the Soviet of Workers' Deputies must be regarded as an embryo of a *provisional revolutionary government.* It seems to me that the soviet must proclaim itself to be a provisional revolutionary government of all Russia as soon as possible or (the same thing, but only in a different form) it must create a provisional revolutionary government."[11]

While the Mensheviks saw in the soviet the realization of workers' self-government without any reference to the problem of power, and while the Petersburg Bolsheviks dismissed the soviet as dangerous to the proletarian movement, Lenin's notion of the soviet as the embryo of a provisional revolutionary government offered a unique possibility for the development of a new revolutionary theory. Nevertheless, one must admit that Lenin's formulation remained extremely tentative, leaving many ambiguities concerning both the relationship between the soviet and a provisional revolutionary government and that between the soviet and the party. Should the soviet be considered a revolutionary government as such, or should it be a transitional institution merely to create a provisional revolutionary government? The statement quoted above indicates that Lenin did not clearly think through these questions. The ambiguities were even more pronounced in his treatment of the relationship between the soviet and the party. On the one hand, he recognized the importance of drawing broader sections of the population into the soviet, advocating the inclusion of not only the workers but also the sailors, soldiers, peasants, and even the "revolutionary bourgeois intelligentsia." On the other hand, he added: "This will be a temporary alliance for clearly defined, immediate practical tasks. The independent and uncompromising Russian Social Democratic Labor party will unbendingly stand for still more important, fundamental interests of the socialist proletariat and its still more important ultimate aims."[12]

Lenin's writings between the end of 1905 and 1907 attested to his vacillation about the soviet. He consistently treated it as an organ of insurrection, and as such he succeeded in convincing his party of the necessity of participating in and even of taking the initiative of creating the soviet. Nevertheless, the crucial questions regarding its role in

11. Lenin, *Sochineniia* 10: 5. Lenin wrote this article abroad in the form of a letter to the editor of *Novaia zhizn'*, the Bolshevik newspaper. This article did not appear until 1940. Lenin qualifies the entire article with the remarks that he might be mistaken and that he should have the right to withdraw any statements. His formulation of the theory was tentative. It is possible that *Novaia zhizn'* rejected the publication of this article.

12. Ibid., p. 8.

the creation of a provisional revolutionary government and its relationship with the party remained unclear.[13]

It was Trotskii who advanced the most positive evaluation of the revolutionary potentialities of the soviet. In fact, his concept of the soviet was central to his theory of permanent revolution. Free from the mistrust of the spontaneity of the mass movement and directly involved in the Petersburg Soviet as its vice-chairman, Trotskii came to regard the soviet, without reservations and qualifications, as the most direct, genuine form of democracy. And yet Trotskii went further than his fellow Mensheviks, who could not see in the soviet anything but an organ adjunct to formal, legal institutions. He arrived at the same conclusion as Lenin, only in a more direct and unqualified manner, that the soviet should be an organ of insurrection as well as forming a provisional revolutionary government charged with the task of fulfilling a bourgeois-democratic revolution.[14]

The Socialist Revolutionary party did not develop a consistent policy toward the soviet, partly because the SRs' influence among the urban workers was less strong than the two factions of the Social Democratic party. The Party Congress held in December 1905 did not even mention a soviet. One can see, however, the basic attitude of the SRs in the leaflet issued by its Central Executive Committee, after the dissolution of the First Duma. In this leaflet, the SRs appealed to the workers to create an interparty, militant Soviet of Workers' Deputies for the general leadership of the struggle among the workers. It should be noted that the SRs envisioned the soviet merely as a center of the various revolutionary forces. In 1906, however, a radical left wing of the SR party, known as Maximalists, together with the anarchists, advanced a slogan calling for the establishment of soviet communes (kommunal'nye sovety) in cities and villages. The union of these soviets would proclaim a dictatorship and organize a provisional revolutionary government.[15]

After the 1905 Revolution was defeated, the revolutionary parties ceased mentioning the soviet, incorporating it no further in their revolutionary theory. But the idea of its creation was revived during the war. Faced with the first signs of the revival of the workers' movement after the Ivanovo massacre in August 1915, the revolutionary leaders recognized the need of a center to coordinate the workers'

13. Anweiler, Die Rätebewegung in Russland, pp. 100-104; Wada Haruki, "Nigatsu kakumei," in Roshia kakumei no kenkyū, ed. Eguchi Bokuro, pp. 369, 380-81.

14. Anweiler, Die Rätebewegung in Russland, pp. 108-9; Isaac Deutscher, The Prophet Armed (New York, London: Oxford University Press, 1954), pp. 149, 163-68.

15. Anweiler, Die Rätebewegung in Ru ːland, pp. 113-16.

movement in Petrograd. According to an Okhrana report, at a series
of the Socialist Revolutionaries' meetings in August and September,
they adopted a slogan to establish a Soviet of Workers' Deputies from
the representatives of the factory committees. This should include
all the representatives of the Socialist parties and should strive for the
convocation of a constituent assembly. The Mensheviks also supported
the creation of the soviet. In the Organization Committee's leaflet to the
workers distributed during the election campaign for the workers'
group in the War Industries Committee, the Mensheviks appealed to
the workers to take advantage of all means to advance the interests
of the proletariat. These means included the election of the workers'
group and the creation of the workers' committees for assistance for
the evacuees, trade unions, cooperatives, the Soviet of Workers' Deputies, and the Workers' Congress.[16] To the Mensheviks and the Socialist
Revolutionaries the soviet was a coordinating body of the workers'
representatives for the over-all leadership of the workers' movement,
an interparty organization to include all the Socialist parties.

The Bolsheviks also revived the notion of the creation of the soviet
in the summer and the fall of 1915. When the Petersburg Committee
discussed at the end of August how to react to the election of the
workers' group, it decided to transform the election campaign into
an election to a Soviet of Workers' Deputies.[17] The Petersburg Committee's position was further elaborated in its instructions to the
electors, written by Bogdatiev. In these instructions, the Petersburg
Committee advocated "organizing a provisional revolutionary government to replace the existing institutions of the state power, preparing by the democratic organizations and by the revolutionary
government for the convocation of the All-Russian Constituent
Assembly, and proclaiming in the Constituent Assembly the abolition
of the tsarist monarchy and the introduction of the Russian democratic
republic." As a practical step, the Petersburg Committee instructed
the electors to declare their meeting as a Soviet of Workers' Deputies,
and lead "a decisive mass offensive of the proletariat and democracy
against the existing autocratic system on the basis of the slogans and
programs of the RSDLP [the Bolshevik party] under the leadership
of the central and local organizations of the RSDLP."[18]

In response to the development of a general strike in September 1915,
the Bolsheviks proposed the creation of the soviet in more concrete
form. At the meeting of the Petersburg Committee on September 2,

16. TsGIA, f. 1405, op. 530, d. 1058, ℓℓ. 42, 84.
17. S. V. Tiutiukin, *Voina, mir, revoliutsiia: Ideinaia bor'ba v rabochem dvizhenii Rossii, 1914-1917 gg.*, p. 209.
18. TsGIA, f. 1405, op. 530, d. 1059, ℓℓ. 4, 5.

in which the representatives of the Narva, Vyborg, and Moscow District Committees also participated, the Bolsheviks decided to create the All-City Strike Committee to coordinate the workers' movement, and to transform the strike committee into the Soviet of Workers' Deputies. Although some factories allegedly conducted elections of their representatives to the soviet, the general strike did not last long enough to create the Soviet of Workers' Deputies.[19] The Petersburg Committee nonetheless continued to support the slogan for the creation of the soviet until November. According to the Okhrana report written in November, the Petersburg Committee intended to call for a general strike in the near future, and to turn this general strike into a political offensive against the regime. For this purpose, it instructed party workers to establish a factory strike committee in each factory. The factory strike committee would send its representatives to the district strike committees, which would in turn send their representatives to the All-City Strike Committee, which would be led by the Petersburg Committee. Such ideas were discussed in various factories and in some factories, for instance, the Petrograd Metal Factory, the workers elected their representatives to the factory strike committee.[20]

In a sense the Bolsheviks' notion of the soviet in the summer and the fall of 1915 was similar to that of the Mensheviks and the Socialist Revolutionaries. They all envisioned it as an organ for the coordination of the workers' movement. Although the Petersburg Committee stood for the creation of a provisional revolutionary government, it failed to elaborate on the role of the soviet in the formation of a revolutionary government. But in another respect the Bolsheviks' notion of the soviet differed from that of the Mensheviks and the Socialist Revolutionaries. They saw the soviet as encompassing all the revolutionary groups; the Bolsheviks maintained that the soviet should be created under the tutelage of the Bolshevik party.

The Petersburg Committee's proposal for the creation of the soviet was criticized by Lenin. In his article, "Several Theses," which appeared in *Sotsial Demokrat* in October, Lenin indicated that "the Soviet of Workers' Deputies and similar institutions should be viewed as an organ of insurrection and as an organ of the revolutionary power," and that the slogan of the soviet should be raised only "in connection with the development of a mass political strike and in connection with an insurrection." The Russian Bureau of the Central Committee,

19. I. P. Leiberov, "Petrogradskii proletariat v gody period pervoi mirovoi voiny," pp. 485-86; idem, "Stachechnaia bor'ba Petrogradskogo proletariata v period pervoi mirovoi voiny," *Sbornik statei: Istoriia rabochego klassa Leningrada* 2: 174.

20. TsGIA, f. 1405, op. 530, d. 1059, ll. 70-71.

restored by Shliapnikov, also opposed the Petersburg Committee's slogan. Nevertheless, the Petersburg Committee seemed to continue its support for the creation of the soviet until November.[21]

Although after the fall of 1915 the revolutionary parties seem to have dropped the notion of creating the soviet as a practical policy, the soviet as a viable organ to coordinate and lead the workers' strike movement appeared to be alive among the activists. It is reported that when the strike movement was stepped up in January 1917, the idea of creating a soviet was proposed by the sick-funds activists who gathered in the Putilov Factory.[22] In fact, the absence of a central coordinating body for the workers' movement in Petrograd continued throughout the war. The workers' group was created, but instead of unifying the workers' movement, its creation further contributed to the split of its leadership. The bitter struggle between the workers' group and the Bolsheviks for influence on the workers' movement in Petrograd throughout 1916 may have made the revolutionary leaders less enthusiastic about the creation of the soviet, but the strike movement that developed after January 9 and culminated in the February Revolution created a totally new situation. The strike was supported by both the workers' group and the Bolsheviks, and it reached a segment of the workers that had never before participated in political movement. It was natural, therefore, that strike leaders advocated the formation of the soviet as a center of the rapidly developing strike movement.

In addition, the two opposing groups of the workers' movement, the workers' group and the Bolsheviks, had a logical reason to welcome the creation of the soviet, because it provided a missing link in their formulation of policy prior to the February Revolution. The central part of the workers' group's policy was the convocation of the All-Russian Workers' Congress, which was never allowed by the tsarist government and the formation of the soviet would be the first step toward this goal. The soviet as the organization to protect the workers' interests could exert its influence in the struggle waged jointly with the bourgeoisie against the remnants of feudalism for the creation of a democratic republic. From the Bolsheviks' point of view, the victory of the insurrection in the February Revolution provided them for the first time with the opportunity to raise the question of the soviet

21. V. I. Lenin, *Polnoe sobranii sochineniia* 27: 49; see the Petersburg Committee's leaflet published in November 1915, in *Listovki Peterburgskikh bol'shevikov* 2: 174-75.

22. G. I. Zlokazov, *Petrogradskii Sovet rabochikh i soldatskikh deputatov v period mirnogo razvitiia revoliutsii*, p. 28. Zlokazov's source is TsGAOR, f. DPOO, 1917 g., op. 5, d. 630, ℓ. 122.

in the context of the formation of a revolutionary power. Thus, the workers' group and the Bolsheviks attempted to create the soviet during the February Revolution, but the two notions of the soviet were bound to clash in its course.

The sudden revolutionary upsurge during the February days that culminated in the soldiers' uprising took the leaders of the revolutionary parties by surprise. V. M. Zenzinov, a leader of the SR party, who worked at the time on the editorial board of the SR-oriented legal magazine, *Severnye zapiski*, noted: "The Revolution struck like lightning from the sky. . . . Let us be frank: it was a great and joyful event, unexpected even by those of us who had been working toward it for many years and waiting for it always." Another SR party member, S. Mstislavskii, makes an oft-quoted phrase in his memoirs: "The revolution caught us, the party men of that time, sleeping like the foolish virgins of the Scriptures."[23] Indeed, the revolutionary leaders were inexperienced, indecisive, and at a loss at the crucial moment when their dreams were about to come true. The Menshevik leaders in the Duma tried to assert their leadership by calling for the creation of the soviet, but "they had no serious influence on the masses." Shliapnikov consistently underestimated the potentialities of the movement that had begun—it never occurred to him that "this would be the last and decisive battle against tsarism." Others, like Zenzinov, "Simply wandered about the streets without plans, going from one street to another, observing the crowds, listening to their conversations." Iurenev (Mezhraionets) and K. S. Grinevich (Menshevik Internationalist) actually joined the demonstrations and made some attempts to lead the crowds, although their leadership could hardly influence the course of events.[24] The actual leaders of the movement were lower level revolutionary activists closely connected with the workers. According to SR workers Mil'chik, "A colossal role was played by the revolutionary party members, organically connected with the crowds. They were internal, moral inspiration, led the masses, and experienced all the peripeteia of the movement with them. Only the workers and a handful of intelligentsia integrally connected with the workers could be such leaders. Wide circles of the Petrograd intelligentsia were only observers from the sideline. This resulted from their alienation from the life of the masses.[25]

23. *Delo naroda*, March 15, 1917; S. Mstislavskii, *Piat' dnei: Nachalo i konets fevral'skoi revoliutsii*, p. 12.

24. N. N. Sukhanov, *Zapiski o revoliutsii* 1: 35; A. Shliapnikov, *Semnadtsatyi god* 1: 87; V. Zenzinov, "Fevral'skie dni," *Novyi zhurnal* 34 (1953): 200, 201; Burdzhalov, *Vtoraia russkaia revoliutsiia*, p. 146.

25. I. Mil'chik, *Rabochii fevral'*, p. 84.

One of the few leaders who saw beyond the events in the streets was N. N. Sukhanov (Gimmer), an editor of Gorky's journal, *Letopis'*, who, though he did not officially belong to the party, took a position close to the Menshevik-Internationalists. Convinced by the second day that a revolution had started, he began formulating a program of revolution. He immediately concluded that a government established after the overthrow of tsarism should be a solely bourgeois government, since the "democracy" that was in a state of total disintegration under the autocracy could not effectively govern a nation tormented by war and the destruction of national life resulting from it. Under these conditions the only way to establish a viable governmental power would be to control the state machinery, which would be organized only by the bourgeoisie, since any socialist government would alienate the bureaucracy. Moreover, a socialist government would have to face the task of ending the war immediately, a task that could not be realized in the face of all the other difficulties of internal transformation. In Sukhanov's opinion, it was "absolutely indispensable to lay the problem of foreign policy temporarily on the shoulders of the bourgeoisie." To put this idea into realization, it was necessary to know how other Socialists were reacting to the crisis. Sukhanov telephoned N. D. Sokolov, a Socialist lawyer, to arrange a meeting of the representatives of different Socialist groups on the following day. The meeting called at Sokolov's apartment on February 25, however, disappointed Sukhanov, since far from being a meeting of the representatives of all the various Socialist groups, only a small handful of the radical populist intelligentsia gathered there.[26]

In addition to Sokolov's, the apartments of Gorky and Kerenskii became the gathering centers of various Socialist intellectuals. On each of the three days of the uprising following February 23 Gorky called "information meetings" that a wide spectrum of Socialists ranging from Shliapnikov, Iurenev, Aleksandrovich on the Left to Peshekhonov and Ehrlich on the Right attended. According to Iurenev, these meetings held in "the comfortable dining room of Gorky's apartment" were devoted merely to academic conversations of what he termed "chatterboxes." Only two practical moves resulted: the publication of an illegal leaflet and the decision to continue periodic meetings of the liberal and revolutionary activists.[27] On February 26 the "in-

26. Sukhanov, *Zapiski o revoliutsii* 1: 25, 39.
27. Zenzinov, "Fevral'skie dni," p. 207. According to Iurenev's memoirs, Skobelev, Chkheidze, Kerenskii, Peshekhonov, and Gorky hosted the meeting, and from the illegal organizations, Grinevich (initiative group), Iurenev (Mezhraiontsy), and Pozhello (Bolshevik) attended the meeting. I. Iurenev, "Mezhraionka," *Proletarskaia revoliutsiia* 25, no. 2 (1925): 136-37.

formation meeting" moved to Kerenskii's apartment, where Kerenskii, Zenzinov, Iurenev, Aleksandrovich, Ehrlich, and others attended. The turn of events resulting from the troops' shooting put them in a pessimistic mood. Ironically, it was the right wing, Kerenskii, Zenzinov, and Ehrlich, who insisted on the continuation of the struggle, whereas the most radical of all, Iurenev, advocated an immediate halt to the movement, declaring: "There will be no revolution. The movement among the troops is dwindling down to nothing. We must prepare for a long period of reaction."[28] Toward the end of this meeting Sokolov brought the startling news that the Pavlovskii Regiment had mutinied. A flicker of hope flared up, but no one dreamed that this would be the harbinger of the large-scale uprising of the soldiers on the following day.

Although these informal meetings of the Socialist intelligentsia were far from what Zenzinov calls "the general staff of the revolution,"[29] it is important to note that the future soviet leaders began coalescing into one group during the February uprising through their personal acquaintances and the exchange of information. Despite their great political differences, these radical intelligenstisa had more in common with one another than with the masses in the streets.

Aside from the gatherings of the Socialist intelligentsia, a small group of the extreme Left attempted to create a united front. To coordinate the illegal activities of these organizations, the Mezhraiontsy proposed to the Bolshevik Petersburg Committee, the Menshevik initiative group, and the SR Maximalists that an interdistrict bureau be formed. The first meeting held on February 24 or February 25 was attended by Iurenev (Mezhraionets), Sokolovskii (initiative group), Pozhello (pseudonym Vladimir, Bolshevik), and Aleksandrovich (SR). This coalition immediately encountered difficulty when discussing what slogan should be presented to the masses. While the initiative group called for the convocation of a constituent assembly, Pozhello advocated the creation of the Soviet of Workers' Deputies in the form of the 1905 model. Iurenev, though expressing theoretical agreement with Pozhello's proposal, considered the appeal for the creation of the soviet still premature.[30] Pozhello and Sokolovskii never bothered to attend the other meeting. Far from its original intention, the attempt to form a united front thus did not go beyond a mere

28. Zenzinov, "Fevral'skie dni," p. 209; A. Kerensky, *The Catastrophe*, p. 6; TsGAOR, f. POO, op. 5, d. 669, l. 363.
29. Zenzinov, "Fevral'skie dni," p. 208.
30. Iurenev, "Mezhraionka," pp. 138-39. Pozhello's participation does not appear to have had the official approval of the Russian Bureau Central Committee.

coalition of the two radical groups, Mezhraiontsy and the SR Maximalists.

Although the Petrograd Soviet was not created until February 27, the appeal for its creation was heard widely in the factories as well as in the streets during the first four days of the strike movement. A fourteen-year-old high-school student, Pavel Slovatinskii, heard this slogan shouted at a rally at Znamenskaia Square on February 25. A Bolshevik worker, Gordienko, also heard an orator screaming from a lamp post: "Comrades, the time we were waiting for has finally come! The people have risen against their oppressors. Don't waste a minute! Create the workers' district soviets! Draw the representatives of the soldiers into them!"[31] A member of the Mezhraiontsy, Kovnator, also heard the appeal to create a soviet at Znamenskaia Square. Some workers returned to the factory to elect their representatives. The new development was intercepted by the sensitive antennae of the Okhrana agents, one of whom reported: "The election to the Soviet of Workers' Deputies will take place in the factories, evidently, tomorrow morning. By tomorrow evening the Soviet of Workers' Deputies may already begin its function." Some factories allegedly immediately elected their delegates—it is reported that the Franco-Russian Factory and Promet elected theirs on February 24.[32] It is also noted that on February 26 the workers of the Armaturnyi Factory in Vyborg District elected a Bolshevik worker, P. A. Alekseev, deputy to the Petrograd Soviet. Sukhanov also confirms that the elections had begun on February 24 in some factories. But if there were indeed such elections before February 27, we have no information of their details: how these elections were held, who was elected, and if those who were elected continued to serve as their delegates after February 27.[33]

Who, then, advanced the slogan for the establishment of the soviet?

31. Iurii Trifonov, "Mal'chik vel dnevnik," *Literaturnaia gazeta*, November 6, 1965; I. Gordienko, *Iz boevogo proshlogo*, p. 58.

32. R. Kovnator, "Nakanune 'fevralia': Otryvki iz vospominanii," *Revoliutsionnoe iunoshestvo, 1905-1917*, p. 189. "Fevral'skaia revoliutsiia i okhrannoe otdelenie," p. 175. The contents of the Okhrana report indicate that the author based his observations on an analysis of the events on February 25, although the report itself was dated February 26. Thus, "tomorrow" should be taken as February 26 rather than February 27. Zlokazov, *Petrogradskii Sovet rabochikh i soldatskikh deputatov*, p. 34; Idem, "Sozdanie Petrogradskogo Soveta," *Istoriia SSSR*, no. 5 (1964), p. 105.

33. *Geroi Oktiabria: Biografii aktivnykh uchastnikov podgotoviki i provedeniia Oktiabr'skogo vooruzhennogo vosstaniia v Petrograde* (2 vols.; Leningrad, 1967) 1: 63; Sukhanov, *Zapiski o revoliutsii* 1: 35; Iu. S. Tokarev, *Petrogradskii Sovet rabochikh i sodatskikh deputatov v marte-aprele, 1917 g.*, pp. 21-22.

It is known that the Menshevik-Defensists close to the Duma Mensheviks and the worker's group of the Central War Industries Committee had supported this slogan at least by February 25. Skobelev states that the delegates from factories came to the Duma pressing for establishment of the soviet and begging for instructions from the Socialist leaders in the Duma. He adds: "We made a concrete proposal to them to create the factory centers and factory committees, and prepare for the election to the Soviet of Workers' Deputies from each factory."[34] The Menshevik activists, upon the advice of their Duma leaders, invited other Mensheviks to a meeting on February 25 at the office of the Workers' Consumer Cooperatives. Thirty to thirty-five delegates from all districts in Petrograd, in addition to the leaders of the labor and cooperative movement and the Duma deputies, attended this meeting.[35] F. A. Cherevanin's proposal to create the Soviet of Workers' Deputies was unanimously approved. The participants decided to use the workers' cooperatives and sick-funds boards in each district as the district center to which the workers would send their delegates. The Petrograd Union of Workers' Cooperatives would become the all-city center to coordinate activities. All the participants would return to their districts to inform the factories of this decision. The first meeting of the soviet would be held on the following day, February 26. It appears certain that the Mensheviks' decision was the first appeal emanating from a revolutionary organization that called for the creation of the soviet as a practical, urgent necessity. Nevertheless, this did not have an immediate effect upon the masses of workers.[36] The police arrested more than half of the participants in that meeting, those who attended another meeting at the office of the workers' group of the War Industries Committee. Those who escaped arrest may have engaged

34. M. Skobelev, "Gibel' tsarizma," *Ogonek*, no. 11 (1927).

35. N. S. Chkheidze (Menshevik Duma Deputy), F. A. Cherevanin (Menshevik-Defensist), I. G. Volkov and N. Iu. Kapelinskii (both leaders of the cooperative movement in Petrograd) are known to have attended this meeting.

36. "Kak obrazovalsia Petrogradskii Sovet," *Izvestiia Soveta rabochikh i soldatskikh deputatov* (hereafter *Izvestiia*), no. 155 (August 27, 1917), pp. 6-7. The Okhrana agent's report cited above corresponds with the decision taken at this meeting. Sukhanov states: "The directive of elections originated from the initiative meeting of the leaders of the labor movement. This directive was immediately picked up by party organizations and, as is known, was successfully carried out in the factories in the capital during these days." Sukhanov, *Zapiski o revoliutsii* 1: 34-35. Sukhanov's contention notwithstanding, documentary evidence is lacking to indicate how widely elections were held on February 25 and 26 and to what extent these elections were the direct results of this "directive."

in propaganda for the creation of the soviet, but the government's brutal suppression of the demonstrators on the following day rendered the creation of the soviet of secondary importance.[37]

While the Mensheviks took the lead in directing the amorphous desire among the masses for the creation of a center of the movement in their pragmatic slogan of the establishment of the soviet, the other revolutionary parties lagged behind the spontaneous initiative of the masses. The Mezhraiontsy considered the adoption of the slogan calling for the creation of the Soviet as yet premature. On February 25, the Russian Bureau of the Central Committee of the Bolshevik party drafted a leaflet that appealed to the workers: "Organize for the struggle! Create committees of the Russian Social Democratic Labor party in each factory, each district, each city and oblast', each barracks and in all Russia. These will be committees for the struggle, committees for freedom."[38] The leaflet did not mention the soviet, and by calling for the creation of revolutionary committees at the time when the slogan for the soviet was widespread its attitude toward it was, by implication, negative. It also showed that the Russian Bureau of the Central Committee had reverted to the parochial position taken by the Petersburg Bolsheviks in 1905— a position that put committees organized by the party instead of the soviet as the main organ of struggle. Moreover, the leaflet lacked both urgency and reference to direct, specific actions and could not have satisfied the activists' craving for directions from above.[39]

The leaflet composed by the Russian Bureau did not satisfy even the members of the Petersburg Committee. At the meeting held on the evening of February 25, the committee responded to the cry for the creation of the soviet by deciding to establish party factory committees, which would be directed to send their delegates to the "Information Bureau for the guidance of the factory committees. This 'Information Bureau' would be subordinated to the Petersburg Committee and would in the future become the Soviet of Workers' Deputies."[40]

37. Wada dismisses any relationship between the appeals for the creation of the soviet at Znamenskaia Square and the Mensheviks' decision. Nevertheless, one cannot completely deny a possible connection. Wada Haruki, "Nigatsu kakumei," p. 405.

38. See p. 258; Listovki peterburgskikh bol'shevikov 2: 250. Also see Proletarskaia revoliutsiia 13, no. 1 (1923): 284-85; Shliapnikov, Semnadtsatyi god 1: 101-2. This leaflet was issued in the name of the Petersburg Committee, but actually drafted by Shliapnikov.

39. Tsuyoshi Hasegawa, "The Bolsheviks and the Formation of the Petrograd Soviet in the February Revolution," Soviet Studies 29, no. 1 (1927): 91-92.

40. TsGAOR, f. DPOO, op. 5, ch. 57/1917 g., ℓ. 32; TsGAOR, f. DPOO,

In this decision the Petersburg Committee specifically mentioned the creation of the soviet, but as something in the future rather than as a task of urgent necessity. Moreover, like the Russian Bureau's leaflet, it adopted the position that the party be recognized as the driving force of the revolutionary struggle. By counterposing the factory committees to the soviet, the Petersburg Committee also displayed hostility toward the spontaneous desires of the masses.[41]

Despite the hostility by its leadership to the idea of the soviet, some Bolsheviks responded to it more positively. A member of the Vyborg District Committee, Sveshnikov, notes: "In the factories there emerged a tendency to elect representatives to the Soviet of Workers' Deputies. The District Committee attempted to take the elections of the deputies into its hands." As noted above, a Lithuanian Bolshevik lawyer, Pozhello (Vladimir) proposed to adopt the slogan for the creation of the soviet at the meeting with other radical left-wing groups. It is unlikely, however, that this proposal, made independently of the regular Bolshevik organizational structure, had any direct impact on the masses of workers.[42]

If no political parties could make exclusive claim for initiating the slogan for the creation of the soviet, then who was responsible for its ·wide circulation? One can speculate that the idea of the soviet had been deeply rooted in the minds of the Petrograd workers, particularly among the politically conscious, experienced activists.[43]

---

d. 341, ch. 57/1917, ℓ. 42; E. K. Bartshtein and L. M. Shalaginova, "Departament politsii o plane petrogradskikh bol'shevikov v fevrale 1917 g.," *Vopros arkhivovedeniia*, no. 1 (1962), pp. 111-12. Tokarev cautions about the reliability of the Okhrana report. Tokarev, *Petrogradskii Sovet rabochikh i soldatskikh deputatov*, pp. 19-20.

41. Hasegawa, "The Bolsheviks and the Formation of the Petrograd Soviet," pp. 92-93.

42. N. Sveshnikov, "Otryvki iz vospominanii," *Petrogradskaia pravda*, March 14, 1923; idem, "Vyborgskii raionnyi komitet RSDRP (b) v 1917 g.," *V ogne revoliutsionnykh boev: Raiony Petrograda v dvukh revoliutsiiakh 1917 g.: Sbornik vospominanii starykh bol'shevikov-pitertsev*, p. 84. See p. 325. Although Iurenev does not mention that Pozhello proposed the creation of the soviet in the context of the problem of power, it might be the case, because the Menshevik initiative group opposed the Bolshevik proposal and presented a counterproposal of a constituent assembly. Wada speculates that the Bolshevik Lithuanian organization led by Pozhello may have taken the initiative in presenting the slogan for the soviet. Wada, "Nigatsu kakumei," pp. 404-5. There was no evidence to deny this contention, but it seems unrealistic to attribute a slogan of such wide circulation to such a small and obscure group.

43. On January 30, 1917, the meeting of the workers' sick funds of the Putilov Factory passed a resolution calling for the creation of a leading center in the form of the soviet in 1905. See above, p. 322.

As the strike movement gained momentum, these activists felt the need to create a center to coordinate activities throughout the city. The slogan was presented to solve practical difficulties stemming from the lack of organization and cohesion of the strike movement. At this stage no one related it to the problem of power, since the seizure of power was believed to be still a remote possibility. The argument whether the initiative belonged to the Mensheviks or the Bolsheviks is futile; either may well have, but at this stage of the strike movement the demarcation of party lines had little significance.

The victory of the insurrection on February 27 placed the importance of the soviet in a different context. Revolutionary leaders were now faced with the urgent need to create a revolutionary power; and the creation of the soviet became integrally related to the problem of power. Of all the revolutionary leaders it was again the Mensheviks who made the first move for its establishment, recognizing the need to organize the insurgent masses. About noon on February 27, the insurgents attacked the Kresty Prison and released the political prisoners. Two of the leaders of the workers' group of the Central War Industries Committee, K. A. Gvozdev and B. O. Bogdanov, made their way to the Tauride Palace, where other Menshevik leaders had assembled. Bolshevik V. Zalezhskii, a former member of the Petersburg Committee, who had just been released from the House of Detention, met Gvozdev and Breido on Liteinyi Bridge on his run to the Vyborg District—a symbolic encounter, where a Bolshevik hurried to the workers' section to join the armed struggle, while the Mensheviks concerned themselves first with the organization of the insurgents.[44] The Socialist Duma Deputies, Chkheidze, Skobelev, and Kerenskii arranged Room 12, a room usually used for the Finance Committee, for the use of the Socialist intelligentsia who gathered in the Duma. These Socialists, predominantly Mensheviks, immediately formed a Provisional Executive Committee of the Soviet of Workers' Deputies,[45] and around two o'clock in the afternoon issued an appeal to insurgent workers and soldiers to elect delegates to the soviet.

Citizens! The representatives of the workers, soldiers, and other people of Petrograd, who are meeting in the State Duma, announce that the first meeting of their representatives will be held tonight at seven o'clock in the evening at a room

44. "Kak obranzovalsia Petrogradskii Sovet," p. 7; V. N. Zalezhskii, *Iz vospominanii podpol'shchika*, pp. 158–59; idem, "Pervyi legal'nyi Pe-Ka," *Proletarskaia revoliutsiia* 13, no. 1 (1923): 139.

45. The members of the Provisional Executive Committee cannot be definitely established, but the following persons seemed to be its members: Chkheidze, Skobelev, Volkov, Kapelinskii, Grinevich, Sokolov, Gvozdev, Bogdanov, and Frankorusskii. All except Sokolov, Kapelinskii, and Frankorusskii were Mensheviks.

of the State Duma. All troops that took the side of the people immediately elect their own representatives, one person per one company. Factories elect their own deputies, one person per one thousand people. Factories with fewer than a thousand workers elect one deputy from each factory.[46]

Ironically, these Menshevik intelligentsia, who called themselves "representatives of the workers, soldiers, and other people of Petrograd," although they had stood outside the strike movement and the insurrection, took the most decisive initiative to organize the insurgent masses. The prescribed election procedures of the workers' deputies followed the pattern of those adopted for the election to the workers' group of the War Industries Committee. Although the initiators adopted the name "the Soviet of Workers' Deputies," the nature of the insurrection demanded the inclusion of the soldiers in this body. Despite the opposition raised by some Menshevik leaders, who wished to keep the soviet purely a representaive body of the workers, it was practically impossible to ignore the soldiers who provided the insurrection with decisive strength, both in number as well as with their rifles and machine guns.

This appeal was printed in the first issue of *Izvestiia komiteta zhurnalistov Petrograda* (later to be renamed *Izvestiia revoliutsionnoi nedeli*), the only newspaper that appeared on this day, and which was widely circulated. Members of the Provisional Committee also took advantage of the legal network of the War Industries Committee and the cooperatives to spread information. Gvozdev, for instance, visiting from factory to factory in an automobile made available by his liberal colleague in the Central War Industries Committee, Baron Maidel', directly appealed to the workers to elect their delegates to the soviet.[47]

The Provisional Committee's proclamation designated the location of the soviet at the Tauride Palace. It was consistent with the initiators' idea that the State Duma should be the main instrument for the struggle against tsarism. This decision, moreover, well suited the newly developing situation. The insurrection was no longer confined to the workers' strike movement but now involved a wide segment of the population and the prestige of the Duma had a great appeal to these newcomers in the political movement. But the proclamation remained totally silent on the nature of the soviet in the context of the problem of power.[48] The Menshevik leaders, who took it for granted that

46. *Izvestiia revoliutsionnoi nedeli,* February 27, 1917.

47. N. I. Iordanskii, "Voennoe vosstanie 27 fevralia," *Molodaia gvardiia,* no. 2 (1928), p. 169.

48. Hasegawa, "The Bolsheviks and the Formation of the Petrograd Soviet,"

the liberals would form a government, were concerned primarily with organizing the revolutionary forces. This assumption, however, was challenged by a small group of radical Left Socialists, who openly advocated the establishment of a provisional revolutionary government in the form of the soviet. Thus, the two views on the nature of the soviet—that it should be an organization center of the insurgents or that it should be a revolutionary power—came into direct conflict as early as February 27.

After learning the news of the soldiers' insurrection, the Mezhraiontsy held an emergency meeting at two P.M. in their headquarters in the Moscow District, and unanimously decided to issue a leaflet calling for general insurrection and the election of workers' and soldiers' representatives to the soviet. This leaflet stated: "The die is cast. You cannot retreat. You have nowhere to go. In case of defeat a merciless reprisal from the tsarist autocracy will wait for the rebels."[49] The Mezhraiontsy sent agitators to the Narva, Vyborg, and Vasilievskii districts to propagate their views among the workers. They held another meeting at five in the evening, at which they decided to issue two other leaflets. The first leaflet, written by Iurenev and addressed to the soldiers, called for the election of soldiers' delegates to "the provisional revolutionary government." What they meant by that was made clear by the second leaflet, written by Glezarov, that stated: "The place of the tsarist government is being taken by the Provisional Revolutionary Government. It must be created by the representatives of the proletariat and the army. Comrades! Immediately undertake the elections to the Soviet of Workers' Deputies. The army is already conducting elections of their representatives. Tomorrow the Provisional Revolutionary Government will finally be formed." More than thirty thousand copies of these leaflets were distributed late at night throughout the city in the name of the Mezhraiontsy and the SRs.[50] The Mezhraiontsy, supported by a small group of the Socialist Revolutionaries, were thus one of the first revolutionary groups to formulate the demand of the creation of a provisional revolutionary government in the form of the Soviet.

---

pp. 95-96; Tokarev, *Petrogradskii Sovet rabochikh i soldatskikh deputatov*, pp. 29-30.

49. Iurenev, "Mezhraionka," p. 142; *Shestoi s'ezd RSDRP (Bol'shevikov), avgust 1917 g.: Protokoly* (Moscow, 1958), p. 149. The entire text of this leaflet has not been made public. I am not certain if this leaflet called for the establishment of the soviet as a provisional revolutionary government.

50. *Izvestiia*, February 28, 1917; Burdzhalov, *Vtoraia russkaia revoliutsiia*, p. 211; Iurenev, "Mezhraionka," p. 143; *Shestoi s'ezd*, p. 149.

The Russian Bureau of the Central Committee of the Bolshevik party lagged behind the quickly developing events. It had had considerable pressure from the Vyborg District Committee to issue a manifesto outlining the general policy of the Bolsheviks. Frustrated with the Russian Bureau's reluctance, Kaiurov and other members of the Vyborg Bolsheviks composed a draft proposal of a manifesto and brought it to the Russian Bureau, which finally approved it with minor changes. The manifesto, "To All the Citizens of Russia," defined "the task of the working class and the revolutionary army" as the creation of a provisional revolutionary government, "that must stand at the head of the newly born republican state." It further urged the workers and the soldiers "to elect immediately your representatives to the provisional revolutionary government that must be created under the protection of the revolutionary people and troops who have revolted."[51] Although the Russian Bureau raised the problem of power as the pressing question—unlike the Mensheviks, who avoided it—the manifesto mentioned absolutely nothing about the Soviet. Unlike the Mezhraiontsy's slogan, the Bolsheviks' manifesto counterposed a provisional revolutionary government to the Soviet—an unrealistic position at a time when the workers were favorably responding to the establishment of the Soviet.

Nevertheless, the Russian Bureau's negative attitude toward the Soviet did not keep the lower echelon of the Bolsheviks from advancing a different position. Approximately at the same time of the Mensheviks' Provisional Committee's proclamation, the Vyborg District Committee issued an appeal to the workers to create a provisional revolutionary government by electing their deputies to the Soviet and to establish Finland Station as revolutionary headquarters.[52] Although its origin was not certain, the Bolsheviks, presumably the Vyborg District Committee or some members of the defunct Petersburg

51. *Izvestiia*, supplement, February 28, 1917; *Pravda*, March 5, 1917; *Revoliutsionnoe dvizhenie v Rossii posle sverzheniia samoderzhaviia* (Moscow, 1957), pp. 3-4. Some Soviet historians argue that by "provisional revolutionary government" the Russian Bureau actually meant the soviet, and that, therefore, the Russian Bureau took the initiative of creating the soviet. To argue this, however, one must accept their contention that the manifesto was issued before the creation of the soviet around two o'clock in the afternoon on February 27. Whether one approves the February 27 theory or the February 28 theory, it is not likely that the manifesto was published before that time. For more detailed discussions see Hasegawa, "The Bolsheviks and the Formation of the Petrograd Soviet," pp. 100-107.

52. Hasegawa, "The Bolsheviks and the Formation of the Petrograd Soviet," pp. 98-100, 106; Tokarev, *Petrogradskii Sovet rabochikh i soldatskikh deputatov*, pp. 24-25.

Committee, issued another leaflet sometime late in the afternoon: "Start immediately in factories the elections to the factory strike committees. Their representatives will compose the Soviet of Workers' Deputies, which will create a Provisional Revolutionary Government."[53]

The call for the establishment of the Soviet as a provisional revolutionary government, however, did not carry much influence among most of the insurgents, except perhaps among a small minority of politically conscious radical workers. The Vyborg Bolsheviks' attempts to establish revolutionary headquarters at Finland Station could not divert the massive procession of insurgents to Tauride Palace. And yet this small group of radical Socialists had significance for the future course of the revolution, although their slogans were ignored by most of the Socialist leaders. This was the only group that provided an alternative to the Soviet as interpreted by the Menshevik leaders— the same alternative that was presented by Lenin on his arrival in Russia in April.

Despite the original intention of the Provisional Executive Committee, its very existence, in the absence of any other authority in Petrograd, imposed two practical tasks on it. One was the creation of the Food Supply Commission. The shortage of food, which had touched off the popular outburst on February 23, was compounded by the insurrection. The presence of thousands of hungry soldiers in the streets, soldiers who had nothing to eat since the previous evening, was ominous, indeed. Lest the insurrection should turn into large-scale pogroms and drunken orgies, the Socialists who gathered in Tauride Palace were forced to take some action. The Food Supply Commission was headed by V. G. Groman, a Menshevik statistician, who was a member of the Special Council for Food Supplies as a representative of the Union of Towns. Volkov (Menshevik leader of the cooperative movement) and the specialists on food distribution, N. Novorusskii and Frankorusskii, also joined the commission. It issued an appeal to the people to help feed the insurgent soldiers, since the Food Supply Commission alone could not immediately cope with this task.[54] The Petrograd populace responded favorably. Viktor Shklovskii, famous literary critic, who was an officer in the Armored Car Division at that time, noted: "We were fed at food stations, where they concocted an incredibly rich fare out of geese,

53. Hasegawa, "The Bolsheviks and the Formation of the Petrograd Soviet," pp. 96-98, 106; Tokarev, *Petrogradskii Sovet rabochikh i soldatskikh deputatov,* pp. 25-26.

54. Tokarev, *Petrogradskii Sovet rabochikh i soldatskikh deputatov,* pp. 50-51; *Izvestiia revoliutsionnoi nedeli,* February 27, 1917.

sausage, and whatever else turned up. I was happy with these crowds. It was like Easter—a joyous, naïve, disorderly carnival paradise."[55] Although the Food Supply Commission took the first step in organizing the food distribution mechanism, it had no intention of usurping a governmental function, nor could it expect to bring about a successful solution to the problem by itself, since a majority of its members had neither experience nor connections. The only experts included in the commission, representatives of the Central Cooperatives of the Association of Wholesale Purchase, immediately demanded the formation of a unified Food Supply Commission composed of the members of both Soviet and of the Duma representatives. By the evening of February 27, Shingarev, the expert on food supply in the liberal camp, joined the commission, representing the Duma Committee. The name of the commission was changed to the Food Supply Commission of the Duma Committee and the Petrograd Soviet.[56]

Another task the Provisional Executive Committee took upon itself was organization of the Military Commission. To avoid degeneration of the insurrection into bloody carnage and to prepare for the expected counterrevolution, those soldiers roaming around the city had to be organized into disciplined revolutionary military units. One of the members of the Provisional Executive Committee, Kapelinskii, telephoned officers known to be Socialists or Socialist sympathizers. Shortly afterwards, Colonel S. D. Mstislavskii, an SR member, who worked at that time as a librarian in the Military Academy of the General Staff, soon appeared in Tauride Palace. With the assistance of Lieutenant V. M. Filippovskii, who also responded to Kapelinskii's telephone call, Mstislavskii began organizing the Military Commission in Room 13, next to the headquarters of the Provisional Executive Committee (Room 12). P. I. Pal'chinskii, a civil servant in the Artillery Administration, became secretary of the Military Commission. Later they were joined by SR officer M. M. Dobranitskii, but at the initial stage most of its members were noncommissioned officers, and with the exception of those mentioned above, no commissioned officer volunteered.[57] Kerenskii maintained constant contact with the Military Commission.

Mstislavskii soon found the situation extremely unsatisfactory

55. Viktor Shklovsky, *A Sentimental Journey: Memoirs, 1917-1922*, p. 16.

56. M. Rafes, "Moi vospominaniia," *Byloe* 19 (1922): 190; A. V. Peshekhonov, "Pervyia nedeli: Iz vospominanii o revoliutsii," *Na chuzhoi storone* 1 (1923): 261.

57. Tokarev, *Petrogradskii Sovet rabochikh i soldatskikh deputatov*, pp. 54-55.

and his assignment hopelessly difficult. It is true that a large number of soldiers joined the insurrection, but the moment they abandoned their positions, the Petrograd garrison units ceased to be capable military bodies. The insurgent soldiers were as much against military discipline and organization as against the old regime, for they envisioned the officers as an embodiment of the regime. The soldiers in the streets lost military cohesion, obeyed no leaders, and acted completely on their own. Moreover, it was impossible to obtain any accurate information about the loyal troops, the immediate threat Mstislavskii presumed. The chief of staff of the revolutionary forces described the discouraging situation as follows:

Our situation was catastrophic. It is true that Khabalov made an essential, gross mistake by withdrawing his troops from the center of the city and giving the "rebels" a chance to surround them from all directions. . . . But was there really a revolutionary atmosphere in the city? . . . I remember the crowds of unarmed soldiers roaming about the city, juveniles engaged in arson, and automobiles driven madly about the streets. If only we had one cohesive unit which maintained its entire composition. We had neither artillery, nor machine guns; neither commanding officers, nor communications. With the exception of Filippovskii . . . who had arrived fifteen minutes after me, there were no officers.[58]

Mstislavskii desperately tried to form a military unit from the soldiers who had gathered in Tauride Palace. Some completely ignored his plea, while others, who at least had the decency to reply, responded with hostility: "We are tired and hungry." Even those soldiers who were persuaded to assemble in Room 13 soon left for the Soviet session held in the next room. Only a handful of despairing people remained in the deserted "headquarters" of the revolutionary army. At this point, Mstislavskii decided to move the Military Commission from Room 13 to Rooms 41 and 42, the office of the vice-chairman of the Duma, Nekrasov, and its adjacent room, in the right wing of Tauride Palace—a decision prompted by his judgment that the Socialists alone could not organize these unwieldy soldiers. Mstislavskii concluded that a wide segment of the officers, sympathetic to the liberal circles in the Duma, though not to the revolutionaries, should be mobilized for that purpose. These officers had begun to assemble in Room 41. Thus, even before the Military Commission organized by the Soviet was taken over by the Duma Committee, cooperation with the liberals was a foregone conclusion.

The transfer of the room, however, did not immediately improve the situation. All the officers assembled in Room 41 turned out to be noncommissioned officers from the front who happened to be in

58. Mstislavskii, *Piat' dnei*, pp. 20-21.

Petrograd on leave. They could not be expected to be effective in establishing contact with mutinying troops. Moreover, four machine guns the Military Commission had managed to obtain proved to be unworkable. As a last resort, Mstislavskii sent officers alone to such strategic positions as Nikolaevskii and Tsarskoe Selo stations, instructing them to pick up the necessary soldiers along the way. To make his order look official, he grabbed from Nekrasov's desk piles of official forms with the impressive letterhead of the vice-chairman of the Duma and the emblem of the State Duma at the top. Although he finally managed to form a detachment of about fifty soldiers under the command of an ensign, this was obviously not enough to respond to the flood of requests for military protection that started pouring in. Aware of the powerlessness of their forces, the leaders of the Military Commission feared every moment that loyal troops led by Khabalov would launch a counterattack upon Tauride Palace—a comical situation, considering that only a few miles away from Tauride Palace, General Khabalov, equally convinced of the military powerlessness of his forces, awaited the moment when the rebels would attack the loyal troops.[59] Between the two headquarters insurgent soldiers controlled the streets, heeding no authority. The outcome of the revolution now depended on a single question: Who would control the troops in the streets?

The Socialist intelligentsia began to gather in Tauride Palace to attend the first soviet session scheduled at seven P.M. In addition to the original members of the Provisional Executive Committee, there were G. S. Khrustalev-Nosar', the former chairman of the St. Petersburg Soviet of 1905; N. N. Sukhanov, who anxiously awaited the moment when he could put his ideas into practice; Iu. Steklov, a former Bolshevik publicist, who now stood close to the Menshevik-Internationalists; G. Ehrlich, a Jewish Bund leader; M. Rafes, another Bund leader, who had just come out of Kresty Prison; and A. Shliapnikov, leader of the Bolshevik party. The "revolutionary democracy," as the Socialist leaders called a coalition of various Socialist factions in the Soviet, was beginning to form. In contrast to the Socialist intelligentsia, very few elected delegates from factories and military units attended the first session, although many soldiers and workers began to assemble in Room 12 to hear the discussions of the Soviet. Under the circumstances it was, of course, impossible to expect the workers to conduct orderly elections of their deputies with only a few hours' advance notice. Most of the workers were in the streets, and it was extremely doubtful that they would return to their factories

59. Ibid., pp. 23-26.

to have an election. A small group of Nobel workers gathered in the street and elected an SR worker deputy to the Soviet in a perfunctory manner. In the Putilov Factory a workers' cooperative was sent to Tauride Palace as its representatives. Some members, Sokolov for instance, argued for immediate opening without waiting for the arrival of duly elected delegates, but the opening of the session was delayed until nine o'clock on Shliapnikov's insistence.[60]

Disturbed by the absence of the Bolshevik delegates, Shliapnikov got in touch with some of the activists by telephone, urging them to attend the Soviet session. The party activists on the lower levels, however, refused to respond to Shliapnikov's appeal, explaining that they were occupied with the struggle against tsarism in the streets.[61] In the Vyborg District the Bicycle Battalion had effectively resisted an attack by insurgents. Naturally, the Bolshevik activists, who had demonstrated a proclivity for concrete action more than for a rational analysis of the situation, placed more emphasis on the attack of what they conceived as one of the last citadels of tsarism in Petrograd than on attendance at the Soviet session. They wanted action rather than words. Their refusal, moreover, revealed their bitter suspicion and hostility to a Soviet created on the initiative of the Mensheviks. It was these activists who had led the workers' movement for the past five days in the factories as well as in the streets, putting their lives on the line, and suddenly the intelligentsia, who had stood aloof from the movement, stole the leadership from them. Kaiurov reminisced that the news of the Soviet put him in a pessimistic mood. "These gloomy thoughts," he states, "brought back the memory of October of 1905, when the workers' friends came out in the rainy road as if from underneath the earth, but no sooner had the workers' movement been defeated than they disappeared as quickly."[62] With resentment and contempt for these "chatterboxes," they stubbornly remained in the streets, where the outcome of the struggle had been long before determined. Their resentment, at the same time, concealed their painful awareness that the leadership was finally slipping out of their hands. They did not want to admit it, but the revolution had, indeed, reached a stage where politics at a higher level played a more decisive part in determining its outcome.

Finally at nine P.M. a short, stocky, half-bald man in a cutaway

60. Tokarev, *Petrogradskii Sovet rabochikh i soldatskikh deputatov*, p. 31; Shliapnikov, *Semnadtsatyi god* 1: 144.

61. Shliapnikov, *Semnadtsatyi god* 1: 144.

62. V. Kaiurov, "Shest' dnei fevral'skoi revoliutsii," *Proletarskaia revoliutsiia* 13, no. 1 (1923): 169.

with a flashing pince-nez and dark bushy beard—a man who would fit better in a well-mannered intellectual salon—approached the podium of Room 12 in Tauride Palace. This Socialist lawyer, Sokolov, called the meeting to order. By that time about fifty voting representatives and two hundred observers packed the room, while new groups kept pouring into the hall.[63] It was impossible to check the credentials of each representative. Shliapnikov notes: "A minority of delegates, if not all, had merely 'oral' credentials without any other certificates from their factories. But who could check on it? It was decided that the meeting of that day was merely an initiative meeting, and that the real meeting with normal representation would be held later."[64] This decision, however, was a mere formality, for the later "formal" sessions reversed nothing established at the first session. It is important to note that most of the voting members at the first session were actually the self-appointed intelligentsia rather than elected delegates from the factories and the military units. Sukhanov describes the haphazard manner in which the voting members were recognized as follows: "N. D. Sokolov was running around, giving orders and seating the deputies. In an authoritative way, but without any discernible justification, he explained to these present what sort of vote they had, whether consulting or deciding, and who had no vote at all. He explained to me, in particular, that I had a vote." At least thirty-one to thirty-five members belonged to the intelligentsia, whose voting rights were acquired through personal acquaintanceship rather than as a result of election in the factories or military units.[65]

The meeting proceeded in the midst of confusion and intoxicated pandemonium, often interrupted by soldiers' reports that a new company had decided to join the revolution. Sukhanov described the scene:

Standing on stools, their rifles in their hands, agitated, stammering, and straining

63. According to Shliapnikov, there were 40 to 50 voting delegates. Shliapnikov, *Semnadtsatyi god* 1: 146. Sukhanov gives the figure of 250, while the anonymous author of "Kak obrazovalsia Petrogradskii Sovet," *Izvestiia Soveta rabochikh i soldatskikh deputatov*, Aug. 27, 1917, cites 125 to 150. Neither author specifies how many were voting members. Peshekhonov's figure is 40 to 50, who were mostly intelligentsia. A. V. Peshkhonov, "Pervyia nedeli: Iz vospominanii o revoliutsii," *Na chuzhoi storone* 1: 262. Judging from the votes cast for the election of various officers, the figure given by Shliapnikov and Peshekhonov appears to be accurate. Also see Tokarev, *Petrogradskii Sovet rabochikh i soldatskikh deputatov*, pp. 32-34.

64. Shliapnikov, *Semnadtsatyi god* 1: 147.

65. Sukhanov, *Zapiski o revoliutsii* 1: 125-26; Marc Ferro, "Les débuts du Soviet de Petrograd (27-28 février 1917—ancien style)," *Revue historique* 223, no. 2 (1960): 370.

all their powers to give a few entrusted messages coherently, with their thoughts concentrated on the process of their story itself, in unaccustomed and half-fantastic surroundings, without thinking, and perhaps, unaware of the whole significance of the facts they were reporting, in simple, clumsy language, infinitely strengthening the impression by the absence of emphasis—one after another the soldiers' delegates told of what had happened in their companies. Their stories were primitive, and repeated each other almost word for word. The audience listened as children listen to a wonderful, enchanting tale they know by heart, holding their breaths, with craning necks and dreamy eyes. . . .

Dreadful rifles, hateful overcoats, strange words! Theoretically, all this has been already known, known since morning. But in practice the events that turned everything upside down were not understood, not made aware of, nor digested.[66]

Despite all this exuberance, the Soviet session concerned itself exclusively with mundane organizational issues, avoiding the most fundamental questions—what kind of revolutionary power should be created and what relationship should the Soviet have with this power? Naturally, the Mensheviks had no intention of discussing this matter, but this was not even raised by the Bolsheviks or the Mezhraiontsy or the SR Maximalists. These groups were "weak and unprepared, without initiative, and incapable of orienting themselves in the situation."[67]

The session took up the election of officers as the first order of business. Khrustalev-Nosar' was nominated as if to tie the broken thread with the 1905 Soviet, but this sentimental nostalgia did not work. This man of the past with dubious integrity as a Socialist was soundly defeated.[68] Instead, the chairmanship went to Chkheidze, a Georgian Menshevik and a deputy to the Fourth Duma, while two other Socialist deputies to the Duma, Skhobelev and Kerenskii, were elected vice-chairmen. The election of these three Socialist Duma deputies indicated that their visibility rather than their political creed had greater meaning at the initial stage. Chkheidze, a slender Georgian with a bearded, dark, thin face and a hooked nose, noted for his oratory as well as his dogmatic adherence to Marxist principles, occupied the position of chairman of the Petrograd Soviet until September, when he was replaced by Trotskii. He represented the Soviet in the same manner that Prince L'vov represented the Provisional Government —a figurehead rather than an active, dynamic promoter of policies.

66. Sukhanov, *Zapiski o revoliutsii* 1: 130-31.
67. Ibid., p. 127.
68. Shliapnikov, *Semnadtsatyi god* 1: 146-47: Shliapnikov denounced Khrustalev-Nosar' as anti-Semitic as well as for his connections with the reactionary paper, *Novoe vremia*.

Together with Kerenskii, Chkheidze was a member of the Duma Committee, but after his election to the chairmanship of the Soviet he devoted all his energies to the fulfillment of this ceremonial position.

Aleksandr Kerenskii, with his flamboyant theatrics and flowery oratory, became the unquestionable leader of the revolution overnight. While Chkheidze resisted or even resented the seduction of power, what drove Kerenskii was his ambition for power. It is almost incongruous to find Kerenskii's name associated with the Soviet, since he not only remained in the Duma Committee, but also spent most of his time in the right wing of the Tauride Palace. Yet he knew that his usefulness in the Duma Committee stemmed from his popularity among the masses and his official connections with the Soviet. Thus, his election to vice-chairman of the Soviet carried immense political implications not only to Kerenskii personally but also to the relationship between the Soviet and the Duma Committee. Unlike Chkheidze and Kerenskii, Skobelev's role during the February Revolution remained minor.

After the election of the chairman, Chkheidze delivered a short speech in which he stressed the significance of the revolution, appealing to .the Soviet and the "democracy" to complete the revolutionary transformation and concluding his speech with "Long live the revolution!" "Long live the revolutionary army!" Kerenskii's speech followed, but after uttering "a few meaningless phrases . . . he immediately vanished into the right wing, not to appear again in the Soviet."[69]

After the election of the Presidium, the Soviet session proceeded to the election of the Secretariat, to which Gvozdev, Sokolov, Grinevich, and Pankov were elected. Three were Mensheviks (Gvozdev was a Menshevik defensist, and Grinevich and Pankov were Menshevik internationalists). After the election of the Secretariat. Frankorusskii reported in the name of the Food Supply Commission on the critical food situation in Petrograd, and moved that the commission be given the authority to confiscate all private and public food stocks, including those in the Army Commissary Department, so as to insure the distribution of food to the soldiers as well as to the general populace in Petrograd. The Soviet approved the creation of the already existent Food Supply Commission, headed by Groman, and passed Frankorusskii's motion unanimously.

The session moved on to military matters. It was necessary to

69. "Kak obrazovalsia Petrogradskii sovet," p. 7; Sukhanov, *Zapiski o revoliutsii* 1: 128-29.

establish the relationship between the Soviet and the Military Commission, which had already begun its function. Although the commission was organized at the initiative of the Provisional Executive Committee, it now showed a strong inclination to cooperate with liberal circles by relocating its headquarters "topographically" in the right wing of Tauride Palace. The Soviet approved the creation of the Military Commission and decided to place all its activities under the direct control of the Soviet by demanding the automatic inclusion within it of the Executive Committee members. This decision received an immediate approval from the commission.[70] A Menshevik, M. A. Braunstein, then moved to organize a militia in every city district to "restore order and direct the struggle against anarchy and pogroms." Every factory was to form a militia of one hundred workers out of every thousand while the district committees were to be formed under the commissars dispatched by the Executive Committee. It is important to note that the maker of the motion defined restoration of order as the primary purpose of the militia rather than further struggle against the remnants of tsarism. According to Sukhanov, who seconded the motion: "The proposal did not encounter any opposition, since its rationale was obvious, but it provoked some misunderstanding and practical amendments. In particular, [some amended] to add the function of offensive actions against the remaining forces of tsarism to this proposed organization. I defended Braunstein's notion, reminding the audience of the existence of the Military Commission and cautioning against the confusion of functions and authorities."[71] The motion was accepted, but no machinery existed to implement it.

The measure approved by the Soviet about food supply and the military situation indicated that the Soviet assigned to itself the tasks that under ordinary circumstances belonged to a government. It was not a conscious attempt by the Soviet leaders to usurp governmental power, but rather, inevitable measures they were forced to adopt. These problems were presented as practical necessities demanded by the situation, without any bearing, they believed, on the problem of power. The Soviet leaders conceived of these measures as merely temporary, to be transferred in due course to a legitimate government.

During the discussion on the defense of the city from anarchy the need to address the general populace of Petrograd in a proclamation was voiced. For that purpose a Literary Commission composed of

70. Sukhanov, Zapiski o revoliutsii 1: 128-29.
71. Ibid., p. 132.

Sokolov, Peshekhonov, Steklov, Grinevich, and Sukhanov was created. According to Sukanov, "No directives were given to the commission. It was obvious to everyone (or must have been obvious) that the proclamation would be accepted in the form that the commission would present it. The first act of the Soviet with political significance was accomplished in such a way." The members of the Literary Commission immediately left the assembly hall to compose the draft proclamation. The Soviet session also charged the Literary Commission with the publication of the newspaper *Izvestiia*. A Bolshevik, V. D. Bonch-Bruevich, who had engineered the occupation of one of the largest printing offices in Petrograd, Kopeika, offered its services for publication of the Soviet newspaper. Steklov became the chief editor, assisted by the Bolshevik intellectuals Avilov, V. Bazarov, G. Tsyperovich, Bonch-Bruevich, and I. Goldenburg.[72] The first issue of *Izvestiia* appeared on February 28.

The Soviet session dealt with one last important item, the election of the Executive Committee. It was agreed that three members of the Presidium and the four members of the Secretariat would be automatically included in the Executive Committee. In addition to these seven, eight more members were elected. Three nonparty intellectuals, Sukhanov, Steklov, and Kapelinskii, were the first elected, receiving from thirty-eight to forty-one votes. Realizing that their factions had no possibility of gaining a majority on their own, both the right wing and the left wing supported the nonparty intellectuals in the hope that they could be won over to their side.[73] Kapelinskii, little known activist of the cooperative movement, received one of the highest votes because of the active involvement of the cooperatives in the election of the Soviet deputies. Shliapnikov and Aleksandrovich, representing the left wing, barely managed to obtain the minimum twenty to twenty-two votes necessary for election. In addition to these five, three more were added: E. Sokolovskii, P. Krasikov (Pavlovich), and Zalutskii.[74] The newly elected Executive Committee included

72. Ibid., pp. 134-35; OR GBL f. 369, p. 16, ed. khr. 30; V. D. Bonch-Bruevich, "Pervye revoliutsionnye gazety fevral'skoi revoliutsii: Izvestiia i Pravda," ll. 1-2; Iu. Steklov, "Po povodu stat'i A. G. Shliapnikova: Pis'mo v redaktsiiu," *Proletarskaia revoliutsiia* 16, no. 4 (1923): 180-81; idem, *Vospominaniia i publitsistika*, pp. 78-79.

73. Tokarev, *Petrogradskii Sovet rabochikh i soldatskikh deputatov*, p. 37.

74. Steklov, "Po povodu stat'i A. G. Shliapnikova," p. 177; Sukhanov, *Zapiski o revoliutsii* 1: 148-49; "Kak obrazovalsia Petrogradskii Sovet," p. 7. Precisely speaking, the Executive Committee created on February 27 called itself the "Provisional Executive Committee." The reelection of the Executive Committee members, however, never took place. On February 28, the Executive Committee

two Bolsheviks (Shliapnikov and Zalutskii), two Socialist Revolutionaries (Aleksandrovich and Kerenskii), six Mensheviks (Chkheidze, Skobelev, Gvozdev, Grinevich, Sokolovskii, and Pankov), and five nonparty intellectuals (Steklov, Sukhanov, Sokolov, Krasikov, and Kapelinskii).[75] Although Steklov, Sokolov, and Krasikov, the nonparty intellectuals, were former Bolsheviks, it is obvious that the Menshevik party dominated the committee.

However, party affiliations were somewhat misleading in indicating the political leaning of the Executive Committee—it is necessary to classify the members of the Executive Committee on a political spectrum. The right wing was represented by Kerenskii and Gvozdev, while Shliapnikov, Zalutskii, and Aleksandrovich formed the left-wing bloc. All the rest were situated in between these two extremes. Among these ten members, Chkheidze and Skobelev were Menshevik Duma deputies and represented the moderate internationalist position. Grinevich, Pankov, and Sokolovskii were members of the Menshevik initiative group. Kapelinskii's political leaning cannot be clearly established, but he appears to have taken a position similar to the initiative group. Former Bolsheviks Steklov, Sokolov, and Krasikov were naturally closer to the Bolsheviks than to the right wing, and Sukhanov espoused an internationalism close to the Menshevik initiative group.[76] Contrary to the often reiterated evaluation of the Executive Committee as being dominated by moderate Mensheviks, its left-wing leaning was obvious in its composition. In the first place, despite the presence of Bogdanov, Zenzinov, and Rafes, the right wing managed to send only two representatives. Although the workers' group played a crucial part in taking the initiative in forming the Soviet, Gvozdev was the only one who was elected to the Executive Committee, and even his election provoked a strong protest. Secondly, in the context of the political realignment that had developed during the war, the composition of the Executive Committee meant a victory of the left-wing alliance. The left wing, combined with the Menshevik initiative group and the nonparty intellectuals who stood for internationalism, were represented by ten members, an overwhelming majority of the Executive Committee.[77]

But the left wing could not capitalize on this strength. This was partly because of ideological disunity and confusion among its members, and partly because of the lack of leadership by the Bolshevik party. Although the left wing was unanimous in its opposition to

further expanded its members while maintaining the original members elected on February 27. Zlokazov, *Petrogradskii Sovet*, p. 55.

75. Tokarev, *Petrogradskii Sovet rabochikh i soldatskikh deputatov*, p. 37.
76. Wada, "Nigatsu kakumei," p. 433.
77. Tokarev, *Petrogradskii Sovet rabochikh i soldatskikh deputatov*, p. 38.

the war and in its support of the proletariat's struggle against the tsarist regime, there existed within it disagreements on the question of the political power to be formed. And as a result of the victorious insurrection, it was precisely the question of power that became the most urgent question of the moment and that led to the disintegration of the left-wing bloc. The Bolshevik party was also split on the question of power. Although the Russian Bureau and the lower echelon activists advocated the establishment of a provisional revolutionary government, they disagreed on the question of what role the Soviet should play. In addition, the Petersburg Committee, which had provided a driving force in the loose alliance of the antiwar groups during the war, had been destroyed by police arrests since February 25. As a result, instead of the left-wing alliance, Sukhanov, Steklov, and Sokolov emerged as the main spokesmen of the Executive Committee. Although their position on the war was internationalist, their response to the question of power was similar to the Mensheviks', and at the inception of the Executive Committee, the rest of the members with the exception of the extreme Left gravitated to their leadership.

After the election of the Executive Committee, Shliapnikov made a strategic mistake. Apparently dissatisfied with the extreme minority the Bolsheviks occupied in the Executive Committee, he moved to include in the committee two representatives from each Socialist party, one from its central organization and another from its city organization. This motion was approved. As a result by the next day, the following representatives entered the Executive Committee: Bramson and Chaikovskii (Trudovik), Peshekhonov and Chernoluskii (Popular Socialist party), Ehrlich and Rafes (Bund), Bogdanov and Baturskii (Menshevik), Zenzinov and Sviatitskii (Socialist Revolutionary), Iurenev (Mezhraiontsy), and Molotov and Shutko (Bolsheviks). With the exception of the last three all were right-wing Socialists. Shliapnikov's resolution clearly contributed to strengthening the Executive Committee's right wing.[78]

Ironically, no deputies duly elected from factories were elected to the Executive Committee, and the soldiers' deputies were not included in it until March 1. The self-appointed intelligentsia completely dominated the highest decision-making body of the Soviet. The predominance of intellectuals clearly distinguished the Petrograd Soviet of 1917 from its predecessor of 1905, which never lost the character of a workers' self-government.[79]

78. Wada, "Nigatsu kakumei," p. 434; Sukhanov, *Zapiski o revoliutsii* 1: 179; Tokarev, *Petrogradskii Sovet rabochikh i soldatskikh deputatov*, pp. 46-47.

79. Anweiler, *Die Rätebewegung in Russland*, p. 173; idem, "The Political Ideology of the Petrograd Soviet in the Spring of 1917," in *Revolutionary Russia*, ed. Richard Pipes, pp. 116-17.

After the election of the Executive Committee, Shliapnikov raised the question of establishing district soviets in Petrograd. However, recognizing the lateness of the hour and the importance of the delegates' immediate return to their districts to inform the broader section of the populace of the decisions adopted by the Soviet, the plenary session decided to refer this matter to the Executive Committee. The chaotic, yet exuberant first session of the Soviet of Workers' Deputies adjourned at midnight. Passionate speeches were delivered, the revolution enthusiastically hailed, and the organizational structure of the Soviet firmly laid down. Yet the first session curiously kept silent on the most important issue of the moment—the problem of power.

Immediately after the Soviet session, the Executive Committee held its first meeting. Concerning the establishment of local soviets, the Executive Committee decided to dispatch "commissars for establishing popular power in the districts of Petrograd."[80] Shliapnikov (Vyborg District), Peshekhonov (Petrograd District), Surin (SR, Lesnoi District), and seven other commissars were appointed. These commissars, however, had little influence as liaison between the Petrograd Soviet and the district soviets. Shliapnikov mentions that the meeting of the commissars held immediately after the Executive Committee "bore a theoretical character," since they had no experience and did not know how to go about their business.[81] Very few district soviets were created immediately after the February Revolution: in addition to the Vyborg District Soviet created on the initiative of a Mezhraionets worker from the Petrograd Cartridge Factory, Maksimov, they were established only in Vasilievskii Island, Nevskii District, and the Narva District in the early days of March. The commissars appointed by the Executive Committee in any event do not appear to have played a major part in their creation.[82]

The Executive Committee proceeded to discuss the creation of the militia. Confirming the resolution passed by the Soviet session, it established a headquarters in each district, where soldiers and workers were urged to gather for creation of the militia. Concerning the rela-

80. *Izvestiia*, supplement, February 28, 1917.

81. Surin was later discovered to be a former tsarist Okhrana agent and arrested. Zenzinov, "Fevral'skie dni," *Novyi zhurnal* 35 (1953): 220. Peshekhonov was not informed of this decision until the afternoon of the following day. Peshekhonov, "Pervyia nedeli," p. 226. The names of the rest of the commissars are not known. Shliapnikov, *Semnadtsatyi god* 1: 154. According to Tokarev, the commissars remained only on paper. Tokarev, *Petrogradskii Sovet rabochikh i soldatskikh deputatov*, pp. 69-70.

82. Gordienko, *Iz boevogo proshlogo*, p. 70; *Raionnye sovety Petrograda* (3 vols.; Moscow, 1966), 2: 59.

tionship between the Soviet and the Military Commission, the Executive Committee decided to make the latter directly responsible to the Executive Committee and to send Sokolov and Aleksandrovich to watch over its activities.[83]

Turning next to the relationship between the Soviet and the Duma Committee, the Executive Committee elected Kerenskii and Chkheidze as the Soviet's official representatives to the Duma Committee, although both actually had been included in that committee even before this decision. According to Shliapnikov, the two Soviet representatives were to watch over the activities of the Duma Committee lest the latter should "compromise with the remnants of tsarism behind the back of the people who had stood up for the revolution."[84] In this decision one can see the genesis of the Soviet's basic attitude toward the Duma Committee, and eventually toward the Provisional Government. Implied in it was the conclusion that a governmental power would emerge from the Duma Committee, while the Soviet would limit itself to exerting pressure upon the Duma Committee so as to make sure that the latter would not deviate from the expected course of actions. On this basic assumption, at least at the first Executive Committee meeting, all the members including Shliapnikov had no disagreement.[85]

When the Executive Committee finished the first meeting, it was past five in the morning. The second day of the revolution was about to start. The leaders of the Soviet, totally exhausted, stayed in the Tauride Palace to catch catnaps on unoccupied chairs and in corners of assembly halls. It had been a good day for them; many of them had emerged from obscurity to mount the crest of the revolutionary wave --vicissitudes so incredible they could not have been dreamed of in the morning. Yet the actions of the Soviet were yet to be tested by the reactions of the insurgents. Would they accept its authority? Or would they drag it in a more radical direction than the intellectual leaders intended to go? The die was cast, but what awaited them was not known.

83. Shliapnikov, *Semnadtsatyi god* 1: 152; *Izvestiia*, February 28, 1917.

84. Shliapnikov, *Semnadtsatyi god* 1: 153.

85. Rafes states that the Bolsheviks from the beginning raised objections to cooperation with the Duma Committee. M. G. Rafes, "Moi vospominaniia," *Byloe* 19 (1922): 190. On the basis of this statement, Burdzhalov contends that the Bolsheviks refused to support the general policy of the Executive Committee toward the Duma Committee. Burdzhalov, *Vtoraia russkaia revoliutsiia*, p. 215. There is no evidence, however, to indicate that Shliapnikov raised any objection to the Executive Committee's decision at the first meeting. He could not have formulated a clear-cut policy toward the problem of power by this time.

18

THE FORMATION OF
THE DUMA COMMITTEE

 Angered by the imperial decree of prorogation in-
voked late at night on February 26, the Duma deputies
gathered in the Tauride Palace early next morning.
On the previous night, under the pressure of some
leading Duma liberals, Rodzianko had reluctantly
agreed to hold a meeting of the Progressive Bloc and
the *senioren konvent,* a council of the representatives of each party
in the Duma.[1] By eight o'clock in the morning, many deputies had
already appeared in the Duma, and news of the soldiers' insurrection
soon drove the remaining deputies out of bed. By noon the Duma
deputies and other liberal activists wandered about the corridors
of the Tauride Palace with concerned looks, gathered in small groups,
and argued heatedly on what action the Duma should take. Should
the Duma defy the order of the tsar to prorogue the Duma—an act
tantamount to joining the ranks of the insurgents? Or should it obey
the order and quietly disperse while the insurrection was threatening
to throw the entire city into chaos and anarchy? Shul'gin described
the dilemma of the Duma deputies: "On the one hand [there was]
the imperial decree of dissolution (prorogation of session) and on the
other, an approaching storm. . . . Inside ourselves respect for the throne
was entangled with protest against the path the tsar was following,
for we knew that this was the path leading to an abyss."[2]

A Kadet, S. V. Panina, stepdaughter of a famous zemstvo activist
and a founder of the Kadet party, Ivan Petrunkevich, tried to per-

1. TsGIA, f. 1276, op. 8, d. 679, ch. III, ℓ. 110.
2. V. V. Shul'gin, *Dni,* pp. 154-55.

suade colleagues in her party to assume leadership of the insurrection, but her suggestion was met with silence. Afraid of involvement, the Kadet deputies shrugged their shoulders, and one remarked, "Let them arrest the ministers first." Contrary to the liberals, some ecclesiastical deputies, who usually belonged to the right wing, boldly demanded the opening of the Duma, "If the ministerial scum ran away, we must organize the ministry." The Socialist deputies also insisted that the Duma session should immediately be called. According to Kerenskii: "My first thought was that the Duma must be kept in session at all costs and that close contact between the armed forces and the Duma must be established."[3] While the voices demanding the opening of the Duma grew louder, Rodzianko sat in his office. At one point Guchkov came in and conferred with him. About noon War Minister Beliaev telephoned and proposed to Rodzianko that in the name of national interest the Duma and the government act together to suppress the insurrection. Rodzianko indignantly replied "What joint action is possible, when you are proroguing the Duma? There cannot be a common language from now on."[4]

Rodzianko remained adamant in his refusal. The opening of the regular session in defiance of the imperial decree, in his opinion, would be tantamount to the Duma's assumption of the role of a constituent assembly.[5] Totally frustrated, Kerenskii rang the bell himself, without Rodzianko's permission, to summon the deputies to the assembly hall, but few responded. A popular Socialist, Chernolusskii, who had just arrived at the Tauride Palace, reported to Rodzianko that the entire city had fallen to the insurgents, and strongly recommended that the Duma take power into its own hands. Refusing to take Chernolusskii seriously, Rodzianko locked himself in his office, and began composing a telegram to the tsar.[6]

3. Diary of A. Tyrkova, quoted by E. N. Burdzhalov, *Vtoraia russkaia revoliutsiia: Vosstanie v Petrograde*, p. 226. D. Zaslavskii, "V Gosudarstvennoi dume," *Krasnaia panorama*, March 11, 1927. Alexander F. Kerensky, *Russia and History's Turning Point*, p. 195.

4. TsGIA, f. 1276, op. 8, d. 679, ch. III, ℓ. 110.

5. "Lichnyi fond M. Polievktova: Materialy komissii oprosov, beseda s M. Rodzianko," quoted in Burdzhalov, *Vtoraia russkaia revoliutsiia*, p. 226. Immediately after the February Revolution a historical commission to study the process of revolution was organized under Professor A. E. Presniakov. A number of students and professors interviewed participants. Part of the materials have come into the personal collection of Professor M. A. Polievktov, and are preserved by his widow, Professor R. N. Nikoladze. Burdzhalov used the materials extensively, but no other historians have made use of them. I did not obtain access to these materials on my recent trip to the Soviet Union. See E. N. Burdzhalov, "Istochniki i literatura po istorii vtoroi russkoi revoliutsii," *Sverzhenie samoderzhaviia*, pp. 245-55.

6. Burdzhalov, *Vtoraia russkaia revoliutsiia*, p. 228.

Since the convocation of the *senioren konvent* scheduled at noon was sabotaged by Rodzianko, a group of deputies held an informal meeting under the chairmanship of Nekrasov. Kerenskii and Skobelev repeated their demand that the Duma should take over leadership of the insurrection. Soon Rodzianko rushed to the meeting, fulminating about gathering illegally and without his permission. Somewhat soothed by the explanation that this was merely an informal meeting of deputies in a private capacity, Rodzianko finally agreed to hold an official meeting of the *senioren konvent* in his chamber, where it was decided that while the Duma should accept the imperial decree, its members should also assemble unofficially.[7]

At 12:40 P.M. Rodzianko sent a second telegram to the tsar, in which he deplored the imperial decree of prorogation that deprived Petrograd of "the last bulwark of order" in face of the total powerlessness of the government "to suppress the disturbances"—civil war had begun in the streets in which the soldiers were killing their officers. Rodzianko then begged the tsar to cancel the decree and to grant a ministry of confidence. "Sire, do not delay. If the movement spreads to the army, the Germans will triumph and the ruin of Russia, and with her [the ruin] of her dynasty, will be inevitable. . . . The hour that will decide the fate of Yourself and of the fatherland has come. Tomorrow it may already be too late."[8] It was the last telegram Rodzianko sent to the tsar.

At half past two in the afternoon, a third of the Duma deputies "privately" assembled, not in the regular assembly hall, but in the Semicircular Hall. The right-wing deputies had disappeared from the Tauride Palace. The private meeting was the Duma's answer to its dilemma between the old regime and the insurrection; it did not violate the law, nor did it take a stand against the insurrection. In

7. Shul'gin, *Dni*, pp. 156-57. There is an extremely important record on the discussions and decisions made in the Duma Committee, *Protokoly sobytii*, recorded by Ia. Glinka, head of the chancellery of the Duma. It includes the critical period from February 27 to March 2, that is, from the formation of the Duma Committee to the formation of the Provisional Government. It was submitted for publication once, but was never published. The original of this record is deposited in fond Vershinin (TsGAOR, f. 5990, op. 1, dd. 1-3). Since the members of the Duma Committee speak little about their discussions and decisions in their memoirs and when they do their accounts frequently conflict one another, this material is of extreme importance. My request to use the material was denied.

8. "Fevral'skaia revoliutsiia 1917 goda," *Krasnyi arkhiv* 21, no. 2 (1927): 6-7. According to Chermenskii, Guchkov also took part in the composition of this telegram. E. D. Chermenskii, *IV gosudarstvennaia duma i sverzhenie tsarizma v Rossii*, p. 282.

fact, the meeting was mistakenly taken by many insurgents as the Duma's determination to stand against the old regime. The only newspaper published on this day by a committee of Petrograd jounalists recorded that the *senioren konvent* "has resolved that the State Duma shall not disperse, and that all deputies shall remain in their place."[9] This inaccurate report contributed to the insurgents' misunderstanding.

The "private" nature of the meeting, though important in explaining the indecisiveness of the Duma liberals, thus mattered little in actuality; the Duma took its first step outside legal boundaries. Regardless of how they explained their actions to themselves, decisions made at this meeting would have no legal authority. Then from what sources did their actions derive authority? The fundamental weakness of the Duma Committee, and later of the Provisional Government, rested on this question of legitimacy.

Rodzianko stated in the opening speech that "we cannot as yet express ourselves definitely, because the correlation of forces is not yet known to us."[10] The first speaker, Nekrasov, said that since there was no government, it was necessary to create one. Since "the governmental machinery is still in the hands of the old regime," a half-way solution would be necessary. He proposed establishing a military dictatorship headed by General A. A. Manikovskii, who had allegedly sympathized with the idea of a palace coup. This proposal, however, met with strong objections. Kovalenko argued that it was tantamount to placing power again in the hands of the old regime. Chkheidze called the proposal "a false road," and stressed the necessity of destroying the old regime and creating a new one. A Trudovik, Dziubinskii, argued that the *senioren konvent* should take power now and announce this move immediately to the people. Later, he amended his proposal and argued that since the Duma had no alternative other than to create a new power, it should proclaim itself a constituent assembly. Kerenskii requested that he and Chkheidze be given authority to announce to the insurgent troops in the streets in the name of the Duma that "the Duma had taken the responsibility into its own hands and that it stands at the head of the movement."[11]

Moderate liberals opposed these demands for immediate seizure

9. *Izvestiia revoliutsionnoi nedeli*, February 27, 1917.
10. "Iz zametok o pervykh dniakh russkoi revoliutsii," *Volia Rossii*, March 15, 1921. These are the minutes of the meeting recorded by an undisclosed attendant. The translation can be found in R. P. Browder and Alexander F. Kerensky, eds., *The Provisional Government* 1: 45-46. Apparently the minutes are identical with those in part of *Protokoly sobytii*.
11. "Iz zametok o pervykh dniakh russkoi revoliutsii," p. 4.

of power by the Duma. Octobrist Savich stated: "A mob cannot hand us authority. For the people the Duma represents the last refuge, and if the Duma should take some illegal step, then it could not [remain] a legislative institution; it would no longer be the Duma." He proposed that the chairman and the Secretariat of the Duma should be entrusted with organization of the government. Shul'gin warned of the danger of yielding to popular pressures—"Imagine that the insurgents would wish to end the war—we could not agree to accept this." Karaulov proposed the election of an executive commission charged with organization of the government. Miliukov outlined the three proposals presented and rejected each one. He could not agree with the proposal of the election of a committee, since such a committee cold not have dictatorial power. Nekrasov's proposal would simply be inappropriate. The idea of creating the new government proposed by Dziubinskii and Chkheidze would be premature. "Personally, I have no concrete suggestion. So, what can we do? To go [to the streets], as suggested by Kerenskii, and appease the troops? But this would hardly appease them; we must look for something more tangible."[12] Miliukov was keenly aware of the predicament in which the liberals found themselves. He knew that no government and no committee that might grow out of the Duma and liberal circles alone would be effective in controlling the masses. The solution, in his opinion, would not be found in identifying with the insurgents. Then, what would be the solution? What did Miliukov mean by "something more tangible?" He had in mind the possibility of suppression of the insurrection by tsarist military forces. He was advocating a wait-and-see policy until the revolution and the counterrevolution fought it out.

An unexpected incident occurred at that time. A chief of the guard of the Duma rushed into the hall and declared that insurgent forces had entered the Tauride Palace. The deputies halted discussions and flew to the windows to see them pouring into the palace court, while Kerenskii, Chkheidze, and Skobelev rushed out of the hall to greet them.[13] Rodzianko urged that they reach a conclusion promptly by voting on four proposals: (1) transfer of power to the *senioren konvent;* (2) the formation of a special committee; (3) a proclamation of the Duma as a constituent assembly; and (4) the election of a commission to be charged with organization of the government. While any of the proposals except the second would have committed the Duma to assume power, which would be necessarily associated with the insurrection under the circumstances, the advantage of the second proposal

12. Ibid.
13. S. I. Shidlovskii, *Vospominaniia* 2: 53; Shul'gin, *Dni*, p. 159.

was in its noncommittal stand. Miliukov supported this proposal, because "while satisfying the tasks of the moment, it did not predetermine anything for the future."[14] Despite strong objections from the Left, the majority approved the second proposal, the formation of a special committee, the selection of the members of which was entrusted to the *senioren konvent.* By five o'clock in the afternoon, "the Provisional Committee of the members of the State Duma for the restoration of order in the capital and the establishment of relations with public organizations and institutions" was created with the following members: Rodzianko (Octobrist), V. Z. Rzhevskii (Progressist party), Shul'gin (Nationalist), Miliukov (Kadet), Nekrasov (Kadet), Kerenskii (Trudovik), Chkheidze (Menshevik), A. I. Konovalov (Progressist party), V. N. L'vov (Centrist), and S. I. Shidlovskii (Octobrist).[15] Later Colonel B. A. Engelhardt (Octobrist) was added to the list. Basically the Duma Committee consisted of the representatives of the Progressive Bloc with two notable additions: Kerenskii and Chkheidze. The Duma liberals considered the inclusion of these two Socialists essential to establishing contact with the insurgents. The participation of Kerenskii, Nekrasov, and Konovalov—members of the conspiratorial masonic organization—had significance in forming a solid bloc in the committee. Through them Guchkov, Tereshchenko, and Prince L'vov later joined the activities and discussions of the Duma Committee, although they were not its official members. Rodzianko became chairman of the Duma Committee by virtue of his position as chairman of the State Duma and for the first few days of its existence all activities of the Duma Committee revolved around Rodzianko's personal decisions. But it was Miliukov, with his keen political intelligence, who towered higher than any of his colleagues and who steered the course of the Duma Committee after Rodzianko's influence began to wane. Ironically, these two men almost did not join the committee. Afraid that his participation might be construed as defiance of the imperial decree, Rodzianko at first refused to take part. Miliukov in turn refused to join without Rodzianko, since he was fully aware that without the prestige of the Duma's chairman, the Duma Committee would have no chance of survival. But Rodzianko changed his mind when he learned of the formation of the Petrograd Soviet, and decided to head the Committee.[16]

14. "Iz zametok o pervykh dniakh russkoi revoliutsii," p. 4; P. N. Miliukov, *Vospominaniia, 1859-1917* 2: 292-93.

15. *Izvestiia revoliutsionnoi nedeli,* February 28, 1917.

16. M. Skobelev, "Gibel' tsarizma: Vospominaniia M. I. Skobeleva," *Ogonek,* no. 11 (1927).

The difference in political views held by the members of the Duma Committee was immense. A deep gulf separated Kerenskii, representing the left wing, from Shul'gin of the right wing. Kerenskii unquestioningly welcomed the insurrection, in which he saw "the spirit of unity, fraternity, mutual confidence, and self-sacrifice, welding all of us into a single fighting body." He believed that the Duma, in obtaining the confidence of the people, had reached the highest point of its strength. On the other hand, Shul'gin felt "a malicious fury" when he witnessed the "disgusting" scene of insurgents pouring into the Tauride Palace. "Machine guns—that is what I wanted," he reminisced. "Only the language of machine guns was accessible to the crowds in the streets . . . only it, the lead, could drive this dreadful beast back to its den." He held a more realistic view than Kerenskii of the real strength of the Duma. According to Shul'gin, the Duma's pretense of holding power had developed simply because "the people hailed the Duma as a *symbol of the revolution,* but not from respect for the Duma itself."[17] Despite this wide range of political differences, the members of the Duma Committee had one common goal: to prevent the revolution from going beyond controllable limits. At this moment the dilemma of the liberals in wartime politics manifested itself in the sharpest form. Led by Miliukov, the liberal mainstream had refused to take decisive action against the government for fear that such action might touch off a revolution from below. The radical wing of the liberals had advocated more active cooperation with the mass movement so as to contain it within reasonable limits. Out of desperation a small group headed by Guchkov had plotted a palace coup. A common thread running through all these differing liberal stances was to try to prevent a revolution, but if it were to come, to keep it within reasonable bounds. Moderate Socialists, who had gathered in the Left Bloc, had been in complete agreement with this goal. According to Kerenskii, "We believed that the elementary revolutionary movement was unacceptable at the time of war. Therefore we considered it our task to support the moderate or even the conservative groups, parties, and organizations, which could prevent a catastrophe of the explosion of *stikhiia* by a palace coup."[18] But on the afternoon of February 27 the insurrection was an established fact. The little space that the liberals and the moderate Socialists

17. Alexander F. Kerensky, *The Catastrophe,* p. 21; Shul'gin, *Dni,* pp. 163, 177-78.

18. *Dni,* May 22, 1917, quoted in E. N. Burdzhalov, "Nachalo vtoroi russkoi revoliutsii," *Uchenye zapiski Moskovskogo gosudarstvennogo pedagogicheskogo instituta imeni Lenina: Materialy i issledovaniia po istorii SSSR,* p. 155.

had chosen during the war was quickly becoming smaller and smaller, squeezed in between the revolution and the old regime. Shingarev stated. "The Duma was still standing between the 'people' and the 'government.' Both sides still recognized it for the time being."[19] But on the afternoon of February 27, despite the creation of the Duma Committee, the liberals continued to take the line persistently advocated by Miliukov during the war—abstention from decisive action for the support of the revolution and overthrow of the government. The "private" meeting simply passed the resolution that "the members of the Duma, regardless of their party affiliations, should give promise to support and extend cooperation with the Provisional Committee in all actions which it should take in the future."[20] But they did not know what actions the Duma Committee was to take.

By late afternoon on February 27 the Duma deputies were witness to an unprecedented scene. Usually impeccable order and decorum ruled in the Duma. Couriers always stood at the doors of the large halls, and guards of the palace walked ceremoniously in the corridors. But on that afternoon Tauride Palace became an extension of the streets in turmoil. The sumptuous Ekaterina Hall, Circular Hall, and all corridors were filled with soldiers, workers, and students. In the Circular Hall weapons taken from regimental arsenals and those confiscated from the police were piled up. There was a broken machine gun, and next to it lay a corpse of a soldier of Semenovskii Regiment with a bullet hole in his temple. Against the wall all sorts of plunder was stacked up. On a heap of sacks of barley and flour lay a carcass of a pig. The noise was incredible. The members of the Duma stood appalled at the gigantic crowds that had violated Tauride Palace and who were behaving as though it were the site of a great festival.[21]

Soldiers who had joined the insurrection arrived in a continuous stream, to be greeted by Skobelev and Kerenskii at the doorstep. The soldiers welcomed their speeches with approving shouts, but asked repeatedly: "Where is the new power? Where is the new government?" Skobelev replied, "The members of the State Duma have not decided to take power in their hands. We are putting pressure on them. Have patience, because . . . it is an extremely difficult task to create a new government."[22]

Rodzianko believed that the establishment of a ministry of confi-

19. Quoted in Shul'gin, *Dni*, p. 153.
20. *Protokoly sobytii*, p. 9 quoted in Burdzhalov, *Vtoraia russkaia revoliutsiia*, p. 233.
21. OR GBL, d. 218, B.A. Engel'gardt, "Potonuvshii mir," ℓ. 104.
22. Skobelev, "Gibel' tsarizma"; *Izvestiia revoliutsionnoi nedeli*, February 27, 1917.

dence would be the only way to solve the crisis. He tried to persuade Nicholas's brother, Grand Duke Mikhail Aleksandrovich, to assume a temporary dictatorship in Petrograd with the help of the Duma and to establish such a ministry. This approach appears to have had the support of the rest of the Duma Committee members at its initial stage. The grand duke had been in the capital since February 25 on Rodzianko's request and on February 27, Rodzianko, Nekrasov, and other representatives of the Duma Committee met the grand duke at six o'clock in the evening at the Tauride Palace. They explained that the anarchy in the streets was threatening the very existence of the monarchical system. The sole solution would be to transfer power to the Duma, the only institution that could save the country from anarchy. Nekrasov suggested that for that purpose the grand duke assume "the regency temporarily until the arrival of the emperor from the Stavka, dismiss the Council of Ministers, and place at the head of the administration a Provisional Government consisting of the men of society with a popular general at its head." Rodzianko also urged the grand duke to establish a dictatorship in Petrograd "on his own initiative," and to demand from the emperor "a manifesto for the formation of a responsible ministry of confidence."[23]

Mikhail, however, declared that he had no right to take such a measure without conferring with the Council of Ministers. The Duma representatives and Mikhail then drove to Marinskii Palace to meet the cabinet members. Golitsyn agreed to resign, but refused to transfer power either to the Duma Committee or to the grand duke without a specific order from the tsar. Rodzianko decided to compromise, and together with Mikhail, Golitsyn, and Beliaev, began composing a text of the demand that the grand duke would present to the tsar.[24] Finally, the grand duke called the Stavka through the Hughes apparatus at ten o'clock, but Nicholas refused to answer directly, sending General Alekseev, instead. Mikhail politely requested the dismissal of the present members of the Council of Ministers and the appointment of a ministry of confidence headed by Prince L'vov to avoid the intensification of anarchy. When Alekseev commented that the tsar was

23. "Lichnyi fond M. Polievktova: Materialy komissii oprosov, beseda s N. Nekrasovym," quoted in Burdzhalov, *Vtoraia russkaia revoliutsiia*, pp. 233-34; *Protokoly sobytii*, p. 10, quoted in ibid.; Rodzianko, "Gosudarstvennaia duma i fevral'skaia 1917 goda revoliutsiia," *Archiv russkoi revoliutsii* 4 (1922): 57. For Rodzianko's role in this attempt, see Tsuyoshi Hasegawa, "Rodzianko and the Grand Duke's Manifesto 1 March 1917," *Canadian Slavonic Papers* 18, no. 2 (1976): 160-61.

24. *Protokoly sobytii*, p. 10, quoted in Burdzhalov, *Vtoraia russkaia revoliutsiia*, p. 234.

scheduled to leave for Tsarskoe Selo on the following day, Mikhail replied that the departure should be delayed for a few days. Nicholas had Alekseev thank the grand duke for his consideration, but to reject each demand categorically, though politely. The emperor did not consider it possible to postpone his departure and would decide on the dismissal of the cabinet members when he returned to the capital. As for the suppression of disorders in Petrograd, General Ivanov would be sent to the capital for that purpose, and would be assisted by reliable troops from the northern and western fronts. The grand duke, unnerved by this rejection, did not press further. Rodzianko blamed the failure of the Duma Committee's first move on Mikhail's lack of determination. "Instead of taking active measures," Rodzianko complained, "and gathering around himself the units of the Petrograd Garrison whose discipline was not yet shattered, Grand Duke Mikhail Aleksandrovich started to negotiate by direct wire with Emperor Nicholas II."[25]

A few hours after the formation of the Duma Committee, two central figures, one representing the Duma Committee and the other a leader of the Petrograd Soviet, met accidentally in a corridor of the Tauride Palace. Sukhanov, pointing out that the Soviet was being formed a few rooms away and was ready to take power, warned that popular demands might be expanded to extreme limits. To keep them within set bounds, Sukhanov argued, it would be imperative that the Duma Committee take state power into its hands. Miliukov replied, however: "We, as a responsible opposition, without doubt, have strived for power and moved toward it, but not along the path of revolution. We have rejected this path; this path is not ours."[26] The Duma Committee was still playing a waiting game.

By late at night, however, the victory of the insurrection became obvious. Crowds continued to gather in the Tauride Palace, where the Socialist intelligentsia had taken the initiative of organizing the insurgents by forming the Petrograd Soviet. The representatives of the Duma Committee, who came back to the Tauride Palace from the Marinskii Palace, saw with their own eyes that the streets of Petrograd were now completely in insurgent hands. Even to Miliukov the situation was clear enough to justify a modification of the Duma Committee's position. Shul'gin stated the motive behind the change of policy: "If we do not take power, others will take it, those who

25. "Fevral'skaia revoliutsiia 1917 goda," *Krasnyi arkhiv* 21, no. 2 (1927): 10. Through these recorded telegraphic conversations the Duma leaders learned of the approach of General Ivanov's punitive detachment for the first time. Rodzianko, "Gosudarstevennaia duma i fevral'skaia 1917 goda revoliutsiia," p. 57.

26. N. N. Sukhanov, *Zapiski o revoliutsii* 1: 118-19.

have already elected some scoundrels in the factories."[27] The only obstacle was Rodzianko's opposition.

Octobrist deputy Engelhardt spent most of February 27 in the officers' New Club, near the Winter Palace. After learning of the formation of the Duma Committee, he finally sent for civilian clothes, took off his officer's uniform, and walked quickly through the bitter, freezing night to the Tauride Palace. Entering the chairman's chamber, Engelhardt saw twelve members of the Duma Committee assembled. Miliukov was whispering something to Shidlovskii in a corner; V. L'vov was pacing back and forth in the room. Rodzianko was sitting behind the large table. "On his usually self-confident face agitation and irresolution were visible." Joining the twelve, Engelhardt urged the committee to take power in order to avoid anarchy. Rodzianko objected and shouted: "Gentlemen, what you are demanding from me is to take power in my hand. This is a direct revolutionary act. How can I agree with that?" Someone suggested that Karaulov, a Cossack, should persuade the Cossacks to suppress the insurgents. Karaulov refused. "I cannot act independently. I could call the Cossacks for action only in the name of an organized power, and such could be now only the Provisional Committee of the State Duma."[28] Rodzianko still hesitated, but was obviously weakening. He asked for fifteen minutes to deliberate and retired to his office.

At this moment, Shidlovskii, who had stepped out for an urgent telephone call, burst into the room. In an agitated voice he announced to Rodzianko: "Mikhail Vladimirovich, I have extraordinarily important news. My nephew, Captain Meshcherskii, informed me officially in the name of the commander of the Preobrazhenskii Regiment that the entire regiment subordinates itself to the disposition of the State Duma." The deputies surrounded Shidlovskii and from all sides voices were heard, "Now there is nothing to think about." "It's time to decide." Rodzianko sat behind the table, staring at the ceiling and pretended not to listen to the voices around him. Miliukov came in front of him across the table. The eyes of Miliukov and Rodzianko met. Miliukov nodded three times significantly. Rodzianko straightened himself on the chair, struck the table loudly with his hands, and declared: "All right, gentlemen, I have decided. I consent to take power. But only on one condition. I demand—and this refers especially to you, Aleksandr Fedorovich [Kerenskii]—that

27. "Lichnyi fond M. Polievktova: Materialy komissii oprosov, beseda s N. Nekrasovym," quoted in Burdzhalov, *Vtoraia russkaia revoliutsiia*, p. 235; Miliukov, *Vospominaniia* 2: 293; Shul'gin, *Dni*, p. 179.

28. Engel'gardt, "Potonuvshii mir," *ll.* 104-5.

all members of the committee . . . unconditionally and blindly subordinate themselves to my command." The members of the Duma Committee, embarrassed by Rodzianko's pompous speech, kept silent, but Kerenskii modestly reminded Rodzianko that he was still vice-chairman of the Soviet.[29]

The Duma Committee issued two proclamations at two o'clock in the morning of February 28, but dated February 27, in the name of Rodzianko. The first proclamation appealed to the populace to protect state and public institutions, factories and mills, "for the damage and destruction of institutions and property benefit no one and cause enormous harm to the state as well as to the people as a whole."[30] The second proclamation stated:

The Provisional Committee of the members of the State Duma under the difficult conditions of internal chaos created by the measures of the old regime has found itself compelled to take upon itself the task of the restoration of state and social order. Recognizing the vast responsibility that this decision carries, the committee expressed its conviction that the people and the army will assist it in the difficult task of creating a new government, in accordance with the wishes of the people and capable of enjoying their confidence.[31]

The Duma Committee finally decided to take power for the purpose of restoring order in Petrograd. Rodzianko explained, "The State Duma did not have any alternative but to take power into its own hands and attempt to arrest the prevailing anarchy in this way."[32] But would the measure it chose and the goal it pursued not be contradictory? By their decision the Duma Committee plunged into the midst of an irreversible revolutionary movement, but the restoration of law and order would definitely require its halt. Moreover, what guarantees could this policy promise in avoiding military confrontation with the forces of the old regime? These difficult questions suddenly faced the Duma Committee.

Immediately after the Duma Committee's decision to assume power, Sukhanov again met Miliukov. The ubiquitous leader of the Soviet Executive Committee described his impression:

At this moment Miliukov came into the room from Rodzianko's chambers. . . . He seemed triumphant, with a restrained smile on his lips.
"A decision has been made," he said, "We are taking power."
I sensed a new situation, a new favorable conjuncture for the revolution and

29. Ibid., ll. 105-6; Miliukov, *Vospominaniia* 2: 298.
30. *Izvestiia revoliutsionnoi nedeli*, February 28, 1917.
31. Ibid.; *Revoliutsionnoe dvizhenie v Rossii posle sverzheniia samoderzhaviia*, p. 402; Browder and Kerensky, *The Provisional Government* 1: 50.
32. Rodzianko, "Gosudarstvennaia duma i fevral'skaia 1917 goda revoliutsiia," p. 41.

new tasks for democracy that were now on the agenda of the moment. I felt that the ship of the revolution, thrown about in those hours by a squall and at the mercy of the elements, had spread its sails, had regained complete stability and regularity of the movement in the midst of the terrible storm and toiling, and between the shoals and reefs had taken a definite course toward a distant point, invisible in the mist but known with certainty. Now the rigging is in order, the engines are working, the only thing needed is to steer the ships skillfully.[33]

It would not take long for Sukhanov to realize how mistaken he was when he praised this moment as the happy beginning of the successful voyage of the Russian Revolution.

33. Sukhanov, *Zapiski o revoliutsii* 1: 142.

19

THE FIRST STEPS
OF THE DUMA COMMITTEE

 On February 28 the revolution in Petrograd accelerated. Insurgent soldiers attacked units that remained loyal to the government; they did not tolerate neutrality. Petrograd fell completely into their hands, and in the meanwhile insurrection spread to the outskirts of the capital. Anarchy and lawlessness were rampant and the Duma Committee was faced with a dilemma. It would be impossible to restore order unless it stemmed the tide of the revolution, but it would be equally impossible to establish a stable government acceptable to the insurgents if it stood in opposition to the revolution. Late on the night of February 27 the Duma Committee had been compelled, in spite of itself, to take power, but this decision pushed the Duma Committee further in a revolutionary direction on February 28. The gap between its goal and the method became wider.

Early in the morning workers and soldiers gathered on Sampsonievskii Prospekt in front of the barracks of the Bicycle Battalion, which remained the only army unit actively resisting the insurrection. The insurgents appealed to the cyclists to join them, but the answer was a volley from a machine gun. The angry insurgents then set the wooden barracks on fire. Stubbornly rejecting pleas from some officers to surrender, the commander of the battalion, Colonel Balkashin, ordered his officers to gun down any deserting cyclists. But when the insurgents brought forward heavy artillery and fired upon the barracks, the demoralized cyclists ran out of the barracks to surrender. The crowds treated them as prisoners rather than welcoming them as comrades. Colonel Balkashin and other officers were executed on the spot. The Bicycle Battalion made the only substantial stand in the city in support of the old regime.[1]

Only the forces that had locked themselves up in the Admiralty remained loyal to the tsar. A curious fact of the insurrection was that while the insurgents viciously attacked police headquarters, they never attacked headquarters of the military establishments—the Admiralty, the General Staff, and the Ministry of War. It was partly because they believed that this area was protected by a large contingent of loyal forces, and partly because the insurgent soldiers were not psychologically prepared to take that risk. It was one thing to leave barracks and pledge allegiance to the Duma, but it was totally another matter to launch an attack on the very source of military authority. But the final blow to the loyal forces came from unexpected quarters. In the morning an aide-de-camp of Navy Minister Grigorovich came to Khabalov with the minister's demand that the loyal troops be evacuated immediately from the Admiralty, lest the building should be damaged by crossfire in a military confrontation. Khabalov decided to avoid bloodshed and ordered the officers and the soldiers to return to their barracks. Abandoning their weapons in one room, the loyal troops slipped out of the building one by one. Khabalov, Balk, and a few of their assistants remained in the Admiralty to be arrested by the insurgents, while Beliaev and Zankevich escaped before their arrival.[2] Within twenty-four hours Zankevich was to cooperate with the Duma Committee's Military Commission "to protect the revolution from a counterrevolutionary attempt."

The insurgents also surrounded the Fortress of Peter and Paul, which they regarded as the symbol of tsarist oppression, although at the time in this vast fortress only nineteen soldiers of Pavlovskii Regiment were imprisoned. To avoid confrontation, Shul'gin of the Duma Committee and Skobelev of the Soviet Executive Committee were dispatched to negotiate with the commandant of the fortress, who was eager to reach a settlement. Setting all the prisoners free and inviting representatives of the insurgents to tour the prison to make sure that all the prison cells were empty, the commandant recognized the authority of the Duma Committee.[3]

Finland Regiment and the 180th Infantry Regiment on Vasilievskii

1. E. I. Martynov, *Tsarskaia armiia v fevral'skom perevorote*, pp. 120-21; "Dnevnik soldata na Vyborgskoi storone," *Pravda*, March 11, 1917.

2. Martynov, *Tsarskaia armiia v fevral'skom perevorote*, pp. 119-20; Deposition of Khabalov, *Padenie tsarskogo rezhima* 1: 302.

3. V. V. Shul'gin, *Dni*, pp. 201-3; M. Skobelev, "Gibel' tsarizma: Vospominaniia M. I. Skobeleva," *Ogonek*, no. 11 (1927).

Island had maintained neutrality. But on February 28 these soldiers, too, joined the insurrection. When workers appeared in the barracks of the Finland Regiment early in the morning and appealed to the soldiers to join the revolution, the soldiers attacked the regimental arsenal and went out to the streets. The insurgent soldiers and workers moved to the barracks of the 180th Infantry Regiment with a musical band leading the way. The soldiers of this regiment also abandoned their position. The insurgents next moved down to Deriabinskii barracks, where the Second Baltic Fleet's depot troops were stationed. There, sailors turned guns on the officers and joined the insurgents.[4]

The cruiser *Aurora* was anchored in the maintenance yard of the Franco-Russian Factory, where the crew had protested the imprisonment of three workers in the ship's stockade on February 27. During confrontation between the sailors and the officers one sailor was fatally shot and some others wounded. In the morning of February 28 workers gathered on the shore, appealing to the sailors to join the revolution. The sailors killed the commander of the ship, elected a new commander, organized the ship's committee, and sent their delegates to the Petrograd Soviet.[5]

The fiercest battle was fought in Hotel Astoria. Some months previously the Astoria was requisitioned by military authorities for officers on leave, with their families, and for officers of the Allies. On February 28 a deputation was sent from the insurgents, who demanded that hotel administrators surrender officers living in the hotel. While negotiations were going on, a Russian general fired into the crowd from one of the windows. As if on a prearranged signal, a machine gun on the rooftop was fired into the dense masses of people below. The infuriated insurgents returned machine-gun fire and many of those with arms stormed the building. The worst fighting took place in the vestibule—in a short time the big doors at the hotel entrance were revolving in a pool of blood. Overcoming the officers' resistance, the insurgents soon began a door-to-door search. They left foreign officers and their families unharmed, as well as the wives and children of the Russian officers. But the arrested Russian officers were dragged down into Marinskaia Square in front of the hotel and a number were shot on the spot, among them the general who fired the first shot. His body was unceremoniously thrown in the canal. Luckier officers were taken to a place of detention. The mob then

4. Vasilii Starkov, "Prisoedinenie Finlandtsev," *Pravda*, April 1917.

5. *Baltiiskie moriaki v podgotovke i provedenii Velikoi Oktiabr'skoi sotsial-isticheskoi revoliutsii: Sbornik dokumentov* (Moscow, 1957). Quoted in E. N. Burdzhalov, *Vtoraia russkaia revoliutsiia: Vosstanie v Petrograde*, p. 252; Martynov, *Tsarskaia armiia v febral'skom perevorote*, p. 122.

looted the hotel and broke into its rich wine cellars. One of the soldiers who could drink no more poured wine into his boots and wandered away.[6]

On the outskirts of Petrograd, the soldiers of the First Machine Gun Regiment in Oranienbaum revolted on the evening of February 27, when they learned of the insurrection in Petrograd. Seizing rifles, machine guns, and cartridges from the armory, they began marching toward the city and arrived early on the morning of February 28, pulling heavy artillery, disorganized and tired, but spirited. Soldiers of the Second Machine Gun Regiment in Strel'na and of the 176th Infantry Regiment in Krasnoe Selo also joined the insurgents in Petrograd.[7]

The rebellion spread to the supposedly reliable soldiers in Tsarskoe Selo. First the soldiers of the reserve battalion of the First Guard Regiment, and then the heavy artillery division and other units defected. Two thousand sailors of the Guard's ship, which had been brought in from the front only ten days before, abandoned their posts and marched to Petrograd, ignoring the command to block the road in case insurgents from Petrograd attacked Tsarskoe Selo. Many units remained faithful to the oath, but refused to take action against the rebels.[8]

On this day, almost all military units in Petrograd and its vicinity joined the insurrection, and the insurgents marched to the Tauride Palace in military formation. The palace yard and the massive Ekaterina Hall suddenly became a large military camp. Among other, Nicholas's cousin, Grand Duke Kirill Vladimirovich, led the crew of the Guard's ship to the Tauride Palace and declared his allegiance to the Duma. He was the first member of the royal family to break his oath to the tsar. He read aloud his telegram to all commanders of military units in Tsarskoe Selo. "I and the Guard's ship have joined to support the Provisional Government. I hope you and your units will do the same." But as soon as he retired to Engelhardt's room, he lost all the boldness and majesty of a grand duke and sat gloomily, his

6. Stinton Jones, *Russia in Revolution, Being the Experiences of an English-man in Petrograd during the Upheaval* (London: Herbert Jenkins, 1917), pp. 163-66.

7. For the rebellion of the First Machine Gun Regiment, see A. Tarasov-Rodionov, *February 1917: A Chronicle of the Russian Revolution*, pp. 56-79; Martynov, *Tsarskaia armiia v fevral'skom perevorote*, p. 122; F. I. Matveev, *Iz zapisnoi knizhki deputata 176 pekhotnogo polka* (Moscow and Leningrad, 1932), p. 13.

8. Martynov, *Tsarskaia armiia v fevral'skom perevorote*, p. 122; Burdzhalov, *Vtoraia russkaia revoliutsiia*, pp. 256-57.

face pinched. He muttered, "I was their chief, and I had to follow them."[9]

Workers on the outskirts of Petrograd also responded to the insurrection in the city. In the Sestroretsk Weapons Factory in Sestroretsk, a resort area along the Gulf of Finland fifty miles north of Petrograd, workers abandoned posts and held a meeting. They took over the factory, elected two Bolshevik delegates to the Petrograd Soviet, and created a militia and a food supply commission. The weapons they seized from the factory were handed over to the workers in Petrograd. Also on February 28, workers of Schlüsselburg Gunpowder Factory, joined by others from small mills, attacked Schlüsselburg Fortress, notorious as the prison for political prisoners since the Decembrists were incarcerated there, and freed all the political prisoners.[10]

The crowds celebrated their victory by knocking off the Romanov's coat of arms—the double eagle—from buildings and palaces. On the second day of the insurrection, the Circuit Court and the massive Aleksandr-Nevskii Police Station were still burning, sending up dark clouds to the sunny sky. Automobiles and trucks full of soldiers careened about the city. Soldiers wore red armbands around the sleeves of their overcoats and some carried machine-gun cartridges around their shoulders. A gymnasium student was walking along the Fontanka, and noticed black smoke curling up from one house at the Fontanka and Gorstkina. Masses of papers and ashes were thrown from windows of the second floor, and then books, other papers, boxes, and finally furniture flew from the windows to the crowds tending a bonfire in the streets below. It was the apartment of Police Chief Zariutskii. A young soldier with a red armband approached on a horse and was surrounded and questioned by the crowd. He told them that Shcheglovitov and Protopopov were arrested and someone asked about Khabalov. The soldier answered somewhat sullenly that it was not soldiers' business to arrest the military. In speaking to the crowd, the young soldier called everyone "comrade"—the revolution was creating new manners among the insurgents. Near Nikol'skii Lane, several drunken soldiers were trying to break into wine cellars. Soldiers guarding the building barred the entrance, but brought a couple of bottles from the cellar before chasing them away. A truck passed by full of soldiers holding a carcass of a calf and some geese.[11]

Faced with the new wave of revolution, the Duma Committee found itself compelled to accommodate itself to the mood of the

9. OR GBL, d. 218, B. A. Engel'gardt, "Potonuvshii mir," l. 112.

10. V. A. Tsybul'skii, "Rabochie Sestroretskogo zavoda v 1917 g.," Istoriia SSSR, no. 4 (1957), pp. 143-44; Burdzhalov, Vtoraia russkaia revoliutsiia, p. 258.

11. TsGIA, f. 1101, op. 1, d. 1195, ll. 5-6.

masses, first timidly, but later more boldly, to forestall further deterioration into anarchy. The first revolutionary step of the Duma Committee began inadvertently and accidentally. The insurgents spontaneously and without the sanction of any organization started arresting supporters of the old regime, ranging from former tsarist ministers and generals to petty police officers. While other Duma Committee members hesitated, Kerenskii personally sanctioned these arbitrary acts in the name of revolutionary justice. The first to be arrested was the former minister of justice and the present president of the State Council, Shcheglovitov. Legally, any member of the State Council or of the Duma enjoyed personal immunity and some members of the Duma Committee urged Rodzianko to have him released. Rodzianko went to the prisoner held in custody by the agitated crowd, and amid the protests of the insurgents amicably invited him into his office as a guest. Kerenskii rushed to the scene and said to Rodzianko, "No, Shcheglovitov is not a guest and I refuse to have him released." Declaring that he was under arrest and that his safety would be guaranteed, Kerenskii led the prisoner to the Ministerial Pavilion, the luxurious chambers that had been used by the tsarist ministers. Shul'gin ironically remarked: *"Ecclesia abhoret sanguinem.* Thus spoke the father-inquisitors, while burning their victims. . . . Likewise, while burning Russians on the altar of 'freedom,' Kerenskii declared: 'The Duma does not shed blood.'"[12] During the day Sukhomlinov, Stürmer, Dobrovol'skii (minister of justice), Kriger-Voinovskii (minister of transport), Klimovich (former director of the police department), and others were brought to the Tauride Palace and ushered into the luxurious prison.

Hiding in the servants' quarters of the State Controller's Office, Protopopov learned from a newspaper that insurgents were conducting a door-to-door search for former ministers. Panicked, the " former" minister of internal affairs immediately abandoned his hideout, walked straight to the Tauride Palace, and announced at its doorstep to student who happened to be there that Protopopov had decided to turn himself in. The news created an immediate sensation among the crowds in the palace. Protopopov was immediately surrounded, and would have been lynched brutally had it not been Kerenskii, who rushed to the scene, ordered everyone in his high-pitched voice not to touch Protopopov, declared that he was under arrest, and ushered him safely to the Ministerial Pavilion.[13] As the number arrested in-

12. Alexander Kerensky, *Russia and History's Turning Point,* pp. 197-98; Shul'gin, *Dni,* p. 171.

13. TsGAOR, f. ChSK, d. 466, ℓ. 181; *Izvestiia revoliutsionnoi nedeli,* February 28, 1917.

creased, the other members of the Duma Committee accepted and even appreciated Kerenskii's initiative, officially entrusting him with the management of the Ministerial Pavilion. To prevent arbitrary arrests, the Duma Committee declared that none should be made without written permission from the Duma Committee. On March 1, M. Karaulov, commissar dispatched to the Ministry of Justice, issued a guideline on who was to be arrested. Despite these efforts, the crowd continued to make arbitrary arrests. To house the numbers in custody, the Duma Committee had to convert the Historical-Philological Institute at Petrograd University, the *gradonachal'stvo,* and six other buildings into temporary prisons.[14] With the exception of the former ministers and police officers, a majority of the arrested were released as soon as the arresting insurgents had left the buildings.

The Duma Committee took other measures that bore a revolutionary character in the sense that they directly aimed at the removal of the old regime, although they were designed to blunt the edge of the revolutionary movement of the masses. On the night of February 27, Bublikov urged the members of the Duma Committee to occupy the Ministry of Transport to control the railway network and telegraphic communications along the railway. Rodzianko first opposed this measure, but early on the morning of February 28, finally gave Bublikov approval for takeover of the Ministry of Transport, at the same time making state funds available for the operation.[15]

Supported by a detachment of fifty soldiers and two trucks furnished by the Military Commission, Bublikov marched into the Ministry of Transport and declared occupation of the ministry by the Duma Committee. He placed all the officials under arrest, including the minister of transport, Kriger-Voinovskii, who refused to pledge allegiance to the Duma Committee, and sent them to the Ministerial Pavilion in the Tauride Palace. The first vice-minister, General Kisliakov, and the second vice-minister, Kozylev, although they were staunch monarchists, decided to cooperate with Bublikov.[16]

Bublikov's first act was to dispatch a telegram to all railway stations

14. TsGAOR, f. 3348, op. 1, d. 129, ℓ. 15; *Izvestiia revoliutsionnoi nedeli,* February 28, March 1, 1917; TsGIA, f. 1278, op. 10, d. 3, ℓ. 70.

15. A. A. Bublikov, *Russkaia revoliutsiia: Vpechatleniia i mysli ochevidtsa i uchastnika,* pp. 20-21; TsGIA, f. 1278, op. 10, d. 3, ℓ. 1.

16. Bublikov, *Russkaia revoliutsiia,* pp. 21-22; "Fevral'skaia revoliutsiia v Petrograde (28 fevralia-1 marta 1917 g.), " *Krasnyi arkhiv,* 41/42, no. 4/5 (1930): 88; A. I. Spiridovich, *Velikaia voina i fevral'skaia revoliutsiia 1914-1917 gg.* 3: 240-41.

in Russia informing them of the revolution in Petrograd. The text, issued in the name of Rodzianko, read:

Railroad workers! The old regime, which created chaos in all aspects of state affairs, has proved powerless. The State Duma took the formation of a new government into its own hands. I appeal to you in the name of the fatherland that it now depends on you to save our native land, that it expects from you more than fulfillment of your duties, and that it expects sacrifices from you. The movement of trains must be carried on without interruption and with doubled energy. Technical weaknesses and insufficiencies must be offset by your selfless energy, love for your native land, and your awareness of the importance of transport for the war and the welfare of the rear.[17]

This announcement was the first nation-wide statement of the Duma Committee that told of the transfer of power. Bublikov's telegram certainly overstated the authority of the Duma Committee, for far from having taken power, it actually held control of no more than the following: the telegraph system, the Petrograd water station, the electrical station, tramways, railways, the State Bank, and all governmental and administrative institutions. The attitude of the two crucial groups, the workers and the soldiers, on whose allegiance the strength of a new government would depend, remained yet unknown. Nevertheless, the impact of Bublikov's telegram was far-reaching. Every single railway station in Russia, "from the front of the war to Vladivostok, from Murmansk to the Persian border," received this news and spread it to the people. All Russia now accepted the revolution as an accomplished fact. "After this the abdication of Nicholas II and Mikhail," Bublikov's assistant, Professor Iu. Lomonosov, wrote, "seemed only a secondary formality. From Bublikov's telegram all knew that by February 28 power was actually in the hands of the Duma."[18] The telegram was calculated to appease those, particularly the military leaders, who feared the destructive elements of the revolution. It assured them that power was now in responsible hands. Bublikov's telegram thus became one of the important factors behind the change of attitude of the military leaders.[19]

The intention of the Duma Committee in sending Bublikov's tele-

17. "Fevral'skaia revoliutsiia 1917 goda," *Krasnyi arkhiv* 21, no. 2 (1927): 32-33. The original draft of this appeal prepared by Bublikov had begun with the phrase: "The old regime has fallen." But, met with Rodzianko's strong objections, Bublikov had to soften the tone. For the Duma Committee's attempts to maintain the normal function of the railway movement see also TsGIA, f. 1278, op. 10, d. 3, ℓℓ. 7-8.

18. Iu. Lomonosov, *Vospominaniia o martovskoi revoliutsii 1917 g.*, p. 27. Only the director of the Southern Line did not immediately inform the railway workers of this telegram.

19. See chap. 24.

gram can be made clear by its subsequent circular telegram to the commanders of all fronts and to the Stavka. Rodzianko informed them that the resignation of the cabinet ministers compelled the Duma Committee to assume power and assured them that no change in external or internal policy would be effected. The telegram continued, "The Duma Committee in cooperation with the military units and the population in the capital will in the immediate future restore peace in the rear and resume the normal activity of governmental institutions."[20] A difference in emphasis between Bublikov's public announcement and Rodzianko's classified telegram to the military leaders illustrated the predicament of the Duma Committee in trying to steer through the narrow passage between the two conflicting forces.

The decision to take over the Ministry of Transport was followed by a series of appointments of commissars to other administrative machinery of the tsarist regime. The Duma Committee's commissars, mainly Kadets, Octobrists, and Progressists, were dispatched to the Ministries of Internal Affairs, Army, Navy, Agriculture, Justice, Trade and Industry, Finance, Education, and such offices as the State Controller, Government Printing Office, Organization for the Wounded and Sick, Petrograd *gradonachal'stvo,* Post and Telegraph, Special Council for Food Supplies, Director of Imperial Theaters, Red Cross, and others.[21] With the exception of a few staunch monarchists, most of the bureaucrats accepted the authority of the Duma Committee, some even with enthusiasm. Continuity of government functions was thus assured.

The success of the Duma Committee's policy depended on whether it could control the insurgents, and for that the Duma Committee decided on two decisive measures: to take over the Military Commission organized by the Petrograd Soviet and to appeal directly to soldiers and officers to restore order.

Those who sought refuge in the Duma were not only soldiers who had mutinied, but also officers who had fled from their units for fear of attack by soldiers. Those officers assembled in Room 1B, office of the journal *Narod i armiia.* To them as well as to the members of the Duma Committee, the presence of the aimless insurgent soldiers in the Tauride Palace was dangerous.[22] No sooner had the Duma

20. *Protokoly sobytii,* p. 14, quoted in Burdzhalov, *Vtoraia russkaia revoliutsiia,* p. 238.

21. TsGIA, f. 1278, op. 10, d. 3, ℓℓ. 4, 9, 11, 13, 18, 22, 37, 38, 42, 48, 49, 51, 54, 55, 60, 62; *Izvestiia revoliutsionnoi nedeli,* March 1, 1917. For some reason no commissar was appointed to the Ministry of Foreign Affairs.

22. TsGIA, f. 1278, op. 10, d. 19, ℓ. 78.

Committee decided to take power than it began the task of organizing the insurgent soldiers. Interestingly, it chose to take over the Military Commission that had been created by the Petrograd Soviet rather than form a separate organization. Around two o'clock on the morning of February 28, Rodzianko and Colonel Engelhardt, whom the Duma Committee had just appointed commander of the Military Commission, appeared in Room 42, the headquarters of the Petrograd Soviet's Military Commission. Rodzianko announced to those present that the Duma Committee placed the functions of the Military Commission under its authority. Sokolov, whom the Soviet Executive Committee had elected as liaison between the Petrograd Soviet and the Military Commission, strongly protested the Duma Committee's arbitrary decision. "What is important now," he stated, "is not to restore order, but to destroy Khabalov and Protopopov." The Military Commission needed the revolutionaries, not those officers appointed by the Duma Committee. "It is completely inadmissible that the Petrograd Soviet, this Soviet of the revolutionary workers and insurgent soldiers, which is at the present moment the only real force, be completely eliminated from the staff that the very Soviet had created and from the tasks that it had been carrying out." Sokolov did not object to the inclusion of the members appointed by the Duma Committee in the Military Commission, but demanded that the majority of the staff unconditionally belong to the Soviet. Rodzianko's high-handed declaration and Sokolov's vehement rebuttal appeared to signal an inevitable clash between the Duma Committee and the Petrograd Soviet, but the majority of the Soviet representatives in the Military Commission, who knew very well the limitations of their own organization, welcomed the participation of the Duma Committee. Mstislavskii persuaded Sokolov to accept the authority of the Duma Committee, guaranteeing watchful supervision by the revolutionary representatives over the activities of the new Military Commission.[23] Neither the Executive Committee nor the general session of the Petrograd Soviet raised any question about this transfer of authority, a flagrant violation of the resolution passed at the first general session on February 27. Nor did Mstislavskii, appointed by the Petrograd Soviet to head the Military Commission, or Sokolov and Aleksandrovich, whom the Executive Committee had sent to watchdog its activities, report their arbitrary decision to the Soviet. The Executive Committee acquiesced in the Duma Committee's gamble and decided to keep silent on its capitulation lest the insurgents should react to it violently.

23. S. Mstislavskii, *Piat' dnei: Nachalo i konets fevral'skoi revoliutsii*, pp. 29-31; Engel'gardt, "Potonuvshii mir," *l*. 106.

The transfer of authority, however, did not immediately involve a drastic change in the function of the Military Commission, since the newly appointed leaders were compelled to take some measure against the remnants of the old regime and their predecessors of the Petrograd Soviet had also assumed the task of restoring order in the streets. But a subtle change of emphasis did occur with the transfer of leadership. A memorandum submitted to the Military Commission under the Petrograd Soviet suggested the following measures: (1) reassembling the soldiers in the barracks; (2) appointing temporary commanders and junior officers; (3) establishing guards and occupying streets, railway stations, and other important public and state institutions: (4) stopping unnecessary traffic of automobiles; (5) organizing food supply in the barracks; (6) establishing contact between the general food centers and the regimental food network; (7) not leaving the soldiers long in the barracks without attention, guidance, and information from the insurgents; (8) making the Fortress of Peter and Paul a major base for all of Petrograd; (9) making the regimental barracks district bases; and (10) isolating officers who had not joined the insurrection from the barracks and arresting officers with a particularly harmful influence on the soldiers.[24] It is clear from this memorandum that the Military Commission under the Soviet emphasized the organization of revolutionary forces.

On the other hand, the report prepared by the Duma Committee's Military Commission after the February Revolution on its activities during the revolution stressed restoration of order in the streets and harmony between soldiers and officers as its primary function, although it did not discount its role as protector of the revolution. According to this report, the Military Commission, "created at the initiative of the Provisional Committee of the State Duma," in conjunction with the Petrograd Soviet, functioned as the "staff of the revolution." Its main tasks consisted of "restoration, construction, and support of the administrative mechanism," unification of the insurgents with the Provisional Government, security of persons and property, security of national treasures, railways, post, and telegraphs, and the establishment of communications with the army at the front and with Allied governments.[25] The most important difference lay in the question of the relationship between officers and soldiers.

An analysis of the Military Commission's orders issued from February 28 to March 3 indicates that it concerned itself with four tasks:

24. TsGAOR, f. 3348, op. 1, d. 170, ℓℓ. 6-7, quoted in Burdzhalov, *Vtoraia russkai revoliutsiia*, p. 275. My request to use this archival material was refused.
25. TsGIA, f. 1278, op. 10, d. 19, ℓℓ. 3-4.

(1) occupation and protection of strategically important positions and buildings; (2) restoration of military order in army units; (3) disarming the military forces of the old regime, and (4) combating lawlessness in the streets.[26]

The first order of the new leadership was issued at eight o'clock on the morning of February 28 in the name of the commandant of the Tauride Palace, Iurevich, to occupy Tsarskoe Selo Railway Station, the electric power station, the Savings Bank, the Technological Institute and to restore order in the surrounding districts. Ten minutes later, Engelhardt ordered a detachment of Preobrazhenskii Regiment to occupy the State Bank, the telephone station, and to establish guards at the Hermitage and the Museum of Alexander III.[27] The occupation of these strategic positions and places of cultural importance had a double meaning; while it bore a revolutionary character by taking control from the functionaries of the old regime, it was also an attempt to assure normal functioning of these places by preventing the insurgents from effectively extending their influence. In this respect, the occupation and protection of military supply depots and the weapon and cartridge factories had a particular importance— the new leadership of the Military Commission was attempting to keep weapons from the insurgents. Lieutenant Stavin of the First Infantry Regiment, assigned to protect a weapon factory, requested the Military Commission to give him special authorization since "the crowd reacted to him suspiciously." Filippovskii immediately complied with that request.[28]

Another important concern of the Military Commission was reorganization of military forces under the authority of the Duma Committee. Order No. 54 of the Military Commission, for instance, instructed all troops of the Petrograd Garrison, and officers and soldiers of the Officers' Electrotechincal School and Reserve Electrotechnical Battalion to return immediately to their companies and detachments

26. The Military Commission's orders issued on February 28 and March 1, "Fevral'skaia revoliutsiia v Petrograde," pp. 62-102; I used also TsGAOR, f. 3348, d. 129 (Pal'chinskii Papers), and TsGIA, f. 1278, op. 10, dd. 3, 6, 9, 55. The last archival materials include the Military Commission's orders issued from February 28 through March 4.

27. Orders No. 1 and No. 2, "Fevral'skaia revoliutsiia v Petrograde," pp. 78-79. The Military Commission issued similar orders to occupy various strategic positions. See Orders No. 4, 28, 29, 35, 48, "Fevral'skaia revoliutsiia v Petrograde," pp. 79, 84, 85, 88. Also see TsGIA, f. 1278, op. 10, d. 3, ll. 19, 39, 61; TsGIA, f. 1278, op. 10, d. 9, l. 19; TsGAOR, f. 3348, op. 1, d. 129, ll. 1, 2, 9, 10.

28. Report 5 and Order No. 19, "Fevral'skaia revoliutsiia v Petrograde," pp. 64, 82. Also see Reports No. 2, 21, 28, 79, ibid., pp. 64, 67, 69, 76; TsGAOR, f. 3348, d. 129, ll. 2, 6, 11.

for fulfillment of the task to be assigned by the Duma Committee. This order signed by Captain Chikolniki later developed into Rodzianko's famous order, which provoked a violent reaction from the insurgents. The Military Commission also dispatched reliable officers —mostly lower rank ensigns and lieutenants—to various military units to restore order and discipline.[29]

The Military Commission also took measures to remove the resistance of the old regime. Officers of the Second Baltic Fleet's depot troops were ordered to remove and replace the imperial guard at the Winter Palace, occupy the palace, and maintain order on the Nevskii, Moika, and in the Admiralty area. They were ordered to arrest former ministers and other agents of the former government. The Military Commission received numerous reports on machine-gun fire from rooftops and windows of tall buildings—actions, people believed, taken by remnants of the police or by officers still hostile to the insurrection.[30]

Reports on lawlessness—particularly looting of wine cellars and illegal searches of houses of the well-to-do, which always ended in pillaging and looting—were also rampant. Numerous orders signed by the Military Commission or by the Duma Committee to stop such acts indicate the extent of the lawlessness prevailing in the capital. The Military Commission issued an order on February 28 to arrest those found pillaging or looting and announced that persons apprehended would be brought to the military tribunal.[31] But this order remained ineffective because, occupied with tasks of higher priority and suffering from the inadequate military support, the Military Commission actually did little to solve these problems. Since it was impossible to cope with lawlessness in the streets, the Military Commission asked the city duma to create a city militia.[32]

When Engelhardt took over the Military Commission, he brought a host of officers from the General Staff. These officers—Tumanov, Tugan-Baranovskii, Polovtsov, Iakubovich—became the driving force of the commission, and officers with connections with the Socialist parties were pushed to the background. The Soviet representatives in the Military Commission fully cooperated with the new leadership.

29. Order No. 54, "Fevral'skaia revoliutsiia v Petrograde," p. 89. See also Orders No. 3, 10, 11, 29, 32, 55, 62, and 106, in ibid., pp. 79, 80, 81, 85, 89, 91.
30. TsGAOR, f. 3348, op. 1, d. 129, ℓ. 4; Reports No. 2, 6, 8, 17, 70, 71, 73, 80, in "Fevral'skaia revoliutsiia v Petrograde," pp. 63, 64, 65, 67, 75, 77.
31. Reports No. 9, 11, 13, 15, 43, 64; "Fevral'skaia revoliutsiia v Petrograde," pp. 65, 66, 71; TsGIA, f. 1278, op. 10, d. 6, ℓℓ. 2, 9, 11, 12, 16, 18; TsGIA, f. 1278, op. 10, d. 55, ℓ. 2.
32. See below, p. 377.

It was Filippovskii who ordered Lieutenant Stavin to protect weapon factories from the insurgents, who were demanding the surrender of weapons. Also Filippovskii made an automobile available for the future prime minister of the Provisional Government, Prince G. E. L'vov. The Soviet Executive Committee appealed to the soldiers not to disobey the orders of the Military Commission and to cooperate with it for the struggle against the old regime.[33]

In addition to the Military Commission's efforts to organize the military, some members of the Duma Committee personally appealed to soldiers to maintain discipline. Rodzianko, addressing cadets of Mikhailovskii Artillery Military Academy who had arrived at the Tauride Palace, asked them to obey their officers and wait for instructions from the Duma Committee, for "only the unity of the army, the people, and the State Duma will guarantee our strength and power." To the soldiers of Preobrazhenskii Regiment, he declared: "You know better than I do that without officers, soldiers could not exist. I implore you to subject yourselves to the officers and believe them, as we believe them. Return peacefully to your barracks to be ready at the first request to come here when you will be needed." Miliukov also delivered speeches to soldiers gathering in the Tauride Palace, emphasizing that the Duma Committee was the only power. He declared: "There can be no dual power."[34] This term, dual power, which later acquired wide currency during the Russian Revolution, was used for the first time.

The Duma Committee also issued a series of proclamations and orders and appealed to soldiers and officers to restore order and discipline in military units. In the appeal addressed to officers, it urged them not to leave the masses of soldiers without commanders and to receive necessary information and instructions from the Duma Committee. The Military Commission ordered officers of Preobrazhenskii Regiment to appear at the Tauride Palace for instructions.[35] In addition, the Duma Committee and the Military Commission jointly issued an order to all officers in Petrograd to attend a meeting of the army and fleet to be held on March 1 and March 2 "for the purpose of receiving a certificate of all-purpose pass and new registration, for receiving instructions from the [Military] Commission to organize the soldiers who had joined the representatives of the people, and for defense of the capital." The order continued: "It is essential at

33. TsGAOR, f. 6, op. 1, d. 1722, ℓ. 26; Engel'gardt, "Potonuvshii mir," ℓ. 110; Orders No. 19, 72, "Fevral'skaia revoliutsiia v Petrograde," pp. 82, 93; Burdzhalov, *Vtoraia russkaia revoliutsiia,* pp. 291-92.

34. *Izvestiia revoliutsionnoi nedeli,* February 28, 1917.

35. Quoted in Burdzhalov, *Vtoraia russkaia revoliutsiia,* p. 253; TsGAOR, f. 3348, op. 1, d. 129, ℓ. 11.

the present moment to devote all our strength to organization of the military units. The strength of the army and the guarantee of the final victory will depend on this." Another proclamation reiterated the Duma Committee's efforts to restore a normal relationship between officers and soldiers, and appealed to officers to cooperate with the Duma Committee in this difficult task.[36] Officers who had kept a noncommittal neutrality since the outbreak of the insurrection by hiding in officers' quarters or in apartments of their acquaintances, welcomed these appeals of the Duma Committee and the Military Commission.

Nevertheless, these proclamations, received with enthusiasm by the officers, further alienated the insurgent soldiers. With the insurrection the relationship between officers and soldiers was completely broken; many soldiers never returned to their barracks after once abandoning their posts. However, as officers returned and began taking command, the soldiers' fear of retaliation mounted. Since their rebellion was directed against military discipline and the hierarchy as much as against the old regime, returning to barracks and obeying orders of their officers again seemed to reduce their entire action to nothing. A leaflet distributed among insurgent soldiers appealed to them: "Retreat is impossible! Either freedom or death! Don't disperse to the barracks! Don't leave the city! Achieve the participation of all who have not yet joined the struggle in the revolution!"[37] Orders and proclamations issued by the Military Commission and the Duma Committee calling for restoration of orders and discipline in military units aggravated their hostility and their suspicions of these bodies.

Engelhardt and Bublikov were concerned with the soldiers roaming around the streets. They believed that the Duma Committee should recall them to their barracks and place them under their commanding officers. They jointly composed an order to all officers and soldiers and issued it in the name of Rodzianko: (1) all the individual soldiers and all military units should return to their barracks immediately; (2) all officers should return to their units and take necessary measures to restore order; and (3) commanders of units should appear at the Tauride Palace at eleven o'clock in the morning of March 1 to receive further instructions.[38] Rodzianko's order clearly intended to restore

36. Quoted in Burdzhalov, *Vtoraia russkaia revoliutsiia*, pp. 253-54; *Izvestiia revoliutsionnoi nedeli*, February 28, 1917.

37. Quoted in Burdzhalov, *Vtoraia russkaia revoliutsiia*, p. 243.

38. Engel'gardt, "Potonuvshii mir," ℓℓ. 106-7; M. G. Rafes, "Moi vospominaniia," *Byloe* 19 (1922): 193; N. N. Sukhanov, *Zapiski o revoliutsii* 1: 207.

order and discipline in the military units under the authority of the old commanding officers, and, although not specifically mentioned, it implied surrender of weapons to the officers. As we shall see later, this order provoked a violent reaction not only among the soldiers but also among the workers, and drove the insurgents decisively to the side of the Petrograd Soviet.[39]

While heading the Military Commission, Engelhardt clearly saw that its operation under the constant influence of the Petrograd Soviet would eventually conflict with the authority of the War Ministry to be organized by the future Provisional Government. Therefore, he suggested the amalgamation of the Military Commission with the War Ministry. For the first step in this direction, he offered his resignation and suggested that the Military Commission be headed by Guchkov, already the unanimous candidate for the post of war minister in the Provisional Government.[40] Thus, late at night on February 28, Guchkov took over. The appointment of Guchkov, who had a large number of acquaintances among the military establishment and enjoyed undisputed authority over military matters, enhanced the authority of the Military Commission in its relations with the officers; but his strong view on military discipline and his undisguised hostility to the insurgents' demands earned the hatred of the masses of soldiers. Guchkov drove around the city from one regimental barracks to another in an effort to organize a new military force strong enough to counter both the crowds in the streets and counterrevolutionary forces. He managed to incorporate the military establishment of the imperial army in Petrograd under his authority. Zankevich, for instance, who had been a commander of loyal forces only a day before and who had narrowly escaped arrest in the Admiralty, was now asked by Guchkov to stay on as head of the General Staff for the Military Commission. This policy, however, had its price. While driving in the city, Guchkov was shot at by a sniper, a shot that narrowly missed Guchkov, but instantly killed his trusted aide, Prince D. M. Viazemskii.[41]

As the tsarist police system was completely annihilated and lawlessness reigned in the city, the creation of some kind of police force by the Duma Committee was an urgent necessity. The Military Commission alone could not do it, since it had to devote itself to assignments of higher priority. Yet any delay in organization of a police force could not be tolerated, since the Duma Committee's rival, the

39. See chap. 20.
40. Engel'gardt, "Potonuvshii mir," &. 114.
41. Burdzhalov, *Vtoraia russkaia revoliutsiia*, pp. 277-78.

Petrograd Soviet, had already taken the initiative of forming a workers' militia. If the Petrograd Soviet succeeded in establishing effective control over police power, it would gravely undercut the authority of the Duma Committee.

On February 28, the Duma Committee dismissed Major-General Balk as the Petrograd *gradonachal'nik* and appointed Professor V. Iurevich of the Military Medical Academy as his successor. To signify the break with the past, the new office was renamed society's *(obshchestvennyi) gradonachal'nik*, the task of which, Iurevich declared, was to "insure the personal safety of citizens and of their property," and to establish committees for "security of order and food for citizens."[42] It turned out to be impossible, however, to establish a militia on the basis of the administrative structure of the *gradonachal'stvo*, which had become completely disrupted by destruction of the police. Iurevich had to entrust D. A. Kryzhanovskii, a member of the city duma and an architect, with this task. Thus the responsibility of creating a militia was transferred from the *gradonachal'nik* to the city duma, which decided on a city militia "in the interest of assuring the life and property of the population," at an emergency meeting held on the evening of February 28. This meeting confirmed the appointment of Kryzhanovskii as head of the city militia and approved appropriations from the city budget for its expenses. At the same time, the city duma appointed district representatives to initiate creation of a city militia and designated specific location for district headquarters. Most of the district representatives were selected from the city duma members, but for the Vyborg District two students of the Military Medical Academy, V. G. Botsvadze and a certain Shvakhtsaboi, together with two city duma members, received authorization—a recognition that the city duma members alone could not carry much influence in the workers' section.[43] Responding to the appeal of the city duma, many educational and technical institutions supported the creation of a city militia. Establishing its headquarters in the newly elected mayor's office, the city militia created the initial contingent of a police force composed mainly of civil servants and university and high school students.

42. *Izvestiia revoliutsionnoi nedeli,* February 28, 1917; TsGIA, f. 1278, op. 10, d. 3, ℓ. 24. For detailed analysis of the formation of the militia organizations during the February Revolution, see Tsuyoshi Hasegawa, "The Formation of the Militia in the February Revolution: An Analysis of the Origins of the Dual Power," *Slavic Review* 32, no. 2 (1973): 303-22.

43. Hasegawa, "The Formation of the Militia in the February Revolution," pp. 305-6; Z. Kel'son, "Militsiia fevral'skoi revoliutsii: Vospominaniia," *Byloe* 29, no. 1 (1925): 162.

By March 1, thus, two centers of militia came into existence in Petrograd, one organized by the Petrograd Soviet and the other by the city duma in close cooperation with the Duma Committee. Both authorities, however, envisaged the militia as a police power designed to restore order in the streets. It was only after the intervention of the insurgent workers in the creation of the militia organizations that conflicting goals split the militia in Petrograd into two separate organizations—the city militia and the workers' militia. The tripartite relationship among these two militia organizations and the Petrograd Soviet vividly illustrated in microcosm the complexities of the power play during the February Revolution.[44]

In addition to the organization of the city militia, the city duma closely cooperated with the Duma Committee in the matter of supplying food. The Duma Committee had on February 27 sent its delegates, Shingarev and S. Vostorgin, to the Food Supply Commission created by the Petrograd Soviet. Compared with the Duma Committee's similar approach to the Military Commission, the takeover of the Food Supply Commission went smoothly because of the extreme willingness of the Soviet members to cooperate with Duma delegates. On February 28 "the Food Commission of the Soviet of Workers' Deputies and the Executive Committee of the State Duma" announced that it had assumed the central leadership of all food supply matters. It decided to introduce a ration system for bread and to reorganize the distribution network. On March 1, the entire matter of food in Petrograd was now transferred to the City Duma Food Supply Commission.[45]

On the first day of its existence the Duma Committee took some important steps in the name of revolution to put a brake on the revolutionary process. Engelhardt commented, "We accepted the revolution as an accomplished fact and for three days we looked as though we were leading it. But actually we dragged ourselves along behind events, while making at the same time hopeless attempts to arrest its development."[46] But the Duma Committee failed to capture the support of most of the insurgents, since its ultimate goal of restoration of order did not correspond to their wishes and aspirations. To mobilize the support of the masses, therefore, the Duma Committee had to rely on other methods.

44. Hasegawa, "The Formation of the Militia in the February Revolution," pp. 303-22.
    45. *Izvestiia*, March 1, 1917, March 2, 1917; P. V. Volobuev, *Ekonomicheskaia politika vremennogo pravitel'stva*, p. 390.
    46. Engel'gardt, "Potonuvshii mir," *l*. 108.

20

THE PETROGRAD SOVIET
AND THE MASSES

 The insurgents responded with enthusiasm to the Petrograd Soviet's call for election of deputies to the Soviet. Their overwhelming support quickly changed the nature of the Soviet from what the leaders had originally envisaged. It was becoming a central organ of the insurrection, through which the masses of insurgents freely expressed their opinions and by virtue of this support the Soviet unexpectedly acquired authority in Petrograd that no other political group matched. When the masses carried their leaders on this buoyant upsurge, the original initiators of the Soviet began to feel frightened by their own creation. The masses who had come to rally behind the Soviet might push them to the forefront of power, which they were neither prepared for nor capable of assuming. The Soviet leaders thus began looking for an escape from this predicament. Their willingness to cooperate with the Duma Committee, even abandoning authority already established, was their first step in solving this difficulty.

On February 28 *Izvestiia* printed the first proclamation of the Petrograd Soviet to the populace of Petrograd and all Russia. After noting that the old regime "led the country to complete chaos and the people to hunger," the proclamation urged a final struggle against autocracy, which "must be overthrown once and for all." It announced the creation of the Petrograd Soviet, which had taken upon itself the struggle for political freedom, the formation of a people's government, and the organization of the people as its main objectives. Emphasizing the importance of establishing a government based on the will of the people, the proclamation called for the convocation of a

"Constituent Assembly elected on the basis of universal, secret, equal, and direct suffrage."[1] The importance of this document consisted in what it did not mention rather than what it actually did state. It skirted around all the important questions that would inevitably confront postrevolutionary Russia. The problems of land and peace, on which the views of the Soviet leaders irreconciliably differed, were totally ignored. More importantly, the proclamation was silent on the problem of power. Stressing the importance of establishing a government based on the will of the people, it did not specifically mention how such a government should be formed. Although it urged the convocation of a constituent assembly, it failed to explain who should take power in the meantime. It did announce the creation of the Soviet, but it remained completely silent as to the part that this organ should play. The document reflected the ambiguous position the Executive Committee took on the matter of power. Yet intensification of the revolutionary movement from below on February 28 and March 1 compelled the Executive Committee to take a definite position on this problem.

The election of Soviet delegates in major factories and military units began on February 28. Although complete lists of the factories and military units that conducted the election and the breakdown of the party affiliations of the elected delegates do not exist, it is clear that the Mensheviks and the SRs composed a majority.[2] With the exception of Rosenkrantz and New Lessner, the Bolsheviks did not do well even in the factories where they had built their strengths during the war. For instance, they managed to gain fewer than ten out of forty delegates in the election of the Putilov Factory held on March 1. The radical Socialists combined (Bolsheviks, SR Maximalists, and Mezhraiontsy) won less than 10 percent of the total of nearly six hundred deputies.[3]

1. *Izvestiia*, February 28, 1917.

2. For a list of factories that held elections on February 28 and March 1, see G. I. Zlokazov, *Petrogradskii Sovet rabochikh i soldatskikh deputatov v period mirnogo razvitiia revoliutsii*, pp. 38-40; E. N. Burdzhalov, *Vtoraia russkaia revoliutsiia: Vosstanie v Petrograde*, p. 223; I. P. Leiberov, *Petrogradskii proletariat v Fevral'skoi revoliutsii* 2: 509-11; Wada Haruki, "Nigatsu kakumei," *Roshia kakumei no kenkyu*, ed. Eguchi Bokuro, pp. 441-42.

3. S. A. Artem'ev, "Sostav Petrogradskogo Soveta v marte 1917 g.," *Istoriia SSSR*, no. 5 (1964), p. 126; G. I. Zlokazov, "Sozdanie Petrogradskogo Soveta," *Istoriia SSSR*, no. 5 (1964), pp. 106-8; Wada, "Nigatsu kakumei," pp. 441-42. Ozno-bishin lists only thirty-eight Bolsheviks in the first days of the Soviet. P. V. Oznobishin, "Bor'ba bol'shevikov s soglashateliami v Petrogradskom Sovete, mart, 1917 g.," *Istoricheskie zapiski*, no. 73 (1963), p. 113. Leiberov adds another ten to Ozno-bishin's list. Leiberov, *Petrogradskii proletariat v Fevral'skoi revoliutsii* 2: 509-11.

This indicated that although Bolsheviks and Mezhraiontsy had a strong base in the underground revolutionary movement, they did not command great influence in the broader section of workers and soldiers who had suddenly plunged into political life. Particularly, the inclusion of nonfactory workers such as city and hospital employees, druggists, cab drivers, teachers, and so on, in the composition of the Soviet as well as the predominance of soldiers over workers with a ratio of 2.3 to 1 contributed to the relative weakness of the extreme Left in the Soviet.[4] The people who supported the Soviet had divergent expectations as to what function the Soviet should fulfill. While workers in Stetinin Factory called the Petrograd Soviet a provisional revolutionary government, the workers of Petrograd Cartridge Factory referred to it as the temporary workers' committee in the State Duma. Workers of Northern Weaving instructed their delegate to convey these instructions to the Soviet: "The war should be carried out to the end, if we cannot come to an agreement with the German people. The form of the political system should be a democratic republic. The actions agreed upon between the Soviet of Workers' Deputies and the committee elected from the State Duma are desirable."[5] The instructions that accompanied the elections of the Soviet deputies at the Pipe Factory referred to "the danger of the actions of those who insist on the Provisional Government." Although Leiberov takes this to mean a criticism of Menshevik leadership in the Executive Committee, it is possible to argue that the criticism was leveled against the Bolsheviks and the Mezhraiontsy, who advocated the establishment of a provisional revolutionary government. The instructions criticized Kerenskii for calling for the subordination of soldiers to the officers. "Since the soldiers are not yet sufficiently [politically] conscious, they should have contact with the workers." The most urgent task was the "necessity of organizational unity of the proletariat," and for that purpose "it was necessary to elect deputies to the Petrograd Soviet, factory committees, and residents' committees." But the instructions stated that the workers should "not at this moment revolt against other classes of the population."[6]

4. For the various arguments by Soviet historians as to why the Bolsheviks did not gain a majority in the Soviet, see Artem'ev, "Sostav Petrogradskogo Soveta," pp. 116-28; Zlokazov, "Sozdanie Petrogradskogo Soveta," pp. 109-11; idem, *Petrogradskii Sovet*, pp. 35-36; Burdzhalov, *Vtoraia russkaia revoliutsiia*, pp. 223-25. The First Don Cossack Regiment sent its delegates in the ratio of one out of every eighty to ninety soldiers. Oznobishin, "Bor'ba bol'shevikov," p. 113.

5. Zlokazov, *Petrogradskii Sovet*, p. 39; Burdzhalov, *Vtoraia russkaia revoliutsii*, pp. 223-25; Leiberov, *Petrogradskii proletariat v Fevral'skoi revoliutsii* 2: 511.

6. Leiberov, *Petrogradskii proletariat v Fevral'skoi revoliutsii* 2: 515-16.

It appears, therefore, that the Soviet delegates consisted of insurgents with divergences of political opinions ranging from the radical Marxian socialism of committed revolutionaries to the political unsophistication of people thrown into the center of political movement overnight. Yet the Soviet provided a focal point for their political activities. Although during the February Revolution the political opinions of the Petrograd masses had not crystallized into a definite, consistent program for radical action, their latent radicalism clearly manifested itself on a number of occasions. In the course of the further development of events in 1917, disillusionment with the speed and the contents of changes in postrevolutionary society, magnified by their newly acquired sense of freedom and constant exposure to propaganda from the radical Left, caused this radicalism to build into explosive political action against all authority.

The workers' enthusiastic reaction to the Soviet's appeal to create a militia intensified the confusion of the revolutionary power play. As has been seen before, the Soviet as well as the Duma Committee envisioned the role of the militia as the restoration of order.[7] The insurgent workers defiantly challenged this consensus in creating the workers' militia, emphasizing its role as the instrument of furthering the revolutionary process and of establishing the workers' self-government. Even before the Soviet's decision, the workers had taken the initiative to form a workers' militia. As early as February 25 the factory committee in the Putilov Factory passed a resolution calling for the formation of a detachment of armed workers (boevaia druzhina) to "establish order and disarm the police in the Narva District." On February 27 at least three cases are recorded where insurgent workers attempted to create a militia, and in two cases out of these three the militia resulted directly from the workers' struggle against the police.[8] This militant desire to destroy the old order and to establish autonomy underscored the primary purpose of the workers' militia hereafter, a purpose far more important in their minds than the mere restoration of order and the struggle against lawlessness and anarchy.

The Petrograd Soviet's decision served as a catalyst that directed vaguely existing desires of the workers into definite action. On February 28 and March 1 the workers' militia was organized in various districts of Petrograd.[9] The formation of a militia in the Vyborg

7. See chaps. 17 and 19.

8. I. P. Leiberov, "Petrogradskii proletariat vo vseobshchei politicheskoi stachke 25 fevralia 1917 g.," Oktiabr' i grazhdanskaia voina v SSSR: Sbornik statei, p. 39; V. I. Startsev, Ocherki po istorii Petrogradskoi Krasnoi gvardii i rabochei militsii, pp. 43-44.

9. For a detailed discussion of the formation of the militia, see Tsuyoshi Hase-

District was already reported at the second session of the Soviet on February 28, although it began to take definite shape only on March 1 with the participation of workers from major factories. The militia organized by about 250 workers of Rosenkrantz absorbed similar militia organizations formed in the neighboring factories—Petrograd Metal, the Arsenal, Phoenix, and others—and established the First Vyborg Subdistrict Commissariat, appointing V. G. Botsvadze, dispatched by the city duma, as the first commissar.[10] Botsvadze had gained great popularity and trust among the workers because he had participated with them in attacks on Kresty Prison and the House of Detention on February 27. Since the rest of the representatives appointed by the city duma quickly lost their effectiveness, one can safely assume that Botsvadze's appointment as commissar stemmed from his ability to identify with the workers rather than from the authority of the city duma. Later, however, as the conflict between the workers' militia and the city militia sharpened, the presidium of the commissariat dismissed Botzvadze.[11]

Also on March 1 major factories in the Second Vyborg Subdistrict along Sampsonievskii Prospekt organized militia. In New Lessner about 50 workers registered, and the militia immediately engaged in patrols in neighboring streets; in Old Lessner the militia, joined by more than 250 workers, occupied Sampsonievskii Bridge and adjoining streets. These militia organizations merged with others formed in such major factories as New and Old Parviainen, Erikson, Aivaz, and created the Second Vyborg Subdistrict Commissariat. It is reported that some soldiers from the Reserve Battalion of the Moscow Regiment and the First Machine Gun Regiment joined the workers' militia in this subdistrict.[12] A workers' militia was organized in Porokhovye District north of Okhta and Vyborg District outside the city limits, where two large gunpowder factories were located. On

gawa, "The Formation of the Militia in the February Revolution," *Slavic Review* 32, no. 2 (1973): 303-22. The passages from p. 382 to the first paragraph of p. 390 are taken from my article, pp. 307-14, with slight revisions, with the permission of *Slavic Review*.

10. Zlokazov, "O zasedanii Petrogradskogo Soveta rabochikh i soldatskikh deputatov," in *Oktiabr' i grazhdanskaia voina v SSSR: Sbornik statei*, p. 50; Startsev, *Ocherki po istorii Petrogradskoi Krasnoi gvardii i rabochei militsii*, pp. 43-44; Z. Kel'son, "Militsiia fevral'skoi revoliutsii: Vospominaniia," *Byloe* 29 (1925): 175.

11. Kel'son, "Militsiia fevral'skoi revoliutsii," p. 175; Startsev, *Ocherki po istorii Petrogradskoi Krasnoi gvardii*, p. 56.

12. Startsev, *Ocherki po istorii Petrogradskoi Krasnoi gvardii*, p. 44. The formation of a militia in the factories Aivaz and Old Parviainen was reported in *Izvestiia*, March 2, 1917.

February 28 the workers of these factories formed the Executive Commission of the district soviet, which organized the militia, "immediately occupying the posts of paralyzed local power, disarming police, factory officials, and removing sentinel posts."[13]

The workers completely controlled the militia organizations in Vyborg District but on Vasilievskii Island the workers' militia co-existed with the city militia. On February 28 the Military Commission of the Duma Committee appointed Professor V. V. Nikitin of the Mining Institute to organize a militia on Vasilievskii Island "for the restoration and the maintenance of order."[14] Whether Professor Nikitin's influence had a direct bearing or not, the students of the Mining Institute formed an organizational committee composed of fifteen students and three professors at a general meeting held on February 28. This committee formed a militia among other specifically designated commissions. Although its chairman expressed a wish to keep contact with the Petrograd Soviet, it appears likely that this militia was absorbed into the city militia, which established the First Vasilievskii Commissariat under its head, Judge Drozdov. This commissariat restored order in the area along Bol'shoi Prospekt and regularly dispatched patrols, each composed of ten soldiers under the leadership of one student. In three other subdistricts, however, the workers' militia took the upper hand.[15] In the second Vasilievskii Subdistrict, where large factories were concentrated, the militia organized by the workers of the large plants—the Pipe Factory, Siemens-Haliske, Vasilievskii Railway Cars, Possel', and others—occupied the police station on Line Five and established the commissariat there. A Bolshevik, Sergeev, became the first commissar.[16] Although the workers' militia controlled the Third Vasilievskii Subdistrict as well, with an SR student named Medvedskii as it first commissar, its strength appears to have been less than its counterparts in the Second and Fourth Subdistricts. The Cable Factory constituted the major force in the militia organization in the Fourth Vasilievskii Subdistrict, also known as the Harbor Subdistrict. The workers of this factory selected militia members at a general meeting held on March 1 and passed a resolution demanding that the Petrograd Soviet transfer weapons to the district

13. *Raionnye sovety Petrograda v 1917 godu* (Moscow, 1966) 3: 180-81.

14. "Fevral'skaia revoliutsiia v Petrograde," p. 96.

15. *Izvestiia*, March 1, 1917; Startsev, *Ocherki po istorii Petrogradskoi Krasnoi gvardii*, p. 43; *Raionnye sovety Petrograda* 1: 365; *Izvestiia*, March 3, 1917. It is significant that *Izvestiia* elected to describe the formation of the city militia and totally ignored the workers' militia in Vasilievskii Island.

16. Startsev, *Ocherki po istorii Petrogradskoi Krasnoi gvardii*, p. 45.

soviet.[17] The workers' militia on Vasilievskii Island worked in close cooperation with the Vasilievskii District Soviet, which appointed an SR member, Alekseev, chief of its Military Commission. The coexistence of the workers' militia and the city militia inevitably led to friction. Under the pressure of the workers' militia, the Executive Commission of the District Soviet established a supervisory commission specifically to watchdog the activities of the city militia in the first subdistrict.[18]

The situation was even more complicated in the Petrograd District, where not only the workers' militia and the city militia but also the militia organized by the commissar appointed by the Soviet Executive Committee competed with one another. The machinists of Langenzippen Machine Factory constituted the nucleus of the workers' militia in this district, but its strength hardly matched the two competing organizations. The workers' militia here failed even to create an independent commissariat. At first it established a militia center at Number 15 Oranienbaum Street, but soon the Second Petrograd Subdistrict Commissariat of the city militia moved in, establishing its headquarters there. Having lost its center, the workers' militia decided on a commissariat and moved into one room of Number 18 Bol'shaia Beloozerskaia Street, where the First Petrograd Subdistrict Commissariat of the city militia, and its All-District Commissariat, had established their headquarters.[19] The transfer of the office of the workers' militia to the headquarters of the city militia strongly indicates that either it completely merged with the city militia or at least it maintained very close cooperation with it.

Neither the workers' nor the city militia, however, had great influence in Petrograd District. These two militias were eventually absorbed into the commissariat organized by A. V. Peshekhonov, the commissar appointed by the Soviet Executive Committee. Peshekhonov, a member of the Popular Socialist party as well as a member of the Soviet Executive Committee and of its Literary Commission, represented the right wing of the Executive Committee. When he accepted the appointment as commissar of Petrograd District on February 28, he sought to obtain authority from the Duma Committee as well. But Duma Committee leader Miliukov refused this authorization for, according to Peshekhonov, the Duma Committee had not come to grips with the importance of extending its authority to the

17. *Revoliutsionnoe dvizhenie v Rossii posle sverzheniia samoderzhaviia* (Moscow, 1957), pp. 455-56.

18. *Raionnye sovety Petrograde* 1: 73.

19. Startsev, *Ocherki po istorii Petrogradskoi Krasnoi gvardii*, p. 44.

local level.[20] It is unlikely that Miliukov failed to appreciate this problem; in fact, he was keenly aware of the dangers of dual power.[21] His refusal stemmed not from his ignorance but from his determined efforts not to support the authority of the Petrograd Soviet.

After establishing his headquarters in a movie theater, the Elite, at the corner of Kamenoostrovskii and Bol'shoi Prospekts, Peshekhonov immediately issued a proclamation to the populace in Petrograd District in which he appealed to them "to maintain calm despite the developing events, to react with trust to the district commissars appointed by the new power [which he did not specify, probably intentionally] and execute their orders, and to fulfill the obligations necessary for public service."[22] The proclamation also urged factories, mills, and other social organizations to send their delegates to the commissariat. It is apparent that Peshekhonov mainly concerned himself with the restoration of order. Responding to the proclamation, which was distributed throughout the district, a few hundred volunteers, including intelligentsia, workers, and soldiers, assembled at the commissariat, and formed a militia.[23]

Peshekhonov's commissariat established itself as the most influential authority in Petrograd District by absorbing some organizations and subordinating others. He entered into negotiations with a group of intellectuals who had organized a commissariat on February 28 and occupied the building of the city administration (gorodskaia uprava) as their headquarters. This group agreed to be incorporated into Peshekhonov's commissariat. A similar organization, which came into existence on Krestovskii Island, pledged allegiance to the commissariat while maintaining its separate entity.[24] Another organization by the name of the "residents' committee" also claimed autonomous local power. This committee was organized by liberal intellectuals calling themselves "the progressive-democratic group," who had undoubtedly originated from the radical wing of the Kadets and other liberals who had been involved in the unsuccessful campaign for the residents' committees in the fall of 1915. The entire district was divided into sixteen to eighteen subdistricts, each of which held residents' meetings. The residents—men and women over twenty—elected their representatives

20. A. V. Peshekhonov, "Pervyia nedeli: Iz vospominanii o revoliutsii," *Na chuzhoi storone* 1 (1923): 266-67.

21. In his speeches addressed to the soldiers on February 28 he warned of the danger of "dual power." See chap. 19, p. 374.

22. *Izvestiia*, March 1, 1917. The same proclamation with a slight change was also printed in *Izvestiia*, March 2, 1917.

23. Peshekhonov, "Pervyia nedeli," p. 271.

24. Ibid., pp. 304-5.

to the residents' committee. Peshekhonov did not attempt to take over this organization, believing that he could come to terms with it in case of conflict.[25] Peshekhonov also negotiated with the commandant appointed by the Military Commission of the Duma Committee, an aristocratic officer of the Grenadier Regiment with a lethargic personality. The authority of this commandant remained negligible, to the extent that Peshekhonov had no knowledge of his existence until a few days after his appointment. Peshekhonov declared to him that, not wishing to create a dual power, he was prepared to accept his authority on the condition that the commandant's office be transferred to the commissariat and that the commandant work in constant contact with Peshekhonov. The commandant gladly accepted these conditions and never interfered in the work of the commissariat.[26]

Thus in Petrograd District the commissariat that had been created from above by the Petrograd Soviet established the most effective police power—a result made possible largely by Peshekhonov's energetic leadership and initiative. Yet the commissariat found itself under continual pressure from the revolutionarized masses. In fact, its survival depended on constant accommodation to the mood of the "crowd." When Peshekhonov refused to surrender weapons in the commissariat to a group of soldiers, he faced rifles pointed at him by the surrounding soldiers. When he released innocent victims charged with counter-revolutionary activities, he could not maintain authority "as the representative of the revolutionary power" unless he treated the accused harshly. It is interesting to note that the most powerful commissar in Petrograd District had to write in his memoirs: "All the power in essence completely rested in the hands of the crowd. The crowd executed it in the form of self-government, and many undoubtedly were convinced that this was truly the people's power."[27]

Many factories in other districts also responded to the appeal of the Petrograd Soviet by electing militia according to the prescribed ratio. Thus the Putilov Factory formed the workers' commissariat on February 28. A workers' militia was created also in Neva Shipyard, San-Galli, the Obukhov Factory, Dinamo, Siemens-Schückert, and

25. See chap. 3. It is not known how widespread the election for the residents' committee was in the district, what relations it established with the Duma Committee or the city militia, what happened to it subsequently, or whether similar organizations existed in other districts in Petrograd. Peshekhonov, "Pervyia nedeli," p. 305.

26. Ibid., p. 306.

27. Ibid., pp. 288-89, 299.

388 THE PETROGRAD SOVIET AND THE DUMA COMMITTEE

Pobeda.[28] In Kolomenskaia and Moscow districts, however, the workers' influence remained weak, and the city militia established effective control. Thus, generally in the industrial sections of the city the workers influenced the formation of militia organizations, but in the administrative and business centers of Petrograd the city militia almost exclusively dominated. Although workers also participated in it, the city militia mainly attracted the middle-class elements, particularly students. For instance, the militia in Kolomenskaia District was created by soldiers and "citizens."

Representatives of the "workers from factories and mills, representatives of the sick funds, consumer associations, city health department, and other social organizations" in Rozhdestvo District who met on March 2 called for "securing in the district order and safety of the population and organizing a special detachment (militia) for that purpose."[29] Thus Petrograd was divided into two areas under conflicting police power: one area under the authority of the workers' militia that pledged allegiance to the Petrograd Soviet or under the commissariat directly created by the Soviet, and the other under the authority of the city militia created by the city duma in close cooperation with the Duma Committee. This conflict of power at the local level indeed constituted the most fundamental reason for the birth of dual power.

As early as February 28 the Soviet Executive Committee made clear its intention to cooperate with the Duma Committee in solving this conflict by sacrificing the independence of the workers' militia. At the second Soviet session held on this day a keynote speaker, Steklov, representing the Executive Committee, stated that to achieve intended goals it was necessary "to rely not only on workers," but also on other groups, without whose cooperation Soviet power would not be able to hold out.[30] Since tension between the Executive Committee and the general deputies mounted to an explosive point at the second general session on the issue of Rodzianko's order, it appears that the Executive Committee decided not to present its policy about the conflict of militia authorities at the second session.[31] Instead, it issued a proclamation on the following day that stated: "The Executive

28. Startsev, *Ocherki po istorii Petrogradskoi Krasnoi gvardii*, pp. 45-46; Kel'son, "Militsiia fevral'skoi revoliutsii," p. 172.

29. With the exception of the Rozhdhestvo and Kolomenskaia districts, it is not known in detail how the city militia extended its authority to the districts. *Izvestiia*, March 2 and 3, 1917.

30. Zlokazov, *Petrogradskii Sovet*, p. 53; Iu. S. Tokarev, *Petrogradskii Sovet rabochikh i soldatskikh deputatov v marte-aprele, 1917 g.*, pp. 517-18.

31. See below.

Committee of the Soviet of Workers' Deputies decided to unify the central organ of the workers' commissariats with this Duma organization [the city militia]. . . . Remember, comrades, that you take part in the militia at the instruction of the Soviet of Workers' Deputies. Remember that the Soviet of Workers' Deputies is your highest authority."[32] This decision to subordinate the workers' militia to the city militia while upholding its ultimate allegiance to the Soviet foreshadowed the famous policy formulated later by the Executive Committee of "conditional support" *(poskol'ku-postol'ku)* for the Provisional Government.

Nevertheless, the mere publication of a proclamation could not convince the workers to accept the authority of the city militia. On March 2, the Executive Committee appointed two Mensheviks, V. P. Piatiev and Chernov (not to be confused with the famous leader of the Socialist Revolutionary party), as liaison between the Executive Committee and the city militia. These two together with the city militia's secretary, Z. Kel'son, visited headquarters of the workers' militia in various workers' districts in an effort to persuade them to merge with the city militia.[33] At the same time, to introduce some uniformity in the procedures of all the militia organizations and, more importantly, to prevent the workers' militia from committing revolutionary excesses, these three men drafted "instructions" regulating the procedures concerning arrest, use of firearms, and appropriation of automobiles, as well as clarifying the aims of militia activities. Article 1 of the draft instructions read: "The duty of a militiaman is to defend each and every one from all violence, offense, and arbitrariness," a statement clearly intended to restrain excesses. On the other hand, the same article stipulated in the latter part of the paragraph that "A militiaman must understand that he is an executive organ of new Free Russia and is obligated to combat all attempts at counterrevolution," a statement designed to lure the workers' militia to the city militia by emphasizing common purpose. On March 3 the city militia convened the first general meeting of the district commissars in the city duma, into which the representatives of the workers' militia were also invited. More than fifty commissars who attended this meeting approved the draft instructions as well as the incorporation of the workers' militia into the city militia.[34] With the unification of the two militia organizations the city militia was renamed the people's city militia *(gorodskaia narodnaia militsiia).*

32. *Izvestiia*, March 1, 1917.
33. Kel'son, "Militsiia fevral'skoi revoliutsii," p. 167.
34. Ibid., pp. 167-68; Startsev, *Ocherki po istorii Petrogradskoi Krasnoi gvardii,* p. 48.

The workers' reluctance to accept the unification provoked a series of protests at the beginning of March. An episode at a meeting of the commissars on March 3 demonstrated their hostility when Kryzhanovskii carelessly addressed the workers as "gentlemen." Angry protests that no gentlemen were there forced Kryzhanovskii to use the unaccustomed word "Comrades."[35] The workers accepted the unification only because of strong pressure from the Soviet Executive Committee. Yet unification remained only theoretical; the workers' militia for all practical purposes maintained its independence and autonomy, continuing to control the workers' sections of the city exclusively, with no interference from the city militia.[36]

Together with the problem of militia the soldiers' ultimate allegiance was another crucial issue for the solution of the problem of power. Rodzianko's order, written actually by Engelhardt and Bublikov and issued on February 28, that directed officers and soldiers to return to the barracks, provoked a violent reaction from the insurgents, who took it as a call for restoration of the old order.[37] Not only did Rodzianko's order attempt to subordinate soldiers to officers in the old way, but the insurgents interpreted it also as an attempt to confiscate their weapons. V. D. Shatov, who volunteered for the newly created district food supply committee in Vyborg District, reported an alarming situation there. Agitators, mostly soldiers, were going around the district, attacking Rodzianko's order. They claimed that the order, not issued by the Petrograd Soviet but by Rodzianko personally, was an attempt to disarm the soldiers and then shoot them with machine guns. The agitators demanded Rodzianko's arrest, and appealed to the crowds to support the Soviet.[38]

The dissatisfaction of the insurgents with Rodzianko's order was clearly expressed in the second general session of the Petrograd Soviet held on February 28. It was dominated by deputies from the factories, since very few military units had elected their deputies. Yet the worker-deputies took Rodzianko's order as aimed directly at themselves. Bogdanov, representing the Executive Committee, explained to the agitated audience that the Duma Committee had already rescinded Rodzianko's order, with a guarantee to the Executive Committee that it would not be circulated. His attempt to cut the discussions short, however, was unsuccessful. Although some deputies counselled

35. Kel'son, "Militsiia fevral'skoi revoliutsii," p. 174.
36. See Hasegawa, "The Formation of the Militia in the February Revolution," pp. 315-22.
37. See pp. 375-76.
38. TsGAOR, f. 3348, op. 1, d. 129, ll. 15-16.

reason and caution, lest the relationship between the Petrograd Soviet and the Duma Committee should deteriorate, a majority of speakers denounced the order as an attempt to restore the old order. Deputy Pavlov accused Rodzianko of betraying the revolution and demanded his personal appearance at the Soviet session. Molotov, representing the Bolsheviks, declared that the Soviet should take appropriate measures for this kind of counterrevolutionary action and demanded Rodzianko's public retraction. Deputy Sakharevskii proposed that all orders and proclamations be issued by the Soviet. Faced with these extreme demands and denunciations, members of the Executive Committee tried to placate the anger of the deputies by warning them of the danger of extreme measures. Expressing agreement with the necessity of tighter control over the Duma Committee, Rafes considered the worsening relations between the two bodies unnecessary and dangerous.

Bogdanov introduced a motion to delegate Kerenskii and Chkheidze to register a protest to the Duma Committee about Rodzianko's order and to entrust the Executive Committee with the task of clarifying the relationship between the Soviet and the Duma Committee and of defining the role of the Duma Committee in relation to the army. Considering the eagerness with which the Executive Committee had surrendered the Military Commission to the Duma Committee, Bogdanov's motion was obviously intended to cushion the anger of the deputies by taking the entire matter out of their hands. This motion, however, did not satisfy the audience. Deputy Savinkov (not to be confused with the famous Socialist Revolutionary terrorist) declared that what the Soviet should do was not to send Kerenskii and Chkheidze to the Duma Committee, but to receive the Duma Committee's immediate reply, and not to demand clarification, but to nullify the order, since there was no question but that Rodzianko had indeed issued it. This speech virtually killed Bogdanov's motion. Steklov's appeal not to take action until Kerenskii registered a protest in the Duma Committee went unheeded. Some even demanded Rodzianko's arrest. Only the news brought by Skobelev at the end of the session that the Fortress of Peter and Paul had fallen to the side of the revolution softened the tense situation. The Executive Committee barely managed to postpone the decision.[39] It is indicative of the Executive

39. Zlokazov, "O zasedanii Petrogradskogo Soveta rabochikh i soldatskikh deputatov 28 fevralia 1917 g.," pp. 57-60. This article is based on a draft copy of the minutes he discovered in LGAORSS, which was believed to be nonexistent. LGAORSS archives were closed to me during my stay in Leningrad. See also M. G. Rafes, "Moi vospominaniia," *Byloe* 19 (1922): 193; Burdzhalov, *Vtoraia russkaia revoliutsiia*, p. 290.

Committee's dilemma that the minutes of this meeting printed in *Izvestiia* on the following day mentioned no word about the discussion of Rodzianko's order except for a vague reference to the discussion on "the organization of the army" and "the relationship between the Committee of the State Duma and the Soviet of Workers' Deputies."[40]

Rodzianko's order created tension between the Soviet representatives and the Duma Committee leaders in the Military Commission. At five o'clock in the morning Engelhardt was awakened by members of the Military Commission and told that Rodzianko's order was creating an angry reaction among the soldiers. Engelhardt wrote later, "My attempt to bring the soldiers within the confines of discipline was regarded, not without foundation, as an attempt to stop the development of revolution." For the first time Engelhardt was accused of being a "counterrevolutionary." Copies of Rodzianko's order were seized by members of the Soviet and destroyed. Additional printing of the order was halted.[41]

A rumor spread that officers were disarming and arresting soldiers in the barracks. Engelhardt dispatched his representatives to various barracks, who found the rumor false. Steklov and some soldiers, presumably after the stormy general session of the Soviet assembly, came to the Military Commission, and strongly protested Rodzianko's order. Engelhardt explained that he had no intention of disarming the insurgent soldiers, and that rumors about the officers confiscating soldiers' weapons were totally false. Steklov asked Engelhardt to put his words in the form of proclamation. Engelhardt readily complied with this request, and issued the following:[42]

On March 1 a rumor is spreading among the soldiers of the Petrograd Garrison that the officers in the regiments are confiscating weapons from the soldiers. These rumors have been checked in two regiments and turned out to be false. As chairman of the Military Commission of the State Duma I declare that the most decisive measures including the execution of the guilty shall be taken not to tolerate such actions on the part of the officers.[43]

This proclamation was printed on the first page of *Izvestiia* on March 2 in bold print and on March 1 Bonch-Bruevich made the printing office of Kopeika available to print 100,000 copies.[44] This concerted effort to publicize the proclamation attested to the seriousness that both the Duma Committee as well as the Soviet Executive Committee attached to the violent and widespread reaction to Rodzianko's order.

40. *Izvestiia*, March 1, 1917.
41. OR GBL, f., 218, B. A. Engel'gardt, "Potonusvshii mir," ll. 107-8.
42. Ibid., l. 116.
43. *Izvestiia*, March 2, 1917.
44. Burdzhalov, *Vtoraia russkaia revoliutsiia*, p. 291.

On the issue of the relationship between officers and soldiers, the Executive Committee of the Petrograd Soviet took a position similar to its attitude toward the conflicting authorities of the militia organizations. Sukhanov stated: "The Executive Committee of the Soviet made every effort to see that officers returned to their own units and to their duties and that soldiers should again recognize the officers. In this relationship the Executive Committee was in complete agreement with the goals of the Duma Committee."[45] It also issued a proclamation:

The Provisional Committee of the State Duma under the assistance of the Military Commission is organizing the army and appointing the commanders of its units. Not wishing to hinder the struggle against the old regime, the Executive Committee of the Soviet of Workers' Deputies do not recommend that soldiers refuse the maintenance of the strong organization and the fulfillment of the measures by the Military Commission and the commanders appointed by it.[46]

Engelhardt's proclamation and the Executive Committee's appeal notwithstanding, soldiers began to take matters into their own hands. The "sorting out" of officers unsympathetic to the revolution had already started on March 1 in some units. The soldiers began electing new commanders from among officers who joined the revolution with the soldiers. In Moscow Regiment the soldiers went even further, disarming and arresting officers who disappeared during the insurrection. Guard soldiers who escorted the arrested officers shot one of the prisoners on the way to the Tauride Palace. In some other units, for instance in the 18th Service Corps (ekipazh), several officers who attempted to disarm soldiers in carrying out Rodzianko's order met with brutal deaths at the soldiers' hands.[47]

Thus, the soldatskii vopros (the problem of soldiers) became one of the most critical questions facing the Soviet and the Duma Committee by March 1. They had to be calmed and prevented from committing large-scale pogroms against the officers, yet to create a stable government, the disorganized rabble had to be reorganized into a military force and made subordinate to the orders of this government.

Rodzianko's order facilitated the election of delegates to the Soviet by the insurgent soldiers so they could air their protest. Late February 28 and early March 1 soldiers of various units, some in their barracks and others in the Tauride Palace, where they had been bivouacking since February 27, conducted elections. The third general

45. N. N. Sukhanov, Zapiski o revoliutsii 1: 162.
46. Burdzhalov, Vtoraia russkaia revoliutsiia, pp. 291-92.
47. "Dnevnik soldata na Vyborgskoi storone," Pravda, March 11, 1917; Burdzhalov, Vtoraia russkaia revoliutsiia, pp. 292, 300-301.

session of the Petrograd Soviet was scheduled at noon on March 1. The Executive Committee, however, decided to postpone the opening of the session so as to reach a decision on the problem of power, which it had been debating since that morning.[48] Skobelev, sent by the Executive Committee for this maneuver, managed to have the delegates vote for postponement, despite some bitter resentment, when suddenly the doors of the assembly hall flung open and a large group of soldiers burst into the hall. Overwhelmed by the number of soldiers, who for the first time appeared in the Soviet session en masse, and panic-stricken by their anger, Skobelev immediately announced that the session was open. The soldiers turned this general session to an exclusive meeting of soldiers, not allowing other delegates to speak. Skobelev, unable to cope with the situation, begged Sokolov to preside over the meeting.[49]

The Soviet session discussed the following three issues: (1) whether the soldiers should obey the orders of the Military Commission of the Duma or of the Petrograd Soviet; (2) how to react to Rodzianko's demand to surrender arms; and (3) the soldiers' attitude toward officers.[50] In his opening speech, Sokolov for the first time explained the Duma Committee's takeover of the Military Commission. According to Sokolov, the representatives of the Duma Committee did not wish to take part in the Military Commission at the critical moment, when the situation was not clear. But when the insurrection triumphed, "the Military Commission entered into contact with Engelhardt of

48. See chap. 21.

49. M. Skobelev, "Gibel' tsarizma: Vospominaniia M. I. Skobeleva," *Ogonek,* no. 11 (1927). According to Shliapnikov and Sadovskii, whose unpublished memoirs are used by Miller, the soldiers held a separate preliminary meeting before the general session, at which Sokolov presided. It is not clearly established whether or not this meeting was indeed held, and if it was, what was actually discussed. A. Shliapnikov, *Semnadtsatyi god* 1: 206; V. I. Miller, "Nachalo demokratizatsii staroi armii v dni fevral'skoi revoliutsii," *Istoriia SSSR,* no. 6 (1966), p. 28.

50. The following account of the general session is based on Miller, "Nachalo demokratizatsii staroi armii," which utilizes the hitherto unknown draft minutes written in pencil at the meeting. As for Order No. 1 and the *soldatskii vopros,* see V. I. Miller, "Iz istorii prikaza No. 1 Petrogradskogo Soveta," *Voenno-istoricheskii zhurnal,* no. 4 (1966), pp. 109-13; John Boyd, "The Origins of Order No. 1," *Soviet Studies* 19 (1968): 359-72, which is primarily based on Miller's articles; Shliapnikov, *Semnadtsatyi god* 1: 206-14; N. N. Sukhanov, *Zapiski o revoliutsii* 1: 264-67; N. D. Sokolov, "Kak rodilsia prikaz No. 1," *Ogonek,* no. 11 (March 13, 1927); A. Paderin, "Pis'ma v redaktsiiu," *Proletarskaia revoliutsiia* 31-32, no. 8-9 (1924): 401-2; E. S. Mikhailov, "Prikaz No. 1,"*Voprosy istorii,* no. 2 (1967), pp. 208-11; V. I. Miller, *Soldatskie komitety russkoi armii v 1917 g.,* pp. 16-35; Tokarev, *Petrogradskii Sovet rabochikh i soldatskikh deputatov,* pp. 57-59.

the Duma Committee, a participant in the Russo-Japanese War and a foremost expert on military matters. He agreed to become the chairman of the commission."[51] Sokolov thus justified the Duma Committee's takeover of the Military Commission by implying that the Petrograd Soviet had begged their participation. But Sokolov saw a danger in the political leaning of the officers. Some had not completely taken the side of the revolution, and many still openly spoke against it. In the Military Commission there were no soldiers, and without them it would be difficult to carry on revolutionary measures in the Military Commission. The important task of the moment was to draw the soldiers more closely into the commission's task.

Sokolov did not exclude the possibility of a direct confrontation between the Soviet and the Duma Committee, but considered one undesirable and defended compromise with the Duma Committee as the only course open to the Soviet. "We are having a democratic revolution with the bourgeoisie. Until our common enemy is completely eliminated, we must cooperate with each other." As long as the Duma Committee carried out the struggle against tsarism, and as long as the Military Commission, which was the only organ with experience and connections, had plans to combat counterrevolutionary attempts from the front, the Soviet should support cooperation with the Duma Committee. Sokolov thus argued that the soldiers should send their delegates to the Military Commission and lead it in a revolutionary direction rather than divorce themselves from it hastily.[52]

The first speaker, S. A. Klivanskii (Maksim, SR), sharply disagreed with Sokolov in his attitude toward the Duma Committee and the Military Commission. Assailing Rodzianko as a landlord and a leader of the "party of order" dominated by "those who want the workers and the peasants to be like a herd of animals and themselves to be masters," he expressed the fear that once the Duma Committee succeeded in disarming the soldiers and mobilizing the support of the most reliable regiments, it would be able to take all the power

51. Tokarev, *Petrogradskii Sovet rabochikh i soldatskikh deputatov*, p. 57.
52. Ibid., pp. 57-58. Tokarev criticizes Miller for an inadequate account of Sokolov's ambivalent attitude toward the officers' question. Unlike Miller, who sees in Sokolov a typical representative of the Soviet Executive Committee, who wished to achieve peace between the officers and the soldiers, Tokarev argues that Sokolov clearly saw the danger of the officers' political orientation. Although Sokolov ultimately supported the Executive Committee's policy to achieve a compromise with the Duma Committee, Sokolov seems to have emphasized the importance of the consolidation of the Soviet by actively organizing the insurgents more than his colleagues, Sukhanov and Steklov.

for the interests of "landlords and capitalists," and smother the revolution. Klivanskii argued that the only way to prevent this would be to create a joint soviet of workers' and soldiers' deputies or a soviet of soldiers of the Petrograd Garrison, to which alone the soldiers should subordinate themselves. They should not obey the orders of the Military Commission and should even abolish it. Sokolov and F. F. Linde (Menshevik deputy from Finland Regiment) supported Klivanskii's proposal to create a united soviet of workers' and soldiers' deputies. Linde also rejected the idea of subordinating themselves to the Military Commission. A deputy from Lithuanian Regiment, possibly I. G. Borisov, not only opposed recognition of the authority of the Military Commission, but also expressed dissatisfaction with the Soviet's support for it. He complained of the ambiguities of the situation: "I don't know whom to deal with, whom to listen to. Everything is unclear. Let's have some clarity." Another SR soldier, Iu. A. Kudriavtsev, representative from the automobile section of the Red Cross, persuasively argued against the previous speakers in support of Sokolov's position. The most urgent question before the soldiers, he stated, was not whom to listen to, but what to do and how to organize. While arguing that the question about whom to obey was already answered, since "we sanction, we are the forces," he nevertheless did not believe that the Military Commission should be liquidated; rather the Soviet should send its representatives and control its action. Sokolov's and Kudriavtsev's arguments apparently prevailed and the meeting passed the following resolution: "The soldiers should be organized in the Soviet of Soldiers' and Workers' Deputies. The opinion of the Military Commission shall be recognized as long as it does not deviate from the opinion of the Soviet. The soldiers' deputies shall be sent to the composition of the Military Commission."[53] The Soviet session formally changed its name to the Petrograd Soviet of Workers' and Soldiers' Deputies.

Discussions on the second point—whether the soldiers should surrender their arms to the officers—was brief. Klivanskii proposed that "weapons not be surrendered." Kudriavtsev, who supported a moderate position on the previous issue, fully endorsed the proposal. A deputy from the Eger Regiment further proposed that the regimental committee elected by the lower ranks should control the weapons. All these proposals were synthesized into the following resolution: "The weapons should not be surrendered to the officers, but the battalion committees."[54]

53. Miller, "Nachalo demokratizatsii staroi armii," pp. 31-33.
54. Ibid., p. 34.

The soldiers' representatives had their most heated debate on the third point—attitude toward the officers. Anger was primarily directed toward those officers who, having left the barracks during the insurrection, had returned to resume command on Rodzianko's order. The first soldier to speak on this issue, Marchenko, reminded the audience that returning officers were calling soldiers, as before, "a herd of sheep," trying to "put the soldiers under the thumb and behaving even worse than before." A soldier from Semenovskii Regiment, Melenchuk, commented, "A herd of officers come in order to deceive us. They join us in order to go around us." A deputy from the First Reserve Infantry Regiment (V. I. Badenko?) also noted that although the officers wore red bands on their sleeves, they still remained monarchists at their own meetings, thinking about disarming workers and shooting insurgents. Some speakers complained in general of officers' treatment of soldiers in prerevolutionary days. Soldier Konovalov pointed out that soldiers had even had to take care of officers' children, suffering punishment for the slightest offense not only from the officers, but also from their children and wives. Referring to Guchkov's appeal to the soldiers of Preobrazhenskii Regiment to forget old accounts, Linde interjected with a shout: "Bastard, who could forget the old?"

The discussion centered around one point—if the soldiers should accept some of the officers or not accept them at all. Two different opinions emerged. Badenko and Linde proposed to reject all returning officers. In Linde's words, "We should not accept those who did not take part in the revolution. We will show our will and elect the new." Badenko went as far as to say, "We will kick out from the battalions those who did not join." A soldier from Preobrazhenskii Regiment, however, complained that if they refused to accept returning officers, there would be "no officers left even for instruction." Another solider from Preobrazhenskii Regiment (A. N. Paderin?), relating experiences in his battalion, introduced a new idea—election of officers. In his battalion all the officers had disappeared during the insurrection and when they had returned, the soldiers refused to recognize their authority, electing a committee of four from their ranks to administer the battalion. Klivanskii, representing a moderate view, stated that the officers were needed for combat, but their rights should be limited to military duties. "When duty ends, an officer is a citizen like a soldier." He emphasized the common goal between officers and soldiers in the struggle against the external enemy. Yet Klivanskii was the only speaker to argue the necessity of cooperation with some of the officers in order to continue the war. The rest of the speakers who also advocated acceptance of returning officers based their argument on the practical reality of the impossibility of the other alternative. Borisov, agreeing with Klivanskii's proposal to retain the officers, nevertheless considered it necessary to regulate conditions in such a way that the officers should command "politely, not using derogatory words." He added, "If we eliminate all the coarse officers, then there will remain no officers. Not a single one, even a student, who would not use derogatory words." He then proposed to create committees elected by the soldiers to control the officers. The discussion of returning officers now shifted to creation of soldiers' committees. Klivanskii, who took the floor for the second time on this issue, stressed the need of maintaining discipline, while in principle agreeing with the idea of soldiers' committees. He introduced a draft resolution synthesizing the various arguments given on the floor. This draft resolution entitled Order to the Garrison of Petrograd consisted of five points: (1) elected representatives from the units are to form a soviet of soldiers' deputies and join the Soviet of Workers' Deputies; (2) all the troops must send their representatives to the Soviet; (3) weapons should not be surrendered; (4) the soldiers' committees would assume control of the weapons as well as economy of the units; and (5) discipline should be maintained as previously while on military duty. The soldiers' representatives adopted this draft resolution by an overwhelming majority after adding to it two points they had already passed: (1) the opinion of the Military Commission shall be recognized as long as it does not deviate from the opinion of the Soviet, and (2) the soldiers will send their representatives to the Military Commission.[55]

Somewhat incongruous with the resolution they had adopted, however, the soldiers agreed to present this decision to the Military Commission for its approval. Apparently those who supported the continuing relationship with the Military Commission successfully persuaded the audience to make one last try to keep the tie between the Military Commission and the soldiers unbroken. Soldiers representing about twenty army units in the Petrograd Garrison appeared in the Military Commission on the evening of March 1 to meet Engelhardt. They declared that they could "not trust the officers who did not take part in the revolutionary offensive, and therefore, demand the publication of an order" regulating the election of officers, soldiers' control of the economy of the units, and the new relationship between the commanding officers and the lower ranks. The draft proposal presented by the soldiers to Engelhardt "affected much less the foundations of military discipline than Order No. 1, concerned itself only

55. Ibid., pp. 39-40.

with the elections of the junior officers, and established some control by the soldiers over the economy in the military units."[56] Although Engelhardt recognized that it was natural that the soldiers turned to the Military Commission, which had grown out of the revolution and which had taken obvious revolutionary measures, to issue such an order, he could not bring himself to agree to publish it in the name of the commission. Thus Engelhardt transmitted the demands to the Duma Committee, but Rodzianko and Guchkov categorically rejected them. Engelhardt managed with difficulty to placate the excited soldiers by promising them that the Military Commission and the Duma Committee would set up a new commission for investigating the entire sphere of soldiers' life and specifically the problems presented by the soldiers. Later on in the evening, however, the soldiers' representatives authorized by the Soviet called again on Engelhardt and stated: "The delegates of many units are demanding that new regulations of the military organization should be established. The Soviet is very much interested in this problem and proposed to the Provisional Committee of the Duma to work them out jointly." Met with Engelhardt's repeated rejection, the soldiers left the room with the words, "So much the better, we will write them ourselves."[57]

The soldiers' meeting elected the following ten representatives to the Executive Committee: A. D. Sadovskii (Sixth Engineer Battalion, former railway engineer, Bolshevik), A. N. Paderin (Preobrazhenskii Regiment, former student and sick-funds activist, Bolshevik), V. I. Badenko (First Infantry Regiment, Menshevik-Internationalist), F. F. Linde (Finland Regiment, Menshevik-Internationalist), Iu. A. Kudriavtsev (Red Cross automobile section, former engineer, Socialist Revolutionary), A. P. Borisov (Lithuanian Regiment, former forester, Menshevik), I. G. Barkov (First Rifle Regiment, former worker), Vakulenko (Eger Regiment, former worker), Klimchinskii (Izmailovskii Regiment, former Putilov worker), and Sailor Sokolov (Baltic Fleet, Kadet).[58] The contrast between the singularity of the soldiers' complaints aired at the meeting and the wide variety of their party affiliations is striking. The soldier representatives, who did not have a deep understanding of the ideological leanings of their respective parties, had similar political outlooks on issues bearing on their lives as soldiers despite

56. Engel'gardt, "Potonuvshii mir," л. 118; TsGIA, f. 1278, op. 10, d. 5, л. 36.
57. TsGIA, f. 1278, op. 10, d. 5, л. 36; Engel'gardt, "Potonuvshii mir," л. 118.
58. Miller, "Nachalo demokratizatsii staroi armii," p. 41.

the differences in their political affiliations. Furthermore, this list presents another interesting point. Despite the repeated assertions that the army was constituted of peasants in uniform, a majority of the representatives elected to the Executive Committee were former workers and intelligentsia. Judging from their established political affiliations with the revolutionary parties, their political consciousness and experience can be assumed as significantly high. It was these groups who articulated into political programs the deeply felt sense of oppression of the common soldiers. As the proceedings of the soldiers' meeting on March 1 clearly indicated, they formulated their own political demands by themselves without help from outside.

The Executive Committee had no choice but to accept the representatives of the soldiers as members. After discussion of the problem of power, it took up the demands presented by the soldiers' delegates late in the evening. Many members—Chkheidze, Sukhanov, Steklov, for instance—seem to have been absent during the debate on this issue. After a brief discussion, the Executive Committee decided to publish these demands in a single order and entrusted "a group of comrades, members of the Executive Committee working in the Military Commission, and the soldiers who had been elected to the Executive Committee, with the composition and editing of the order."[59] The soldier delegates who went to see Engelhardt for the second time this evening may have been sent to the Military Commission on the basis of this decision. Since the Military Commission rejected any possibility of working out a compromise on the soldatskii vopros, Sokolov and the soldiers' representatives, retiring to a small room next to the headquarters of the Executive Committee, began composing a draft order.

Surrounded by Paderin, Borisov, Kudriavtsev, and other soldier representatives, Sokolov sat at a desk and wrote down what the soldiers dictated—a scene that reminded Sukhanov of Tolstoy narrating a story to the children in Iasnaia Poliana. The already adopted demands were quickly written in a readable style by Sokolov's pen. The only debate was on the question of whether this document should be called a proclamation or an order. The soldiers' insistence that they were more likely to obey an order than a proclamation prevailed.[60] The entire document, known as Order No. 1, was composed within half an hour. Having received the Executive Committee's quick approval, it was

59. Shliapnikov, Semnadtsatyi god 1: 211.
60. Sukhanov, Zapiski o revoliutsii 1: 265; Paderin, "Pis'mo v redaktsiiu," p. 401.

presented to the general meeting, which was still in session. "The soldiers and the workers," Shliapnikov writes, "listened to the order in triumphant silence. To understand the revolutionary significance of this order, it was enough to see the faces of the soldiers. Thunderous voices of approval then spread throughout the stuffy, packed room of the Soviet." Order No. 1 was printed in leaflets and distributed throughout the city on the night of March 1. *Izvestiia* also published it on March 2.[61]

Order No. 1 contained seven points: (1) election of the soldiers' committees in the military units; (2) election of soldiers' representatives to the Soviet; (3) subordination of the soldiers to the Soviet in political actions; (4) subordination to the Military Commission in so far as its orders did not deviate from those of the Soviet; (5) control of weapons by company and battalion committees, and no surrender of weapons to officers in any case; (6) maintenance of military discipline when on duty, but the guarantee of full civil rights of the soldiers when off duty; and (7) abolition of both honorary titles of officers and of the convention of addressing soldiers in coarse and familiar terms.[62] Quite obviously Order No. 1 was based on the decision of the soldiers' meeting on March 1 with only minor changes. Abolition of honorary titles, coarse addressing habits, standing at attention, and compulsory saluting when off duty does not appear in the resolution of the soldiers' meeting, but the need of this action was clearly pointed out during the debate. One point in the resolution that called for sending soldiers' representatives to the Military Commission was dropped, since Engelhardt's refusal to comply with the soldiers' demands made this meaningless.

The provisions of Order No. 1 were a product of "practical rather than theoretical considerations," resulting from the soldiers' response to "the circumstances in which they found themselves."[63] Most of the provisions were therefore inspired by the specific situation in the capital on March 1. Nonetheless, the impact of Order No. 1—its spirit rather than the practical application of specific provisions—spread far beyond the confines of Petrograd. It introduced the principle of control by committees of soldiers—of weapons, of the economy of the military units, of the "sorting out" of undesirable officers

61. Shliapnikov, *Semnadtsatyi god* 1: 212; Sokolov, "Kak rodilsia Prikaz No. 1"; Miller, "Nachalo demokratizatsii staroi armii," p. 43; *Izvestiia*, March 2, 1917.

62. For the complete text, *Izvestiia*, March 2, 1917. Also *Revoliutsionnoe dvizhenie v Rossii posle sverzheniia samoderzhaviia*, pp. 190-91.

63. John Boyd, "The Origins of Order No. 1," *Soviet Studies* 19 (1968): 371-72.

from the units—a principle irreconcilable with military discipline and
hierarchical organizations. As General A. I. Denikin states, Order
No. 1 "gave the first and chief blow to the disintegration of the army."
For the same reason, to Soviet historians it is hailed as the beginning
of the "democratization of the old army."[64]

More importantly, Order No. 1 put an end to the hitherto ambiguous question of to whom the insurgent soldiers would pledge
allegiance. By rejecting the authority of the Military Commission and
hence of the Duma Committee, a decisive majority of the insurgent
soldiers now rallied solidly behind the Petrograd Soviet. Sokolov
writes: "Since the publication of Order No. 1 the situation of the
Soviet of Workers' Deputies sharply improved. The Soviet suddenly
established itself as a real authority relying on a genuinely real force—
the Petrograd Garrison."[65] Order No. 1 thus made it impossible for
the Duma Committee to regain the support of the insurgent soldiers.
Since the formulation of the provisions of Order No. 1 was based on
the soldiers' practical rather than ideological considerations, it would
have been theoretically possible for the Duma Committee to acquire
their allegiance, had it accepted the soldiers' demands. The acceptance of these demands, however, was contradictory to the ultimate
aim of the Duma Committee—the creation of the political basis on
which a stable government could be established.

From the Executive Committee leaders' point of view, Order No. 1
was a hot potato in their hands. On one hand, they had tried to avoid
exclusive concentration of the insurgents' support for the Soviet,
which might inevitably lead to the demand that the Soviet take power.
On the other, they found it necessary to dispel the intense anger and
fear felt by the soldiers, which might trigger large-scale slaughter of
officers. For the latter reason, the Executive Committee members reluctantly accepted Order No. 1. It is doubtful that the leading members
of the Executive Committee, Sukhanov, Steklov, and Chkheidze, who
participated in negotiations with the Duma Committee, fully acquainted
themselves with its contents and implications, since they did not
attend the Executive Committee meeting when it was presented.[66] The

64. A. I. Denikin, *Ocherki russkoi smuty* 1, pt. 1: 66. Miller, "Nachalo demokratizatsii staroi armii," p. 26; Mikhailov, "Prikaz No. 1," p. 208; Burdzhalov,
Vtoraia russkaia revoliutsiia, pp. 298-99.

65. Sokolov, "Kak rodilsia Prikaz No. 1."

66. Steklov declared at the Executive Committee meeting on March 28 that
Order No. 1 was issued despite the Executive Committee: "The representatives
of the army forced us to accept it." Quoted in Zlokasov, *Petrogradskii Sovet*,
p. 62. Sukhanov also states that the Executive Committee had nothing to do with
Order No. 1; Sukhanov, *Zapiski o revoliutsii* 1: 263.

Duma Committee members had no knowledge about the issuance of such a document at the time of the negotiations, although they were aware of the extent of the soldiers' dissatisfaction. Thus, negotiations between the Duma Committee and the Soviet Executive Committee for the purpose of placing a provisional government on popular support were from the beginning futile, since Order No. 1, which preceded them, virtually nullified their purpose.

Order No. 1 in its final form as published did not include the principle of the election of officers, but it is possible to argue, as Tokarev does, that this principle was included in its original version.[67] At any rate, it did not deny the principle, as the Executive Committee later explained. During the debate at the soldiers' meeting on March 1 a representative from Preobrazhenskii Regiment (possibly Paderin) advocated election of officers. The Mezhraiontsy and the SR Maximalists developed this demand in their jointly published leaflet on March 1, which appealed to the soldiers: "Take power into your hands. Elect platoon, company, and regiment commanders. Elect company committees for management of food supply. All the officers must be under the company committees. Accept only those officers whom you know as friends of people. Obey only the deputies dispatched by the Soviet of Workers' Deputies."[68] There was actually little difference between Order No. 1 and this leaflet except that the latter clearly mentioned the principle of election of officers' corps. It was quite likely that the common soldiers understood Order No. 1 as implying election of officers. In fact, election of officers occurred in a number of military units.[69]

The Executive Committee, however, found the leaflet of the Mezhraiontsy and the SR Maximalists too provocative and decided to confiscate all copies before distribution. It took pains to explain this act in an article entitled "Officers and Soldiers" in *Izvestiia* on March 3. This article began with the contrast between Order No. 1, which was alleged to have positively determined a mutual relationship between officers and soldiers, and the leaflet of the two extreme

67. Some Soviet historians argue that Order No. 1 in its original form included the provision concerning the election of officers, but that this provision was dropped by the Executive Committee. See Mikhailov, "Prikaz No. 1," p. 209; Tokarev, *Petrogradskii Sovet rabochikh i soldatskikh deputatov*, pp. 64-65. Miller argues that there is no basis for this contention; Miller, "Iz istorii prikaza No. 1 Petrogradskogo Soveta," pp. 339-40.

68. Shliapnikov, *Semnadtsatyi god* 1: 339-40.

69. Miller, "Iz istorii prikaza No. 1 Petrogradskogo Soveta," pp. 111-13. TsGIA, f. 1278, op. 10, d. 10, ll. 1, 12, 14. Also see Miller, *Soldatskie komitety russkoi armii*, pp. 33-43.

Left Socialists, who "attempted to disrupt the unity achieved by many precious sacrifices." Order No. 1 placed officers in the proper place, giving them power only while on duty. In time of war all soldiers should observe military discipline. The significance of the order, the article continued, lies in its declaration that the soldiers were citizens and no longer slaves. While the order clearly and correctly understood the relationship between officers and soldiers, the proclamation of the radical Socialists contained a strange resentment and blanket accusations against all officers, including those who had joined the revolution.[70] The article purposely magnified the differences between Order No. 1 and the radical Socialists' proclamation, unfairly characterizing the latter as a provocation. More importantly, however, one can detect in this article a clear shift of emphasis. During the debate at the soldiers' meeting, suspicion and hatred against officers dominated the general atmosphere among the soldiers, while the article written by an anonymous Executive Committee member emphasized the unity between soldiers and officers and the importance of maintaining discipline. Later, met with strong protests from commanders at the front as well as the war minister of the Provisional Government, the Executive Committee further retreated, issuing Order No. 2, which denied the principle of the election of officers, while affirming Order No. 1.

Directly related to the problem of militia and the *soldatskii vopros* and equally important in the context of the problem of power is the issue of weapon control. During the insurrection of February 27 the soldiers went to the streets, emptying regimental arsenals. The insurgents acquired more weapons after they occupied the Arsenal, weapon and cartridge factories, and police stations. According to I. I. Mints, weapons captured by insurgents from the Arsenal alone numbered 40,000 rifles and 30,000 revolvers, not to mention the weapons taken from the various regimental armories. More than 2,000 shells and 2,000,000 cartridges fell into the hands of the masses. In addition, workers of the Sestroretsk Weapon Factory handed most of the weapons they had captured from the factory stock to the insurgents in Petrograd, which included 1,247 rifles, 48 sporting guns, 64 revolvers, and 100,000 cartridges. Moreover, despite opposition from the Duma Committee as well as from the Soviet Executive Committee, the Military Commission was compelled to surrender to the insurgents the weapons that came under its control. Zlokazov states that the Military Commission gave the workers 24,000 rifles and

70. *Izvestiia*, March 3, 1917.

400,000 cartridges between March 2 and March 4.[71] Undoubtedly many weapons fell into the hands of irresponsible citizens, and even criminals, thus creating a public menace. The Duma Committee, the Petrograd Soviet, and the insurgents differed in their approaches to dealing with the problem of weapon control.

The Duma Committee felt that the greatest danger lay not in the possession of weapons by a small group of irresponsible citizens and criminals, but in the arming of the masses of insurgents in the streets.[72] In its opinion, only a few authorized institutions—the Military Commission and the city militia—should possess weapons. The Duma Committee therefore consciously treated this problem as a part of the question of power. The successful removal of weapons from the hands of the insurgents would assure the creation of a stable government strong enough to steer its course without yielding too much to popular pressure. Thus, as soon as the Duma Committee took over the Military Commission, it quickly took measures to protect military supply depots and munition factories from the insurgents.[73] Rodzianko's order did not specifically mention confiscation of weapons from the soldiers, but restoration of order and discipline it intended to achieve clearly implied that, and the soldiers understood Rodzianko's order to lead to such a conclusion. As we have already seen, Rodzianko's order angered the insurgents. Met with a strong protest from the Executive Committee as well as from the insurgents, Engelhardt had to declare that officers who attempted to confiscate weapons from soldiers would be executed. During the discussion on March 1 the soldiers' delegates unanimously decided that no weapons should be surrendered to officers under any circumstances, and ultimately their decision was incorporated into one part of Order No. 1, which stated that weapons should be controlled by the soldiers' committees.

On March 1 the head of the city militia, Kryzhanovskii, issued a proclamation appealing to citizens to voluntarily surrender weapons to the city militia.[74] Unlike Rodzianko's order, this was an appeal for cooperation and did not imply any punitive action. Only a small

71. I. I. Mints, *Istoriia Velikogo Oktiabria*, vol. 1, *Sverzhenie samoderzhaviia*, p. 538; V. A. Tsybul'skii, "Rabochee sestroretskogo zavoda v 1917 g.," *Istoriia SSSR*, no. 4 (1957), p. 144; Zlokazov, *Petrogradskii Sovet*, p. 55.

72. For a detailed discussion of the problem of weapon control, see Tsuyoshi Hasegawa, "The Formation of the Militia in the February Revolution: An Analysis of the Origins of Dual Power," *Slavic Review* 32, no. 2 (1973): 317-21. These passages are taken from various parts of the article with the permission of the *Slavic Review*.

73. See chap. 19.

74. *Izvestiia*, March 4, 1917.

number of citizens responded; most simply ignored it. The city militia acquired by voluntary surrender only 108 rifles and 307 revolvers and pistols. Compared with the enormous number of weapons that had fallen into insurgent hands, these figures represented no more than a drop in a bucket. Of the 300 persons who surrendered their weapons, 223 did so in the central districts of the city (Admiralty, Spasskaia, Kazan, Liteinaia, and Kolomenskaia), while only 15 persons in Petrograd District and 7 persons in Vyborg District responded to Kryzhanovskii's appeal.[75] Thus it was apparent by March 1 that attempts by the Duma Committee and the city militia to confiscate weapons from the masses had failed. They realized that without antagonizing them to the extent that a military showdown would be inevitable, they could not disarm the population at large. Having burned their fingers, they now proceeded to reach a modus vivendi with the workers' militia and ultimately with the Soviet Executive Committee in the hope that the Soviet leaders would accomplish what they were unable to do.

How, then, did the Executive Committee react to this conflict? On February 28, when delegates of the workers' militia in Vyborg District approached the Executive Committee with a request for weapons, they met a flat rejection on the grounds that the Military Commission itself did not possess sufficient weapons.[76] In the official proclamation published in Izvestiia on March 1, the Executive Committee appealed to the insurgents to surrender weapons to the "commissars appointed by the Soviet" in various districts or to the Executive Committee in the Tauride Palace. Yet the Executive Committee did not go so far as to demand the transfer of weapons to the Military Commission or the city militia, since it could not dispel its fear that the "bourgeoisie" might turn the weapons against the revolution. Hence, on this issue as well, the Executive Committee took a middle road; while maintaining that individual insurgents should surrender their arms, it nevertheless advocated control of weapons by the Soviet or by the commissars appointed by the Soviet. But attempts by the Duma Committee and the city militia as well as the Executive Committee to dispossess the masses of weapons were frustrated by the workers' stubborn resistance. Both the Petrograd Soviet and the city militia soon began to yield to the persistent pressure of the workers' militia for more weapons.[77]

An inherent weakness of the Duma Committee and the city militia was clearly revealed by their failure to carry through on their original

75. Startsev, *Ocherki po istorii Krasnoi gvardii*, pp. 50-51.
76. G. I. Zlokazov, "O zasedanii Petrogradskogo Soveta," p. 52.
77. Hasegawa, "The Formation of the Militia," pp. 320-21.

intention of disarming the people. Only one measure could have accomplished this goal—a military showdown and neither the Duma Committee nor the city militia was prepared to take this risk. Once they abandoned their original policy their only choice was to accept the existence of the workers' militia and the soldiers' committees, hoping to exert some control over them, if not to dominate. This policy, however, left the Duma Committee and the city militia wide open to popular pressure. The Executive Committee of the Petrograd Soviet also advocated seizure of weapons from insurgents, although it refused to support the bid of the Duma Committee and the city militia for the exclusive right to control weapons. This position was consistent with the Executive Committee's implicit assumption that a provisional government should be formed from the "bourgeoisie" without the participation of the "proletariat." Yet its actions were motivated not only by its desire to help the "bourgeois" forces organize a new government but also by its fear that popular pressure might push it to seize power—a course that it was not capable of pursuing and had no intention of following.

An examination of the Executive Committee's attitude toward the conflict of police power between the city militia and the workers' militia, toward the *soldatskii vopros,* and toward the problem of weapon control reveals two interesting points. First, despite the overwhelming support of the insurgents, whose self-governing forces in the workers' militia and the soldiers' committees could have formed a nucleus of the incipient Soviet power, the Executive Committee leaders not only had no intention of seizing power, but also helped its rival organization, the Duma Committee, to increase its strength even to the point of endangering its own power base. Its willingness to cooperate with the Duma Committee was so persistent as to give one the impression that the Executive Committee even feared the spontaneous popular movement expressed in the formation of the workers' militia and in Order No. 1. Secondly, while it was cooperating with the Duma Committee, the Executive Committee qualified its support by demanding the ultimate allegiance of the insurgents to the Soviet. This was partly due to the popular pressure; to have the masses accept the unpopular policy of compromise, the Executive Committee needed to assure them that it was not betraying their expectations. At the same time, the Executive Committee was well aware that the strength of the Soviet largely stemmed from the support of the masses. While it was anxious to see a "bourgeois" social order established, it was not interested in diminishing its strength and losing its effectiveness as a pressure group. Hence, the Executive Committee took a contradictory position. On the other hand, it lent its support to the Duma

Committee to smooth the way for the latter to form a stable govern-ment, but on the other hand it jealously guarded its ultimate claim to the allegiance of the insurgents. Nor was there total unanimity among the leading members of the Executive Committee on this issue. There existed a difference in nuances between Sukhanov, who emphasized the necessity of cooperating with the Duma Committee, and Sokolov, who was more interested in consolidating the power base of the Soviet—a difference that was reflected in the contradiction of the policies of the Executive Committee.

The analysis of the formation of the militia, the *soldatskii vopros,* and the problem of weapon control lead us to some important con-clusions concerning the birth of dual power. The essential nature of dual power was not the conflict between the Duma Committee and the Executive Committee of the Petrograd Soviet, as it has been hitherto argued, but rather the conflict between the authority emanat-ing from the Duma Committee and the self-government established by the insurgents in the form of the workers' militia and the soldiers' committees. The Duma Committee, and subsequently the Provisional Government, suffered an inherent weakness. It could not rely on the institutional structure of the old regime, which had been greatly dis-rupted by revolutionary upheaval, and it also failed to establish direct connections with the masses. Decrees and proclamations were limited in their effectiveness; the naked force of coercion was unavailable. Quite in contrast, the incipient self-government of the workers and the soldiers came into existence right in the midst of the daily life of the masses, and therefore had promising revolutionary vitality and potentiality. Yet its force was extremely limited on a national scale, particularly when the attitude of the soldiers at the front still remained in question. Nor had the majority of workers and soldiers, who had established an enclave of autonomy in the capital, yet begun to translate their immediate feelings and grievances into conscious revolutionary programs. The workers and soldiers, with a few excep-tions, could not offer an alternative to the Executive Committee's policy toward the problem of power, despite the manifestation of their latent radicalism on a number of specific issues. The Duma Com-mittee could not destroy even the incipient forces of the insurgents' self-government, since it had sought from the very beginning to attain revolutionary legitimacy. Thus, the fundamental conflict between the two powers was, peculiarly, not immediately disrupted by one side's bid to devour the other. The Soviet Executive Committee's policy provided a crucial clue to the temporary stalemate in this conflict. Refusing to strive for the seizure of power by relying on the overwhelming support of the insurgents in Petrograd, it willingly assisted its opponent to establish power.

21

THE TRANSFER OF POWER

 By March 1 the insurgents were beginning to establish a self-government. In the industrial sections of Petrograd the workers created the workers' militia, taking police power into their hands. The soldiers' committees, which Order No. 1 urged the soldiers to create, would assert incontestable self-governing power in military units. It seemed almost a logical step from this for the insurgents, who now came to rally solidly behind the Petrograd Soviet, to demand that the Petrograd Soviet should seize power in opposition to the Duma Committee. A small group of the radical Left had already demanded that the Soviet should become a provisional revolutionary government— a dangerous demand, which might find eager audience among many of the insurgents. The leaders of the Executive Committee, sensing the danger of drifting away with popular pressure to an unwilling destination, desperately tried to adhere to their original plan. They chose to appeal directly to the Duma Committee to form a provisional government immediately. Thus, the historic negotiations conducted in the small hours of March 2 were less like a hard-fought bargaining than an anointment of a provisional government by the leaders of the Soviet Executive Committee.

The Executive Committee, which had thus far avoided a discussion of the problem of power, was forced to make a decision on this matter on March 1. By then three different opinions had developed within the Executive Committee. The right wing, represented by the Bund and the Popular Socialists and joined by some Mensheviks and the SRs, advocated the formation of a coalition government composed of the members of the Duma Committee and of the Soviet Executive Committee. The left wing, represented by the Bolsheviks, the Mezhraiontsy, and the SR Maximalists, rejecting cooperation with the "bourgeois" Duma Committee, called for the establishment of a provisional revolutionary government, although they differed in how this government should be created. Faced with these two extremes, the majority of the Executive Committee members took the middle road, advocating the creation of a provisional government by the "bourgeoisie," but not allowing the "revolutionary democracy," as the Socialists gathering in the Executive Committee called themselves, to participate in the government.

At eleven o'clock on the morning of March 1 the Executive Committee for the first time discussed the problem of power, while excited Soviet delegates began to gather in the next room, Room 13, to discuss the *soldatskii vopros* at the third general session. This was the first time that various factions within the Soviet faced each other on a major issue. The meeting, which had begun amicably, quickly became tense with the sharp exchange of opinions. Chkheidze, "unnecessarily excited and threatening with ultimatum," argued against participation of the Socialists in a provisional government. The right wing presented its demand for a coalition government. Their argument, however, was not particularly effective since its strongest advocates, Bogdanov and Peshekhonov, absented themselves for other engagements. The center of discussion thus shifted to the *"conditions of the transfer of power to the Provisional Government which was being formed by the Duma Committee"* (emphasis in original). Despite the presence of Shliapnikov, Molotov, and Zalutskii, the Executive Committee took it for granted that the provisional government would be formed by the Duma Committee.[1] In the meantime, the delegates in the assembly hall became restless as they waited for the opening of the general session past the scheduled time. Unable to reach a conclusion, the Executive Committee sent Skobelev to Room 13 to delay opening the session. Further interrupted by new business that needed immediate decision, the Executive Committee finally postponed discussion of the problem of power until that evening.

The evening session of the Executive Committee, which began at six o'clock, was attended by almost all its members. In the middle of the meeting the soldiers' deputies, who had been just elected to represent the Petrograd Garrison in the Executive Committee, also participated in the discussion. The agenda was set as follows: (1) character and class composition of the first revolutionary government; (2) demands to be presented to this government; and (3) composition

1. N. N. Sukhanov, *Zapiski o revoliutsii* 1: 241.

of the cabinet.[2] The right wing attacked the majority opinion with increased force, pleading the case for the establishment of a coalition government. Bund leader Rafes argued: "The working class of Russia is taking such an active part in the development of the revolution that without its direct participation in the creation of state life, the revolution would hardly be carried out to be a favorable end. It is indispensable to lead the active work of the working class in the direction of revolutionary state construction." Another Bund leader, Ehrlich, while agreeing that in general theoretical terms the participation of Soviet leaders in the new government would be harmful, pointed out nevertheless that "the first Provisional Government had not yet developed its character of correctly organized power." To influence this government in a revolutionary direction, the leaders of the Soviet should join it.[3] SR Zenzinov also supported this position. In contrast to the offensive from the Right, the left-wing members of the Executive Committee remained curiously silent, without presenting their demand for the establishment of a provisional revolutionary government. At the end of heated discussion, the following motion, moved by the majority, passed by thirteen to eight: "We should not send representatives of democracy to the ministry of Miliukov and should not demand participation therein."[4]

2. Ibid., p. 255.

3. M. G. Rafes, "Moi vospominaniia," *Byloe* 19 (1922): 194.

4. Sukhanov, *Zapiski o revoliutsii* 1: 255-56; V. Zenzinov, "Fevral'skie dni," *Novyi zhurnal* 35 (1953): 220. According to Shliapnikov, the Bolsheviks and other left-wing members of the Executive Committee proposed to "take the administrative affairs of the country into the hands of the revolutionary democracy by means of selecting a provisional revolutionary government from the composition of the majority of the Soviet." In his opinion, the discussion of the Executive Committee centered around whether the Soviet should approve the provisional government composed by the Duma Committee, while the major opponents in the debate were the left wing, on the one hand, and the united front of the right wing and the center on the other. He further states that "only eight members stood for revolutionary democracy." A. Shliapnikov, *Semnadtsatyi god* 1: 216-17. Many Soviet historians, citing Shliapnikov, argue that the Bolsheviks stood for a provisional revolutionary government created from the Petrograd Soviet. For instance, see E. N. Burdzhalov, *Vtoraia russkaia revoliutsiia: Vosstanie v Petrograde*, p. 314. This account completely contradicts other evidence supplied by Sukhanov, Rafes, and Zenzinov. It is true that the Bolsheviks had called for the establishment of a provisional revolutionary government in the manifesto issued on February 27 and 28, but this was presented not as an urgent, practical solution to the problem of power, but as a doctrinal statement of their position. Shliapnikov himself admits that the Bolsheviks shared with the Mensheviks the belief that the revolution was a bourgeois-democratic revolution. Shliapnikov, *Semnadtsatyi god* 1: 220. Further, according to Tarasov-Rodionov, Shliapnikov supported the formation of the provisional government as a matter of fact and stated that from an objective point of view the Duma was helping the workers destroy tsarist power.

The discussion moved to the next topic—what conditions to impose on the provisional government. Sukhanov argued that the most urgent task of the Soviet was to compel the "bourgeoisie" to take power, not to undermine their authority. Thus the conditions should be restricted to the absolute minimum lest they should disrupt the accord between the Duma Committee and the Soviet. Then he presented three such conditions: guarantees of political freedom, amnesty, and the convocation of a constituent assembly.[5] Sukhanov's proposal was accepted in general terms, but further elaborated upon and supplemented. Again, the left wing did not raise objections; in fact, the decision was reached in a surprisingly short time. The conditions finally agreed upon consisted of nine points: (1) complete and immediate amnesty for all political and religious prisoners; (2) freedom of expression, publication, unions, meetings, and strikes; (3) immediate introduction of a democratic republic; (4) immediate measures for the convocation of a constituent assembly on the basis of universal, equal, direct, and secret suffrage; (5) replacement of the police by a people's militia; (6) election to organs of local administration, also on the basis of four-tailed suffrage; (7) abolition of all organizations discriminatory on the basis of class, religion, and nationalities; (8) construction of the army on the basis of self-government, including the election of the commanding officers; and (9) no disarmament and no withdrawal from Petrograd of the army units that took part in the revolutionary movement.[6] The seventh condition was added at the insistence of the Bund leaders.

Most of the demands were quite moderate, as Sukhanov argued that they should be. The demands for amnesty, guarantees of basic freedoms, election of local administration, and abolition of all discriminatory organizations, were more or less identical with those of the Progressive Bloc. The Duma Committee would easily accept the demands for a constituent assembly and the replacement of the police by a people's militia, since the former had been one of the dearest

---

A. Tarasov-Rodionov, *February 1917: A Chronicle of the Russian Revolution* p. 214. Thus, it is safe to assume that Shliapnikov's account is false and that the left wing did not object to the position of the majority at the Executive Committee meeting on March 1.

5. Sukhanov, *Zapiski o revoliutsii* 1: 232-35.

6. No minutes were taken for this meeting so it is not certain how the final form of conditions was drafted. The above list is reconstructed from the accounts of Sukhanov, *Zapiski o revoliutsii* 1: 256-60; *Izvestiia*, March 3, 1917; Rafes, "Moi vospominaniia," p. 220; Iu. S. Tokarev, *Petrogradskii Sovet rabochikh i soldatskikh deputatov*, p. 89. Sukhanov does not mention the seventh condition, while *Izvestiia* omits the third. The conditions published in *Izvestiia* were those that the provisional government had agreed upon as a result of the negotiations on the transfer of power. Tokarev uses the minutes of the general session of the

demands of the liberals, and the tsarist police were also repugnant to the leaders of the Duma Committee, who had, in fact, taken the first step toward their replacement in Petrograd without pressure from the Left. However, point three, the establishment of a republican form of government, could cause some difficulty, given the existence of monarchists in the Duma Committee. Also points eight and nine, the demands for the soldiers' rights, radically departed from an otherwise inoffensive list of demands. Obviously it was the soldiers' representatives, fresh from drafting Order No. 1, that injected this radicalism into the Executive Committee's demands. While the soldiers' representatives remained silent during the discussion on these general questions, they were adamant on the inclusion of their rights as a part of the demands for the transfer of power. Their argument apparently troubled the majority leaders of the Executive Committee, who tried to keep the demands minimal and acceptable to the Duma Committee. Sukhanov later wrote: "Now all this group, which had suddenly appeared from behind the curtains and filled the small room of the Executive Committee, of course, could not join in the course of already begun deliberations, and, trying actively to participate in the discussions, they only hindered the work."[7]

During the discussions, there arose another problem: should the Executive Committee support the provisional government even if it did not accept some of the demands? While the right wing argued that the Soviet should back up the future government as long as it stood for the general spirit of the revolution, a majority favored Sukhanov's argument that these conditions constituted the absolute minimum, the fulfillment of which would be the only guarantee of the success of the revolution. As for the last item of the agenda, the composition of the cabinet of the provisional government, the Executive Committee quickly decided not to interfere in the selection of its personnel.[8]

The Executive Committee thus came to adopt a contradictory position. While it decided to let the bourgeoisie form a provisional government and even not to interfere in the selection of the cabinet, it wrote a platform for this government. The provisional government should perform according to the scenario given to it, while the Soviet should function as a director, who, not wishing to act, was interested nevertheless in monitoring every move within his production. According to Rafes, however, this decision was not final. The Executive Committee considered the resolutions adopted at this meeting tempo-

---

Soviet on March 2, in which Steklov outlined the process of the negotiations.

7. Sukhanov, *Zapiski o revoliutsii* 1: 255.

8. Ibid., pp. 260-61.

rary, to be ratified by the Soviet general session on March 2. Before the general session another Executive Committee meeting would be held, where representatives of each party would present the result of the deliberations of their parties.[9] The majority leaders might have given this promise to assuage the right-wing opposition, but fulfillment of this promise was virtually impossible, since open discussion of the negotiating terms in the general session was impractical, though satisfying to democratic principles. In addition, by March 1 the radical demand for the establishment of provisional revolutionary government by the Soviet had been presented in the workers' sections of the city.

The Bolshevik Vyborg District Committee convened its first legal meeting on March 1 in the building of the Sampsonievskii Brotherhood. K. Shutko's passionate appeal for the establishment of a provisional revolutionary government organized by the Petrograd Soviet was received with enthusiastic applause from the audience, which packed a large assembly hall. The Vyborg District Committee adopted a resolution that called for: (1) the establishment of a provisional revolutionary government; (2) the reorganization of the revolutionary army; (3) the proclamation by the Soviet as being a provisional revolutionary government; (4) the subordination of the Duma Committee to the Soviet; and (5) the separation of the people's government from the State Duma.[10] This resolution, circulated among the workers in the Vyborg District, presented an alternative to the Executive Committee's compromising policy. It had, admittedly, only a few followers and its influence was restricted to the most politically conscious elements of the working class. Yet in view of the upsurge of the revolutionary temper precipitated by Rodzianko's order, it was like a time bomb in a powder keg. The majority leaders of the Executive Committee found it necessary to forestall the acceptance of this radical program by large segments of the insurgents by presenting them with an established fact.

It was therefore not surprising that the negotiations between the Duma Committee and the Soviet Executive Committee started on the latter's initiative.[11] Ignoring the understanding agreed upon at the last Executive Committee meeting, Sukhanov went to the right

9. Rafes, "Moi vospominaniia," p. 220.

10. *Revoliutsionnoe dvizhenie v Rossii posle sverzheniia samoderzhaviia,* p. 6; also see *Pravda,* March 8, 1917; F. N. Dingel'stadt, "Vesna proletarskoi revoliutsii," *Krasnaia letopis'* 12, no. 1 (1925): 193.

11. According to Shliapnikov, the Duma Committee's official proposal for negotiations preceded the Executive Committee's discussions on the problem of power. Shliapnikov, *Samnadtsatyi god* 1: 216. Shul'gin also states that the negotiations originated from the Duma Committee's offer to the Executive Com-

wing of the Tauride Palace "at his own responsibility and risk" to arrange a meeting with the Duma Committee. He first approached Kerenskii, who refused to relay Sukhanov's offer to his colleagues of the Duma Committee. He then went directly to their headquarters and announced to Nekrasov the Executive Committee's proposal to negotiate with the Duma Committee on the matter of power. Half an hour later, Nekrasov, returning from consultation with his colleagues, told Sukhanov that the Duma Committee and the candidates for the provisional government would meet with the representatives of the Soviet at midnight. From the Duma Committee's point of view, it was necessary to insure the Executive Committee's full support for the provisional government so as to obtain allegiance of the insurgent masses in Petrograd; thus, Sukhanov's offer was more than welcome. Using lack of time as an excuse, Sukhanov, Chkheidze, Steklov, and Sokolov delegated themselves to participate in the negotiations without formal authorization and in violation of the agreement reached at the last Executive Committee meeting.[12]

The negotiations began at midnight in the headquarters of the Duma Committee. From the Duma Committee and the provisional government, Rodzianko, Miliukov, Nekrasov, Prince G. E. L'vov, Godnev, Adzhemov, Shidlovskii, V. L'vov, Shul'gin, and Kerenskii were present. Most of the participants from the Duma Committee remained silent during the negotiations. Rodzianko, now crushed by the eclipse of his personal influence, yet still occupying the largest table at the head of the room, kept himself busy drinking soda except when he made a few irrelevant comments. The future prime minister, Prince L'vov, sat impassively, without uttering a word. Kerenskii, too, despite his proclivity to theatrics, remained curiously indifferent to the negotiations as if immersed in melancholy reflection. Only Miliukov actively participated in the whole process, busily taking notes, asking questions, and retorting to the remarks of the Executive Committee representatives.

Rodzianko, Nekrasov, and Miliukov complained about the worsening anarchy in the capital and pleaded for the cooperation of the Petrograd Soviet in restoring order. Seizing this moment, Sukhanov emphasized the necessity of establishing the provisional government immediately. He declared:

The Provisional Committee of the State Duma, which has taken the executive power

---

mittee. V. V. Shul'gin, *Dni*, p. 228. The main figures in the negotiations, Sukhanov and Miliukov, however, state that the Executive Committee had made the first move.

12. Sukhanov, *Zapiski o revoliutsii* 1: 271-72.

into its hand, is not a *government*, not even "provisional." It is necessary to create this government and on this account there undoubtedly exist definite intentions and plans on the part of the leading group of the State Duma. The Soviet of Workers' Deputies supports on its part the privileged elements to form a provisional government, considering that it follows from the general situation at hand and corresponds to the interests of the revolution. However, as the organizational and the ideological center of the popular movement, as the only organ capable at present of keeping this movement within limits and of directing it into certain channels, and as the only organ which has the real force at its disposal in the capital, it wishes to speak on its relations to the government formed in the right wing, explain how it sees its tasks, and in order to avoid complications, to state the demands that it presents to the government created by the revolution in the name of all democrats.[13]

After Sukhanov's speech, Steklov read the demands from a slip of paper, and explained each point as if he were giving a popular lecture in a workers' circle. As Steklov explained the Executive Committee's demands, Sukhanov observed the anxiety on the faces of the Duma Committee leaders, but "Nekrasov kept completely calm and on the face of Miliukov one could even catch the signs of complete satisfaction."[14]

Miliukov responded to the Executive Committee's demands. Most of the conditions were completely acceptable, he stated, since they had been included already in the program of the provisional government. Nevertheless, Miliukov had to raise objections on two points, first concerning the future form of the political system, and secondly, concerning soldiers' rights.[15] Rejecting the Executive Committee's demand for the introduction of the republican form of government, Miliukov argued that the question of the future form of government could be determined by the Russian people alone. Until the constituent assembly freely elected by the people expressed its opinion on this matter, neither the Executive Committee nor the Duma Committee should impose a republican or monarchical form of government on the nation. The immediate introduction of the republican form of government would mean the beginning of a new Time of Troubles. Therefore, in the transitional period until the convocation of the constituent assembly, the preservation of the monarchy in the form of the new tsar, Aleksei, under the regency of Grand Duke Mikhail Aleksandrovich, was necessary. According to Steklov, Miliukov stated that this position was final, and that without agreement on this point, there would be no agreement at all.[16] Chkheidze and Sokolov

13. Ibid., pp. 274-75.
14. Ibid., p. 278.
15. P. N. Miliukov, *Vospominaniia* 2: 306.
16. Tokarev, *Petrogradskii Sovet rabochikh i soldatskikh deputatov*, p. 92.

objected, and tried to convince the Duma Committee members of
the absurdity of their position in view of the total loss of prestige
of the Romanov dynasty and the monarchical system in general in
the eyes of the people. But Miliukov did not change his opinion.
While monarchists such as Rodzianko and Shul'gin remained silent,
Miliukov's militant stand on this issue surprised the Executive Committee's delegates. The Kadet leader was keenly aware of the powerlessness
of a provisional government with no legal or institutional foundations
to rely on. For this reason he was vitally interested in establishing
a constitutional monarchy before any discussions of the future form
of the political system could take place. Miliukov's perspective went
far beyond the revolutionized capital, and focused on the conservative
forces in the nation as a whole. He hoped that "the balance of national
forces would be called in to redress the balance of forces in the capital." To persuade the Executive Committee delegates to accept this
position, Miliukov even went as far as to say that "one is a sick child,
the other is a thoroughly stupid man."[17]

Also there was the immediate threat of the counterrevolutionary
forces that had been sent from the front to suppress the revolution
in the capital. The Duma Committee was determined to avoid confrontation between the revolution and the counterrevolution, but
the preservation of the monarchy appeared to be a necessary prerequisite to having the military leaders withdraw the troops.[18]

Although the Soviet delegates could not accept the preservation
of the monarchy as a matter of principle, they were prepared to drop
point three from their demands. Until March 1 the idea of the abolition
of the monarchy was considered too radical. Sukhanov even told
Zenzinov privately that the candidacy of Mikhail as regent would
be favorable "to the future struggle for democracy."[19] As long as
the Duma Committee and the provisional government pursued their
policy toward the monarchy independently without implicating the
Soviet, they saw nothing wrong with its result. They thus agreed
to leave the future form of government undecided, and the Duma
Committee would not be required to accept point three.

Miliukov raised another objection concerning the soldiers' rights.
Having learned a lesson from the violent reaction caused by Rodzianko's order, Miliukov had to swallow point eight, which promised to

17. Bryan Cartledge, "The Russian Revolution: February, 1917," *St. Anthony's
Papers* (June 1956), p. 39; Sukhanov, *Zapiski o revoliutsii* 1: 279.
18. See chaps. 23 and 24.
19. D. O. Zaslavskii and V. A. Kantorovich, *Khronika fevral'skoi revoliutsii*,
pp. 43-44; Zenzinov, "Fevral'skie dni," p. 226.

take no measure to disarm or withdraw from the capital any units that had taken part in the revolution. He argued, however, that to give soldiers full civil and political rights would be tantamount to destruction of the armed forces. Above all, he objected to the demand of the election of the officers. After some exchange of opinions, Miliukov accepted the demand for soldiers' civil rights "within the limitation permitted by military-technical conditions," while the Soviet representatives dropped the demand for the officers' election.[20]

Although the Executive Committee purposely excluded any demand concerning the war, Sokolov pointed out that he had heard a rumor that the new chairman of the Military Commission, Guchkov, was preparing a proclamation to the army with the appeal to fight the war to the victorious end. The Soviet representatives expressed their fear that such a proclamation would cause difficulty in the Executive Committee in its attempt to convince the masses of the necessity to reach an agreement with the Duma Committee. Sukhanov requested that such a proclamation should be stopped, and the Duma Committee, not interested in a confrontation with the Soviet, readily agreed.[21]

When the arguments on the conditions were exhausted, Sukhanov pleaded for complete acceptance of the Executive Committee's demands as modified by the Duma Committee as the program of the provisional government. He stated his reasons:

Among the masses, with every day and hour, an incomparably broader program was developing, which the masses were following and would follow. The leaders were straining all their energies to direct the movement into a definite channel, and keep it within reasonable limits. But if these limits were, under the complicated circumstances, to be settled imprudently and not in accordance with the swing of the movement, then spontaneous energy would sweep them away together with all the designed governmental "unity." Either we could stop this spontaneous energy or nobody could. The real power therefore was either ours or nobody's. Only one conclusion is possible: to agree to our conditions and accept them as the governmental program.[22]

There was actually no need for Sukhanov to make this plea, for the Duma Committee members, who had expected tougher negotiating terms from the Socialists, encompassing demands on socioeconomic problems and foreign policy, found them moderate enough to accept easily.

After the discussion of the Executive Committee's conditions,

20. Sukhanov, *Zapiski o revoliutsii* 1: 279; Miliukov, *Vospominaniia* 2: 307; Shul'gin, *Dni*, p. 231; Tokarev, *Petrogradskii Sovet rabochikh i soldatskikh deputatov*, pp. 64-65, 93.

21. Tokarev, *Petrogradskii Sovet rabochikh i soldatskikh deputatov*, p. 93.

22. Sukhanov, *Zapiski o revoliutsii* 1: 281.

Miliukov presented the Duma Committee's demands: (1) the Executive Committee should immediately take action to restore peace and order, and, in particular, to establish contact between soldiers and officers; and (2) the Executive Committee must proclaim that the provisional government was formed as a result of the argreement between the Duma Committee and the Soviet Executive Committee and that this government should be recognized as the sole legitimate government by the citizens. He also demanded that the declaration of the Soviet to that effect should be printed side by side with the government's proclamation. From Miliukov's point of view, this was precisely the purpose of the negotiations. The Duma Committee sought to reach an agreement with the Executive Committee to mobilize the support of the masses for the new government—a goal that all the attempts of the Duma Committee had so far failed to attain—by using the authority of the Petrograd Soviet.[23]

The Executive Committee representatives accepted these two demands readily. Having achieved his goal, Miliukov "did not even think of concealing his satisfaction and pleasant surprise." The meeting adjourned at three o'clock in the morning, satisfying all its participants. Two hours later, Miliukov, Sokolov, and Sukhanov met again to reach final agreement on the text of the proclamation. As for the Soviet's point three, they agreed that "they abstain from all activities that might determine the form of the future political system." According to Sukhanov this was a "middle-way compromise decision" to solve the contradiction between two diametrically opposing views by shelving the matter temporarily until the convocation of a constituent assembly.[24] The draft proposal Sokolov had prepared satisfied neither Miliukov nor Sukhanov. Miliukov rewrote the entire draft of the Soviet's proclamation, which was accepted by the Soviet representatives with minor changes. His draft appealed to the people to restore order and to avoid anarchy for the consolidation of the revolu-

23. Ibid., pp. 281-83. Schapiro states that the Duma Committee's acceptance of the Executive Committee's demands "predetermined the impotence of the government and laid the foundations for future anarchy." Leonard Schapiro, "The Political Thought of the First Provisional Government," in *Revolutionary Russia*, ed. Richard Pipes, p. 103. One must realize, however, that most of the conditions would have been included in the programs of the Provisional Government without any pressure from the Soviet. The agreement with the Soviet was precisely the measure by which the Duma Committee hoped to bolster the strength of the new government and to prevent further anarchy. The failure of this policy did not stem from its acceptance of the conditions, but from the more fundamental political relations at the time.

24. Sukhanov, *Zapiski o revoliutsii* 1: 258-59, 283.

tion. Miliukov writes: "This is almost the same thing that I had been telling the soldiers from the platform of the regiment barracks. And it was accepted for publication in the name of the Soviet!" His jubilation, however, was a little premature, as Steklov later changed the content of the proclamation entirely by exercising his editorial discretion.[25]

The negotiations between the Duma Committee and the Soviet Executive Committee appeared to have achieved the goals that both sides desired. The self-appointed delegates of the Executive Committee succeeded in having the Duma Committee accept their demands as the programs of the Provisional Government, while the Duma Committee gained the support of the Executive Committee for the creation of the Provisional Government. The success of the negotiations, however, was illusory, since both sides overestimated the influence of the Executive Committee among the insurgent masses. The Duma Committee falsely assumed that the Executive Committee and the insurgent masses who supported the Soviet were an unseparable unit. The leaders of the Executive Committee wishfully hoped that the presentation of the established fact would sway the allegiance of the masses to the Provisional Government. Yet the insurgent masses were not robots that moved in every direction that the Executive Committee leaders dictated. Within twenty-four hours after the negotiations, the Duma Committee as well as the leaders of the Executive Committee had to witness the fruit of the negotiations violently snatched out of their hands. Order No. 1, of which the Duma Committee members had little inkling during the negotiations, shattered any hope of the Duma Committee's chance of regaining the support of the soldiers. Steklov's editorial discretion and his speech at the fourth general session of the Soviet on March 2 substantially changed the Executive Committee's assurance of full-fledged support for the Provisional Government into a half-hearted, wishy-washy endorsement, which fostered suspicion rather than trust among the masses for the Provisional Government.

The discrepancies between the Executive Committee's original purpose to support the Provisional Government even to the point of weakening its power base and the later shift of policy in response to popular pressure were one of the most important causes for the birth of dual power. The Executive Committee chose to take an ambiguous, inconsistent position on the problem of power without giving the Provisional Government its full-fledged support or seeking to seize

25. Miliukov, *Vospominaniia* 2: 308. Also see Sukhanov, *Zapiski o revoliutsii* 1: 298; Miliukov, *Istoriia vtoroi russkoi revoliutsii* 1: 48. See chap. 27.

power on its own. Trotskii asks: "The insurrection triumphed. But to whom did it hand over the power snatched from the monarchy? We come here to the central problem of the February Revolution: Why and how did the power turn up in the hands of the liberal bourgeoisie?" His answer is that the moderate Socialists who stood at the head of the Soviet voluntarily surrendered the Soviet's already established power to the Provisional Government, for they believed, for ideological reasons, that power ought to pass to the bourgeoisie.[26] Since this interpretation enjoys wide circulation among historians both in the Soviet Union and in the West, one must closely examine its assumptions.

Trotskii assumes that the Soviet *was* already a revolutionary power. It is undoubtedly true that the Petrograd Soviet exerted more influence on the insurgent masses in Petrograd than its rival, the Duma Committee. An episode in which Rodzianko refused to leave the headquarters of the Duma Committee without a military escort authorized by the Soviet Executive Committee illustrated the relative influence of the two bodies. It is also true that the Petrograd Soviet took a series of executive measures that ranged from the food supply and the organization of the military forces to tramway fares and permission to publish newspapers.[27] Yet, one cannot conclusively say on this basis that the real governmental power rested with the Petrograd Soviet. In the first place, it did not possess the coercive power to execute its policy. The support of the insurgent soldiers for the Soviet, particularly after Rodzianko's order, was not immediately translated into a concrete military force capable of enforcing the will of the Soviet. In fact, as Mstislavskii's testimony introduced above vividly describes, the military forces available to the Soviet were indeed small. The insurgent soldiers constituted formidable forces for street demonstrations and lynching officers, but not nearly strong enough to counter any systematic attempt at counterrevolution. The workers did create the workers' militia, but its forces were not well incorporated into the Petrograd Soviet.

Nor did the Petrograd Soviet consciously attempt to seize the administrative machinery. For instance, it was not the Petrograd Soviet, but rather the Duma Committee, that seized the Ministry of Transport, that controlled railway transportation and the communications attached to it throughout Russia. Likewise, the Duma Com-

---

26. Leon Trotsky, *History of the Russian Revolution* 1: 153, 159.

27. Sukhanov, *Zapiski o revoliutsii* 1: 284; Tokarev discusses the Soviet's control over the city's transportation, postal system, and state financial matters. Tokarev, *Petrogradskii Sovet rabochikh i soldatskikh deputatov*, pp. 74-76.

mittee took over all the governmental machinery and were controlling not only the railways, but the telephones, telegraphs, banks, power stations, and other strategic positions. The Soviet even failed to cut off communication lines between Petrograd and the front, over which the Duma Committee assumed full control. Thus, if the Petrograd Soviet had any semblance of power, it was solely because the insurgents overwhelmingly supported it. The masses had established self-government in the workers' sections of the city in the form of the workers' militia as well as in the military units in the soldiers' committees. These self-governing forces still existed outside the Soviet, although the masses who created them pledged allegiance to the Soviet. It could have sought to seize power on the basis of these already established self-governing forces. The leaders of the Executive Committee, however, refused to take this forceful action. The Petrograd Soviet, therefore, was never a power and never meant to be such. Its leaders did not surrender state power to the Duma Committee but, rather, they simply refused to compete for this power.

Why did they refuse to strive for power? As Trotskii states, the ideological imperatives of Menshevism that a bourgeois-democratic revolution should precede a socialist revolution and that the bourgeoisie should carry out the task of this revolution no doubt played an important part. Sukhanov was the main architect of this policy, providing the theoretical foundations for it. According to Sukhanov, although the revolution was accomplished by the proletariat, it had neither real strength nor the indispensable prerequisites for an immediate socialistic transformation of the country. The immediate task of the revolution was to eliminate the feudal remnants and to transform the social, political, and economic systems of the country into democratic ones. This task, however, would be unachievable without the cooperation of the bourgeoisie.

> The revolution, which did not bring Russia immediately to socialism, must be led *straight to it* and guarantee complete freedom of socialistic construction in Russia. For this purpose it is indispensable to establish immediately the proper *political prerequisites:* ensure and consolidate the *dictatorship* of the democratic classes. . . .
> The Soviet democracy has to entrust power to the privileged elements, its class enemy; it cannot handle the technique of administration in these desperate conditions of disintegration, nor can it cope with the forces of tsarism without the participation [of this class] or if the forces of the bourgeoisie are completely opposed to it.[28] (Emphasis in the original)

28. Sukhanov, *Zapiski o revoliutsii* 1: 230-31.

Any attempt on the part of the Soviet to deprive the bourgeoisie of hopes of winning power would be detrimental to the interests of the revolution. Rather, the Soviet must encourage them to take power. Hence, the conditions that the Soviet imposed on the Provisional Government should be minimal. Basically "the assurance of complete political freedom in the country, and absolute freedom of organization and agitation" would be sufficient. The inclusion of any other issues would be harmful, since it might discourage the bourgeoisie from assuming power.[29]

The importance of the ideological imperatives notwithstanding, this was not the only reason why they failed to strive for power. According to Viktor Chernov, the leader of the SR party, "neither theory nor doctrine triumphed in the ranks of the Soviet democracy, but it was the direct sensation of the *burden of power* that triumphed, when doctrinaires proposed—with the corresponding theoretical basis —to lift this burden from their shoulders to the shoulders of the privileged class" (emphasis in the original).[30] Chernov further points out five organizational weaknesses of the Executive Committee, which contributed to its refusal to take power. First, its members gravely differed in their opinions on a number of fundamental issues. They could not have brought up these issues, which a future government would inevitably face, without risking a serious organizational crisis among themselves. Second, while the Duma Committee was represented by the most capable leaders in Russia, the best men of the "Soviet democracy" were absent from the capital. The lesser caliber of Socialist leaders, who took the task of leading the Soviet, shrank from the grave responsibilities, "which would perhaps have been unbearable even for their leaders." Third, while the leaders of the Duma Committee were well known throughout Russia, few people except in small circles of the labor movement and Socialist groups knew the leaders of the Soviet. Fourth, in contrast to the Duma Committee leaders, who were experts in the technique of administration, the Socialists in the Soviet were without experience. Finally, the "bourgeois parties" had had more than ten years of public existence, but the revolutionary parties, thrust upon the open stage from the obscure underground, could not quickly adjust themselves to legal procedures.[31] Chernov certainly overstates the last two points. One should not overlook the importance of the legal activities of the Socialist parties, while one

29. Ibid., pp. 225 ff.

30. Viktor Chernov, *Rozhdenie revoliutsionnoi Rossii: Fevral'skaia revoliutsiia*, pp. 246-47.

31. Ibid., pp. 243 ff.

must recognize that the Socialist deputies in the Duma as well as the labor leaders in the Central War Industries Committee had developed expertise in administrative technique as much as their colleagues in these bodies. Nevertheless, Chernov's argument in general is well taken. The undisputed leaders of the revolutionary parties—Lenin, Trotskii, Martov, Tseretelli, Chernov, Dan, and many others—had to hear the news of the February Revolution abroad or in Siberia. Such obscure figures as Sukhanov, Steklov, and Sokolov took the reins of leadership of the Soviet, avoiding any controversial issues so as to insure the fragile unity of the "revolutionary democracy," and transferring the handling of executive matters to the Duma Committee.

Their refusal to strive for power was made more determined by their fear of popular pressure from below as much as awareness of their organizational weaknesses. The overwhelming support of the insurgent masses, which showed every sign of driving the Soviet to the pinnacle of power, while granting to it powerful influence, frightened the Soviet leaders. The Russian revolutionary intelligentsia, who had worked tirelessly for more than half a century to incite a mass uprising against autocracy, shrank from the destructive forces suddenly unleashed. Their sense of alienation from the masses in victory equaled the alienation they had felt in setbacks. Sukhanov warned Miliukov on February 27 of the danger that "the popular demands . . . would inevitably be expanded to the most extreme limits," and that "the movement would turn into an uncontrollable explosion of *stikhiia*."[32] Mstislavskii noted that both the leaders of the Soviet Executive Committee and of the Duma Committee had a common fear of the masses. The day before yesterday, he stated, it had been easy to be leaders of the working class and to make speeches "in the name of the proletariat," but "when . . . this theoretical proletariat stood here, side by side, in full height, in full power of its emaciated flesh and of revolting blood . . . unintentionally the words of inquietude, instead of militant slogans, began to be mumbled from the pale mouths of the 'leaders.' They grew frightened."[33] It would not be unreasonable to assume that the leaders of the Executive Committee found it more comfortable to talk with the representatives of the Duma Committee than to deliver speeches in front of the masses in the general sessions of the Soviet.

Nevertheless, it would be unfair to picture the Soviet leaders during the February Revolution merely as naïve pipe dreamers who missed the opportunity to receive power presented to them for the

32. Sukhanov, *Zapiski o revoliutsii* 1: 118.
33. S. Mstislavskii, *Piat' dnei: Nachalo i konets fevral'skoi revoliutsii*, pp. 56-57.

sake of their ideological purity or as soft-kneed cowards who ran scared at the prospect of power. Their decision was partly based on a realistic evaluation of political relations at the time. Skobelev later stated that when he had made speeches to the first group of soldiers who arrived at the Tauride Palace, he was certain that he was making one of his last speeches, and that in a few days he would be shot or hanged. Peshekhonov accepted the position in the Executive Committee, although the thought occurred to him that it might lead him to the gallows.[34] All the leaders were painfully aware of the powerlessness and the disorganization of the revolutionary forces. Steklov described the general sentiment of the Soviet leaders at the Soviet Conference held on March 30 as follows:

Why was the problem of immediate seizure of power into our hands not raised before us at that moment? . . . The first reason is that when an agreement was planned, it was quite uncertain whether the revolution would triumph, not only in the form of revolutionary democracy but even in a moderate bourgeois form. Comrades, you who were not here in Petrograd and have not experienced this revolutionary fever cannot imagine how we lived. Surrounded in the Duma by isolated platoons of soldiers who did not have even noncommissioned officers, and who had not even succeeded in formulating any political programs of the moment, we knew at the moment that the ministers were meeting at leisure somewhere either in the Admiralty or in the Marinskii Palace. The atmosphere of the troops in general and the atmosphere of the Tsarskoe Selo Garrison were not known to us and we were informed that they were marching to us. We heard the rumor that from the north five regiments were dispatched, that General Ivanov was leading twenty-six echelons and that in the streets shots were exchanged. We thought that this weak group who surrounded the palace would be crushed. Every moment we expected that they would come and arrest us, if not shoot us. We, like the ancient Romans, sat and spoke with an air of importance, but there was no complete certainty of success of the revolution at that time.[35]

The members of the Executive Committee shared this deep fear of counterrevolution—which an episode that took place in the middle of the Executive Committee meeting on February 28 illustrates. A few machine-gun shots were heard in the courtyard of the palace. Someone shouted: "Cossacks!" Taken by sudden panic, some flung themselves onto the floor, while others started running away from the room. Kerenskii shouted in his shrill voice: "Get ready! Defend the Duma! Listen! I tell you, I, Kerenskii, tell you—defend your freedom! Defend the Revolution!" Sukhanov writes: "There could be no doubt; if Cossacks or any sort of organized unit had really

34. Quoted in A. I. Denikin, *Ocherki russkoi smuty* 1, pt. 1: 47; A. V. Peshekhonov, "Pervyia nedeli: Iz vospominanii o revoliutsii"; *Na chuzhoi storone* 1 (1923): 262.
35. *Izvestiia*, April 5, 1917 g., p. 4.

been attacking us, however negligible their number might have been, we could not have looked anywhere for salvation and they would have conquered the revolution with their bare hands."[36] It turned out, however, that the shots had been fired by a noncommissioned officer of the machine-gun regiment to find his lost leader in the quickest way, which made Kerenskii's hysterical speech look embarrassingly silly. Sukhanov told Kerenskii, "Perhaps it would have been wise if you had not spoken. Your words came nearer precipitating a panic than shots did." Kerenskii did not quite appreciate this friendly advice. He jumped up, face distorted and lips trembling with fury, and shouted: "I ask everyone to do his duty and not to interfere with me when I give orders." After these words he left the room hurriedly.[37]

The fear of counterrevolution, however, was by no means only a paranoia on the part of the Soviet leaders. Steklov's information on the counterrevolutionary forces was not an illusion, but reality. The Soviet leaders realistically believed that the undisciplined soldiers and untrained workers would have been impotent before a large-scale military suppression. The only alternative for the survival of the revolution appeared to the Soviet leaders to lie in the possibility of broadening its base so as to include the liberal opposition. If the liberals stood at the forefront of the revolution, it would disguise the intense class contents of the revolution, and it would appear as if it were a patriotic, national revolution, one more palatable to the military leaders. This judgment was quite sound. The Soviet could not have established a revolutionary government without inviting a counterrevolution; and had the Soviet government faced determined resistance from the army in the front, in view of the disorganization of the insurgents and the ideological disunity among its leaders, it would not have stood for a day. The Executive Committee leaders' decision to help the Duma Committee to form a provisional government thus saved the revolution from taking a precipitous course to a civil war.

Trotskii called the transfer of power by the Soviet leaders to the Provisional Government "a paradox of the February Revolution." Yet close examination of the relations of the political forces demonstrates that there was nothing paradoxical about their refusal to strive for power. They did not have power, nor did they intend to take power. Even if they had so intended, they could not have taken power without risking the future of the revolution.

36. Sukhanov, *Zapiski o revoliutsii* 1: 200; Tarasonov-Rodionov, *February 1917*, pp. 115-16; Shliapnikov, *Semnadtsatyi god* 1: 189.
37. Sukhanov, *Zapiski o revoliutsii* 1: 200.

PART V

The Abdication
of Nicholas II

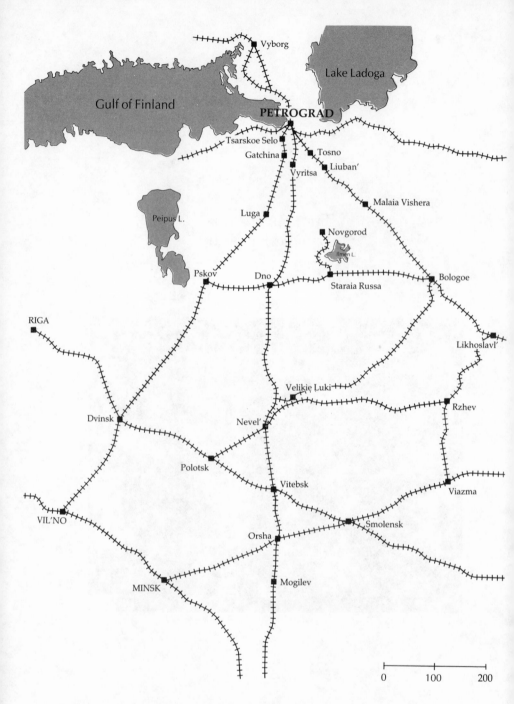

Railways of northwestern Russia; *preceding page,* the abdication of Nicholas II by an unknown painter (*from left to right,* Count Fredericks, General Ruzskii, V. V. Shul'gin, A. I. Guchkov, K. A. Naryshkin, Nicholas II [State Historical Museum, Moscow])

22

NICHOLAS II

AND THE REVOLUTION

 Tsar Nicholas left Tsarskoe Selo on February 22 to resume his duties at the front as supreme commander in chief, and arrived in Mogilev on the next day. The intolerable loneliness resulting from his separation from his family overwhelmed Nicholas in the Stavka, although he felt a sense of relief in being emancipated from the burdens of political problems in the captial and in being able to resume a quiet, secluded life. He wrote in one of his letters to Aleksandra: "My brain takes rest here—no ministers, no troublesome problems requiring my attention. I think this is good for me, but only for my brain. My heart aches from the separation. I hate this separation, particularly at such a time! I shall not stay here for long."[1] His life in the Stavka went uneventfully, as he resumed his routine schedule, methodically dividing his time between ceremonious teas and suppers, holding audiences to hear formal reports, daily outings, and games of dominos. One member of his entourage, A. Mordvinov, noted that "One day after another passed like two drops of water."[2]

During the first few days after his arrival in Mogilev, Nicholas's mind was mainly occupied by his concern for his children, who, he learned after his arrival, had been stricken with measles. The condition

1. "Perepiska Nikolaia Romanova s Aleksandroi Fedorovnoi," *Krasnyi arkhiv* 4, no. 4 (1923): 207-8.
2. A. Mordvinov, "Otryvki iz vospominanii," *Russkaia letopis'* 5 (1923): 86. For Nicholas's daily schedule see A. Tal', "Memuary ob otrechenii ot prestola rossiskago gosudarstva Imperatora Nikolaia II," pp. 4-5.

THE ABDICATION OF NICHOLAS II

of the sick children was reported in detail in Aleksandra's daily letters to her husband. Among the minutiae of family affairs, however, there soon appeared a discordant commentary on what was happening outside their family. In a letter dated February 24, Aleksandra noted the disturbances in Petrograd, and urged Nicholas to "expel Kedrenskii [Kerenskii] from the Duma because of his dreadful speech—this is necessary (military law in wartime) and will set an example." On the next day she wrote: "This is a hooligan movement: little urchins are running and shouting that they have no bread, simply to create confusion. Workers are hampering others from working. If the weather were very cold, probably they all would stay home. But this will be all over and will calm down if only the Duma behaves itself well. They are printing the worst speeches, and I think that those anti-dynastic speeches should be *immediately* and very severely punished, all the more so since it is now a time of war." She further suggested that the strikers should be punished by deportation to the front as soldiers.[3]

By February 25 the news of labor unrest in Petrograd had reached the Stavka from other sources. The palace commandant, General V. N. Voeikov, received reports from Protopopov and the director of the palace police, Colonel Geradi. The entourage began discussing the disturbing news. On this day Nicholas reacted to the crisis by issuing an order to Khabalov to stop the unrest by the next day. Nicholas's letters, telegrams, and diary do not explain his thinking behind this decision, since absolutely nothing is mentioned about the political situation in Petrograd. Nor is there any evidence to indicate that he consulted anyone in reaching this decision. It appears likely that he took this step without seriously deliberating its consequences.

On February 26 government troops began their offensive against the demonstrators. All the reports that reached the Stavka indicated an improving situation in Petrograd. Aleksandra noted that the government had taken "rigorous measures," including the arrest of the ringleaders of the movement, and predicted that everything would return to normal by the next day. As if this optimism had relieved his concern, Nicholas broke his silence and for the first time commented on the crisis in Petrograd in his letter to his wife: "I hope that Khabalov can immediately halt these street disorders. Protopopov must give him clear and definite instructions. I only hope that old Golitsyn will not lose his head."[4] In this optimistic atmosphere,

3. "Perepiska Nikolaia Romanova," pp. 207-9.
4. Ibid., pp. 209, 212.

Rodzianko's telegram to the tsar, which emphasized the danger of the spontaneous mass movement and the powerlessness of the government, struck Nicholas as being strange. Accustomed to Rodzianko's alarmism in the past, he immediately dismissed his recommendation to grant a ministry of confidence and told Count Frederiks: "That fat Rodzianko wrote to me all kinds of nonsense, to which I will not even reply."[5] Despite the flippancy of the statement, given the political philosophy of Nicholas, his reaction to Rodzianko's telegram was understandable. If he had found it unnecessary to grant political concessions in the past, there was absolutely no reason why Nicholas should have suddenly changed his policy on the basis of Rodzianko's distorted information, which contradicted all other reports he had received.

Rodzianko not only appealed directly to the tsar to grant a ministry of confidence, but also attempted to convince the high command to prevail upon Nicholas to make this desired political move. Only two generals, Brusilov and Ruzskii, responded favorably to Rodzianko's telegrams. Brusilov wrote to Alekseev, "In view of the approaching storm of the times I do not see any other alternative."[6] General Ruzskii sent his telegram directly to the tsar, and urged him to consider the "adoption of urgent measures, which could appease the population and instill in them confidence, courage, and faith in themselves and their future." He concluded, "Under existing circumstances repressive measures could only aggravate the situation rather than accomplish the necessary, lasting peace."[7] Brusilov's recommendation had no impact whatever, since Nicholas did not consider the situation in Petrograd serious enough to warrant such drastic action, while Ruzskii's advice, which reached the tsar late in the evening of February 27, likewise fell on deaf ears. By this time Nicholas had made up his mind to solve the crisis in Petrograd by force.

The first news of the soldiers' uprising in Petrograd reached the Stavka early in the afternoon of February 27. Khabalov's special telegram to the tsar informed the Stavka for the first time of the spread of the insurrection from Volynskii Regiment to the Lithuanian

5. See chap. 15.

6. "Fevral'skaia revoliutsiia 1917 goda: Dokumenty stavki verkhovnogo glavnokomanduiuschego i shtaba glavnokomanduiuschego armiiami severnogo fronta," *Krasnyi arkhiv* 21, no. 2 (1927): 7.

7. Ibid., p. 13. Although this telegram was sent from Pskov at 9:15 P.M. on February 27, its contents indicate that Ruzskii had not received the news of the soldiers' insurrection in Petrograd, nor did he have any knowledge of Rodzianko's second telegram.

and Preobrazhenskii Regiments, and requested the immediate dispatch of reliable troops from the front. The Stavka, however, did not take the matter seriously as yet, since a telegram from Beliaev, which immediately followed Khabalov's, optimistically assured that every conceivable measure had been taken to suppress the disorder rigorously and that the government maintained complete calm.[8] It was not until that evening, when alarming news started pouring in, that the high command began to realize the magnitude of the crisis in Petrograd.

After learning of the soldiers' insurrection, Nicholas made two decisions: to send reliable troops to Petrograd to suppress the disorder and to leave the Stavka for Tsarskoe Selo on the next day. It is not known exactly how and when the first decision was made, but it appears that the appointment of General Ivanov as commander of the punitive detachment was made before seven o'clock in the evening, before the Stavka realized the seriousness of the situation in Petrograd. Nicholas wrote to his wife: "After yesterday's news from the city I see here many frightened faces. Fortunately, Alekseev is calm, but I think it is necessary to appoint a very energetic person to compel the ministers to work for the solution of such problems as food supply, railway transportation, and fuel, etc."[9]

Nicholas also made the decision to leave Mogilev before he fully realized the seriousness of the situation in the capital. He wrote in his diary on February 27: "After lunch I decided to return to Tsarskoe Selo." He informed his wife in the telegram sent at seven o'clock in the evening, February 27, that he would leave Mogilev at 2:30 in the afternoon of the following day.[10] News of the deterioration of the crisis in Petrograd, however, changed his original schedule. After

8. Khabalov to the tsar, no. 56, "Fevral'skaia revoliutsiia 1917 goda," p. 8; Beliaev to Alekseev, no. 196, ibid.

9. "Perepiska Nikolaia Romanova," p. 213. The contents of the letter, which referred to the food supply and other problems as the major points at issue, strongly indicate that this letter was written before he received the news of the deterioration of the situation in Petrograd. Nicholas and Alekseev therefore made the decision to send the punitive detachment before they knew how serious the uprising in Petrograd was. Katkov's assertion that this decision was made late at night appears to be inaccurate. George Katkov, *Russia 1917: The February Revolution*, p. 307. Ivanov clearly stated that this appointment was made before dinner, which took place usually at seven-thirty. See S. P. Mel'gunov, *Martovskie dni 1917 goda*, pp. 143-44.

10. "Dnevnik Nikolaia Romanova," *Krasnyi arkhiv* 20, no. 1 (1927): 137. "Perepiska Nikolaia Romanova," p. 213. Palace Commandant Voeikov instructed Colonel von Thal to prepare the imperial trains so as to be able to leave by 2:30. Tal', "Memuary ob otrechenii," p. 7.

ten o'clock in the evening, Voeikov received a telegram at Tsarskoe Selo from the grand marshal of the Imperial Court, Count Bencken-dorff, who conveyed a message from the empress, who, on the verge of nervous exhaustion, sought her husband's advice as to the advisa-bility of her leaving Tsarskoe Selo with her sick children for Mogilev. While instructing Aleksandra to stay in Tsarskoe Selo, Nicholas immediately had arrangements made for an early departure.[11] The disturbing news of the situation in Petrograd, however, made the high command realize the risk of the tsar's trip to Tsarskoe Selo. The imperial train would hinder transportation of reinforcement troops from the front to the capital—the main concern of the high command at that moment—while Tsarskoe Selo was dangerously close to the heart of the trouble, where Nicholas might not expect to find many reliable troops. Moreover, the tsar's departure from Mogilev would inevitably create difficulties in communication between the Stavka and the emperor. But Nicholas was not in the mood to listen to Alekseev's objections. General Bazilii sarcastically remarked: "He was first of all an excellent husband and a good father. In these moments of anguish he was anxious about his own family and desired above all to be with them."[12]

During the day and evening of February 27 Nicholas continued to receive unsolicited advice from various quarters to seek a political solution. In the afternoon the tsar received another telegram from Rodzianko, which passionately requested the tsar to rescind the decree of prorogation of the Duma and to appoint a new cabinet enjoying the trust of the country.[13] Not realizing the seriousness of the crisis yet, Nicholas treated this telegram as a nuisance. When the news of Petrograd's paralysis reached the Stavka, Nicholas was even more firmly determined to pursue the military solution alone. At half past ten, Grand Duke Mikhail requested from Petrograd a direct telegraphic conversation with the tsar. The grand duke suggested that to bring

11. Paul Benckendorff, *Last Days at Tsarskoe Selo*, p. 2; V. A. Voeikov, *S tsarem i bez tsaria: Vospominaniia posledniago dvortsovago komendanta gosudaria Imperatora Nikolaia II*, pp. 200-201. According to Spirodovich, this suggestion actually originated from Rodzianko. A. I. Spiridovich, *Velikaia voina i fevral'skaia revoliutsiia, 1914-1917 gg.* 3: 150.

12. Nicolas de Basily, *Diplomat of Imperial Russia, 1903-1917: Memoirs*, p. 110.

13. Rodzianko to the tsar, "Fevral'skaia revoliutsiia 1917 goda," *Krasnyi arkhiv* 20, no. 1 (1927): 6-7. Alekseev, who showed this telegram to Nicholas, confided to Bazilii: "Again I did everything possible to convince him to take the road to salvation at last. Again, I ran against a wall." Basily, *Diplomat of Imperial Russia*, p. 106.

the anarchy to an end it would be necessary to dismiss the present ministry and to organize a new cabinet that could enjoy the trust of the emperor as well as command the respect and confidence of the nation. He then requested the tsar's permission for the issuance of a manifesto to that effect in the tsar's name, and suggested that Prince L'vov would be the most suitable candidate for the head of the future cabinet.[14] To General Alekseev's reply that the tsar would leave the Stavka on the next day for Tsarskoe Selo, Mikhail said that it might be wise to delay his departure for a few days. When Nicholas received his brother's message, he refused to communicate directly with him, as Mikhail requested, and had General Alekseev convey his reply. The tsar, through Alekseev, thanked the grand duke for his "thoughtful suggestions," but bluntly rejected them one by one. First, the tsar did not consider it possible to postpone his departure for Tsarskoe Selo. Second, concerning the dismissal of the Council of Ministers, the tsar himself would decide on this matter pending his return to the capital. Third, with regard to the suppression of the disorder in the capital, General Ivanov would be sent to Petrograd for that purpose. Fourth, on the next day reliable troops would be sent to the capital from the northern and the western fronts.[15]

Although General Alekseev fully endorsed Nicholas's policy for military suppression of the disorder in Petrograd, he nevertheless considered it equally important to seek a political solution acceptable to the Duma liberals. In his telegraphic conversations with Mikhail, Alekseev implied his agreement with Mikhail's recommendation and promised to urge the emperor to "take some measures" when he reported to the tsar on the next morning.[16] Shortly after this conversation was over, a telegram from Golitsyn arrived, reporting to the emperor that the cabinet found itself unable to function in the face of the prevailing anarchy, and imploring the tsar to relieve the ministers of their duties and to appoint a new ministry enjoying the confidence of the nation. Despite the high fever from which he was suffering, Alekseev got out of his bed and implored the tsar "on his knees" to seek the political solution recommended by Golitsyn. His request, however, was again to no avail. Returning from the frustrating audience, Alekseev told General Lukomskii: "The Emperor was very displeased with the contents of Golitsyn's telegram and stated that he would write the reply by himself. . . . The Emperor simply did not want to talk to me." A few hours later Nicholas appeared

    14. "Fevral'skaia revoliutsiia 1917 goda," p. 11. Also see chap. 17.
    15. "Fevral'skaia revoliutsiia 1917 goda," p. 12.
    16. Ibid.

in person in Lukomskii's room and handed a copy of the imperial order to Golitsyn. In this telegram Nicholas rejected Golitsyn's request for resignation and informed him of the appointment of the new commander of the Petrograd Military District. The tsar declared: "This is my final decision, which I shall not change, and therefore, it is useless to report to me further on this issue."[17] Early in the morning, shortly before his departure, Nicholas received General Ivanov in the salon car of the imperial train, and appointed him military dictator of the Petrograd Military District by extending his power to civilian affairs. As firm as ever in his rejection of compromise, Nicholas and his entourage left Mogilev at five o'clock on the morning of February 28. He had no inkling of what was in store for him on this fateful journey. As the train left the station, soldiers assembled on the platform for departure to the front shouted enthusiastic hurrahs. Spontaneously they began singing a hymn.[18]

Since the direct line between Mogilev and Tsarskoe Selo was reserved for General Ivanov's expedition, the tsar and his entourage traveled along the longer, roundabout way through Orsha, Smolensk, Viaz'ma, Rzhev, Likhoslavl', and the Nikolaevskii Line from Likhoslavl' through Bologoe, Malaia Vishera, and Tosno, and from Tosno to Tsarskoe Selo from a branch line (see map of northwestern railways on p. 430). For security reasons the tsar always traveled in two trains— the suite train and the imperial train. Train B, which held the entourage, proceeded first and any information they received along the way was relayed in code to Train A, which was moving one hour behind the suite train.[19] The two trains moved slowly through the snow-covered countryside without obstruction. Colonel von Thal, commandant of the railway regiment, who was on board the suite

17. A. S. Lukomskii, *Vospominaniia* 1: 126-27; Basily, *Diplomat of Imperial Russia*, p. 111. Nicholas to Golitsyn, "Fevral'skaia revoliutsiia 1917 goda," p. 13.

18. According to Mordvinov, Naryshkin, who witnessed the scene, whispered to Mordvinov: "Who knows? This might be the last hurrah the emperor might hear." Mordvinov, "Otryvki iz vospominanii," p. 96. This is unlikely, since no one could possibly expect Nicholas's abdication as early as February 28.

19. The emperor's entourage consisted of the following: minister of the imperial court, General Count V. B. Frederiks; Flag Captain General K. D. Nilov; Palace Commandant Major-General V. N. Voeikov; head of military campaign bureau, Major-General K. A. Naryshkin; commander of the convoy of His Majesty, Major-General Count A. N. Grabbe; Count Nitikin; court historian, Major-General D. N. Dubenskii; commander of the railway regiment, Major-General Tsabel'; imperial physician, Professor S. A. Fedorov; military ceremony, Baron Rudolf A. Stakelberg; aide-de-camp to the emperor, Colonel Mordvinov; and marshal of the court, V. A. Dolgorukii. D. N. Dubenskii, "Kak proizoshel perevorot v Rossii: Zapiski-dnevniki," *Russakai letopis'* 3 (1922): 22.

train, noted that "There was absolutely no sign of disturbance or confusion either along the railway or in the cities we passed through.
Everything was quiet and calm."[20] The gendarmes and the troops
protecting the railway stations greeted the imperial trains with loud
hurrahs as they passed through the stations. As they went along,
however, in contrast to the quiet surroundings, they began receiving
disturbing news of the deteriorating situation in Petrograd. The suite
train (B), which arrived at Rzhev at five o'clock in the evening, learned
that in Petrograd a "Provisional Government" (actually the Duma
Committee) had been formed. This news was confirmed four hours
later when Bublikov's telegram to all the railway stations in Russia
reached Train B between Likhoslavl' and Bologoe. Nevertheless, this
did not change Nicholas's plans; in fact, he did not appear to attach
any significance to it at all.[21]

As the suite train approached Bologoe, however, even more disturbing news arrived. At a small station near Bologoe the entourage received
an order signed by a certain Grekov, who assumed the title of commandant of Nikolaevskii Station in Petrograd, to the stationmasters of the
Nikolaevskii Line to reroute the imperial trains directly to Petrograd
and not to allow them to proceed to Tsarskoe Selo. The entourage
immediately discussed what course they should take. The court
historian, Dubenskii, sent a telegram to Voeikov in Train A, outlining
this alarming news and advising that the imperial trains should change
directions at Bologoe towards Pskov rather than risking the danger
of falling into the hands of the rebels. To Dubenskii's disappointment,
however, the telegram from Voeikov that awaited the suite train at
Bologoe instructed Train B to "break through to Tsarskoe Selo at all
costs."[22]

Despite the entourage's deep misgivings, the suite train proceeded as
far as Malaia Vishera, where it arrived at 1:55 A.M. on March 1. When

20. Tal', "Memuary ob otrechenii," p. 20. Colonel von Thal was, as commandant of the railway regiment, responsible for the technical details of the movement
of the trains as well as for general information. His handwritten manuscript in the
Hoover Institution is one of the most important and accurate sources of information regarding the movement of the imperial trains from February 28 to March 1.

21. In neither of two telegrams he sent to his wife on the way nor in his diary
did he mention anything about incoming news. The entry for February 28 in his
diary simply states: "I went to bed at 3:25, since I talked for a long time with
N. I. Ivanov, whom I am sending to Petrograd with troops in order to restore
order. I slept until 10. I left Mogilev at five in the morning. The weather is frosty
and sunny. During the day we went through Viaz'ma, Rzhev, and Likhoslavl'
at nine." "Dnevnik Nikolaia Romanova," p. 137.

22. Tal', "Memuary ob otrechenii," p. 23, 30; Dubenskii, "Kak proizoshel
perevorot," pp. 40-41.

von Thal was giving the stationmaster instructions to make arrangements for departure, an officer of the railway regiment, Lieutenant Geliakh, arrived in the station from the opposite direction, and brought grave news. The stations Liuban' and Tosno had been captured by revolutionary troops led by companies of the Lithuanian Regiment. Armed with machine guns, these rebels had completely destroyed the railway regiment that guarded the stations. The troops that had occupied Liuban' and Tosno were now approaching Malaia Vishera.[23] The imperial train (A) arrived fifteen minutes after this frightening news was brought to the entourage. To the surprise of the worried entourage, however, all the passengers including Voeikov were fast asleep. The news was immediately brought to Voeikov. Some favored returning to Mogilev, but a majority of the entourage proposed to go to Pskov. Voeikov finally made the decision to direct the trains to Pskov—the headquarters of the northern front, where he could expect reliable troops and have access to the Hughes telegraphic apparatus. Nicholas, who was awakened and informed of this decision, readily approved it. He had not abandoned his will to join his family, and Pskov was closer to Tsarskoe Selo than Mogilev was.[24]

The trains left Malaia Vishera at 3:35 back for Bologoe. The trains reversed order, with Train A going first and Train B leaving twenty minutes later. They returned to Bologoe at seven o'clock in the morning, and changed direction to the West. As soon as the imperial trains left the Nikolaevskii Line, new information from the capital ceased to arrive. The emperor's company noticed no signs of disturbance along the line. All security measures were carried out with precision. As the imperial train passed the station at Staraia Russa, they saw a large crowd on the platform taking off their hats and bowing deeply. Dubenskii noted: "Our trains proceeded quietly without the slightest difficulty. The only change in our movement was that we proceeded more slowly since the route was not familiar and we had to slow down our speed."[25]

When the imperial trains reached Dno around half past four in the afternoon, Rodzianko's telegram awaited the emperor. Rodzianko requested an immediate audience with the tsar on "an urgent matter" at Dno Station, where he was expected to have arrived hours earlier. Pacing on the platform with some of his entourage, Nicholas waited for the arrival of the chairman of the Duma patiently. More than half

23. Dubenskii, "Kak proizoshel perevorot," pp. 41-42; Tal', "Memuary ob otrechenii," p. 34.
24. Tal', "Memuary ob otrechenii," pp. 36-37; Dubenskii, "Kak proizoshel perevorot," p. 43; Voeikov, S tsarem i bez tsaria, pp. 204-5.
25. Dubenskii, "Kak proizoshel perevorot," p. 45.

an hour had elapsed, but Rodzianko never showed up. Voeikov telegraphed Petrograd and discovered that although Rodzianko's train
had been prepared for his departure, he had been preoccupied with
some important meeting and had not left Petrograd. At the same
time, Voeikov learned that the railway line connecting the Vindarskii
Line and Tsarskoe Selo had been seized by revolutionary troops.
On this information the tsar abandoned the venture to Tsarskoe Selo
and decided to proceed to Pskov as planned, and wait for Rodzianko
there.[26]

The tsar finally arrived at Pskov at eight o'clock on the evening
of March 1. The absence of ceremony usually accorded to such an
occasion immediately struck the entourage. There was no official
reception, nor was a guard of honor present. On the platform the
governor of Pskov and his subordinates welcomed the emperor, but
conspicuous was the absence of the commander of the northern front,
General Ruzskii, and his staff. Only a few minutes afterwards, Ruzskii
arrived hurriedly "in rubber galoshes" with his chief of staff, General
Iurii N. Danilov, to meet the emperor.[27]

The two days when Nicholas was traveling along the railway line
in the countryside of Russia were crucial moments for the outcome
of the February Revolution. The Duma Committee and the military
leaders had defined their attitude toward the revolution during these
two days. The political atmosphere on the evening of March 1, when
Nicholas arrived in Pskov, was radically different from the one he
had left behind in Mogilev. Nicholas's failure to intervene actively
during these crucial two days was, indeed, important to the outcome
of political developments. That Nicholas lost two valuable days was
not necessarily a historical accident. An important force was at work
to nullify Nicholas's intervention in the course of events. When one
analyzes the information Nicholas received throughout this journey,
one cannot but recognize a certain artificialness in it. Nicholas changed
the direction of the trains based on information supplied by a single
officer of the railway regiment, the accuracy of which was not verified
by any other evidence. In fact, the only evidence of the capture of
Liuban' and Tosno comes from the secondhand information of the
imperial entourage. It is strange also that the tsar's company suddenly
received no further information as soon as the trains changed their
direction at Malaia Vishera, although they had received numerous
reports until then indicating the seriousness of the situation in Petrograd. The report on the seizure of the branch line between the

26. Voeikov, *S tsarem i bez tsaria*, pp. 205-6; Tal', "Memuary ob otrechenii,"
pp. 42-43.
27. Dubenskii, "Kak proizoshel perevorot," pp. 46-47.

Vindarskii Line and Tsarskoe Selo—the report that led Nicholas to abandon the journey to Tsarskoe Selo from Dno—is not corroborated by other historical evidence, either. In fact, General Ivanov had no trouble traveling that route during the day. It is incongruous to assume that Rodzianko's train was arranged without trouble, when the commandant of the station defiantly ordered the capture of the imperial trains. To solve these mysterious circumstances, we must now turn to the policy of the Duma Committee during these two days.

23

THE DUMA COMMITTEE
AND THE MONARCHY

 It is difficult to ascertain exactly how the Duma Committee decided on its policy about the monarchy from February 27 to March 2. Documentary evidence regarding the debates of the Duma Committee is lacking,[1] and the memoirs of the major participants are often contradictory. The difficulty is further compounded by the power struggle among the Duma Committee members, who pursued different approaches. This made it nearly impossible for the Duma Committee as a whole to follow a consistent, united policy. Two ambitious men, Rodzianko and Miliukov, struggled for the position of power,[2] while a third, less conspicuous force—Kerenskii and Nekrasov—quietly extended their influence. Guchkov, though himself not officially a member, loomed around the Duma Committee, and often exerted important yet unobtrusive influence. The Duma Committee's formulation of policy on the dynastic question was closely connected with the power struggle among these men.

At the beginning Rodzianko, as chairman of the Duma as well as the head of the Duma Committee, exerted unquestioned leadership. He pursued his policy in the name of the Duma and the Duma Committee without consulting other members. All the proclamations and orders of the Duma Committee were issued in the name of Rodzianko, chairman of the Duma. At first, his colleagues accepted his leadership,

1. *Protokoly sobytii* used by Burdzhalov and Chermenskii might be an important document on this, but it was unavailable to me.
2. For the rivalry between Miliukov and Rodzianko see George Katkov, *Russia 1917: The February Revolution*, pp. 291-93.

since they found his authority useful in extending the prestige of the Duma Committee, whose legitimacy was questionable. But as the revolution developed further in the capital, Rodzianko's influence slipped considerably, and Miliukov replaced Rodzianko as the Duma Committee's spokesman. With this shift of power, the Duma Committee's policy toward the monarchy took a dramatic twist.

His personal ambition and conservative desire to avoid a drastic political change guided Rodzianko's conduct during the February Revolution. As chairman of the Duma he always considered himself spokesman of the liberal forces, while as a moderate in the liberal opposition he had sought to achieve a compromise between the liberals and the bureaucracy. He thought of himself as a logical candidate to head a ministry of confidence. In fact, his name was often mentioned for the post of the chairman of the Council of Ministers in a list of a possible ministry of confidence circulated among the liberal opposition circles. When Protopopov's appointment to the post of acting minister of internal affairs raised the liberals' hope for a further concession of the bureaucracy, there was a widespread rumor, which Rodzianko himself believed, that the tsar would soon appoint Rodzianko chairman of the Council of Ministers.[3] But Rodzianko never acquired popularity among a majority of the liberals, not to mention the radical liberals. The Kadets did not trust him, suspecting him too eager to compromise with the bureaucracy. Thus, in August 1915, when various opposition circles circulated a list of a possible ministry of confidence, the Kadets supported Prince L'vov rather than Rodzianko. In 1916, when public opinion was radically polarized, the liberal opposition appeared to be divided into two groups. The first group considered Prince L'vov a more suitable candidate for the head of a ministry of confidence, while the more conservative group gravitated to Rodzianko as the last hope of bridging the gap between the liberals and the bureaucracy. Realizing his slipping popularity with the liberals, Rodzianko tried to mobilize the support of the aristocracy to bolster his strength at the end of 1916 and at the beginning of 1917.[4]

When the insurrection triumphed in Petrograd and all governmental authority disappeared, many considered the Duma to be the only organ that could restore order in the streets. Ironically, it was the revolution that thrust Rodzianko's prestige to its pinnacle. When the British military attache, Sir Alfred Knox, visited Rodzianko on February 26, and suggested that Krivoshein might be a good choice to head a government that might allay the dissatisfactions of the

3. See chap. 2.
4. See chaps. 7 and 9.

people, Rodzianko did not agree with Knox. When asked if Rodzianko himself would take on the job, he answered without hesitation that he would.[5]

Until February 28, Rodzianko's proposed solution was the formation of a ministry of confidence. He did not entertain the possibility of the slightest change in the fundamental political structure.[6] In the telegrams dispatched to Nicholas on February 26 and February 27, Rodzianko implored the tsar to grant a ministry of confidence to solve the crisis in Petrograd. The new situation created by the soldier's insurrection convinced him all the more of the necessity of securing this concession. On the evening of February 27 he attempted to use the influence of Grand Duke Mikhail to overcome Nicholas's stubborn opposition and to have him accept the formation of a ministry of confidence. Mikhail's recommendations to Nicholas, however, were rejected by Nicholas.[7] There was one curious interlude in this futile attempt. Urging the tsar to make the political concession, Mikhail recommended Prince L'vov, Rodzianko's rival, as a possible candidate to head a ministry of confidence. It is not clear how L'vov's name came to be adopted. Mikhail had had connections with both Rodzianko and L'vov. The recommendation might have come either from Nekrasov, who accompanied Rodzianko to negotiations with Mikhail, or from Guchkov, who also participated at one time in the negotiations.[8] At any rate, the mention of L'vov's name strongly suggests that opposition to Rodzianko existed on the first day of the Duma Committee.

Rodzianko was undaunted by the failure of his first attempt, and pursued compromise through a different channel. But the rapid development of the revolution in Petrograd must have been a great shock to him. By February 28, he modified his position, now advocating a more fundamental political change involving the establishment of a constitutional system in the form of a responsible ministry. On Feb-

5. Sir Alfred Knox, *With the Russian Army, 1914-1917: Being Chiefly Extracts from the Diary of a Military Attache* 2:531.
6. For Rodzianko's role during the February Revolution, see Tsuyoshi Hasegawa, "Rodzianko and the Grand Dukes' Manifesto on 1 March 1917," *Canadian Slavonic Papers* 18, no. 2 (1976): 154-57.
7. See chaps. 15, 17, and 22.
8. Katkov states that Rodzianko kept his dealings with Mikhail strictly secret from his colleagues of the Duma Committee. Katkov, *Russia 1917*, p. 290. This was not the case. It is known that Nekrasov and the other members of the Duma Presidium also participated in the negotiations with the grand duke. Had Rodzianko acted alone, it would be inconceivable that he voluntarily conceded the premiership to L'vov. According to Shakhovskii, Guchkov was also present during the negotiations. S. P. Mel'gunov, *Martovskie dni 1917 goda*, p. 147.

ruary 28, he established contact with Nicholas's uncle, Grand Duke Pavel Aleksandrovich, who was at the time in charge of the guard units in Tsarskoe Seloe. A lawyer, N. Ivanov, Rodzianko's trusted aid, mediated between Tsarskoe Selo and the Tauride Palace. It was decided that upon Nicholas's arrival at Tsarskoe Selo, Pavel would meet the tsar before the latter had a chance to join his wife, and press upon him the necessity of granting a responsible ministry and of creating a constitutional monarchy. These measures were to be announced in the form of a manifesto. A draft manifesto was written by Prince Putiatin, and approved by Pavel and Rodzianko.[9] When it became known that the tsar would not arrive in Tsarskoe Selo and that no political concessions would be forthcoming from him, Rodzianko and Pavel decided to send the draft proposal of the manifesto in the name of the empress and the grand dukes to the Stavka for the approval of Nicholas. But Aleksandra, considering such a manifesto "idiotic," refused to endorse it. Nevertheless, the manifesto gained the signatures of the three senior grand dukes, Pavel Aleksandrovich, Kirill Vladimirovich, and Mikhail Aleksandrovich. The draft manifesto stated:

We grant the Russian Empire a constitutional system and enjoin to continue the interrupted session of the State Duma and the State Council by Our decree. We entrust the chairman of the State Duma with the immediate formation of a temporary cabinet which relies on the confidence of the country and which in agreement with Us is concerned with the convocation of the legislative assembly which is necessary for the urgent reexamination . . . of the draft of the new fundamental laws of the Russian Empire.[10]

In this manifesto Rodzianko restored himself as the candidate for the head of the responsible ministry and promised the scrutiny and reevaluation of the new fundamental laws and the institution of the new legal system. Presumably, even Rodzianko realized that in the face of the rising revolutionary temper the establishment

9. E. N. Burdzhalov, *Vtoraia russkaia revoliutsiia: Vosstanie v Petrograde*, p. 308; Paul Benckendorff, *Last Days at Tsarskoe Selo*, p. 15; Princess Paley, *Memories of Russia, 1916-1919*, p. 53. Burdzhalov's account is based on archival materials, N. I. Ivanov's memoirs, TsGAOR, f. 6439, op. 1, d. 1. My request to see this archival material was refused. Pavel's involvement in the negotiations with Rodzianko is also confirmed by Aleksandra's letter to Nicholas dated March 2, which stated: "Pavel . . . is trying now to work with all his power and is attempting to save us all by a noble, and reckless method: he had composed an idiotic manifesto concerning a constitution after the war, etc." "Perepiska Nikolaia Romanova s Aleksandroi Fedorovnoi," *Krasnyi arkhiv* 4, no. 4 (1923): 215.

10. *Ogonek*, no. 1, 1923; Hasegawa, "Rodzianko and the Grand Dukes' Manifesto on 1 March 1917," pp. 154-55.

of a ministry of confidence alone would not be enough to calm it down. Rodzianko and the grand dukes must have hoped that this manifesto, like the October Manifesto in the 1905 Revolution, would ultimately contribute to the end of the revolution and the opening of a new era. Mikhail, who signed the manifesto on March 1, wrote to his wife, M. Brasova: "Events are developing with dreadful speed. . . . I signed the manifesto, which must be signed by the emperor. It included the signatures of Pavel A. and Kirill, and now mine as elder grand dukes. With this manifesto a new existence of Russia will begin."[11]

Despite this optimism, the manifesto was never signed by Nicholas. According to Burdzhalov, it was brought back to the Duma Committee on March 1 "for its approval." Ivanov carried the manifesto through the Petrograd streets occupied by the excited crowds on the way to the Tauride Palace. According to Ivanov, "I carried the manifesto to the Duma Committee and with each step I was convinced that the cause of the Romanovs was defeated, that Rodzianko's cabinet would not materialize, that the masses would need greater sacrifice. . . . I told [Rodzianko] about the manifesto: 'I think that this was too late.' He answered: 'I am of the same opinion.' "[12] Ivanov brought the manifesto to Miliukov, who jotted down the date of receipt on the copy. The manifesto became a scrap of paper.

The episode involving the draft manifesto raises some unanswered questions. Why was the draft manifesto, which was approved by Rodzianko on February 28, brought back to the Duma Committee on March 1? Why did Rodzianko, who took the initiative in this move, look "crushed," as Ivanov described, on March 1? Why did the draft manifesto turn up in the hands of Miliukov? These questions can be answered only by understanding the power struggle within the Duma Committee about the dynastic question.[13] But before we turn to this subject, we must examine another move Rodzianko made in seeking a compromise solution with Nicholas.

Nicholas's departure from Mogilev gave each faction of the Duma Committee the necessary time to formulate its policy toward the monarchy and the group favoring the abdication of Nicholas a chance to impose its policy upon the Duma Committee. By separating himself from the Stavka, the emperor became isolated from reliable troops during these crucial hours while he and his small entourage in the

11. TsGAOR, f. 622, op. 1, d. 22, ℓ. 87. Also see *Nikolai i velikie kniazia*, pp. 143-44.

12. Burdzhalov, *Vtoraia russkaia revoliutsiia*, p. 310.

13. See Hasegawa, "Rodzianko and the Grand Dukes' Manifesto on 1 March 1917," pp. 156-57.

imperial trains became prey to the manipulations of the self-appointed commissar of transport, Bublikov, and his assistant, Lomonosov, who placed virtually all the railway network in Russia under their control on behalf of the Duma Committee.

It appears that Bublikov and Lomonosov worked closely with Rodzianko. The tsar's departure from Mogilev seemed to make the execution of Rodzianko's policy easier, since he could mobilize support of the military leaders to achieve his goal without Nicholas's interference. At the same time, Rodzianko considered it necessary to isolate the tsar from both Tsarskoe Selo and from Petrograd. In Petrograd his safety might be endangered by the unruly insurgents—an occasion that would inevitably touch off a civil war. Tsarskoe Selo was dangerously close to the revolutionary capital, and furthermore, Rodzianko feared that the reunion of the imperial couple would inevitably reinforce Nicholas's stubborn opposition to political concession. Thus, Bublikov and Lomonosov closely watched the movement of the imperial trains, and took measures to prevent them from approaching either the capital or Tsarskoe Selo.

This plan met obstructions from an unexpected quarter. Between Likhoslavl' and Bologoe the suite train learned of the instructions from the commandant of Nikolaevskii Station, Grekov, to the station-masters in the Nikolaevskii Line to redirect the imperial trains to Petrograd. This obviously ran counter to Bublikov's objectives. Grekov's instructions, which have been believed hitherto to be an individual act of an unknown revolutionary who took over the control of the railway station, probably originated from the Military Commission.[14] Grekov was not a revolutionary, but a lieutenant officially appointed by the Military Commission to seize the Nikolaevskii and Tsarskoe Selo stations.[15] His political orientation was definitely close to the liberals in the Duma Committee. It is not likely that Grekov would have issued an order of such importance that it might determine

14. Katkov states: "The order was signed by 'Grekov,' a Cossack subaltern, but later, when Bublikov's assistant, Lomonosov, made enquiries at the Petrograd terminal, Grekov had disappeared, and was never heard of again." Katkov, *Russia 1917*, p. 311. Relying on the memoirs of Rodzianko and Lomonosov, Mel'gunov argues that Grekov, appointed by the Petrograd Soviet, issued this order "despite the instruction given by the railway engineers under the influence of the Duma." In Mel'gunov's opinion, this chaotic situation, typical of the time, was not the conscious doing of the revolutionary leaders. Mel'gunov, *Martovskie dni*, p. 169.

15. Order no. 29, "Fevral'skaia revoliutsiia v Petrograde: Materialy voennoi komissii vremmennogo komiteta gosudarstvennoi dumy," *Krasnyi arkhiv* 41, no. 4 (1930):24. Later Grekov was appointed head of the security forces of the Neva Gates. TsGIA, f. 1278, op. 10, d. 48, ℓ. 5.

the fate of the emperor without consultation with members of the Military Commission.

Bublikov and Lomonosov immediately took measures to resolve the conflict with the Military Commission. Once Bublikov's objective was explained, Grekov appeared to cooperate wholeheartedly with the commissar of transport. The archival materials in the Military Commission indicate that the Military Commission, the Ministry of Transport, and Grekov worked in harmony to pursue the plan outlined by Bublikov.[16] Early in the morning of March 1, Lomonosov gave the assistant chief of the railway movement at Nikolaevskii Station instructions to change directions of the imperial trains if so instructed.[17] After 3 A.M. Bublikov received a report that the imperial trains had reached Malaia Vishera. Further, a telegram from Liuban' indicated that the imperial trains would soon reach Tosno to change to the route to Tsarskoe Selo and that the commander of the corps of gendarmes had already instructed railway authorities to uncouple locomotives for the imperial trains. If they had to be redirected, it would have to be done quickly. Bublikov immediately asked Rodzianko for instructions, but received only an ambiguous reply that nothing had been determined yet.[18] It was under these circumstances that the entourage on the suite train were informed that Liuban' and Tosno had been captured by the revolutionaries. The entourage based their decision to redirect the imperial trains from Malaia Vishera back to Bologoe, and from Bologoe to Pskov, solely on the information given by Lieutenant Geliakh.[19] Strangely, this information is not corroborated by any other firsthand evidence, and all the documentary evidence of the capture of Liuban' and Tosno comes invariably from the memoirs of the entourage on the imperial trains.

The only incident that took place at Liuban' was minor. An echelon of troops arrived at the station, although it is not known what military unit they belonged to or where they came from. The commander of the unit commandeered a locomotive and four wagons from the railway authorities. The armed soldiers got on board, and left for Petrograd.[20] But this was hardly an occupation of the station by insurgents,

16. See TsGAOR, f. 3348, d. 129, ℓℓ. 17, 21; TsGAOR, f. 6, op. 1, d. 1722, ℓℓ. 3-5, 7, 9.

17. Iu. V. Lomonosov, *Vospominaniia o martovskoi revoliutsii 1917 g.*, p. 29.

18. TsGAOR, f. 2248, d. 129, ℓ. 20; Lomonosov, *Vospominaniia o martovskoi revoliutsii*, p. 30; A. I. Spiridovich, *Velikaia voina i fevral'skaia revoliutsiia, 1914-1917 gg.* 3:203.

19. See chap. 22.

20. The report also stated that the soldiers' mood was against the Provisional Government, but we do not know if they were revolutionaries or monarchists. TsGAOR,

as narrated by Lieutenant Geliakh. After their departure no troops remained at the station, and the soldiers had gone in the direction of Petrograd, not in the direction of Malaia Vishera, as Geliakh indicated. Furthermore, nothing was mentioned about the capture of Tosno by the revolutionaries.

While there is no evidence to prove the seizure of Liuban' and Tosno, archival materials reveal that railway authorities in cooperation with Grekov and Bublikov did everything to change the direction of the imperial trains. Lomonosov had already given instructions to Nikolaevskii Station about changing the route of the two trains, although he did not spell out the details of the instructions in his memoirs. Engineer Karelin of the Ministry of Transport informed Grekov that Malaia Vishera had sworn allegiance to the new government and that all the stations from Petrograd to Bologoe were following its directions for control of the railways. Another telegram from Liuban' reported to Grekov that Count Tatishchev, commander of the corps of gendarmes in Tosno, was conducting negotiations with Malaia Vishera—which indicates that the Duma Committee had succeeded in gaining his support.[21] A telephone call that Lomonosov received from Malaia Vishera after the imperial trains left the station reported: "According to the instructions of engineer Kern [assistant stationmaster] train A left here at 4:40 to return to Bologoe."[22] Another telegram from Bol'shaia Vishera to Grekov reported that the both trains had been redirected from Malaia Vishera back to Bologoe.[23] These materials confirm that Lomonosov, Bublikov, and Grekov had firm control over the events at Malaia Vishera. Thus, unless some new evidence that proves otherwise is discovered, one can reasonably conclude that actually the seizure of Liuban' and Tosno by the revolutionaries had not taken place, and that it was a fabrication concocted by Lomonosov and Bublikov to prevent the imperial trains from approaching either Tsarskoe Selo or Petrograd.[24]

---

f. 3348, d. 129, ℓ. 20; TsGAOR, f. 6, op. 1, d. 1722, ℓℓ. 8-9.

21. TsGAOR, f. 3348, d. 129, ℓℓ. 17, 21; TsGAOR, f. 6, op. 1, d. 1722, ℓℓ. 3-5, 7, 9.

22. Lomonosov, *Vospominaniia o martovskoi revoliutsii,* p. 43. According to Thal, Train A left Malaia Vishera at 3:35 A.M. A. Tal', "Memuary ob otrechenii ot prestola Rossiiskago Gosudarstva Imperatora Nikolaia II," pp. 76-77.

23. TsGAOR, f. 3348, d. 129, ℓ. 18.

24. There is no mention of the capture of the two stations in the two contemporary newspapers *Izvestiia* and *Izvestiia revoliutsionnoi nedeli.* No information other than hearsay can be found in the collections of telegrams in the Stavka and in the headquarters of the northern front in "Fevral'skaia revoliutsiia 1917 goda: Dokumenty Stavki verkhovnogo glavnokomanduiushchego i shtaba

The imperial trains reached Bologoe shortly before seven o'clock on the morning of March 1. The news of their arrival at Bologoe was immediately relayed to Lomonosov, who called up Rodzianko for further instructions. This time, Rodzianko instructed Lomonosov to detain the trains at Bologoe and arrange a special train for him to take to Bologoe. Lomonosov dispatched a telegram to the emperor on Rodzianko's behalf, which requested the emperor to wait in Bologoe for Rodzianko, since the latter wished to talk with him about "the critical situation of the throne."[25] This telegram, however, did not reach Nicholas, since the railway authorities of Bologoe Station let the imperial trains leave for Pskov either by default or on purpose. They even failed to deliver Rodzianko's telegram to Voeikov. This news alarmed Bublikov and Lomonosov, who feared that the imperial trains might either reroute from Dno to Tsarskoe Selo, where the emperor would join Ivanov's troops as well as his family, or proceed to Pskov, where he would be under the heavy protection of the loyal troops of the northern front. In panic, Bublikov issued an order to send freight trains from Dno to jam the track.[26] This measure did not stop the imperial trains, but slowed their movement considerably.

In the meantime, Lomonosov personally went to Nikolaevskii Station to arrange a train for Rodzianko. He encountered no resistance from the insurgent soldiers who had occupied the station, and easily got the train ready. Nevertheless, despite Lomonosov's repeated inquiries to the Duma, Rodzianko did not come to the station. Shortly after half past one in the afternoon, the imperial trains passed Staraia Russa. When Lomonosov received this news, he changed plans, with Rodzianko's approval, so that Rodzianko could meet the tsar at Dno

---

glavnokomanduiushchego armiiami severnogo fronta," *Krasnyi arkhiv* vol. 21, no. 2 (1927), and "Telegrammy i razgovory po telegrafu mezhdu Pskovom, Stavkoiu i Petrogradom, otnoshiashcheisia k obstoiatel'stvam otrecheniia Gosudariia Imperatora, s primechaniiami k nim general-ad"iutanta N. V. Ruzskago," *Russkaia letopis'*, vol. 3 (1922) (hereafter cited "Telegrammy Ruzskago"). The first Soviet historian to turn his attention to the problem of Nicholas's abdication, P. E. Shchegolev, found no evidence to substantiate the "seizure" other than the accounts written by the tsar's entourage. P. E. Shchegolev, *Poslednii reis Nikolaia vtorogo*. The most recent Soviet historians such as Burdzhalov and Leiberov, who used extensive archival materials, did not uncover any archival materials to prove the seizure. If the capture of the two stations was carried out by large forces as indicated in Lieutenant Geliakh's report, the absence of firsthand materials is most strange.

25. Lomonosov, *Vospominaniia o martovskoi revoliutsii*, p. 33.
26. Ibid., p. 34; A. A. Bublikov, *Russkaia revoliutsiia: Vpechatleniia i mysli ochevidtsa i uchastnika*, p. 24.

instead of Bologoe, since it was two hundred miles from Petrograd to Staraia Russa through Dno as compared with two hundred sixty miles through Bologoe.[27]

When Train A arrived at Dno at 4:25 P.M. Rodzianko's telegram was awaiting the tsar: "Your Majesty the Emperor, a special train is leaving now for Dno Station to deliver a report to you, Sire, concerning the general situation and measures necessary for the salvation of Russia. I earnestly implore you to wait for my arrival, for each moment is precious."[28] Precious though each moment might be, Rodzianko failed to come to the station. It was already dark. Lomonosov kept calling the Duma. When he finally received an answer from Rodzianko, the latter instructed him to send another telegram to the tsar, explaining that extenuating circumstances made it impossible for Rodzianko to leave the capital. At the same time, Rodzianko gave Lomonosov permission to let the imperial trains proceed to Pskov without obstruction.[29]

Nicholas, tired of waiting for Rodzianko, had Voeikov call Petrograd railway authorities directly. Voeikov learned that although Rodzianko's train was prepared, he could not leave the capital and that the railway line connecting the Vindarskii Line and Tsarskoe Selo had been seized by revolutionary troops.[30] The latter information, which is not supported by any other evidence, led the emperor's entourage to abandon their intention to reach Tsarskoe Selo. Nicholas had Voeikov send a telegram to Rodzianko saying that the tsar would wait for him in Pskov. Evidently, Rodzianko's last telegram to the emperor, which Lomonosov was instructed to send, did not reach Nicholas.

Rodzianko's failure to meet the tsar at Dno raises two important questions that have direct bearings on the Duma Committee's policy toward the monarchy. First, what was the motive that led Rodzianko to seek a special audience with the emperor? Second, why did he

27. Lomonosov, *Vospominaniia o martovskoi revoliutsii*, pp. 35-38.

28. Shchegolev, *Poslednii reis Nikolaia vtorogo*, pp. 45-46.

29. Lomonosov, *Vospominaniia o martovskoi revoliutsii*, p. 39. The attempts by Bublikov and Lomonosov to obstruct the movement of the imperial trains caused considerable alarm in the Stavka, which intercepted Bublikov's order to the railway authorities of the Vindarskii Line. "Fevral'skaia revoliutsiia 1917 goda," p. 36. Alekseev strongly protested against such measures to Rodzianko and demanded that the Duma Committee take all necessary measures to guarantee the safe arrival of the imperial trains to Pskov. Alekseev to Rodzianko, no. 1845, ibid., pp. 44-45. This threat might be the factor that facilitated Rodzianko's decision to let the imperial trains go to Pskov without obstruction.

30. See chap. 22. It is not clear whom Voeikov talked to, but it seems possible that whoever it might be was with the knowledge of Lomonosov and Bublikov.

cancel the trip? According to Katkov, Rodzianko's purpose in requesting the audience was to arrest the tsar. This contention, which is based on the unreliable memoirs of Shidlovskii, does not seem to make much sense.[31] If Rodzianko had intended to arrest Nicholas, it would not have been necessary for him to travel to Bologoe or Dno. He could have easily redirected the imperial trains to Petrograd, where he could rely on the forces at the disposal of the Military Commission. Actually, in cooperation with Bublikov and Lomonosov, Rodzianko vigorously resisted Grekov's order to that effect, and avoided taking such a drastic action—an incident that might provoke a civil war, which Rodzianko tried to avoid at all cost.

Contrary to Katkov's contention, throughout March 1 Rodzianko resisted the growing sentiment within the Duma Committee that Nicholas should abdicate. In fact, when the Duma Committee finally accepted abdication as necessary during the night of March 1 and 2, Rodzianko still refused to commit himself totally.[32] As Mel'gunov states, "it is impossible to attribute to Rodzianko the idea of going to the tsar with the proposal of abdication from the throne, as is done by Shidlovskii. During the day of March 1, he was not yet psychologically prepared to make such a radical decision."[33] It would make more sense to interpret Rodzianko's motives in seeking an audience with Nicholas as a continuation of all his previous efforts: a plan of compromise with Nicholas that would stop short of abdication.

The isolation of Nicholas from his reliable troops as well as from his trusted advisors seemed to present Rodzianko with a favorable opportunity to press toward his desired goal once again, this time personally to the emperor. He must have thought of presenting the manifesto of the formation of a responsible ministry, which he and the grand dukes had not been able to send to the emperor.[34] The British Ambassador, Sir George Buchanan, noted that on March 1 he had a visit from Grand Duke Mikhail, who told him that Rodzianko would go to Bologoe to request the emperor to "sign the manifesto granting a constitution and entrusting Rodzianko with the selection of a new government."[35]

31. Katkov, *Russia 1917*, pp. 297, 299; Burdzhalov, *Vtoraia russkaia revoliutsiia*, p. 311. See Hasegawa, "Rodzianko and the Grand Dukes' Manifesto on 1 March 1917," pp. 162-65.

32. See chap. 25.

33. Mel'gunov, *Martovskie dni*, p. 57.

34. Shidlovskii might have mistaken this manifesto for a manifesto demanding the abdication of Nicholas. The manifesto of abdication had not been drawn up on March 1.

35. Sir George Buchanan, *My Mission to Russia and Other Diplomatic Memoirs* 2: 68.

Nevertheless, Rodzianko's audience at Dno did not materialize. What prevented him from leaving the capital? It is often attributed to the opposition of the Soviet Executive Committee.[36] It is true that the Executive Committee first opposed the departure of Rodzianko to Bologoe and tried to instruct the railway workers to stop Rodzianko's train. According to Sukhanov, on the morning of March 1, the proceedings of the Executive Committee were suddenly interrupted by the intrusion of a certain colonel in field uniform, who appealed to the Executive Committee to end the railway workers' interference with Rodzianko's train. Temporarily suspending the discussion on the agenda, the Executive Committee directed its attention to the question of whether Rodzianko should be permitted to leave the capital to meet the tsar. After a brief discussion it unanimously decided to refuse Rodzianko's departure and to dispatch Skobelev for propaganda work among the railway workers for this purpose.[37]

It is doubtful, however, that the Executive Committee's opposition was decisive in delaying and finally cancelling Rodzianko's departure. According to Lomonosov, who actually went to Nikolaevskii Station personally to arrange a train for Rodzianko, neither the railway workers nor the insurgents who had occupied the station had shown any signs of resistance.[38] Moreover, the Executive Committee reversed their decision later. According to Sukhanov, after the unanimous decision was taken not to permit Rodzianko to leave the capital, Kerenskii rushed into the room of the Executive Committee in extreme anger and accused the members of the Executive Committee of playing into the hands of the monarchy, since Rodzianko's mission was to force Nicholas's abdication. As a result of Kerenskii's flamboyant performance, all those present "gave in to Kerenskii's hysteria," except for three members.[39] What motivated the Executive Committee to oppose Rodzianko's departure seems to have been the fear that the Duma Committee would negotiate with Nicholas behind the back of the

36. Burdzhalov, *Vtoraia russkaia revoliutsiia*, p. 347.

37. N. N. Sukhanov, *Zapiski o revoliutsii* 1: 241-48; M. Skobelev, "Gibel' tsarizma: Vospominaniia M. I. Skobeleva," *Ogonek*, no. 11 (1927).

38. Lomonosov, *Vospominaniia o martovskoi revoliutsii*, p. 35.

39. Sukhanov, *Zapiski o revoliutsii* 1: 248; Skobelev, "Gibel' tsarizma." It appears strange that Kerenskii, an opponent of Rodzianko's moderate policy, reacted so violently to the Executive Committee's opposition to Rodzianko's departure. Yet, Kerenskii's intervention on Rodzianko's behalf appears to have really taken place, since not only Sukhanov but also Skobelev noted the same incident. It is possible to think that Kerenskii resented the interference of the Executive Committee, which might adversely affect the outcome of the power struggle within the Duma Committee, while seeking to block Rodzianko's departure independently of the Executive Committee.

revolutionary insurgents to suppress the revolution militarily. Once this fear was removed, the Executive Committee no longer interfered in the Duma Committee's dealings with the tsar.

The opposition of the Executive Committee, therefore, was never the direct cause of the cancellation of Rodzianko's departure. The real cause should be sought in the struggle within the Duma Committee and the uncertainty of its policy on the dynastic question. Rodzianko's personal diplomacy and his moderate policy met increased opposition from those who advocated more drastic action favoring Nicholas's abdication. Already on February 28 some openly advocated this action in the Duma Committee meeting. The unofficial minutes of the Duma Committee for February 28 read: "The course of events, the sentiment of the army units and their commanding staff and the masses of people indicate that the act of Nicholas's abdication is absolutely necessary."[40] Rodzianko's influence was still strong enough to suppress this opinion on February 28, but no longer on March 1. Miliukov noted that by March 1 it became evident that Nicholas could no longer occupy the throne, although the Duma Committee had not yet reached a final decision as to how to force Nicholas to abdicate or what kind of government should be formed after his abdication. When the majority of the Duma Committee members learned of Rodzianko's personal move to seek an audience with the tsar and his secret dealings with the grand dukes in composing a manifesto on the establishment of a responsible ministry, they suspected that he was "plotting a conspiracy with the military leaders, considering himself dictator of the Russian Revolution."[41] They must have demanded an explanation from Rodzianko about the purpose of his intended rendezvous with the tsar and the contents of the manifesto he was supposed to bring along. Naturally, it was impossible for Rodzianko to leave the capital in this situation. Confronted with strong opposition from the majority of the Duma Committee members, he could not pursue his compromise with the tsar. Moreover, leaving Petrograd in this precarious situation would mean the loss of his authority as a leader of the liberals.

When the Duma Committee entered into negotiations with the representatives of the Soviet Executive Committee for the transfer of power on the night of March 1 and 2 it was no longer Rodzianko but Miliukov who served as the Duma's spokesman. Rodzianko sat through the negotiations without any active part in them. On the

40. *Protokoly sobytii*, quoted in Burdzhalov, *Vtoraia russkaia revoliutsiia*, pp. 310-11.

41. P. N. Miliukov, *Vospominaniia 1859-1917* 2: 309.

question of the monarchy, Miliukov stated that the Duma Committee stood for the abdication of Nicholas in favor of his son, Aleksei, under the regency of Grand Duke Mikhail Aleksandrovich.[42] Miliukov would not have presented this position to the Executive Committee representatives without the formal acceptance by the Duma Committee, since almost all members of the Duma Committee were present. After the negotiations, the Duma Committee decided to send immediately two representatives, Guchkov and Shul'gin, to Pskov to force this solution—Nicholas's abdication for Aleksei under Mikhail's regency —on the tsar.[43]

That the dynastic problem was finally decided in the meeting on March 1 was confirmed by other sources. The French Ambassador, Paléologue, learned "just before midnight" that "the leaders of the liberal parties held a secret conference this evening—in the absence of the socialists and without their knowledge"—and that "they were of one accord that the monarchy must be retained, but' Nicholas II . . . must be sacrificed to the salvation of Russia." Grand Duke Pavel Aleksandrovich, who kept close contact with Rodzianko through N. I. Ivanov, wrote a letter dated March 2 to Kirill Vladimirovich and referred to "the new tendency" in the Duma circle "yesterday evening" to appoint Mikhail as a regent. Disturbed by this "tendency," Pavel instructed Kirill to get in touch with Rodzianko to try to solve the crisis along the policy outlined in the manifesto signed by the grand dukes.[44]

The shift of the Duma Committee's policy on the dynastic question was accompanied by the shift of political strength of the chief contenders for power within the Duma Committee. During the two days, from February 28 to March 1, Rodzianko's influence declined considerably. Rodzianko's order, which had provoked a violent reaction from the radical workers and the insurgent soldiers, immensely damaged his prestige. Steklov told Engelhardt: "Drop Rodzianko, otherwise, they will start criticizing us."[45] On the other hand, Miliukov's star was rising. It was Miliukov who had set out to make up the list of the members of the Provisional Government, from which Rod-

42. See chap. 21.

43. Deposition of Guchkov, *Padenie tsarskogo rezhima: Stenograficheskie otchety doprosov i pokazanii dannykh v 1917 g. v Chrezvychainoi sledstvennoi komissii vremennogo pravitel'stva* 6: 262-63.

44. Maurice Paléologue, *An Ambassador's Memoirs* 3: 233; "Romanovy v pervye dni revoliutsii," *Krasnyi arkhiv* 24, no. 5 (1927): 208; Paley, *Memories of Russia*, pp. 55-56.

45. OR GLB, f. 218, B. A. Engel'gardt, "Potonuvshii mir: Vospominaniia," ℓ. 117.

zianko's name was conspicuously dropped. Zaslavskii and Kantorovich noted: "The Octobrist [Rodzianko] who created the Duma Committee was eliminated from power in the first two days, and Miliukov, who had been behind Rodzianko's shadow on the 27th, became on the 28th the unquestionable leader, and already, on March 1, had bidden farewell to Rodzianko without regret."[46]

Rodzianko tried to regain his authority by presenting the formation of a responsible ministry under his premiership as an established fact through his personal negotiations with Nicholas. However, his opponents moved more quickly. His manipulations with the military leaders and the tsar were suspected as a conspiracy to establish a dictatorship. It backfired and invited a rebellion of the other members of the Duma Committee who favored Nicholas's abdication. Thus, when the draft manifesto was brought back to the Duma Committee by Ivanov, it was not for its "approval," as Ivanov stated, but for what was tantamount to its confiscation. It was not brought to Rodzianko, but to Miliukov, the foremost critic of Rodzianko. It is no wonder that Rodzianko looked "crushed."

Shortly after the negotiations with the Soviet Executive Committee concerning the transfer of power were over, Rodzianko began the historic communications on the Hughes apparatus with General Ruzskii— the communications that became the immediate cause for the abdication of Nicholas II.[47] Rodzianko began by explaining why he could not fulfill his promise to meet the tsar at Dno and later at Pskov.

Frankly speaking, there are two reasons why I did not go: in the first place, the troops you dispatched mutinied, ran out of the train at Luga, declared that they were going to associate themselves with the State Duma, and decided to take the weapons and not to let anybody pass, not even the imperial trains. Immediately, I took measures so that the track for the train of His Majesty could be freed, but I do not know if I shall succeed or not.

The second reason is that I received the information that my leaving the capital would cause an undesirable result. It was impossible to leave the pent-up anger of the people without my presence, because at that time they believed me and carried out only my instructions.[48]

Rodzianko's explanation revealed the political predicament in which he found himself rather than the real reasons for his failure to keep the appointment. Luga was on the line between Petrograd and Pskov, not between Petrograd and Dno. Therefore, "the mutiny

46. D. O. Zaslavskii and V. A. Kantorovich, *Khronika fevral'skoi revoliutsii*, p. 38.

47. See chap. 25.

48. "Fevral'skaia revoliutsiia 1917 goda," pp. 55-56; "Telegrammy Ruzskago," p. 128.

at Luga" might have been an excuse for his failure to travel to Pskov, but it did not explain why he failed to go to Dno. Actually, the troops sent from the northern front never mutinied at Luga.[49] Rodzianko may well not have had any knowledge of this fact. Even if he had known that, however, Rodzianko himself admitted that the mutineers supported the Duma. Assuming that his claim to his great popularity among the populace was correct, one wonders why they would hinder Rodzianko's train. In fact, when Guchkov and Shul'gin traveled to Pskov through Luga on March 2, they encountered no resistance. Moreover, Rodzianko was familiar with the efforts by Bublikov and Lomonosov to manipulate the movement of the imperial trains. Therefore, his first explanation was as deceitful as irrelevant.

Rodzianko does not fare well in the second explanation, either. The reaction of the masses, particularly of the insurgent soldiers, to Rodzianko's order clearly demonstrated that the authority among the masses he claimed in this statement did not exist. To say that the people "believed me and carried out only instructions" reflected his wishful thinking more than reality.

The importance of Rodzianko's statement lay not in how he concealed the truth from Ruzskii but in why he told him untruth in the first place. As Katkov persuasively argues, Rodzianko was in a difficult plight. On the one hand, he had deeply committed himself to seek a compromise with the tsar—the policy for which he had succeeded in mobilizing the support of the high command. As we shall see in the next chapters, it was partly because of Rodzianko's persuasion that the high command agreed to induce the tsar to grant the political concession prescribed by Rodzianko's project. Therefore, to go to Pskov to demand Nicholas's abdication would be out of the question, since he did not know how the high command would react to the new demand. It would inevitably damage his reputation with the military leaders, whom he could not afford to antagonize, since the military was the only support he had in his effort to regain political influence. On the other hand, he could not go to Pskov to present the old demand for the establishment of a responsible ministry, either, since it would be regarded by his colleagues in the Duma Committee as a conspiracy behind their backs. If he were alienated from his Duma colleagues, no matter what support he might receive from military leaders, he would not be able even to begin the constitutional experiment for which he aspired. Either way, he would not gain anything from the trip to Dno or to Pskov. Thus, as Katkov states brilliantly, Rodzianko "thought it preferable to wait and see how matters would

49. See chap. 25.

develop in Pskov after the meeting between the emperor and Ruzskii, and then try to persuade the army commanders that an immediate abdication was both desirable and necessary."[50] Rodzianko's conversation with Ruzskii was a desperate maneuver to escape this predicament and to stay alive in the power struggle in the Duma Committee without alienating either the high command or his colleagues. Yet, it was this personal maneuver that touched off a train of reactions that ultimately led to the end of the monarchical system.

50. Katkov, *Russia 1917*, p. 320.

24

THE STAVKA AND
COUNTERREVOLUTIONARY ATTEMPTS

 When General Khabalov brought the first news of the soldiers' uprising in Petrograd early afternoon on February 27 to the Stavka and requested an immediate dispatch of troops from the front, Nicholas quickly reacted by appointing an "energetic person" to deal with the crisis. the appointment itself, he believed, would be sufficient to quell the localized unrest, which he attributed to the discontent of the companies of evacuees.[1] Early in the evening the Stavka learned of the alarming situation in Petrograd from the two telegrams dispatched by War Minister Beliaev. His first (no. 197) reported that the insurrection had spread to many army units, and urged Alekseev to send from the front immediately "truly reliable units in substantial numbers." Telegram (no. 198), which immediately followed the first, reported that the Council of Ministers had now declared Petrograd to be in a state of siege, while in view of General Khabalov's confusion, Beliaev was compelled to appoint General Zankevich to assist the commander of the Petrograd Military District.[2] Realizing for the first time the seriousness of the uprising in Petrograd, General Alekseev fully supported Nicholas's decision to suppress the insurrection by force. After supper, Nicholas summoned General N. I. Ivanov, and appointed him commander of the Petrograd Military District to replace Khabalov. Alekseev on his part immediately made

1. "Perepiska Nikolaia Romanova s Aleksandroi Fedorovnoi," *Krasnyi arkhiv* 4, no. 4 (1923): 213.
2. Beliaev to Alekseev, no. 197, 198, "Fevral'skaia revoliutsiia 1917 goda: Dokumenty Stavki verkhovnogo glavnokomanduiushchego i shtaba glavnokomanduiushchego armiiami severnogo fronta," *Krasnyi arkhiv* 21, no. 2 (1927): 9.

arrangements to dispatch counterrevolutionary forces to Petrograd by making available three companies of the St. George Battalion to accompany General Ivanov and further by ordering the commanders of the northern and the western fronts to send reinforcements to support Ivanov's companies.

General Ivanov, a stocky old man with a massive beard, was a strict disciplinarian, but his paternalistic attitude and the unpretentious simplicity with which he treated soldiers made him well liked by his men. In 1906 he had mercilessly suppressed the rising of the sailors in Kronstadt. In 1915 he became a commander of the southwestern front, and at this post he made a scathing attack on the military bureaucracy in Petrograd for its incompetency in producing war supplies. Directly responsible for the Great Retreat in 1915, he was later relieved of the post, and had worked in a sinecure at Mogilev. Ivanov and Alekseev, who were never close to begin with, were no longer on speaking terms. Ivanov confided to his closest friends that he had been dismissed because of Alekseev's intrigue.[3] Despite the animosity between the two men, they shared the view that a political concession would have to accompany military suppression of the revolution.

After he retired from the audience with the tsar, Ivanov discussed with Alekseev the technical details of the punitive expedition. Alekseev granted Ivanov an extraordinary power to enforce martial law by overriding civil authority.[4] At two A.M. on February 28, shortly before the emperor's departure from Mogilev, Ivanov was summoned again to the tsar's car in the imperial train. Apparently not satisfied with the power granted by Alekseev, Ivanov requested that he be given absolute power over four ministries: Internal Affairs, Agriculture, Trade and Industry, and Transport. Nicholas went far beyond Ivanov's request and granted him dictatorial power over all ministers. At the same time Ivanov recommended that since military means alone would not solve the crisis, a political concession in the form of a ministry of confidence be granted.[5] To this Nicholas replied: "Yes, yes. General Alekseev just mentioned it." Ivanov had a distinct impression that the tsar had made up his mind to make this concession. Nicholas,

    3. E. I. Martynov, *Tsarskaia armiia v fevral'skom perevorote*, pp. 130-31.
    4. TsGAOR, f. ChSK, d. 643, ll. 1-2; TsGAOR, f. ChSK, d. 466, l. 130.
    5. Ivanov's deposition, *Padenie tsarskogo rezhima* 5: 317-18; Aleksandr Blok, "Poslednie dni starago rezhima," *Arkhiv russkoi revoliutsii* 4 (1922): 40; "Proval popytki Stavki podavit' Fevral'skuiu revoliutsiiu 1917 goda v Petrograde," *Voprosy arkhivovedeniia*, no. 1 (1962), p. 104; D. N. Dubenskii, "Kak proizoshel perevorot v Rossii, zapiski-dnevniki," *Russkaia letopis'* 3 (1922): 30-31; Nicolas de Basily, *Diplomat of Imperial Russia, 1903-1917: Memoirs*, pp. 108-9.

however, took no such action and continued to reject all suggestions of political concessions. According to Ivanov's testimony before the Extraordinary Investigation Commission, at the last audience with the tsar, he had told Nicholas that he did not intend to bring troops into Petrograd since he wanted to avoid bloodshed. The emperor answered, "Yes, of course."[6] This testimony should be taken with a grain of salt: it is contradicted by Ivanov's determination to assume a dictatorship in Petrograd. The possibility of bloodshed was from the beginning inherent in undertaking the expedition.

Examination of the Stavka's policy also indicates that Ivanov's expedition was conceived as an extremely serious endeavor in which the military leaders clearly meant to use the most reliable forces available against the insurgents in the capital. As it has been discussed in the preceding chapter, General Alekseev favored a political solution to the crisis and was understandably reluctant to commit forces from the front for the suppression of an internal disorder, particularly when the scheduled spring offensive was approaching. Moreover, he was not at all sure of the morale of the soldiers, who would be ordered to fire, not upon the enemy, but upon their fellow countrymen. Despite this reluctance, however, Alekseev fully endorsed Nicholas's decision for a counterrevolutionary offensive. As soon as he realized the seriousness of the insurrection in Petrograd, he made two decisions: to dispatch reliable troops to suppress the revolution by force and to secure the normal function of the railways.

By the evening of February 27 Alekseev had taken measures to move sizable troops from the front. In his conversation with General Danilov, chief of staff of the northern front, Alekseev instructed the northern front to dispatch two infantry regiments, two cavalry regiments selected from the "strongest and most reliable units," and commanded by the "strongest generals, because apparently Khabalov lost his head, and it is necessary to have reliable, capable, and bold assistants at the disposal of General Ivanov." He further stated: "The situation demands the immediate arrival of troops. . . . It is a threatening moment, and it is necessary to do everything to speed up the dispatch of strong troops. The problem of our future depends on this." General Boldyrev, quartermaster of the northern front,

---

6. Ivanov's deposition, *Padenie tsarskogo rezhima* 5: 318; "Proval popytki Stavki podavit' Fevral'skuiu revoliutsiiu," p. 104. Mel'gunov and Katkov take this as the evidence to show that Nicholas and Ivanov intended to aviod bloodshed. S. P. Mel'gunov, *Martovskie dni 1917 goda*, p. 159; George Katkov, *Russia 1917: The February Revolution*, pp. 308-9.

also noted in his diary: "Everything will depend upon whether General Ivanov will succeed." In addition to these four regiments, the northern front was instructed to send one machine-gun detachment and two artillery batteries. Presumably at the same time Alekseev also ordered the western front to send troops of similar size to Petrograd.[7] Thus, the size of the forces initially made available to Ivanov consisted of three companies of the St. George Battalion, four infantry regiments, four cavalry regiments, two machine-gun detachments, and four artillery batteries. Contrary to Katkov's contention, this is a formidable force. The Stavka further instructed the main administration of the General Staff in Petrograd to form a staff for Ivanov's forces and made arrangements to install a field radio station between Orsha and Tsarskoe Selo to coordinate information and activities of Ivanov's forces, the northern front, the western front, and the Stavka.[8]

In the small hours of February 28, the Stavka learned that the situation in Petrograd had changed from bad to worse. Khabalov admitted that he could no longer discharge the obligation to "restore order" and revealed that "by evening the rebels occupied a large part of the capital." Shortly before two o'clock in the morning the Stavka was informed by Beliaev that insurgents had occupied the Marinskii Palace and that the ministers "just in time fled from the palace." As if to bolster the morale of the loyal troops in Petrograd, Alekseev informed Golitsyn of Ivanov's appointment and of the dispatch of counterrevolutionary troops from the front. At the same time, he ordered the northern and western fronts to add one infantry and one cavalry battery each to the reinforcements.[9]

Around 8:30 A.M. another telegram from Khabalov arrived at Mogilev, saying that the number of loyal troops had shrunk to 600 infantry and 500 cavalry, with 15 machine guns, 12 guns, and 80 cartridges. Khabalov commented, with astonishing understatement, "the situation is extremely difficult."[10] Urgent measures were necessary to prevent further deterioration of the situation until the arrival of Ivanov's troops. For this purpose Alekseev ordered Ruzskii

7. Alekseev-Danilov conversation and Evert to Alekseev, no. 6144, "Fevral'-skaia revoliutsiia 1917 goda," pp. 9-10, 17; V. G. Boldyrev, "Iz dnevnika gen. V. G. Boldyreva," *Krasnyi arkhiv* 23, no. 4 (1927): 251; TsGAOR, f. ChSK, d. 466, ℓ. 130.

8. Alekseev to Beliaev, no. 1789, "Fevral'skaia revoliutsiia 1917 goda," pp. 10-11; Lukomskii to Lebedev, no. 1817, ibid., p. 28.

9. Khabalov to Alekseev, ibid., pp. 15-16; Beliaev to Voeikov, no. 200, ibid., p. 16; Alekseev to Ruzskii and Evert, no. 1805, ibid., p. 17.

10. Khabalov to Alekseev, no. 415, ibid., p. 19.

to send the "most reliable battalion" of the Vyborg Fortress Artillery. Also the "two most reliable battalions" of the Kronstadt Fortress Artillery were ordered to march to Petrograd immediately. At 11:30 A.M. the situation became even more hopeless. The Stavka was informed that the rebels "had occupied the most important institutions in all parts of the city," and "normal life of the government had stopped."[11] Approximately at the same time Khabalov's response to a ten-point questionnaire from General Ivanov also reached Mogilev. According to this information, only a small number of troops remained at Khabalov's disposal; the revolutionaries had taken all railway stations as well as all artillery and munition administrations and factories into their hands, and had arrested the ministers; no food supply was available to Khabalov, who had lost contact with all technical and economic institutions connected with military operations. Finally, after two o'clock in the afternoon, the Stavka received news that the loyal troops had completely disintegrated. The soldiers who remained loyal to the last moment surrendered arms on the orders of their commanders and quietly returned to their barracks. This news made Alekseev's resolve to crush the rebellion more determined. He ordered Ruzskii and Evert to send additional reinforcements and requested General Brusilov, commander of the southwestern front, to prepare three guard battalions for possible use by Ivanov.[12]

The Stavka's determination to quell the revolution by force was indeed a serious one. Each time it received information that the situation was worsening in Petrograd, it stepped up military commitment to the counterrevolutionary attempt. This response emanated from the belief that Petrograd had fallen into the hands of irresponsible, anarchical masses, influenced by left-wing elements—an alarming situation that, if allowed to develop further, would inevitably undermine the integrity of the army and seriously hamper military operations at the front. The Stavka was given to understand that no forces were at work to restore peace and order. Even worse, there were some indications that radical left-wing elements were forming a revolutionary government.[13] In his circular telegram to all the commanders outlining the situation in Petrograd, Alekseev stated this fear: "In the State Duma a Soviet of leaders of the parties was formed for [establish-

11. Alekseev to Ruzskii, no. 1807, Alekseev to Grigorovich, no. 1809, ibid.; Beliaev to Alekseev, no. 201, ibid., p. 20.
12. Khabalov to Alekseev, ibid., pp. 20-21; Beliaev to Alekseev, no. 9157, p. 27; Alekseev to Ruzskii and Evert, no. 1819, Alekseev to Brusilov, no. 1912, ibid., p. 24.
13. Kapnist to Rasin, no. 2704; ibid., pp. 14-15, direct conversation between the Naval Staff at the Stavka and the main Naval Staff in Petrograd, ibid., p. 29.

ing] relations with institutions and persons, and additional elections from the workers and the rebel troops have been called for."[14] Actually, the proclamation for "the establishment of relations with institutions and persons" was issued by the Duma Committee, not by the Soviet. Alekseev's telegram shows that in his mind these two were not as yet distinguished.

In addition to sending troops to Petrograd, the Stavka was extremely concerned about the security of the railways. Katkov states that it was one of Alekseev's gravest mistakes to have the Duma Committee control railway movement, thereby surrendering "an important instrument of power, which he could well have used to influence the political issue at that critical juncture."[15] The Stavka, however, never conceived control of the railways as a political instrument, but solely as a means of transporting troops, food supplies, and war materiel. From its standpoint it mattered little who controlled the railways, as long as normal function was guaranteed. In midday of February 28, when the Stavka learned of the paralysis of the government in Petrograd, Alekseev inquired of Beliaev about the fate of the minister of transport, Kriger-Voinovskii, and asked the war minister if in the present situation it might be advisable to transfer control of the railways to the deputy minister of transport, General Kisliakov, who was in charge of railways in the theater of war. At Beliaev's answer that the transfer should be done as quickly as possible, Alekseev decided that he would assume the entire responsibility for railway movement through Kisliakov.[16] But it was easier said than done. Kisliakov himself pointed out the impossibility of this measure. His operation was part and parcel of the entire operation of the Ministry of Transport, and it would be totally impossible to schedule the entire railway network anew, independent of the railway administration in Petrograd. He justifiably recommended that the Stavka's decision to assume the responsibility for the railway should be postponed until serious disruptions actually did take place. In the meantime, operations of the Ministry of Transport were taken over by the Duma Committee's new commissar, Bublikov. Although Kisliakov has been maligned by monarchists for having joined the intrigues of the Duma Committee,[17] his action was in concert with the goal of the Stavka.

14. Alekseev's circular telegram, no. 1813, ibid., p. 24.

15. Katkov, *Russia, 1917*, p. 316.

16. Alekseev to Beliaev, no. 1811; Lukomskii to Kisliakov, no. 1818, "Fevral'skaia revoliutsiia 1917 goda," pp. 25-26.

17. Kisliakov to Lukomskii, no. 1, ibid., p. 26; A. I. Spiridovich, *Velikaia voina i fevral'skaia revoliutsiia 1914-1917 gg.* 3: 240-42; Katkov, *Russia, 1917*, p. 315.

Without reliable forces to enforce his decision, Kisliakov could not have resisted the Duma Committee's takeover. Detaching his operation to set up a completely new system of railway control would have been a hopeless endeavor, and even if he had succeeded, it would have irreparably disrupted normal function of the railways—the situation that he and the Stavka tried to avoid at all cost. Thus, Kisliakov chose the best course of action available under the circumstances and continued to work under Bublikov to ensure that railway movement would proceed as usual.

In the meantime, General Ivanov was organizing his expedition. Before his departure from Mogilev, Ivanov instructed Ruzskii and Evert to assemble the reinforcements from the northern front at Aleksandrovskaia, near Tsarskoe Selo, and those from the western front at Tsarskoe Selo, where he was scheduled to arrive around eight o'clock on the morning of March 1.[18] The first reinforcements from the northern front were expected to arrive at Aleksandrovskaia late on the night of February 28 and March 1, and the last troops from the western front not earlier than March 2.[19] To acquaint himself with the situation in Petrograd, he attempted to talk with Khabalov directly, but the latter was unable to come to the Hughes apparatus at the Admiralty. Ivanov then sent the ten-point questionnaire and received Khabalov's answer at 11:30 on the morning of February 28, an answer that revealed a situation far worse than he had expected.[20] Ivanov concluded that suppression of the revolution would not be achieved quickly and that he had no choice but to wait for the massive reinforcements before initiating military action against Petrograd.

The St. George Battalion left Mogilev at eleven o'clock on the morning of February 28, and General Ivanov himself two hours later. Ivanov's delay in leaving Mogilev has often been taken as evidence to prove his lack of seriousness in his counterrevolutionary attempt.[21] Considering the slowness with which the reinforcements were scheduled to assemble in Tsarskoe Selo, however, there actually was no need

18. Ivanov to Ruzskii, no. 2, "Fevral'skaia revoliutsiia 1917 goda," p. 21; Ivanov to Evert, no. 1, ibid. At the same time Ivanov ordered the commandant of Tsarskoe Selo to billet 13 battalions, 16 squadrons and 4 artillery batteries. TsGAOR, f. ChSK, d. 643, ℓ. 14; TsGAOR, f. ChSK, d. 466, ℓ. 127.

19. TsGAOR, f. ChSK, d. 643, ℓ. 18.

20. For Ivanov's attempt to talk directly with Khabalov and his subsequent telegram with the ten-point questionnaire, see TsGAOR, f. ChSK, d. 643, ℓℓ. 9-13; Khabalov to Alekseev, "Fevral'skaia revoliutsiia 1917 goda," p. 20.

21. For instance, A. S. Lukomskii, Vospominaniia 1: 125; Mel'gunov, Martovskie dni, p. 94.

for Ivanov to leave earlier. His special train caught up with the advancing battalion at Orsha. His force proceeded along the Vindarskii Line with no trouble, and arrived at Dno, approximately one hundred and thirty miles from Tsarskoe Selo, around seven o'clock on the morning of March 1—at about the same time that the imperial trains were approaching Bologoe to change their direction to Pskov. However, from Dno Ivanov's troops proceeded with excruciatingly slow speed. It took eleven hours to travel from Dno to Vyritsa, some one hundred ten miles. By the time they arrived at Vyritsa, twenty miles south of Tsarskoe Selo, it was already six o'clock in the evening.[22]

The stationmaster of Vyritsa refused to let Ivanov's trains go further. When Ivanov threatened force, however, the stationmaster easily capitulated and made arrangements to let the trains proceed.[23] When Ivanov and his troops finally arrived at Tsarskoe Selo at nine o'clock in the evening, the situation was the following: Nicholas had already arrived at Pskov; the Tarutin Company of the 67th Infantry Regiment sent from the northern front had arrived at Aleksandrovskaia, and the first echelon of the Borodin Company of the same infantry regiment had reached Luga. The rest of the reinforcements were on the way as scheduled.

It is often argued that Ivanov's safe arrival at Tsarskoe Selo was possible only with the connivance of the Duma Committee, which wished to use Ivanov's forces to suppress the revolution in Petrograd.[24] When the Duma Committee first learned of the dispatch of the counterrevolutionary forces late on the evening of February 27, there was great apprehension, even panic, among its members. Not only was the prospect of a bloody confrontation abhorrent, but a counterrevolutionary offensive against the insurgents would make its position precarious. It had openly sided with the rebellion against legitimate authority. It wished for peace and order to be restored, but not in the form of a bloody military suppression, which would make its long-awaited chance for internal reforms practically impossible. Moreover, a confrontation between the insurgents and the tsarist army would completely obliterate the middle ground that it tried to occupy, and force it to take the side of either the revolution or the

22. Ivanov's deposition, *Padenie tsarskogo rezhima* 5: 321.
23. Iu. V. Lomonosov, *Vospominaniia o martovskoi revoliutsii 1917 g.*, p. 40.
24. William Henry Chamberlin, *The Russian Revolution, 1917-1921* 1: 86; Martynov, *Tsarskaia armiia v fevral'skom perevorote*, p. 146. This is the accepted opinion of Soviet historians. See V. S. Diakin, *Russkaia burzhuaziia i tsarizm v gody pervoi mirovoi voiny*, p. 345; E. D. Chermenskii, *IV gosudarstvennaia duma i sverzhenie tsarizma v Rossii*, p. 297.

tsar. For these reasons the Duma Committee members were determined to avoid confrontation and stop the counterrevolutionary forces led by Ivanov. Bublikov gave the railway authorities instructions to hinder and obstruct any military train coming within 250 versts of Petrograd.[25] This was why Ivanov's trains moved so slowly after they passed Dno. But at Vyritsa, when Ivanov was determined to proceed to Tsarskoe Selo, if necessary with the use of force, Bublikov had no choice but to let him go. But this decision was made against Bublikov's wish. Despite some Soviet historians' contention, it did not represent "the Duma Committee's tacit approval" of Ivanov's forces. The Duma Committee's opposition to Ivanov's forces can be also confirmed by Grekov's order to hinder the movement of troops to Petrograd.[26]

As soon as Ivanov arrived at Tsarskoe Selo Station, he was greeted by the assistant commandant of the palace, Groten, and the Tsarskoe Selo police chief, Osipov, who reported that the Tsarskoe Selo Garrison had taken the side of the Duma, although the palace itself was protected by loyal troops. Ivanov immediately issued an order, which announced his position as dictator of the Petrograd Military District, that all citizens, military personnel, and clergy were to subordinate themselves to Ivanov. He took measures to assemble all troops in the headquarters he established in Tsarskoe Selo.[27] This bold stand, however, was not destined to continue very long. Soon Colonel Domanevskii and Lieutenant Colonel Tille arrived at the station. They had been dispatched by General Zankevich, chief of the main administration of the General Staff in Petrograd.

Soviet historians claim that the Domanevskii mission was engineered by the Duma Committee for negotiations with Ivanov to utilize Ivanov's troops for suppression of the revolution. Actually, it originated from Alekseev's instruction to Zankevich to create a staff for Ivanov from the main administration of the General Staff.[28] Until the pre-

25. A. A. Bublikov, *Russkaia revoliutsiia: Vpechatleniia i mysli ochevidtsa i uchastnika*, p. 40.

26. Lukomskii-Kvetsinskii conversation, "Fevral'skaia revoliutsiia 1917 goda," p. 33.

27. Ivanov's deposition, *Padenie tsarskogo rezhima* 5: 321-22; TsGAOR, f. 6, op. 1, d. 1722, ℓ. 18; Spiridovich, *Velikaia voina fevral'skaia revoliutsiia* 3: 221.

28. Martynov, *Tsarskaia armiia v fevral'skom perevorote*, p. 147; E. Genkina, "Fevral'skii perevorot," *Ocherki po istorii Oktiabr'skoi revoliutsii*, ed. M. N. Pokrovskii, 1: 75; Diakin, *Russkaia burzhuaziia*, p. 345; Chermenskii, *IV gosudarstvennaia duma*, p. 297; Alekseev to Beliaev, no. 1789, "Fevral'skaia revoliutsiia 1917 goda," p. 11.

vious day Zankevich had assumed the hopeless task of commanding
loyal troops against the insurgents. After their disintegration, he returned to the General Staff. In the meantime, Engelhardt and Guchkov
succeeded in recruiting some officers from the General Staff for the
work of the Duma Committee's Military Commission.[29] This development, coupled with his unsuccessful, frustrating experience of trying
to organize the loyal troops against the insurgents, must have convinced Zankevich of the necessity of reaching a compromise with
the Duma Committee. This opinion was widely shared by officers
in the General Staff. Late on the night of February 28, Domanevskii
went to the Tauride Palace to tell Engelhardt that he had been appointed chief of staff for Ivanov's forces. To Engelhardt the aim of
Ivanov's mission was clear: "Ivanov went to Petrograd to restore
tsarist power. In this relation my lot was cast: I openly acted against
the tsar and no excuse nor any agreement could be possible here."
But he said to Domanevskii, "Ivanov could also, on the other hand,
help to contain the revolution within those limits that seemed at
that time acceptable. We could become allies and co-workers only
on that basis. However for the agreement it was necessary to obtain
a concession from Ivanov. He must recognize the accomplished fact,
recognize the legal power of the Provisional Committee of the State
Duma." Engelhardt's point was understood by Domanevskii and
"he even allowed a possibility of agreement on the part of Ivanov."
But Domanevskii expressed doubt that restoring tsarist power and
imposing order could be separated in the minds of the soldiers. In
general "faith in the success of Ivanov's mission did not exist in
him."[30]

Engelhardt's statement should not be taken as the Duma Committee's intention to turn Ivanov's troops against the revolution, as
Soviet historians would have us believe. At that time, although the
Military Commission made contact with some officers of the General
Staff, it did not know the over-all attitude of the General Staff toward the revolution. After all, it was part of the military machinery
that was committed to counterrevolution. Since the General Staff
continued to maintain constant contact with the Stavka, it was
necessary for the Duma Committee to present itself as a champion
of law and order to persuade the military to reverse its plan for
counterrevolution. On the other hand, General Staff officers wanted

29. TsGAOR, f. 6, op. 1, d. 1722, ℓ. 26. Also see chap. 9.
30. OR GBL, f. 218, B. A. Engel'gardt, "Potonuvshii mir: Vospominaniia," ℓ.
112.

to avoid the appearance of official recognition of the Duma Committee, which accepted the revolution, as long as they were under the Stavka's order to cooperate with Ivanov's counterrevolutionary expedition. The Domanevskii-Engelhardt conversation was, therefore, delicate diplomatic negotiation, during which the true intentions of both sides were camouflaged in carefully worded opinions. But at the end both understood the wishes of the other side. Ivanov's counterrevolutionary offensive should be stopped and peaceful settlement with the Duma Committee should be sought as the only available means to solve the crisis.

Although the ultimate goal of the Duma Committee in general and the Military Commission in particular was the restoration of order, they were too deeply committed to the revolution to support Ivanov's expedition. On the contrary, they believed that it would contribute to the spread of revolution and anarchy, and that for the restoration of order the counterrevolutionary attempt should be stopped. A short outline of the activities of the Military Commission, written after the February Revolution, listed one activity "the organization of the efforts against the echelons dispatched from the army under the command of General Ivanov for the struggle with the revolution."[31]

Having secured tacit approval from the Duma Committee for the course of action they intended to take as well as safe passage to Tsarskoe Selo, Domanevskii and Tille went to Tsarskoe Selo to meet General Ivanov.[32] In the name of the chief of the General Staff, Domanevskii reported to Ivanov that all troops as well as officers in Petrograd had fallen under the influence of the Provisional Government formed by the Duma. The Provisional Government was making efforts to restore order, and "the reserve battalions support only the orders issued by the Provisional Government." Some members of the ministry were arrested, but most of the ministries, the War Ministry, for instance, continued to function only in agreement with the Provisional Government. In Domanevskii's opinion, "it is difficult to restore order by force in the armed struggle against the insurgents and the Provisional Government." Armed intervention would require an enormous number of troops, and it would encounter difficulties in provisioning, billetting, and transporting—tasks that could not be carried out without the cooperation of the Provisional Government. Aside from these practical difficulties, Domanevskii also presented political considerations. There were two points of

31. TsGIA, f. 1278, op. 10, d. 19, ℓ. 4.
32. TsGAOR, f. ChSK, d. 643, ℓ. 24.

view among the insurgents: one group, which swore allegiance to the Provisional Government, remained faithful to the monarchical principle, wished only limited internal reforms, and intended to eradicate disorder as quickly as possible to continue the war. But the other group, which supported the Petrograd Soviet, was willing to overthrow the existing state structure and to end the war. "Until March 1 the prestige of the Duma government stood high and in fact it looked master of the situation, at least in the capital. But it is clear that with each day the situation of the Duma government, which is not supported by law, is getting more difficult and that there is an increasing possibility that power could go to the extreme Left." All this would lead to the conclusion that "at the present moment an armed struggle would only complicate and worsen the situation, that each hour is precious, that order and normal state of affairs could be restored most easily by the agreement with the Provisional Government." It is not clear what effect this report had on Ivanov's mind, although his subsequent testimony indicates that he did not seem to attach much importance to Domanevskii's recommendation.[33]

After he heard Domanevskii's report, Ivanov was summoned by the tsarina to the palace. By this time the revolution had spread to Tsarskoe Selo. On February 27 everything was quiet in Tsarskoe Selo, but at 10 o'clock in the evening Beliaev informed Groten that a revolution had broken out in the capital, and recommended that since the empress was in danger she and her family should immediately leave the palace. Groten immediately relayed this news to Voeikov in Mogilev and asked for the tsar's advice. Nicholas replied that his family should stay in Tsarskoe Selo, and he would join them on March 1.[34]

The next day, on February 28, Princess Paley, Grand Duke Pavel Aleksandrovich's wife, woke up in the morning. "Then I glanced out of the window: a pure blue sky, the snow sparkling and scintillating in the sun's rays, not a sound to disturb the calm of the nature."[35] But this was not to last long. Count Apraksin walked all the way from Petrograd to Tsarskoe Selo on foot, and arrived at the palace in the morning to tell Aleksandra that the revolution had taken over the capital. Apraksin and Benckendorff, grand marshal of the court, met the empress at 10 o'clock in the morning and advised her to leave the palace. Before this meeting the empress had entertained the notion of leaving for Gatchina, and ordered Gilliard, Aleksei's

33. Ibid., ℓ. 29; deposition of Ivanov, *Padenie tsarskogo rezhima* 5: 323.
34. Paul Benckendorff, *Last Days at Tsarskoe Selo*, pp. 2-3.
35. Princess Paley, *Memories of Russia, 1916-1919*, pp. 48-49.

French tutor, to prepare a train. But she quickly changed her mind. She told Benckendorff and Apraksin that "in no case would she consent to leave by herself, and that owing to the state of her children's health, especially that of the Heir Apparent, departure with them was completely out of the question." It was decided to stay and wait for the arrival of the emperor.[36]

The afternoon was quiet, but many cars carrying soldiers arrived from Petrograd. By the evening of February 28, revolution had finally begun in Tsarskoe Selo. Soldiers broke out of the barracks. Armed with rifles, and singing revolutionary songs, insurgents attacked prisons, pillaged stores, and marched toward the palace. But the imperial palace was heavily guarded by loyal troops: two battalions of His Majesty's private regiment, one battalion of the guard regiment, 1,200 strong, two squadrons of the Cossacks of the emperor's escort, one company of the First Railway Regiment, and one heavy artillery battery. The troops were under the command of General Groten. The insurgents would approach the guarded enclosure of the palace and then withdraw, but never launched a serious attack. The loyal troops spent the night awaiting an attack, but nothing occurred except a skirmish between a patrol and some hooligans. Although the Cossacks and the private regiment were ready to do their duty, the morale of the guard regiment, artillery, and the railway regiment was not high. The empress was persuaded to inspect the troops who were assembled in the courtyard. As she went out, "some of the troops answered in a surly fashion." Faced with the physical danger threatening her children, the empress's concern was for their safety alone. At night she slept dressed on her bed. Groten considered confrontation with the insurgents extremely dangerous to the imperial family, and entered into negotiations with the rebels with the empress's approval. By promising that the palace guard would send two truce emissaries to the Duma, he gained the insurgents' assurance that they would not attack the palace.[37]

The empress and her entourage still hoped that the situation would improve with Nicholas's arrival at Tsarskoe Selo. But at 5 o'clock in the morning on March 1 she learned that the imperial trains had been detained and that Nicholas would not be coming. She sent the following telegram to her husband, but did not know where he was: "The thoughts of prayers will not desert you. Lord will save. The temperatures of the children are still high. They are coughing badly. All

36. Benckendorff, *Last Days at Tsarskoe Selo*, p. 5.

37. Ibid., pp. 6-9; Spiridovich, *Velikaia voina i fevral'skaia revoliutsiia* 3: 196-203.

firmly kiss you." The telegram never reached the emperor; instead it fell into the hands of the Military Commission.[38] Alone and helpless, the empress instructed Groten to enter into negotiations with Rodzianko to insure the avoidance of bloodshed and to learn the whereabouts of her husband. Rodzianko promised to send the members of the Duma to calm the insurgents, but pleaded ignorance of the whereabouts of the tsar—a lie, since Bublikov and Lomonosov constantly apprised him of the location of the imperial trains. Despite her hatred of Rodzianko, the empress was beginning to look upon him as "the only person who could do a lot."[39] At 11 o'clock in the morning, however, telephone and radio communications between Tsarskoe Selo and the Stavka were cut off on the order of Engelhardt.

On the afternoon of March 1, V. A. Stepanov and I. Demidov, two Duma deputies, arrived at Tsarskoe Selo.[40] They went around the barracks, and succeeded in calming the insurgents by having them pledge their allegiance to the Duma. As requested by General Groten, they did their best to prevent an attack on the imperial palace. By the time General Ivanov arrived in Tsarskoe Selo, therefore, the empress and palace authorities found it necessary to surrender the entire garrison to the Duma Committee to secure the safety of the imperial family.

From the point of view of the empress and her entourage, Ivanov's arrival was, ironically, not welcome, since the security of the imperial family hung by a thread. They had gone through the dreadful night and barely managed to achieve a precarious peace with the insurgents, but if the insurgents learned of the arrival of Ivanov's troops, this peace might be broken at any moment. Thus Groten at the railway station and the empress at the palace hinted to Ivanov that his forces were not welcome in Tsarskoe Selo. The empress summoned Ivanov for a single reason, to learn from him where her husband was located. It was from Ivanov that she first learned that Nicholas's train had been diverted from Bologoe to Dno, from where he was to proceed to Pskov. Aleksandra asked Ivanov if he might send a message on her behalf to her husband, since she was deprived of all other means of communicating with him. Ivanov refused her request on the grounds that he did not possess personnel to carry such a message. The rest of the empress's talk was incoherent and depressed. She talked about

38. TsGAOR, f. 3748, d. 129, ℓ. 19.
39. Spiridovich, *Velikaia voina i fevral'skaia revoliutsiia* 3: 218-19.
40. I. Demidov, "Tsarskoe Selo 1-go marta 1917 goda," *Poslednie novosti*, March 12, 1927.

her sick children and then bitterly about the proposed solution of a responsible ministry.[41]

When General Ivanov retired from the palace and returned to the station, he learned that insurgents from the Tsarskoe Selo Garrison were approaching. He immediately withdrew his troops to Vyritsa to avoid confrontation with the insurgents. There he learned that only fifteen minutes after their withdrawal the insurgent soldiers and the crowds had occupied the station.[42] The withdrawal of Ivanov's troops from Tsarskoe Selo was not quite a rout nor was it caused by the dissolving loyalty of his troops, as often argued.[43] As long as the presence of his troops might endanger the safety of the imperial family and as long as his duty did not specifically include defense of the palace and the imperial family, he had no desire to defy the express wish of the empress. Until the very end of Ivanov's operation, his forces showed no signs of faltering loyalty.[44]

Yet, one cannot but notice haphazardness in Ivanov's moves. The officers who accompanied Ivanov, Captains Kapustin and Lodyzhenskii, for instance, had a distinct impression that Ivanov had "neither definite goals nor definite plan of action, and they could not understand what measures he would undertake in the near future."[45] But the true cause for the failure of Ivanov's offensive lay neither in the reliability of his troops nor in the lack of definite plans. It was rather due to the change of policy of the Stavka. When he was still in Tsarskoe Selo, Ivanov received two telegrams, one from Alekseev and another from Nicholas, which fundamentally altered the nature of his expedition. Both telegrams ordered a halt until further notice. Nicholas ordered Ivanov "not to take any action until my arrival."[46]

Alekseev's telegram (no. 1833), to General Ivanov, which was sent early on March 1, but not received until late at night stated:

According to the latest information, on February 28, complete peace was restored

41. Ivanov's deposition, *Padenie tsarskogo rezhima* 5: 322-23.

42. Ibid., p. 323.

43. Chamberlin, *The Russian Revolution* 1: 86.

44. A commander of the St. George Battalion, Pozharskii, testified at the Extraordinary Investigation Commission that he had declared that he would not give his soldiers an order to shoot at the people, even if Ivanov had given him instructions to do so. Blok, "Poslednie dni starago rezhima," pp. 41, 46; "Proval popytki Stavki podavit' Fevral'skuiu revoliutsiiu," p. 105. But this testimony made after the revolution may not be reliable.

45. "Proval popytki Stavki podavit' Fevral'skuiu revoliutsiiu," p. 106.

46. TsGAOR, f. ChSK, d. 643, л. 36; TsGAOR, f. ChSK, d. 466, л. 30; the tsar to Ivanov, "Fevral'skaia revoliutsiia 1917 goda," p. 53.

474 THE ABDICATION OF NICHOLAS II

in Petrograd. The troops that had joined the Provisional Government in entire composition have been brought in order. The Provisional Government under the chairmanship of Rodzianko, meeting in the State Duma, asked the commanders of the military units to obey orders for the restoration of peace. The proclamation to the populace issued by the Provisional Government mentions the immutability of the monarchical basis of Russia, necessity of a new basis for election and appointment of a government. They are waiting with impatience for the arrival of His Majesty, to present the aforementioned demands and to request his acceptance of the aspirations of the people. If this information is correct, then the method of your action will be changed, and the negotiations will lead to pacification, to avoid disgraceful fratricide, which our enemy has long awaited, and to preserve institutions and to get the factories operating. The proclamation of the new minister of transport, Bublikov, to the railway workers, which I received in a roundabout way, appeals to all to intensify work to remedy the disorganization of transportation. Let His Majesty know all this and also the conviction that it is possible to bring everything to a peaceful end, which will strengthen Russia.[47]

If the Stavka's determination to organize a counterrevolutionary offensive was based on its judgment that Petrograd was thrown into complete anarchy, from which the radical elements were emerging to control the insurgents, the news of the Duma Committee's control over the situation immediately produced a change of attitude. Even before the revolution military leaders had sympathized with the moderate wing of the liberals so it would be psychologically difficult to direct arms against those with whom the military leaders had no substantial disagreement. Such an intervention, even if successful, would totally isolate the army from the rest of the population and would render the continuation of the war impossible. In the eyes of the public the army and its leaders would inevitably be associated with the reactionary "dark forces." Moreover, if the Stavka were to involve the army in a counterrevolutionary attempt not only against the insurgents but also against the Duma, it could no longer count on the reliability of the officers, not to mention the soldiers.[48] Thus the Stavka welcomed with a sigh of relief the news that the Duma Committee was exerting its influence, with some measure of success, to restore order in the capital.

47. Alekseev to Ivanov, "Fevral'skaia revoliutsiia 1917 goda," p. 31.
48. Soviet historians claim that the Stavka's fear of the spread of the revolution in the army was the most important cause for the failure of Ivanov's counterrevolutionary attempt, and minimize the importance of the Duma Committee's alleged control of the situation in Petrograd. This fear became a factor only when the Stavka realized the extent of the revolution, which was broad enough to include the Duma Committee. The two factors are not mutually exclusive, as Soviet historians contend, but integrally related.

From a strictly legalistic point of view, there was no question that the Duma Committee had revolted against legitimate authority, and as long as the supreme commander in chief's order to suppress it stood effective, the Stavka should have had no other choice but to pursue it. But for the sake of a broader national interest, the Stavka saw catastrophe for the nation and for the army in pursuing such a policy, and decided to defy the imperial order and halt Ivanov's offensive without the emperor's permission.

The source of information on the basis of which the Stavka made this decision is not clear. Because the stiuation in Petrograd as described in this telegram was not quite the same as actuality, there has been developed a conspiracy theory, that the Duma Committee deceived the Stavka to stop Ivanov's offensive.[49] The telegram referred to the Duma Committee's proclamation, but inaccurately described its contents, which indicates that the Stavka had not obtained the two proclamations that the Duma Committee had issued on February 28. One of the proclamations did state that order was being restored, but did not say that complete peace was restored. Neither of the proclamations had mentioned anything about the "immutability of the monarchical basis of Russia." It is doubtful that the information came directly from the Duma Committee. It is known that Rodzianko sent two telegrams to the commanders at the front on March 1. The first telegram informed Alekseev that "due to the removal of all the former Council of Ministers from administration governmental power was transferred at the present moment to the Provisional Committee of the State Duma." But it did not reach the Stavka until shortly before six o'clock in the morning. The other telegram stated that the Duma Committee's task was to "create normal conditions of life and administration" in the capital. However, this telegram apparently did not reach the Stavka. Alekseev was irritated by Rodzianko's frequent dispatch of telegrams to commanding officers without due consideration for the normal chain of command in the army and wrote a telegram of protest to Rodzianko, requesting that this practice be

---

49. Spiridovich cites two sources that intentionally attempted to mislead the Stavka with false information. The first was the deputy transport minister, Kisliakov, who talked with Alekseev and dissuaded him from taking counterrevolutionary measures. The second source was Rodzianko, who recommended Nicholas's abdication to Alekseev. Katkov also implies that this was the case. Spiridovich, *Velikaia voina i fevral'skaia revoliutsiia* 3: 240-41; Katkov, *Russia, 1917*, p. 315. There is no evidence to support this contention. As for Kisliakov's activities, see above, pp. 464-65. Rodzianko, on the other hand, could not have made such a proposal on the night of February 28.

immediately discontinued.[50] Alekseev's reaction to Rodzianko leads one to doubt that there were direct negotiations between Alekseev and Rodzianko before the Stavka decided to stop Ivanov's expedition.

Although existing evidence is not conclusive, it appears that Alekseev made the decision from information supplied by the military hierarchy in Petrograd, particularly by the Naval Staff and the main administration of the General Staff. The Stavka's contact with these staffs was maintained without interruption, and they provided the Stavka with valuable details about the situation in Petrograd. The solution suggested in Alekseev's telegram (no. 1833) closely resembled the line taken by Zankevich, Domanevskii, and other officers of the general staff. Their close contact with Rodzianko, Guchkov, and Engelhardt indicates that they had a quite accurate reading of the Duma Committee's position at the moment. Justifiably, Alekseev considered their judgments more reliable than those that came from other sources. Their suggested solution resembled the line pursued by Rodzianko at that moment, but it does not necessarily mean that the military was deceived by Rodzianko and the Duma Committee.

Alekseev mentioned one specific source of information: Bublikov's telegram to the railway workers. This celebrated telegram was so hostile in tone to the monarchy that it should have aroused suspicion among the military leaders of the Duma Committee's intention to stand on the principle of the "immutability of the monarchical basis of Russia." That it did not and that the Stavka rather welcomed Bublikov's telegram as a sign of the Duma Committee's intention to maintain the normal functioning of the railway characterized the Stavka's general thinking during the February Revolution.[51] The High Command was more concerned with the war effort than with preservation of the monarchy. The Stavka's decision to halt Ivanov's offensive was a decisive turning point of the February Revolution. The Stavka was prepared to accept the Duma Committee as a legitimate government and to seek a negotiated settlement. Although it did not

50. Rodzianko to Alekseev, "Fevral'skaia revoliutsiia 1917 goda," p. 36; G. P. Perets, *V tsitadeli russkoi revoliutsii: Zapiski komendanta Tavricheskogo dvortsa 27 fevralia—23 marta 1917 g.*, pp. 41-42. When Evert mentioned that he had two teelgrams from Rodzianko, Lukomskii replied that the Stavka was aware of only one of them. Evert-Lukomskii conversation, "Fevral'skaia revoliutsiia 1917 goda," pp. 36-37; Alekseev to Rodzianko, no. 1845, ibid., pp. 44-45.

51. When Klevetskii at the western front informed Lukomskii of the contents of Bublikov's telegram, Lukomskii said, "The telegram is known to us, but it is not bad, since it is calling for order." Lukomskii-Klevetskii conversation, "Fevral'skaia revoliutsiia 1917 goda," p. 33.

completely abandon the possibility of military intervention, it did not feel the need for military suppression as urgently as before.

If the news of the Duma Committee's control over the situation in Petrograd was decisive in changing the Stavka's policy, the spread of the revolution to Moscow and to other army units convinced the Stavka all the more of the urgent necessity to conclude a peaceful settlement. By 11 o'clock in the morning the Stavka learned that revolution had broken out in Moscow and Kronstadt. The situation as described in the dispatches of telegrams from Moscow followed the familiar pattern: in the morning it was reported that while the workers took to the streets, the armed units remained at their posts.[52] Shortly after three o'clock in the afternoon, however, the first news of the soldiers' uprising in Moscow reached the Stavka. One hour later, General Mrozovskii, commander of the Moscow Military District, reported: "In Moscow, a complete revolution. The armed units are going over to the side of the revolutionaries." In the afternoon, the news from Kronstadt was even gloomier. Rebels took over the fortress and cut off communication with outside. It was reported that the commander of the fortress had been killed and that insurgents were arresting the officers.[53] Around the same time the Stavka received news that the revolution had now spread to the Baltic Fleet, where Admiral Nepenin was compelled to recognize the authority of the Duma Committee without sanction from the Stavka, since "such a direct and straightforward method is the only way that I could maintain the discipline and the military preparedness of the units entrusted to me."[54]

This news hastened the Stavka to recognize the Duma Committee and to attempt frantically to pressure Nicholas into granting the concession of a responsible ministry. How Nicholas finally acquiesced under this pressure will be discussed in the next chapter. It suffices to say here that, together with the concessions of a responsible ministry, Nicholas agreed to halt Ivanov's offensive and sent him a telegram, ordering the general "not to take any action" until his arrival at Tsarskoe Selo.[55] Ivanov thus received two telegrams—one from Alekseev and another from the tsar himself—ordering the temporary halt of his offensive. If Domanevskii's recommendation had no

52. Lukomskii-Evert conversation, ibid., p. 37; Baranovskii-Mediokritskii conversation, ibid., p. 39.

53. Mrozovskii to Alekseev, nos. 8196, 8197, ibid., p. 45; Lukomskii to Danilov, ibid., p. 43.

54. Lukomskii to Danilov, ibid., p. 43.

55. TsGAOR, f. ChSK, d. 643, л. 36; TsGAOR, f. ChSK, d. 466, л. 130; Nicholas to Ivanov, "Fevral'skaia revoliutsiia 1917 goda," p. 53.

tangible effects, Ivanov had no choice but to obey the two orders. He decided to wait in Vyritsa until further instructions from the Stavka.

The halt of the counterrevolutionary operation, however, did not mean that the Stavka decided to discontinue Ivanov's operation entirely. Shortly after Alekseev sent his telegram (no. 1833) to Ivanov, Lukomskii stated to General Kvetsinskii of the western front, "Of course, it is necessary to take all measures to ensure that the echelons will proceed without interruption." At one o'clock on the afternoon of March 1, more than thirteen hours after Alekseev's telegram (no. 1833), the western front still continued to dispatch troops to support Ivanov.[56] At 6:30 in the evening General Klembovskii instructed Ruzskii to have a battalion of the Vyborg Fortress Artillery march to Petrograd, if it proved to be impossible to reach there by rail. In addition, a reliable unit of the 106th Infantry Division was to be prepared to support this battalion.[57] During the night of March 1 and 2, however, the northern front, presumably with the approval of the tsar, began recalling the reinforcements without explicit approval of the Stavka. The battalion of the Vyborg Fortress Artillery and the Tarutin Company, which had already arrived at Aleksandrovskaia —the two units located closest to Ivanov—were the first to be recalled. At the same time without the prior approval of Alekseev Ruzskii ordered the western and the southwestern fronts to detain the dispatched troops at the nearest railway stations.[58] The Stavka accepted

56. Lukomskii-Kvetsinskii conversation, ibid., p. 33; Lebedev to Lukomskii, no. 6157, ibid., p. 41.

57. Klembovskii to Ruzskii, no. 1857, ibid., p. 47. The fate of the Vyborg Fortress Artillery battalion offers an interesting insight into the relationship between Alekseev and Ruzskii. When the situation in Petrograd grew worse on February 28, Alekseev ordered Ruzskii to dispatch a battalion of the Vyborg Fortress Artillery to Petrograd. Its commander, General Gulevich, learned that the Duma Committee had been formed in Petrograd and asked the Stavka to which authority in Petrograd he should subordinate himself. Gulevich to Alekseev, no. 525, ibid., p. 35. For this action Gulevich was reprimanded by Ruzskii, who reminded Gulevich of his duty to obey his immediate superior officer (Ruzskii) and not to jump over the commanding hierarchy. Ruzskii to Gulevich, no. 1183/B, ibid., p. 35. On March 1, Ivanov received a telegram from Gulevich, who informed Ivanov that transport of the Vyborg Fortress Artillery would be possible only as far as Beloostrov, since the railway further down from Beloostrov was occupied by the rebels. TsGAOR, f. ChSK, d. 643, l. 17. It is difficult to establish if the occupation of the railway line between Petrograd and Beloostrov was true, but it appears that Ruzskii halted Gulevich's advance without the Stavka's authorization. Later, the Stavka ordered the northern front to have the battalion march to Petrograd on foot, if railway transportation was impossible.

58. Danilov to commander of the 42nd Corps, no. 1221/B, "Fevral'skaia revoliutsiia 1917 goda," p. 54; Danilov to commander of the 5th Army, no.

the established fact and sent its instructions to the northern and the western fronts: "In view of the impossibility of moving the echelons of troops directed to Petrograd beyond Luga, the emperor's permission for the commander of the northern front to enter into negotiations with the chairman of the State Duma, and imperial consent to recall the troops sent from the northern front back to the Dvinsk region, the chief of staff requests that the measures be taken immediately not to transport those units not yet dispatched and to hold those units that are on the way at the nearest large stations."[59] As if to make sure that this decision would not be reversed by the Stavka, the northern front secured imperial sanction of the recall and cancellation of the reinforcement troops.[60]

What made the military finally abandon the effort of intervention? The northern front learned during the night of March 1 and 2 that Luga Garrison had taken the side of the Duma Committee. In his telegraphic conversation with Ruzskii, Rodzianko informed the commander of the northern front that troops dispatched from the northern front had revolted at Luga, occupied the station, and pledged to stop military trains.[61] If this information proved to be true, it would be ominous, the first sign that revolution had spread to the very troops sent to suppress it. Furthermore, the occupation of Luga posed a serious question about effective transportation of the reinforcements, since Luga was situated in the middle of the line between Pskov and Petrograd. The "mutiny at Luga" was another decisive turning point for the military.

The revolution had spread to the Luga Garrison on March 1, when the soldiers left the barracks, attacked the arsenal, and began arresting the officers. The officers corps was split into two groups: one group led by N. Voronovich advocated supporting the Duma Committee and organizing the insurgent soldiers along this line, while the other,

---

1216/B, "Telegrammy i razgovory po telegrafu mezhdu Pskovom, Stavkoiu i Petrogradom, otnoshiashcheisia k obstoiatel'stvam otrecheniia Gosudariia Imperatora, s primechaniiami k nim general-ad"iutanta N. V. Ruzskago," *Russkaia letopis'* 3 (1922): 126 (hereafter cited as "Telegrammy Ruzskago"); Danilov to Alekseev, no. 1220, ibid., p. 127; Kvetsinskii to the chief of military communications of the western front and the commander of the 2nd Army, no. 6176, "Fevral'skaia revoliutsiia 1917 goda," p. 55.

59. Lukomskii to Kvetsinskii and Danilov, no. 1869, "Fevral'skaia revoliutsiia 1917 goda," p. 60.

60. Danilov to Alekseev, no. 1227/B, ibid., p. 64. Alekseev accepted the imperial decree to recall the troops. Alekseev to Evert and Brusilov, no. 1877, ibid., p. 64.

61. Boldyrev to Lukomskii, ibid., p. 61; Ruzskii-Rodzianko conversation, ibid., pp. 55-56; "Telegrammy Ruzskago," p. 126.

represented by the commander of the garrison, General Mengden, refused to join the revolution. It was at the officers' initiative that a Military Committee was formed, which immediately established contact with the Duma Committee. The formation of the Military Committee subdued the flaring temper of the insurgents, who having shot to death several officers including General Mengden, had tasted blood. Voronovich, who assumed chairmanship of the Military Committee, and his colleagues managed to disarm the insurgents and convince them to return to barracks.[62]

The Luga Military Committee received instructions from "Petrograd" to "stop and disarm the Borodin Company without fail in order to avoid the possibility of useless bloodshed."[63] There was another telegram, which was dispatched by Nekrasov to the "Luga District Committee": "You have promised to discontinue the movement of the troops for the pacification of Petrograd. I request that you report the details."[64] It was a difficult task, indeed. In the approaching Borodin Company there were 2,000 disciplined soldiers with eight machine guns, while the Luga Military Committee could gather only 300 to 400 undisciplined, untrained soldiers and the available guns in the reserve artillery divison were for training purposes only and no use in actual battle. Against all odds, however, the members of the Military Committee decided at an emergency meeting to follow instructions. Machine guns with no cartridge belts and the training weapons were displayed on the platform. As soon as the train entered the station, three members of the Military Committee issued a strict order to the soldiers on the train to remain inside. They then hurried into the officers' car and solemnly handed to the commanders an ultimatum in the name of the Duma Committee. They demanded unconditional surrender and voluntary disarmament of officers and soldiers and declared that noncompliance would mean that artillery fire would fall on the trains.

There was no effort to resist by the Borodin Company. The commanders easily gave in, surrendered their arms, and ordered their soldiers to do the same. In fifteen minutes the entire company was disarmed.[65] Whether the commanders of the Borodin Company really believed the threat of the Luga Military Committee or pretended to

62. N. Voronovich, "Zapiski predsedatelia soveta soldatskikh deputatov," *Arkhiv grazhdanskoi voiny* 2 (1921): 17-18, 23-30.

63. Ibid., p. 31. Although Voronovich does not spell out who in Petrograd gave this order, we can assume that this came from the Duma Committee, either Bublikov or Nekrasov, with whom the Luga Military Committee kept communications.

64. TsGIA, f. 1278, op. 10, d. 5, ℓℓ. 5, 6.

65. Voronovich, "Zapiski predsedatelia soveta soldatskikh deputatov," pp. 32-33.

believe it for a good excuse not to fulfill the onerous obligation of putting down the revolution will never be known. If the latter is true, they must have decided to have a little fun in this revolutionary vignette, when they told the representatives of the Military Committee that they would wait for the arrival of the Duma Committee's representatives—a proposal that made the members of the Military Committee extremely nervous, since they feared that approaching dawn would reveal the dummies ostentatiously displayed on the platform. The proposal was rejected and Borodin Company was ordered to return to the northern front immediately. The news of the disarmament of the Borodin Company was immediately dispatched to the Duma Committee, which in the name of Bublikov sent a telegram thanking the Military Committee for its successful operation.[66]

Thus, there never was a mutiny at Luga by the reinforcement troops sent from the northern front, as Rodzianko stated in his conversations with Ruzskii. Rodzianko may not have known the details of the "mutiny," but must have known the Military Committee's general direction. He made use of the episode to impress on Ruzskii the impossibility of continuing the counterrevolutionary attempt and the necessity of bringing about the political solution he suggested. Ruzskii knew that Rodzianko was telling him an untruth. The northern front learned before one o'clock in the morning of March 2 that the Luga Garrison had taken the side of the Duma Committee. This news, not the "mutiny of the reinforcement troops" as told by Rodzianko, led the northern front to reevaluate the wisdom of continuing the counterrevolutionary attempt. Soon the northern front received a report from the Borodin Company: "Before the arrival at the Luga Station, echelon No. 1 of the regiment entrusted to me, consisting of a battalion and a machine-gun unit, was surrounded by the units of the Luga Garrison . . . and the soldiers were disarmed." Nonetheless, the northern front continued to feed the Stavka with the inaccurate information that reinforcement troops had revolted at Luga.[67] As Rodzianko used this untruth to convince the northern front of the necessity to discontinue the counterrevolutionary attempt, the commanding officers of the northern front in turn did the same to shake the resolve of the Stavka by concealing the true information. In the meantime, the northern front went ahead in the recalling of

66. Ibid., pp. 32-33, 92.

67. Boldyrev to Lukomskii, no. 1215/B, "Fevral'skaia revoliutsiia 1917 goda," p. 61; Danilov to Alekseev, no. 1224/B, ibid., p. 62; Boldyrev to commander of the 5th Army, "Telegrammy Ruzskago," p. 126. This telegram is not included in the Stavka's telegrams in Krasnyi arkhiv.

troops without approval of the Stavka. It is characteristic of Ruzskii that he recalled the troops closest to Ivanov to preclude any possibility of linking them up with Ivanov's forces. The Stavka at first had no choice but to accept established fact.

However, the Stavka had not completely abandoned its intention of a military intervention. The disagreement between the Stavka and the northern front on this issue became pronounced on the morning of March 2. At 10 o'clock in the morning Alekseev sent the northern front a telegram, in which he ordered Ruzskii to dispatch officers "in order to make sure of the true sentiment of the troops" at Ivanov's disposal, since Alekseev now had "a basis not to trust entirely the information of Rodzianko." Alekseev explained that he had come to learn the information on March 1 that Luga had been occupied by the representatives of the "Provisional Government," who had definite instructions not to let the imperial trains pass.[68] The commanding officers of the northern front questioned the wisdom of this instruction, and delayed its execution. Danilov expressed his doubt about the advisability of the instruction. Receiving the repeated order from the Stavka, Boldyrev asked for specific instructions as to what message to convey to Ivanov, while still expressing the doubt whether a special emissary could reach Ivanov because of the difficulties with railway movement. But after the Stavka insisted on the execution of its order for the third time, the northern front finally, though reluctantly, appointed the officers, but delayed their departure until March 4.[69] By this time, the Stavka had committed itself to seek Nicholas's abdication, and had abandoned the idea of military intervention.

When General Ivanov was ordered by Alekseev and the emperor to halt his operation, he did not think that his mission was over, either. After he retreated to Vyritsa, Ivanov requested General Tikhmenev at the Stavka to speed up the arrival of the rest of the St. George Battalion at Vyritsa. Also he wished to communicate with the the commanders of the Tsarskoe Selo Garrison and Tarutin Company at Alesandrovskaia and to request the Tsarskoe Selo railway administration to make the arrangements necessary for his trip to Aleksandrovskaia. This request was immediately relayed to Lomonosov and Bublikov, who frantically attempted to block the linkage of Ivanov's forces with the Tarutin Company. Ivanov managed to

    68. Alekseev to Danilov, no. 1871, "Fevral'skaia revoliutsiia 1917 goda," p. 65.
    69. Boldyrev to Lukomskii, no. 1229/B, ibid.; Lukomskii to Boldyrev, no. 1881, ibid.; Sutin-Sergeev conversation, ibid., p. 66.

reach Susashino when he received a telegram from Bublikov: "Your persistent wish to go further is causing an insurmountable difficulty for the august wish of His Majesty to reach Tsarskoe Selo immediately. I most urgently request that you remain in Susashino or return to Vyritsa."[70] The train he occupied was led off the main track of the Warsaw Line on the pretext of opening the line for another train, which never came. Ivanov was stuck there for several hours.[71] Unable to go further, Ivanov finally returned to Vyritsa. To the Duma Committee, which was not aware of the change of policy by the military, Ivanov's forces continued to pose a threat. It was, therefore, imperative to isolate them from both the remaining forces dispatched from the front and the emperor. The resistance of the railway authorities aggravated the general, who threatened them with arrest if his order met with delay. At Vyritsa he received another telegram from Bublikov: "It became known to me that you are arresting and terrorizing the employees of the railway who serve my administration. With the approval of the Provisional Committee of the State Duma I warn you that you bring grave responsibility on yourself by this. I recommend that you not move out of Vyritsa, otherwise in accordance with my instructions your regiment will be fired upon by the artillery of the people's army."[72]

Ivanov was completely isolated from the troops that had been made available to him. In the meantime, no reinforcement troops promised for him arrived. He had received no information from the Stavka since Alekseev's telegram on the previous day.[73] Outraged, Ivanov sent Alekseev a rather irate telegram: "Until now I have no information about the movement of the units assigned at my disposal. I have secret information about my train being stopped. I request that you take extraordinary measures for the restoration of order in the railway administration, which is undoubtedly receiving instructions from the Provisional Government." After this telegram was dispatched, Ivanov received the first telegram since Alekseev's telegram (no. 1833). It informed the general of the Stavka's decision to recall reinforcements.[74]

70. TsGAOR, f. ChSK, d. 643, ℓℓ. 35, 38, 40.

71. "Proval popytki Stavki podavit' Fevral'skuiu revoliutsiiu," p. 107.

72. TsGAOR, f. ChSK, d. 643, ℓ. 41; "Proval popytki Stavka podavit' Fevral'skuiu revoliutsiiu," p. 108.

73. Two telegrams were written to be dispatched to Ivanov, but they were never sent to Ivanov. Klembovskii to Ivanov, no. 1844, "Fevral'skaia revoliutsiia 1917 goda," p. 38; Klembovskii to Ivanov, ibid., p. 61.

74. TsGAOR, f. ChSK, d. 643, ℓℓ. 39, 42; Ivanov to Alekseev, no. 9, "Fevral'skaia revoliutsiia 1917 goda," Krasnyi arkhiv 21, no. 3 (1927): 30-31.

While at Vyritsa, Ivanov received a telegram from Guchkov, who wished to see the general either in Pskov or at Gatchina on his way to Pskov. Guchkov and Shul'gin were entrusted by the Duma Committee to persuade Nicholas to accept abdication.[75] The reason Guchkov wanted to meet Ivanov was not mentioned in his telegram. Soviet historians argue that Guchkov intended to negotiate with Ivanov for a possible use of his forces to suppress the insurgents in Petrograd.[76] It is unlikely, however, that Guchkov had such an intention. The Duma Committee, which was divided on Nicholas's abdication, was united in opposition to the counterrevolutionary expedition. Bublikov's consistent attempt to isolate Ivanov's forces has been detailed and we have also seen Rodzianko's effort to talk Ruzskii out of Ivanov's offensive. When the Duma Committee finally decided to seek Nicholas's abdication, it is unlikely that the Duma Committee schemed to use Ivanov's forces against the revolution. It makes more sense to think that Guchkov's appointment with Ivanov was made for the same purpose as the Domanevskii mission and Rodzianko's conversation with Ruzskii—to convince the general of the uselessness of the counterrevolutionary attempt.

Ivanov, as we have seen, was unable to move out of Vyritsa, and cabled to Guchkov that he would wait for him there. Guchkov immediately promised to see the general either at Vyritsa or Gatchina, if Ivanov could reach there, on his way back from Pskov to Petrograd. But on March 3, after the negotiations with Nicholas, Guchkov returned directly to Petrograd, and expressed regret in a telegram to Ivanov that he did not have a chance to meet him.[77] Since Guchkov learned in Pskov that the reinforcements had been recalled and that the military leaders had finally decided to call off the counterrevolutionary attempt, he had no reason to waste time by seeing the general.

After Ivanov learned that the Stavka had decided to recall the reinforcement troops, he received a telephone call from the commander of the Tarutin Company, who told him that his company had received instructions to evacuate from Aleksandrovskaia and return to the front.[78] After this Ivanov was left in the dark as to what the Stavka intended to do with his forces. On March 3, he received Rodzianko's telegram saying that General Alekseev had appointed General Kornilov commander of the Petrograd Military District, and that Ivanov was relieved of his post.[79] Rodzianko demanded his immediate return to

75. TsGAOR, f. ChSK, d. 643, ℓ. 31. See chap. 25.
76. For instance, Diakin, *Russkaia burzhuaziia*, p. 345.
77. TsGAOR, f. ChSK, d. 643, ℓℓ. 32, 33.
78. "Proval popytki Stavki podavit' Fevral'skuiu revoliutsiiu," p. 108.
79. TsGAOR, f. ChSK, d. 643, ℓ. 45.

Mogilev. After he inquired about the accuracy of this information, Ivanov received a one-sentence telegram from the Stavka: "You and the St. George Battalion are ordered to return to Mogilev."[80] Ivanov left Vyritsa with his troops at 3 o'clock in the afternoon and at Dno Station he learned of Nicholas's abdication. On March 5 he arrived at Mogilev, and reported to Alekseev. After he was officially relieved of his duty, he reviewed his troops. He thanked each company of the St. George Battalion, which remained intact and loyal to their commander throughout his unfortunate journey, and expressed his hope that they would loyally serve the new government.[81]

General Ivanov's counterrevolutionary attempt represented a serious intention on the part of the military leaders to suppress the revolution in Petrograd. As long as the Stavka believed that the capital was thrown into complete anarchy and that there was a real possibility of a take-over by the extreme radical elements, it was prepared to pour massive troops from the front to put it down. But as soon as it learned that the Duma Committee was successfully restoring order, it immediately ordered the halt of Ivanov's operation. It hoped that it would be possible to reach a negotiated settlement with the Duma Committee without involving troops from the front. The news of the spread of revolution in Moscow and other units of the armed forces convinced the military of the necessity to reach an agreement with the Duma Committee as quickly as possible. The military was split, however, over what to do with Ivanov's forces. Both the Stavka and the northern front attempted to isolate them lest Ivanov should unilaterally act against Petrograd, and wreck the carefully orchestrated effort to reach a political setttlement. But while the commanding officers of the northern front considered it wise to call off Ivanov's offensive once and for all, the Stavka did not completely relinquish the possibility of military intervention and it was not until it finally committed itself to Nicholas's abdication that the Stavka agreed to cancel Ivanov's offensive.

As long as Ivanov depended on the support of the reinforcement troops from the front to initiate an operation against Petrograd, his small forces had no practical effect on the course of the revolution. It should be pointed out, however, that contrary to popular interpretation, Ivanov's forces never disintegrated. If Ivanov's offensive failed, it was not due to the unreliability of his forces, but to the change of policy made by the Stavka.

80. Klembovskii to Ivanov, no. 1940, "Fevral'skaia revoliutsiia 1917 goda," *Krasnyi arkhiv* 21, no. 3 (1927): 44. This telegram was sent to Ivanov after the general had already left Vyritsa at 3 P.M. on March 3.
81. "Proval popytki Stavki podavit' Fevral'skuiu revoliutsiiu," p. 109.

The existence of Ivanov's forces near Petrograd, however, created serious concern among the members of the Duma Committee. Realizing that a military confrontation between the insurgents and organized forces of the tsarist army would jeopardize the very existence of the Duma Committee, it made a frantic attempt to stop Ivanov's expedition. Bublikov and Lomonosov took advantage of control over the railway and ordered railway authorities to block military trains. Bublikov had the Luga Military Committee stop the approaching reinforcements from the front. Rodzianko tried to talk Ruzskii out of the counterrevolutionary attempt by exaggerating an episode about the "mutiny at Luga." But one of the most important moves of the Duma Committee was to mobilize the support of the officers of the Naval Staff and the General Staff in Petrograd.

Thus, the military finally accepted the Duma Committee's position that resolution of the crisis required a political, not a military solution. But as to what this political solution ought to be, there was a serious disagreement between the military and the Duma Committee.

25

THE ABDICATION

During the preceding few years the military leaders had been painful witnesses to internal deterioration of the government. They had come to have serious doubts about its competency in organizing such crucial matters as food supplies, transport, and war industries. Political instability and increasingly bitter conflicts between the government and the opposition began to affect morale of soldiers and officers by the end of 1916. The military leaders, as professional soldiers, considered the prosecution of war to a victorious end their first and foremost duty. Although few dared to push the argument to its logical conclusion, they had secretly come to regard Nicholas and his policies as a hindrance rather than an asset to successfully carrying out the war. Some officers were drawn into a plot for a palace coup, but the military leaders on the whole had so far demonstrated a remarkable restraint in not intervening in internal political matters. However, during the unprecedented crises caused by the revolution in Petrograd, they were faced with a choice between their blind oath to the emperor and their patriotism. Ultimately, the military leaders almost unanimously believed that Nicholas should be sacrificed for the welfare of the nation.

Important to an understanding of the formulation of policy by the military leaders is their failure to comprehend the real situation in Petrograd. When the disturbance broke out, neither Khabalov nor Beliaev let the Stavka know how serious the situation was. General Ruzskii later suspected that this delay had been intentional: "I am very sorry that from the 24th to 27th we were not informed as to what was going on in Petrograd. I have to think that by the 24th there were signs of beginning discontent and of agitations among the workers of the Petrograd Military District. They did not bother to tell us about these things, either; perhaps with the intention of not informing the front."[1] This delinquency was caused not by any calculated desire on the part of security authorities in Petrograd, but rather partly by their ineptitude and partly by the rivalry between the Petrograd Military District and the army at the front. After Beliaev and Khabalov were arrested, it became difficult for the military leaders at the front to obtain accurate information about Petrograd.

What the military leaders at the front did hear was received from different channels and was often conflicting, tinged with the political inclinations of the informer. The first source of information was the Duma Committee. After Bublikov's takeover of the Ministry of Transport, the railway network came under the control of the Duma Committee. The information given by the Duma Committee to railway personnel reached the military leaders at the front indirectly. Bublikov's famous telegram was a notable example of such information. In addition, Rodzianko sent telegrams and on a few occasions talked directly with the military leaders at the front. Although the theory that the military was completely outwitted by false information manipulated by the Duma Committee may be an exaggeration, it is undeniable that the Duma Committee deliberately sent information in such a way to accomplish its political goals. The military leaders, at least some of them, were not completely unaware of the Duma Committee's manipulation of the news but the rapidly changing situation and the necessity of dealing with the Duma Committee to bring the crisis to a peaceful conclusion blinded the critical judgment of the military leaders.

The military relied also on two other sources: the Naval Staff and the General Staff in Petrograd. Despite the near-complete collapse of government authorities in the capital and the takeover of government agencies by the insurgents, the Admiralty and the General Staff had not been occupied by the insurgents, which suggests that, having vented their anger at their immediate superior officers, the insurgents were not yet prepared to strike the military establishment itself. The Hughes telegraphic apparatuses available in these two military ad-

1. "Telegrammy i razgovory po telegrafu mezhdu Pskovom, Stavkoiu i Petrogradom, otnoshiashcheisia k obstoiatel'stvam otrecheniia Gosudariia Imperatora, s primechaniiami k nim general-ad''iutanta N. V. Ruzskago," *Russkaia letopis'* 3 (1922): 8 (hereafter cited as "Telegrammy Ruzskago").

ministrative offices provided an important means of communication between Petrograd and the front. The Military Commission, which cut off communication between Tsarskoe Selo and the Stavka, did not attempt to obstruct communication between the front and military authorities in Petrograd. Nevertheless, after the Okhrana and the police network had been eliminated, it was impossible to gather accurate information so the dispatches from the officers in the Naval and the General Staffs were haphazard in nature. In addition, their political opinions on the crises inevitably colored information sent to the front.

Not to be overlooked either was the physical condition of both Alekseev and Ruzskii. After his convalescence from his illness, Alekseev had returned to duty only a few days before the outbreak of the revolution. During the crucial days, unable to take the necessary rest, Alekseev was suffering from a high fever. After February 27, Ruzskii hardly slept, either: exhaustion and illness obviously dulled the judgment of both men. The combination of the lack of accurate information from Petrograd and fatigue contributed to the lag between the military leaders and the rapidly changing events in the capital.[2]

As news of the revolution spread to the front, Alekseev received many questions from local commanders concerning his attitude toward the Duma Committee. Whether these local commanders should support the Duma Committee or remain loyal to the emperor more or less depended on Alekseev's decision.[3] By halting Ivanov's operation, Alekseev took the first major step toward recognition of the Duma Committee at about 11 P.M. on February 28. On the afternoon of March 1, several disheartening news dispatches arrived at Mogilev. Moscow had fallen into the hands of the insurgents, and mutiny was spreading

2. The impact of technology on revolution is an interesting subject for research. If, for instance, instead of a few Hughes apparatuses, a long-distance telephone network had connected the front with Petrograd, the military leaders would have had more accurate information and their reaction to the revolution might have been somewhat different. The influence of technology is also an important issue in understanding the art of insurgency and counterinsurgency. The February Revolution was the first revolution, as far as I can see, in which automobiles, armored cars, and machine guns were used for an insurgency. Even the Hughes apparatuses and telephone communications within the city seem to be new. But tanks and airplanes were not used. A comparative study of the role of technology in revolution might be a fascinating topic.

3. Gulevich to Alekseev, no. 525, "Fevral'skaia revoliutsiia 1917 goda: Dokumenty Stavki verkhovnogo glavnokomanduiushchego i shtabla glavnokomanduiushchego i shtaba glavnokomanduiushchego armiiami severnogo fronta," *Krasnyi arkhiv* 21, no. 2 (1927): 35; Evert-Lukomskii conversation, ibid., pp. 36-37.

to the Baltic Fleet and Kronstadt. Admiral Nepenin of the Baltic Fleet urged the tsar to come to terms with Rodzianko immediately: he himself had unilaterally recognized the authority of the Duma Committee without sanction from the Stavka. General Brusilov urged the tsar to recognize "the accomplished fact" and emphasized "the necessity of solving the terrible situation peacefully and quickly."[4] Such news hastened Alekseev to seek a compromise with the Duma Committee.

In late afternoon Alekseev sent the tsar a telegram in care of the northern front that reached Pskov before Nicholas's arrival there. It told the tsar of the spread of the revolution to Moscow. Since the army was closely connected with life in the rear, Alekseev reported, "It can be said with certainty that a disturbance in the rear will provoke the same in the army." When the revolution was taking place in the rear, it would be impossible to ask the army to keep fighting, since the social composition of the soldiers and officers "will not give any basis to consider that the army will not react to what goes on in Russia." Alekseev concluded: "The suppression of the disorders by force is dangerous under the present conditions and will lead Russia and the army to ruin." It would be necessary to take measures that would quiet the population and restore normal life in the country. If the Duma Committee's attempt to restore order was not accompanied by the emperor's "act quieting the population," the power would inevitably go to the "hands of the extreme elements tomorrow." Thus, Alekseev recommended: "I beg you, for the sake of salvation of Russia and the dynasty, place at the head of the government a person whom Russia would believe and entrust him with the formation of a cabinet. At the present moment this is the only salvation. It is impossible to delay, and it has to be done immediately. To report Your Majesty otherwise will unconsciously and criminally bring Russia to ruin and shame, and create a danger for the dynasty of Your Imperial Majesty."[5]

By the time Nicholas arrived at Pskov, however, Alekseev's position had drastically changed. Until then all he had asked for was the formation of a ministry of confidence. On this point Alekseev had maintained the same position prior to Nicholas's departure from Mogilev. But some time early on the evening of March 1 he had come to advocate the establishment of a responsible ministry. On the basis of the existing sources we can only speculate the exact time of this crucial decision and the circumstances behind it. Telegram 1857, in which he still clung

4. See chap. 24; Brusilov to Frederiks, no. 744, "Fevral'skaia revoliutsiia 1917 goda," p. 47.
5. Alekseev to Nicholas, no. 1847, ibid., pp. 39-40. This telegram was written before the news of the revolution in Kronstadt and the Baltic Fleet reached the Stavka.

to a ministry of confidence, was sent shortly before 4 P.M. The first official document that confirmed Alekseev's change of policy was his telegram 1865 to the tsar, which was not sent from the Stavka until 10:20 P.M.[6] But in all likelihood Alekseev made this decision sometime before 7:30 P.M., shortly before Nicholas's arrival at Pskov.

It appears that two events were responsible for Alekseev's change of policy. First, around 6 P.M. the news of the revolution in Kronstadt and the Baltic Fleet reached the Stavka. Spread of the revolution to Moscow was alarming enough, but it now threatened the very existence of the armed forces. Although there is no direct evidence to link this news with Alekseev's change of policy, it seems clear that the Stavka took it extremely seriously. General Klembovskii, under Alekseev's instruction, sent telegrams to the commanders at the front and explained that the spread of the revolution to Moscow, Kronstadt, and the Baltic Fleet had forced the Stavka to request that the tsar "issue an act capable of calming the population and ending the revolution." Klembovskii then continued: "General Alekseev reports that the salvation of Russia and the possibility of continuing the war will be achieved only when at the head of the government stands a person who can enjoy the confidence of the population and who can form a corresponding [sootvetstvuiu-shchii] cabinet."[7] Klembovskii's telegram indicates that the Stavka had not quite made up its mind to pursue the establishment of a responsible ministry but was strongly leaning toward it. An imperial decree significant enough to calm the population, which the Stavka decided to request of the tsar, seems to go a little further than a ministry of confidence. The awkward term, "corresponding cabinet," curiously sounds similar to "responsible [otvestvennyi] cabinet."

Klembovskii's telegram was sent sometime between 6 and 7:30 P.M., while the imperial trains were traveling between Dno and Pskov. During this period another event took place. It appears that Alekseev had direct communication with Ruzskii through the Hughes apparatus, although the existing sources do not record any such conversations. Klembovskii's telegram no. 1854/718 was sent to all the commanders except General Ruzskii since, as noted on the margin of the original telegram, the commander of the northern front was separately "oriented."[8] It is likely that the possibility of seeking a political solution to the crisis by granting a responsible ministry was discussed by the two military leaders. We do not know whether it was Ruzskii who pressured Alekseev to accept this position or it was Alekseev himself who sounded out this possibility to Ruzskii. In either case in this unrecorded but crucial conver-

6. Alekseev to Nicholas, no. 1865, "Fevral'skaia revoliutsiia 1917 goda," pp. 53-54.
7. Klembovskii to commanders, no. 1854/718, ibid., pp. 40-41.
8. Ibid., p. 40.

sation both military leaders seem to have agreed to pursue the formation of a responsible ministry.

The difficult task of persuading the emperor to grant the concession of a responsible ministry thus fell upon General Ruzskii, commander of the northern front. From the very beginning of the revolution, Ruzskii's sympathy lay with the liberal opposition. He later stated that he was neither Right nor Left politically, but that he believed it was impossible for a tsar like Nicholas to reign over such a vast empire as Russia.[9] As early as February 27, when the outcome of the disturbances in the streets was not yet clear, Ruzskii dispatched a telegram to the tsar imploring him to take measures to quiet the country. He was the first military leader to align himself with the Duma opposition during the crisis. While the tsar and the Stavka were determined to suppress the revolution by force, Ruzskii recommended to the tsar not to take military measures but instead to grant political concessions.[10] As long as he believed Petrograd to be in chaos, he fully cooperated with the Stavka in its military intervention and complied with Alekseev's order to dispatch reinforcements from the northern front. But when he learned of the formation of the Duma Committee he began to have serious doubts about the wisdom of intervention. While Alekseev only temporarily halted Ivanov's operation, Ruzskii had recalled the troops he had dispatched to Petrograd without the Stavka's prior approval. Nicholas thus spent the most crucial two days of his life under the influence of the military commander who was most decisively against the emperor.

Two days after his departure from Mogilev, Nicholas finally arrived at Pskov at 7:30 P.M. on March 1. He was greeted by the governor of Pskov, but the customary inspection of the guard of honor did not take place. To the consternation of the entourage, Ruzskii and his important subordinates failed to appear at the station on time to meet the emperor. A few minutes after the arrival, Ruzskii appeared with his chief of staff, Danilov, and his aide-de-camp, Count Sheremetiev. According to an eyewitness: "Stooping, grey, and old, Ruzskii walked in rubber galoshes; he was in the uniform of the general staff. His face was pale and sickly, and his eyes under the glasses revealed hostility." Nicholas, on the other hand, maintained his usual calm. The tsar told Ruzskii that he expected to meet Rodzianko at Pskov, since he had failed to come to Dno as he had promised. He explained that he had left Mogilev since the situation was serious and he hoped that he could be closer to the

9. Andrei Vladimirovich, "Iz dnevnika A. V. Romanova za 1916-1917 gg.," *Krasnyi arkhiv* 31, no. 1 (1928): 208.
10. E. I. Martynov, *Tsarskaia armiia v fevral'skom perevorote,* pp. 90-91; Ruzskii to Nicholas, no. 1147/B, "Fevral'skaia revoliutsiia 1917 goda," p. 13; S. N. Vil'chkovskii, "Prebyvanie Gosurdaria Imperatora v Pskove, 1-i marta 1917 goda, po razskazu general-ad"iutanta N. V. Ruzskago," *Russkaia letopis'* 3 (1922): 163-64.

scene, where he could talk personally with the necessary people. Ruzskii then asked for an audience before Rodzianko arrived so that he could give the tsar an important report entrusted to him by Alekseev. The appointment was set at nine o'clock. Ruzskii talked with the emperor's entourage for a little while and discovered that they were oblivious to the seriousness of the situation. They blamed Khabalov and Balk for incompetence, but hoped that Ivanov, with reliable troops, would soon put down the revolt.[11]

This was more or less what Nicholas had in mind also. Isolated from events in Petrograd while he was traveling in the countryside, he had no knowledge of the Stavka's halt of Ivanov's operation and its recognition of the Duma Committee. When he read the piles of telegrams, which shattered his naïve notion, his shock must have been great. For the first time he learned of the revolution's spread to Moscow, the Baltic Fleet, and Kronstadt. Alekseev, who had strongly endorsed Nicholas's plan to suppress the revolution by force, now urged the tsar to stop Ivanov's operation. General Brusilov, Grand Duke Sergei Mikhailovich, artillery inspector at the Stavka, and his own brother, Grand Duke Mikhail Aleksandrovich, all appealed to the tsar to accept Alekseev's recommendations. There was no news from his wife or from Tsarskoe Selo.

Ruzskii was well aware that convincing the emperor of the necessity of the concession to the Duma Committee would be difficult. Thinking nervously of the historical role he was to play, he felt himself extremely ignorant of events in Petrograd and of the Stavka's intentions. He finally went to the tsar's salon car, but had to wait for an hour in the corridor, since Voeikov, "busy with smoking a cigar and straightening out the pictures on the wall," neglected to tell the emperor of Ruzskii's arrival. Finally, at ten o'clock he was received by the emperor.

Ruzskii began with a general outline of events as reported by the Stavka. He made it clear that what he intended to report was not concerned with military matters, but matters of state structure, which would go beyond his competence. He expressed fear that the emperor might not wish to listen to his report, since he might not have much confidence in the commander of the northern front and was accustomed to the report of General Alekseev, with whom Ruzskii had many disagreements and with whom Ruzskii had a strained relationship. But Nicholas told Ruzskii to state his opinion frankly. Immediately getting to the point, Ruzskii urged the tsar to grant a responsible ministry. But, as expected, the tsar rejected this suggestion "quietly, coolly, but with the feeling of a deep conviction." Ruzskii was persistent. As he later reminisced, he had "enough nerve to tell the emperor all that I thought

11. D. N. Dubenskii, "Kak proizoshel perevorot v Rossii: Zapiski dnevniki," *Russkaia letopis'* 3 (1922): 46-47; Vil'chkovskii, "Prebyvanie Gosudaria Imperatora v Pskove," p. 167; Andrei Vladimirovich, "Iz dnevnika A. V. Romanova," p. 204.

about individual persons who occupied responsible posts in the last years, and who seemed to me the greatest mistakes . . . both in the government and in the Stavka." Nicholas told Ruzskii that he was opposing a responsible ministry not from personal interests nor for any concealed purposes, but "he was not entitled to give up the whole matter of governing Russia to the hands of those who, today in the government, could cause such blunders to the fatherland and tomorrow wash their hands, and send in their resignations from the cabinet." Ruzskii reminded Nicholas that under the existence of the State Council and the State Duma, autocracy was merely a fiction. Nicholas declared: "I am responsible before God and Russia for everything that has happened and will happen. Whether ministers are responsible before the Duma and the State Council, it is all the same to me." To Nicholas, autocracy was not a "fiction," but the essence of his moral and religious responsibility. Ruzskii emphasized: "The emperor reigns, but a government governs." But Nicholas retorted that he could not understand such a formula and that he would have had to be brought up differently to understand it. He repeated that he was not clinging to power for personal interest, but simply could not take measures against his own conscience. The conference was, indeed, stormy and completely at cross purposes. Ruzskii's persuasion seemed to no avail.[12]

Ruzskii objected, disputed, and argued. About 11 o'clock the long-awaited telegram from Alekseev finally arrived at Pskov. This telegram suggested to the tsar that in view of the "disorganization of the army and the impossibility of continuing the war," the only possible solution would be to "recognize a responsible ministry, the composition of which should be entrusted to the chairman of the State Duma." According to Alekseev, the Duma Committee could still stop the complete breakdown of authority. A further loss of time would diminish the chances for restoration and maintenance of order and create circumstances favorable to the extreme radical elements. Finally, Alekseev proposed that the emperor sign a manifesto drafted by the Stavka for a responsible ministry.[13]

To Nicholas Alekseev's desertion was a great blow. His stubborn resistance to Ruzskii can be explained partly by his belief that at least Alekseev had not advocated a responsible ministry. Alekseev's telegram revealed that what Ruzskii had advocated was not merely the personal opinion of the general he did not trust, but also the opinion of the entire army. As Katkov observes, Nicholas could not oppose their demand without preparing "a drastic purge of the Army High Command"—an impossibility in time of war. Thus, Nicholas finally agreed

12. Vil'chkovskii, "Prebyvanie Gosudaria Imperatora v Pskove," pp. 167-70.
13. Alekseev to Nicholas, no. 1865, "Fevral'skaia revoliutsiia 1917 goda," p. 53.

to issue the manifesto sent by Alekseev without the slightest change and without studying it carefully, and in addition also agreed to recall all troops sent from the front. Ruzskii himself later confessed: "I do not know if I would have been successful in convincing the emperor, had it not been for Alekseev's telegram."[14]

Retiring to his office, Ruzskii immediately dispatched a telegram to let Alekseev know of Nicholas's consent to the manifesto. But when he received a draft copy of the telegram Nicholas was supposed to send to Rodzianko, he discovered with shock that it mentioned nothing about a responsible ministry and merely authorized Rodzianko to form a cabinet with the exceptions of the ministers of war, navy, and foreign affairs. Dumfounded, Ruzskii asked Voeikov to tell the emperor that this telegram would not be acceptable. He asked for another audience.[15] It was already past midnight. Finally Ruzskii was summoned to the emperor's salon car again. This time Nicholas asked him about the details of the text of the manifesto. A dreadful suspicion crossed Ruzskii's mind that Nicholas might have changed his mind. He asked the emperor if he had acted in an unacceptable way by having already informed the Stavka of the emperor's agreement with the manifesto. This was another way of telling the tsar that his acceptance of a responsible ministry was already an established fact. The tsar answered that he had made up his mind to grant a responsible ministry for the good of Russia, since Ruzskii and Alekseev, who could hardly agree with anything, were of the same opinion.[16] Reassured, Ruzskii dispatched a telegram to Ivanov ordering him to halt his operation. At the same time, he made arrangements to speak directly to Rodzianko through the Hughes apparatus rather than to send him a telegram, to tell him the news of the emperor's acceptance of a responsible ministry. Ruzskii was completely exhausted and could hardly stand up. He went to bed to take a catnap with the conviction that this hard-won concession of a responsible ministry would once and for all quiet the nation.

About three-thirty in the morning of March 2 Ruzskii was awakened with the news that Rodzianko was at the Hughes apparatus in the General Staff in Petrograd. This conversation between Ruzskii and Rodzianko was one of the most important incidents in the February Revolution, one that led directly to the abdication of Nicholas II.[17]

14. George Katkov, *Russia, 1917: The February Revolution*, p. 323; Vil'chkovskii, "Prebyvanie Gosudaria Imperatora v Pskove," p. 170; Andrei Vladimirovich, "Iz dnevnika A. V. Romanova," p. 204.

15. Andrei Vladimirovich, "Iz dnevnika A. V. Romanova," p. 204.

16. Vil'chkovskii, "Prebyvanie Gosudaria Imperatora v Pskove," pp. 170-71.

17. Ruzskii-Rodzianko conversation, "Fevral'skaia revoliutsiia 1917 goda,"

Ruzskii began by asking Rodzianko why he had canceled the promised trip to Pskov. Rodzianko gave two reasons: first, the troops sent from the front had revolted at Luga, and had declared that they would block the passage of any train, including the imperial trains. Although he immediately took measures to free the path for the imperial trains, he did not know if they would be successful. Secondly, he feared that his departure would bring about undesirable results in Petrograd. It was impossible "to leave the people's rekindled passions without my personal presence, since until now they believe only in me and carry out only my orders."

Ruzskii then told Rodzianko that the tsar had finally agreed to grant a responsible ministry, the formation of which would be entrusted to Rodzianko. Rodzianko's reply, however, was a great shock to Ruzskii. Rodzianko answered: "It is obvious that His Majesty and you did not take into account what was going on here." The picture Rodzianko presented as the real situation in Petrograd was completely different from what Ruzskii had been led to believe. According to Rodzianko, "one of the most terrible revolutions is approaching, the course of which is impossible to reverse." Soldiers were roaming about in the streets, randomly killing officers. The ugly passions of the insurgents were unleashed to such an extent that it would be almost impossible to control them. Rodzianko was forced to take the side of the insurgents "to avoid anarchy and demoralization, which might bring the state to downfall." He was obliged even to "imprison all the ministers except for the ministers of war and navy in the Fortress of St. Peter and Paul, to avoid bloodshed." Agitation was now directed against anyone who tried to counsel moderation. Rodzianko then concluded, "I consider it necessary to tell you that what you have proposed is not enough; the problem of the dynasty has been put point blank."

The gloomy news presented by Rodzianko must have surprised Ruzskii, who had been assured that the capital had resumed normal functions since the Duma Committee had taken power. In fact, only several hours before Ruzskii had received a telegram from Rodzianko himself, which assured him that order was being restored. This telegram had said: "All measures for security of order in the capital are taken. Information concerning the railway is maintained carefully and without interruption. There is no danger for transportation of food supplies. Measures are taken. The disorder which had erupted is being liquidated. Calm is being restored, although with great difficulty."[18] The Duma

pp. 55-59; "Telegrammy Ruzskago," pp. 127-33.
    18. Rodzianko to Ruzskii, "Fevral'skaia revoliutsiia 1917 goda," p. 52.

Committee's control of the situation was the most important factor behind the change of policy by the Stavka in halting counterrevolutionary action and seeking peaceful settlement with the Duma Committee. Both Ruzskii and Alekseev believed that the manifesto granting a constitutional government, on which Rodzianko had insisted, could bring the crisis to a peaceful end. But Rodzianko's new information destroyed whatever optimism remained in Ruzskii. He confessed that the situation described by Rodzianko was totally different from what he had believed. Such anarchy would imperil continuance of the war. "Having lost so many lives in the struggle with the enemy, we cannot stop half way, and we must carry it out to the end suitable for our great fatherland. We must find a way to bring peace in the country." He then asked what kind of solution Rodzianko had in mind for the dynastic question.

Rodzianko answered that despite the determination by all the insurgents that "the war should be carried out to be a victorious end," and that all the troops and the insurgents "remain on the side of the Duma." Hatred toward the dynasty had reached extreme limits, and had led the insurgents to present the formidable demand for the abdication of Nicholas in favor of his son, under a regency of Mikhail Aleksandrovich. Rodzianko went on to say that Ivanov's expedition would pour fuel onto the fire, and would lead inevitably to a civil war. Thus he asked the commander of the northern front to recall the troops. Ruzskii answered that the emperor had already sent Ivanov an imperial order not to take any measure until his arrival, and that the tsar had agreed to recall the other troops sent from the front. Ruzskii stated: "You see that His Majesty is taking such measures as are possible. If the initiative of His Majesty would be responded to in the hearts of those who have the power to extinguish the fire, it would be desirable for the interests of the fatherland and the patriotic war we are carrying out." He then read the draft manifesto. To Ruzskii's desperate effort to limit the concession to the formation of a responsible ministry, Rodzianko replied: "Power is slipping from my hands. The anarchy has reached such a degree that I am compelled tonight to announce the formation of the Provisional Government. Unfortunately, the manifesto was too late; it should have been issued immediately after my first telegram. . . . Time was wasted and there is no return."

Rodzianko's statement was a strange yet shrewd juxtaposition of two contradictory positions. On the one hand, he held an extremely pessimistic view of the anarchy prevailing in the capital, while, on the other, he firmly believed that the people were united under the Duma Committee. Anarchy had reached the point that "power was slipping from the hands" of the chairman of the Duma, and the Duma Committee's effort to restore order was "far from successful." And yet "all the troops joined the State Duma" and "there was no disagreement" between the Duma and the people. On the one hand, there was anarchy, in which "soldiers are killing the officers," but on the other, there was order and unity in which "everywhere the troops remain on the side of the Duma and the people."

We have already seen the predicament in which Rodzianko found himself in the Duma Committee. He had staunchly opposed abdication for the past few days, but by March 1 the Duma Committee finally rejected moderation and adopted abdication as its official demand. With the shift of policy concerning Nicholas's future, Rodzianko's personal power considerably declined. Rodzianko's statement reflected more accurately his personal power within the Duma Committee than the general situation in Petrograd. When he stated that power was slipping from his hands, that people with moderate demands were losing ground, and that the question of abdication was put point blank, he was not very far off the mark, if these referred to the political situation within the Duma Committee. He had been put in an extremely delicate position. To avoid civil war, he had presented the picture to the Stavka and the military leaders at the front with emphasis on the Duma Committee's control of the situation and with assurance that the concession of a responsible ministry would be enough to quiet the insurgents and restore order. The Duma Committee was now advocating Nicholas's abdication and in a few hours, its official delegates would confront the emperor with this demand. The reaction of the military would be hard to guess, but there was a real danger of its stepping up military intervention. Personally as well, Rodzianko's reliability would be irrevocably damaged in the eyes of the military leaders. Rodzianko's conversation with Ruzskii was therefore a master stroke by which he tried to prepare the military for the bad news as well as to prevent further erosion of his personal influence among them. It is interesting that while he presented the abdication as the aspiration of the masses, he himself remained noncommittal. When Ruzskii asked whether or not the issuance of the manifesto was needed, Rodzianko answered: "I really do not know how to answer. It will all depend upon the course of events, which are developing with terrific speed." Not knowing the military's next move, it was better for Rodzianko to leave a little room for retreat should the high command reject the demand for abdication.

Was Ruzskii aware of the contradictions in the information given by Rodzianko? It is difficult to attribute, as Ruzskii's subordinate

Vil'chkovskii does, his blindness totally to physical and psychological exhaustion after the long and violent encounter with the emperor.[19] If the decisions of the high command hinged on the Duma Committee's ability to contain the anarchy, Rodzianko's simultaneous emphasis on the Duma Committee's control of the insurgents and on the danger of the prevailing anarchy must have struck him as being strange. Moreover, the contrast between Rodzianko's previous telegram and his information during the conversation was so obvious that Ruzskii could not have failed to question the reliability of Rodzianko's information. In addition, what really happened at Luga Station must have been relayed to him by this time.[20] Thus, Ruszkii possessed ample grounds to suspect Rodzianko's truthfulness. Yet in the conversation Ruzskii showed no hint of such suspicions. He might have been careful in covering himself, as Katkov speculates, because the text of the conversation would be inevitably relayed to the Stavka and to the emperor.[21] More importantly, however, his silence on Rodzianko's contradictions was based on political calculations. As soon as he learned of the existence of the Duma Committee in Petrograd, he seemed to draw a conclusion that counterrevolutionary measures should be avoided at all costs and that a political settlement should be reached through the Duma Committee. For him the most important task at hand was the continued prosecution of the war, for which everything else should be sacrificed. As long as the insurgents in Petrograd had sworn allegiance to the Duma Committee, any military intervention would mean a civil war within the nation, which would undoubtedly render the continuance of the external war impossible. Thus, he began recalling the troops sent from the front without the Stavka's permission. He wished that peaceful settlement could be reached with the concession of a responsible ministry, but if it was impossible, he was willing to accept Nicholas's abdication. True, there is no indication that he supported the abdication during the conversation with Rodzianko, but he never forcefully rejected this idea, either. From his point of view, therefore, there was no sense in pointing out Rodzianko's contradictions. It would serve no political purpose; it would be better to pretend to believe in Rodzianko and to let him be the initiator of the demand for abdication.

While the conversation between Ruzskii and Rodzianko through the Hughes apparatus was still in progress, General Danilov of the northern front began conveying its contents to the Stavka shortly

19. Vil'chkovskii, "Prebyvanie Gosudaria Imperatora v Pskove," pp. 175-76.
20. See chap. 24.
21. Katkov, Russia, 1917, pp. 320-21.

before 6 o'clock in the morning. Three hours later Alekseev instructed
Lukomskii to call the northern front and to have Ruzskii inform the
tsar of the contents of his conversation with Rodzianko.[22] What
Alekseev did during these three hours is not clear, but his reaction
does not seem to have been an instant acceptance of Rodzianko's
explanations. The Stavka's official position as conveyed by Lukomskii
at 9 o'clock did not indicate Alekseev's acceptance of the abdication.
On the contrary, in the telegram sent to the northern front, Alekseev
cast serious doubt on the authenticity of Rodzianko's information
concerning the revolt at Luga Station and ordered the northern front
to dispatch reliable officers to contact General Ivanov.[23] This telegram,
however, also indicated that he was asking other commanders for their
attitudes toward abdication. The direct conversations the Stavka
conducted in the morning with the commanders indicate that by this
time Alekseev had made up his mind to support abdication. It is unlikely that Alekseev made such a crucial decision merely on the basis
of the information given by Rodzianko, whose reliability he suspected.
Although existing sources do not clear up this matter, it is possible
to surmise that during these three hours Alekseev tried to check the
veracity of Rodzianko's information, possibly through channels to
the Naval or the General Staffs. The result of this contact might have
been mixed. On the one hand, it revealed the mendacity of Rodzianko's
tale of the "revolt at Luga," but on the other hand, this source might
have generally accepted the general situation in Petrograd as outlined
in Rodzianko's conversation, and it might even have recommended
to accept the abdication. Thus, by 10 o'clock in the morning, Alekseev
also came out in favor of abdication, although he did not completely
abandon the possibility of military intervention.

    The Stavka knew well that it would not be easy to persuade
Nicholas to abdicate. Alekseev therefore decided to mobilize all the
commanders at the front solidly behind him. Between 10 and 11
o'clock in the morning, the Stavka dispatched telegrams to commanders
of all fronts—Grand Duke Nikolai Nikolaevich (Caucasian front),
General Evert (western front), General Brusilov (southwestern front),
General Sakharov (Romanian front), Admirals Nepenin and Kolchak
(Baltic Fleet and the Black Sea Fleet). Describing the situation in
Petrograd as described by Rodzianko, Alekseev stated:

The situation apparently does not permit other solution, and every minute of

    22. Danilov to Alekseev, no. 1224/B, "Fevral'skaia revoliutsiia 1917 goda,"
pp. 62-63; Lukomskii-Danilov conversation, ibid., pp. 74-75; "Telegrammy Ruzskago," pp. 133-34.
    23. Alekseev to Evert, no. 1871, "Fevral'skaia revoliutsiia 1917 goda," p. 65.

further vacillation will only enhance these demands, which are based on the fact that the existence of the army and the work of railways are actually in the hands of the Petrograd Provisional Government. It is necessary to save the active army from disintegration, to continue to the end the struggle with the external enemy, and to save the independence of Russia and the future of the dynasty. This needs to be put into the highest priority even at the sacrifice of costly concessions.[24]

It is interesting that to Alekseev the integrity of the army and continuation of the war had higher priority than preservation of the monarchy. Alekseev further emphasized the necessity of maintaining unity among the commanders of the active army and of saving the army from "instability and possible occasions of treason to duty." There was a danger of a split within the army in its attitude toward abdication. Alekseev must have foreseen the possibility of a civil war in which army units swearing allegiance to the emperor and others supporting the Duma Committee would be involved in an armed clash. While Ruzskii's willingness to cooperate with the Duma Committee was apparent to him by the northern front's hasty recall of the troops, communications with Evert and Sakharov in the past few days had indicated that they were not enthusiastically disposed to the Stavka's support of the "rebel" Duma Committee. The best course of action seemed to Alekseev to take the posture of noninterference in internal politics, while putting pressure on the tsar to sacrifice himself for a peaceful settlement of the crisis. Alekseev stated: "The army must fight with all its strength against the external enemy, and the decision concerning the internal affairs must spare it the temptation to take part in the coup, which will be less painfully carried out under the decision from above."[25]

This circular telegram was conveyed to the most important commanders in personal telegraphic communications by the representatives of the Stavka. General Klembovskii dealt with Evert, who expressed his general agreement with Alekseev in that the issue should be resolved only from above, by the imperial decision to abdicate. He feared that otherwise there would be some elements hostile to either the abdication or its refusal, and probably "those who wish to fish in troubled waters." He then asked Klembovskii if he had time to consult other commanders on this matter. Klembovskii answered that there

24. Alekseev to Evert, no. 1872, in Evert-Klembovskii conversation, ibid., p. 67; Alekseev-Brusilov conversation, ibid., p. 69; "Telegrammy Ruzskago," pp. 135-36.

25. Alekseev to Evert, no. 1872, in Evert-Klembovskii conversation, "Fevral'skaia revoliutsiia 1917 goda," p. 67; Alekseev-Brusilov conversation, ibid., p. 69; "Telegrammy Ruzskago," p. 136.

502   THE ABDICATION OF NICHOLAS II

was not time for consultation. Only the unanimous opinion of the military leaders would be able to overcome Nicholas's hesitation.[26] Alekseev himself asked Brusilov to send the tsar a telegram to persuade him to accept the abdication. Brusilov completely agreed with Alekseev and promised to do so. Lukomskii talked to Sakharov, who replied that however sad it might be, he, too, had to agree with the unanimous opinion. All the commanders were requested to send their reactions to the Stavka rather than to the emperor directly. Since Ruzskii's opinion was known to the Stavka, he was not consulted.[27] The answers from the commanders reached the Stavka by half-past two in the afternoon.

While Alekseev tried to persuade the generals to endorse his policy, he instructed Bazilii to look into the legal implications of Nicholas's abdication. Bazilii immediately presented to Alekseev his report, in which he stated that although the law did not envision abdication, it stipulated the order of succession to the throne, according to which the oldest son of the emperor should succeed him.[28]

Ruzskii's conversation with Rodzianko through the Hughes apparatus continued until half-past seven in the morning. Having instructed his aide to awaken him in one hour to report the conversation to the emperor, Ruzskii collapsed in bed, completely exhausted. At 9 o'clock in the morning Lukomskii conveyed Alekseev's order to Danilov to wake up the tsar "ignoring all the etiquettes," and to inform him of the contents of the Rodzianko-Ruzskii conversation.[29] Ruzskii went to the tsar's salon car at 10 o'clock. The tsar read the text of the conversation, silently stood up, and looked out of the window. There was a dreadful silence. Returning to his desk, he gestured to Ruzskii to sit down, and quietly began. "He again remembered that his conviction that he was born for unhappiness was true, that he had brought Russia unhappiness, and said that even last night he was clearly aware that any manifesto would not help." The em-

26. Evert-Klembovskii conversation, "Fevral'skaia revoliutsiia 1917 goda," p. 68.
27. Nicolas de Basily, *Diplomat of Imperial Russia, 1903-1917: Memoirs*, p. 121.
28. Ibid., p. 119.
29. The exact time of Ruzskii's report to the tsar is not firmly established. According to Vil'chkovskii, it was about 10:15 A.M. ; according to Andrei Vladimirovich, 9:30; according to Martynov, who used archival materials of Spiridovich, 10:45. If Martynov is correct, Ruzskii received Alekseev's telegram before he met the emperor. Vil'chkovskii, "Prebyvanie Gosudaria Imperatora," p. 177; Andrei Vladimirovich, "Iz dnevnika A. V. Romanova," p. 206; Martynov, *Tsarskaia armiia v fevral'skom perevorote*, p. 152.

peror went on to say: "If it is necessary that I should abdicate for the good of Russia, I am ready for it. But I am afraid that the people will not understand it. Old Believers would not forgive me for the breach of the oath taken on the day of the Holy Coronation. The Cossacks will blame for abandoning the front."[30] Ruzskii consoled the emperor by saying that there was still hope that the manifesto might settle the situation, and urged the tsar to wait for the instructions from General Alekseev, although he did not conceal Lukomskii's opinion that indicated that the Stavka was already leaning toward the acceptance of abdication. About half-past ten, Alekseev's circular telegram finally arrived. Turning pale, he read the telegram aloud to the tsar, and then said: "The problem is so serious and so dreadful that I ask Your Majesty to think over this dispatch before answering it. This is a circular telegram. Let us see what the other commanders would say. Then the situation will be clear."[31] Nicholas stood up for a lunch break. Attentively and sadly looking at Ruzskii, he said: "Yes, I have to think." Declining the luncheon invitation, Ruzskii returned to his headquarters to study closely the instructions from the Stavka and to learn the reactions of the other commanders. After finishing lunch with his entourage in an awkward silence, the emperor walked silently on the platform.

About half-past two, Ruzskii was summoned by the emperor. By this time the telegrams of the commanders had arrived in Pskov. Having studied their contents, Ruzskii braced himself for the graveness of the meeting with the tsar. This time he asked permission to be accompanied by Danilov and Savvich. In addition to these three generals, the minister of the imperial court, Count Frederiks, also attended the meeting. The three generals entered the emperor's car. All the windows were closed. Nicholas smoked incessantly.[32] Ruzskii first made a short routine report about all the telegrams he had received since he left the tsar that morning. When Alekseev's telegram, which included all the answers of the commanders, came up, Ruzskii put the sheaf of telegrams on the desk and asked the tsar to read them for himself.[33]

All the generals had answered in favor of abdication. Brusilov

30. Vil'chkovskii, "Prebyvanie Gosudaria Imperatora v Pskove," p. 178. Nicholas was referring to the two most conservative elements in society.

31. Ibid.

32. S. S. Savvich, "Priniatie Nikolaem II resheniia ob otrechenii ot prestola," in *Otrechenie Nikolaia II: Vospominanii ochevidtsev, dokumenty*, ed. P. I. Shchegolev (Leningrad, 1927), p. 176.

33. Iu. N. Danilov, "Moi vospominaniia ob Imperatore Nikolae II-om i Vel. Kniaze Mikhaile Aleksandroviche," *Arkhiv russkoi revoliutsii* 19 (1928): 230.

outspokenly suggested to the emperor that "at the present moment the only solution that could save the situation and make possible the continuation of the struggle with the external enemy . . . is abdication of the throne in favor of the Heir Tsarevich under the regency of Grand Duke Mikhail Aleksandrovich." Evert urged the emperor to accept Rodzianko's declaration "as the only measure which apparently can halt the revolution and thus save Russia from the horrors of anarchy."[34] The most damaging telegram to Nicholas was that of Grand Duke Nikolai Nikolaevich: "As a faithful subject I consider it necessary, in accordance with the duty as well as the spirit of my oath of allegiance, to implore on my knees Your Imperial Majesty to save Russia and Your Heir, knowing the feeling of Your sacred love to Russia and to Him." Concluding the point of view of the high command, Alekseev asked Nicholas "without delay to make a decision, as God inspires you." He implored, "For the sake of the security and independence of the fatherland, and for the sake of its achievement of victory, please make the decision that can provide a peaceful and satisfactory way out of the situation."[35] Later Sakharov's telegram also arrived. Although upset by "the small gang of bandits called the State Duma, treacherously exploiting a convenient moment to carry out their criminal designs," Sakharov was nevertheless "compelled to state that perhaps the least painful solution for the country and for the preservation of the possible chance to fight the external enemy would be to meet the conditions already stated."[36]

After the tsar finished reading the telegrams, Ruzskii asked him to listen to the opinion of the two other generals who were with him. The emperor granted Danilov and Savvich permission to express their frank opinions. First, Danilov stated that he saw no way out except for his abdication. Savvich was entirely confused and simply answered: "I am a simple person, and therefore, I entirely agree with what was said by General Danilov.[37] For a few minutes there was a dead silence. Suddenly, the emperor spoke. "I have made up my mind. I have decided to abdicate from the throne in favor of my son, Aleksei." After finishing his words, Nicholas crossed himself. The generals followed his example. The emperor turned to Ruzskii, thanked him for his "valorous and faithful service," and kissed him.

34. Alekseev to Nicholas, no. 1878, "Fevral'skaia revoliutsiia 1917 goda," p. 73.

35. Ibid., pp. 72-73.

36. Sakharov to Ruzskii, no. 03317, ibid., p. 74.

37. Danilov, "Moi vospominanii ob Imperatore Nikolae II-om," p. 231; Savvich, "Priniatie Nikolaem II resheniia ob otrechenii ot prestola," p. 177.

He then retired to his car, where he wrote two telegrams: one to Alekseev and the other to Rodzianko. To Alekseev he wrote, "In the name of the good, peace, and salvation of Russia, which I passionately love, I am ready to abdicate from the Throne in favor of my son. I ask you all to serve him loyally and sincerely." The telegram to Rodzianko, however, set one condition for his abdication: "There is no sacrifice I would not bear for the sake of the real welfare and for the salvation of our own Mother Russia. Therefore, I am ready to abdicate from the Throne in favor of my son on the condition that he can remain with me until he comes of age."[38]

The news of a possibility of Nicholas's abdication angered his entourage, who saw conspiracy and treason in Ruzskii's pressure on the emperor. For the past two days, the entourage felt that the emperor had become a prisoner at the northern front. They bitterly complained that neither Voeikov nor even the emperor were allowed to have access to the Hughes apparatus.[39] While the emperor met with the three generals, the entourage gathered in Voeikov's car. Finally, Count Frederiks returned from the meeting and told them of the abdication. They exploded with anger. Nilov declared that he would arrest Ruzskii and execute him on the spot.[40] Voeikov darted off into Nicholas's car. The tsar, showing the piles of telegrams on the desk, said: "What else can I do, when all have betrayed me? Even Nikolasha [Nikolai Nikolaevich]. . . ."[41] Voeikov asked where the text of abdication was. Nicholas gave him permission to retrieve the telegrams that he had already given Ruzskii. By this time Ruzskii had already sent the tsar's telegram to Alekseev, but when he learned that the two delegates of the Duma Committee were headed to Pskov to negotiate with the emperor, he withheld the telegram to Rodzianko. When K. A. Naryshkin, who was dispatched by the entourage to retrieve the telegrams, demanded their return, Ruzskii had an officer of the telegraph section answer that both telegrams had already been dispatched. When the emperor and his entourage learned

38. Savvich, "Priniatie Nikolaem II resheniia ob otrechenii ot prestola," pp. 177-78; "Telegrammy Ruzskago," p. 140. Ruzskii later added a phrase: "under the regency of my brother, Grand Duke Mikhail Aleksandrovich."

39. V. N. Voeikov, S tsarem i bez tsaria: Vospominaniia posledniago dvortso-vogo komendanta Gosudariia Imperatora Nikolaia II, p. 209; Dubenskii, "Kak proizoshel perevorot," p. 52.

40. A. Mordvinov, "Otryvki iz vospominanii," Russkaia letopis' 5 (1923); 109; Voeikov, S tsarem i bez tsaria, p. 212.

41. Dubenskii, "Kak proizoshel perevorot," p. 49. But Dubenskii confuses the date. The entourage was outraged with the news of abdication, not with the news of granting a responsible ministry.

of this news, someone said, "It is all over."[42] Some of the entourage began to weep.

As soon as the Stavka received the emperor's telegram consenting to abdicate, Alekseev entrusted Bazilii to write an act of abdication. The draft of the abdication manifesto was approved by Alekseev with minor alterations and quickly sent back to the northern front about 7 P.M. for the approval of the emperor.[43]

Nicholas's personal reaction, his internal turmoil, and his perception of events that forced his abdication are left for the speculations of historians. He did not reveal his opinions and feelings either in his letters or in his diary. On the day of his abdication, he wrote in his diary:

> March 2. Thursday. In the morning, Ruzskii came and read to me the long conversation by direct wire with Rodzianko. In his words, Petrograd was in such a state that a cabinet [formed] from the members of the State Duma will be powerless to do anything, for the SR-Socialist-Democratic parties are competing with it in the form of a workers' committee. My abdication is necessary. Ruzskii transmitted this conversation to Alekseev in the Stavka and to all General Headquarters. At 12:30 the answers came. For the salvation of Russia and the preservation of the army at the front, I decided to take this step. I conceded, and from the Stavka a draft for the manifesto was sent. In the evening, from Petrograd came Guchkov and Shul'gin, with whom I had a talk and to whom I handed the manifesto, which was drawn up and signed. At one o'clock at night I left Pskov with gloomy feelings.
>
> Treachery, cowardice, and deception all around.[44]

Although he allowed suppressed anger to slip into the diary, on the whole it revealed amazing indifference to the catastrophe that had struck him. In fact, throughout the drama of abdication at Pskov the calm and indifference Nicholas demonstrated impressed the participants with an eerie unbelievability in contrast to the gravity of the historic moment. Even at this critical moment, he did not forget the decorum to embrace and say a few kind words to Ruzskii, the most likely candidate for Nicholas's "treachery, cowardice, and deception." How was it possible for Nicholas, who had stubbornly refused to make the slightest concession to the liberals' most modest demands for the past two years, to acquiesce so easily and calmly to his own abdication? It appears that external events—the revolution in Petrograd, Moscow, and other units of the armed forces—had little

42. Danilov, "Moi vospominaniia ob Imperatore Nikolae II-om " pp. 234-35; Mordvinov, "Otryvki iz vospominanii," pp. 110-11.

43. Withold S. Sworakowski, "The Authorship of the Abdication Documents of Nicholas II," *Russian Review* 30, no. 3 (1971): 282.

44. "Dnevnik Nikolaia Romanova," *Krasnyi arkhiv* 20, no. 1 (1927): 136.

impact on Nicholas. Miliukov said, "The tsar gave the impression of a withdrawn person who has ceased to understand what must be done in order to find a way out of the situation."[45]

Nicholas's world was far removed from the real world, which he refused to comprehend. The more complicated internal politics became and the more vociferous and widespread his critics became, the more Nicholas escaped into his simple, highly personalized notion of autocracy. Thus, when he made the concession to limit his power by granting a responsible ministry, his world had been already shattered, and he had been defeated. According to Grand Duke Andrei Vladimirovich, it took from nine to twelve-thirty at night to gain the concession of a responsible ministry from the tsar, but it took him only forty-five minutes to agree on the abdication.[46] Vil'chkovskii also noted that the first round was stormy, but that Ruzskii's audience with the tsar, when he decided on abdication, was marked by Nicholas's air of resignation. Katkov contends that to Nicholas the abdication seemed "a solution far more morally acceptable" than a responsible ministry that restricted his autocratic power.[47] But it seems that the abdication was a logical conclusion of the concession of a responsible ministry. He had breached the sacred duty ordained by God and sworn to at his father's deathbed. His personal and moral world had been completely destroyed by this concession. He must have felt compelled to seek absolution of his sin by willingly accepting his abdication.

45. Quoted in Mel'gunov, *Martovskie dni*, p. 181.
46. Andrei Vladimirovich, "Iz dnevnika A. V. Romanova," p. 181.
47. Katkov, *Russia, 1917*, p. 323.

26

THE DUMA COMMITTEE'S
DELEGATES

 Early in the morning on March 2 the Duma Committee finally rejected Rodzianko's continued effort to confine the reforms to the establishment of a responsible ministry, and decided to seek Nicholas's abdication. Rodzianko was forced first to cancel his trip to Dno and later to Pskov to meet the tsar, since the majority of the Duma Committee members suspected that he might strike a secret bargain with Nicholas and the military leaders. Guchkov and Shul'gin volunteered to go in his stead to present the tsar with the Duma Committee's request to abdicate

From the Duma Committee's point of view, Guchkov was a perfect emissary for the job. For the past few months he had striven to achieve a palace coup without much success. A plot to depose Nicholas and install the regency of Mikhail had been opposed by a majority of the liberal leaders and had not gained much support from the military leaders. But once the revolution began, Guchkov's idea of a palace coup quickly gained the support of the majority of the Duma Committee members as the only viable action to stem the tide of the revolution. Kerenskii, Nekrasov, and Konovalov—the members of the masonic organization— had already either supported or been actively involved in Guchkov's plot. Miliukov and Shul'gin, who had rejected the plot before the revolution, strongly advocated its implementation. Thus, it is possible to argue that the February Revolution combined two forces: the revolution from below and the plot for a palace coup.

The Duma Committee, however, did not make the terms of conditions for the abdication specific except for its demand for Nicholas's abdication for his son under the regency of Grand Duke Mikhail Aleksandrovich. It did not even discuss a draft act of abdication, which was composed by Shul'gin in a hasty manner in the train on their way to Pskov. The Duma Committee's delegates left Petrograd around 3 A.M. on March 2. Since Rodzianko's train had been ready at Warsaw Station, they did not have any trouble in arranging the special train. But on their way the train stopped at various stations and Guchkov and Shul'gin had to deliver short speeches before the people who gathered on the platforms. Particularly, the train had to stop for a long time at Gatchina and Luga, where the soldiers who had joined the revolution welcomed the Duma delegates with enthusiasm.[1] Because of these interruptions the Duma Committee's emissaries arrived at Pskov at 9 P.M., two hours later than scheduled.

Guchkov's mission seemed to be an anticlimax to the intense drama of abdication, which had been already enacted. When Guchkov and Shul'gin departed from Petrograd, they believed that the tsar and the high command were still intent on military suppression of the revolution. It was for the purpose of dissuading General Ivanov from taking a military action against the revolution that Guchkov requested an appointment with the general on his way to Pskov.[2] Both Guchkov and Shul'gin were nervous at the thought of a violent encounter with the emperor and insurmountable difficulty in obtaining consent for his abdication. The thought of being arrested on the spot might have crossed their minds, but this danger appealed all the more to their sense of heroism. Particularly for Guchkov, the opportunity had finally come to put into realization the idea of a palace coup, of which he had talked and dreamed. They had no idea that Rodzianko had stolen their thunder by talking directly with Ruzskii, that this conversation had led the military to mount pressure on Nicholas, and that the emperor had already agreed to abdicate.

After learning that the Duma Committee's delegates would arrive in Pskov, General Ruzskii withheld the dispatch of the emperor's telegram to Rodzianko and awaited their arrival. He instructed the railway commandant to direct the Duma Committee's delegates immediately to him before they went to the emperor. It was necessary for Ruzskii to inform Guchkov and Shul'gin of Nicholas's decision to abdicate. The general wanted to "salvage as much as possible the

1. Guchkov's letter to Bazilii, quoted in Nicolas de Basily, *Diplomat of Imperial Russia, 1903-1917: Memoirs*, pp. 127; V.V. Shul'gin, *Dni*, pp. 243-44.
2. See chap. 24.

prestige of the emperor in such a way that it would show that he had not abdicated under their pressure, but voluntarily before their arrival."[3] Also Ruzskii feared that the direct pressure from Nicholas's personal enemy might be counterproductive, and contribute to Nicholas's change of mind. The general had already suspected Nicholas of wavering from the repeated attempts by his entourage to retrieve the emperor's telegrams.

The tsar, indeed, changed his mind on one of the conditions for his abdication, but he did not bother to tell Ruzskii about it. After he agreed to abdicate, Nicholas summoned his private physician, Professor Fedorov, and asked for his opinion about the possible length of Aleksei's life. Fedorov frankly answered that given the powerlessness of modern science in curing hemophilia, he was pessimistic about the possibility of a long life for Aleksei. Nicholas remarked that he hoped to stay with his family in Livadia and that he could not part with his son. Since assumption of the throne by Aleksei would make it impossible for Nicholas to live with him, he decided to abdicate not only for himself but also for his son in favor of Grand Duke Mikhail Aleksandrovich. It was for this reason that Nicholas sent his aide to retrieve his previous telegrams so that he could correct the terms of his abdication.[4]

The Succession Law clearly stipulated that succession to the throne was to be assumed by the eldest son. Nicholas's decision was, therefore, from a strictly legal point of view, illegal.[5] Nicholas as well as other members of the imperial family were aware of this. But his overriding desire to live with his family had priority over the legality. Some liberal critics later impugned Nicholas's motivation and saw in this change of heart a secret desire to complicate the situation or even to make a comeback after the storm.[6] It appears, however, that Nicholas was incapable of such intrigue. In view of the great sacrifice he had made, he felt justified in demanding a small concession to meet his personal desires. Unable to retrieve the telegrams, Nicholas himself wanted to see the Duma Committee's delegates before they had a chance to talk with Ruzskii.

Upon their arrival Guchkov and Shul'gin were immediately ushered

3. Andrei Vladimirovich, "Iz dnevnika A. V. Romanova," p. 206.

4. E. I. Martynov, *Tsarskaia armiia v fevral'skom perevorote*, p. 160; Pierre Gilliard, *Le tragique destin de Nicolas II et sa famille* (Paris: Payot, 1921), p. 165.

5. Paul Gronsky, "La chute de la monarchie en Russie," *Revue politique et parlementaire* 116 (1923): 97.

6. P. N. Miliukov, *Vospominaniia, 1859-1917* 2: 314-15; V. Nabokov, "Vremennoe pravitel'stvo," *Arkhiv russkoi revoliutsii* 1 (1922): 18-19; A. A. Bublikov, *Russkaia revoliutsiia: Vpechatleniia i mysli ochevidtsa i uchastnika*, p. 27.

into the emperor's salon car, although they, too, intended to speak with Ruzskii first to orient themselves with the tsar's attitude. They had no knowledge whatever of the emperor's decision until they faced him. In the salon car they found Count Frederiks and Major-General Naryshkin. In a few minutes Nicholas entered in a Cossack uniform. According to Guchkov, "his expression was calm; as usual his eyes were clear; his gestures tranquil and calculated. There was no trace of agitation."[7]

After pleasantries were exchanged, Guchkov began. He explained that both Shul'gin and Guchkov were dispatched by the Duma Committee to inform the emperor of the real situation in Petrograd and to give him advice on action that the Duma Committee considered necessary in order to escape from the complicated situation. "The situation is extremely threatening. This is not a result of some conspiracy or premeditated coup, but movement exploded from the very bottom." The movement had immediately taken an anarchical turn, and to prevent the further spread of anarchy the Duma Committee had been formed. But in addition to the Duma Committtee, "a committee of the workers' party is having a meeting in the Duma and we found ourselves under its influence and its censorship." The first danger was that anarchy led by these extremists, who espoused the concept of a "socialist republic," might sweep away the moderate elements. Secondly, the revolution might spread to the armed forces at the front.[8] He stated that troops dispatched from the front had mutinied and declared their allegiance to the Duma Committee. Ruzskii, who had joined the meeting in the middle of Guchkov's speech, supported Guchkov and declared that the army could no longer afford to send a single soldier from the front for suppression of the revolution.[9] By then it should have been clear to both Ruzskii and Guchkov that the revolt of troops sent from the front had never taken place at Luga, but they both considered it convenient to use this fiction as a leverage to put pressure on the tsar.

Guchkov came to the important point: "The only way out is to transfer the burden of the highest government to other hands. It is possible to save Russia, save the monarchical principle, and save the dynasty if You, Your Majesty, declare that you transfer power to

7. Guchkov's letter to Bazilii, quoted in Basily, *Diplomat of Imperial Russia,* p. 127. Shul'gin also noted his tranquillity. Shul'gin, *Dni,* p. 267.

8. S. P. Mel'gunov, *Martovskie dni 1917 goda,* pp. 190-91. This is based on the official minutes taken by Naryshkin, which were published by Strozhev in *Nauchnaia izvestiia* in 1922.

9. Guchkov's deposition, *Padenie tsarskogo rezhima* 6: 264; Guchkov's letter to Bazilii, quoted in Basily, *Diplomat of Imperial Russia,* p. 128.

your small son, if You give the regency to Grand Duke Mikhail Aleksandrovich, and if in your name or in the name of the regent a new
government is formed." Guchkov continued to state that even this
solution would not guarantee the successful conclusion of the crisis,
since the moderate elements were losing ground to the extremists
every moment. He further added that the tsar should think it over
before he made up his mind, but he should not wait too long, since
"we shall not be in a situation to give you any advice, even if you
ask us, if too much time were wasted."[10] Ruzskii interrupted, told
the Duma Committee's delegates that the emperor had already made
that decision, and handed to the emperor the signed telegram that
included the draft version of the manifesto of abdication. Ruzskii
considered it necessary to cut off Guchkov's speech before it went
too far. It had already taken an ominous turn toward intimidation.
By handing the telegram to the tsar, Ruzskii also hoped to preclude
further discussion and force the issue to an end. He was astounded
to see the emperor fold the telegram without reading it aloud to the
Duma Committee's delegates and put it in his pocket.[11]

Without paying attention to Ruzskii, Nicholas spoke calmly to
Guchkov and Shul'gin: "Before your arrival and after General Ruzskii's
conversation with the chairman of the State Duma by direct wire, I
deliberated during the morning and was ready for abdication from the
throne in favor of my son in the name of good, peace, and salvation of
Russia." Ruzskii must have felt sick with the premonition that his
worst fear would be confirmed. As for Guchkov and Shul'gin, they
heard for the first time about the conversation Rodzianko had had
with Ruzskii. Nicholas continued: "But now, reconsidering the situation, I have come to the conclusion that because of his illness, I must
abdicate at the same time for my son as well as for myself, since I
cannot part with him." He softly added: "I hope you will understand
the feelings of a father."[12] This answer was so unexpected that the
delegates could not immediately decide what to say. They looked at
each other incredulously. Guchkov then replied, rather ridiculously:
"We were hoping that the tender age of Aleksei Nikolaevich would have
a softening effect on the situation at the transfer of power." Shul'gin
saved his colleague from making a further embarrassing remark by
requesting a recess.[13]

Guchkov at first opposed the emperor's proposal, since "no one

10. Mel'gunov, *Martovskie dni*, p. 191.
11. Andrei Vladimirovich, "Iz dnevnika A. V. Romanova," p. 207.
12. Mel'gunov, *Martovskie dni*, p. 192; Shul'gin, *Dni*, p. 269.
13. Mel'gunov, *Martovskie dni*, p. 192.

could agree to entrust the fate and the education of the future emperor with those who had brought the country to the present condition."[14] Ruzskii, who also took part in the consultation, asked if it would be possible for the tsar legally to abdicate for his son. But neither knew the answer. The general exploded: "How could you come here to decide on such an important matter of the state without bringing a single volume of the Fundamental Laws or even a jurist?" Shul'gin justified this oversight by saying that they had not expected such an answer from the emperor. Shul'gin further argued that the formula proposed by the emperor should be accepted, for "whether or not the emperor had the right does not matter." The most important point at the moment was not the legality of the abdication, but the fact of abdication. Guchkov finally gave in.[15]

The Duma Committee's delegates returned to the tsar's salon car. Guchkov gave the emperor his consent: "Your Majesty, human feelings of a father have spoken in you, and politics has no place in it. Therefore, we cannot object to your proposal." Nicholas sarcastically asked him: "Do you want to think more about it?" Guchkov replied: "No, I think we can immediately accept your proposal."[16] In this exchange one can sense a delicate shift of attitude by the Duma Committee's delegates. They had come to "inform the emperor of the real situation and to give him proper advice." But they now elevated themselves to a position where they "accepted" the emperor's proposal, like generals of a conquering army.

To Nicholas the whole process must have been intolerably humiliating. The abdication itself was bad enough, but a situation in which his personal enemy should accept its terms added insult to injury. If he felt humiliated, however, he disguised his emotions. He occasionally threw oblique sarcasms at his opponents, but on the whole maintained a quiet dignity throughout the meeting. This struck Guchkov, who later testified: "Such an important act in history of Russia . . . was conducted in such a simple, ordinary form. And I would say that there was such a profoundly tragic lack of understanding of all the events by the very person who was the main character of this scene that I even wondered if we were dealing with a normal person."[17] Guchkov, of course, did not know that Nicholas was already resigned to the necessity of abdication before they came to negotiate with him and

14. Guchkov's deposition, *Padenie tsarskogo rezhima* 6: 265.
15. Andrei Vladimirovich, "Iz dnevnika A. V. Romanova," p. 207; Shul'gin, *Dni*, pp. 270-71; Guchkov's letter to Bazilii, quoted in Basily, *Diplomat of Imperial Russia*, pp. 128-29.
16. Mel'gunov, *Martovskie dni*, p. 194.
17. Guchkov's deposition, *Padenie tsarskogo rezhima* 6: 268-69.

that to Nicholas the meeting with the Duma Committee's delegates was nothing more than a ceremony that he had to go through to get the whole odious affair over with. Nicholas refused to give his conquerors the satisfaction of knowing the depths of his humiliation and disappointment.

Guchkov then stated that since they could not stay more than an hour and a half in Mogilev, they should have in their hands a signed manifesto of Nicholas's abdication. Shul'gin presented his version of the manifesto, but Nicholas offered his draft as a point of departure. That was the draft manifesto that had been composed by Bazilii on Alekseev's instructions and sent to Pskov around 7 o'clock in the evening, but handed to the emperor by Ruzskii during the meeting. Reading the highly polished, dignified draft, Shul'gin, embarrassed with his own version, immediately withdrew his. Bazilii's original formula—Nicholas's abdication in favor of his son, Aleksei, under Mikhail's regency—had been corrected by the emperor: "Not wishing to be parted from Our Beloved Son, We hand over Our Succession to Our Brother, Grand Duke Mikhail Aleksandrovich."[18] Guchkov and Shul'gin requested two changes: first, a phrase to the effect that the new emperor would pledge allegiance to the constitution should be inserted; second, to avoid the impression that the Duma Committee forced Nicholas to abdicate, Shul'gin asked the tsar to write the time of abdication at 3 P.M., when the emperor had made his decision, rather than the actual time when the manifesto was finally signed, at 11 P.M. Nicholas accepted these requests without protest. The emperor signed the manifesto. Thus ended Nicholas II's twenty-three year reign.

The abdication manifesto was in a way a step backward from the manifesto for a responsible ministry, since it made no reference to the government responsible for the legislative assembly. In general the abdication manifesto did not specifically state the relationship between the tsar and the legislative assembly except in the phrase inserted on the Duma Committee's delegates' demand that the new emperor should be bound by the "constitution." Neither Guchkov nor Shul'gin realized that Nicholas had already given his consent to the responsible ministry. Nor did the abdication manifesto clarify the position of the emperor in relation to the Provisional Government. Unlike the manifesto for the responsible ministry, the abdication manifesto changed nothing in the legal structure of the state. Nicholas was gone, but the monarchical system remained. This was to change overnight.

18. Withold S. Sworakowski, "The Authorship of the Abdication Documents of Nicholas II," *Russian Review* 30, no. 3 (1971): 282.

On that night, Nicholas, the "former" emperor of the Russian Empire, left Pskov for Mogilev. The journey was the first page of his tragedy, which was to end with the violent death of his entire family by the Bolsheviks.

The news of Nicholas's abdication reached Tsarskoe Selo on March 3. Busy with nursing the sick children in the palace, Aleksandra did not know until 11 o'clock in the morning, when Grand Duke Pavel Aleksandrovich brought the news to her. None of her entourage had had the courage to tell her. The empress received the grand duke in a hospital nurse's uniform. When Pavel broke the news, "the Empress trembled and bent down her head, as though she were uttering a prayer." Then she burst into tears.[19] But without a moment's hesitation, she accepted her husband's decision.

19. Princess Paley, *Memories of Russia, 1916-1919*, pp. 60-61; Paul Benckendorff, *Last Days at Tsarskoe Selo*, pp. 16-17.

PART VI

THE END OF THE MONARCHY:
THE PROVISIONAL GOVERNMENT

Izvestiia, a special issue announcing the abdication of Nicholas and Mikhail (Hoover Institution); *preceding page*, members of the Provisional Government: *clockwise from top*, I. V. Godnev, A. I. Shingarev, A. A. Manuilov, N. N. Nekrasov, F. I. Rodichev, M. I. Tereshchenko, P. N. Miliukov, V. N. L'vov, A. I. Guchkov, A. F. Kerenskii, A. I. Konovalov, G. E. L'vov (Hoover Institution)

27

THE FORMATION OF THE
PROVISIONAL GOVERNMENT

 The Duma Committee decided to take power on the eve-
ning of February 27. But it did not immediately proclaim
itself as a provisional government. In fact the Provisional
Government was not formed until March 2, and when it
was created, its composition was significantly different
from that of the Duma Committee. The delay of its formation and the differences in composition between the Duma Committee and the Provisional Government resulted from the intense power
struggle among the liberals and the question of legitimacy of the Provisional Government—the question integrally connected with this struggle.

The question of legitimacy involved two crucial points: the policy
toward the revolution and the policy toward the monarchy. It was
here that the dilemma of the liberals during the war was most vividly
revealed. They had stood between revolution and tsarism during the
preceding years and, sensing the approaching storm from below, had
tried in vain to convince the tsar of the necessity of instituting internal
reforms. Met with intransigent rejection of their demands, some liberals
had sought to utilize the revolutionary movement and others had
plotted a palace coup to force the tsarist government to accept their
demands. But a majority of the liberals led by Miliukov had stubbornly
refused to take either course for fear that such action by the liberals
might induce the outbreak of a revolution.

The February Revolution completely changed the situation. The
revolution that they had feared all along had actually taken place.
Once it became a reality, the liberals' position shifted to that of the
Left liberals, which the majority had previously consistently refused

to endorse. Their immediate goal was not the elimination of the revolution, but rather its containment. To arrest the further development of the revolution, the liberals were compelled both to accept the revolution and to stand at its forefront. In fact, it was the revolution that granted the Duma Committee the authority to enforce its will. From the moment it decided to seize power on the evening of February 27, it was clear that the future liberal government would seek a source of legitimacy in the revolution itself. But the liberals' ultimate goal of stopping the revolutionary process proved contradictory to the aspirations of the people. Furthermore, their conscious effort to keep a distance from the mass movement during the preceding years rendered them ineffective at the crucial moment, and most of the insurgents refused to endorse the liberals as the sole representatives of the revolution. Therefore, the liberals needed the support of the Executive Committee of the Petrograd Soviet, which they expected to serve as a bridge connecting the deep gulf between the future Provisional Government and the insurgent masses—a function that the Executive Committee was more than willing to perform.

But the revolution was not the only source of legitimacy that the liberals sought for the future government. They finally activated Guchkov's plot for a palace coup, which they had rejected before. To the majority of the liberals Rodzianko's limitation of reform to a responsible ministry seemed inadequate to close the floodgate of the revolution. They thus advocated Nicholas's abdication. But it was not as a revolutionary government that the liberals forced Nicholas to abdicate, but in the context of a palace coup—within the framework of the old regime. Nicholas not only agreed to abdicate, but also granted Prince L'vov the permission to form a government. In other words, the liberals attempted to gain sanction for the Provisional Government from the tsar. The simultaneous pursuit of legitimacy from the revolution as well as from the old regime was logically as well as politically impossible and was doomed to fail.[1]

By March 1 various liberal organizations put pressure on the Duma Committee to form a provisional government. On March 1, the Central War Industries Committee held a meeting, in which representatives of various liberal organizations also participated, and passed a resolution calling for "the immediate organization of civil and military power." The resolution stated: "Such power of the provisional administration must be single, firm, and authoritative in the eyes of

---

1. For the discussion of legitimacy of the Provisional Government, see Tsuyoshi Hasegawa, "The Problem of Power in the February Revolution in Russia," *Canadian Slavonic Papers* 14, no. 4 (1972): 622-32.

the army and the entire country and can originate only from the only center of entire Russia—the State Duma."[2] The delay of the formation of a provisional government and the continuation of the existing indefinite situation would be intolerable, since the absence of power was harmful both to the army and to the people. Furthermore, the Central War Industries Committee considered the most pressing tasks of the Provisional Government as: (1) immediate takeover of the government apparatus to insure an uninterrupted administrative mechanism; (2) subordination of all military forces in Petrograd to the government organization and a single commanding hierarchy; (3) resumption of production in the factories engaged in war production by appealing to workers to return to work and by insuring workers' rights to elect representatives for protection of their interests; and (4) restoration of a normal working life for the entire population by appealing to the populace to observe safety of life and property.[3]

After Rodzianko's influence was beginning to decline, the Kadet party assumed leadership of the Duma Committee.[4] The Central Committee of the Kadet party decided to place itself at the disposal of the Duma Committee and instructed its secretaries to compose a list of persons who could assist. At the same time, the Central Committee of the Kadets recommended that the Duma Committee take the following measures: (1) appoint commissars of the Duma Committee to provinces, (2) publish the resolutions of the Duma Committee in *Izvestiia* of the Petrograd Soviet as well as in the official organ of the Duma Committee; (3) announce amnesty to political and religious offenders; and (4) secure the safety of the embassies. On March 2, the Central Committee decided to demand Nicholas's unconditional abdication and advocated the immediate proclamation of the official composition of the Provisional Government.[5] It is presumed that the Kadets also exerted pressure on the Duma Committee to hasten the formation of the Provisional Government on March 1.

Within the Duma Committee itself the demand for the formation of a provisional government was raised on March 1. According to Miliukov, "It was necessary to hasten the final formation of a government. In view of this, by March 1 the Provisional Committee [the Duma Committee] initiated the composition of the cabinet, to which it should transfer its power.[6] Shul'gin had urged Miliukov to nominate

2. TsGIA, f. 1278, op. 5, d. 1252, ℓ. 3.
3. Ibid.
4. V. S. Diakin, *Russkaia burzhuaziia i tsarizm v gody pervoi mirovoi voiny*, p. 346.
5. *Vestnik partii narodnoi svobody*, no. 1 (March 11, 1917), p. 13.
6. P. N. Miliukov, *Istoriia vtoroi russkoi revoliutsii* 1: 45.

the members of the Provisional Government and emphasized that only Miliukov could perform the task. While the others were bustling about, Miliukov was compiling the list of ministers at the corner of the Duma Committee's room: this roster of ministers was born "from the head of Miliukov." The Duma Committee approved this list on March 1.[7]

Miliukov's list was composed of the following: Prince G. E. L'vov (chairman of the Council of Ministers and minister of internal affairs), Miliukov (minister of foreign affairs), Guchkov (minister of war and navy), Kerenskii (minister of justice), Chkheidze (minister of labor), Nekrasov (minister of transport), Tereshchenko (minister of finance), Shingarev (minister of agriculture), Konovalov (minister of trade and industry), A. A. Manuilov (minister of education), I. V. Godnev (state comptroller), and V. N. L'vov (procurator of the holy synod).[8]

After the crisis in the summer of 1915, various opposition circles had compiled possible ministries of confidence. According to Astrov, every liberal organization including the Union of Zemstvos, the Union of Towns, the War Industries Committees, and various political parties had assembled such a list. Chermenskii reproduced four of such lists circulated around various political parties in August 1915.[9] Kuskova told Mel'gunov that the liberal leaders who gathered at Prokopovich's apartment in April 1916 discussed acceptable names for a ministry of confidence. According to Diakin, the left-wing liberals composed a list of a cabinet headed by Prince L'vov in January 1917, but this list met with strong opposition from the right wing of the Progressive Bloc.[10] Presumably these lists reflected the wishful thinking of various liberal groups, among whom there was no solid agreement on candidates for the ministerial posts. A comparison of these compilations with the actual composition of the Provisional Government, however, may help us determine the nature of the Provisional Government. The earlier lists of a ministry of confidence and the composition of the Provisional Government are give in table 7.

One of the most important disagreements among the liberals prior

7. V. V. Shul'gin, *Dni*, pp. 210-11, 223; E. Krivosheina, "Prichiny peredachi vlasti Petrogradskim sovetom rabochikh i soldatskikh deputatov burzhuazii v fevral'skuiu revoliutsiiu," *Sovetskoe gosudarstvo i revoliutsiia prava*, no. 2 (1931), p. 131. Krivosheina quotes from the Duma Committee's resolution on March 1, which must have come from archival sources.

8. *Izvestiia revoliutsionnoi nedeli*, no. 6 (March 2, 1917). Chkheidze's name was not included, although it was on Miliukov's list.

9. S. P. Mel'gunov, *Na putiakh k dvortsovomu perevorotu*, p.176; E. D. Chermenskii, *IV gosudarstvennaia duma i sverzhenie tsarizma v Rossii*, p. 98.

10. Mel'gunov, *Na putiakh*, pp. 171-72; Diakin, *Russkaia burzhuaziia*, p. 291.

TABLE 7

GOVERNMENTAL MINISTERS:
THOSE PROPOSED EARLIER AND THOSE INCLUDED IN PROVISIONAL GOVERNMENT

	Progressists (August 1915)	Kadets (August 1915)	Octobrists (August 1915)	Progressive Bloc/ State Council (August 1915)	Kuskova- Prokopovich (April 1916)	Provisional Government (March 1, 1917)
Premier	Rodzianko	G. E. L'vov	Guchkov	Shcherbatov	G.E. L'vov	G. E. L'vov
Internal Affairs	Guchkov	G. E. L'vov	G. E. L'vov	V. I. Gurko		G. E. L'vov
Foreign Affairs	Miliukov	Miliukov	Sazonov	Miliukov	Miliukov (Pr. Trubetskoi)	Miliukov
Finance	Shingarev	Pokrovskii	Shingarev	Shingarev		Tereshchenko
Transport	Nekrasov	Dobrovol'skii	Nemeshev	Nemeshev		Nekrasov
Trade and Industry	Konovalov	Konovalov	Konovalov	Konovalov	Konovalov	Konovalov
Agriculture	Krivoshein			Shingarev	Shingarev	Shingarev
War	Polivanov	Polivanov	Guchkov	Polivanov	Guchkov	Guchkov
Navy	Savich	Savich	Savich			Guchkov
State Comptroller	Efremov					Godnev
Procurator Holy Synod	V. N. L'vov	V. N. L'vov	V. N. L'vov			V. N. L'vov
Education	Ignatiev	Ignatiev	Kovalevskii	Ignatiev	Gerasimov (Manuilov)	Manuilov
Justice	V. Maklakov	Maklakov	Manukhin	Manukhin	Maklakov (Nabokov)	Kerenskii
Labor						Chkheidze*

*Chkheidze was included in Miliukov's list, but refused to join the Provisional Government.

to the February Revolution was whether Rodzianko or Prince L'vov should head a ministry of confidence. In August 1915, Rodzianko was accepted as a possible candidate even by the Progressists. But as the relationship between the liberals and the tsar became increasingly strained in 1916, Rodzianko's moderation and conservatism disillusioned the radical wing of the liberals, who had come to support Prince L'vov as a more suitable candidate. For the first two days after the insurrection Rodzianko's prestige was boosted to its height. As chairman of the Duma and the Duma Committee, he imposed his will on the other members of the Duma Committee and pursued a policy of moderation in the name of the Duma Committee. But Rodzianko's order to the soldiers irretrievably damaged his prestige in the eyes of the insurgents. The other members of the Duma Committee believed that his participation in the Provisional Government would make its relationship with the Soviet and the insurgent masses extremely difficult. According to Shul'gin, when Rodzianko's name was mentioned, the members of the Duma Committee "all shouted at once: 'the Left will not accept Rodzianko.' "[11]

But Rodzianko continued to negotiate independently with the military leaders. His middle-of-the-road approach and independent action caused the other members of the Duma Committee to suspect that he was plotting to make himself dictator with the help of the military and through a secret bargain with the tsar. In Miliukov's words, "He [Rodzianko] continued to think of himself as leader and savior of Russia in this transitional stage. He had to be removed from that place; and I was given the task of removing him—a mission that was in agreement with my own intentions."[12]

Miliukov achieved his goal by two means. First, he created the Provisional Government separate from the Duma Committee, and secondly, he removed Rodzianko's name from its composition. Rodzianko considered the Duma not only still in existence, but also the only source of authority, one that stood higher than the Provisional Government itself. Anxious to get rid of Rodzianko's influence, Miliukov and his colleagues were ready to write off the Duma as a "shadow of the past." On March 3 the Central Committee of the Kadet party passed a resolution, which recognized "that the Provisional Government is considered as possessing legislative and executive power and that the Provisional Committee of the State Duma should be left inactive."[13] Once the Provisional Government was formed, its leaders considered other competing authorities as useless hindrances.

11. Shul'gin, *Dni*, p. 225.
12. P. N. Miliukov, *Vospominaniia, 1859-1917* 2: 274-75.
13. *Vestnik partii narodnoi svobody*, no. 1 (March 11, 1917), p. 13.

Prince L'vov had emerged as a hero of the opposition through his activities in the Union of Zemstvos. When the Duma had remained inactive in its struggle with the tsarist government, L'vov had often spoken out sharply. At the end of 1916, he became involved in a plot to stage a palace coup, although the plot was deadlocked at the initial stage. From the end of 1915 he was mentioned by various opposition groups as a possible candidate to head a ministry of confidence. At the end of December 1916, and at the beginning of January 1917, Klopov, in agreement with Grand Duke Mikhail Aleksandrovich, had petitioned to the tsar for the formation of a ministry of confidence headed by Prince L'vov.[14] When the February Revolution broke out, L'vov was in Moscow, but at the request of Miliukov he arrived in Petrograd on March 1, and was seen in the Tauride Palace on this day. By the evening of March 1 it became clear to the members of the Duma Committee that L'vov would head the Provisional Government.[15]

But during the crucial three days from March 1 to 3, L'vov left no distinct impression on events. A Kadet, Nabokov, who became the secretary of the Provisional Government, remarked, "He sat in the driver's box, but did not even try to pick up the reins."[16] But it was precisely because of his lack of dynamic personality that Miliukov chose L'vov rather than Rodzianko. L'vov was meant to be a figurehead, and Miliukov expected to establish himself as undisputed leader of the Provisional Government. But Miliukov was to be disappointed. He wrote in his memoirs: "He arrived and got acclimated, as was his custom. Hence came the undecisiveness which at my first encounter caused my disappointment. We did not know 'whose' he would be, but we felt that he was not 'ours.' "[17]

The appointments of Miliukov and Guchkov as minister of foreign affairs and of war and navy respectively were natural choices. Miliukov was known as an expert on foreign relations, had close connections with diplomats, and had been selected by the opposition groups as a suitable candidate for the post. Guchkov, on the other hand, had contributed to military reforms as a member of the military committee of the Third Duma, was the chairman of the Central War Industries Committee, and had replaced Engelhardt as the head of the Military Commission of the Duma Committee. He had established close rela-

14. See chap. 10; T. E. Polner, *Zhiznennyi put' kniaziia Georgiia Evgenievicha L'vova*, p. 225.

15. OR GBL, f. 218, B. A. Engel'gardt, "Potonuvskii mir: Vospominaniia," ℓ. 114.

16. Quoted in Miliukov, *Vospominaniia* 2: 299.

17. Ibid., p. 302.

tionships with the officers of the General Staff and the Naval Staff in Petrograd. On March 1 he was busy visiting regimental barracks in the attempt to restore order in the military units.

One of the most striking features of the composition of the Provisional Government was the inclusion of two Socialists, Kerenskii and Chkheidze. Aware of the impossibility of liberals persuading the workers to obey the Provisional Government's orders, Miliukov created a new ministry dealing with labor and offered the post of the new minister to the chairman of the Petrograd Soviet, Chkheidze. He hoped that through the mediation of the Petrograd Soviet the Provisional Government could achieve peace with the workers. But Chkheidze, faithful to the Executive Committee's decision not to participate in the "bourgeois" government, declined to accept the post. In contrast to Chkheidze, Kerenskii was at home with the Duma Committee, although he held the position of vice-chairman of the Petrograd Soviet. Kerenskii himself later admitted: "Even after my election by chance [as vice-chairman] of the Soviet I rarely attended the Soviet meetings or those of its Executive Committee. From the first days of the Revolution my relations with the Soviet leaders were strained. They could not abide me, as I was compelled to fight continually against the academic, dogmatic socialism of the Soviet, which from the very beginning tried to thwart the normal development and sound forces of the revolution."[18]

Kerenskii was offered the post of minister of justice. He was well aware that "in Duma circles it was considered imperative that I be included in the Provisional Government."[19] According to Rodzianko, Kerenskii "had to be included in the composition of the cabinet in view of the demands of the democratic elements, without whose consent there was no possibility either to restore even the likeness of order or to establish a popular government." The Provisional Government needed the vice-chairman of the Soviet "as the link between the government and its critics." Unlike Chkheidze, Kerenskii wanted to be a minister. But on the same day the ministerial post was offered, the Soviet Executive Committee decided that no Socialists should take part in the new cabinet.[20] What the Provisional Government wanted was not merely Kerenskii's personality, but his link with the Soviet. Also to exert influence in the Provisional Government, Kerenskii had to join the cabinet as a "hostage of the revolution."

18. Alexander F. Kerensky, *The Catastrophe*, p. 29.
19. Ibid., p. 57.
20. M. V. Rodzianko, "Gosudarstvennaia duma i fevral'skaia 1917 goda revoliutsiia," *Arkhiv russkoi revoliutsii* 4 (1922): 29; Polner, *Zhiznennyi put'*, pp. 232-33; see chap. 21.

He began carefully preparing a way out of this dilemma. During the negotiations between the Duma Committee and the Soviet Executive Committee on the conditions for the transfer of power Kerenskii took no part in the discussion—although he sat in on negotiations—lest he should be embroiled in a conflict between the two sides.

The Executive Committee's decision seemed to Kerenskii absurd, and he described his dilemma: "I was confronted with a painful question, having to choose between leaving the Soviet and remaining in the government or remaining in the Soviet and refusing to take part in the government. Both alternatives seemed impossible to me. The dilemma buried itself deep in my mind and the decision ripened somehow by itself, for there was no time or opportunity to think over the problem in the turmoil of the day."[21] To Kerenskii the night of March 1-2 was the most painful night he had ever experienced. After lying in a semiconscious, semidelirious state, he suddenly found an escape. The decision of the Executive Committee was not final, but had to be ratified by the general session of the Soviet on March 2. He decided to appeal to the delegates directly, ignoring the Executive Committee's decision. As soon as he thought of this solution, he telephoned Miliukov and accepted the post in the Provisional Government.[22] Kerenskii's charismatic influence was still great among the masses and he had every reason to count on the success of his plan.

Another curious feature of the Provisional Government was the inclusion of Tereshchenko as minister of finance. His name had not been mentioned in any list of candidates for a ministry of confidence before. Miliukov himself, who composed the list of the cabinet members, curiously cast doubt on how some of the names of this list came to be included. He wrote in his memoirs: "On what 'list' did he [Tereshchenko] 'come into' the Ministry of Finance? I did not know then that the source was the same one from which Kerenskii had a post thrust upon him, from which the republicanism of our Nekrasov came, and from which also the unexpected radicalism of the Progressists, Konovalov and Efremov, came. About this source I learned much later."[23] In another book, he alleged that Tereshchenko and Nekrasov were included in this list because of their personal intimacy with Kerenskii and because of their proximity to the conspiratorial circles that prepared the revolution.[24] But Miliukov did not clearly spell out what kind of conspiratorial organization it was. We now know

21. Kerensky, *The Catastrophe*, p. 53.
22. Ibid., p. 59.
23. Miliukov, *Vospominaniia* 2: 311-12.
24. Miliukov, *Istoriia vtoroi russkoi revoliutsii* 2: 45-46.

that it was the masonic organization of which Kerenskii, Nekrasov, Konovalov, and Tereshchenko were important members. According to Katkov, Prince L'vov had personal connections with this group, though he was not formally a member.

Katkov emphasized the importance of the Masons in the Provisional Government, and argues as if the entire Provisional Government was the product of a conspiracy on their part.[25] Certainly, the four (Kerenskii, Nekrasov, Konovalov, and Tereshchenko) out of the eleven-member cabinet constituted a large block. But the lack of evidence makes it virtually impossible to make an intelligent conclusion on the role played by the masonic element during the February Revolution. It is known that these four were a part of it, but was the pressure Katkov refers to exerted by the organization as a whole or at the individual initiative? Did they meet one another during the February Revolution? If they did, where and what decisions did they make? Were the other members, Kuskova and Prokopovich, for instance, involved in the "conspiracy"? How exactly did they put pressure on Miliukov, who compiled the list of the cabinet members? Katkov offers no answers to these questions, and the existing evidence provides no clues, either. We know little about Kerenskii's and Nekrasov's activities during the revolution, and on Konovalov's activities there is nothing at all.

On the other hand, an argument could be made to minimize the significance of the masonic influence on the selection of the cabinet ministers. If there was a conspiracy of the masonic organization, it is difficult to explain why Efremov's name, which was included in the Progressists' list in August 1915, was withdrawn. Kerenskii was chosen, not because he was a Mason, but because he was needed as a link between the Provisional Government and the Petrograd Soviet. Konovalov had been on everyone's list for the minister of trade and industry, and his selection seemed to have little to do with his masonic ties, as Katkov admits. Nekrasov's appointment to the post of the minister of transport was not unexpected, either. His name had been mentioned already for that post in the Progressists' list in August 1915. Nekrasov had been consistently arguing for the necessity of making an alliance with the mass movement. The liberals' acceptance of the revolution vindicated his argument, and Nekrasov's appointment reflected the relative increase of strength of the left-wing liberals. Also the deposed commissar of transport of the Duma Committee, Bublikov, may have been associated too closely with Rodzianko. That leaves only Tereshchenko, whose appointment may be questioned

25. George Katkov, *Russia, 1917: The February Revolution*, pp. 163-74 377-83.

as strange. But Tereshchenko was not unknown, as Miliukov unfairly indicated in his memoirs. He was the chairman of the Kiev War Industries Committee, and had been actively involved in the political activities of the Central War Industries Committee. In fact, Miliukov had some difficulty in finding a good candidate for finance minister. Shingarev, an acknowledged expert on food supply, who had been mentioned often for the post of finance minister, was more needed for the post of minister of agriculture.[26] Thus, anyone who was appointed to this post must have been a surprise. Masonic ties aside, it is possible to think of two important factors that contributed to Tereshchenko's appointment. The first was geographical. The Provisional Government needed someone to represent the south of Russia. Another might be the influence of the War Industries Committees. The Central War Industries Committee had put pressure on the Duma Committee to form the Provisional Government, and it is conceivable that its delegates might have pushed Tereshchenko's candidacy. But definitive conclusions on the role of the masonic organization in the selection of the members of the Provisional Government cannot be drawn at this stage of historical research.

The composition of the Provisional Government indicated that it was more radical than the Duma Committee. By party affiliations, the Provisional Government consisted of six Kadets (Miliukov, Shingarev, Tereshchenko, Nekrasov, and Manuilov), two Progressists (Prince L'vov and Konovalov), two Octobrists (Guchkov and Godnev), one Centrist (V. N. L'vov), and one Socialist (Kerenskii). The Octobrists, Nationalists, and Centrists, who provided the majority of the Duma Committee, lost significant strength in the Provisional Government. Furthermore, the radical liberals, represented by Konovalov and Nekrasov, who also counted Kerenskii's support, outnumbered the moderate liberals led by Miliukov and Shingarev. This was necessitated by the Provisional Government's need to be recognized by the insurgent masses.

So far, preparations for the creation of the Provisional Government had been made in secrecy. But by the early morning of March 2, the liberals had solved the question of legitimacy. They had reached agreement with the Soviet Executive Committee on the transfer of power, and the Duma Committee's delegates were on the way to Pskov to force Nicholas's abdication. Therefore, it was necessary to break the news of the formation of the Provisional Government to the masses. Miliukov decided to test their reaction by informally announcing the

26. Shul'gin, *Dni,* pp. 273-74.

creation of the Provisional Government to the crowds who were still gathering in the Ekaterina Hall of the Tauride Palace.[27]

He began with attacks on the old regime and announced that the first cabinet of society *(obshchestvennyi)* was being formed. He stressed the necessity of organizing the revolutionary forces under the new government and the unity of the people, particularly the unity between soldiers and officers. According to Miliukov, this speech was welcomed with enthusiasm, but Sukhanov stated that a substantial part of the audience was hostile and that the speaker sometimes found himself in difficulty. When Miliukov announced the formation of the Provisional Government, one of the audience shouted: "Who elected you?" Miliukov answered, "No one elected us, for if we began to wait for popular elections, we could not have wrung the power from the hands of the enemy. While we were arguing whom to elect, the enemy would have succeeded in organizing itself and won over you and us. It was the Russian Revolution that elected us."[28] Although the Duma Committee had virtually acted as a revolutionary power, in spite of itself, and its members had delivered speeches praising the activities of the insurgents, it was the first time that the Duma Committee and the Provisional Government explicitly acknowledged that the Provisional Government was created by the revolution and would stand for the revolution. According to Miliukov, "This simple reference to the historical process that had led us to power shut the mouths of the most radical opponents. This was later often cited as the canonical source of our power." Did Miliukov really mean that the legitimacy of the Provisional Government was derived from the revolution itself? Or was this statement merely an improvised gesture to win the support of the insurgents? In his memoirs, Miliukov justifies his actions by saying that the revolution was the only conceivable source of power, since the majority of the Duma Committee members believed that under the new circumstances the Duma was no longer a viable institution.[29] Miliukov had, indeed, traveled very far in a few days— from the staunch moderate who had adamantly refused to align himself with the revolutionary forces to the new position of accepting the revolution.

Miliukov continued his speech. After promising that the new government would convene the Constituent Assembly, he began to introduce the names of the ministers of the Provisional Government.

27. For Miliukov's speech see *Izvestiia revoliutsionnoi nedeli*, March 2, 1917; Miliukov, *Istoriia vtoroi russkoi revoliutsii* 1: 51-52; idem, *Vospominaniia* 2:310-12; N. N. Sukhanov, *Zapiski o revoliutsii* 1: 321-28.

28. *Izvestiia revoliutsionnoi nedeli*, March 2, 1917.

29. Miliukov, *Vospominaniia* 2: 303, 311.

"From the people there should not be any secrets. All Russia will know this secret in a few hours and, of course, we did not become ministers to hide their names in secret. I will tell them to you right now. At the head of our ministry we put the person whose name signifies the organized Russian society . . . G. E. L'vov." Immediately a voice was raised, "The privileged class!" Miliukov hastened to answer: "You say the privileged class. Yes, but the only organized class that will later give the other strata of Russian society the possibility of organizing themselves." To placate the masses, Miliukov introduced the name of Kerenskii. "But, gentlemen, I am happy to tell you that also the nonprivileged class has its representative in our ministry. I have just received the acceptance of my colleague, A. F. Kerenskii, to occupy a post in the first Russian cabinet of society." Kerenskii's name was welcomed with enthusiastic applause. The speaker next told the audience that Miliukov himself was entrusted with the Ministry of Foreign Affairs. This announcement was also welcomed with "stormy and prolonged applause, growing into an ovation for the speaker," who bowed in all directions. Miliukov solemnly swore that while he was in office confidential matters would not fall into the hands of the enemy—an insinuation that the tsarist government had been infiltrated by German spies. The speaker expected to have some opposition to the war minister, and he slightly distorted the truth so that the audience should accept the name of Guchkov. "While I am speaking to you in this hall, Guchkov is in the streets of the capital organizing our victory." Actually, at this moment Guchkov was on his way to Pskov to force the tsar to abdicate. Then Miliukov introduced the names of Konovalov and Tereshchenko. The audience asked "Who is Tereshchenko?" Miliukov answered, "Yes, ladies and gentlemen, this is a famous name in southern Russia. Russia is vast and it is hard to know everywhere the names of all our best people." He quickly introduced the rest of the names of the cabinet.[30] Miliukov must have felt relieved to see that the list of the names of the Provisional government was accepted with little opposition from the audience.

But trouble came from a different direction. Someone in the audience wanted to know what program the Provisional Government intended. Miliukov stressed the agreement that the Provisional Government had reached with the representatives of the Soviet Executive Committee as a result of an all-night conference. He was about to begin an explanation of the program, when someone interrupted him: "How about the dynasty?" It was at this moment that Miliukov

30. *Izvestiia revoliutsionnoi nedeli*, March 2, 1917.

for the first time revealed the policy of the Duma Committee and the Provisional Government concerning the monarchy. Miliukov declared: "The power will be transferred to the regent, Grand Duke Mikhail Aleksandrovich. Aleksei will be the successor." According to a reporter who happened to be at the Ekaterina Hall, there were "prolonged bursts of indignation, exclamations: 'Long live the republic,' 'Down with the dynasty!' Weak applause was drowned out by new bursts of indignation."[31] They shouted, "This is the old dynasty!" Miliukov tried to placate the outraged masses:

Yes, gentlemen, you don't like the old dynasty. I may not like it, either. But now the question is not who likes what. We cannot leave the question of the constitution of the state without making a decision. We can see it as a parliamentary, constitutional monarchy. Perhaps others see it differently, but if we start arguing about this now instead of reaching an immediate decision, then Russia will find herself in a state of civil war that will only revive the ruined regime. Neither you nor we have the right to do this. However, this does not mean we have solved the problem for good. You will find a point in our program, in accordance to which, as soon as the dangers disappear and order is securely restored, we will proceed to the preparation for a convocation of the Constituent Assembly which will be convened on the basis of universal, direct, equal, and secret suffrage.[32]

Cleverly, Miliukov had shifted from the dynastic question to the problem of a Constituent Assembly. He was loudly applauded there. When he finished his speech, the excited audience lifted Miliukov several times, and carried him out of the Ekaterina Hall.[33]

Although Miliukov's speech was generally well received, one of the most important points of the policy of the Provisional Government, the question of the monarchical system, provoked a violent reaction from the audience. It was in the Ekaterina Hall of the Tauride Palace that the intention of the Provisional Government to obtain dual legitimacy—from both the revolution and the old regime—faced its most critical challenge. The news of the retention of the monarchical system spread quickly. According to Sukhanov, tens of thousands of people stood outside the Tauride Palace and demanded to see some delegates from the Soviet Executive Committee to inquire about the program of the Provisional Government with regard to the preservation of the old dynasty.[34] Although Sukhanov's account might be a slight exaggeration, it appears certain that Miliukov's revelation touched off violent actions by the insurgents against the privileged class in general

31. Ibid.
32. Ibid.
33. Ibid.
34. Sukhanov, *Zapiski o revoliutsii* 1: 328.

and by soldiers against officers in particular. The attack by soldiers against officers may also have been induced by the issuance of Order No. 1.

The archival materials of the Duma Committee indicate that on March 2 there was a sudden increase of soldiers searching and plundering apartments occupied by officers and members of the privileged class.[35] Soldiers arrested those officers they considered monarchists and hounded out those hiding in hotels and in the apartments of their acquaintances. On March 2 the commandant of the Fortress of Peter and Paul requested the Duma Committee's intervention to prevent illegal arrests of officers by soldiers.[36] Some officers, dissatisfied with the lack of direction and strength of the Provisional Government on dynastic issues, passed a resolution demanding that the Provisional Government should more forcefully argue that only the Constituent Assembly could determine the future form of government and that it should silence propagandists advocating republicanism. But the majority of officers were frightened by the violence of the soldiers. Officers, if they had still maintained neutrality, suddenly pledged their allegiance to the Duma Committee.[37] Miliukov noted: "later in the evening a crowd of extremely excited officers made its way into the Tauride Palace and declared that they could not return to their units unless P. N. Miliukov retracted his words."[38] According to officer Tugan-Baranovskii of the Military Commission, insurgent soldiers burst into the Military Commission and demanded to know whether there would be a monarchy or a republic. Rodzianko demanded that Miliukov declare that his speech concerning the dynasty was only his personal opinion.[39] Although his influence was severely undercut by the formation of the Provisional Government and by the adoption by the Duma Committee of the policy of abdication, Rodzianko jumped on this opportunity to undermine Miliukov's prestige. Miliukov considered his retraction a matter of formality to cool the temper of the masses, but the other members of the Duma Committee and the Provisional Government thought otherwise, and concluded that for the survival of the Provisional Government the monarchy should be sacrificed once and for all.

35. TsGIA, f. 1278, op. 10, d. 6, ll. 9-12, 16, 18.
36. TsGIA, f. 1278, op. 10, d. 9, l. 21.
37. TsGIA, f. 1278, op. 10, d. 5, ll. 22, 23.
38. Miliukov, Istoriia vtoroi russkoi revoliutsii 1: 52.
39. Lichnyi fond Polievktova: Materialy komissi oprosov, beseda s Tugan-Baranovskim, quoted in E. N. Burdzhalov, Vtoraia russkoi revoliutsii: Vosstanie v Petrograde, pp. 325-26; Miliukov, Vospominaniia 2: 312-13; Izvestiia, March 3, 1917.

While the Duma Committee and the Provisional Government retreated from their original plan regarding the monarchy in the face of the violent protest of the insurgents, they experienced another serious setback in their attempts to secure legitimacy from the masses through the endorsement of the Soviet Executive Committee. As the liberals had to accommodate themselves to the sentiments of the masses, the leaders of the Soviet Executive Committee, too, had to surrender to their radicalism.

On the basis of the agreement reached between the Duma Committee and the Soviet Executive Committee early on March 2, Miliukov wrote a proclamation that was to be issued in the name of the Petrograd Soviet. The Petrograd Soviet was to support the Provisional Government in its efforts to restore order in the capital and to normalize the relationship between soldiers and officers. However, two significant developments had taken place before this proclamation was ratified at the general session of the Soviet. The first was the issuance of Order No. 1, and the second was mounting pressure from both the Left and the Right within the Executive Committee to denounce the agreement that its representatives had reached with the Duma Committee. By urging the soldiers to subordinate themselves ultimately to the authority of the Petrograd Soviet, Order No. 1 destroyed any possibility of the Provisional Government's establishing itself as the sole authority of the revolution and broadened even further the gap between the Provisional Government and the insurgent soldiers. The leaders of the Executive Committee had to retreat from the original full-fledged support of the Provisional Government to a conditional support to have the agreement it had reached with the Duma Committee ratified by the insurgents at the plenary session.

As mentioned earlier, the Executive Committee's decision on March 1 not to participate in the Provisional Government remained to be approved by the general session on March 2. Both the Right and the Left of the Executive Committee therefore organized meetings to plan strategy to overturn the decision. To prevent this, Chkheidze, Sukhanov, Steklov, and Sokolov conducted negotiations with the Duma Committee for the transfer of power. They considered it imperative to present the result of the negotiations as an established fact before their critics attacked their policy.

On the morning of March 2, when Sukhanov went to the room of the Soviet Executive Committee, one of the right-wing members of the Executive Committee burst into the room with a leaflet published jointly by the Mezhraiontsy and the SR Maximalists. Written by Iurenev and Aleksandrovich, this leaflet appealed to the soldiers in inflammatory language to act against the Duma Committee and against officers. Pointing out that for the two days since the formation of the Duma Committee, neither Rodzianko nor Miliukov had mentioned anything about land for the peasants and the workers' rights, the leaflet appealed to the soldiers to go to the Duma and ask them if there would be land, rights, and peace. It further stated: "Soldiers! Now that you have revolted and triumphed, you are approached not only by your friends, but also your former enemy—officers, who are calling themselves your friends. Soldiers, the fox's tail is more dangerous than the wolf's teeth." To protect themselves from the deception of the nobles and the officers, they should take power into their hands by forming company committees and electing platoon, company, and regiment commanders. "All officers must be under the control of these company committees." Urging the soldiers to send their delegates to the Petrograd Soviet, it continued, "Your representatives and the workers' deputies must become the provisional revolutionary government of the people."[40]

Although its language was inflammatory, its contents had nothing contradictory with the letter and the spirit of Order No. 1. In fact, at the first glance Shliapnikov concluded that the leaflet responded to the concerns expressed by the soldiers at their plenum on March 1. Nowhere did it "sanction violence" against the officers, as Sukhanov mentioned.[41] Yet when Shliapnikov arrived at the Executive Committee, Sukhanov, Steklov, and Kerenskii were indignant about the leaflet, and demanded its confiscation. Their indignation was understandable. Anxious to keep the fast-developing revolution within reasonable limits, they themselves wished to restore a normal relationship between officers and soldiers. But the most dangerous point of this leaflet was its appeal to transform the Soviet into the provisional revolutionary government—the demand that Steklov and Sukhanov had tried to avoid at all costs. Thus, they demanded informal discussion of the leaflet at the Executive Committee, where the majority decided to confiscate all copies.[42] Neither Iurenev nor Aleksandrovich was present at the meeting. Shliapnikov did not raise strong objections. To counter the confiscated leaflet, the Executive Committee printed a proclamation in *Izvestiia*:

Comrade soldiers and workers! The Executive Committee of the Soviet of Workers' and Soldiers' Deputies has learned that rumors are going around the city and an appeal urging violence against officers is being posted. The Executive Committee

40. A. Shliapnikov, *Semnadtsatyi god* 1: 339-40. See also A. Tarasov-Rodionov, *February 1917: A Chronicle of the Russian Revolution*, pp. 129-30.

41. Sukhanov, *Zapiski o revoliutsii* 1: 292.

42. Shliapnikov, *Semnadtsatyi god* 1: 231-32.

has no doubt that the workers and the soldiers not only will not follow such scandalous appeals, but also will oppose their distribution, since they are new attempts to sow trouble and destroy the revolutionary forces.[43]

The confiscation of the leaflet was not necessarily an overreaction of the leading group of the Executive Committee. There existed a real possibility of a left-wing alliance of the Bolsheviks, the Mezhraiontsy, the SR Maximalists, and the Menshevik initiative group, united with a demand for the establishment of a provisional revolutionary government by the Petrograd Soviet. That such a coalition did not materialize was largely because of the confusion within the Bolshevik leadership about the problem of power.

The Vyborg District Committee called for the Bolsheviks in the Vyborg District to hold their first legal meeting at the Sampsonievskii Brotherhood on Sampsonievskii Prospekt on March 1. About two hundred party activists, who came out of the underground for the first time, took part. There were also many nonparty workers, who, despite explanations by the Vyborg District Committee that only party members had the right to speak and vote, actively participated in the discussion and voted for a resolution. At the end the Vyborg Bolsheviks passed the following resolution: (1) immediate formation of a provisional revolutionary government from the insurgent workers and soldiers; (2) new organization of troops to complete the overthrow of the tsarist regime; (3) immediate proclamation of the Petrograd Soviet as the Provisional Revolutionary Government and subordination of the Duma Committee to this Provisional Revolutionary Government; and (4) withdrawal of the people's representatives from the Duma, "which is based on the electoral law serving as a foundation of the overthrown tsarist regime."[44] Another version of the resolution, which reached Shliapnikov, stated that "all power must be concentrated in the hands of the Soviet of Workers' and Soldiers' Deputies as the single Revolutionary Government until the convocation of the Constituent Assembly," and further that "the army and the population must execute only the measures of the Soviet of Workers' and Soldiers' Deputies and consider the measures of the Executive Committee of the members of the State Duma inactive."[45] In both versions of the resolution the idea of transformation of the Soviet into a provisional revolutionary government was clearly expressed. This

43. *Izvestiia*, March 2, 1917.

44. *Revoliutsionnoe dvizhenie v Rossii posle sverzheniia samoderzhaviia*, p. 6; F. Dingel'stadt, "Vesna proletarskoi revoliutsii: Iz vpechatlenii agitatora v marte 1917 g.," *Krasnaia letopis'* 12, no. 1 (1925): 193.

45. Shliapnikov, *Semnadtsatyi god* 1: 236.

idea was consistent with the proposals that the Vyborg District Committee had advanced on February 27 with regard to the formation of the Petrograd Soviet and provided a basis for the potential alliance with the Mezhraiontsy and the SR Maximalists, who had stood for the same principle. Although the Menshevik initiative group supported the leading center of the Executive Committee and opposed the assumption of power by any revolutionary group, they were disturbed by the Executive Committee's close cooperation with the Duma Committee. In fact, one of its leaders, Ermanskii, supported the Bolsheviks at the general session of the Soviet on March 2.[46] Thus, Sukhanov's fear that the left wing might present a demand for the transformation of the Soviet into a provisional revolutionary government was justifiable, and it was possible that if such a cry had been made, the masses might have been swayed to support it.

But the Vyborg District Committee's demand was not accepted by the Russian Bureau and the Petersburg Committee, which was reconstructed again on March 1 at the meeting held at the office of L. M. Mikhailov, assistant director of the Labor Exchange in the Petrograd District.[47] Both the Russian Bureau and the Petersburg Committee, considering the demand for the transformation of the Soviet into a provisional revolutionary government dangerous, ordered the Vyborg District Committee to stop circulating the leaflet containing the resolution.[48] The Russian Bureau "did not advance the notion of the Soviet power as a special system of administration of the state," but it rather considered the Soviet "as an organ of the revolutionary democracy, which alone is competent to give the country a provisional revolutionary government."[49] Thus, it theoretically stood for "the establishment of a provisional revolutionary government from the composition of the Petrograd Soviet." But since the leadership of the Petrograd Soviet disagreed with the formation of a provisional revolutionary government and Bolshevik strength was not yet pronounced, Shliapnikov and his colleagues of the Russian Bureau concluded that it was still premature to adopt even their own slogan. For the time being it was necessary for the Bolsheviks to concentrate on organizational work and agitation among the masses and achieve a majority in the Soviet. Moreover, according to Tarasov-Rodionov, Shliapnikov believed that the gravest danger for the revolution still

46. Ibid., 1: 219; D. O. Zaslavskii and V. A. Kantorovoch, *Khronika fevral'skoi revoliutsii*, p. 45.

47. *Pervyi legal'nyi PK bol'shevikov 1917 g.*, p. 5; Shliapnikov, *Semnadtsatyi god* 1: 236.

48. *Pervyi legal'nyi PK*, pp. 11-12; Shliapnikov, *Semnadtsatyi god* 1: 236.

49. Shliapnikov, *Semnadtsatyi god* 1: 236-37.

lay in the possibility of the restoration of tsarism and that from the objective point of view the Duma and the Provisional Government were helping the workers to destroy tsarist power.[50]

The Petersburg Committee, which came out of underground existence, was in a confused state. At first, it was dominated by those party activists who had not worked in the party underground, and followed Shliapnikov's policy. Alarmed by the dominance of intellectuals, the former underground activists had to contact and recruit the underground revolutionaries in the works of the Petersburg Committee. K. I. Shutko served as liaison between the Russian Bureau and the Petersburg Committee. Before the general session of the Soviet on March 2, Shliapnikov, Molotov, Zalutskii, and Shutko discussed what strategy they should take to oppose the Executive Committee's transfer of power to the Provisional Government. They decided to attack such a capitulation and to stand for the eventual establishment of a provisional revolutionary government, but refused to adopt the slogan of the Vyborg District Committee.[51]

The challenge to the position advocated by the center of the Executive Committee came not only from the Left but also from the Right, which advocated formation of a coalition government consisting of the members of the Duma Committee and the Soviet Executive Committee. According to Rafes, the Organization Committee of the Menshevik party met on the night of March 1 and 2 and decided to push forward the policy of "coalition" against the decision of the Executive Committee. Prior to the general session of the Soviet on March 2, the Mensheviks were to have a caucus to plan their strategy.[52] The *Izvestiia* of the Soviet printed an article on March 2 written by a right-wing Menshevik, Bazarov. In this article Bazarov stressed that "the energy and solidarity of the revolutionary democracy have already compelled the bourgeoisie to make a series of steps beyond the limits that the ruling class would not otherwise have crossed." Recognizing that the Duma Committee had taken revolutionary measures against the old regime, Bazarov went on, "Lest we should turn this revolutionary path into a counterrevolution, democracy must participate in the further reconstruction of the country with unabated energy and must join the composition of the Provisional Government."[53] Also the conference of the Petrograd Socialist Revolutionaries held on the morning of March 2 approved Kerenskii's participation

50. *Pervyi legal'nyi PK*, pp. 3-4; Tarasov-Rodionov, *February 1917*, p. 214.
51. Shliapnikov, *Semnadtsatyi god* 1: 228.
52. M. G. Rafes, "Moi vospominaniia," *Byloe* 19 (1922): 195.
53. *Izvestiia*, March 2, 1917.

in the Provisional Government and condemned the leaflet written by Iurenev and Aleksandrovich.[54]

The slogans of both the Right and the Left, "coalition government" and "Soviet government," which originated from totally different ideological contexts, advocated participation of the Soviet leaders in the new government directly or indirectly. The center feared that in the confused state of most of the Soviet deputies on ideological matters, these slogans might lead to the demand for the establishment of a Soviet government. The primary aim of the leading group of the Executive Committee was therefore to prevent the demand for a Soviet power from gaining wide support among the rank-and-file Soviet deputies. Thus, pointing out the growing danger from the Left, Sukhanov persuaded Ehrlich, the most staunch advocate of a coalition government, not to oppose the transfer of power to the Provisional Government. Ehrlich promised that he would not intervene in the policy of the Executive Committee.[55] At the same time, Sukhanov instructed Steklov, who was to introduce the Executive Committee's resolution and to explain the results of the negotiations with the Duma Committee at the general session, to make his report as full and lengthy as possible to cut the time for discussion to a minimum.

The general session of the Petrograd Soviet on March 2 began with Steklov's long speech. He explained the conditions for transfer of power adopted by the Executive Committee and how the Duma Committee reacted to each point of these conditions. The Duma Committee did not object to the demands for amnesty, political freedom, people's militia, removal of religious, class, and national restrictions, and nonremoval of the Petrograd garrison troops, but Steklov explained that the Duma Committee revised the demand for the soldiers' right for self-government, and opposed the introduction of the republican form of government. He then urged the deputies to ratify these conditions and expounded for the first time the famous formula for the Soviet's conditional support of the Provisional Government in so far as it carried out democratic reforms.[56] According to this plan, the Petrograd Soviet was not to seek power by itself, but rather to stand behind and watch every activity of the Provisional

54. *Delo naroda*, March 15, 1917, quoted in Iu. S. Tokarev, *Petrogradskii sovet rabochikh i soldatskikh deputatov v marte-aprele, 1917 g.*, p. 96; Tarasov-Rodionov, *February 1917*, p. 215.

55. Sukhanov, *Zapiski o revoliutsii* 1: 308, 310.

56. See chap. 21, also *Izvestiia*, March 3, 1917, and Zaslavskii and Kantorovich, *Khronika fevral'skoi revoliutsii*, p. 43.

Government so that the latter would not go astray from the path that the Petrograd had mapped out for it. This policy discredited rather than augmented the authority of the Provisional Government; it alienated the masses from the government rather than uniting them around it. Miliukov noted that "the embryo of future difficulties and complications was already reflected in this initial formulation of the mutual relations between the government and the highest organization of the revolutionary democracy."[57]

When Steklov's long-winded speech was finally finished, the Executive Committee's plan was disrupted from a completely unexpected direction. Kerenskii stood up, rushed to the platform, and asked for the floor. Despite Chkheidze's hesitation, this move was welcomed by the audience. Pale, trembling, in a mystical half-whisper, Kerenskii began his speech. "Comrades! Do you trust me?" Enthusiastic exclamations roared in the assembly hall: "We do, we do!" Kerenskii went on to say: "At the present moment the Provisional Government has been formed, in which I was appointed to the post of minister of justice. Comrades! I had to give an answer in five minutes and therefore I did not have any possibility of receiving your consent before my decision was made regarding the participation in the Provisional Government. In my hands the representatives of the old regime were detained and I am determined not to let them out of my hands."[58] Actually he had been offered the post by Miliukov on March 1 and it was not until the morning of March 2 that he accepted. He continued: "Immediately after I became the minister of justice, I ordered the liberation of all political prisoners." This order had been given by V. Maklakov, the Duma Committee's commissar to the Ministry of Justice, before Kerenskii's appointment. Kerenskii breathing heavily, came to the crucial point: "Comrades! Since I took upon myself the duties of minister of justice before being formally authorized by you, I resign from the duties of the vice-chairman of the Soviet. But I am ready to accept that title from you again if you acknowledge the necessity of it." The crowd enthusiastically responded: "We do, we do!" Without a formal vote and only by the stormy applause, Kerenskii obtained the consent of the Soviet deputies for his participation in the Provisional Government. Once his goal was accomplished, the rest of his speech was an emotional eulogy of the people and the revolution. At one point of his speech, he shouted, leaning forward with a helpless gesture, waving his arms

57. Miliukov, *Istoriia vtoroi russkoi revoliutsii* 1: 49.

58. *Izvestiia revoliutsionnoi nedeli*, March 3, 1917; *Izvestiia*, March 3, 1917; Tarasov-Rodionov, *February 1917*, pp. 187-88.

convulsively in the air: "I cannot live without the people, and if you doubt it, at this moment, kill me!" This rather effusive sentimentalism, typical of Kerenskii's oratorical style, appealed to the temper of the time. As soon as he finished his speech, he left the hall in a hurry without giving his opponents a chance to counteract his action. His colleagues of the Executive Committee, speechless, marveled at Kerenskii's audacity in manipulating the emotions of the masses with half-truths but did not dare contradict him for fear that such an action might provoke a dangerous discussion on the problem of power. Thus Kerenskii completed his coup d'état.

After Kerenskii's performance, the general session moved to the discussion on the problem of power. As Sukhanov expected, the Bolsheviks attacked the Executive Committee's proposal. Zalutskii spoke first against the formation of the Provisional Government. He accused the bourgeoisie of making a deal with tsarism. "Crucial questions were skirted. A revolutionary provisional government has not been formed in the name of the people. What really happened? We marched in the streets, spilled blood, but what do we get today? A tsarist counterrevolution against the people." He bitterly complained that none of the basic questions such as the land question, the eight-hour working day, and the question of peace had been solved. Molotov declared: "The Provisional Government is not revolutionary. Guchkov, factory owners, Rodzianko, and Konovalov would make a mockery out of the people. Instead of land they will throw rocks at the peasants." Shutko proposed the formation of the Provisional Revolutionary Government "from the composition of the Soviet." Shliapnikov supported Shutko's proposal, saying that the introduction of a democratic republic, eight-hour working day, and the democratic election of officers by the soldiers would be included in the program of such a government.[59] Iurenev supported the Bolshevik position and opposed the formation of the Provisional Government.

Although most of the leaders of the Right refrained from attacking the Executive Committee's proposal, some still advocated the formation of a coalition government. Kantorovich, a Menshevik, argued that the success of the revolution would depend on whether it could bring all segments of the population into it. For this purpose, the formation of a coalition government was a necessary prerequisite. Zaslavskii, accusing the opponents of the coalition government of being "a child with a burn who dreads fire," argued that since other

59. Tokarev, *Petrogradskii sovet rabochikh i soldatskikh deputatov*, p. 97. Tokarev uses the hitherto unused minutes of the general session on March 2, which he discovered at LGAORSS.

classes of society had already joined the workers and the soldiers, cooperation would be possible also at the governmental level. In fact, coalition would be the only guarantee to save the revolution from its isolation from the people. Other Menshevik deputies stated that without sending the Soviet's representatives to the Provisional Government, it would be impossible to control the activities of the Provisional Government.[60]

The Menshevik initiative group did not like the formation of the Provisional Government, which they considered "a sad fact," and whose members were "clearly servants of reaction." But they did not see any alternative but to accept the conditions presented by the Executive Committee. In A. E. Diubua's words, "If we were to transform the Soviet of Workers' Deputies into a Provisional Revolutionary Government, there will be a dual power and a civil war. Comrades, it is not clear if that part of the people, who will not support [the proletariat], will support the Provisional Revolutionary Government of the workers and the soldiers. They are prepared to act against the tsarist government and to overthrow the tsarist government, but are they willing to go further?"[61] To insure that the Provisional Government should faithfully carry out the democratic program, deputy Smirnov proposed the creation of a watchdog committee to monitor the activities of the Provisional Government. Deputy Anin, who represented the Lithuanian organization, and Deputy Grigoriev proposed to include a demand for the nationality minorities' rights for self-determination and cultural autonomy.

After the discussion the motion of the Executive Committee was presented:

The Soviet of Workers' Deputies, taking into account the program of reforms announced in the Provisional Government's proclamation to the populace, and recognizing that the realization of these reforms can be achieved only by way of the constant pressure of the working class [on the Provisional Government], organizes propaganda and agitation among the soldiers for this purpose. The Provisional Government at the same time as it carries out desirable reforms [must in the future] fulfill the demand of the working class for [the introduction] of a democratic republic. The [Soviet] expresses regrets that [the government] does not [wish] to introduce it immediately, and appeals [to the workers and the soldiers] to [struggle] indefatigably for the democratic republic as well as for the other [demands. The Soviet] approves the appeal to the population [concerning] the cessation of disorders and entrusts its [representatives to insure] the inclusion of the government's Manifesto in the text assuring that the government would not make the military situation an excuse to postpone the reforms. The

60. Ibid., p. 98.
61. Ibid.

Soviet of Workers' and Soldiers' Deputies, recognizing the Provisional Government [as legal power], proposes for the preservation of the interests [of democracy] to create a committee, which will serve the function of observing [the government].[62]

As a counterproposal, the Bolsheviks offered the following resolution: "In view of the fact that the Provisional Government is organized by antipeople circles and landlords of Guchkov's type, whom the revolutionary workers and soldiers cannot trust, we protest against every attempt at agreement [with them]. We express no confidence in Kerenskii. Also we recognize that only the Provisional Revolutionary Government can fulfill the popular demands."[63]

The Executive Committee' resolution indicated that to gain the approval of the deputies it had to retreat further from its original full-fledged support of the Provisional Government to a conditional support. The main tone of the resolution was no longer support of the Provisional Government, but rather suspicion of the intention and the ability of the Provisional Government to carry out reforms. On the other hand, the Bolsheviks' resolution mentioned nothing about the position of the Soviet in relation to the proposed Provisional Revolutionary Government. Zaslavskii and Kantorovich also noted that the Bolsheviks did not advocate the seizure of power by the Soviet, thereby failing to provide an alternative to the Executive Committee's policy. The result of the vote was overwhelming victory for the Executive Committee. Of approximately four hundred deputies present at the general session, of whom there were at least forty Bolsheviks, only fourteen voted for the Bolshevik resolution.[64]

The crushing defeat brought the Bolsheviks into further disarray. While the Russian Bureau continued to advocate the establishment of a provisional revolutionary government from the composition of the Soviet, it did not consider it possible to achieve immediately.[65] On the other hand, the Petersburg Committee moved in a more conservative direction and adopted a resolution that stated that the Petersburg Committee would not obstruct the activities of the Provisional Government "in so far as its actions correspond to the interests of the proletariat and the wide masses of democratic people." Although

62. Ibid., p. 100.
63. Ibid., pp. 96-97.
64. Zaslavskii and Kantorovich, *Khronika fevral'skoi revoliutsii*, p. 45; Tokarev, *Petrogradskii sovet rabochikh i soldatskikh deputatov*, p. 98; Shliapnikov, *Semnadtsatyi god* 1: 240-41. According to Zaslavskii and Kantorovich, the resolution obtained about fifteen votes; according to Shliapnikov, nineteen votes. Tokarev's figure, fourteen, which is based on the minutes, seems to be most accurate.
65. Shliapnikov, *Semnadtsatyi god* 1: 254.

frustrated, the Vyborg District Bolsheviks continued to advocate their radical position. This confusion was to last until Lenin's return in April.[66]

After the Soviet session Sukhanov, Steklov, and Chkheidze met again with Miliukov to reach final agreement on the content of the proclamation of the Provisional Government that was to be printed in the newspapers the next day. Miliukov again demanded the elimination of the demand for the immediate introduction of a democratic republic. Sukhanov agreed to withdraw this demand. According to Sukhanov, "The question of the 'third point' was resolved in the following way: we agreed not to include [this point] in the government declaration as an official obligation. . . . We agreed to leave the question open and to allow the government, or more correctly, its individual elements, to work for the Romanov monarchy. But we categorically declared that the Soviet would be relentlessly engaged in the broad struggle for the democratic republic on its side."[67]

With the concession of the Executive Committee on the question of the future form of government, full agreement was reached between the new government and the Soviet Executive Committee. The draft of the proclamation of the government had been already written by Miliukov on the previous night. It declared that the Provisional Government would not try to find an excuse in wartime conditions for delaying the internal reforms it had agreed to carry out through the negotiations with the Soviet, and listed the contents of the reforms. After the final agreement, Miliukov collected the signatures from the members of the Provisional Government. The conservative member, Godnev, refused to sign it, but his opposition mattered little. As the general session of the Soviet stipulated, the proclamation also obtained Rodzianko's signature. On March 3, the Soviet newspaper, *Izvestiia,* and the *Izvestiia revoliutsionnoi nedeli* printed the Provisional Government's proclamation.[68]

However, when the proclamation was printed in *Izvestiia,* the reader also saw in the adjacent column the following announcement:

Comrades and citizens!

The new government, which was created from socially moderate elements of society, today has announced all the reforms it pledges to carry out, partly in the process of the struggle with the old regime, partly upon the conclusion of this struggle. These reforms include some which should be welcomed by wide

66. *Pervyi legal'nyi PK,* p. 11; David Longley, "The Divisions in the Bolshevik Party in March 1917," *Soviet Studies* 24, no. 1 (1972): 61-76.

67. Sukhanov, *Zapiski o revoliutsii* 1: 340.

68. *Izvestiia,* March 3, 1917; *Izvestiia revoliutsionnoi nedeli,* March 3, 1917.

democratic circles: political amnesty, the obligation to make preparations for the Constituent Assembly, the realization of civil freedoms, and the abolition of nationality restrictions. And we believe that, in so far as the emerging government acts in the direction of realizing these obligations and of struggling resolutely against the old regime, the democracy must lend its support.[69]

That was the formulation of the conditional support of the Provisional Government. It nullified the results obtained by the Provisional Government, which had expected the Soviet Executive Committee to persuade the insurgents to pledge their support to the Provisional Government. Despite Miliukov's bold pronouncement that the Provisional Government was a product of the revolution, in the eyes of the insurgents it remained illegitimate.

69. *Izvestiia*, March 3, 1917; *Izvestiia revoliutsionnoi nedeli*, March 3, 1917.

28

THE ABDICATION
OF GRAND DUKE
MIKHAIL ALEKSANDROVICH

 The abdication of Nicholas II in favor of Aleksei under Grand Duke Mikhail Aleksandrovich's regency was the original intent of the Duma Committee and the Provisional Government. However, two significant events took place after the departure of Guchkov and Shul'gin to Pskov that impaired the original plan. The first was the angry reaction of the masses to Miliukov's revelation that the monarchy was being preserved. Succumbing to their opposition, the Provitional Government came to the conclusion that they should do without the monarchy.

The second incident was the unexpected abdication by Nicholas II for Aleksei as well as for himself in favor of Mikhail. This news was first brought by Guchkov and Shul'gin early on the morning of March 3. They telegraphed Rodzianko from Pskov before their departure: "The emperor has agreed to abdicate the throne in favor of Grand Duke Mikhail Aleksandrovich, who is obligated to swear allegiance to the constitution. Prince L'vov was charged with the formation of a new government. At the same time, Grand Duke Nikolai Nikolaevich was appointed supreme commander in chief. The manifesto will follow immediately. Inform Pskov immediately of the situation in Petrograd."[1]

These new developments again changed the pattern of liberal political alliances. Those who had sought and won Nicholas's abdication,

1. Guchkov and Shul'gin to chief of staff, "Fevral'skaia revoliutsiia 1917 goda: Dokumenty Stavki verkhovnogo glavnokomanduiushchego i shtaba glavnokomanduiushchego armiiami severnogo fronta," *Krasnyi arkhiv* 21, no. 3 (1927): 15-16.

rather than accepting Rodzianko's limited constitutional reform, were an alliance of the two diverse points of view. The first was represented by Miliukov, who considered it crucial to obtain legitimacy of the Provisional Government from the old regime and to secure continuity of the legal and institutional framework between the new and the old regimes, while he was compelled to recognize the revolution as an established fact. Kerenskii and Nekrasov headed the second group, which might have been joined by Tereshchenko, Konovalov, and possibly Prince L'vov. Although there is no evidence to prove their "conspiracy," it appears that at least those masonic members who joined the Provisional Government shared the idea of republicanism. They welcomed the revolution and sought legitimacy for the Provisional Government in the revolution itself, but in the political context of March 1, they were compelled to accept retention of the monarchical system in the form of Nicholas's abdication and Mikhail's regency.

The new developments on March 2 contributed to the split of the alliance that had stood for abdication on the previous day. They pushed the second group further to the Left. They openly advocated the abolition of the monarchical system by taking advantage of Nicholas's deviation from the original plan as an excuse to justify their change of policy. But to Miliukov, the preservation of the monarchical system was necessary for the survival of the Provisional Government. He feared that the possibility of the development of a constitutional monarchy would not be as easy under the tsardom of Mikhail as under that of a young boy, Aleksei, but he was prepared to defend the monarchy even under Mikhail.[2] It was Rodzianko, however, who tipped the balance in this split. March 1 had been a humiliating day for Rodzianko: his policy had been vetoed by the majority of the Duma Committee members, and his name had been bounced off the list of the Provisional Government. But Rodzianko had not relinquished his political ambition nor hopes for the restoration of his influence. To make the best of a bad situation, therefore, he had sanctioned the formation of the Provisional Government in the name of the Duma Committee, thereby attempting to maintain a fiction that the Duma Committee was the parent body of the Provisional Government.[3] When the insurgents protested against the retention of the monarchical system, Rodzianko was frightened by the extent of the popular resentment to the monarchy, but at the same time, he saw in the new development an opportunity to undermine the prestige of his rival, Miliukov. Thus,

2. P. N. Miliukov, *Istoriia vtoroi russkoi revoliutsii* 1: 23.
3. Rodzianko to Alekseev, no. 158, "Fevral'skaia revoliutsiia 1917 goda," p. 9.

Rodzianko made a 180-degree turnaround and supported Kerenskii and Nekrasov. From Kerenskii's and Nekrasov's point of view, Rodzianko's participation in their rank was welcome, since they had to pursue their goals in such a way that the segments of society that might support the monarchy, particularly the military leaders, should be convinced of the necessity of abolishing the monarchical system. Rodzianko was a suitable candidate for the negotiator with the military.

As soon as the Duma Committee and the Provisional Government received the telegram from Guchkov and Shul'gin, Rodzianko rushed to the Hughes apparatus in the War Ministry and called Alekseev at the Stavka. It was six o'clock on the morning of March 3. Rodzianko demanded that in view of the new development in the capital Alekseev should not circulate the manifesto of Nicholas's abdication until further instructions from Rodzianko. Irritated with Rodzianko's commanding tone, Alekseev answered that the Stavka had already sent the manifesto to the commanders in chief of all fronts and that it was not only undesirable but also impossible to halt its circulation. He promised to send a supplementary explanation, but expressed fear that despite his efforts the contents of the manifesto would become known sooner or later. He added: "Apparently, A. I. Guchkov telegraphed to you the essence [of the manifesto] from Pskov. I would prefer to have been oriented by you earlier as to what should have been detained." What Rodzianko said next was a total shock to Alekseev. Rodzianko replied that what had been agreed before Guchkov and Shul'gin's departure was the accession to the throne by Aleksei under Mikhail's regency. But this solution was not adopted, and therefore it was necessary to wait for the decision of the Constituent Assembly. During the interim "the Supreme Committee and the Council of Ministers" were to assume power. The use, or rather the misuse of the terms, "Supreme Committee" for the "Provisional Committee of the State Duma," and "Council of Ministers" for the "Provisional Government," was not accidental. The "Supreme Committee" sounded like an organ that could have been entrusted by the Duma to function as supreme power, and the "Council of Ministers" suggested continuity from the old regime. Rodzianko continued that "the promulgation of the manifesto should be prevented, because the proposed combination [of the abdication of Nicholas and Aleksei in favor of Mikhail] may lead to civil war, and because the candidacy of Mikhail Aleksandrovich for emperor is acceptable to no one."[4]

What was being suggested by Rodzianko was the abolition of

4. Rodzianko-Alekseev conversation, ibid., p. 26.

the monarchical system, at least until the Constituent Assembly decided to restore it. But this point was not clearly understood by Alekseev. Nonetheless, Alekseev's reply was no less threatening. He stated that Rodzianko's information was far from pleasing. "The uncertainty [of the dynastic question] and the Constituent Assembly are two dangerous toys for the active army." He further declared that the Petrograd Garrison had become "harmful for the fatherland, useless for the army, and dangerous for all." Although Alekseev assured Rodzianko that as a soldier all his thoughts were concentrated on the struggle with the external enemy, the threat of a military intervention was obviously implied.[5]

If such a plan were contemplated, it was necessary to destroy it. For this purpose, Rodzianko talked to Ruzskii two hours later through the Hughes telegraphic apparatus. Prince L'vov also stood by Rodzianko at the end of the Hughes apparatus, but it was only Rodzianko who spoke. Rodzianko began with the request to withhold the manifesto of Nicholas's abdication, since "we succeeded in confining the revolutionary movement within more or less reasonable limits, but the situation has not returned to normal and a civil war is still possible."[6] Ruzskii promised that he would do his best, but complained about the Duma Committee's delegates' lack of familiarity with the situation. Rodzianko then explained the situation in Petrograd as follows: Another soldiers' uprising had broken out with a destructive force such as he had never seen before. They were no longer soldiers, but *muzhiks*—simple, ignorant peasants—who found a good opportunity to declare *muzhiks'* demands. The crowds were shouting only: "Land and liberty!" "Down with the dynasty!" "Down with the Romanovs!" "Down with the officers!" Officers were massacred in many army units, and anarchy reached its climax. To prevent further development of anarchy, "we had to come to an agreement with the deputies of the workers," and promise the convocation of a constituent assembly to enable the people to express their opinion about the form of government. "Only then did Petrograd take a long breath and the night passed relatively peacefully. During the night order was gradually being restored in the army. However, the proclamation of Grand Duke Mikhail Aleksandrovich as emperor will pour oil onto the fire and touch off a merciless destruction of everything that can be destroyed. Power is slipping out of our hands and no one could possibly allay the popular unrest." Rodzianko assured Ruzskii that the possibility of return to monarchy was not lost completely, since the

5. Ibid., p. 27.
6. Ruzskii-Rodzianko conversation, ibid., pp. 27-28.

people would be able to voice their opinion in its favor in the Constituent Assembly. But in the meantime, until the end of the war, the "Supreme Soviet" and the Provisional Government should continue to rule. When Ruzskii asked what was meant by "Supreme Soviet," Rodzianko immediately hastened to correct the mistake and said that he meant the State Duma. Rodzianko then expressed his hope that "under these conditions [of the proposed solution] peace will rapidly be restored and a decisive victory will be secured, since undoubtedly patriotic sentiments will rise and everybody will work hard at an intensified tempo."[7]

It is true that popular resentment of Miliukov's speech was expressed in a number of incidents of illegal searches, arrests, and reprisals on officers by soldiers. But it would be an obvious exaggeration to call these incidents "another soldiers' uprising" and "a large-scale massacre." Rodzianko was curiously silent about another factor that led to the soldiers' violence against the officers—Order No. 1. Rodzianko must have known the existence of Order No. 1 by then, but he did not tell the military leaders of the document that was to have a far-reaching effect on the integrity of the military, lest the high command should take action against the revolution. Rodzianko clearly wished to prevent the manifesto of Nicholas's abdication from being made public before Mikhail was compelled to abdicate also. Unlike the previous conversation that Rodzianko had conducted with Ruzskii in his personal capacity, this conversation appears to have had the knowledge of the supporters of Mikhail's abdication. Prince L'vov's presence at the telegraphic apparatus, although he had nothing whatever to say to Ruzskii, is an indirect piece of evidence to substantiate this. Later on the same day, Alekseev stated that Rodzianko was controlled by the left-wing parties, although it is not clear on what basis he made this judgment.[8]

In the meantime, the Naval Staff at the Stavka contacted at Alekseev's instructions the Naval Staff in Petrograd through another Hughes apparatus to verify Rodzianko's information. According to the informant, Altfater, in Petrograd, "the situation is rather quiet, and everything is gradually returning to normal." Goncharov at the Stavka asked about the rumor that a slaughter of officers had taken place on the previous day. Altfater answered: "It is all sheer nonsense." Altfater further ascertained that the authority of the Duma Committee was increasing rather than diminishing.[9] This information was immediately brought to Alekseev.

7. Ibid., p. 28.
8. Alekseev to Ruzskii, Evert, Brusilov, Sakharov, no. 1918, ibid., p. 23.
9. Ibid., p. 32.

Alekseev had suspected before that Rodzianko had not been altogether candid, but because of the lack of contradictory information, he had accepted his recommendation on Nicholas's abdication and decided to withdraw General Ivanov's troops. Also it was on Rodzianko's recommendation that Alekseev had agreed to appoint General Kornilov against General Brusilov's opposition to replace General Ivanov, thereby making it impossible to reverse the decision to discontinue military intervention. Although he was skeptical about Rodzianko's further demand to withhold the manifesto of Nicholas's abdiction, he nonetheless complied by ordering all commanders not to make it public.[10] But the information brought by the Naval Staff for the first time made him realize clearly that Rodzianko had been manipulating the information all along and that Alekseev and the military had been duped. Angered by Rodzianko's duplicity and terrified that he might have irretrievably led the military into the muddle, he took immediate action. At 1:30 P.M. on March 3 he dispatched telegrams to the commanders in chief at all fronts. In this telegram Alekseev at first outlined the conversation he had had with Rodzianko and the conversation between Rodzianko and Ruzskii, the copy of which had just been sent to him. After introducing Rodzianko's demand to delay circulation of the manifesto of Nicholas's abdication among the army units, Alekseev pointed out that the manifesto had already been widely distributed and insisted that such an important document intended for the public should not be kept secret. Indeed, the alleged "concealment" of the abdication manifesto—the action Admiral Nepenin did not desire—had led to the sailors' uprising against the officers in the Baltic Fleet.[11]

Alekseev then expressed his opinion about Rodzianko's information. First, Alekseev learned that there was no unity within the Duma nor within the Duma Committee itself and that the Soviet was acquiring strong influence. Second, "the left-wing parties and the workers' deputies are exerting tremendous pressure on Rodzianko and in the information supplied by Rodzianko there is neither frankness nor sincerity." Third, the political solution proposed by Rodzianko emanated from the aims of the left-wing parties, whose prisoner Rodzianko had become. Fourth, the troops of the Petrograd Garrison had finally fallen completely under the influence of the propaganda of the workers' deputies and had become "harmful and dangerous to all, including

10. Alekseev to commanders, no. 1913, ibid., p. 19.
11. Ibid., pp. 22-23; for the insurrection of the sailors in the Baltic Fleet at Helsingfors, see David Longley, "The February Revolution in the Baltic Fleet at Helsingfors: *Vosstanie* or *Bunt?" Canadian Slavonic Papers* 20, no. 1 (1978): 1-22.

the moderate elements of the Provisional Committee." Thus characterizing Rodzianko's information, Alekseev concluded that "the outlined situation constituted a danger more serious than any other for the active army," since he expected that "uncertainty, vacillation, and change of the manifesto" would have staggering effects and deprive the army of "the fighting capacity," which in turn would result in "the hopeless misery of Russia, territorial loss, and the takeover by the extreme Left elements."[12] He then made the following recommendation:

Since I received the order from His Majesty the emperor to consult with Grand Duke Nikolai Nikolaevich at serious moments by urgent telegrams, I report all this to him, and ask for his instructions, adding: first, it is urgent to communicate to the chairman of the Duma the essence of my present conclusions and demand the realization of the manifesto in the name of salvation of the homeland and of the active army; second, to restore unity in all cases and all circumstances [it is necessary] to convene a meeting of the commanders at Mogilev. If the supreme commander [now Nikolai Nikolaevich] is willing to attend this meeting, the date will be determined by his Majesty; if the grand duke considers it impossible to attend personally, then it will be held on March 8 or 9.[13]

His reference to "uncertainty, vacillation, and change of the manifesto" indicates that Alekseev had not realized that the majority of the Duma Committee and the Provisional Government had already decided to do away with the monarchical system itself by forcing Mikhail's abdication. Nevertheless, this telegram made it clear that Alekseev wished the military to stand behind his decision to present an ultimatum to Rodzianko that the military would not tolerate any concessions beyond Nicholas's abdication. The proposal for a conference of commanders in chief clearly indicated his intention to revive the plan of military intervention against Petrograd. Finally to confirm his analysis, Alekseev repeated the information he had obtained from the Naval Staff, and stated: "Consequently, the basic motives of Rodzianko cannot be trusted and must be directed to compel the representatives of the active army to accept the decision of the extreme elements as an established and inevitable fact." Although in his recommendation to Nicholas to abdicate, Alekseev insisted upon the necessity of the army's staying out of internal politics, he now advocated that the military should actively intervene in the course of events. He urged the commanders in chief to consult the army commanders and to let them know of both the situation and the proposed conference.[14]

12. Alekseev to Ruzskii, Evert, Brusilov, Sakharov, no. 1918, "Fevral'skaia revoliutsiia 1917 goda," p. 23.
13. Ibid.
14. Ibid., pp. 23-24.

However, the commanders in chief, with the exception of Sakharov, reacted to Alekseev's proposal coldly. Brusilov considered it unwise for commanders in chief to abandon their posts under the present circumstances. He did not mention specifically anything about Rodzianko's attitude toward the monarchical system, but merely declared that "the problem is extremely difficult to solve, though obviously extremely necessary to discuss."[15] While Brusilov avoided the issue on grounds of technicality, Ruzskii completely opposed Alekseev's proposal to convene a military conference for military action against the Provisional Government. Ruzskii also considered it necessary to make the manifesto of Nicholas's abdication public, but disagreed with Alekseev on all other points. In Ruzskii's opinion, the military should come to terms with the Provisional Government. Since the military was the only authoritative power in places other than Petrograd, the commanders in chief should remain at their posts. As for notifying subordinates of the situation, Ruzskii did not see any merit in consulting with them.[16] Thus, the distinct possibility of the end of the monarchy and Rodzianko's duplicity, which Ruzskii might have been aware of long before Alekseev, did not deter Ruzskii from the conclusion he had drawn when he learned of the formation of the Duma Committee—the necessity of cooperating with the Duma Committee and the Provisional Government.

Sakharov was the only commander who agreed with Alekseev's proposal to convene a military conference, but even Sakharov did not express his opinion about the wisdom of military intervention and the danger of making further concessions to the liberals.[17] Evert considered it necessary for the military to act decisively and immediately. In his opinion, both the absence of the official announcement and the convocation of a constituent assembly would be dangerous. The only alternative would be to change the form of government by imperial decree and to have this change accepted by the Duma and the Provisional Government. In any case the proposed conference on March 8 or 9 would be too late.[18] If Alekseev did not quite understand Rodzianko's implied message that the monarchical system would be abolished, he at least felt the danger in any deviation from Nicholas's abdication manifesto. With the possible exception of Ruzskii, who was aware of the implication of Rodzianko's policy, none of the commanders appears to have grasped the danger to the monarchical system.

15. Brusilov to Alekseev, no. 782, ibid., p. 24.
16. Ruzskii to Alekseev, no. 1254/B, ibid., p. 24.
17. Sakharov to Alekseev, no. 03411, ibid., p. 25.
18. Evert to Alekseev, no. 6245, ibid., pp. 43-44.

But the most decisive blow to Alekseev's proposal came from Grand Duke Nikolai Nikolaevich. The grand duke answered Alekseev that the convocation of a constitutent assembly would be unacceptable and that the transfer of power to Mikhail Aleksandrovich rather than the tsarevich would lead to bloodshed. But he further stated that he could not attend the meeting suggested by Alekseev since he would need several days for orientation as the new supreme commander with the new government.[19] From the grand duke's point of view, to accept Alekseev's invitation for a military conference and military intervention against the Provisional Government would mean to risk the new post. Since in Alekseev's plans for military action against the Provisional Government Nikolai Nikolaevich was to play a central part, the grand duke's refusal to attend the military conference destroyed Alekseev's plan. It would be difficult to try to save the Romanovs when the most important member of the Romanovs opposed the attempt.

Finally Brusilov's direct conversation with Alekseev dealt the coup de grâce to Alekseev's attempt to intervene. Brusilov argued that at a time when there was an omnipresent danger from the Left, it was necessary for the military to support the Provisional Government and not to interfere in politics while the latter was trying its best to alleviate its danger.[20] Although Alekseev declared that he would no longer play into the hands of Rodzianko, he nonetheless promised to obey any instructions of the new supreme commander. Thus, Alekseev's plans for military suppression were finally frustrated by other military leaders. It is interesting to point out that as early as March 2 the two Petrograd newspapers had printed the allegiance pledged by Ruzskii, Brusilov, and Nikolai Nikolaevich to the Duma Committee.[21] Although we lack definitive evidence on this, we can presume that after Rodzianko discovered Alekseev's intention, he and those colleagues who pursued Mikhail's abdication must have exerted pressure on the commanders. Rodzianko's conversation with Ruzskii was a part of their efforts to achieve this purpose. Later Alekseev bitterly complained to Guchkov that the Duma Committee, violating the commanding hierarchy, had entered negotiations with other military personnel without his knowledge.[22] Also contributing to the demise of Alekseev's policy was the news that the sailors' up-

19. Nikolai Nikolaevich to Alekseev, no. 3318, ibid., p. 24.

20. Alekseev-Brusilov conversation, ibid., p. 25.

21. *Izvestiia*, March 3, 1917; *Izvestiia revoliutsionnoi nedeli*, March 2, 1917.

22. Alekseev-Guchkov conversation, "Fevral'skaia revoliutsiia 1917 goda," p. 37.

rising had spread to the entire Baltic Fleet. Nepenin declared that the Baltic Fleet as a fighting unit "does not exist."[23] The military was thus prepared to accept the latest news—the abolition of the monarchical system—with resignation and without protest.

On March 3 the members of the Duma Committee and the Provisional Government discussed the problem of the monarchy. The majority favored the abdication of Grand Duke Mikhail. The staunchest advocate of abdication was Kerenskii, but Rodzianko also supported it. It seemed to the chairman of the Duma "that it was quite obvious to us that the grand duke would not have reigned more than a few hours and that terrible bloodshed, marking the beginning of a general civil war, would have immediately started within the walls of the capital."[24]

Ironically, it was Miliukov, Nicholas's personal enemy, who fought a lone fight to preserve the monarchy. Miliukov realized that for the consolidation of the new order a strong power would be needed, and that a strong power was, under the circumstances, guaranteed only when it was based on a symbol that could attract the support of the masses. The monarchy was such a symbol. "The Provisional Government alone without the fulcrum of this symbol could not survive until a constituent assembly. It will turn out to be a fragile boat that will sink in the ocean of mass disturbances."[25] While other members of the Duma Committee and the Provisional Government succumbed to the radicalism of the Petrograd masses, Miliukov alone could see beyond the insurgents of Petrograd and comprehend the cold reality of the problem of power. Only Miliukov understood that support for the Provisional Government would not come from the revolutionized Petrograd masses, but from the vast majority of the Russian people who had remained neutral to the revolution in Petrograd. Miliukov suggested that the Provisional Government should leave Petrograd and establish its headquarters in Moscow, where he assumed the situation was more calm. Despite the persuasive efforts of his colleagues, Miliukov stood firm and stubbornly refused to give in. The discussion was deadlocked, and they decided to leave the decision to the grand duke himself.

23. Nepenin to Rusin, no. 285/op, ibid., p. 35; Nepenin to Rusin, no. 286/op, ibid., p. 36. Also see David Longley, "The February Revolution in the Baltic Fleet," pp. 1-22; Norman E. Saul, *Sailors in Revolt: The Russian Baltic Fleet in 1917*, pp. 59-80.

24. M. V. Rodzianko, "Gosudarstvennaia duma i fevral'skaia 1917 goda revolutsiia," *Arkhiv russkoi revoliutsii* 4 (1922): 62.

25. P. N. Miliukov, *Vospominaniia, 1859-1917* 2: 316.

After the joint meeting of the Duma Committee and the Provisional Government Kerenskii telephoned Grand Duke Mikhail Aleksandrovich at 5:55 on the morning of March 3 and requested that he be good enough to receive the representatives of the Duma Committee and the Provisional Government. The grand duke had been in Petrograd since February 27, since the revolution had made it impossible for him to return to his home in Gatchina by train. On the night of February 27 he had stayed in the Winter Palace, but left the next day when, at the Military Commission's order, all the guards in the Winter Palace were removed. Since then he had been staying at Princess Putiatina's apartment on Millionnaia Street, not far from the Winter Palace, and across the street from the Hermitage and the palace of Grand Duke Nikolai Mikhailovich. Pogroms by the insurgents had begun on March 1 in this aristocratic neighborhood, but soon the Military Commission posted guards to secure the safety of the grand duke. Mikhail had been in touch with political developments through Duma member Count I. I. Kapnist and through Rodzianko.[26] On March 1 he had signed the manifesto sent by Grand Duke Pavel Alexandrovich in Tsarskoe Selo. On the next day Mikhail learned from Rodzianko that the proposal for Nicholas's abdication and Mikhail's regency had been made. But he had not known the outcome of this proposal. When Kerenskii's telephone call came the grand duke naturally assumed that the Duma Committee and the Provisional Government would come to offer him the regency, and he was prepared to accept the offer.[27]

At 9:15 A.M. the members of the Duma Committee and the Provisional Government gathered at Princess Putiatina's apartment at Millionnaia 12 to attend the last ceremony of the passing of the Russian monarchy. From the Provisional Government Prince L'vov, Miliukov, Kerenskii, Nekrasov, Tereshchenko, Konovalov, Godnev, and V. L'vov, and from the Duma Committee Rodzianko, Efremov, Karaulov, Shidlovskii, and Rzhevskii attended the meeting. It is interesting to note the presence of the five members of the masonic organization—Kerenskii, Tereshchenko, Nekrasov, Konovalov, and Efremov. Kerenskii was the most outspoken proponent of Mikhail's abdication, and Tereshchenko, Konovalov, and Nekrasov actively supported his opinion. It is reported that before the meeting Nekrasov had prepared a draft manifesto of Mikhail's abdication.[28] It is also known that Prince

26. Ibid.; see chap. 23.

27. A. S. Matveev, "Vel. Kniaz' Mikhail Aleksandrovich v dni perevorota," *Vozrozhenie* 24 (1952): 144.

28. According to S. P. Mel'gunov, Kerenskii, Tereshchenko, Nekrasov, and Efremov attended the meeting; *Martovskie dni 1917 goda*, p. 223. According

L'vov, who, according to Katkov, stood close to the masonic members, also supported his abdication.

Prince L'vov and Rodzianko expressed the majority opinion of the Provisional Government and the Duma Committee. They stated that in view of the danger to his person and the Provisional Government's inability to insure his safety, his abdication was desirable. Their statement must have been a great shock to the grand duke, who had not known that by the act of Nicholas he had suddenly been thrust upon the throne.[29] According to the agreement reached before the meeting, Miliukov then presented the minority opinion. He insisted upon the preservation of the monarchy as a necessary prerequisite for the survival of the Provisional Government and asked the grand duke to take the grave task of leadership upon himself. Finally, Guchkov and Shul'gin arrived at the conference at 9:45, and a recess was declared for the exchange of information.[30]

When Guchkov and Shul'gin had arrived at Warsaw Station in Petrograd, they were welcomed by insurgent soldiers and the railway workers. Guchkov was asked by the representatives of the railway workers to attend their meeting and bring them up to date with the recent developments. In the meantime, Shul'gin delivered a passionate speech to the crowds gathered at the station and read the manifesto of Nicholas's abdication without realizing the hostile reaction of the insurgents to the preservation of the monarchy. He appealed to the people to unite for the salvation of Russia in the face of the external enemy by rallying around the new emperor, Mikhail, and ended his speech with the words: "Long live Emperor Mikhail II!"

---

to Guchkov's account, which he dictated to Bazilii, Konovalov was also present and energetically supported Rodzianko. Nicolas de Basily, *Diplomat of Imperial Russia, 1903-1917: Memoirs*, p. 143.

29. For the meeting at Princess Putiatina's apartment, see Miliukov, *Istoriia vtoroi russkoi revoliutsii* 1: 53-55; idem, *Vospominaniia* 2: 316-18; Alexander Kerensky, *The Catastrophe*, pp. 68-71; idem, *Russia and History's Turning Point*, pp. 215-16; deposition of Guchkov, *Padenie tsarskogo rezhima: Stenograficheskie otchety deprosov i pokazanii dannykh v 1917 g. v Chrezvychainoi Sledstvennoi Komissii Vremennogo Pravitel'stva* 6: 266-68; Guchkov's account in Basily, *Diplomat of Imperial Russia*, pp. 143-45; Rodzianko, "Gosudarstvennaia duma i fevral'skaia 1917 goda revoliutsiia," pp. 61-62; Matveev, "Vel. Kniaz' Mikhail Aleksandrovich," pp. 141-45; V. V. Shul'gin, *Dni*, pp. 295-307; S. V. Iablonovskii, "Vstrecha s v. kn. Mikhailom Aleksandrovichem," *Golos minuvshago na chuzhoi storone* 14, no. 1 (1926): 137-46; Mel'gunov, *Martovskie dni*, pp. 222-41; Andrei Vladimirovich, "Iz dnevnika A. V. Romanova za 1916-1917 gg.," *Krasnyi arkhiv* 31, no. 1 (1928): 200-201; Maurice Paléologue, *An Ambassador's Memoirs* 3: 239-42.

30. Matveev, "Vel. kniaz' Mikhail Aleksandrovich," p. 144.

Fortunately for Shul'gin, the crowds responded to his speech with shouts of "Hurrah!"[31]

After this speech, Shul'gin was called to the telephone at the station, where Miliukov asked him not to make the manifesto public, explaining the rapid deterioration of the situation in the capital and the general mood of the Duma Committee members favoring Mikhail's abdication. He asked Shul'gin and Guchkov to come immediately to the meeting with the grand duke at Princess Putiatina's apartment. Bublikov sent Shul'gin his aide-de-camp, to whom Shul'gin handed the manifesto of Nicholas's abdication, since he was afraid it might be confiscated by the insurgents.[32]

Guchkov was not so fortunate as Shul'gin. The railway workers were extremely hostile. A speaker accused the Provisional Government of consisting of rich capitalists and landlords, and asked the audience if their revolution had been accomplished to install a prince and an owner of tens of sugar factories into the revolutionary government. The speaker went as far as to demand the arrest of Guchkov. But a certain engineer stood up and delivered a persuasive speech against arrest and calmed the excited audience. Thanks to this intervention, Guchkov returned safely from the meeting after his brief speech. From the station Guchkov and Shul'gin rushed to Millionnaia 12 in the car made available by a sympathetic soldier.[33]

After the recess Kerenskii spoke first: "Your Highness. I am by conviction a republican. I am against a monarchy. But now I do not wish nor can I. . . . Permit me to speak to you as a Russian to a Russian. Pavel Nikolaevich Miliukov is wrong. By assuming the throne you do not save Russia. I know the mood of the masses—the workers and the soldiers. At present sharp dissatisfaction is directed at the monarchy. Precisely this issue will become the cause for bloodshed." Russia would need unity in the face of the external enemy, but the assumption of the throne by Mikhail would lead to civil war. At the end Kerenskii threateningly reminded the grand duke: "I cannot vouch for the life of Your Highness."[34] Next Guchkov spoke. He appealed to the patriotism and courage of the grand duke and pointed out that the Russian people would need the "living embodiment of a national leader." "If you are afraid to take up the burden of the imperial crown, you should at least agree to exercise supreme authority as 'Regent of the Empire' during the vacancy of

31. Shul'gin, *Dni*, p. 286.
32. Ibid., p. 288.
33. Ibid., pp. 289-94.
34. Ibid., pp. 299-300.

the throne."[35] Mikhail then asked for Shul'gin's opinion. Shul'gin replied that when a majority of the Provisional Government members were opposed to Mikhail's assumption of the throne, he did not have the courage to advise the grand duke to take the throne.[36] Miliukov responded to Kerenskii's statement. Although it was true that the assumption of power would mean to risk the personal safety of the grand duke, and for that matter of the ministers, "such a risk must be taken for the interest of the fatherland." Moreover, he pointed out that there was still a possibility of gathering a military force necessary to protect the grand duke. With white hair, his face gray from sleepless nights, he "croaked" in a hoarse voice for a long time, more than an hour, without having anyone interrupt him.[37]

Mikhail Aleksandrovich, who by then had shown signs of impatience, asked for half an hour to deliberate the matter quietly by himself. As he retired, Kerenskii leapt up and called out: "Promise us not to consult your wife." There had been a persistent rumor that his wife, Countess Brasova, had been active on behalf of her husband. The grand duke answered with a smile: "Don't worry, Aleksandr Feodorovich, my wife isn't here at the moment. She stayed behind at Gatchina."[38] A few minutes later the grand duke invited Rodzianko and Prince L'vov to his room. While waiting for the decision, Guchkov tried to telephone his wife to tell her that he had returned from Pskov. But no sooner had he started to speak than Kerenskii rushed to him and inquired: "Where are you telephoning? Whom do you want to talk to?" Kerenskii suspected that Guchkov was contacting a detachment to arrest the members of the Provisional Government. Only after Guchkov explained that he was talking with his wife did Kerenskii suspiciously let him continue on the telephone.[39]

The grand duke asked Rodzianko and L'vov whether his life would be guaranteed if he were to accept the throne. Rodzianko bluntly gave him a negative answer. Mikhail made up his mind to abdicate. Actually, there was not much else he could do. Rodzianko and L'vov, with whom he had maintained close political contact for the past few months, advised against the assumption of the throne. A majority of the Provisional Government did not support him. Moreover, he must have been aware of the illegality of his succession. Mikhail also knew the opposi-

35. Deposition of Guchkov, *Padenie tsarskogo rezhima* 6: 267; Basily, *Diplomat of Imperial Russia*, p. 144; Paléologue, *An Ambassador's Memoirs* 3: 240.

36. Shul'gin, *Dni*, p. 310.

37. Mel'gunov, *Martovskie dni*, p. 227; Shul'gin, *Dni*, p. 297.

38. Paléologue, *An Ambassador's Memoirs* 3: 240-41; Basily, *Diplomat of Imperial Russia*, p. 144.

39. Basily, *Diplomat of Imperial Russia*, pp. 144-45.

tion of other grand dukes to his assumption of power.[40] Returning before the members of the Duma Committee and the Provisional Government, Mikhail announced that he would refuse to take the throne. Kerenskii, overwhelmed with joy, said to the grand duke: "Your Royal Highness, you have acted nobly and like a patriot. I assume the obligation of making this known and of defending you."[41] It was 1 o'clock in the afternoon.

From the legal standpoint Mikhail's refusal to take the throne was far graver than Nicholas's abdication itself, since the former meant the end of the monarchical system. Gronskii concludes: "One must assume that it was exactly with the refusal of Mikhail Aleksandrovich to assume power that the fall of the monarchy in Russia took place."[42] Maklakov argues that the revolution could have been stopped at Nicholas's abdication and blames the abdication of Mikhail for the further development of anarchy. To Maklakov Nicholas's abdication represented the realization of the demands of the Progressive Bloc. First, the emperor finally sanctioned the constitutional regime by urging Mikhail to govern "in complete accordance with the representatives of the country" and to take an inviolable oath to the legislative assembly. Secondly, because Nicholas had entrusted Prince L'vov with the formation of a responsible cabinet, not only the continuity of legal power was assured but also an agreement with the national representation was realized.[43] On this basis "an era of peaceful and legal evolution would have been possible" under the parliamentary monarchy. The authority of the Provisional Government was still enormous, compared with the prestige of the revolutionary leaders who headed the Petrograd Soviet. The Provisional Government had control over the administrative machinery and the armed forces. "The forces of the state could have overcome the movements in the streets, though through compromise. The sympathies of the masses of the country would have gone to the new government in its struggle against the disorder. Thus, a conflict between it and the upheaval had every chance of success." Maklakov blames the members of the Provisional Government and the Duma Committee who compelled Mikhail to abdicate. His abdication "corresponded not to the conception of the Duma, but to that of the 'revolutionary democracy.' "[44]

40. Princess Paley, *Memories of Russia, 1916-1919*, p. 57. Grand Duke Nikolai Mikhailovich, who had been banished from Petrograd on January 1, returned to the capital on March 2 and met Mikhail.

41. Kerensky, *The Catastrophe*, p. 70.

42. P. Gronsky, "La chute de la monarchie en Russie," *Revue politique et parlementaire* 116 (1923): 100.

43. V. Maklakov, Introduction, *La chute du régime tsariste*, p. 10.

44. Ibid., pp. 12-13.

Mikhail's manifesto was a proclamation of the revolution. It assured the disappearance of the monarchy, the constitution, and the Duma. As a result, the old regime collapsed and revolutionary forces came to the forefront.

Another Kadet lawyer, Nabokov, makes the same argument. Mikhail's acceptance of the throne "would have maintained the continuity of the governmental apparatus and structure." Mikhail's straightforwardness and nobleness would have facilitated the development of the constitutional monarchy. A constitutional government on the basis of solid legal grounds could have been established and it would not have been necessary to convene a constituent assembly in the time of war. "In short, the upheaval could have been arrested within certain limits and probably the international position of Russia could have been maintained. There might have been chances of preserving the army."[45]

However, these legal arguments are academic rather than practical. Actually, what had taken place before Mikhail's abdication was not an upheaval, but a revolution. It had defied and negated the old order and created the new. There was little middle ground between the revolution and the old order. Standing between them, the liberals had attempted to mediate the two by choosing the side of the revolution facing the insurgents on the one hand and acting as a defender of the old order, on the other in dealing with the military and the holders of the old system. Mikhail's abdication was the expression of a bankruptcy of this policy. Theoretically, as Makakov argues, it might have been possible for the Provisional Government to ally itself with the army, the bureaucracy, and large segments of the population in the country who remained neutral. But this choice would have meant clearly that the liberals should have stood for the counterrevolution on the side of the old regime against the insurgents in Petrograd. Psychologically as well as ideologically, it was impossible for the liberals to take such an action.

It was necessary to make public a written statement announcing Mikhail's refusal to assume the throne. Nekrasov had already written the first draft of the manifesto, but it was unsatisfactory since it mentioned nothing about the position of the Provisional Government.[46] But the members of the Duma Committee and the Provisional Government, after many sleepless nights, were not in any condition to compose a coherent statement. Most of the participants in the meeting, declining the invitation by Princess

45. V. Nabokov, "Vremennoe pravitel'stvo," *Arkhiv russkoi revoliutsii* 1 (1922): 19.
46. B. E. Nol'de, *Delekoe i blizkoe: Istoricheskie ocherki*, p. 144.

Putiatina for a late breakfast, had left the apartment. It was decided that two jurists, V. Nabokov of the General Staff at Petrograd and Baron B. E. Nol'de in the Ministry of Foreign Affairs, should be summoned to assist the grand duke to compose the proclamation.

Nabokov and Nol'de were joined by Shul'gin and set out to write a draft. The most important question that occupied the attention of the authors of the manifesto was its political implication. Nabokov stated: "Under the conditions of the moment, it appeared to be essential to utilize this act, without limiting ourselves to its negative aspect, to confirm solemnly the plenitude of power of the Provisional Government and its continuing tie with the State Duma." For this purpose they inserted the phrase in the manifesto: "I ask all citizens of the Russian State to pledge allegiance to the Provisional Government, which came into being at the initiative of the State Duma and which is endowed with full power." Thus, two sources of power were indicated: the State Duma and Grand Duke Mikhail Aleksandrovich. But the Duma Committee and the Provisional Government had no institutional and legal connections, whereas Mikhail did not possess supreme power to hand over to the Provisional Government. According to Nabokov, however, the authors of the manifesto "did not see at that time the center of gravity in the juridical significance of the formula, but rather in its moral-political significance." In fact, the manifesto of Mikhail's abdication was the only legal document that defined the scope of the power of the Provisional Government.[47]

Finally, the draft manifesto was approved by Mikhail at 4:30 in the afternoon and sent to the Tauride Palace for the Provisional Government's approval. At the same time Bublikov's assistant, Lomonosov, brought the copy of the manifesto of Nicholas's abdication, which Shul'gin had handed to Bublikov's aide-de-camp. The Provisional Government decided to issue the two manifestos side by side. But Nabokov and Miliukov began arguing the form of Mikhail's manifesto heatedly. Miliukov insisted that it should be issued in the name of Mikhail II, the emperor, as the manifesto of abdication, but Nabokov did not accept this argument and insisted that Mikhail's title as emperor would not only invite suspicion from the members of the imperial family but also would sanction the illegal decision by Nicholas II to transfer supreme power to Mikhail. As a result of long discussion, Miliukov finally yielded and it was decided that it should not be a manifesto of abdication but rather a manifesto to decline to take

47. Nabokov, "Vremennoe pravitel'stvo," p. 21.

the supreme power.[48] Lomonosov sarcastically remarked that on the top of the two manifestos one might add: "The results of the first six hours of the work of the Provisional Government."

When Mikhail decided to refuse the throne, Miliukov and Guchkov resigned from the Provisional Government. Prince L'vov asked Miliukov's trusted colleague, Nabokov, to persuade Miliukov to stay. L'vov said, "It is not a misfortune that Guchkov resigned. It turned out that he is not liked in the army and the soldiers simply hate him. But we have to persuade Miliukov without fail to remain. It is the task of you and your friends to help us."[49] The Kadet Central Committee members, Vinaver, Nabokov, and Shingarev, went to Miliukov's home on Baseinaia Street. They argued that Miliukov had no right to quit and deprive the Provisional Government of the authority that he alone could grant. Finding this argument difficult to refuse, Miliukov changed his mind, and decided to remain in the government. He went to the evening session of the ministers, where he found Guchkov, too.[50]

The meeting at Princess Putiatina's apartment on March 3 was kept secret from the military leaders until the abdication of Mikhail became an established fact. General Alekseev kept trying all day to get hold of Rodzianko to no avail. Since their conversation in the morning Rodzianko had refused to accept any call from Alekseev. Finally, at 6 P.M. Guchkov appeared at the Hughes apparatus in the War Ministry. Alekseev, ignorant of Mikhail's abdication, demanded that the manifesto of Nicholas's abdication be made public immediately and that the Provisional Government promptly take measures to enable the soldiers of the active army to take an oath of allegiance to the new emperor. Guchkov replied:

The manifesto of March 2 was given to me by the emperor last night at Pskov. Its promulgation met with difficulties in Petrograd because Grand Duke Mikhail Aleksandrovich, who consulted with the members of the Council of Ministers, decided to refuse the throne despite my and Miliukov's opinions. It is supposed that the manifestos of March 2 and March 3—the refusal of Mikhail Aleksandrovich—will be promulgated simultaneously. The promulgation of the two manifestos will be made during the night. The Provisional Government will remain at power with Prince L'vov at its head and with the composition which is already known to you until the convocation of a constituent assembly, to which the right to determine definitely the problem of the state structure belongs. The date of convocation has not been decided upon.[51]

48. Ibid.; Iu. V. Lomonosov, *Vospominaniia o martovskoi revoliutsii 1917 g.*, p. 70.
49. Nabokov, "Vremmenoe pravitel'stvo," p. 17.
50. Miliukov, *Vospominaniia* 2: 318.
51. Alekseev-Guchkov conversation, "Fevral'skaia revoliutsiia 1917 goda," pp. 36-37.

Alekseev was crestfallen, and hurriedly suggested: "Is it not possible to persuade the grand duke to accept the power temporarily until the convocation of the [constituent] assembly?" He emphasized that to maintain the cohesion and morale of the army the retention of the monarchical system would be essential. Guchkov agreed with Alekseev, but stated that no one believed him and that the decision of the grand duke was voluntary and final. "We must submit ourselves to the established fact of extremely grave historical importance and honestly and conscientiously try to consoldiate the new system and not to allow serious damage to the army. It was with this intention that I have assumed the proposed post and that I shall exert all my power for the fulfillment of this task." Alekseev did not pursue the matter further.[52]

No one knows what came to Alekseev's mind at that moment, since he left no personal records to reveal his reactions to the crucial events during the February Revolution. But it is possible to surmise that, isolated from the rest of the military commanders who had decided to make peace with the Provisional Government and realizing that he was intentionally and hopelessly left in the dark as to the situation in Petrograd, he finally renounced any further active participation in the events. If the news of Mikhail's abdication greatly shocked him, what followed it was a Kafkaesque absurdity. Immediately after he finished his telegraphic communications with Guchkov, he wished to speak again either with Guchkov or Rodzianko. But at the end of the Hughes apparatus in the War Ministry, Engelhardt appeared and announced that Rodzianko was busy with urgent matters and that Guchkov had resigned. Engelhardt was assuming the post of the War Ministry temporarily. Alekseev explained that he had just finished talking with Guchkov and that he not only had not indicated anything about this resignation but also he had specifically stated his intention to fulfill the task of war minister.[53] Although this confusion was a result of the misunderstanding of Guchkov and Engelhardt who did not know that Guchkov had changed his mind, this episode must have increased Alekseev's sense of hopelessness.

If Alekseev had been faced with the demand for the end of the monarchical system before March 1, when he forced Nicholas's abdication, he would have mobilized the military decisively against the revolution, even if it had meant to take arms against the Provisional Government. He could have counted on Nicholas's support for this attempt, and with Ivanov's forces still near Tsarskoe Selo and other

52. Ibid., p. 38.
53. Alekseev-Engel'gardt conversation, ibid., p. 39.

units on the way to join Ivanov, he could have reactivated the plan for military intervention easily. But on March 3 it was too late. Ivanov had been ordered to return to Mogilev, and a new commander of the Petrograd Military District, General Kornilov, had been appointed. There were no longer any Romanovs available to head the attempt to preserve the monarchy. Nicholas had abdicated; Mikhail had refused to succeed; and Nikolai Nikolaevich had flirted with the Provisional Government. Since all the counterrevolutionary forces had been recalled and Ruzskii and Brusilov were adamantly opposed to military intervention, there was no longer a possibility of mobilizing the military forces against the revolution. Thus, Alekseev decided to concentrate all his energy on one single goal—the preservation of the active army.

At 10 P.M. Rodzianko, who did not know that Guchkov had already informed Alekseev of the news of Mikhail's abdication, finally called Alekseev. Rodzianko stated that because of the negotiated settlement with the Petrograd Soviet the Provisional Government had succeeded in containing the anarchy. "The soldiers' uprisings have been liquidated. The soldiers are returning to the barracks, and the city is gradually returning to a decent appearance." He then requested that the manifesto of Nicholas's abdication finally be made public, together with the manifesto of Mikkail's abdication. Although this was the first time Rodzianko informed Alekseev of the news of Mikhail's abdication and, therefore, the end of the monarchical system, no explanation as to how this decision had been reached was given. Rodzianko added that although the official announcement of the end of the monarchy had not yet been made, rumors were spreading around the city and 101 salvos were sounded in the Fortress of Peter and Paul. Alekseev by then, of course, knew how manipulative Rodzianko's information was, but if he was upset, he did not show his anger in any outward fashion. His suppressed irritation could only be guessed at in his couched language. He informed Rodzianko that the Baltic Fleet had been completely taken over by the rebels, and added: "This was the result of the delay in announcing the contents of the act of March 2 to the sailors." He further stated that the Petrograd Garrison was out of commission because of the propaganda of the workers, "against whom apparently no measures have been taken." All the other reserve regiments, which were infested with the spirit of rebellion, might as well be written off until the restoration of order and discipline. "I believe that the new government must come to the aid of the army, restore order in the scattered army units, and above all place a limit on the propaganda of the workers. The further stability of the army and the possibility of victory will depend upon this." Further, Alekseev informed Rodzianko that he had sent the manifesto of Mikhail's abdication to Grand Duke Nikolai Nikolaevich, as the latter had instructed him not to make it public to the army until its publication by the legal notice. Alekseev then tried to end the communication: "I have nothing further to add except the words: Lord, save Russia!"[54]

Rodzianko's further comments added insult to injury. "I sincerely regret that Your Excellency is in such a gloomy and depressed mood that you cannot take advantage of a favorable factor for the victory. Here we are all in a bold, decisive mood." According to Rodzianko, the information he possessed about the Baltic Fleet was not as gloomy as Alekseev had indicated, and the army commanders were as bold and decisive as they had been. He was convinced that the people would come around to unite themselves again with the army. He then insisted upon the necessity of publishing the two manifestos immediately. He added: "Here we also explain: Lord, save Russia, but we also add: Long live strong, great mother Russia, and her glorious, brotherly army and great Russian people!"[55] Alekseev was provoked by Rodzianko's paternalistic smugness. He introduced the two telegrams from the Baltic Fleet, which had informed the Stavka that the revolt had spread to all ships, and that the killing of officers had begun. "You see how quickly events are developing," Alekseev added, "and how careful we must be in evaluating events." He sharply pointed out that both senior and junior officers were exerting their utmost effort to maintain the strength of the army. "As for my mood, it has resulted from the fact that I have never allowed myself to be led to an error by those on whom at this moment lies the responsibility before the country. To say that everything was all right and that serious work would not be necessary for recovery would mean to say the untruth."[56] One must admire Alekseev's courage and restraint in containing his personal feelings. Even this flash of anger at Rodzianko in the telegraphic conversation was restrained. To save the army from disintegration, he did not accuse nor recriminate the person who was most responsible for having made a fool of him.

Late on the night of March 3, the two newspapers in Petrograd— *Izvestiia* of the Petrograd Soviet and *Izvestiia revoliutsionnoi nedeli*, unofficial organ of the Duma Committee, printed special issues in which large Gothic headlines told the sensational news of the abdication of Nicholas and Mikhail. The Romanov dynasty had fallen. At dawn, the first day of the Provisional Government's existence had

54. Rodzianko-Alekseev conversation, ibid., p. 41.
55. Ibid., pp. 41-42.
56. Ibid., p. 42.

begun. Prince L'vov issued the following proclamation to all the provincial governors, city mayors, zemstvo officials, all the army units at the front as well as in the rear and to General Alekseev:

On March 2 Emperor Nicholas II abdicated from the Throne for himself and for his son in favor of grand Duke Mikhail Aleksandrovich. On March 3, Mikhail Aleksandrovich refused to take the supreme power until the Constituent Assembly determined the form of government. [The Grand Duke] appealed to the populace to subordinate themselves to the Provisional Government that was created at the initiative of the State Duma and granted all the power [to the Provisional Government] until the convocation of the Constituent Assembly, which will express the will of the people with regard to the form of government.[57]

On March 3 thousands of people again appeared in the streets, but their mood was festive. They greeted the news of the end of the monarchy with enthusiasm. The Provisional Government issued an order to shopowners and banks to reopen, and some actually began operation on this day. The general situation in the city was quickly returning to normal. During the night of March 3 the temperature dropped sharply. And Saturday morning dawned with a fierce Russian blizzard raging. It was the first bad weather since the beginning of the revolution. According to an English eyewitness, the blizzard did more than the militia to restore order. On March 4, thanks to an act of God, the streets were deserted for the first time since February 23. When in the afternoon the weather changed to beautiful sunshine, people reappeared in the streets, not for demonstration, but to resume normal life. Many stores were open, cabs were in sight, and newspapers reappeared. Red banners hung from buildings and windows. The first day of New Russia had begun.[58]

According to Leiberov's study, the February Revolution claimed the lives of 433 persons in Petrograd, 313 of whom were insurgents and 120 of whom were police, gendarmes, officers, and loyal soldiers. An additional 1,214 were wounded, of whom 1,136 were insurgents; and 300 were crippled, of whom 291 were insurgents. Of the total of 1,740 killed, wounded, and crippled insurgents, 535 or 30 percent were workers and 832 or 48 percent were soldiers.[59] These figures prove that contrary to popular belief the February Revolution in Petrograd was by no means bloodless. The victims of the revolution were later buried in Mars Field in a solemn ceremony.

Nicholas II, the deposed emperor and now citizen Romanov, arrived at Mogilev shortly after 8 o'clock on the evening of March 3.

57. *Izvestiia revoliutsionnoi nedeli,* March 4, 1917.
58. Stinton Jones, *Russia in Revolution: Being the Experiences of an Englishman in Petrograd during the Upheaval,* pp. 218-19.
59. I. P. Leiberov, *Petrogradskii proletariat v Fevral'skoi revoliutsii* 2: 503, 507.

Two hours before his arrival, he had been informed by Bazilii, who met the imperial trains at Orsha at Alekseev's instructions, that Mikhail had also abdicated from the throne. As the imperial trains approached the station, the personnel of the Stavka were assembled at the station. Nicholas got out of the train, approached Alekseev and embraced him. Then he walked past the persons present. According to Bazilii, "In silence he saluted each one of us with a handshake, looking into our eyes. All were greatly moved, and stifled sobs could be heard. The emperor kept his apparent calm. From time to time he threw back his head in a movement customary to him. A few tears formed in the corners of his eyes and he brushed them away with a gesture of his hand." Bazilii thought that Nicholas accepted his tragedy with great courage and dignity.[60] On March 4 the Stavka requested the Provisional Government's permission to arrange Nicholas's trip to Tsarskoe Selo to join his family.[61] In Tsarskoe Selo, Prince Putiatin, Colonel Geradi of the police, and General Groten (assistant commandant of the palace) were arrested on the order of the newly appointed commandant on March 4. The soldiers who guarded the palace and the imperial family requested that they be relieved of the oath of allegiance to the tsar and decided to subordinate themselves to the Provisional Government. Grand Duke Mikhail Aleksandrovich left Petrograd early in the morning on March 4 for his home in Gatchina.[62] On the same day the new commander in chief, Nikolai Nikolaevich, instructed the army to swear allegiance to the new government. But on March 3 the Executive Committee of the Petrograd Soviet had already decided to arrest the members of the Romanov family.[63]

On March 4 Ruzskii became for the first time acquainted with Order No. 1. Admiral Nepenin in the Baltic Fleet was shot to death. The disintegration of the imperial army spread to the front.

The February Revolution in Petrograd was completed, but it was only the beginning of a larger social and political upheaval.

People celebrated the end of the monarchical rule by hoisting flags in buildings. An old lady approached the city's main street. Noting the red flags decorating the street, she talked aloud to herself: "What's this? There are so many flags. Is today a tsarist holiday?"[64]

60. Basily, *Diplomat of Imperial Russia*, p. 140.

61. Alekseev to L'vov, no. 55, "Fevral'skaia revoliutsiia 1917 goda," p. 54.

62. Paul Benckendorff, *Last Days at Tsarskoe Selo*, pp. 18-19; Mel'gunov, *Martovskie dni*, p. 241.

63. Nikolai Nikolaevich to Alekseev, no. 4138, "Fevral'skaia revoliutsiia 1917 goda," p. 45; A. Shliapnikov, *Semnadtsatyi god* 1: 246-47.

64. TsGIA, f. 1101, op. 1, d. 1195, ℓ. 10.

29

CONCLUSION

The February Revolution was the explosion of the two fundamental contradictions in Russia—the revolt of the masses against established order and the irreconcilable conflict between "society" and "state." The process of what Haimson describes as dual polarization had steadily progressed after 1905 under the impact of the successful modernization undertaken by Russia. The outbreak of the First World War at first appeared to halt this process—the liberals pledged to support the government in its effort to win the war and the "sacred union" seemed to close the gap between state and society. The workers' strike movement that had appeared to be approaching a clash with the regime was silenced at the outbreak of war. But internal peace did not last more than a year. Once a crack appeared in the monolith after the first humiliating defeat of the Russian army, the war that had initially cemented all segments of society together began to rip them apart with ferocious force.

The working class provided the most important source of social instability in Russia. Never integrated into the established order, workers lived segregated geographically as well as culturally and socially. At the outbreak of war, the modicum of independence that had existed previously had been brutally taken away. Unlike other classes in society that had formed national organizations to advance their class interests, workers were deprived of such privilege. Whatever modest legal organizations they maintained during the war were severely curtailed by the police. And yet the workers' labor lay at

569

the foundation of the war effort. As Russian industry rapidly expanded and created a shortage of skilled workers, the workers' confidence grew in proportion. It was precisely the combination of resentment stemming from their exclusion from privileged society and their growing pride as a distinct and vital class that made the working class in Russia explosively dangerous.

The strike movement was suddenly revitalized in the summer of 1915, and from then on grew in size and militancy. It was by no means a linear development constantly moving upward toward a climax, but characterized by peaks and valleys. But as time went on peaks became constantly higher and valleys less deep. At the vanguard of the strike movement stood the metalworkers in factories that employed between 1,000 and 8,000 workers, and it was the metalworkers in the Vyborg District who provided the major impetus. Workers in the largest munition plants and in large textile factories participated in economic strikes, but they generally stayed out of political strikes until the end of 1916. As the new wave of strikes began in January 1917, even these workers merged with the militant metalworkers in Vyborg District in strikes for political reasons. Moreover, the new wave began to involve workers who had not participated in strikes since the war began. The basic trend of the wartime strike movement—to grow ever larger and wider—culminated in the February Revolution.

Wartime conditions had changed the composition of the working class in Petrograd. But in accounting for the sharp rise in the strike movement during the war, it must be stressed that changes were less drastic in Petrograd than elsewhere in Russia. The skilled metalworkers, from whom the major source of working-class radicalism in Petrograd came, were highly urban, literate, relatively highly paid, and confident and proud of their abilities. Even with the enormous influx of new labor and the rapid expansion of the number of workers, more than half of the workers in Petrograd in January 1917 had been working since the prewar period. To this core of the proletariat were added the displaced skilled workers from Poland and the Baltic provinces, the urban youths who had grown into adulthood during the war, and the women who had returned to work after the war began. Thus, Petrograd workers maintained an urban outlook despite the enormous influx into their ranks. Whether the newly recruited peasants contributed to the radicalism of the workers' movement is difficult to ascertain. Although they might have stayed out of the strike movement, it is possible to assume that the militant workers might have influenced them in a radical direction. An element of *buntarstvo* became apparent by the end of 1916 and in the beginning of 1917, not in the strike movement itself, but in the attacks on food stores. It is plausible that these attacks were made by those unorganized segments of workers and artisans who had found no way to express their pent-up anger. The organized strike movement and the *buntarstvo* were to merge into one in the February Revolution.

Just as the workers themselves were alienated from the existing order of society, the workers' movement developed independent of the conflict within established society. With the exception of a brief moment immediately after the declaration of war, the workers on the whole were relatively indifferent to its outcome. What drove them out of the factories in the first major strike during the war was not the defeat of the Russian army but the massacre of fellow workers in Ivanovo. The prorogations of the Duma and the government's other repressive measures against liberal organizations had little effect on the workers' movement. But the workers showed their class solidarity in the January 9 strikes and in a series of sympathy strikes in protest against the arrest of their leaders.

No doubt such wartime miseries as decline in real wages, inflation, long working hours, deterioration of working conditions, and above all food shortage contributed to the development of the strike movement. But these were only the immediate manifestations of the established order, and it was toward that established order that their deep-seated resentment was directed. There was no possibility of establishing a united front between the liberal opposition and the workers' movement during the war. All such attempts made either by the leaders of the workers' movement or by the liberals ended in failure.

The growth of the strike movement was not entirely spontaneous. In fact, it would be impossible to organize "spontaneously" such strikes as happened in August and September 1915, January, March, and October 1916, and January and February 1917. These strikes involved many factories in the entire city. Strikes required organizers who planned strategy, agitators who appealed to the workers, orators who spoke at factory rallies, and a network of communications that coordinated activities with other factories. Amorphous grievances of the workers had to be defined in simple slogans. Demonstrations had to be directed to a certain destination through specific routes. Although no single political group could claim exclusive leadership of the workers' movement and it is impossible to measure accurately the influence of the underground revolutionary activists, it is certain that it was the underground activists at the factory level who provided the workers' movement with important leadership and continuity. Although activists who were official members of the revolutionary parties were few, they were assisted by nonparty sympathizers who came to support the hard-core activists. The government's repressive measures did not eradicate such activists, but created more of them.

During the war the revolutionary parties were basically split into two groups: the antiwar alliance of left-wing Socialists centered around the Bolsheviks and the moderate Socialists that gravitated toward the workers' group of the Central War Industries Committee. The differences between the two groups revolved around two issues. On the issue of war the antiwar group took a militant internationalist position, while the workers' group qualified that position by allowing a possibility of national defense against aggression. A more important difference was their respective methods for achieving a revolution. While the Bolsheviks advocated a revolution carried out by the workers and the soldiers alone, the workers' group conceived revolution to be a united struggle against tsarism by all segments of society, one in which the liberal opposition was to play a leading role. The workers' movement should be subordinated to the broader struggle of the entire society. For two fundamental reasons the workers' groups' concept of revolution did not correspond to Russian reality. First, the Russian liberals, on whom the sole hope of the workers' group for revolution rested, had ceased to be revolutionary. They were frightened by the prospect of revolution from below and were more willing to accommodate themselves to the tsarist regime than to form a united front with the workers against it. Second, the workers' movement developed outside the liberal forces in society. They had no common ground on which to establish a united front.

In the latter half of 1916 the Bolsheviks and the antiwar alliance intensified their influence among the Petrograd workers at the expense of the workers' group. This is not to say that the Bolshevik programs were wholeheartedly accepted by the masses of workers. But it does indicate that the Bolsheviks' most militant antiwar stand and their equally militant rejection of the established order were beginning to strike a responsive chord among the worker-activists. As wartime reality hit the workers hard, the Bolsheviks' antiwar propaganda was not incomprehensible to the workers. The Bolsheviks' insistence on the insurrection of the masses without the help of any other class in society appealed to the workers' sense of independence and was compatible with their resentment of privileged society.

Alarmed by the loss of influence, the workers' group finally turned in a radical direction in December 1916. It began a massive campaign appealing to the workers to take action to overthrow the tsarist regime. The workers' group's new direction was taken still in the framework of the over-all struggle of the entire society against the tsarist regime. But the drastic shift from its previous policy restraining the workers' radicalism into one that encouraged the workers' action against the regime had a significant implication. On the eve of the February Revolution both groups that influenced the workers' movement advocated violent action against the regime. In this sense, the conflict between the two groups did not hinder, but rather hastened the development of the revolutionary crisis.

The workers' group also created an important buffer between the liberals and the workers—a buffer that deceptively concealed the basic antagonism between the two. The liberal movement and the workers' movement during the war and subsequent developments after the February Revolution amply demonstrated that the two were fundamentally in opposition. The liberals desperately tried to the last moment to avoid a revolution from below. The existence of the workers' group, however, contributed to the liberals' psychological acceptance of the revolution, if a revolution were inevitable. Instead of choosing a course of a civil war against the workers' movement, the liberals could count on the moderating influence of the workers' group to contain the revolution within acceptable limits. In this sense, the workers' group provided a vital link between the liberals and the revolution.

Although the workers' strike movement developed during the February Revolution into a general strike that involved virtually all the workers in Petrograd, it did not ensure the victory of the insurrection by itself. One of the crucial differences between the 1905 Revolution and the February Revolution was the soldiers' loyalty. In 1905 there were sporadic attempts by the soldiers to rise against the regime, but on the whole they remained loyal. But the impact of the world war drastically changed the morale of the officers as well as the soldiers.

The reasons for the soldiers' insurrection were not identical with those for the workers' strike movement. If the workers demanded bread, peace, and the overthrow of tsarism, the soldiers' grievances were more immediate and were directed against the officers and military discipline. The barrier between soldiers and officers—common in any military force—was even more magnified in the Russian army because of the peculiar social tensions that existed outside the military units. Barracks life reminded the soldiers—mostly "peasants in uniform"—of the servile life on the landlords' estates in pre-Emancipation days. They were at the mercy of the officers, subject to beatings, theft, and extortion by them, and detailed more often to act as servants in the officers' club or their households than to actual military training. Officers treated soldiers as landlords treated serfs. Officers had little contact with the soldiers, did not speak the same language, and did not understand them. Left alone, the soldiers managed their barracks life by forming their own self-governing communal organizations without much interference from the officers.

The morale of the reserve units was low. Unlike the front, where there was a possibility of establishing a common bond between officers and soldiers in the face of danger, boredom and regimentation in the rear made the reserve soldiers restless. The influx of older recruits and the existence of sick and wounded soldiers who had been temporarily removed from the front also contributed to declining morale. Moreover, the government's policy of drafting strike organizers into the army was like throwing matches around on a dry field. But organized revolutionary activities in the military units were negligible, although revolutionary literature was occasionally smuggled into the barracks. More significant was the influence of the general political deterioration in the rear. The trial of Miasoedov, the arrest of Sukhomlinov, rumors of the government's treason, and sensational tales of Rasputin and the empress eroded the hypnotic hold of the sacred oath of allegiance to the tsar. As Colonel Engelhardt observed, soldiers in the reserve battalions became "rather reserves of flammable material than a prop of the regime . . . capable at any moment of exercising their own will and their demands." In fact, there were some instances during the war in which the soldiers openly supported demonstrators against the police. Though sporadic, these instances foreshadowed the danger in the future.

If the oath of allegiance ceased to have magical hold over the soldiers, prestige of officers—another important factor to tie the soldiers to descipline—had declined. The most capable officers of the Russian army had either been killed in the first few months of the war or sent to the front where they were most needed. The shortage of officers contributed to the creation of a host of newly commissioned officers with dubious qualifications. It also meant the influx of a new breed of officers who brought into the military units acute political consciousness. Unlike the professional officers of the old generation, they could no longer be indifferent to political developments outside the military. Many openly sympathized with the liberal opposition, and even a few revolutionaries were in the officers' corps. The "transfer of allegiance" had taken place among the officers long before the February Revolution.

Crucial to the soldiers' loyalty to the regime at the time of crisis was the attitude of noncommissioned officers, since unlike the officers,

NCOs had daily contact with the soldiers and the detachments designed to train the NCOs were supposed to be the main instrument
of suppression of disturbances. It is known that the NCOs treated
the soldiers most brutally, but at the same time they were much closer
to the soldiers in their social and cultural background. Just as the
workers who came closest to the established order of society most
resented it, the NCOs were more keenly conscious of the oppressive
wall that separated them from the officers. Combined with this resentment was initiative and leadership—attributes that had led them to
NCO status and that made them particularly dangerous.

But the revolt of the masses was but one aspect of the February
Revolution. If the basic confrontation in the February Revolution
was between the masses and privileged society, why did it not immediately lead to a civil war? The answer lies in another aspect of
wartime politics: the relationship between state and society. The
revolution from below provided the general framework, but the
specific course of the February Revolution was determined by the
conflict within established society.

The internal peace that the liberal opposition had promised at
the outbreak of war did not last beyond the summer of 1915. After
the Russian army suffered a humiliating defeat, the liberals began
criticizing the government. The voluntary organizations became increasingly involved in political questions, while in the Duma liberals
formed the Progressive Bloc. After the political crisis of the summer
of 1915, the liberals and the tsarist government drifted apart. But
contrary to what Katkov claims, the liberals never attempted to take
over the tsarist government apparatus. In fact, they never wished
a far-reaching political reform in the time of war. The most the Progressive Bloc wished to accomplish was the formation of a ministry
of confidence. The mainstream of liberal opposition led by Miliukov
had persistently refused to take drastic action against the government,
partly because they feared that such action might provoke a revolution
from below, and partly because during the war, despite political animosity, the liberals and the bureaucracy had created a web of inter-
dependent organizations in support of the war effort. The liberals
and the government hated and distrusted each other, but they needed
each other for survival. Faced with the growing movement from below,
the government's intransigence from above, and constant danger
of internal split within the fragile liberal coalescence, the liberals remained inactive and powerless. Only a minority attempted to break
away from this impasse. The radical wing of the liberals had insisted
upon the need of an alliance with the mass movement to keep it within
reasonable bounds. At the lower level a certain cooperation was

achieved between liberal activists and the moderate Socialists in the practical work of labor exchange, cooperative movements, and food supply committees. But these liberals had no tangible influence on the masses of workers. Another group of liberals became involved in a conspiracy for a palace coup to forestall the outbreak of revolution. But this course was not accepted by the majority of liberals as a viable alternative, and even those who advocated it did not seriously attempt to implement it.

From the very beginning of the war Nicholas excluded two radical actions he might have taken in dealing with the liberal opposition. On one hand, he never seriously entertained the proposal made by his reactionary advisors (including his wife and Nikolai Maklakov) that he should break completely with the liberals. On the other, he adamantly stood on his imperial prerogatives, refusing to yield to public pressure to grant a ministry of confidence willing to cooperate with the Duma. Nicholas's political actions during the war were skillful maneuvers in the narrow passage between these two extremes. When liberals raised their voices, Nicholas gave them concessions sufficient to defuse their radicalism. Dismissals of unpopular ministers, the creation of special councils, the opening of the Duma in the spring and the summer of 1915, Goremykin's dismissal and Stürmer's appointment in the aftermath of Miliukov's "stupidity or treason" speech, and even Protopopov's appointment as acting minister of internal affairs—each of these measures was taken at a time the liberals heightened the tone of criticism. And each time these measures succeeded in keeping the conservative elements of the Progressive Bloc clinging to the illusion that more concessions would follow. But Nicholas never intended to grant what the liberals wanted. As soon as he weathered a storm, he would return to reaction. Instead of forming a ministry of confidence in the summer of 1915 (which he could have done easily by replacing Goremykin with Krivoshein), he fired the "rebellious" ministers one by one. By assuming supreme commandership, he let the Aleksandra-Rasputin clique influence the appointments and dismissals of ministers. He never agreed to drop Protopopov, and never listened to the advice from various quarters to get rid of the unsavory influence of his wife and her spiritual advisor. As soon as the Duma quietly accepted the prorogation, Trepov was dismissed. Thus, in his struggle with the liberal opposition, Nicholas took the upper hand and won many tactical victories. These maneuvers themselves had a great deal to do with the liberals' powerlessness.

But these small victories ultimately led to Nicholas's downfall. The *krizis verkhov* (the crisis of power) was further deepened by them. It would be a mistake to characterize the entire tsarist cabinet as inept and corrupt—to the last moment it included capable ministers. But there was no question that following the crisis in the summer of 1915 the over-all quality of the government declined sharply. "Ministerial leapfrogging" was but one manifestation of the erosion of the government's competency. Such scandals as Khvostov's plot to assassinate Rasputin and the arrest of Manasevich-Manuilov lowered the prestige of the government. Rasputin's frolicking and the unfounded, sensational rumors about Rasputin, the empress, and the "dark forces" fed the basest popular imagination and invited the indignation of the decent public. It is true that the liberals were incapacitated by Nicholas's maneuvers. But psychologically they deserted the government. Nicholas and his government thus irretrievably alienated an ally with whom they could have combated the approaching storm from below.

The crack in the dike that let in a deluge was the supply of food. The crisis was the result of a panic rather than a real shortage of bread itself. After the news of the introduction of the ration system was announced, the number of food riots suddenly increased. At the same time the workers' strikes also sharply increased. On the eve of the February Revolution the Putilov Factory and the Izhora Factory were closed, and numerous other factories began economic strikes.

The February Revolution began with the strike in the textile mills in the Vyborg District when women workers went out into the streets with a single demand—"bread"—on February 23, to commemorate International Women's Day. The strike immediately spread to neighboring metal factories, and its leadership was quickly taken over by more experienced activists. At least 78,000 workers of fifty factories joined the strike. Although the total number of strikers was much smaller than the January 9 and February 14 strikes of this year, and the strike movement was limited in the main to the Vyborg District, its militancy far surpassed any of the previous wartime strikes. The strikers systematically employed a tactic of forcible removal, not allowing other workers to continue working. Almost all the major factories in Vyborg District employing more than 1,000 workers were shut. The strikers staged a massive demonstration in the major streets in Vyborg District, but the police succeeded in dispersing the demonstrators who attempted to cross the Neva to the center of the city.

On the second day, February 24, the strike was no longer confined to Vyborg District, but spread to all the districts in Petrograd. At least 158,000 workers participated and 131 factories were struck, more than doubling the size of the strike on the previous day. Almost all the metal and textile factories with more than 100 workers were struck, and for the first time in the war workers of other branches of industry—paper, printing, wood processing, mineral processing, leather, food processing, tobacco, and chemicals—joined the strike. For the first time during the war massive demonstrations were staged along Nevskii Prospekt. The demonstrators no longer passively waited for police assault, but instead, counterattacked. Although on this day as well, the police and the Cossacks still managed to disperse the crowds, the demonstrators became more difficult to deal with. The Cossacks were not enthusiastic in fulfilling the order to attack.

The general strike on February 25 paralyzed normal functions in the capital. The strike participants surpassed 200,000, the largest figure since the 1905 Revolution. Almost all factories were closed. Newspapers did not come out, trams and cabs stopped, many stores, restaurants, and cafes were closed, banks did not open, and schools were canceled. The demonstrators became more vicious in their attacks on the police. Revolver shots were fired, bombs thrown, and police chiefs Shalfeev and Krylov were brutally murdered. Cossacks and soldiers remained halfhearted in their task of suppressing the demonstration. In some cases soldiers openly sympathized with the crowd and attacked the police. For the first time since February 23 the crowds completely controlled Nevskii Prospekt. Political rallies were held continuously on Kazan and Znamenskaia Squares, where orators spoke freely, without much harassment from the police. The demonstrators boldly hoisted red banners lettered with "Down with the War," "Down with the Government." The workers' strike movement induced unorganized workers to come into the streets. Suddenly an element of *buntarstvo* was injected into the movement. Some demonstrators, mostly youths and women, rampaged in the streets, "trashing" stores along the way. Armed robberies, including one spectacular bank robbery, were committed in the heart of the city.

Who led the revolution? Was it spontaneous, as often claimed by Western historians? Or was it led by the Bolshevik party as Soviet historians argue? It would be a mistake to characterize the February Revolution, as Chamberlin does, as "one of the most leaderless, spontaneous, anonymous revolutions of all time."[1] Historians in the West have long considered the Russian mass movement as controlled by *stikhiia*—that mysterious, savage, elemental force that defies rational analysis.[2] This belief has led them to refrain from examining the

1. William Henry Chamberlin, *The Russian Revolution, 1917-1921* 1: 73.

2. For instance, Bertram D. Wolfe's "Comment" on Leonard Schapiro's and Oskar Anweiler's papers in *Revolutionary Russia*, ed. Richard Pipes, pp. 128-38.

dynamics of the mass movement. But on the other hand, it is difficult
to subscribe to the theory of Bolshevik leadership. The Bolshevik
party as a whole failed to react to the workers' strike movement
quickly and imaginatively. The Russian Bureau led by Shliapnikov
was constantly behind the developing events and grossly underestimated the revolutionary potentialities of the movement. The Petersburg Committee was more actively involved in leadership of the strike
and demonstration, but it, too, failed to exert strong influence among
the masses, partly because its attempt to expand the movement met
constant objections from the Russian Bureau, and partly because it
lacked the resources and a close communication network to coordinate
the activities in various districts. On the night of February 25 a majority of the Petersburg Committee was arrested and it became defunct.
Thus, the 3,000 Bolsheviks scattered around Petrograd were left pretty
much on their own to interpret the significance of events and exert
their influence among the workers without much direction from
above.

Nonetheless, in such an explosive situation as the February Revolution the existence of 3,000 committed revolutionaries cannot be
easily dismissed. The most important Bolshevik organization, the
one that exerted a significant influence on the workers, was the Vyborg
District Committee. Headed by militant Chugurin and led by such
experienced party activists as Kaiurov and Sveshnikov, the Vyborg
District Committee had placed its 500 to 600 members in strategically
important factories. It met frequently from the beginning of the strike
movement on February 23, and from the very beginning worked
to expand the movement to its maximum limit. They were the strike
organizers at the factory level, stood at the head of the demonstrations,
talked the Cossacks out of punitive action against the demonstrators,
and led the attack on the police. Considering the important role played
by the metal factories in the Vyborg District, these Vyborg Bolsheviks
must have contributed to the rapid acceleration of the strike movement. In this sense, Trotskii was partially correct in stating that the
February Revolution was led by the lower-rank Bolshevik activists.[3]

However, the Bolsheviks were but one part of a much larger group
of activists. There were 400 to 500 members of the initiative group,
150 Mezhraiontsy, and 500 to 600 left-wing Socialist Revolutionaries who were scattered in various factories. These activists formed
a united front with the Bolsheviks and took concerted action. Not
only these antiwar activists but also the moderate Socialists who

3. Leon Trotsky, *The History of the Russian Revolution* 1: 136-52.

supported the workers' group actively organized the strike movement. Despite ideological differences, there emerged a common goal among the activists at the factory level: the transformation of labor unrest into a revolution against the tsarist regime. Trotskii was wrong to exclude such activists from the role of leadership.

To be sure, the February Revolution was not organized in the sense that the revolution in October was. There existed no central headquarters from which all directives emanated. Nor did these activists control all aspects of the movement. But it is important to recognize the existence of these activists, who had acquired experience in strike organization under the difficult repression that existed in wartime and whose concern was no longer the solution of immediate economic problems but the ultimate overthrow of the tsarist regime itself. Moreover, these activists with affiliations with the revolutionary parties were not isolated from the masses of workers, although their number was small. Surrounding this core of activists were those nonparty activists who had not committed themselves to join the underground revolutionary parties, but who were sympathetic with the causes they espoused. Beyond these activists there were the rank-and-file workers. But many of them already had experience in strikes during the war. Taking these factors into consideration, one must reject the "spontaneity theory," according to which the masses of workers poured onto the streets spontaneously, trusting only their own destructive instincts.

It is true, however, that the February Revolution gave many workers the opportunity to join the strike movement for the first time. Certainly the sudden appearance of great numbers of workers who had been thrust into the political movement injected an element of "spontaneity" in the sense that these newcomers were more difficult for the seasoned veteran organizers to control. The uncertainty of their political allegiances contributed to the blurring of the distinct social content of the February Revolution.

By February 25 the strike movement had reached its height. But it did not lead to a revolution. It became clear that the workers' movement alone was insufficient to overthrow the regime. On February 26 security authorities in Petrograd, having adopted a stance of restraint for the three days, changed to active suppression of the unrest. Government troops systematically fired upon the demonstrators. This measure seemed successful. Demonstrators disappeared from Nevskii Prospekt. Even the veteran leaders of the strike movement pessimistically predicted that the movement was coming to an end. But the firing order inevitably pushed the soldiers to a choice between conscience and obedience. On the night of February 26, the Fourth Company of

Pavlovskii Regiment revolted. This was still isolated and easily put down, but it was an ominous sign.

On February 27 the revolt of the Volynskii Regiment led by a few noncommissioned officers quickly spread to the Preobrazhenskii and Lithuanian Regiments and the Sixth Engineers Battalion. The soldiers' insurrection had begun. Insurgent soldiers crossed the Neva and were united with the workers in Vyborg District who, on their own, had attacked weapon factories and the police station. The insurgents soon occupied the entire Vyborg District. They attacked Kresty Prison, occupied Finland Station, burned the police station, and armed themselves after they occupied the weapon factories. While insurgents continued to attack the barracks of the Moscow Regiment and the Bicycle Battalion, others crossed the Neva and marched to the Tauride Palace. On their way they occupied the Arsenal, seized enormous quantities of weapons and ammunition, and burned the Circuit Court. From then on the insurrection spread to all parts of the city, and by late night almost all the reserve battalions in the city joined or were forced to join the insurrection. Lawlessness and chaos reigned in the streets. Trucks, automobiles, and armored cars full of soldiers with red armbands zoomed madly around the city, while people armed to the teeth experimented with their newly acquired toys.

The ineptitude of the security authorities contributed to the insurrection's quick spread. Khabalov lost his nerve and stood aimless and ineffectual. The punitive detachment under the command of Colonel Kutepov was isolated from the other loyal troops and disintegrated by evening. Beliaev meddled in the commanding hierarchy and heightened the confusion by issuing conflicting orders. While the insurrection spread in the city, Khabalov, Beliaev, and Zankevich moved the loyal troops that had gathered to defend the government aimlessly back and forth between the Winter Palace and the Admiralty. Disgusted by the ineptitude of the commanding hierarchy, the loyal troops disappeared; some marched to the Tauride Palace to join the insurrection. But the greatest mistake made by Khabalov and Beliaev was that they concealed the extent of the crisis in Petrograd from the Stavka until it was too late. By the time the Stavka realized the necessity of dispatching troops from the front, Petrograd was under the control of the insurgents.

The insurrection had triumphed in Petrograd. Cabinet ministers were arrested and loyal troops disintegrated. But the revolution was far from over. Nicholas II was still alive and well in Mogilev, determined to suppress the revolution by force, and the Stavka wholeheartedly endorsed his decision. In the meantime, the insurrection created anarchy in the streets, but not a revolutionary government to consolidate its gains.

One of the most curious characteristics of the February Revolution was that the insurgents who revolted against the old regime failed to create their own revolutionary government. The two organs that came into being—the Petrograd Soviet and the Duma Committee—had little to do with the insurrection itself. The masses of insurgents still continued to influence the course of events, but their influence was no longer direct. Their continued existence and radical actions provided the general framework, which the political leaders could neither ignore nor defy, but the specific course of the revolution was now determined by groups other than the insurgents themselves.

The Petrograd Soviet was created at the initiative of the Menshevik leaders, whose goal was to form a center for the movement to coordinate and organize the activities of the insurgent masses. Despite the strong left-wing preponderance in the Executive Committee, the antiwar groups were not united on the question of power. Particularly important was the confusion of the Bolshevik leadership. As a result the most important policy of the Soviet Executive Committee was formulated by Sukhanov, Steklov, and Sokolov. These Socialist intellectuals were ideologically more Left than the workers' group, but on the question of power they consistently maintained that a provisional government to be created by the revolution ought to be a bourgeois government composed of the representatives of the liberal opposition. This basically Menshevik notion that had been most persistently pursued by the workers' group during the war and that seemed to have gradually lost relevancy in the wartime political reality was ironically espoused by a majority of the Petrograd Soviet leaders and infected even the Bolshevik leaders like Shliapnikov. The new situation created by the revolution seemed to these leaders to justify the plan to transfer power to the "bourgeoisie." There was a basic confrontation between the masses and established order, and this confrontation became even clearer as the revolution became older. But the Petrograd Soviet leaders accurately judged that revolutionary power emanating solely from the insurgent masses could not possibly survive. It seemed foolhardy to rest the future of the revolution on those soldiers roaming around the street defying all order and discipline and the armed workers who did not even know how to use weapons. A civil war, if initiated by an organized military unit, would surely crush the young revolution. The leaders of the Soviet Executive Committee thus concluded that, for its survival, the revolution would have to be expanded to include the rest of society. Although its basic content was the social conflict between the masses and privileged society, the revolution would have to make itself appear *obshchestvennyi*—a political revolution involving all segments of society against the tsarist regime.

The challenge to this notion came from two different directions. First, the overwhelming support that the Petrograd Soviet received from the insurgent masses began to transform its nature into something more than the initiators had envisaged. The masses supported the Soviet, not the Duma Committee, thereby accentuating the social content of the revolution. The workers' militia in the workers' districts effectively established its police power, and the district soviets were quickly extending their self-governing authority. The soldiers formed soldiers' committees in their units, controlled weapons and the economy of their units, and began electing their officers. In other words, the insurgent masses began taking care of administrative matters on their own without reference to any outside authority. The source of "dual power" was derived, not from the conflict between the Provisional Government and the Petrograd Soviet, but from the most fundamental conflict—between the insurgents' self-assumed authority and the authority emanating from the privileged element of society. The majority of insurgents, however, had not yet begun to translate their feelings into conscious revolutionary programs. They could not offer an alternative to the Executive Committee's policy toward the problem of power, despite occasional manifestations of their latent radicalism on a number of specific issues.

The second threat to the Soviet leaders' policy toward the problem of power came from a small group of radical antiwar Socialists led by the Bolshevik Vyborg District Committee and Mezhraiontsy. From the moment the insurrection triumphed, this group called for the establishment of a provisional revolutionary government in the form of a soviet, and after the Petrograd Soviet was formed, they advocated the transformation of the Soviet into a revolutionary government. Unlike the Bolshevik leaders led by Shliapnikov, who considered the establishment of a provisional revolutionary government a task of the distant future, these activists proposed this as one of the most urgent tasks of the moment. Although the Vyborg Bolsheviks and the Mezhraiontsy were still isolated from the masses of insurgents, there were signs that their proposal might receive wide acceptance. Alarmed by this possibility, the Soviet leaders decided to hasten the formation of a bourgeois provisional government by negotiating directly with the liberal representatives before the militant insurgents could push them into a position where they would have no choice but to assume power.

The liberals played a crucial role in the February Revolution. During the war, pushed by two conflicting forces—the government's intransigence and the approaching storm from below—the liberal opposition was rendered powerless. But when the revolution came, it was the liberals who tipped the balance between the two forces and who had the most telling effect on the specific course of events during the Revolution.

The liberals had attempted to avoid a revolution at any cost during the war, but when the revolution became a reality, their goal was not to crush it but to contain it. As the insurrection threw the capital into chaos, and eliminated all sources of authority, the liberals formed the Duma Committee, which was forced to assume power to restore order. From that moment, at first gingerly and later more actively, the liberals became involved in the revolutionary process. The revolutionary situation no longer allowed the liberals to stand in the neutral territory between the old regime and the revolution. But the actions of the liberals during the February Revolution represented their desperate but ultimately futile effort to create such a middle ground. The two courses of action that the liberals had rejected during the war were adopted during the revolution. First, they accepted the revolution as legitimate to prevent further intensification of the revolutionary process. Second, they reactivated the plan for a palace coup.

The most difficult question that the liberals faced during the February Revolution was the problem of legitimacy of the Provisional Government. On the one hand, they sought to make the revolution itself the source of legitimacy. In fact, they had to take some revolutionary actions despite themselves to contain the further intensification of the revolution. The Duma Committee sanctioned the arrest of the former ministers, officials, and the police, while it took over the government apparatus in the name of the revolution but actually to ensure the continuity of government functions. It created the city militia to replace the old police, which had disappeared, and took over the Military Commission created by the Petrograd Soviet to exert its influence among the insurgent soldiers. Nevertheless, because there existed an unbridgeable class barrier between the liberals and the insurgents and more importantly because their ultimate goals—the restoration of order and the prevention of further intensification of revolution—were basically contradictory to the aspirations of the insurgents, they failed to gain their acceptance. It was for this reason that they chose to negotiate with the leaders of the Petrograd Soviet for the conditions of the transfer of power in the hope that the Soviet would persuade the insurgents to support the Provisional Government.

But the Duma Committee's plan to use the Soviet leaders as agents for the Provisional Government failed. Its basic assumption that the insurgents could be swayed by the mere directives of the Soviet Executive Committee proved to be false. The insurgents were not robots moving in any direction that their leaders ordered but unmistakably imposed their will on their leaders. Despite their intention to help out the Provisional Government, the Soviet leaders could not give it their unconditional support without risking the loss of their own prestige among the masses. What the insurgents wanted was not crystallized into political programs, but on specific issues they unceremoniously overruled the Executive Committee's policy and enforced their will without much consideration of the leaders' intentions and ideological niceties. The process in which the soldiers issued Order No. 1, the insurgents' reaction to the question of weapon control, and the reaction of the workers' militia to the merger with the city militia all indicated the futility of the Provisional Government's reliance on the Soviet leaders to gain the support of the insurgents.

On the other hand, the liberals sought legitimacy for the Provisional Government in legal and institutional continuity with the old regime. A palace coup was conceived as the last defense against the intensification of the revolution and as a measure to ensure that continuity. In dealing with the tsar and military leaders the liberals always presented themselves as defenders of law and order against anarchy. They never demanded Nicholas's abdication in the name of revolution, but for the purpose of stopping the revolution. Ultimately it proved impossible to pursue two contradictory policies. The middle ground that they sought between the old regime and the revolution did not exist. The Provisional Government did not gain the full endorsement of the Petrograd Soviet. The insurgents were effectively expanding their self-governing authority in the factories and the military units, thereby undermining the authority of the Provisional Government. But the Provisional Government could not even muster the strength of privileged society, since they were forced to accept the abolition of the monarchical system. The tsarist government and the liberals had needed each other for their mutual survival. Forced to remove the monarchical system surgically, the liberals were left in a vacuum, with no solid foundation.

Another important factor that prevented a civil war in the February Revolution was the action of the military leaders. They had refused to be involved in internal politics prior to the revolution, but even among the highest leaders in the military the "transfer of allegiance" had been slowly taking place. At the beginning of the revolution the military supported Nicholas's counterrevolutionary measures, because they believed that the capital had been taken over by radical elements. But as soon as they were assured that power had been transferred to the liberal forces, they fully cooperated with the Duma Committee— some like Ruzskii and Brusilov, because they agreed with their general goals; others, like Alekseev, because they were outwitted by the Duma Committee's manipulation of information. What ultimately determined the actions of the military leaders was their concern with the continuation of war and the preservation of the fighting capacities of the armed forces. For these goals they were willing to sacrifice the monarchical system. Fearing that forceful intervention by the military to suppress the revolution might provoke the expansion of revolution in the armed forces, the military leaders were also willing to accept the revolution to contain it. What they did not foresee was that the February Revolution was in its essence directed against the integrity of the armed forces themselves. They did not receive the news of the issuance of Order No. 1 until after the February Revolution.

Nicholas had to pay the price for his intransigence. He had irretrievably alienated the forces that could have come to his rescue against the threat of revolution. When he allowed the creation of a responsible ministry under the collective pressure of the commanders and against all his moral and religious convictions, Nicholas was already a broken man. The acceptance of his abdication demanded by the liberals and supported by the military leaders was easier for Nicholas after that concession. Once Nicholas accepted his abdication, it was impossible in the revolutionary crisis for other members of the dynasty to attempt to preserve the monarchical system. It was indicative of the extent of the erosion of tsarist authority that during the entire course of the revolution only one military commander declared his willingness to sacrifice his life for the tsar. Despite its three centuries of history, tsarism had failed to create a mystical symbol of the tsar even among its most faithful subjects.

The February Revolution was complete. The old regime no longer existed, but all the important issues—now out in the open—remained unsolved. The February Revolution was thus merely the beginning of a more violent revolutionary process.

APPENDIXES

APPENDIX 1. CHRONOLOGY IN BRIEF

1917	Masses	Revolutionary leaders and Petrograd Soviet	Government and security authorities	Duma and Duma Committee	Military leaders	Nicholas
Feb. 23	International Women's Day triggers strike for women textile workers. Strike spreads to metal-workers in Vyborg District. Demonstration in Vyborg District.	Vyborg District Committee decides to expand the movement. Representatives of labor movement meet.	Cossacks show reluctance to interfere. Security authorities decide to move to second stage of contingency plan.	Duma meets and passes motion to organize supply of food.		
Feb. 24	Strike burgeons; strikers cross the Neva; all districts in city involved. Demonstration in Nevskii Prospekt.	Gap widens between Bolshevik activists and Russian Bureau. Leaders of labor movement continue to meet.	Cossacks again fail to act forcefully and even chase away some police.	Great agitation in Duma. Rodzianko urges meeting with government on food supply crisis.		
Feb. 25	General strike. Almost all workers including Putilov workers join. City is paralyzed.	Call for establishment of soviet becomes widespread. Revolutionary intelligentsia meet.	A few soldiers defect. Rifle fire is used by police under provocation, 9 persons killed. Police chiefs Shalfeev and Krylov killed by demonstrators. Khabalov receives Nicholas's telegram to quell disturbance. Police arrest more than 100 leaders. Government begins negotiations with Duma.	Duma still discusses food distribution. Joint meeting of Duma representatives and government decide to transfer food distribution to city duma. City duma meets in revolutionary atmosphere.		News finally reaches Nicholas and the Stavka. Nicholas orders Khabalov to quell disturbance. Beliaev assures that measures are being taken.
Feb. 26	Demonstrators meet with systematic firing by troops. More than 50 killed.	Revolutionary leaders predict that with troops firing the movement will come to an end.	Troops begin firing on demonstrators. One company of Pavlovskii Regiment deserts, but are arrested. Government discontinues negotiations with Duma and hands down decree of prorogation.	Rodzianko wires tsar, recommending ministry of confidence. He receives notice of Duma's prorogation.		Nicholas dismisses Rodzianko's telegram as coming from an alarmist.

Feb. 27	Soldiers' insurrection begins. Revolt begun by Volynskii Regiment spreads. Strikers seize arms. Insurgents take over prisons, release prisoners. Anarchy spreads. Insurgents march to Tauride Palace; begin to arrest ministers.	Socialists form Soviet of Workers' Deputies; ask insurgents to elect delegates. Military Commission and Food Supply Commission are formed. First Soviet session begins. Executive Committee elected.	Khabalov improvises counterinsurgency measures, but loyal troops quickly disintegrate. Government resigns. Arrests of ministers begin. Khabalov asks Stavka for reinforcements.	Duma forms Duma Committee.	Stavka receives contradictory messages.	Nicholas refuses Mikhail's recommendation. Dismisses Khabalov, appoints Ivanov. Decides to leave Mogilev for Tsarskoe Selo.
Feb. 28	All military units join insurrection, which spreads to Tsarskoe Selo. Insurgents continue to march to Tauride Palace. Workers' militia is formed in Vyborg District. Insurgents begin electing deputies to Soviet.	First issue of *Izvestiia* prints Petrograd Soviet's proclamation. Second Soviet session denounces Rodzianko's order.	Loyal troops disintegrated. Khabalov arrested. Protopopov surrenders.	Duma Committee decides to take power: sanctions arrest of ministers; takes over Ministry of Transport; Bublikov sends telegram to railway stations; takes over Military Commission. Rodzianko's order is issued; city militia is formed. Rodzianko advocates responsible ministry and mobilizes support of grand dukes.	Stavka commits itself to counterrevolution. Calls more reinforcements for Ivanov. Ivanov leaves Mogilev.	Nicholas leaves Mogilev.
March 1	Workers' militia formed in parts of city. Soldiers attend Petrograd Soviet session, formulate demands, which develop into Order No. 1. Revolt of soldiers in Luga.	Executive Committee discusses problem of power. Right advocates coalition government; extreme Left calls for provisional revolutionary government. Executive Committee accepts Order No. 1, calls for surrender of weapons, confiscates Mezhraiontsy -SR leaflet.		Lomonosov and Bublikov manipulate movement of tsar's train. Duma Committee seeks Nicholas's abdication. Rodzianko's influence wanes; Miliukov's increases. Miliukov begins list of Provisional Government members.	Stavka learns of existence of Duma Committee. Ivanov arrives at Tsarskoe Selo. Alekseev orders halt of Ivanov's operations. Stavka is alarmed by spread of revolution to Moscow, Kronstadt, and the Baltic Fleet. Alekseev advocates responsible ministry.	Nicholas changes direction of his trains at Bologoe, arrives at Pskov at 8 P. M. Ruzskii asks for responsible ministry; Nicholas accedes, and halts Ivanov's operation.

APPENDIX 1 —*Continued*

1917	Masses	Revolutionary leaders and Petrograd Soviet	Government and security authorities	Duma and Duma Committee	Military leaders	Nicholas
March 2	Luga Military Committee disarms Borodin Company. The masses react to Miliukov's announcement of monarchy with hostility. Soldiers' attacks on officers increase. Search and looting rampant.	In early morning, Executive Committee negotiates with Duma Committee for transfer of power. Decides to merge workers' and city militias. Results of negotiation with Duma Committee approved by Soviet session with overwhelming majority. Kerenskii obtains sanction to join Provisional Government. Steklov formulates Soviet conditional support for Provisional Government.		Duma Committee conducts negotiations with Executive Committee on conditions for transfer of power. Sends Guchkov and Shul'gin to Pskov to gain Nicholas's abdication. Bublikov and Lomonosov try to hinder Ivanov's movement. Miliukov announces formation of Provisional Government and transfer of power to Mikhail.	Rodzianko reveals to Ruzskii that Nicholas's abdication is necessary. Military leaders now recommend Nicholas's abdication.	Ruzskii recommends abdication. Nicholas accepts. Later, meeting with Duma Committee delegates, abdicates not only for himself but also for his son in favor of Mikhail.
March 3	Streets begin to return to normal.	*Izvestiia* prints both Provisional Government and Soviet proclamations. Steklov formulates Soviet's conditional support for Provisional Government. Abdication of Nicholas and Mikhail is printed late at night.		Duma Committee and Provisional Government meet with Mikhail. Miliukov fights to retain monarchy but Mikhail responds to pressure from others to abdicate. L'vov's first proclamation as head of Provisional Government.	Rodzianko asks Alekseev to postpone distribution of Nicholas's abdication manifesto. Alekseev learns that he has been outwitted by Rodzianko and proposes a military conference, but other commanders reject Alekseev's proposal. Ivanov relieved of post.	Nicholas leaves Pskov, arrives in Mogilev.

APPENDIX 2. INVOLVEMENT OF PETROGRAD FACTORIES IN STRIKES, 1914–1917

The classification of industries and the number of workers are based on *Spisok fabrichno-zavodskikh predpriiatii Petrograda* with slight modifications. The totals following each group indicate the number of such factories in Petrograd. Since factories employing fewer than 100 workers are not listed, the figure may not agree with the number of factories listed. The total number of workers in each group also includes workers in factories with less than 100 employees. *Spisok* did not list the total number of workers in Kahn Paper.

Sources for the strikes were (1914–16) *Rabochee dvizhenie v Petrograde*; (Jan. 9, 1917)

TsGAOR, f. POO, op. 5, d. 669, *ll.* 41–42; (Feb. 14, 1917) TsGAOR, f. DPOO, op. 341, ch. 57/1917, *ll.* 31–32; TsGIA, f. 1282, 1917 g., op. 1, d. 741, *ll.* 4, 7; (Jan.-Feb, 1917) TsGAOR, f. DPOO, op. 341, ch. 57/1917g.; TsGAOR, f. POO, op. 1917, d. 669a; TsGAOR, f. POO, op. 5, d. 669; (Feb.-23-25, 1917) TsGIA, f. 1282, 1917 g., op. 1, d. 741; TsGIA, f. 23, op. 16, d. 253.

NOTE: e indicates an economic strike.

Industry	Number of workers	1914-15 Aug. '14–July '15 (e)	Aug. 17-19	Sept. 2-4	Aug.-Dec. (e)	1916 Jan. 9	March 1-3	Jan.-Aug. (e)	Oct. 17-19	Oct. 26-28	Sept.-Dec. (e)	1917 Jan. 9	Feb. 14	Jan.-Feb. (e)	Feb. 23	Feb. 24	Feb. 25
METALS/HARDWARE																	
General Production																	
Neva Shipbuilding	6,141	•		•		•		•			•	•	•	•			•
Obukhov	10,600	•			•			•				•	•	•			•
Petrograd Metal	6,704	•		•	•		•	•			•	•	•	•	•		•
Putilov	24,449			•	•	•	•					•	•			•	
Franco-Russian Factory	6,656					•		•				•			•		
TOTALS 5	54,550																
Foundries																	
Aleksandrov	165																
Vitt & Bruns	105																
Liteishchik	291																
Ozoling	129					•						•					
Parviainen	206															•	
Smolenkov	104								•							•	
Trud	151															•	
TOTALS 24	1,706															•	
Metal Rolling																	
Donetsko-Iurievskii	287																
Petrograd Copper (Rosenkrantz)	3,773			•		•		•				•			•		•

APPENDIX 2 —*Continued*

Industry	Number of workers	1914-15				1916						1917					
		Aug. '14–e July '15	Aug. 17-19	Sept. 2-4	Aug.–e Dec.	Jan. 9	March 1-3	Jan.–e Aug.	Oct. 17-19	Oct. 26-28	Sept.–e Dec.	Jan. 9	Feb. 14	Jan.–e Feb.	Feb. 23	Feb. 24	Feb. 25
Northern Society of Pipe Rolling	228																•
TOTALS 4	4,333																
Machine Construction																	
Aivaz	4,086		•	•		•	•	•	•		•	•	•			•	•
Anchar	600										•	•	•			•	•
Arsenal of Peter the Great	3,958											•	•		•	•	•
Atlas-Petrograd	523							•	•	•	•	•			•		•
Baranovskii, I	300															•	•
Baranovskii, II	1,296		•	•		•									•	•	•
Beier	170				•									•			•
Veltz	121							•	•		•	•	•		•	•	•
Ventilo	320												•			•	•
Westinghouse	415			•	•	•						•	•			•	•
Vulkan	1,094		•	•	•	•						•					
Gil'zovoi Pipe	666																•
Glukhoozerskii (Pulemet)	870																
Dekhtelev	125			•	•	•		•	•		•	•	•		•	•	•
Dinamo, I	514							•			•	•				•	•
Dinamo, II	2,109																•
Zabaikan	190																
Zelenov	785																
Zigel'	592			•								•					•
Kerting	210																
Kravtsovich	146																
Kreinin	147																
Krug	191																
Langenzippen	2,583			•					•		•	•	•	•	•	•	•
Mantel'	215																•
Miklitskii	110																•
Nobel	1,597			•	•	•	•	•	•	•	•	•	•	•	•	•	•
Ekval'	300						•	•	•	•		•				•	•

Odner	279
Orudinskii	3,500
Ouf	262
Pastor	198
Petrograd Cartridge, I	8,292
Petrograd Cartridge, II	3,788
Petekerov	171
Pneumatic Machine	248
Promet, I	719
Promet, II	2,985
Prelovskii	115
Reikhel'	250
Ressora	117
Russian Renault	1,670
Russian-Baltic Machine	389
Parviainen	7,316
San-Galli	1,168
Semenov	705
Siemens-Schückert	3,091
Old Lessner	1,111
New Lessner	6,511
Northern Machine & Boiler	1,469
Technological Institue	1,472
Petrograd Pipe	19,046
Tunel'd	265
Faians	245
Phoenix	1,940
Franco-Russian, Railway signal	187
Khessein	100
Shkilin & Kirt	128
Stein	345
TOTALS 118	94,877

Metal Fitting

TOTALS 8	286

APPENDIX 2 —Continued

Industry	Number of workers	Aug. '14-[e] July '15	Aug. 17-19	Sept. 2-4	Aug.-[e] Dec.	Jan. 9	March 1-3	Jan.-[e] Aug.	Oct. 17-19	Oct. 26-28	Sept.-[e] Dec.	Jan. 9	Feb. 14	Jan.-[e] Feb.	Feb. 23	Feb. 24	Feb. 25
		1914-15				**1916**						**1917**					
Fitting: Repair & Assembly																	
Petrograd Artillery Warehouse	1,222																
TOTALS 6	1,298																
Wire and Nail																	
Aristov	123																•
Military Horse-shoes	2,645															•	•
Petichev	493															•	•
Donetsko-Iurievskii	1,852							•									•
Northern Wire & Nail	116																•
TOTALS 12	5,395																
Tin Soldering																	
Blagodarev	504																•
Wolfson	200															•	•
Granata	430																•
Koka & Birman	258																
Molodtsov	202																
Nikiforov	319																
Trainin	300															•	
Elektrozhest	123															•	•
TOTALS 20	2,698																
Electrotechnics																	
Bip & Saveliev	106															•	•
Geisler	746															•	•
Diuflon & Konstan-tinovich	823	•		•	•	•	•		•		•	•	•		•	•	•
Armaturnyi	960					•	•		•			•	•		•	•	•
Petrograd Electro-technical, III	631																

technical, IV	211
Petrograd Electro-technical, V	237
Reks	104
Russian Society of Wireless Tel. & Tel.	495
Siemens-Haliske	1,560
Siemens-Schückert	1,968
United Cable	2,274
Electromechanical	266
Tudor	215
Electrical Energy	176
Erikson	2,212
TOTALS 28	13,366

Shipbuilding

Admiralty Shipyard, I	4,476
Admiralty Shipyard, II	254
Baltic Shipyard	7,645
Grebnyi Port	286
Johanson	446
Okhta	117
Putilov Shipyard	4,178
Finland Steamship	200
TOTALS 11	17,667

Wagon

Aleksandrovskii Machine	1,965
Koppel	625
Petrograd Wagon	2,004
International Assn. of Sleeping Wagon	286
Northern Assn. of Railway Construction	1,000
TOTALS 5	5,880

APPENDIX 2 —Continued

Industry	Number of workers	1914-15				1916						1917					
		Aug. '14-e July '15	Aug. 17-19	Sept. 2-4	Aug.-e Dec.	Jan. 9	March 1-3	Jan.-e Aug.	Oct. 17-19	Oct. 26-28	Sept.-e Dec.	Jan. 9	Feb. 14	Jan.-e Feb.	Feb. 23	Feb. 24	Feb. 25
Automobile																	
Avto-otdel, Orudin-skii Factory	240																
Puzyrev	227		•	•		•	•	•	••	•		•		•	•	•	•
Russian Baltic Motor	370			•		•	•		•	•						•	•
TOTALS 4	902																
Aeronautic																	
Lebedev	1,085	•	•	•		•		•	•	•		•	•	•	•	•	•
Russian-Baltic	500		•	•		•	•	•	•			•	•	•	•	•	•
Sliusarenko	227		•	•			•		•			•	•			•	•
Stetinin	2,162					•	•		•	•			•		•	•	•
TOTALS 6	4,048																
Automobile-Airplane Repair																	
Armored Car Garage	769																
Nikolaev Station	193																
Petrograd Park	844																
Staledub	180																
TOTALS 14	2,253																
Others																	
Mint	894					•											•
Eduward	185				•												
Buch Brothers	152																
TOTALS 12	1,670																
TEXTILES/PAPER																	
Textile																	
Aukh	198																
James Beck	1,176					•			•		•	•			•	•	•

APPENDIX 2 —*Continued*

Industry	Number of workers	1914-15					1916						1917					
		Aug. '14-e July '15	Aug. 17-19	Sept. 2-4	Aug.-e Dec.	Jan. 9	March 1-3	Jan.-e Aug.	Oct. 17-19	Oct. 26-28	Sept.-e Dec.	Jan. 9	Feb. 14	Jan.-e Feb.	Feb. 23	Feb. 24	Feb. 25
Triumph	254														●	●	
Tiulevaia	369																
Sherst'	112																
TOTALS 45	36,848																
Weaving																	
Alafuzovskii, I	407																
Alafuzovskii, II	108																
Garmsen	108																
Glikin	750																
Kebke	763													●		●	
Kirikov	224																
Red Cross	627																
Mars	117																
Parusinovykh	399																
Pogranichnaia	350																
Rubakhin	259																
Russian Mfg. of Maple	306																
Social Aid	154																
Triumph	190																
Fain	106																
TOTALS 26	5,226																
Paper																	
Batel't	101													●	●	●	●
Bolodaevskaia	797															●	●
Kartontol	128																●
Kibbel'	524																●
Otto Kirchner	986																●
Kulymanov	184																●
Levinson-Shaub	103																
Neva Writing Paper	420																
Kahn	620															●	●

Progress	162
Russian Printing	572
Shaplygin	138
TOTALS 30	4,829

PRINTING/PUBLISHING

Brockhaus-Efron	131
Vefers	398
Vladimirskii	165
War Commissariat	335
Heller	181
Gerol'd	210
Halix & Viloborg	335
Gov't Printing Press	873
Dom Pechati	266
Ekaterinogof Printing	104
Ivanov	100
Commissariat of Social Aid	566
Novoe vremia	461
Kopeika	338
Lapiner	104
Lehman	825
Marks	690
New Petrograd Newspaper	120
Prosveshchenie	210
Rabochee delo	321
Slovo	181
Expedition of Gov't Papers	5,784
Iakovlev	130
TOTALS 148	14,560

WOOD PROCESSING

Brandt	158
Beliaev	155
Volkovyskii	130
Grigoriev	200

APPENDIX 2 —Continued

Industry	Number of workers	1914-15				1916						1917					
		Aug. '14-e July '15	Aug. 17-19	Sept. 2-4	Aug.-e Dec.	Jan. 9	March 1-3	Jan.-e Aug.	Oct. 17-19	Oct. 26-28	Sept.-e Dec.	Jan. 9	Feb. 14	Jan.-e Feb.	Feb. 23	Feb. 24	Feb. 25
Gromov, I	259															•	•
Gromov, II	289															•	•
Zass	135																
Lebedev, D. N.	100																•
Mel'tser	228						•		•			•	•			•	•
Rusanov	104																
Russkaia Fanera	280																
Semenov, I. A.	651							•									•
Sokolova	172																
Shreder	225	•				•		•			•	•	•			•	•
TOTALS 52	**4,956**																
MINERAL PROCESSING																	
Glukhoozerskii Cement	338																
Denfer	244																
Zhelezno-Tsement	169																
Morgan	175																
Petrograd Glass	367																
Struk	286		•	•	•	•	•					•			•	•	•
Farforovyi	463													•		•	•
TOTALS 18	**4,854**																
LEATHER/SHOES																	
Brusnitsyn	391															•	•
Neva Shoes, I	111															•	•
Osipov	1,281								•								
Paramonov	331																•
Petrograd Leather	436															•	•
Bystrokhod	111																
Veis	145															•	•
Neva Shoes, II	1,260			•				•	•			• •	•			• •	• •
Skorokhod	4,909				•												•

Stoliarov	121	
Kharmadzhev	122	
Sampsonievskii		
Trade	178	
Sanov	180	
Bekhli	248	
Trezor	676	
TOTALS	35	11,181

FOOD/LIQUOR/TOBACCO

Food and Liquor

Ivanov Macaroni	103	
Blinken & Robinson	352	
George Borman	685	
Karl Bezdek	409	
Konradi	320	
Kraft	149	
Mignon	179	
Shuvalov	200	
Kenig Sugar	967	
Gutuevskii State		
Liquor	105	
Keller	100	
Bavaria Beer	176	
Kalinin Beer	349	
Astra	158	
Salolin	111	
TOTALS	40	5,208

Tobacco

Bogdanov, I	1,899	
Bogdanov, II	459	
Havana	379	
Kolobov & Bobrov	841	
Laferm	2,362	
Shaposhnikov	1,831	
TOTALS	6	7,771

CHEMICALS

Pel' Chemical Lab.	148

APPENDIX 2 —Continued

Industry	Number of workers	1914-15				1916						1917					
		Aug.'14-[e] July '15	Aug. 17-19	Sept. 2-4	Aug.-Dec.	Jan. 9	March 1-3	Jan.-[e] Aug.	Oct.-[e] 17-19	Oct. 26-28	Sept.-[e] Dec.	Jan. 9	Feb. 14	Jan.-[e] Feb.	Feb. 23	Feb. 24	Feb. 25
Petrograd																	
Chemical Lab.	156																
Perun	727									•	•	•	•			•	•
Tentelev	1,119																
Zhukov	174																
Kurganskii	128																
Neva Detergent	1,173																
Petrograd City Gas	550																
Okhta Explosives	10,200																
Okhta Gunpowder	5,725																•
Petrograd Matches	420																•
Vacuum Oil	134																
Rezvyi	235																
TOTALS 55	22,515																
RUBBER																	
Protivogaz	1,890																
Treugol'nik	15,338						•			•						•	•
TOTALS 2	17,228																
OPTICAL/SURGICAL INSTRUMENTS																	
Main Hydrographic Admin.	117																
Optico-Mechanical	987																
Petrograd Optical	500												•		•	•	•
TOTALS 24	2,458																

BIBLIOGRAPHY

ABBREVIATIONS

ARR: *Arkhiv russkoi revoliutsii*
KA: *Krasnyi arkhiv*
KL: *Krasnaia letopis'*
PR: *Proletarskaia revoliutsiia*
RL: *Russkaia letopis'*
TsGIA: Tsentral'nyi gosudarstvennyi istoricheskii arkhiv SSSR (Leningrad)
TsGAOR: Tsentral'nyi gosudarstvennyi arkhiv Oktiabr'skoi revoliutsii i sotsiali-
sticheskogo stroitel'stva SSSR (Moscow)
LGIA: Leningradskii gosudarstvennyi istoricheskii arkhiv SSSR (Leningrad)
OR GBL: Otdel rukopisi gosudarstvennoi biblioteki imeni V. I. Lenina (Moscow)
f.: fond
op.: opis'
d.: delo
ll.: listy
l. list

ARCHIVES

TsGIA, f. 23 (Ministry of Trade and Industry)
    op. 16, d. 253, Svedeniia statistiki (doneseniia) fabrichnogo inspektura o
    zabastovochnom dvishenii.
TsGIA, f. 150 (Petrograd Association of Factory Owners)
    op. 1, d. 207, Perepiska s MT i Pr., Voennym ministerstvom i predpriiatiiami
    po voprosu predostavleniia ot srochek rabochim i sluzhashchim v sviazi s
    mobilizatsiei ratnikov opolcheniia l-go i 2-go razriada.
    op. 1, d. 215, Perepiska s ministrom prodovol'stviia, uchrezhdeniiami i pred-
    priiatiiami po voprosu snabzheniia rabochikh i sluzhashchikh produktami
    pitaniia.

op. 1, d. 669, Statisticheskie svedeniia o khode zabastovok na zavodakh i fabrikakh Petrogradskogo promyshlennogo raiona.

op. 1, d. 673, Perepiska s raznymi predpriiatiiami o zabastovkakh rabochikh s prilozheniem iz trebovanii.

TsGIA, f. 457 (Special Council for Food Supplies)

op. 1, d. 10, O khode rabot Osobogo soveshchaniia.

op. 1, d. 67, O poezdkakh Ministra zemledeliia.

op. 1, d. 78, Ob"iasneniia v Gosudarstvennoi dume upravliaiushchego M-vom zemledeliia senatora A. A. Rittikha o polozhenii prodov dela v imperii po zaprosami ot 19/XI, 1916 g.

op. 1, d. 487, Materialy soiuza gorodov o regulirovanii snabzheniia armii i naseleniia prodovol'stviem.

op. 1, d. 209, Po pis'mu MVD Preds.: Jateliu Soveta Ministrov o vzaimootnosheniiakh MVD i gubernatorov.

op. 2, d. 5, O tverdykh tsenakh.

op. 2, d. 6, Osobyi zhurnal soveta Ministrov ot 27 marta, 28 aprelia, i 8 maia 1915 goda.

TsGIA, f. 892 (Balashovs)

op. 1, d. 1581, Proekt rezoliutsii s popravkami, priniatymi v zasedanii postoiannogo soveta za noiabria 1916 goda.

TsGIA, f. 1099 (A. A. Klopov)

op. 1, d. 3, Pis'mo A. A. Klopova vel. Kniaziu Mikhailu Aleksandrovichu s pros'boiu peredat' pis'ma o perezhivaemom momente i o kn. G. E. L'vove imp. Nikolaiu II.

op. 1, d. 15.

op. 1, d. 16, Proekt reskripta Imp. Nikolaia II, sostavlennyi A. A. Klopovym.

op. 1, d. 17, Biograficheskaia spravka o Kn. L'vove.

op. 1, d. 20, Konspekt razgovora A. A. Klopova s Im. Nikolaem II.

TsGIA, f. 1090, (A. I. Shingarev)

op. 1, d. 163, Poslanie k Shingarevu ot vremennogo komiteta gorodskoi dumy.

TsGIA, f. 1093, op. 1, d. 372, Vypiski iz rezoliutsii Nikolaia II na vsepodanneishikh otchetakh gubernatorov i ministrov i dr. dokumentakh za 1894-1916 gg.

TsGIA, f. 1101 (Various personal papers)

op. 1, d. 1195, Dnevnik gimnazista o sobytiiakh v Petrograde 23 fevralia-1 marta, 1917 g.

TsGIA, f. 1276 (The Council of Ministers)

op. 5, d. 16, Podlinnyia bumagi po zasedaniiu Osobago soveshchaniia 12-go oktiabria 1916 g.

op. 8, d. 679, ch. III, delo materialy nabliudenii za deliatel'nost'iu fraktsii i otdel'nykh chlenov Gosudarstvennoi dumy.

op. 10, d. 7, Perepiska s predsedatelem Gos. dumy i ministrami po otdel'nymi voprosam deiatel'nosti Gosudarstvennoi dumy.

op. 11, d. 975, O merakh k uporiadochniiu prodovol'stvennogo dela v Imperii.

op. 12, d. 1288b, Delo kantseliarii soveta ministrov po voprosu o merakh k uporiadochniiu dela snabzheniia prodovol'stviem armii i naseleniia.

op. 12, d. 1790, Protokol zasedaniia Soveta ministrov, 15 oktiabria, 1916 goda.

op. 12, d. 1806, Perepiska predsedatelia Soveta ministrov s raznymi uchrezhdeniiami po raznym voprosam: ob organizatsii i snabzhenii armii i tyla prodovol'stviem i toplivom: snabzhenii armii, Petrograda i naseleniia dr. raionov prodovol'stviem i toplivom.

op. 12, d. 1818, Doklady, A. F. Trepova Nikolaiu II o zapreshchenii sozyva rasporiaditel'nogo s''ezda Vserossiiskogo gorodskogo soiuza, prodovol'-stvennogo soveshchaniia gorodskogo i zemskogo soiuzov.

op. 13, d. 21, Perepiska predsedatelia Soveta ministrov s ministrom vnutrennikh del o polnomochiiakh ego po razresheniiu s''ezdov i sobranii.

op. 13, d. 33, Predstavleniia Tsentral'nogo voenno-promyshlennogo komiteta s protestom protiv razgroma rabochei gruppy Komiteta i s khodataistvom o vostanovlenii v dolzhnosti gorodskogo inzhenera predsedatelia Permskogo oblastnogo voenno-promyshlennogo komiteta.

op. 13, d. 34, Zaiavlenie 30 chlenov Gosudarstvennoi dumy po povodu nezakonomernykh deistvii chinov administratsii po otnosheniiu k rabochim i ikh professional'nym organizatsii.

op. 13, d. 36, Telegramma ministra vnutrennikh del na imia dvortsovogo komendanta o nachale revoliutsii v Petrograde.

op. 13, d. 48, Po voprosu ob obespechenii prodovol'stvennykh nuzhd g. Petrograda.

TsGIA, f. 1278 (The State Duma)

op. 5, d. 266, Gosudarstvennaia duma, stenograficheskii otchet, sozyv IV, sessia V. Zasedanii 1-oe, noiabria, 1916 g.

op. 5, d. 330, Stenograficheskii otchet, zasedanii biudzhetnoi komissii za 1916 g.

op. 5, d. 331, Biudzhetnaia komissiia. Stenograficheskii otchet, zasedanii komissii, 24 ianvaria 1917 g.- 21 fevralia, 1917 g.

op. 5, d. 446, Zhurnal komissii po voennym i morskim delami.

op. 5, d. 1252, S raznogo roda zaiavleniiami i khodataistvami kasaiushchimisia· organizatsii vlasti eia deiatel'nosti i sozyva uchreditel'nogo sobraniia.

op. 10 (The Duma Committee and the Military Commission)

op. 10, d. 3, Prikazy i rasporiazhenii predesedatelia Vremennogo komiteta Gos. dumy o besprekoslovnom vypolnenii uchrezhdeniiami i vedomstvami rasporiazhenii komissarov Vremennogo komiteta Gos. dumy.

op. 10, d. 4, Telegramma i dokladnye zapiski gorodskikh dum, glavnokomanduiushchikh okrugov, komendantov krepostei i professional'nykh soiuzov i dr. Vremennomu komitetu Gos. dumy ob organizatsii vlasti na mestakh, o nastroenii i sostoianii voinskikh chastei na fronte i v tylu, o rabote metallurgicheskikh zavodov na Urale i na iuge i dr.

op. 10, d. 5, Telegrammy predsedatelia Vrem. Kom. Gos. Dumy M. V. Rodzianko v Stavku i glavkomam vsekh frontov o sverzhenii samoderzhaviia.

op. 10, d. 6, Komandirovochnye i okhrannye udostovereniia i svidetel'stva vydannye raznym litsam Vremennym Komitetom Gosudarstvennoi dumy.

op. 10, d. 7, Prikazy i telegrammy o naznachenii komissarov Vremennogo komiteta gosudarstvennoi dumy dlia organizatsii vlasti o podavlenii zabastovochnogo dvizheniia v gorodakh Sestroretske, Revele, na Kavkaze i dr.

op. 10, d. 8, Perepiska predsedatelia Vremennogo komiteta Gosudarstvennoi dumy M. V. Rodzianko so Stavki i glavkomom Severnogo fronta po povodu naznacheniia gen. Kornilova glavkomom Petrogradskogo voennogo okruga, rezoliutsii sobranii soldat i ofitserov s privetstviiami Vremennomu pravitel' stvu.

op. 10, d. 9, Prikazy, rasporiazheniia i tsirkuliary Vremennogo pravitel'stva.

op. 10, d. 10, Delo Voennoi komissii Vremennogo pravitel'stva o vybore komandirov i registratsii voinskikh chastei.

op. 10, d. 11, Delo o pozhertvovaniiakh otdel'nykh lits, organizatsii i uchre-
zhdenii Vremennomu pravitel'stvu: spiski zhertvuiushchikh.

op. 10, d. 12, Vozvanie Vremennogo komiteta Gosudarstvennoi dumy k
naseleniiu, soldatam i t. d. v sviazi so sverzheniem samoderzhaviia.

op. 10, d. 19, Delo o reorganizatsii Voennoi komissii pri Vremennom komitete
Gosudarstvennoi dumy.

op. 10, d. 48, Voennaia komissiia. Prikazy po voprosam naznacheniia i per-
emeshcheniia militsionerov i vydacha im oruzhiia.

op. 10, d. 46, Voennaia komissiia. Voennye soobshchenii.

op. 10, d. 55, Prikazy ob arestakh raznykh lits.

op. 10, d. 56, Prikazy i tsirkuliary voennoi komissii; protokoly zasedanii
batalionnogo komiteta.

TsGIA, f. 1282. Chancellery of the Ministry of Internal Affairs.

op. 1, 737, Spravki i doneseniia o zabastovkakh na predpriiateliakh gorodov
Peterburga i Ivanovo-Voznesenska, Moskovskoi i Viatskoi gubernii v 1915-
1917 gg.

op. 1, d. 738, zapiska neustanovlennogo litsa o deiatel'nosti rabochikh grupp
voenno-promyshlennykh komitetov i ob ispol'zovanii ikh bol'shevikami
dlia legal'noi revoliutsionnoi raboty.

op. 1, d. 741, raporty nachal'nika Okhrannogo otdeleniia MVD, ad"iutanta
Petrogradskogo zhandarmskogo diviziona i politseiskikh pristavov o rev-
oliutsionnom dvizhenii v Petrograde v polednikh chislakh fevralia 1917
goda.

op. 1, d. 1165, O sozyve Glavnym komitetom Vserossiiskogo soiuza zemstv
i gorodov soveshcheniia po prodovol'stvennomu voprosu.

TsGIA, f. 1405, The Ministry of Justice

op. 177, d. 1972, Delo pervogo departamenta ministerstva iustitsii, ugolovnoe
otdelenie, I deloproizvodstvo o zabastovke vagonovozhatykh i konduk-
torov gorodskogo tramvaia v Petrograde.

op. 530, d. 1058, Doklady i zapiski Okhrannogo otdeleniia v Departament
politsii o revoliutsionnykh vystupleniiakh rabochikh na predpriiatiiakh
Petrograda za ianvar'-sentiabr', 1915 g.

op. 530, d. 1059, the same, za oktiabr'-dekabr', 1915 g.

op. 530, d. 1066, the same, za 1916-1917 gg.

TsGAOR, f. 6. Chancellery of the Provisional Government.

op. 1, d. 1722.

op. 2, d. 120, Zhurnal zasedaniia Vremennogo komiteta chlenov Gosudarstvennoi dumy.

TsGAOR, f. DPOO (102) (The Department of the Police, 4th Division)

d. 5, ch. 57/1917 g.

d. 27, ch. 46, 1916 g.

op. 17, d. 45, 1917 g., O dostovlenii voennoi tsenzury

d. 61, ch. 2, 1B, 1917 g.

d. 158/1917 g., O prazdnovanii 9-go ianvaria.

d. 307a, t. 2-i, 1916 g.

d. 341, ch. 57/1917 g., O brozhenii sredi rabochikh na ekonomicheskoi po-
chve.

d. 343ZS, 57 ch/1917 g., O Vserossiiskom zemskom i gorodskom soiuzakh i
o Voenno-promyshlennom komitete.

d. 347/1917, O rabochei gruppe pri VPK.

d. 347, 54/1917 g., O rabochei gruppe pri VPK.

d. 347, 46/1917 g., O rabochei gruppe pri VPK.

No. 171/1917, Zapiski o vazhneishikh sobytiiakh v oblasti razyska predstav-
liaemy g. Ministru D.

TsGAOR, f. POO (111), The Petrograd Okhrana Department.

op. 5, d. 669 (1917 g.), Delo s donoseniiami i telefonnymi soobshcheniiami
POO ob obshchestvennom dvizhenii.

d. 669a, Delo s donoseniiami nachal'nika Petrogradskogo okhrannogo otdeleniia ob obshchestvennom polozhenii.

TsGAOR, f. 579 (P. N. Miliukov)

op. 1, d. 878, Zaiavleniia v TsK KD partii D. Protopopova o neobkhodimosti
obratit'sia k tsariu s pros'boi naznachenii novogo pravitel'stva.

op. 1, d. 2235, Deiatel'nosti rabochei gruppy TsVPK, 15 fevralia 1917 g.

op. 1, d. 2844, Obzor politicheskoi deiatel'nosti obshchestvennykh organizatsii za period vremeni s 1 marta po 16 aprelia.

TsGAOR, f. 601. (Nicholas II)

op. 1, d. 1003, Proekt manifesta o rospuske Gosudarstvennoi dumy, ianvar',
1917 g.

TsGAOR, f. 622, op. 1, d. 22, Pis'ma b. vel. kn. Romanova, Mikhaila Aleksandro-
vicha Brasovoi, Natal'e Sergeevne.

TsGAOR, f. 670, op. 1, d. 439, Pis'mo V. V. Shul'gina Nikolaiu Mikhailovichu.

TsGAOR, ChSK (1467). The Extraordinary Investigation Commission.

d. 41, Protokola doprosa V. N. Voeikova.

d. 460, Protokola doprosa A. D. Protopopova, Khabalova, M. I. Tiazhel'-
nikova.

d. 466, Protokola doprosa Beliaeva, Protopopova, Lodyzhenovskogo, Go-
litsyna.

d. 643, Prilozhenie k delu generala N. I. Ivanova.

LGIA, f. 1229. The Factory Inspectorate.

d. 944, Fabrichnogo inspektora 10-go uchastka Petrogradskoi gubernii.

d. 995, Aktsionnoe obschchestvo elektro-mekhanicheskikh soobruzhenii.

d. 991, Perepiska s Russko-Baltiiskim zavodom.

d. 999, Metalicheskii i mekhanicheskii zavod Zelenova i Zimina.

LGIA, f. 1278, The Petrograd Association of Factory Owners.

op. 1, d. 183, Tsirkuliary obshchestva zavodchikov i fabrikantov.

OR GBL, f. 15, P. A. Bazilevskii.

papka IV, edinitsa khraneniia 1, Dnevnik P. A. Bazilevskogo.

OR GBL, f. 218. B. A. Engel'gardt.

No. 306, edinitsa khraneniia, 1-3, B. A. Engel'gardt, "Potonuvshii mir: Vospominaniia."

OR GBL, f. 369, B. D. Bonch-Bruevich.

No. 16, edinitsa khraneniia, 33, Kak nachalas' Fevral'skaia revoliutsiia.

No. 16, edinitsa khraneniia, 34, Fevral'skaia revoliutsiia.

No. 16, edinitsa khraneniia, 30, Pervye revoliutsionnye gazety Fevral'skoi
revoliutsii: Izvestiia i Pravda.

No. 16, edinitsa khraneniia, 36, Pervye dni Pevral'skoi revoliutsii.

Hoover Institution.

Balk, A., "Poslednie piat' dnei tsarskago Petrograda: Dnevnik posledniago
Petrogradskago gradonachal'nika" (Belgrade, 1929), typewritten.

Garvi, P., "Professional'nye soiuzy Rossii v pervye gody revoliutsii" (n.p., 1935), typewritten.
Naglovskii, A. D., "Zheleznodorozhniki v russkoi revoliutsii, 1917-1921 gg." (n.p., 1935), typewritten.
"Faksimili akta otrecheniia Nikolaia II."
Rodichev, F. I., "Vospominaniia o 1917 g." (Lausanne, 1924), typewritten.
Rogers, Leighton W., "An Account of the March Revolution" (n.p., n.d.).
Winnerton, C. T., "Letter from Petrograd" (March 12/27, 1917).
Tal', von G. A., "Memuary ob otrechenii ot prestola Rossiiskago Gosudarstva Imperatora Nikolaia II" (n.p., n.d.), handwritten.
London School of Economics.
S. P. Mel'gunov archives.

NEWSPAPERS AND CONTEMPORARY JOURNALS

Birzhevyia vedomosti (liberal newspaper, Petrograd)
Delo naroda (SR newspaper, Petrograd)
Gorodskoe delo (liberal journal devoted to the issues of urban self-government, Petrograd)
Izvestiia Petrogradskago Soveta rabochikh i soldatskikh deputatov (central organ of the Petrograd Soviet; before March 2 it was published as *Izvestiia Petrogradskago Soveta rabochikh deputatov)*
Izvestiia revoliutsionnoi nedeli (published by the committee of journalists in Petrograd; liberal leaning; Petrograd)
Poslednye novosti (émigré newspaper published by Miliukov, Paris)
Petrogradskaia pravda (Bolshevik local newspaper, Petrograd)
Pravda (central organ of the Bolshevik party, Petrograd)
Rabochaia gazeta (Menshevik newspaper, Petrograd)
Rech' (Kadet newspaper, Petrograd)
Russkii invalid (published by the Ministry of War, Petrograd)
Trud (journal devoted to cooperatives, Petrograd)
Utro Rossii (Progressists' newspaper, Moscow)
Volia Rossii (émigré SR newspaper, Prague)
Voprosy strakhovaniia (journal under Bolshevik influence devoted to insurance problems, Petrograd)

SOURCES AND CHRONICLES

Akhun, M. I. "Revoliutsionnoe dvizhenie v armii nakanune burzhuazno-demokraticheskoi revoliutsii." *Istoricheskii zhurnal,* 1937, no. 1.
Alekseev, S. A., ed. *Fevral'skaia revoliutsiia v opisaniiakh belogvardeitsev.* Moscow and Leningrad, 1926.
Avdeev, N., ed. *Revoliutsiia 1917 goda: Khronika sobytii,* vol. 1. 6 vols. Moscow, 1923-1930.
——. "Pervye dni fevral'skoi revoliutsii." *PR,* vol. 13, no. 1 (1923).
Bol'sheviki Petrograda v 1917 godu: Khronika sobytii. Leningrad, 1957.
Browder, R. P. and A. F. Kerensky, eds. *The Russian Provisional Government: Documents.* 3 vols. Stanford, Calif.: Stanford University Press, 1961.
Bunyan, James and H. H. Fisher. *The Bolshevik Revolution, 1917-1918: Documents and Materials.* Stanford, Calif.: Stanford University Press, 1934.
"Documents sur la Révolution russe." *Le monde slave,* no. 1 (July); no. 2 (August), 1917.

"Dokumenty Biuro TsK RSDRP v Rossii (iiul' 1914 g.-fevral' 1917 g.)." *Voprosy istorii KPSS*, 1965, no. 9.

"Dokumenty k 'Vospominaniiam' gen. Lukomskago." *ARR*, vol. 3 (1921).

Drezen, A. K. *Bol'shevizatsiia petrogradskogo garnizona 1917 goda: Sbornik materialov i dokumentov.* Leningrad, 1932.

"Fevral'skaia revoliutsiia i okhrannoe otdelenie." *Byloe*, vol. 29, no. 1 (1918).

"Fevral'skaia revoliutsiia 1917 goda: Dokumenty Stavki verkhovnogo glavno-komanduiushchego i shtaba glavnokomanduiushchego armiiami severnogo fronta." *KA*, vol. 21, no. 2; vol. 22, no. 3 (1927).

"Fevral'skaia revoliutsiia v dokumentakh." *PR*, vol. 13, no. 1 (1923).

"Fevral'skaia revoliutsiia v Petrograde: Materialy voennoi komissii vremennogo komiteta gosudarstvennogo dumy." *KA*, vols. 41-42, nos. 4-5 (1930).

"Fevral'skie dni v Tsarskom Sele." *KL*, vol. 25, no. 1 (1928).

Golder, Frank Alfred. *Documents of Russian History, 1914-1917.* New York, London: The Century Co., 1927.

Gor'kii, M., V. Molotov, et al. *Istoriia grazhdanskoi voiny v SSSR*, vol. 1. Moscow, 1936.

Grave, B. B. *K istorii klassovoi bor'by v Rossii vo godu imperialisticheskoi voiny.* Moscow and Leningrad, 1926.

——, ed. *Burzhuaziia nakanune fevral'skoi revoliutsii.* Moscow and Leningrad, 1927.

"Inostrannye diplomaty o revoliutsii 1917 g." *KA*, vol. 24, no. 5 (1927).

"K istorii poslednikh dnei tsarskogo rezhima (1916-1917 gg.)." *KA*, vol. 14, no. 1 (1926).

Lelevich, G. "Fevral'skaia revoliutsiia v belogvardeiskom opisanii." *PR*, vol. 13, no. 1 (1923).

Listovki peterburgskikh bol'shevikov: 1902-1917 gg. 2 vols. Moscow, 1939.

Nalivaiskii, B. Ia., ed. *Petrogradskii Sovet rabochikh i soldatskikh deputatov: protokoly zasedanii ispolnitel'nogo komiteta i biuro I. K.* Moscow and Lenintrad, 1925.

Padenie tsarskogo rezhima: Stenograficheskie otchety doprosov i pokazanii dannykh v 1917 g. v Chrezvychainoi Sledstvennoi Komissii Vremennogo Pravitel'-stva. 7 vols. Moscow and Leningrad, 1924-27.

Pervyi legal'nyi PK bol'shevikov 1917 g. Moscow and Leningrad, 1927.

"Podpol'naia rabota v gody imperialisticheskoi voiny v Petrograde." *KL*, vols. 2-3 (1922).

"Programma soiuza russkogo naroda pered fevral'skoi revoliutsii." *KA*, vol. 20, no. 1 (1927).

"Politicheskoe polozhenie Rossii nakanune fevral'skoi revoliutsii v zhandarmskom osveshchenii." *KA*, vol. 17, no. 4 (1926).

"Progressivnyi blok, 1915-1917." *KA*, vols. 50-51, nos. 1-2 (1932); 52, no. 3 (1932); 56, no. 1 (1933).

"Proval popytki Stavki podavit' Fevral'skuiu revoliutsiiu 1917 goda v Petrograde." *Voprosy arkhivovedeniia*, 1962, no. 1.

Rabochee dvizhenie v Petrograde v 1912-1917 gg. Leningrad, 1958.

"Revoliutsionnoe dvizhenie v voiskakh vo vremia mirovoi voiny." *KA*, vol. 4 (1923).

"Romanovy v pervye dni revoliutsii," *KA*, vol. 24, no. 5 (1927).

"Russkaia armiia nakanune revoliutsii." *Byloe*, vol 7, no. 1 (1918).

Shchegolev, P. E., ed. *Otrechenie Nikolaia II: Vospominaniia ochevidtsev i doku-*

menty. Leningrad, 1927.

Seminnikov, V. P., ed. *Monarkhiia pered krusheniem.* Moscow, 1927.

"Stavki i ministerstvo inostrannykh del." *KA,* vols. 27, 28, 29, 30 (1928).

"Telegrammy i razgovory po telegrafu mezhdu Pskovom, Stavkoiu i Petrogradom, otnosiashcheisia k obstoiatel'stvam otrecheniia Gosudaia Imperatora, s primechaniiami k nim general-ad"iutanta N. V. Ruzskago." *RL,* vol. 3 (1922).

"V ianvare i fevrale 1917 g.: Iz donesenii sekretnykh agentov A. D. Protopopova." *Byloe,* vol. 13, no. 7 (1918).

V ogne revoliutsionnykh boev: Raiony Petrograda v dvukh revoliutsiiakh 1917 g: Sbornik vospominanii starykh bol'shevikov-pitertsev. Moscow, 1967.

"V Petrograde nakanune fevral'skoi revoliutsii: V osveshchenii Petrogradskogo okhrannogo otdelenia." *KL,* vol. 22, no. 1 (1927).

Velikaia Oktiabr'skaia sotsialisticheskaia revoliutsiia: Khronika sobytii, vol. 1. 4 vols. Moscow, 1957.

Velikaia Oktiabr'skaia sotsialisticheskaia revoliutsiia: Revoliutsionnoe dvizhenie v Rossii posle sverzheniia samoderzhaviia. Dokumenty i materialy. Moscow, 1957.

Velikie dni rossüskoi revoliutsii 1917 g. Petrograd, 1917.

"Verkhovnoe komandovanie v pervye dni revoliutsii." *KA,* vol. 5 (1923).

"Verkhovnoe komandovanie v pervye dni revoliutsii." *ARR,* vol. 16 (1925).

Vserossiiskoe soveshchanie Soveta rabochikh i soldatskikh deputatov: Stenograficheskii otchet. Moscow and Leningrad, 1927.

Zeman, A. A. B. *Germany and the Revolution in Russia, 1915-1918: Documents from the Archives of the German Foreign Ministry.* London: Oxford University Press, 1958.

PRIMARY SOURCES

Akaemov, N. O. "Agoniia starago rezhima." *Istoricheskii vestnik,* vol. 148 (April 1917).

Aleksandr Mikhailovich, *Once a Grand Duke.* New York: Farrar & Rinehart, 1932.

———. *Kniga vospominaniia.* Paris. 1933.

Aleksandrov, P. P. *Za Narvskoi zastovoi: Vospominaniia starogo rabochego.* Leningrad, 1963.

Alekseev, M. V. "Izdnevnika." *Russkii istoricheskii arkhiv,* vol. 1 (1929).

Andrei Vladimirovich, Grand Duke. "Iz dnevnika A. V. Romanova za 1916-1917 gg." *KA,* vol. 31, no. 1 (1928).

Anet, Claude [Jean Schoepher]. *Through the Russian Revolution: Notes of an Eye-Witness from 12th March-30th May.* London: Hutchinson & Co., 1917.

Arefin, S. "Razval armii." *Belyi arkhiv,* vols. 2-3 (1928).

Bark, Sir Peter. "The Last Days of the Russian Monarchy: Nicholas II at the Headquarters." *Russian Review,* 1957, no. 3.

Bazarov, V. "Pervye shagi russkoi revoliutsii." *Letopis',* no. 2, no. 4 (1917).

Basily, Nicolas de. *Diplomat of Imperial Russia, 1903-1917: Memoirs.* Stanford, Calif.: Hoover Institution, 1973.

Benckendorff, Paul. *The Last Days at Tsarskoe Selo.* London: William Heinemann, 1927.

Bogdanovich, T. *Velikie dni revoliutsii, 23 fevralia-12 marta 1917 g.* Petrograd, 1917.

Boldyrev, V. G. "Iz dnevnika gen. V. G. Boldyreva." *KA,* vol. 23, no. 4 (1927).

Bolokonskaia, V. *Tagebuch vor und wärend der St. Peterburger Revolution.* Berlin,

1917.

Bonch-Bruevich, V. D. *Na boevykh postakh fevral'skoi i oktiabr'skoi revoliutsii*. Moscow, 1931.

Borodin, N. A. *Idealy i deistvitel'nost': Sorok let zhizni i raboty riadovogo russkogo intelligenta (1879-1919)*. Berlin, Paris: Petropolis-verlag, 1930.

Brusilov, A. A. *Moi vospominaniia*. Riga, 1929.

Bublikov, A. A. *Russkaia revoliutsiia: Vpechatleniia i mysli ochevidtsa i uchastnika*. New York, 1918.

Bubnov, A. *V tsarskoi Stavke: Vospominaniia admirala Bubnova*. New York: Izd-vo im Chekhova, 1955.

Buchanan, Sir George. *My Mission to Russia and Other Diplomatic Memoirs*. 2 vols. Boston: Little, Brown, 1923.

Buchanan, Muriel. *Krushenie velikoi imperii*. 2 vols. Paris, 1933.

Bulgakov, V. "Revoliutsiia na avtomobiliakh: Petrograd v. fevrale 1917 g." *Na chuzhoi storone*, vol. 4 (1924).

Buryshkin, P. A. *Moskva kupecheskaia*. 1924. New York: Izd-vo im Chekhova, 1954.

Buxhoewden, Baroness Sophie. *The Life and Tragedy of Alexandra Fedorovna, Empress of Russia*. London, New York: Longmans, Green, 1928.

Cherniavskii, Michael, ed. *Prologue to Revolution: Notes of A. N. Iakhontov on the Secret Meetings of the Council of Ministers, 1915*. Englewood Cliffs, N. J.: Prentice-Hall, 1967.

Chernov, V. M. *Pered burei*. New York: Izd-vo im Chekhova, 1953.

Dainskii, I. *Kak proizoshla russkaia revoliutsiia*. Moscow, 1917.

Demidov, I. "Tsarskoe Selo 1-go marta 1917 g." *Poslednie novosti*, March 12, 1927.

Danilov, Iu. N. "Moi vospominanii ob Imperatore Nikolae II-om i Vel. Kniaze Mikhaile Aleksandroviche." *ARR*, vol. 19 (1928).

Denikin, A. I. *Ocherki russkoi smuty*, vol. 1, pt. 1. 5 vols. Paris, Berlin, 1921-26.

——. *The Russian Turmoil: Memoirs, Military, Social and Political*. London: Hutchinson, 1922.

——. *Put' russkogo ofitsera*. New York: Izd-vo im Cheknova, 1953.

Dingel'stadt, F. N. "Vesna proletarskoi revoliutsii: Iz vpechatlenii agitatora v marte 1917 g." *KL*, vol. 12, no. 1 (1925).

"Dnevnik soldata na Vyborgskoi storone." *Pravda*, March 10, 1917.

Dobrovol'skii, O. "Iz vospominanii o pervykh dniakh revoliutsii." *RL*, vol. 3 (1922).

Dolgorukov, Prince Pavel Dmitrievich. *Velikaia razrukha*. Madrid, 1964.

Drabkina, A. K. "Prikas No. 2." *KA*, vol. 37, no. 7 (1929).

Drabkina, F. D. "Vserossiiskoe soveshchanie bol'shevikov v marte 1917 goda." *Voprosy istorii*, no. 9 (1956).

Dubenskii, D. N. "Kak proizoshel perevorot v Rossii: Zapiski-dnevniki." *RL*, vol. 3 (1922).

Dybenko, P. E. *Iz nedr tsarskogo flota v velikom Oktiabriu*. Moscow, 1958.

Egorov, I. "Matrosy-bol'sheviki nakanune 1917 g." *KL*, vol. 17, no. 2; vol. 19, no. 4.

Ermanskii, O. A. *Iz perezhitogo*. Moscow and Leningrad, 1927.

Francis, David R. *Russia from the American Embassy, April 1916-November 1918*. New York: Charles Scribner's Sons, 1921.

Gavrilov, I. "Na Vyborgskoi storone v 1914-1917 gg." *KL*, vol. 23, no. 2 (1927).

Ganetskii, Ia. "Ot fevralia k oktiobriu." *PR*, vol. 24, no. 1 (1924).

Gessen, I. V. "V dvukh vekakh: Zhiznennyi otchet." *ARR*, vol. 22 (1927).

Gilliard, Pierre. *Le tragique destin de Nicolas II et de sa famille*. Paris: Payot, 1921.

Gippius, Z. *Siniaia kniga, Peterburgskii dnevnik, 1914 gg.* Belgrade, 1929.

Glezer, D. "Na fronte v 1917 godu." *KL*, no. 6 (1923).

Golovin, N. N. *Rossiiskaia kontr-revoliutsiia v 1917-1918 gg.* 5 vols. Paris, 1937.

Golubenko, I. "Kak grenadery prisoedinilis' k narodu." *Pravda*, March 12, 1917.

Gordienko, I. "V Kronshtadte v 1917 g." *KL*, vol. 16, no. 1 (1926).

——. *Iz boevogo proshlogo*. Moscow, 1957.

Graf, G. *Na Novike: Baltiiskii flot v voinu i revoliutsii*. Munich, 1922.

Guchkov, A. I. "Vospominaniia." *Poslednye novosti*, September 13, 1936.

Gundorov, A. "Fevral' 1917 goda." *Slaviane*, no. 3 (1957).

Gurevich, V. "Real'naia politika v revoliutsii." *Volia Rossii*, no. 2 (1923).

Gurko, V. I. "Pis'mo gen. Gurko k byvsh. tsariu." *Izvestiia Petrogradskago Soveta rabochikh i soldatskikh deputatov*, September 21, 1917.

——. *Tsar' i tsaritsa*. Paris, 1927.

Hunbury-Williams, Sir John. *The Emperor Nicholas II, as I Knew Him*. London, 1922.

Iablonovskii, S. V. "Vstrecha s v. kn., Mikhailom Aleksandrovichem." *Golos minuvshago na chuzhoi storone*, vol. 14, no. 1 (1926).

Iakhontov, A. N. "Tiazhelye dni: Sekretnyia zasedaniia Soveta Ministrov-16 iiulia-2 sentiabria, 1915 goda." *ARR*, vol. 28 (1926).

Iordanskii, N. I. "Voennoe vosstanie 27 fevralia." *Molodaia gvardiia*, vol. 2 (1928).

Ivanov, Aleksandr. "Volnenie v 1916 godu v 181-om Zap. Pekh. Polku." *KL*, vol. 10, no. 1 (1924).

Ivanov, N. I. "Pis'ma generala N. I. Ivanova A. I. Guchkovu." *Russkii invalid*, March 23, 1917.

Iurenev, I. "Mezhraionka, 1911-1917 gg." *PR*, vol. 25, no. 2 (1924).

"Iz ofitserskikh pisem s fronta 1917 g." *KA*, vols. 50-51, nos. 1-2 (1932).

"Iz zametok o pervykh dniakh russkoi revoliutsii." *Volia Rossii*, March 15, 1921.

Janin, M. "Au G. H. Q. russe." *Le monde slave*, no. 1 (January), no. 2 (February), 1927.

Kaiurov, V. *Petrogradskii proletariat v gody imperialisticheskoi voiny*. Moscow, 1930.

——. "Shest' nei fevral'skoi revoliutsii." *PR*, vol. 13, no. 1 (1923).

"Kak obrazovalsia Petrogradskii Sovet." *Izvestiia Soveta rabochikh i soldatskikh deputatov*, August 27, 1917.

Kel'son, Z. "Militsiia fevral'skoi revoliutsii: Vospominaniia." *Byloe*, vol. 29, no. 1 (1925).

Kerensky, Alexander F. *The Catastrophe: Kerensky's Own Story of the Russian Revolution*. New York: Appleton, 1927.

——. *La révolution russe*. Paris: Payot, 1928.

——. "P. N. Miliukov," *Novyi zhurnal*, vol. 5 (1943).

——. *Russia and History's Turning Point*. New York: Duell, Sloan, and Pearce, 1965.

Krestinskii, N. N. "Iz vospominanii o 1914 gode." *PR*, vol. 7 (1924).

"Khod sobytii." *Pravda*, March 5, March 8, 1917.

Kirpichnikov, T. "Vozstannie 1.-gv. Volynskago polka v fevrale 1917 g." *Byloe*, vols. 27-28, nos. 5-6 (1917).

——. "Vosstanie Volynskogo polka." *Ogonek*, no. 11 (1927).

Knox, Sir Alfred. *With the Russian Army, 1914-1917: Being Chiefly Extracts from the Diary of a Military Attache.* 2 vols. New York: Dutton, 1921.

Kokovtsov, Count V. N. *Iz moego proshlago.* 2 vols. 1933. Paris: Mouton, 1969.

Kondrat'ev, A. "Vospominaniia o podpol'noi rabote v Petrograde." *KL,* no. 5 (1922), no. 7 (1923).

Korotkov, D. S. *Fevral'skaia zabastovka rabochikh Izherskikh zavodov.* Leningrad, 1927.

Kovnator, R. "Nakanune 'fevralia': Otryvki iz vospominanii." *Revoliutsionnoe iunoshestvo, 1905-1917.* Petrograd, 1924.

Krasnov, P. N. "Na vnutrennom fronte." *ARR,* vol. 1 (1921).

———. "Pamiati Imperatorskoi russkoi armii." *RL,* vol. 5 (1923).

Krylenko, N. "Fevral'skaia revoliutsiia i staraia armiia." *PR,* vols. 61-62, nos. 2-3 (1927).

Kuropotkin, A. A. "Iz dnevnika 1917 g." *KA,* vol. 20, no. 5 (1927).

Kutenov, B. G. "Zaniatie departamenta politsii (1-5 marta 1917 goda)." *Golos minuvshago na chuzhoi storone,* vol. 19, no. 6 (1928).

Kutepov, A. P. "Pervye dni revoliutsii v Petrograde: Otryvok iz vospominanii, napisannykh generalom Kutepovym v 1926 godu." In *General Kutepov: Sbornik statei.* Paris, 1934.

Kuznetsov, N. "Okhtenskii raion v fevral'skie dni 1917 g.: Revoliutsionnye kartiny." *KL,* vol. 18, no. 3 (1926).

Lemeshev, F. "Na Putilovskom zavode v gody voiny." *KL,* no. 2 (1927).

Letters of the Tsar to the Tsaritsa, 1914-1917. Stanford, Calif.: Hoover Institution, 1973.

Liubimov, I. "Fevral' na zapadnom fronte i Minskii sovdep." *PR,* vol. 17, no. 5 (1923).

Lockhart, Sir R. H. Bruce. *The Two Revolutions: An Eyewitness Study of Russia 1917.* London: Bodley Head, 1967.

Lomonosov, Iu. V. *Vospominaniia o martovskoi revoliutsii 1917 g.* Stockholm and Berlin, 1921.

Lukash, Ivan. *Pavlovtsy.* Petrograd, 1917.

———. *Preobrazhentsy.* Petrograd, 1917.

———. *Volyntsy.* Petrograd, 1917.

Lukomskii, A. S. "Iz vospominanii." *ARR,* vol. 2 (1921).

———. *Vospominaniia.* 2 vols. Berlin, 1922.

Maklakov, V. A. "Iz proshlogo." *Sovremennye zapiski,* vol. 38. Paris, 1929.

Mannerheim, Baron C. G. *Memoirs.* Translated by Count Eric Lewenhaupt. London: Cassell, 1953.

Mansyrev, Prince S. P. "Moi vospominaniia o Gosudarstvennoi dume." *Istorik sovremennik,* vol. 3 (1922).

Markov, I. "Kak proizoshla revoliutsiia." *Volia Rossii,* 1927, no. 3.

Markov, S. *Pokinutaia tsarskaia sem'ia.* Vienna, 1928.

Materialy po statistike truda severnoi oblasti. Petrograd, 1918.

Mel'gunov, S. P. *Vospominaniia i dnevniki.* Paris, 1964.

Mil'chik, I. *Rabochii fevral'.* Moscow and Leningrad, 1931.

Miliukov, P. N. *Istoriia vtoroi russkoi revoliutsii.* 3 vols. Sofia, 1921-1924.

———. "Pervyi den'." *Poslednye novosti,* March 12, 1927.

———. *Rossiia na perelome, bol'shevistskii period russkoi revoliutsii.* 2 vols. Paris: Imprimerie d'art Voltaire, 1927.

———. *Vospominaniia, 1859-1917.* 2 vols. New York: Izd-vo im Chekhova, 1955.

———. *Political Memoirs, 1905-1917.* Ann Arbor: University of Michigan Press, 1967.

Mordvinov, A. "Otryvki iz vospominanii." *RL*, vol. 5 (1923).

Mstislavskii, S. *Piat' dnei: Nachalo i konets fevral'skoi revoliutsii.* Berlin, Petrograd, Moscow, 1922.

——. "Fevral'skaia revoliutsiia." *Krasnaia panorama*, 1927, no. 11.

Nabokov, V. "Vremennoe pravitel'stvo." *ARR*, vol. 1 (1922).

Narishkin-Kurakin, Elizabeth. *Under Three Tsars: The Memoirs of the Lady-in-Waiting.* New York: E. P. Dutton, 1931.

Nazhivin, I. F. *Zapiski o revoliutsii.* Vienna: Knigoizdatel'stvo "Rus'," 1921.

Nicolas Mikhailovitch. *La fin du tsarisme: Lettres inédites à Frédéric Masson (1914-1918).* Paris: Payot, 1968.

Nikitin, B. V. *Rokovye gody.* Paris: Le Polonais en France, 1937.

Nikolai II, Emperor of Russia. "Perepiska Nikolaia Romanova s Aleksandroi Fedorovnoi." *KA*, vol. 4, no. 4 (1923).

——. "Dnevnik Nikolaia Romanova." *KA*, vol. 20, no. 1 (1927).

——. *Journal intime de Nicolas II.* Paris: Payot, 1934.

Nol'de, Baron B. E. "V. N. Nabokov v 1917 g." *ARR*, vol. 3 (1924).

——. *Dalekoe i blizkoe: Istoricheskie ocherki.* Paris, 1930.

Oberuchev, K. M. *V dni revoliutsii: Vospominaniia uchastnika russkoi revoliutsii 1917 goda.* New York, 1919.

——. *Ofitsery v russkoi revoliutsii.* New York: Pervago russkago izdatel'stvo v Amerike, 1928.

Obzor deiatel'nosti osobogo soveshchaniia dlia obsuzhdeniia i ob"edineniia meropriiatii po prodovol'stvennomu delu. Petrograd, 1916.

Paléologue, Maurice. *La Russie des tsars pendant la grande guerre.* 3 vols. Paris: Plon Nourrit, 1921-1922.

——. *An Ambassador's Memoirs.* Translated by F. A. Holt. 3 vols. New York: George H. Doran, n.d.

Paley, Princess. *Memories of Russia, 1916-1919.* London: Herbert Jenkins, n.d.

Perets, G. P. *V tsitadeli russkoi revoliutsii: Zapiski komendanta Tavricheskogo dvortsa 27 fevralia-23 marta 1917 g.* Petrograd, 1917.

Peshekhonov, A. V. "Pervyia nedeli: Iz vospominanii o revoliutsii." *Na chuzhoi storone.* vol. 1 (1923).

Petrov, F. "Iz zhizni Petrogradskoi organizatsii bol'shevikov, 1905-1917 gg." *KL*, no. 9 (1924).

Polovtsev, P. A. *Dni zatmeniia.* Paris, n.d.

"Poslednii vremenshchik poslednego tsaria." *Voprosy istorii*, 1964, no. 10, no. 12; 1965, no. 1.

Protopopov, A. D. "Iz dnevnika." *KA*, vol. 20, no. 3 (1925).

Rabinovich, S. E. "Deklaratsiia prav soldata." *PR*, vol. 66, no. 7 (1927).

——. "Komissary petrogradskogo Soveta do i posle 1917 g." *KL*, vol. 33, no. 6 (1929).

Rafes, M. G. "Moi vospominaniia." *Byloe*, vol. 19 (1922).

——. *Dva goda revoliutsii na Ukraine: Evoliutsiia i raskol "Bunda."* Moscow: Gos. izd-vo, 1920.

Raskol'nikov, F. F. *Kronshstadt i Piter v 1917 g.* Moscow and Leningrad, 1925.

Rengarten, I. I. "Fevral'skaia revoliutsiia v balticheskom flote." *KA*, vol. 32, no. 2 (1929).

Rodzianko, M. V. "Gosudarstvennaia duma i fevral'skaia 1917 goda revoliutsiia." *ARR*, vol. 4 (1922).

——. "Pis'mo Rodzianko kniaziu G. E. L'vovu: General Alekseev i vremennyi gosudarstvennoi dumy." *KA*, vol. 2 (1923).

——. "Krushenie imperii." *ARR*, vol. 17 (1926).

——. *The Reign of Rasputin: An Empire's Collapse.* 1927. Gulf Breeze, Fla.: Academic International Press, 1973.

Rumiantsev, V. D. "V Shlissel'burgskoi kreposti v fevrale 1917 g.: Vospominaniia." *KL*, vol. 22, no. 1 (1927).

Ryss, P. *Russkii opyt: Istoriko-psikhologicheskii ocherk russkoi revoliutsii.* Paris: Siever, 1921.

Salivachev, V. I. "Iz dnevnika." *KA*, vol. 19 (1923); vol. 20, no. 1 (1924).

Samoilov, F. N. *Po sledam minuvshego.* Moscow, 1954.

Saratov, N. "Fevral' na Shlissel'burgskom porokhovom zavode: Dni revoliutsii 1917 g." *PR*, vol. 13, no. 1 (1923).

Savich, S. S. "Otrechenie ot prestola Imperatora Nikolaia II." *Otechestvo*, 1919, nos. 10, 11, 12.

Semenov, E. "Fevral'skie i martovskie dni 1917 g." *Istoricheskii vestnik*, vol. 147 (1917).

——. "La révolution de Petrograde: Notes d'un témoins." *Le monde slave*, no. 1 (January, 1917).

Shepelev, V. "Fevral'skie dni." *Ogonek*, 1927, no. 7.

Shidlovskii, S. I. *Vospominaniia.* 2 vols. Berlin: O. Kirchner, 1923.

Shklovskii, Viktor. *Sentimental'noe puteshestvie: Vospominaniia 1917-1922.* Moscow and Berlin: Gelikon, 1923.

——. "Zhili-byli." *Znamia*, 1961, no. 8.

——. *A Sentimental Journey: Memoirs, 1917-1922.* Translated by Richard Sheldon. Ithaca, N. Y. : Cornell University Press, 1970.

Shliapnikov, A. "Fev'ral'skii dni v Peterburge." *Petrogradskaia pravda*, March 12, 1920.

——. "Politicheskie svodki i doneseniia." *PR*, vol. 13, no. 1 (1923).

——. *Kanun semnadtsatogo goda.* 2 pts. Moscow and Petrograd, 1923.

——. *Semnadtsatyi god.* 4 vols. Moscow and Petrograd, 1923-1931.

Shmidt, V. "V Krestakh." *Pravda*, March 12, 1927.

Shul'gin, V. V. *Dni.* Belgrade: Novoe Vremia, 1925.

Skalov, S. "27 fevralia 1917 g. v Peterburge: Vospominaniia uchastnika vosstaniia." *Krasnaia nov',* no. 3 (1931).

Skobelev, M. "Gibel' tsarizma: Vospominaniia M. I. Skobeleva." *Ogonek*, 1927, no. 11.

Slonimskii, M. *Kniga vospominanii.* Moscow and Leningrad, 1966.

Sokolov, N. D. "Kak rodilsia prikaz No. 1." *Ogonek*, 1927, no. 11.

Sorokin, P. A. *Leaves from a Russian Diary—and Thirty Years After.* 1924. Boston, 1956.

Spiridovich, A. I. *Velikaia voina i fevral'skaia revoliutsiia, 1914-1917 gg.* 3 vols. New York: Vseslavianskoe izd-vo, 1960-1962.

Spisokfabrichno-zavodskikh predpriiatii Petrograda. Petrograd, 1918.

Stankevich, V. B. *Vospominaniia, 1914-1919.* Berlin: I. P. Ladyzhnikov, 1920.

Stasova, E. D. *Stranitsy zhizni v bor'by.* Moscow, 1957.

"Stavka Verkhovnago Glavnokomandiuushchago: Dva prikaza Gosudaria Imperatora Nikolaia II—raskaz ochevidtsa." *RL*, vol. 1 (1921).

Steinberg, I. *Ot fevralia po oktiabr' 1917 g.* Berlin: Izdatel'stvo "Skify," 1919.

Steklov, Iu. "Doklad Steklova." *Izvestiia Soveta rabochikh i soldatskikh deputatov*, April 5, 1917.

——. "Po povodu stat'i A. S. Shliapnikova: Pis'mo v redaktsiuu." *PR*, vol. 13, no. 4 (1923).

——. *Vospominaniia i publitsistika*. Moscow, 1965.

Sukhanov, N. N. *Zapiski o revoliutsii*. 7 vols. Berlin: Z. I. Grzhebin, 1922-1923.

Sveshnikov, N. "Otryvki iz vospominanii." *Petrogradskaia pravda*, March 14, 1923.

——. "Vyborgskii raionnyi komitet RSDRP (b) v 1917 g." *V ogne revoliutsionnykh boev: Raiony Petrograda v dvukh revoliutsiiakh 1917 g.*

Tarasov-Rodionov, A. *February 1917: A Chronicle of the Russian Revolution*. New York: Covici-Friede, 1931.

Trotskii, Leon. *My Life*. New York: Charles Scribner's Sons, 1930.

Tseretelli, I. G. "Reminiscences of the February Revolution." *Russian Review* 14 (1955): 93-108, 184-200; 15 (1956): 37-48.

——. *Vospominaniia o Fevral'skoi revoliutsii*. 2 vols. Paris: Mouton, 1963.

Tyrkova-Williams, Adriana. *From Liberty to Brest-Litovsk: The First Year of the Russian Revolution*. London: MacMillan and Co., 1919.

Ul'ianov, Ivan. *Kazachestvo v pervye dni revoliutsii: K 3-ei godovshchine Velikoi rossiiskoi revoliutsii*. Moscow, 1920.

Varnack, E., and H. Fisher. *The Testimony of Kolchak and Other Siberian Memoirs*. Stanford, Calif.: Stanford University Press, 1935.

Vasil'ev, A. [Wassilieff]. "Mes souvenirs." *Le monde slave*, 1927, nos. 1-5.

Verkhovskii, A. I. *Rossiia na Golgofe: Iz pokhodnago dnevnika, 1914-1918*. Petrograd, 1918.

——. *Na trudnom perevale*. Moscow, 1959.

Ves' Petrograd na 1917 god: Adresnaia i spravochnaia kniga g. Petrograda. Petrograd, 1917.

Vestnik partii narodnoi svobody, no. 1, March 11, 1917.

Vil'chkovskii, S. N. "Prebyvanie Gosudaria Imperatora v Pskove, 1-i marta 1917 goda, po rasskazu general-ad''iutanta N. V. Ruzskago." *RL*, vol. 3 (1922).

Vinberg, F. V. *Krestyi put'*. Munich, 1921.

Vishniak, M. *Dan' proshlomu*. New York: Izd-vo im Chekhova, 1954.

Voeikov, V. N. *S tsarem i bez Tsaria: Vospominaniia posledniago dvortsovago Komendanta gosudaria Imperatora Nikolaia II*. Helsingors: Tip. O Liter, 1936.

Voitolovskii, L. M. "Fevral' na fronte." *Krasnaia panorama*, 1927, no. 11.

Volin, Iu. *Rozhdestvo svobody: Pobrosok iz al'man: Revoliutsiia v Petrograde*. Petrograd, 1917.

Volkonskii, Sergei. *Moi vospominaniia*. 3 vols. Berlin: Miednyi vsadnik, 1922.

Voronovich, N. "Zapiski predsedatelia soveta soldatskikh deputatov." *Arkhiv grazhdanskoi voiny*, vol. 2. Berlin, 1921.

"Vpechatleniia soldata zapasnogo batal'ona leib-gvardii Litovskogo polka." *Pravda*, no. 5, March 10, 1917.

Vrangel', P. N. "Zapiski: Noiabr' 1916-noiabr' 1920 gg." *Beloe delo*, vol. 5 (1928).

"Vremennoe pravitel'stvo: Opyt analiza." *RL*, vol. 1 (1921).

Vyrubova, A. A. [Taneeva]. "Stranitsy iz moei zhizni." *RL*, vol. 4 (1922).

"Vystuplenie 1-gv zheleznodorozhnogo batal'ona." *Pravda*, March 9, 1917.

Zalezhskii, V. N. "Pervyi legal'nyi Pe-Ka." *PR*, vol. 13, no. 1 (1923).

——. *Iz vospominanii podpol'shchika*. Moscow, 1931.

Zalutskii, P. "V poslednie dni podpol'nogo Peterburgskogo komiteta bol'shevikov v nachale 1917 g." *KL*, vol. 35, no. 2 (1930).

"Zametka soldata o revoliutsionnykh dniakh." *Pravda*, March 10, 1917.

Zaslavskii, D. "Gorod i arkhiv fevral'skoi revoliutsii." *Ogonek*, 1927, no. 11.

——. "V Gosudarstvennoi Dume." *Krasnaia panorama*, 1927, no. 11.

——, and V. A. Kantorovich. *Khronika fevral'skoi revoliutsii*. Petrograd, 1924, Zavadskii, S. V. "Na velikom izlome." *ARR*, vol. 8 (1923).

Zavarzin, P. P. *Rabota tainoi politsii*. Paris, 1924.

——. *Zhandarmy i revoliutsionery: Vospominaniia byvshego nachal'nika Kishinev-skogo, Donskogo, Varshavskogo i Moskovskogo okhrannykh otdelenii*. Paris, 1930.

Zenzinov, V. *Iz zhizni revoliutsionera*. Paris: Tipografiia I. Rirakhovskago, 1919.

——. "Fevral'skie dni." *Novyi zhurnal*, vols. 34-35 (1953).

——. *Perezhitoe*. New York: Izd-vo im Chekhova, 1955.

Zhenevskii, A. F. [Il'in]. "Gel'singfors vesnoi 1917 goda. *KL*, vol. 13, no. 2 (1925).

——. *Ot fevralia k zakhvatu vlasti: Vospominaniia o 1917 gode*. Leningrad, n.d.

Zhizn' soldata zap. batal'ona gvardii grenaderskago polka: Kazarma na obnovlen-nyk nachalakh. Petrograd, 1917.

SECONDARY SOURCES

Abramovich, R. R. *The Soviet Revolution, 1917-1939*. New York: International University Press, 1962.

Akimova, A. S. "Glavnyi po snabzheniiu armii komitet (zemgor) 1915-1918 gg." Kandidat, University of Moscow, 1972.

Alexandrov, Victor. *The End of the Romanovs*. Boston: Little, Brown, 1966.

Antsiferov, Alexis N., Alexander D. Bilimovich, et al. *Russian Agriculture during the War*. New Haven: Yale University Press, 1930.

Anweiler, Oskar. *Die Rätebewegung in Russland, 1905-1921*. Leiden: E. J. Brill, 1958.

——. "The Political Ideology of the Petrograd Soviet in the Spring of 1917." In *Revolutionary Russia*. Edited by Richard Pipes. Cambridge. Mass.: Harvard University Press, 1968.

Aronson, Grigorii. *Rossiia nakanune revoliutsii: Istoricheskie etiudy*. New York, 1962.

——. *Rossiia v epokhu revoliutsii: Istoricheskie etiudy i memuary*. New York, 1966.

Artem'ev, S. "Sostav Petrogradskogo Soveta v marte 1917 g." *Istoriia SSSR*, 1964, no. 5.

Baevskii, D. "Partiia v gody imperialisticheskoi voiny." *Ocherki po istorii Oktiabr'-skoi revoliutsii*, vol. 1.

Bater, James H. *St. Petersburg: Industrialization and Change*. Montreal: McGill-Queen's University Press, 1976.

Blok, Aleksandr. *Poslednie dni imperatorskoi vlasti*. Petrograd, 1921.

——. "Poslednie dni starogo rezhima." *ARR*, vol. 4 (1922).

Boltinov, S. "Rol' mestnykh sovetov sozdanii sovetskoi vlasti." *Sovetskoe gosudar-stvo i revoliutsiia prava* (Moscow, Leningrad), 1931, nos. 5-6.

Boyd, John. "The Origins of Order No. 1." *Soviet Studies*, vol. 19 (1968).

Burdzhalov, E. N. "O taktike bol'shevikov v marte-aprele 1917 goda." *Voprosy istorii*, 1956, no. 4.

——. "Nachalo vtoroi russkoi revoliutsii," In *Ucheny zapiski Moskovskogo gosu-darstvennogo pedagogicheskogo instituta imeni Lenina: Materialy i issledo-vaniia po istorii SSSR*. Moscow, 1964.

——. *Vtoraia russkaia revoliutsiia: Vosstanie v Petrograde*. Moscow, 1967.

——. *Vtoraia russkaia revoliutsiia: Moskva, front, periferiia*. Moscow, 1971.

Bushnell, John. "Peasants in Uniform: The Tsarist Army as a Peasant Society."

Paper presented at Mid-Atlantic AAASS meeting, April 1979.

Cartledge, Bryan. "The Russian Revolution: February, 1917." *St. Anthony's Papers*, June 1956.

Chamberlin, William Henry. *The Russian Revolution, 1917-1921*. 2 vols. New York: Macmillan, 1935.

Chermenskii, E. D. "Fevral'skaia burzhuazno-demokraticheskaia revoliutsiia 1917 goda." *Voprosy istorii*, 1957, no. 2.

———. *Fevral'skaia burzhuazno-demokraticheskaia revoliutsiia 1917 goda v Rossii*. Moscow, 1959.

———. "IV gosudarstvennaia duma i sverzhenie samoderzhaviia v Rossii: K voprosu o zagovorakh burzhuazii i tsarizma nakanune revoliutsii." *Voprosy istorii*, 1969, no. 6.

———. *IV gosudarstvennaia duma i sverzhenie tsarizma v Rossii*. Moscow, 1976.

Chernov, Viktor. *Rozhdenie revoliutsionnoi Rossii: Fevral'skaia revoliutsiia*. Paris, Prague, New York, 1934.

———. *The Great Russian Revolution*. New Haven: Yale University Press, 1936.

Danilov, Youri. *La Russie dans la guerre mondiale, 1914-1917*. Paris: Payot, 1927.

Delage, Jean. *Koutêpoff: La carrière militaire, l'exile, l'enlèvement*. Paris: Librairie Delagrave, 1930.

Deutscher, Isaac. "The Russian Revolution." *The New Cambridge Modern History*, vol. 12. Cambridge: At the University Press, 1968.

Diakin, V. S. *Russkaia burzhuaziia i tsarizm v gody pervoi mirovoi voiny*. Leningrad, 1967.

———. "K voprosu o 'zagovore' tsarizma nakanune Fevral'skoi revoliutsii." In *Vnutrennaia politika tsarizma*. Leningrad, 1967.

Drezen, A. K. "Tsentral'nye matrosskie i ofitserkie organizatsii balticheskogo flota v 1917 g." *KL*, vol. 30, no. 3 (1929).

Dvinov, B. "Pervaia mirovaia voina i Rossiiskaia sotsialdemokratiia." Inter-University Project on the History of the Menshevik Movement, papers, no. 10. New York, 1962.

Dziubinskii, V. "Revoliutsionnoe dvizhenie v voiskakh vo vremia mirovoi voiny." *KA*, vol. 4 (1923).

Fainsod, Merle. *International Socialism and the World War*. Cambridge, Mass.: Harvard University Press, 1935.

Falkova, Zh. Z. "Rabochaia gruppa strakhovogo soveta v gody pervoi mirovoi voiny." In *Sbornik Leningradskogo tekhnologicheskogo instituta pishchevoi promyshlenosti*. Leningrad, 1958.

Fallows, Thomas. "Politics and the War Effort in Russia: The Union of Zemstvos and Organization of the Food Supply, 1914-1916." *Slavic Review*, vol. 37, no. 1 (1978).

Ferro, Marc. "Les débuts du Soviet de Petrograd (27-28 février 1917-ancien style)." *Révue historique*, vol. 223, no. 2 (1960).

———. *La révolution de 1917: La chute du tsarisme et les origines d'Octobre*. Paris: Aubier, 1967.

Fleer, M. G. *Rabochee dvizhenie v Rossii v gody imperialisticheskoi voiny*. Leningrad, 1926.

———. "Rabochaia krasnaia gvardiia vo fevral'skuiu revoliutsiiu." *KL*, vol. 16, no. 1 (1926).

———. "Peterburgskii komitet bol'shevikov v gody imperialisticheskoi voiny."

KL, vol. 19, no. 4 (1926).

Florinsky, Michael T. *The End of the Russian Empire.* New Haven: Yale University Press, 1931.

Futrell, Michael. *Northern Underground: Episodes of Russian Revolutionary Transport and Communications through Scandinavia and Finland, 1865-1917.* London: Faber and Faber, 1963.

Gelis, I. "Ekspeditsiia gen. Ivanova na Petrograd." *KA*, vol. 17, no. 4 (1926).

Genkina, E. "Fevral'skaia perevorot." In *Ocherki po istorii Oktiabr'skoi revoliutsii,* vol. 2. Edited by M. N. Pokrovskii. 2 vols. Leningrad, 1927.

Geroi Oktiabria: Biografii aktivnykh uchastnikov podgotovki i provedenii Oktiabr'-skogo vooruzhennogo vosstaniia v Petrograde. 2 vols. Leningrad, 1967.

Gleason, William E. "The All-Russian Union of Towns and the Politics of Urban Reform in Tsarist Russia." *Russian Review,* vol. 35, no. 3 (1976).

Golovin, N. N. *The Russian Army in the World War.* New Haven: Yale University Press, 1931.

——. *Voennye usiliia Rossii v mirovoi voine.* Paris, 1939.

Gorovtseff, A. *Les révolutions: Comment on les éteint, comment on les attise.* Paris, 1930.

Grenard, Fernand. *La révolution russe.* Paris, 1933.

Gronsky, Paul. "La chute de la monarchie en Russie." *Revue politique et parlementaire,* vol. 116 (1923).

Gronsky, Paul F. and Nicholas J. Astrov. *The War and the Russian Government.* New Haven: Yale University Press, 1929.

Grunt, A. "Progressivnyi blok." *Voprosy istorii,* 1945, nos. 3-4.

Haimson, Leopold. "The Problem of Social Stability in Urban Russia, 1905-1917." *Slavic Review,* vol. 23, no. 4 (1964); vol. 24, no. 1 (1965).

——, ed. *The Mensheviks from the Revolution of 1917 to the Second World War.* Chicago: University of Chicago Press, 1974.

Hamm, Michael. "A Liberal Politics in Wartime Russia: An Analysis of the Progressive Bloc," *Slavic Review,* vol. 33, no. 3 (1974).

Hasegawa, Tsuyoshi. "The Problem of Power in the February Revolution in Russia." *Canadian Slavonic Papers,* vol. 14, no. 4 (1972).

——. "The Formation of the Militia in the February Revolution: An Analysis of the Origins of the Dual Power." *Slavic Review,* vol. 32, no. 2 (1973).

——. "Rodzianko and the Grand Dukes' Manifesto on 1 March 1917." *Canadian Slavonic Papers,* vol. 18, no. 2 (1976).

——. "The Bolsheviks and the Formation of the Petrograd Soviet." *Soviet Studies,* vol. 29, no. 1 (1977).

Hözle, E. "Das Kriegsproblem in der russischen Revolution 1917." *Osteuropa,* vol. 12 (1962).

Iakovlev, Ia. "Fevral'skie dni 1917 g." *PR,* vols. 61-62, nos. 2-3 (1927).

Iaroslavskii, E. "Bol'sheviki v fevral'sko-martovskie dni 1917 g." *PR,* vols. 61-62, nos. 2-3 (1927).

Ignatiev, Count Paul N., D. M. Odinets, et al. *Russian Schools and University in the World War.* New Haven: Yale University Press, 1929.

Ioffe, A. E., and B. A. Boiarskii, eds. *Zarubezhnaia literatura ob Oktiabr'skoi revoliutsii.* Moscow, 1961.

Kakurin, N. E. *Razlozhenie armii v 1917 g.* Moscow and Leningrad, 1961.

Katkov, George. *Russia 1917: The February Revolution.* New York: Harper and Row, 1967.

Keep, John L. H. *The Russian Revolution: A Study in Mass Mobilization.* New York: Norton, 1976.

Kenez, Peter. "A Profile of the Prerevolutionary Office Corps." *California Slavic Studies,* vol. 7 (1973).

Khesin, S. "Lichnyi sostav russkago flota v 1917 g." *Voenno-istoricheskii zhurnal,* 1965, no. 11.

Kikuchi Masanori. *Roshia kakumei to nihon-jin.* Tokyo: Chikuma shobo, 1973.

Kir'ianov, I. I. "Soldatskie pis'ma kak istochniki dlia izucheniia voprosa o soiuze rabochego klassa s krestianstvom v godakh pervoi mirovoi voiny." *Istoriia SSSR,* 1965, no. 2.

Kochakov, B. M. "Petrograd v gody pervoi mirovoi voiny i fevral'skoi burzhuazno-demokraticheskoi revoliutsii." In *Ocherki istorii Leningrada,* vol. 3.

——. "Sostav petrogradskogo garnizona v 1917 g." *Uchenye zapiski Leningradskogo universiteta,* 1956, no. 205.

Koenker, Diane. "Urban Families, Working-Class Youth Groups, and the 1917 Revolution in Moscow." In *The Family in Imperial Russia.* Edited by David L. Ransel. Urbana: University of Illinois Press, 1978.

Kohn, Stanislas. *The Cost of the War to Russia: The Vital Statistics of European Russia during the World War, 1914-1917.* New Haven: Yale University Press, 1932.

Komarov, V. "Dvoevlastie 1917 g." *Sovetskoe gosudarstvo,* vol. 12, no. 4 (1932).

Kondrat'ev, N. D. *Rynok khlebov i ego regulirovanii vo vremia voiny i revoliutsii.* Moscow, 1922.

Krivosheina, E. "Prichiny peredachi vlasti Petrogradskim sovetom rabochikh i soldatskikh deputatov burzhuazii v fevral'skuiu revoliutsiiu." *Sovetskoe gosudarstvo i revoliutsiia prava,* 1931, nos. 1-2.

Kruze, E. E. *Polozhenie rabochego klassa Rossii v 1900-1914 gg.* Leningrad, 1976.

——, and D. E. Kutsentov. "Naselenie Petrograda." *Ocherki istorii Leningrada,* vol. 3.

Krylenko, N. "Fevral'skaia revoliutsiia i staraia armiia." *PR,* vols. 61-62, nos. 2-3 (1927).

Laverychev, V. Ia. "Prodovol'stvennaia politika tsarizma i burzhuazii v gody pervoi mirovoi voiny." *Vestnik moskovskogo universiteta.* Seriia istorii i filologii, 1956, no. 1.

——. "Legendy, predpolozhenie i fakty o podgotovke dvortsovogo perevorota." *Nauchnaia sessiia posviashchennaia 50 letiiu sverzheniia samoderzhaviia,* pt. 3.

Lazitch, Branko. *Lenine et la IIIe Internationale.* Paris, 1951.

Leiberov, I. P. "Petrogradskii proletariat v bor'be za pobedu Fevral'skoi burzhuazno-demokraticheskoi revoliutsii v Rossii." *Istoriia SSSR,* 1957, no. 1.

——. "V. I. Lenin i Petrogradskaia organizatsiia bol'shevikov v period mirovoi voiny." *Voprosy istorii KPSS,* 1960, no. 5.

——. "Rabochee dvizhenie v Petrograde v period pervoi mirovoi voiny." In *Nauchnaia sessiia po istorii rabochego klassa Leningrada.* Leningrad, 1961.

——. "Stachechnaia bor'ba petrogradskogo proletariata v period pervoi mirovoi voiny." In *Sbornik statei: Istoriia rabochego klassa Leningrada,* vol. 2. Leningrad, 1963.

——. "K voprosu o revoliutsionnykh massovykh deistviiakh petrogradskogo proletariata v period Fevral'skoi revoliutsii 1917 g." In *Nauchnaia konferentsiia kafedr obshchestvennykh nauk vuzov Sever-Zapada.* Leningrad, 1963.

——. "O revoliutsionnykh vystupleniiakh petrogradskogo proletariata v gody pervoi mirovoi voiny i Fevral'skoi revoliutsii." *Voprosy istorii*, 1964, no. 2.

——. "O vozniknovenii revoliutsionnoi situatsii v Rossii v gody pervoi mirovoi voiny (iiul'-sentiabr', 1915 g.)." *Istoriia SSSR*, 1964, no. 6.

——. "Petrogradskii proletariat vo vseobshchei politicheskoi stachke 25 fevralia 1917 g." In *Oktiabr' i grazhdanskaia voina v SSSR: Sbornik statei.* Moscow, 1966.

——. "Petrogradskii proletariat v Fevral'skoi stachke (25 fevralia-10 marta, 1917 goda.)" *Nauchnaia sessiia, posviashchennaia 50 letiiu sverzheniia samoderzhaviia*, pt. 2.

——. "Problema podgotovki partiei bol'shevikov vseobshchei politicheskoi stachki protiv voiny i tsarizma v period s iulia 1915 g. po fevral' 1917 g." *Nauchnaia sessiia, posviashchennaia 50 letiiu sverzheniia samoderzhaviia*, pt. 1.

——. "Nachalo Fevral'skoi revoliutsii (sobytiia 23 fevralia 1917 g. v Petrograde." In *Iz istorii velikoi Oktiabr'skoi sotsialisticheskoi revoliutsii i sotsialisticheskogo stroitel'stva v SSSR: Sbornik statei.* Leningrad, 1967.

——. "Revoliutsionnoe studenchestvo Petrogradskogo universiteta nakanune i v period pervoi mirovoi voiny." In *Ocherki po istorii Leningradskogo universiteta*, vol. 2. 2 vols. Leningrad, 1968.

——. "Deiatel'nost' Petrogradskoi organizatsii bol'shevikov i ee vliianie na rabochee dvizhenie v Rossii v gody pervoi mirovoi voiny." In *Pervaia mirovaia voina, 1914-1918.* Moscow, 1968.

——. "Petrogradskii proletariat v Fevral'skoi revoliutsii." Ph.D. dissertation, University of Leningrad, 1970.

——. "Vtoroi den' Fevral'skoi revoliutsii: Sobytiia 24 fevralia 1917 g. v Petrograde." In *Sverzhenie samoderzhaviia.*

——. "Petrogradskii proletariat v gody pervoi mirovoi voiny." In *Istoriia rabochikh Leningrada.* 2 vols. Leningrad, 1972.

——, and O. I. Shkaratan. "K voprosu o sostave petrogradskikh promyshlennykh rabochikh v 1917 godu." *Voprosy istorii*, 1961, no. 1.

Longley, David. "The Divisions in the Bolshevik Party in March 1917." *Soviet Studies*, vol. 24, no. 1 (1972).

——. "The February Revolution in the Baltic Fleet at Helsingfors: *Vosstanie* or *Bunt?*" *Canadian Slavonic Papers*, vol. 20, no. 1 (1978).

Maevskii, Evg. *Kanun revoliutsii.* Petrograd, 1918.

Maklakov, V. Introduction to *La chute du regime tsariste.* Paris, 1927.

Martynov, E. I. *Tsarskaia armiia v fevral'skom perevorote.* Leningrad, 1927.

Mel'gunov, S. P. *Na putiakh k dvortsovomu perevorotu.* Paris, 1931.

——. *Legenda o separatnom mire.* Paris, 1957.

——. *Martovkie dni 1917 goda.* Paris, 1961.

Meyendorff, A. *The Background of the Russian Revolution.* New York, 1928.

Miller, V. I. "Iz istorii prikaza No. 1 Petrogradskogo Soveta." *Voenno-istoricheskii zhurnal*, 1966, no. 5.

——. "Petrogradskii garnizon v fevral'skie dni 1917 goda." *Voenno-istoricheskii zhurnal*, 1967, no. 2.

——. *Soldatskie komitety russkoi armii v 1917 g.* Moscow, 1974.

Mints, I. I. *Istoriia Velikogo Oktiabria.* 3 vols. Vol. 1: *Sverzhenie samoderzhaviia.* Moscow, 1967-1973.

——, L. M. Ivanov, et al. *Sverzhenie samoderzhaviia: Sbornik statei.* Moscow, 1970.

Mittel'man, M. I., Glebov, and A. Ul'ianskii. *Istoriia Putilovskogo zavoda: 1789-1917.* Moscow, 1941.

Moiseev, M. N. "Armiia revoliutsii." *Voprosy istorii KPSS,* 1958, no. 1.

Monkevitz, N. *La décomposition de l'armée russe.* Paris, 1919.

Muratov, Kh. I. *Revoliutsionnoe dvizhenie v russkoi armii v 1917 g.* Moscow, 1958.

Naida, S. F. *Revoliutsionnoe dvizhenie v russkom flote, 1825-1917.* Moscow and Leningrad, 1948.

Nauchnaia sessiia, posviashchennaia 50 letiiu sverzheniia samoderzhaviia v Rossii. 4 pts. Moscow and Leningrad, 1967.

Nolde, Boris. *L'ancien régime et la révolution russes.* Paris, 1928.

——. *Russia in the Economic War.* New Haven: Yale University Press, 1928.

Ocherki istorii Leningrada. 4 vols. Moscow and Leningrad, 1956.

Ol'denburg, S. S. *Tsarstvovanie Imperatora Nikolaia II-go.* 2 vols. Munich, 1949.

Oznobishin, P. V. "Vremennyi komitet gosudarstvennoi dumy i Vremennoe pravitel'stvo." *Istoricheskie zapiski,* vol. 75 (1965).

Pares, Bernard. *The Fall of the Russian Monarchy.* New York: Alfred A. Knopf, 1939.

Pavlov, A. V. "Bol'sheviki Vyborgskoi storony v bor'be za pobedu sotialistiche-skoi revoliutsii," Kandidat dissertation, University of Leningrad, 1973.

Pearson, Raymond. *The Russian Moderates and the Crisis of Tsarism, 1914-1917.* New York: Barnes and Noble, 1977.

Petrov, N. N. "Gorodskoe upravlenie i gorodskoe khoziaistvo Petrograda." *Ocherki istorii Leningrada,* vol. 3.

Pokrovskii, M. "Istoricheskii smysl Fevralia." *PR,* vols. 61-62, nos. 2-3 (1927).

Polner, T. E. *Zhiznennyi put' kniaziia Georgiia Evgenievicha L'vova.* Paris, 1932.

——, et al. *Russian Local Government during the War and the Union of Zemstvos.* New Haven: Yale University Press, 1930.

Potekhin, M. "K voprosu o vozniknovenii i sostave Petrogradskogo Soveta v 1917 g." *Istoriia SSSR,* 1965, no. 5.

Rabinovich, S. E. "Komissary petrogradskogo soveta do i posle 1917 g." *KL,* vol. 33, no. 6 (1929).

Rabinowitch, Alexander. *Prelude to Revolution: The Petrograd Bolsheviks and the July 1917 Uprising.* Bloomington: Indiana University Press, 1968.

——. *The Bolsheviks Come to Power: The Revolution of 1917 in Petrograd.* New York: Norton, 1976.

Radkey, Oliver H. *The Agrarian Foes of Bolshevism: Promise and Default of the Russian Socialist Revolutionaries, February to October, 1917.* New York: Columbia University Press, 1958.

Rauch, G. von. "Russische Friedenfühler 1916/17?" *Internationales Recht und Diplomatie,* 1965.

Riha, Thoma. "Miliukov and the Progressive Bloc in 1915." *Journal of Modern History,* January, 1960.

——. *A Russian European: Paul Miliukov in Russian Politics.* Notre Dame, Ind.: University of Notre Dame Press, 1969.

Rosenberg, William G. *Liberals in the Russian Revolution.* Princeton, N. J.: Princeton University Press, 1974.

Saul, Norman E. *Sailors in Revolt: The Russian Baltic Fleet in 1917.* Lawrence, Kan.: Regents Press of Kansas, 1978.

Schapiro, Leonard. "The Political Thought of the First Provisional Government."

In *Revolutionary Russia*. Edited by Richard Pipes. Cambridge, Mass.: Harvard University Press, 1967.

Schwarz, Solomon. *The Russian Revolution of 1915: The Workers' Movement and the Formation of Bolshevism and Menshevism*. Chicago: University of Chicago Press, 1967.

Seraphim, Ernest. "Der Stürz des Zaren Nikolaus II. und die russische Generalität." *Jahrbücher für Geschichte Osteuropas*, 1937, no. 2.

Shchegolev, P. E. *Poslednii reis Nikolaia vtorogo*. Moscow and Leningrad, 1928.

Sidorov, A. L. "Otrechenie Nikolaia II i Stavka." In *Problemy obshchestvenno-politicheskoi istorii Rossii i slavianskikh stran: Sbornik statei*. Moscow, 1963.

———. *Ekonomicheskoe polozhenie Rossii v gody pervoi mirovoi voiny*. Moscow, 1973.

———, L. M. Ivanov, et al. *Pervaia mirovaia voina, 1914-1918*. Moscow, 1968

Smith, Nathan. "The Role of Russian Freemasonry in the February Revolution: Another Scrap of Evidence." *Slavic Review*, vol. 27, no. 4 (1968).

Startsev, V. I. *Ocherki po istorii Petrogradskoi krasnoi gvardii i rabochei militsii*. Moscow and Leningrad, 1965.

Stepnoi, N. *Etapy velikoi russkoi revoliutsii*. Samara, 1918.

Stone, Norman. *The Eastern Front*. London: Hodder and Soughton, 1975.

Struve, Petr. *Razmyshleniia o russkoi revoliutsii*. Sofia, 1921.

Szeftel, Marc. *The Russian Constitution of April 23, 1906: Political Institutions of the Duma Monarchy*. Brussells: Editions de la libraire encyclopédique, 1976.

Timoshenko, A. I. "Izmeneniia v gosudarstvennoi mekhanizme Rossiiskoi imperii v period pervoi mirovoi voiny." Kandidat dissertation, University of Leningrad, 1968.

Tiutiukin, S. V. *Voina, mir, revoliutsiia: Ideinaia bor'ba v rabochem dvizhenii Rossii, 1914-1917 gg.* Moscow, 1972.

———. "Rabochaia gruppa Ts VPK nakanune Fevral'skoi revoliutsii v Rossii." *Nauchnaia sessiia, posviashchennaia 50 letiiu sverzheniia samoderzhaviia*, pt. 1.

Tokarev, Iu. S. *Petrogradskii Sovet rabochikh i soldatskikh deputatov v marte-aprele, 1917 g.* Leningrad, 1976.

Trotsky, Leon. *Istoriia russkoi revoliutsii*. 3 vols. Berlin, 1931.

———. *The History of the Russian Revolution*. 3 vols. New York: Simon and Schuster, 1932.

Varentsov, O. "Lenin o fevral'skoi revoliutsii." *PR*, vols. 61-62, nos. 2-3 (1927).

Volk, S. S. "Prosveshchenie i shkola v Peterburge." *Ocherki istorii Leningrada*, vol. 3.

Volobuev, P. V. *Ekonomicheskaia politika vremennogo pravitel'stva*. Moscow, 1962.

———. *Proletariat i burzhuaziia Rossii v 1917 g.* Moscow, 1964.

Wada Haruki. "Nigatsu kakumei." In *Roshia kakumei no kenkyū*. Edited by Eguchi Bokuro. Tokyo: Chuokoron-sha, 1968.

Wettig, Gerhardt von. "Die Rolle der russischen armee im Revolutionären Machtkampf 1917." *Forschungen zur osteuropäischen Geschichte*, vol. 12 (1967).

Zagorsky, S. O. *State Control of Industry in Russia during the War*. New Haven: Yale University Press, 1928.

Zaitsev, K. I., and S. S. Demosthenov. *Food Supply in Russia during the War with Introduction of Peter B. Struve*. New Haven: Yale University Press, 1930.

Zlokazov, G. I. "Sozdanie Petrogradskogo Soveta." *Istoriia SSSR*, 1964, no. 5.

———. "O Zasedanii Petrogradskogo Soveta rabochikh i soldatskikh deputatov 28 fevralia 1917 g." In *Oktiabr' i grazhdanskaia voina v SSSR: Sbornik statei.* Moscow, 1966.

——. *Petrogradskii sovet rabochikh i soldatskikh deputatov v period mirnogo razvitiia revoliutsii.* Moscow, 1969.

Zviagintseva, A. G. "Organizatsiia i deiatel'nosti militsii Vremennogo pravitel'-stva Rossii v 1917 godu." Kandidat dissertation, University of Moscow, 1972.

INDEX

Abdication. *See* Nicholas II; Mikhail Aleksandrovich

Abrasimov, V. N., 89, 124, 175, 204, 205-6, 285

Admiralty, 65, 228-309 passim, 362, 376, 426, 465, 488, 581

Adzhemov, M. S., 175-76, 179, 416

Agrarian reform, 82

Aivaz. *See* Petrograd, factories

Akhmatova, Anna, 3, 6

Alcoholism, 201

Aleksandr Garden, 305, 306

Aleksandr Mikhailovich, Grand Duke, 55, 155, 190

Aleksandra Fedorovna, Empress: and patriotism, 4, 157; as tsar's advisor, 12-13, 576; involvement in politics, 29, 31, 37-38, 40, 41, 45, 47, 51-59 passim, 148, 153, 160, 162-63, 181, 230; sentiment against, 29, 58; and grand dukes, 55-56, 147, 154-55; and Rasputin, 58-59, 145, 146, 148; and liberals, 179, 185, 186; and palace coup, 185, 186; and February Revolution, 230, 263, 431-32, 434, 435, 471-72, 493; and grand dukes' manifesto, 445 and n; and Ivanov, 470, 472-73; and revolution in Tsarskoe Selo, 470-72; and Rodzianko, 472; and tsar's abdication, 515; and soldiers' declining morale, 574. *See also* Court camarilla

Aleksandrovich, Petr A., 137, 241, 255, 324-26, 343-44, 347, 370, 534-35, 539

Aleksandrovskaia, 456, 466, 478, 482, 484

Alekseenko, M. M., 183

Alekseev, General N. V.: as chief of staff, 31; ends Great Retreat, 35; proposes dictatorship, 47, 50; and Guchkov, 47, 191, 554, 563-64; and palace coup, 55, 185-86, 191; and Klopov, 156; as dictator, 156, 265; origins of, 170; and L'vov, 185-86; and Rodzianko, 276, 433, 436, 451n, 475 and n, 482, 490, 500, 548-49, 550, 551, 563, 586; and insurrection in Petrograd, 301-2, 459, 462-63; and Mikhail, 356-57, 563-65; and counterrevolution, 436, 459-64, 473-77, 482, 551-54, 565-66; and Duma Committee, 436, 451n, 463-64, 489-91, 494, 586; and Ivanov, 460, 473-74, 478, 483, 484-85, 492, 500, 551; and rail-

PUBLICATIONS ON RUSSIA AND EASTERN EUROPE OF
THE SCHOOL OF INTERNATIONAL STUDIES

1. Peter F. Sugar and Ivo J. Lederer, eds. *Nationalism in Eastern Europe.* 1969. 487 pp., index.
2. W. A. Douglas Jackson, ed. *Agrarian Policies and Problems in Communist and Non-Communist Countries.* 1971. 485 pp., maps, figures, tables, index.
3. Alexander V. Muller, trans. and ed. *The* Spiritual Regulation *of Peter the Great.* 1972. 150 pp., index.
4. Ben-Cion Pinchuck. *The Octobrists in the Third Duma, 1907-1912.* 1974. 232 pp., bibliog., index.
5. Gale Stokes. *Legitimacy through Liberalism: Vladimir Jovanović and the Transformation of Serbian Politics.* 1975. 280 pp., maps, bibliog., index.
6. Canfield F. Smith. *Vladivostok under Red and White Rule: Revolution and Counterrevolution in the Russian Far East, 1920-1922.* 1975. 304 pp., maps, illus., bibliog., index.
7. Michael Palij. *The Anarchism of Nestor Makhno, 1918-1921: An Aspect of the Ukrainian Revolution.* 1976. 428 pp., map, illus., bibliog., index.
8. Deborah Hardy. *Petr Tkachev, the Critic as Jacobin.* 1977. 339 pp., illus., bibliog., index.
9. Tsuyoshi Hasegawa. *The February Revolution: Petrograd, 1917.* 1981. 652 pp., maps, tables, illus., appendixes, bibliog., index.

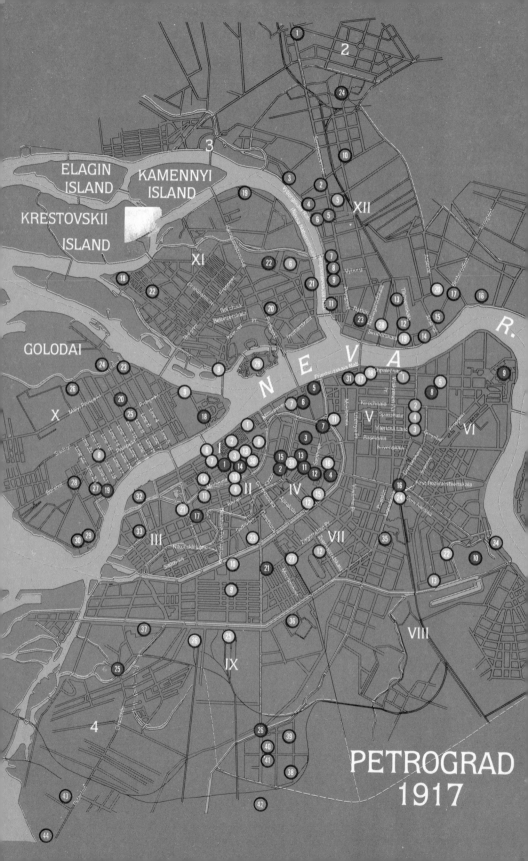

ELAGIN
ISLAND

KAMENNYI
ISLAND

KRESTOVSKII

ISLAND

XI

GOLODAI

X

N E V A   R.

XII

V

VI

I

II

IV

VII

VIII

III

IX

PETROGRAD
1917

4